HANS CHRISTIAN ANDERSEN

BETWEEN CHILDREN'S LITERATURE AND ADULT LITERATURE

The Hans Christian Andersen Center
University Press of Southern Denmark

HANS CHRISTIAN ANDERSEN

BETWEEN CHILDREN'S LITERATURE AND ADULT LITERATURE

Papers from the

**Fourth International
Hans Christian Andersen Conference
1 to 5 August 2005**

**Edited by
Johan de Mylius, Aage Jørgensen and Viggo Hjørnager Pedersen**

Issued by
The Hans Christian Andersen Center,
University of Southern Denmark

University Press of Southern Denmark
2007

Hans Christian Andersen
Between Children's Literature and
Adult Literature

© University Press of Southern Denmark
and the authors 2007

Illustrations:
p. 32 Her Majesty the Queen of Denmark
© Aage Sikker-Hansen, Svend Otto Sørensen,
Werner Wejp-Olsen, Henry Heerup, Axel Mathiesen/billedkunst.dk
p. 457: Lise Ungermann Schmidt-Madsen

Published with support from
HCA 2005 Foundation and
Ministeriet for Videnskab Teknologi
og Udvikling, Exhausto, Fehrs Fond,
Fionia Bank, Fyens Stiftstidende,
Fyns Amt, Sydbank and "Anonymous".

Cover design by
Anne Charlotte Mouret, Unisats ApS
showing original cut by Hans Christian Andersen
from the Hans Christian Andersen Museum

Printed by
Narayana Press, Gylling
ISBN 978 87 7674 256 0

University Press of Southern Denmark
Campusvej 55, DK-5230 Odense M
www.universitypress.dk

Distribution in the United States and Canada:
International Specialized Book Services
920 NEE 58th Ave, Suite 300
Portland, OR 97213
1.800.944.6190 | 503.287.3093
fax: 503.280.8832
www.isbs.com

Distribution in the United Kingdom:
Gazelle
White Cross Mills, Hightown, Lancaster
LA1 4 XS U.K.
www.gazellebooks.co.uk

List of Contents

Preface 9

Plenary Lectures

Caught Between Heaven and Hell: The Two Faces of Hans
    Christian Andersen
    Carola Scanavino... 13
The Queen and I
    Erik M. Christensen 23
Andersen's Poems For and About Children
    Hans Kuhn... 37
Death and The Child
    Johan de Mylius 52
The Language that Stayed at Home: Hans Christian Andersen's
    Ways with Words
    Kirsten Malmkjær 71
Romantic and Modern Metatexts: Commemorating Andersen
    and the Self-Referential Text
    Marianne Stecher-Hansen 88
"Out of a Swan's Egg": Metamorphosis in Hans Christian
    Andersen's Tales and *The Fairy Tale of My Life*
    Maria-Sabina Draga Alexandru 101
Chronotope of Hans Christian Andersen's Fairy Tales and
    Stories
    Andrey Korovin 119
The Shepherdess and the Chimney Sweep
    Martin Lotz... 131

Culture, Travels and Biography

Hans Christian Andersen Tourist? An Investigation of
    Etymology, Social History and Ideology
    Hans Christian Andersen 149
Hans Christian Andersen Was No Hypochondriac, He Was Ill
    Annelies van Hees 166
Hans Christian Andersen's View of the Orient and His Dealing
    with Otherness
    Nina Hintz 174
Children and Moods in Hans Christian Andersen's Travel
    Books
    Lars Bo Jensen 189
Hans Christian Andersen between Rootedness and Modernity,
    with Special Reference to His Fairy Tale "The Dryad"
    Aage Jørgensen 199
Shadow Pictures – Truth or Tale
    Lone Funch Kofoed 216

Medias and Reception

Encyclopaedic "Portraits" of Hans Christian Andersen in
  Contemporary Polish Encyclopaedias and Lexicons
  Zbigniew Baran 225
The Motif of Mermaid in Baltic Literatures (Karlis Skalbe,
  Maironis, Leons Briedis, Aspazija, Kazys Puida, Violeta
  Palčinskaité)
  Silvestras Gaižiūnas 237
Hans Christian Andersen and Evgeny Shwartz — Means of
  Reinterpretation
  Elizaveta Isaeva 244
Hans Christian Andersen in Puppet Theatre
  Rossitsa Minovska-Devedzhieva 250
Life and Death in "The Little Mermaid". Three Contemporary
  Adaptations of Hans Christian Andersen's Fairy Tale
  Elisabeth Oxfeldt 263
"Everything in the Picture Book Was Alive": Hans Christian
  Andersen's Strategy of Textual Animation in His Fairy
  Tales and the Interactive Child Reader
  Jacqueline Reid-Walsh 275

Translation

Translations of Hans Christian Andersen in Latvian and
  Lithuanian (1990-2005)
  Arūnas Bliūdžius 290
Like Roses to a Cow?
  Hans Christian Andersen in English Translations
  Lise Bostrup 297
Hans Christian Andersen and His First Romanian Translators
  Anca Dumitrescu 326
"Prenez garde aux enfants" – Swedish Versions and Varieties of
  Hans Christian Andersen's Eventyr.
  Ivo Holmqvist 332
The Identity and Integrity of the Slovene Andersen in the Post-
  WW2 Period: Translation as the Right of Passage
  Silvana Orel Kos 343
Hans Christian Andersen's Fairy Tales for Estonian Readers
  Mare Müürsepp 360
For Adults Only
  Yoichi Nagashima 369
"Out in The World, Thoughts Come"
  Viggo Hjørnager Pedersen: 374
Dynamism in Perception of Hans Christian Andersen in Saint
  Petersburg, one of the Most Andersenous Cities of the
  World
  Boris Zharov 389
Hans Christian Andersen's Fairy Tales – Children's Literature?
  Anette Øster 398

Children's Aspects

Childishness as Poetic Strategy
   Mogens Davidsen.. 409
Father's Fault Concerning His Daughter
   Asta Ivanauskaité-Gustaitiene 426
Dream and Reality: "The Little Match Girl" Seen in a Socio-
   psychological Perspective
   † *Inger Lise Jensen*.. 443
Hans Christian Andersen's Flair to Communicate Basic Social
   Skills Naturally and Imperceptibly to National and
   International Readers
   Eric J. Jones.. 460
Language for Children? An Examination of the Language and
   Intended Readership of the Fairy Tales
   Tom Lundskær-Nielsen: 466
About Little Gerda, and Her "Moratoria"
   James Massengale... 478
Hans Christian Andersen's Stories: The Southern Africa
   Perspective
   Vincent Mhlakaza.. 505
Hans Christian Andersen – a Young Poet? Considerations
   About a Textbook
   Ivy York Möller-Christensen... 516
Strong Minded and Strong Willed Girls in Hans Christian
   Andersen's Fairy Tales Found in "The Snow Queen"
   (1844); "The Little Match Girl" (1845); "Clod Hans" (1855)
   and "The Swamp King's Daughter" (1858)
   Inger M. Olsen 522
"The Snow Queen" by Hans Christian Andersen:
   "Weltanschauung" and the Imaginative Mind
   Inge Lise Rasmussen 528
Hans Christian Andersen – Writing for Children?
   Torben Weinreich.. 538

Aesthetics, Text, Analysis and Ideas

"Look! Now we'll begin. When we have got to the end of the
   story we shall know more than we do now"
   Ejnar Askgaard 547
The Toll of Andersen's Bell. From Neo-Platonism to New Age
   – Ways of Understanding and Interpreting the Great
   Writer's Spirituality
   Vera Gancheva 570
Trivializing Trauma(s): Carnivalesque-grotesque Elements in
   Hans Christian Andersen's "The Happy Family" (1847,
   1848), "Heartache" (1852), and "The Goblin and the
   Grocer" (1852)
   Ib Johansen 585

The Bed of Procrustes: An Analysis of Hans Christian
    Andersen's "The Fir Tree"
        Lone Koldtoft (and Paul A. Bauer) 599
Approaching Fear in Hans Christian Andersen's Fairy Tales
    Through Sigmund Freud, Julia Kristeva and Melanie Klein
        Cynthia Mikaela Mikkelsen 610
The Soul of Things. Literary Forms and Popular Motifs in the
    Tales of Hans Christian Andersen
        Leander Petzoldt 625
"Now Then! We Will Begin ...": Communicative Strategies in
    Hans Christian Andersen's Fairy Tales
        Margarita Slavova 632

Preface

The international Hans Christian Andersen conferences have been recurrent events since 1991, three years after the foundation of the Hans Christian Andersen Center at what was then Odense University, now University of Southern Denmark. Recurrent, but at suitable intervals: the first two were in 1991 and 1996, both in Odense; in 2000 the conference was in Provo (Brigham Young University, Utah, USA) and in 2005 again in Odense. From 1996 English has been the only conference language.

The conferences have been followed by the publication in book form of papers presented, appearing in respectively 1993, 1999, 2004, and now the most recent, in 2007. The two first conference books (Hans Christian Andersen and the World and Hans Christian Andersen. A Poet in Time) were made available on the Center's web site: www.andersen.sdu.dk a few years after their publication: thus a broad body of material for studying Andersen and his work has been placed at the disposal of potential users all over the world, whereas previously scholarly studies of Andersen in other languages than Danish were few in number or even non-existent. We expect that the conference book from Utah (H.C. Andersen. Old Problems and New Readings) and the present volume will in time also become available via the Center's web site.

Since 1991 there have been many other smaller conferences and seminars, both in Denmark and in many other countries, culminating in a wave of seminars in 2005, the year of Andersen's bicentenary. A number of these seminars and conferences have also produced conference volumes. The rings have spread, and Andersen studies is becoming an international field; for instance, a little offshoot of the Hans Christian Andersen Center at the University of Southern Denmark will open at the University of Sofia (Bulgaria) at the end of 2007.

One of the reasons why Andersen studies has had difficulty for many years in becoming established internationally in spite of the exceptional fame and visibility of this author in much of the world is undoubtedly that outside Denmark he is often regarded as exclusively a children's writer: children's literature is not normally included in serious literary studies but is relegated to a few scattered special centres or departments.

For the same reason it was important for the group of scholars who originally rallied round the international Andersen conferences to focus on the 'grown up' aspects of Andersen's oeuvre, quite simply in order to legitimate it internationally and establish a serious interest among other than Danish scholars.

But in the long run even the most inveterate Andersen scholars cannot very well close their eyes to the fact that, whether we like it or not, it is as a children's writer that Andersen has won world fame and that it is in this area that the overwhelming majority of his audience is found and will continue to be found.

The planners of the 2005 conference realized, therefore, that this time a new approach was required. The 'grown up' aspects of Andersen's work (especially with respect to the tales and stories) had been given sufficient attention in the first three conferences. The time had come to consider his work also as children's literature.

This message did not please all the delegates of the former conferences. Why was it necessary to kowtow to the conception of Andersen as a children's writer? But reality is not easily ignored, and therefore the organizers chose to maintain this thematic approach, whilst allowing for consideration of other aspects in some papers. So both the conference and this book celebrate Andersen in two capacities: as a writer for children and for adults.

In order to underline the specific focus of this conference, the leading authority on children's literature in Denmark, Professor Torben Weinreich (The Danish School of Education – now a branch of the University of Aarhus) – was co-opted to the organizing committee. However, he has chosen not to be a co-editor of this volume, which is therefore under the aegis of the same three scholars as the publications of 1993 and 1999.

A large section of the book appears under the heading "Children's Aspects". But a careful reading of the book will reveal that approaches or topics related to children's literature have also found a place in the majority of the remaining contributions, even if the main focus appears to be different. So the original hesitation about focusing on Andersen as a writer for children has been replaced by a comprehensive and serious examination of this topic from many angles: linguistic, cultural, national, reception-oriented and with regard to traditions and genres: in short the whole gamut of possible approaches to the oeuvre was brought into play. Thus this book may be said to have done full justice to the large and multifaceted oeuvre, and is a fitting celebration of the bicentenary.

The international Andersen conferences have proved able to provide room for more than research in a narrower sense. To a greater extent than is usual with university conferences, they have given an opportunity to hear voices from other cultural spheres, and to become acquainted with the variety of ways in which Andersen and his tales are used. The three Odense conferences in particular have been a meeting ground for research and culture in a broader perspective, and this is indeed reflected in the present conference book. It is a memorial to a multifacetted meeting with Hans Christian Andersen, both in his historical context and in our contemporary world.

Thus in 2007 it appears that Andersen's bicentenary could not spoil the impact of his work. It survives himself, his jubilee – and will indeed survive us, his modern readers and users.

Johan de Mylius   Aage Jørgensen   Viggo Hjørnager Pedersen

Caught Between Heaven and Hell:
The Two Faces of Hans Christian Andersen

Carola Scanavino

The interest taken in Andersen arises from due observation that even well after his death, our feeling of familiarity with the Danish writer has not in the least diminished. Translated into virtually all languages, it is a fact that his fairy tales go on being constantly present in the childhood of many a boy and girl the world over as well as in the recollections of just as many adults. The question that therefore arises here is what the actual reasons for such a long lasting success might be the fact that the times and the audiences the fairy tales were aimed at have been subject to profound changes.

Scientific research has disproved the conviction, widespread amongst the limited number of Italian critics that have dealt with Andersen, of his true image being that of a children's writer; a simple man endowed with a straightforward, positive and profoundly religious view of life. On the contrary, North European research has shed light on the overall complexity of Andersen's personality and, focusing particularly on his striking duplicity, has demonstrated again and again how this feature has veritably nurtured a literary production whose contents are not as sparklingly clear and reassuring as we are accustomed to consider them. In Andersen, there is an inseparable bond linking the man, the artist and his works: so tight a link that the works actually are an extraordinary intimate diary other than a manifest display of poetics in which he gives utterance to the unease he feels in his being an artist and through which, hiding behind a different mask for each different tale and story, he gives us access to his own individual truthfulness concerning art, a truthfulness that is often obscure and uncomfortable.

The philosopher Søren Kierkegaard, one of Andersen's contemporaries, was the first critic to point in this direction in his essay *Af en endnu Levendes Papirer. Udgivet mod hans Villie af S. Kierkegaard*,[1] the content of which conveys some very harsh criticism on Andersen, both as an individual and as a novelist. The philosopher highlights the strong presence of feminine components acting as stumbling blocks to Andersen's personality integration processes, claiming that they would force his personality to waver between contrasting and contradictory issues throughout his entire life. Although to Kierkegaard the said ambiguity was considered as a limitation to both the individual as well as to the artist Andersen, to us, as children of the modern ages that have uncovered all that can be held as being ambiguous and enigmatic behind human behaviour, it is an emblem of fascination, inviting us to ponder on the chance that it is his ambiguity that actually might be, fundamentally, the real reason for his literary successes.

The Danish writer's dual nature is perceived in all the aspects of his life but predominantly so in the sexual and religious aspects that hold a more direct influence on his literary production. Andersen displayed inclinations towards a good number of women, but he also revealed homosexual inclinations and he certainly did have a voyeuristic bent. As to religion, he professed a brand of orthodox and rationalistic Christianity, often overshadowed by an animistic, magic and superstitious faith, typical of his childhood. Andersen's relationships with the cultured and wealthy Danish upper middle classes also display some very strongly contradictory traits. Throughout his life he was committed to endeavouring to accept the ideals of harmony and moral perfection pertaining to a world that he felt he was not entirely a part of, the hypocrisy and cruelty of which he often denounced: of an upper middle class that dictated the rules for respectability in social and artistic circles and that invested the artists, in their capacity as Apollonian creatures, with the noble task granted them of drawing on the Absolute, on the spiritual values of Truth, Beauty and Ethics and to act as intermediaries of their knowledge thereof, for the sake of the public audiences.

The ambiguity of Andersen's disposition and the world around him can be traced back to one major set of opposites, on the one side there being his need for order, for the type of reassuring order reigning in the upper middle class communities where all is rationality, logic and harmony; on the other side the oppressive and obscure inner legacy from his childhood, spent in a poor, dark, uncertain, disorderly and irrational universe, that Andersen never quite found the ability to leave behind him. The Danish writer's poetics therefore were fired by two souls, one a luminous, classicist, Golden Age soul, the other an obscure soul, decidedly closer to the irrational aspects of romanticism. It is thus in this capacity of the spirit that is far more in tune with 19th century European culture than with Danish culture, a spiritual capacity that somehow displays the symptoms proper to literature and art of the second half of the Century, that the typical traits of real modernity in Andersen are evident – features that are the reason for the never ending fascination of his works.

The first marked reference to the author's dual Apollonian-Diabolic guise is his early novel *Kun en Spillemand* (Only a Fiddler), published 1837. Christian, the main character, declares right from the start that his great love for music and his desire to become a violin virtuoso have been instilled into him by his godfather, he too a violinist. Andersen describes the relationship between the youngster and his maestro as follows:

> Naar Christian var hjemme, da gjaldt hans Længsel, da var hans høieste Ønske, at komme til Gudfaderen; og dog følte han hos Ingen, som hos ham, denne uhyggelige Følelse, vi kjende, ved at være ene i det snevre Gravkapel eller i en stor Skov, hvor vi have forfeilet Vei og Sti.[2]

> If he were at home, he unceasingly yearned after his godfather, and it was his greatest wish to go to him; and yet, when he was once there, that strange feeling fell upon him whic oveerpowers us when either we step alone in a fearful valut or find ourselves in a dark wood where we have missed our way.[3]

The godfather is therefore portrayed as being an unsettling, obscure and diabolic character, yet subtly and fascinatingly so, with the diabolic element being knowledgeably camouflaged:

> Det skulde opdrages i Uskyldighed, men om Natten kom Satan og lod Barnet die sin sorte Geed, saa kom der Vildskab i Blodet, men Ingen mærkede det, for det havde alle Dydsfagterne.[4]

> He should be brought up in innocence; but in the night came the Devil, and made him drink the milk of his black goat. The wild desires inflamed his blood, but no one remarked this until he had assumed all the manners of a hero of virtue.[5]

The idea that art does contain a certain diabolical element is confirmed by the fairy tale "The Will-o'-the-Wisps are in Town",[6] in which the main character shows the old man that goes in search of the stories that no longer come a-knocking at his door, the cabinet that is full of bottles filled with poetry of all nations that had been extracted, refined, criticised and reviewed by the Devil's Godmother who, with genius and a little added deviltry, had corked up the bottles so that the essence of poetry could be put to use for all future times. In order to be true to itself, poetry, and more generally art, must therefore contain an element of murkiness and unconsciousness whereby the artist ceases to be a mere Apollonian being in order to regain possession of his body with its passions and non confessable needs.

The same concept is revisited and further clarified in the fairy tale "The Psyche",[7] which tells the tale of an artist who reaches the peak of his genius and is able to accomplish an immortal work of art. Only once he is able to combine his luminous and rational soul with the instinctual and uncontrollable soul dictated by passions. The young sculptor is thus able to mould his Psyche only once after he has fallen in love with the very beautiful maiden, or better, only as a result of his yearning for the Absolute, for eternity, for beauty ideal and pure being all mixed with physical desire within his soul. It would appear that Andersen means to portray the process leading to the Absolute as a downward journey, to meet the flesh, the nethermost regions of one's being, beset with difficulties. Rimbaud, in his *Lettre à Paul Demeny*, provides the poet with some images of that same, difficult journey; an interior process that, through some frightening and unmentionable ordeals will lead him to become "le grand malade, le grand criminel, le grand maudit, et le suprême Savant!"[8]

It is not a coincidence that, in refusing the young man's love, the maiden says "Bort! ned!"[9] ("Away! Out of my sight!")[10], and that the young man himself, staggering desperately under its weight, decides to lower his Psyche into a ruined, dried-up well or hole in the garden whereupon he repeats "Bort! ned!" as his brief burial service.[11] It is equally revealing that one of his friends invites him to recover from the pain of rejection and reproaches him for his eternal dreaming and of not being a man like his friends, with the following words:

> Du faaer tykt Blod i det evige Drømmeri! Vær dog Menneske, som vi Andre, og lev ikke i Idealer, saa knækker man over! [...] jeg lever ikke i Indbildninger, men i Virkeligheden! Kom med! Bliv Menneske![12]

> Why don't you stop your eternal dreaming! Be a man like your friends. Don't be an idealist; if you do you'll have a breakdown. [...] I do not live in imagination; I live in reality. Come along! Be a man![13]

For Andersen, "Kom med! Bliv Menneske!" ("Come along! Be a man!") stands for regaining possession of one's body, the reintegration of passions into their natural order, of freely giving vent to one's desires and the willing acceptance of carnality. Being unable to carry out this step, the young sculptor chooses the peace of the monastery and decides to seek for the Absolute exclusively by becoming a servant of God. This choice too however turns out to be the wrong one for him and having been unsuccessful in rejoining the Absolute, he dies, neither wholly an artist nor fully a man. The inner self is revealed as being incomprehensible and unfathomable just as God is, and, the quest for the Absolute meant as a place of truth where opposites coincide and reconcile themselves harmoniously turns out to be most difficult to accomplish. What Andersen appears to say here is that the artist is suspended between these two opposite poles and is untenably caught there by the fatal attraction generated in between.

The consideration that an artist bears two very distinct and irreconcilable solicitations deep within is also the theme of one of Andersen's less known stories, that in as far as poetics go, nevertheless is brimful of the subject: "Skyggen" ("The Shadow"). In this tale the image of the artist is completely split into a kind of two-faced Janus bearing two opposite truths, one centred on the individual and one centred on art.

It tells the tale of a young and clever scholar from the North, that travels to the hot countries and finds himself living in front of an extremely mysterious house. One night he asks his shadow to step inside and to have a look around but then to be sure to return and tell him what he had seen. Alas, the shadow stays away and from that moment onwards is no more to be seen. One evening, after many, many years, the shadow returns and pays the scholar a visit completely transformed as a very elegant, successful and rich man. The scholar accepts his former shadow's proposal to become in turn his shadow, but, after having taken all that he can bear and having suffered a good number of humiliations, when he is informed that the real former shadow is about to marry a very beautiful princess, he threatens to reveal the whole truth whereupon they simply do away with him.

Even if read superficially, it is obvious that the scholar and his shadow are the two faces of one individual artist, the two roads leading to Poetry, one cast in shadow and the other filled with light. The scholar is a Golden Age Poet, that, as often cited throughout the whole tale, is replete with the True, the Good, and the Beautiful albeit without success. The shadow, on the other hand, represents a poet that has no hesitation of picking the dark corners of his own conscience, other than the conscience of other individuals. He practices "den sorte Kunst",[14] ("black art") as cited in "Nattergalen" ("The Nightingale"). Once it enters the mysterious house, which is then revealed as being the house of Poetry, the shadow becomes extremely powerful. It is the shadow itself that says to the scholar:

> [...] havde De kommet derover, var De ikke blevet Menneske, men det blev jeg! Og tillige lærte jeg at kjende min inderste Natur, mit Medfødte, det Familieskab, jeg havde med Poesien [...][15]

> Had you come over, it would not have made a man of you, as it did of me. Also, I learned to understand my inner self, what is born in me, and the relationship between me and Poetry.[16]

According to Andersen therefore, Poetry is not only the sister of light, it is also closely related to the obscure recesses of conscience, to the unconscious still awaiting to be theorised.

During the extraordinary inversion of roles that then takes place as the tale unfolds whereby the former shadow takes on a body and becomes a man and the scholar is transformed into his shadow, another one of Andersen's points of view concerning artists turns up at this point. It seems that what Andersen wants to get across here is that the artist is now only showing the one face, that of a man that has abandoned all illusions and useless disputes concerning the True, the Good, and the Beautiful and has acknowledged individual proprietorship of that kernel of obscurity thrashing around within himself.

Once the shadow becomes a man, he ventures forth into a city that turns out to be the ideal hunting ground:

> Jeg løb op og jeg løb ned, kiggede ind af de højeste Vinduer, ind i Salen og paa Taget, jeg kiggede, hvor Ingen kunde kigge og jeg saa hvad ingen Andre saae, hvad Ingen skulde se! Det er i Grunden en nedrig Verden! [...] Jeg saa det Allerutænkeligste hos Konerne, hos Mændene, hos Forældrene og hos de søde mageløse Børn [...] Havde jeg skrevet en Avis, den var blevet læst! Men jeg skrev lige til Personen selv, og der blev en Forfærdelse i alle Byer hvor jeg kom. De bleve saa bange for mig! Og de holdt saa overordentlig af mig. [...] og saa blev jeg den Mand jeg er![17]

> Up I ran and down I ran, peeping into the highest windows, into drawing rooms, and into garrets. I peered in where no one else could peer. I saw what no one else could see, or should see. Taken all in all, it's a wicked world. [...]I saw the most incredible behavior among men and women, fathers and mothers, and among those 'perfectly darling' children. I saw what nobody knows but everybody would like to know, and that is what wickedness goes on next door. If I had written it in a newspaper, oh, how widely it would have been read! [...] and so I became the man I am.[18]

Andersen's judgement of man and society of his time is quite merciless. The universe of men is an ugly world and their communities are receptacles of unworthy behaviour. But what is most striking, is the image of the poet that is actually defined by the above description. Having abandoned the serenely clear spheres of the mind, the shadow-poet ventures forth into the city streets, peeping into even the highest windows of the upper middle class wherefrom he observes, unseen, the most incredible behaviour among men and women and amongst the children. Andersen seems to want to get across that the poet is gazing at all that should not be seen, he is a minstrel of all that is obscure and unpronounceable. It is from within and not outside our inner selves, it is from within the most profound and ignored regions of our conscience that poetry must be nurtured. Not only does this view of art and of artists appear to be in tune with the most non-rationalistic sides of romanticism, it also appears to prefigure the poetic sensitivity featured through the last decades of the 20th century. Andersen foretells, albeit with a reduced depth of feeling, the framework of the poetics as granted by *Les fleurs du mal* (1857) by Baudelaire, i.e. the idea that art is simultaneously heaven and hell. Baudelaire in fact writes in his *Hymne à la Beauté*:

> Que tu viennes du ciel ou de l'enfer, qu'importe,
> O Beauté! monstre énorme, effrayant, ingénu!
> Si ton œil, ton souris, ton pied, m'ouvrent la porte
> D'un Infini que j'aime et n'ai jamais connu?[19]

Contrarily to Baudelaire, Andersen is not capable of levering himself down into the abysses of hell. Neither is he capable, if not in metaphoric form, of relaying exactly what lies in the recesses of the hearts of mankind. He limits himself to the observation that the roadway to art is a roadway to heaven as well as to hell. It is man, or better, it is the most secret and forgotten corners of man's conscience that are the new feeding grounds of poetry. And so are the wretchedness of daily life, the absurdity of the events taking place behind the respectable façade of buildings, the many faces of misery.

The idea of the poet as voyeur, albeit with a meaning that lacks any social criticism at all, is also apparent in Andersen's tale "Hvad man kan hitte paa" ("What One Can Invent"), which tells the story of a young man who wants to become a poet but feels that there is nothing in the world left to write about because every subject has been worn out. A wise old lady makes him try on her spectacles and listen through her ear trumpet, and then gives him the following advice: "[…] bed saa til Vorherre og lad være at tænke paa Dig selv!"[20] ("say your prayers, and please, for once in your life, stop thinking about yourself.")[21]

The young man puts on her spectacles and listens through her ear trumpet and thanks to them he finds he has a lot to tell on everything: the story of the potato and its forefathers, of the blackthorn bush, of the bees and finally of the swarms of people he sees, "Historie paa Historie! det snurrer og snurrer!"[22], ("What endless stories I seem to hear in all that buzzing, droning, and confusion.")[23] The young man feels dizzy, his eyes fog over and he starts falling backward in fright. The old lady urges him not to fall backward, but to go straight onwards, "lige ind i Menneskevrimlen"[24] ("right in among the people") and to have "Syn paa den, Øre for den og Hjerte med!"[25], ("Have eyes for all you see, ears for all you hear, and above all throw your whole heart into it").[26] A poet true to himself must therefore not limit himself to mere observation: the ear trumpet and the spectacles are necessary to him so that he can release himself from his inner being, forget his own rational identity and plunge himself completely in with objects or other individuals until he is fully tuned in with them.

Have an ear to hear and the right heart to feel (Dulcken).

In "Skyggen" though, the poet's task as voyeur gives rise to a number of further definitions. It does not merely entail the generic recounting of humanity but it strips off all the barriers of society in order to specifically unmask the false morality of the upper middle classes. The poetics of illumination are thus replaced here with the poetics of unmasking, as further confirmed by the fairy tale "Lygtemændene er i Byen, sagde Mosekonen", ("The Will-o'-the-Wisps are in Town") written 1865. In this tale the old woman tells of the birth of twelve

Will-o'-the-Wisps and how they had been given permission to go out amongst men and to take on their form, to go into the church and to enter "the vicar"[27], to succeed in leading people downward along bad paths in order to receive the highest honour a will-o'-the-wisp can, that "at blive Løber foran Fandens Stadskarreet"[28], ("that of being a runner before the Devil's coach").[29]

In the tale of the Will-o'-the-Wisps, society is described as hypocritical and even diabolic. The old woman of the marsh advises the story teller that he must unmask the truth. Contrarily to "Skyggen" ("The Shadow") though, in the tale of the Will-o'-the-Wisps Andersen has no illusions as to the chance that the poet as a voyeur will actually be heeded and subsequently be honoured and become successful. The end of the tale also tells a bitter truth: the poet will have to keep silent and give up his role to save himself from being subject to the wraths of a world hostile to his clairvoyance, a world wherein there is no longer any more space for the truth.

Notes

1. S. Kierkegaard, *Af en endnu Levendes Papirer*. Udgivet mod hans Villie af S. Kierkegaard, København, Bianco Lunos Forlag 1838.
2. H. C. Andersen, *Kun en Spillemand*, Det danske Sprog- og Litteraturselskab 1988, pp. 30-31.
3. *Only a Fiddler*. New York, 1876 (p. 26).
4. As previously cited, p. 82.
5. *Only a Fiddler*. New York, 1876 (p. 85).
6. Compare H.C. Andersen, "Lygtemændene er i Byen, sagde Mosekonen" (1865), taken from *H. C. Andersens Eventyr*, critical edition by Erik Dal and Erling Nielsen, Det Danske Sprog- og Litteraturselskab, volumes 1-7 1963-70, volume IV, pp. 183-194.
7. Compare H.C. Andersen "Psychen" (1861) taken from *Eventyr...* as previously cited, volume IV, pp. 166-176.
8. A. Rimbaud, *Lettre à Paul Demeny* (1871) from M. Eigeldinger, *La Voyance avant Rimbaud*, Librairie Droz, Genève, Librairie Minard, Paris 1975, p. 137.
9. H.C. Andersen, "Psychen" ... as cited, p. 170.
10. Hersholt, vol 1, p. 107.
11. Compare as previously cited, p. 172.
12. As previously cited, p. 170.
13. http://www.andersen.sdu.dk/vaerk/hersholt/ThePsyche_e.html
14. H.C. Andersen, "Nattergalen" (1843) taken from *Eventyr* ...as previoulys cited, volume II, p. 19.
15. H.C. Andersen, "Skyggen" (1847) taken from *Eventyr* ...as previously cited, volume II, p. 134

16. http://www.andersen.sdu.dk/vaerk/hersholt/TheShadow_e.html
17. As previously cited, page 135.
18. http://www.andersen.sdu.dk/vaerk/hersholt/TheShadow_e.html
19. C. Baudelaire, *Hymne à la Beauté* in *I fiori del male,* Introduction by E. Auerbach, Milano, Feltrinelli, 1991, verses 19-22, p. 44.
20. H.C. Andersen, "Hvad man kan hitte paa" (1869), taken from *Eventyr...* as cited, volume V, p. 109.
21. http://www.andersen.sdu.dk/vaerk/hersholt/WhatOneCanInvent_e.html
22. As previously cited, p. 110.
23. http://www.andersen.sdu.dk/vaerk/hersholt/WhatOneCanInvent_e.html
24. Ibidem.
25. Ibidem.
26. http://www.andersen.sdu.dk/vaerk/hersholt/WhatOneCanInvent_e.html
27. H.C. Andersen "Lygtemændene"... as previously cited, p. 193.
28. As previously cited, p. 191
29. http://www.andersen.sdu.dk/vaerk/hersholt/TheWillOTheWispsAreInTown_e.html

The Queen and I

Erik M. Christensen

"Sneedronningen", "The Snow Queen. A Fairy Tale in Seven Stories", in its first printing dated 1845, was to be had at winter solstice 1844, December 22, at your booksellers' in Copenhagen and bound with "Grantræet", "The Fir-tree". Together, they were Andersen's *Nye Eventyr. Første Bind. Anden Samling* (1845). – "The Snow Queen" has since been called "Andersen's greatest story". I am afraid I do not like it much. "The Fir-tree", that reminder of perishableness, is less dated and more decent fun.

Apart from the way I read "The Snow Queen", and wrote about it in 1999, from that year I shall call as a witness for the defense: the Queen of Denmark, Her Majesty Margrethe II. From our year 2005 I call an English lady, a critic, and – assisting her – a very famous American gentleman, being a scholar and a critic, and finally a couple of young geniuses, authors and theatre people from Copenhagen.

In great art nothing is accidental, everything counts and the smallest detail may one day change your life. In "The Snow Queen" it is only one billionth of an artful mirror, or even less, says our storyteller, and it almost kills the boy. "The Snow Queen" is, however, like much of Andersen's work, about the biggest questions of all, viz. what sort of world are we living in and what can we do about it? "See saa!" begins "The Snow Queen": "Look now!". In Danish "see saa!" is a rather modest expression, in spoken language it almost always means something like "now then" or "all right" or "there". In writing it may, of course, mean just that, but nothing prevents the reader from putting particular stress on the two words "see" and "saa!" meaning as much as: "now, everybody, please *do* take the trouble of taking a close look! this is important! attention! awareness! scrutinize! look!". And that is what the small expression could, and I think should, mean as the first words in "The Snow Queen": "See saa!", exclamation point! This is, you know, a fairy tale about a glass and what you may see and what you must realize. "Look now!" is therefore a requirement and an offer of a special sort, to be defined in a few words: "The Snow Queen" is Religious Drama!

Hans Christian Andersen's oeuvre is often "Religious Drama". "The Snow Queen. A Fairy Tale in Seven Stories", I see as a Black Comedy in Religious Drama in the shape of seven stories.

The late H.D.F. Kitto (1897-1982), who introduced the term in his famous *Form and Meaning in Drama. A Study of Six Greek Plays and of Hamlet* (1956), has the following short definition:

> [Religious Drama is] a form of drama in which the real focus is not the Tragic Hero but the divine background. [p. 231]

Accordingly, I suggest that neither the Snow Queen nor Gerda, nor Kay, nor "Old Grandmother" – Tragic and/or Comic Heroes – are the real focus in "The Snow Queen". The focus is the divine background and the world it willed.

In that world a boy is treated by a grown up, a heavenly beauty, to seducing kisses and warmth under her fur, in such a way that the adult reader must think of eroticism or sex, and the boy gets lost. A young girl is in many other ways repeatedly confronted with sex, talk of sex and allusions to sex, confrontations that she cannot possibly accept or understand. To my mind this is perverse, bordering on literary pederasty towards your own listening child, inducing a horror of sex, fear of life in the world as it is. – The first story in the tale makes it apparent that this is Religious Drama, i.e. a tale with its focus on the divine background, like e.g. "The Book of Job" in The Holy Bible or the Oresteia by Aeschulus in Kitto's reading. In "The Snow Queen" the Devil's great, distorting mirror is broken, disturbing our perception, and we know from St. Paul of such difficult glass (1 Corinthians 13.12). Much later, in her gravest crisis, Gerda repeats "The Lord's Prayer" (HCA 73; Matthew 6.9) and she is thereby saved from the onslaught of legions of killing snowflakes. The last story in "The Snow Queen" also seems to allude to Scripture. It lets us remember – if we know our Bible and St. Matthew – who and where we are, and where we may end, viz. in Hell (Matthew 18.1-10). As already mentioned, the first fairy tale in Andersen's second collection of *Nye Eventyr* is "The Fir-tree". It ends with well worn words of warning after the burning of the Christmas-tree: "All, all over! And so it is with every story!" (224). Now, "The Snow Queen" takes up that warning right after the opening words about seeing: "When we get to the end of the story we shall know more than we know now" (225), but that is an allusion to the end of your own life which is of course much more than a preceding fairy tale by Andersen, if you have ears to hear St. Paul once more:

> For now we see through a glass, darkly; but then face to face: now I know in part; but then shall I know even as also I am known. [1 Corinthians 13.12]

The Religious Drama of this fairy tale will let us know the divine background, the rules of the game, if we are touched by the tale; and vice versa: it is planned to touch us, if we know the rules that we are supposed to accept.

*

Among your conference papers you may find an essay, in Danish, on "The Snow Queen". It was originally published in Copenhagen in an anthology of essays on that particular fairy tale, edited by prizewinning Andersen authority Finn Barlby in 1999 and published the following year 2000. You have, however, for technical reasons received that essay copied from an anthology of mine, its German title is *Zurückbleiben*, printed in Berlin 2001. I consider that essay suitable as a starting point for our discussion, by and large a fair interpretation of Andersen's text – condensed and expressing what he himself might conceivably have been able to read into, or out of, "The Snow Queen" – and what he may thus have seen as the meaning of his tale. For the few of you who do not trust yourselves with a text in Danish I quote the concluding passage (p. 400-401) of that essay in translation:

> I have not discussed every word in this fairy tale, nor everything implied in it today or in 1845, but does "The Snow Queen" make sense and have a meaning as one whole text? Yes, I think it does.
>
> The meaning of "The Snow Queen. A Fairy Tale in Seven Stories" (1845) – understood as one whole text – is that the world, as created by Our Lord, is horrible. A normal human being may be able to stand it, to suffer exposure to life and world as they are, for some time if, and only if, raw reality is pasted over with fairy tales, but in the end our world is essentially as the flowers say. Each flower stands in the sun dreaming "its own fairy tale or story" (240), none other and no way out; and the child, our little Gerda, cannot take it:

> "I'm not a bit interested," said Gerda. "That's no story for me!"
> And with that she ran to the edge of the garden. [243]

To little Gerda it is given to live in a fairy tale, which lets her get what she, as a good girl, desires. She wants to stay fairy-tale-wise childish, evangelic in that sense. She pays the price asked for, and thus, as a grown up she does not enter the world, but stays with Old Grandmother in her rocking chair, and the roses in a big wooden box. The alternative to Gerda is the Robbergirl wearing the revolutionary cap on her head, having a horse between her legs "and pistols in front" (267). They both live in a fairy tale which believes that our world is in a fight between "the very Devil himself" (225) and "Our Lord [...] God and his angels" (227). Such a fight is well known in Christian belief, and in Christian belief "Our Lord" is the one who has made it all, and who knows what we humans deserve. When Gerda in the end asks the Robbergirl how their little helpers are doing now, she receives, as we all know, the message: "nonsense, that's what it is!" (267). That, however, does not shake Gerda and her Kay:

> And looking into each other's eyes, Kay and Gerda at once understood the old hymn:
>
> "Then seek your Saviour down below;
> For roses in the valleys grow!" [268]

Only, "the old hymn" is, as we have seen, a little modern piece of poetry after a model, and itself not older than the fairy tale. A fairy tale it is "The Snow Queen", from one end to the other:

> So there they both sat, grown up and yet children, children at heart; and it was summer – warm and blessed summer. [268]

Is this supposed to be happiness, as long as it may last? It is in order, I think that this fairy tale in its title is named after death in the story.

One cannot envy this couple, which must live in hiding from sex-as-a-sin and from death-by-rationality. The conclusion that I have just quoted rests on a close reading emphasizing the uncanny, quite pederastic interest pressed upon the normal reader's sensibility and resulting in a sort of complicity, perhaps even producing a guilty conscience, since sexual lust and rational interest are never explicit in "The Snow Queen" in an innocent or positive way. Some of you may remember your own smiling or your horrified reaction to one or the other of about 40 to 50 passages more or less reminding the grown up reader of sex, concerning, but not understood by Andersen's children:

It may be as distant as this:

> The peas hung down over the boxes, and the rose trees [...] it was rather like a wedding arch [...]. [228]

– or this:

> In the evening, when little Kay was back home and half undressed, he climbed on to the chairs by the window and peeped out of the little hole. [...] it was a woman [...] so pretty and so delicate [...]. [229]

> [...] he even used to tease little Gerda, who loved him with all her heart. [231]

– or like this:

> The Snow Queen kissed Kay once more, and by this time he had forgotten little Gerda and Granny and everyone at home.
> "That's the last kiss you get!" she said. "Or I'll kiss you to death!" [233]

> "I'm going to put on my new red shoes," she said one morning; "the ones Kay has never seen." [234]

– or this:

> [...] she slept there and dreamt as beautifully as a queen on her wedding day. [238]

> And Gerda put her arms around it, and kissing the roses thought of the lovely roses at home, and with them of little Kay. [238]

– or even this:

The Hindu woman stands in her long scarlet mantle on the bonfire, the flames leaping up around her and around her dead husband. But the Hindu woman's thoughts are on the living person who stands there in the crowd, the man whose eyes burn hotter than the flames which soon will burn her body to ashes. [240]

How softly her silken robe rustles! "Will he never come?" she says. [240]

– or this:

Are the dancing girls asleep, or are they dead? The scent of flowers tells that they are dead, and now the bells are ringing for them! [241]

"I can see myself! I can see myself!" said the narcissus. "Oh, oh, how I smell! ... [...]. Leg up! See how she holds herself on one stalk. I can see myself! I can see myself!" [242f]

Oh, how Gerda's heart throbbed with fear and longing. It was as though she was about to do something wrong, while all she wanted to know was whether it was little Kay. [248]

"They come and fetch the noble people's thoughts out hunting; that's a good thing, for then they're [original: you are better] able to see them in bed. [...]" [249]

Bending aside one of the red leaves, she saw a brown neck. Yes, it was Kay! [249]

The prince resembled him only in the neck, [...]. [250]

– or this:

And the prince got up from his bed and allowed Gerda to sleep in it; it was the most he could do. [250]

"She shall play with me," said the little robber girl. "She shall give me her muff and her pretty dress, and sleep in my bed with me!" [254]

The little robber girl was the same size as Gerda, but stronger, more broad-shouldered, and dark-skinned. [254]

And drying Gerda's eyes, she put both her hands into the fine muff, which was so soft and so warm. [254]

"You shall sleep here tonight with me and all my little pets," said the robber girl. [255]

[...] seizing one of the nearest and holding it by the legs and shaking it as it flapped its wings. "Kiss it!" she cried, slapping Gerda in the face with it. [255]

Every night I tickle his neck with this sharp knife of mine; that frightens him! [255]

And drawing a long knife out of a crack in the wall [...] the robber girl laughed and pulled Gerda into bed with her. [255]

"Are you taking the knife to bed?" asked Gerda, looking at it rather nervously.
"I always sleep with a knife!" said the little robber girl. [255]

– or this:

The little robber girl put her arm round Gerda's neck, and, holding the knife in her other hand, fell into a loud sleep. [255]

"Lie still there!" said the robber girl. "Or you'll get the knife in your tummy!" [257]

The robber girl lifted little Gerda up, and was careful to tie her fast and even give her a little cushion to sit on. "You'll be all right," she said. "There are your furry boots, for it's going to be cold. But I'm keeping the muff; it's far too nice! [...]." [258]

Inside, it was so sweltering hot that the Finn woman herself was almost naked [...]. She at once undid little Gerda's clothes, [...]. [259]

> There [the reindeer] put Gerda off and kissed her on the lips, while big, glistening tears rolled down the creature's cheeks. [261]
>
> [the Snow Queen] would say that she sat on the Mirror of Reason, and that this of all things was the best in the world. [262]
>
> She knew him at once and flung her arms round his neck, holding him tight and crying: "Kay! Dear little Kay! So now I've found you!" [264]
>
> And he held Gerda tight, while she cried and laughed for joy. [265]

– or this:

> Then Gerda kissed his cheeks and they became rosy; she kissed his eyes and they shone like hers; she kissed his hands and feet and he was well and strong. [265]
>
> [the reindeer] had with it another, young reindeer whose udder was full, and it gave the little ones warm milk and kissed them on the lips. [265]
>
> Then they carried Kay and Gerda first to the Finn woman's, where they warmed themselves in the hot room [...]. [265]

– ending like this:

> But as they walked in at the door they felt that they had become grown-up people. The roses from the gutter were blooming inside the open windows, and there stood the little stools; and Kay and Gerda sat down on their own and held each other by the hand. Like a bad dream, they had forgotten [...]. [268]

*

We almost know it by heart, and obviously, in "The Snow Queen" it is of the greatest importance what a female is sitting on: a bonfire, a strong stalk, a costly pearl, a soft cushion, a live horse, a cold mirror, or a child's little stool.

I do not think that the proposed reading of the tale, as Black Comedy of sex and ratio in Religious Drama, is due only to my own very personal and perverse fantasy. At another time and place, such as Andersen's own, where such a reading could not have been discussed, however, one might have thought of one self, perhaps as slightly perverse or worse, especially when as a child you were half understanding the hints. But today?

The Times Literary Supplement, May 20, 2005, on Andersen, subtitles its title essay by Dinah Birch: " – and other perverse fantasies of sorrow", and Dinah Birch writes:

> The ruthless Snow Queen, in Andersen's greatest story, enthrals Kay, but spares the kiss that would kill him. In a rare concession to optimism, Andersen allows her inhuman curse to be lifted by Gerda's warmth and loyalty. Yet Gerda, like the mermaid, suffers for her love, and the story's final happiness has an unearthly quality [...] an imagined paradise.
>
> [...] In shaping these emotions into his uncompromisingly dark stories, Hans Christian Andersen added a new dimension to the scope of fiction.

Emeritus professor Harold Bloom of Yale University is even more outspoken. In *The Wall Street Journal*, April 20, 2005, he says:

> Sexual frustration is Andersen's pervasive though hidden obsession, embodied in his withches and icy temptresses, and in his androgynous princes. [...] Andersen's universe is totally vitalistic, but more malign than not. [...] Andersenian day-dreams, being largely free of history and nature, frequently are cruel, even sadistic, perhaps because of androgynous drives.

In an illustrated Danish edition of "The Snow Queen" from the same year as the first publication of my essay on that fairy tale you may find the perfect picture of Dinah Birch's "perverse fantasies" and Harold Bloom's idea of the cruel, even sadistic Andersenian daydreams because of perhaps androgynous drives. It appears on page 40 of that lavishly illustrated *Sneedronningen. Et eventyr af H. C. Andersen* (2000), illustrated by the Queen of Denmark.

Look at the hands and at the knife! This knife is apparently not *held*, it is simply *coming out* of those clothes. Not stuck into, but protruding. By the strength of this single illustration alone does one dare to say that Her Majesty may have seen, what I have called Black sexual Comedy in the text, or perhaps even what professor Harold Bloom in Wall Street says is the cruel, even *sadistic* Andersenian daydreams because of *androgynous* drives?

All the illustrations in the book are papercuttings, so-called "assemblages" or better "découpages", which is the art of decorating something with cutouts of paper, linoleum, plastic, or other flat material over which varnish or lacquer is applied. The artist here at work is H. M. Queen Margrethe II of Denmark. Her Majesty writes in a short foreword as follows (my translation):

> During the winter of 1999, as we were finishing the film "The Snow Queen", we realized that it would be interesting to publish Hans Christian Andersens fairy tale "The Snow Queen" complete, illustrated by the découpage plates from which the film is created.

> The universe of fantastic pictures that Hans Christian Andersen invented in words I have tried to make visible. I hope that others may enjoy taking part in the dream. [5]

The Queen's filmed edition of "The Snow Queen" told as digital theatre is available to us on one dvd, which is produced by JJ Film, Copenhagen (2000). It has been broadcast by the Danish television station TV2 five years ago and again this year on Andersen's birthday. This dvd may still be ordered from any bookstore at abt. DKK 250. The dvd has two different films in it: (1) The filmed digital theatre, i.e. découpages with a couple of actors (Gerda, Kay, Grandmother, Robbergirl) and a text read by Her Majesty herself, 27 minutes, and (2) A film about the production, the planning, the discussion, the filming of the découpages and the actors and the Queen reading, 26 minutes.

If you wish to see more of, and also read about, Queen Margrethe's artful découpages, – practiced in the footsteps of, among others, Hans Christian Andersen himself – there is an English and a Danish edition of Karen Blixen, *Seven Gothic Tales / Syv fantastiske Fortællinger*. It has many découpages by the Queen and an afterword about them by Frans Lasson, Gyldendal 2002 (DKK 495). I have the book in Danish. Frans Lasson says:

> [...] Queen Margrethe's talent and professionalism as a collage-artist was made apparent to a greater audience by the eminent tv-film on Hans Christian Andersen's "The Snow Queen" [...]. [464, my translation]

Andersen's text has, however, been changed for that film. The more drastic – implicit and explicit – sexuality has been left out, perhaps with one exception. And the robber girl is no longer a drastic, revolutionary alternative, horseriding and with pistols. No other female than Gerda is sitting comfortably in the film. Even the robber girl is NOT sitting with her big knife in the position that we know from the illustration in *the book*. And of the forty to fifty more or less suggestive passages that I have mentioned, only six – I think – are read in the film. As the context is changed they all seem harmless. The film is neat, and the girl Gerda of the film is in fact an attractive, pretty, greatlipped and wide-eyed girl with beautiful thick hair, gracious movements, breasts almost there (or hidden?), almost pubescent. In her person some of the sexuality left out of the film seems latent – perhaps you would call it perverse. The little robber girl is pretty as well, but does not act sexy in my eyes, perhaps she is just too masculine, which cannot be said of Kay, I think. I have done my best, and you should try for yourselves. I have noticed only one short moment of an outspoken grown-up erotic interest in the film. That is when little Gerda is dressed up by the princess, and right behind Gerda a découpé, décolleté, swelling Pre-Raphaelite bosom appears as a memento of what may one day be the case in and out of little Gerda's clothes.

In any case, Her Majesty's film, in contrast to her book, remains Andersen expurgated.

*

We are almost through now. In the media room of our conference you should see the film and then ask to hear a "Radio-satire-musical-serial", eighty minutes in Danish, called *Snedronningen,* recorded as it was broadcast in eight early morning installments on Danish radio P3 at Easter 2005. It is published on one cd by SONY and Danmarks Radio. The price in any bookstore is about DKK 150.

It is not relevant for us, now, to have a complete knowledge of the contents and meaning of this most Danish contemporary work of art, where the Snow Queen – and she is not alone – is heard to practice seduction on television, behind the tv-glass, a media queen. Suffice it to say that Kai – provoked by the Snow Queen behind the glass of the tv-screen – leaves Gerda in the beginning because *she,* Gerda, is not prepared nor willing to have sex before marriage. She finds it great to wait. He, Kai, doesn't, but in the end she gives in and they live happily ever after, together, as we are told, because neither has had sex with any other person than just Gerda, respectively Kai, and they consequently are unable to compare the experience and realize how miserable their sexlife honestly is.

Between the beginning and the end of that musical of rock, rap and romance we enjoy hilariously modernized versions of Andersen, at times a hundred miles from the poet, and at times a parody perhaps destined to live its own life forever, just like that famous Norwegian-Danish parody on bad tragedy *Kierlighed uden Strømper* (*Love without Stockings. A Tragedy in Five Parts)* by Johan Herman Wessel, as it survives from 1772 to this present day at the Royal Theatre in Copenhagen, and in print, one great laugh. Not one moment sentimental!

Do the Royal film's and the Royal book's different transforming loyalties to Andersen's text, and the Queen's découpages, does the Outspoken Popular Satire and Topical Parody, support my understanding of "The Snow Queen"? Do they correspond to my dislike of this particular fairy tale? Do the recent critics corroborate from abroad? I think so. – The British and the American critic generalize, for all of Andersen, what I have found in "The Snow Queen". The Danish satire and parody on "The Snow Queen" grotesquely magnifies the ugly aspect and laughing, makes it sympathetic. The Danish Queen in her film tries to minimize the same aspect and thereby ruins the meaning of it all, the horror, the tragedy and comedy of growing up where sex and ratio remain threats to Eternity.

Thank you!

References

H. C. Andersen, "Sneedronningen. Et Eventyr i syv Historier", in *H. C. Andersens Eventyr. Kritisk udgivet efter de originale Eventyrhefter med Varianter ved Erik Dal og Kommentar ved Erling Nielsen*, vols. I-VII, Hans Reitzels forlag, København 1963-1990. – "Sneedronningen" in vol. II (1964), p. 49-76. "Kommentar efter forarbejder ved Erling Nielsen udarbejdet af Flemming Hovmand" in vol. VII (1990), pp. 91-98. – In this paper quoted as HCA.

Hans Christian Andersen, *Fairy Tales. Translated by Reginald Spink. With Illustrations by W. Heath Robinson,* Everyman's Library. Alfred A. Knopf, New York & Toronto 1992. – The almost exclusive use of this translation (from 1906) throughout my paper is not problematic, as far as the present analysis is concerned.

Finn Barlby (ed.), *Det (h)vide spejl. Analyser af H. C. Andersens "Sneedronningen",* Dråben, København 2000.

Dinah Birch, "The Poker inside him. Snowmen, ducklings – and other perverse fantasies of sorrow", *The Times Literary Supplement,* London, May 20, 2005, pp. 3-4.

Karen Blixen, *Syv fantastiske Fortællinger. Med découpager af Dronning Margrethe II. Billedvalg og efterskrift af Frans Lasson,* Gyldendal, København 2002.

Karen Blixen, *Seven Gothic Tales. With découpages by Queen Margrethe II. Selection and Afterword by Frans Lasson,* Gyldendal, Copenhagen 2002.

Harold Bloom, "Great Dane", *The Wall Street Journal,* New York, April 20, 2005.

Erik M. Christensen, "Een på brillen", in Finn Barlby (see above), pp. 35-53, with a list of errata. – Corrected reprint, quoted here, in Erik M. Christensen, *Zurückbleiben. Tryk 1943-2001* (Hartmut Röhn, ed., *Berliner Beiträge zur Skandinavistik*, Humboldt-Universität zu Berlin, vol. 6), Berlin 2001, pp. 389-402.

The Holy Bible. King James Version, Ivy Books, New York 1991.

H. D. F. Kitto, *Form and Meaning in Drama. A Study of Six Greek Plays and of Hamlet,* Methuen & Co., London 1956.

Snedronningen. Et eventyr af H. C. Andersen fortalt som digitalt teater, dvd, JJ Film, København 2000. – With découpages by Queen Margrethe II. Transmitted by Danish TV2 (2000.04.14 and 2000.04.20, again 2005.04.02)

Snedronningen. Et eventyr af H. C. Andersen. Découpager af Hendes Majestæt Dronning Margrethe II, JJ Film and G. E. C. Gads Forlag, København 2000.

Snedronningen. Radiosatiremusicalføljeton. Manuscript: Nikolaj Peyk, Thomas Hartmann and Oliver Zahle, Sony BMG Music Entertainment Danmark & DR, SM 520218, København 2005. – Broadcast by Danmarks Radio P3 (2005.03.21-28).

Johan Herman Wessel, *Kierlighed uden Strømper. Et Sørge-Spil i Fem Optog*, København 1772.

Andersen's Poems for and about Children

Hans Kuhn

Andersen published his first volume of poetry in 1830, followed in quick succession by three more, and already in 1833 there was a collected edition, which was revised and enlarged in 1846 and 1854. These poems fill 362 pages in the second edition of his Collected Works, followed by an almost 200-page supplement in 1879 of poems that had not appeared in book form before.

Considering this output, and considering how much the general public regard him as a writer primarily for children, it is something of a surprise that his poems for and about children are comparatively few in number, less than thirty. Some of these have become popular in Denmark, especially as songs, while the more narrative ones are less well known. Depending on who the (fictitious) speaker of a poem is, three groups can be distinguished:

(1) The poet/speaker is an observer describing a scene, and he often quotes the persons observed.
(2) The poet/speaker addresses a child in the second person.
(3) The poet writes role poems for a child (the speaker is a child).

The best-known in the first group is "Moderen med Barnet" [Mother and child] (XII 49[1]), first published in *Kjøbenhavnsposten* in August, 1829. It describes a mother outside a ramshackle little house holding her little boy while the sun is setting, a dog is barking, the swallows are chirping and the cat is irritated by a mosquito – a perfect idyll, and we are not surprised that the child dreams about angels when it falls asleep. But sentiment is kept at bay by humorous everyday-language touches: "Døren synker halvt i Knæ" [the door is half on its knee], "Solen synker – og saa vid're" [the sun sets, etcetera], and the mother gives the little boy a gentle beating "paa de søde Pusselanker" [on its sweet legs; *pusselanker* is a playful nursery word]. Gebauer's simple but charming melody assured the poem an enduring place in Danish song.

Hist, hvor Vej-en slår en Bugt, lig-ger der et Hus saa smukt.
Væg-ge-ne lidt skæ-ve staa, Ru-der-ne er gan-ske smaa

A "mother-and-child" poem with a drastic turn is "Tyveknegten" (XII 331), which appeared in November, 1829, in *Nyt Repertorium for Morskabslæsning*. Here it is not a child dreaming about angels but the mother seeing an angel in her little boy and phantasising about his future. But in the third stanza, the raven outside the window predicts a different outcome: "Din Engel bliver en Tyveknegt, / og vi skal Engelen spise" [your angel will turn into a thief, and we will eat up the angel] – namely, once he has ended on the gallows as a criminal. Schumann wrote music for Chamisso's translation in 1840; his title is "Muttertraum" [A mother's dream], which does not give away the unexpected end.

The picture of the thief hanging on the gallows must have followed the poet on his trips during the following two summers. The fourth of his eight "Billeder fra Jylland" [Pictures from Jutland] of 1830 is entitled "Drengen og Moderen paa Heden" [The boy and his mother on the heath] (XII 164), where a boy presses his mother for information about his father, whom he has never met, and he relates a dream where he saw his father under a rainbow, crowned, with a chain around his neck and waving to him. And now the mother comes out with the truth: The boy was born in Hungary, where his father was hanged and she escaped from prison; the ravens would have eaten his body long ago. Jutland, with its stretches of lonely heath and its wandering gypsies, must have struck Andersen as a likely background for such a story. And it turns up again, in a more concise form, the following year, when he returns from his first trip abroad, to Germany, and is travelling through a lonely, sandy stretch of Brandenburg. In the last chapter of his account of that trip, *Skyggebilleder af en Reise til Harzen*, he inserts a poem "Tre Dage i en Tyveknægts Liv" [Three days in a thief's life] (IX 120) where a thief, from his elevated position on the gallows, looks back on three decisive moments of his life: his father being hanged and his mother escaping with him, his girlfriend deceiving him, and he himself ending on the gallows.

A more idyllic picture first appeared in 1830 in Elmquist's periodical *Læsefrugter* (well known for providing a forum for Blicher's tales) under the title "Skizze efter Naturen" [a sketch from nature], later changed to "Studium", finally "Studie efter Naturen" (XII 98), stressing the pictorial element through the title. It describes the sun shining in a neighbour's small backyard, where for once neither the gooseberry bush nor the dungheap are visible because the family's bedding is being aired, and the children are lying on top and falling asleep with their sandwiches, the butter melting in the sun and the rooster crowing. It is not strictly a poem about children, they only figure prominently in a picture reminiscent of genre painting. Carl Nielsen wrote music for it in 1916; it is not one of his better-known songs.

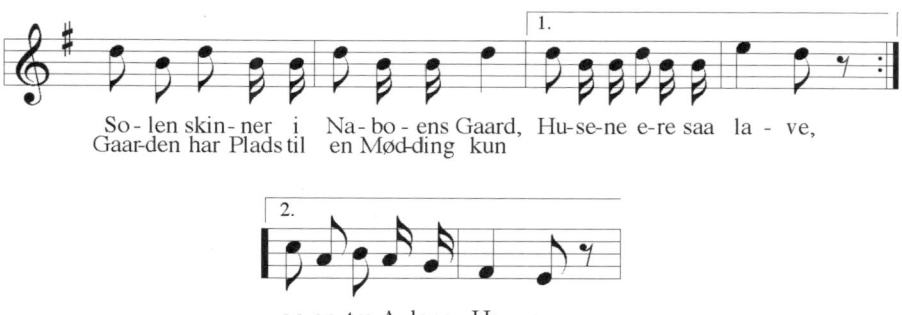

While, in this poem, we are invited to smile, we are meant to be moved to pity, if not tears, in two longer poems of a narrative nature, "Barnet ved Kirken" [The child near the church] (XII 60), first published in a New Year's miscellany for 1832, and "Den lille Pige i Asylet" [The little girl in the orphanage/day-care centre] (XII 214), which appeared, together with an illustration, in the journal *Ny Portefeuille* in January, 1843. With increased mobility and industrialisation, poverty became more visible, was debated as 'the social question' and alleviated by private and public initiatives. Hence, 19th century literature abounds with depictions of scenes of struggling individuals or families, none more touching than where children were the victims. "The child near the church" is a wintery midnight scene; a priest returning home finds a child from a family where the father and all possessions have been taken away to pay for debt and where the rest of the family are starving. The child must have heard of desperate people signing away their souls to the devil; so, as God has not helped them so far, it wants to sign away its soul to God in order to activate Him. This sort of childish naiveté was another touch often found in

19th century literature. The priest's concluding words give us reason to believe that the family will be helped.

"The little girl in the orphange / day-care centre" is even more of a tearjerker – she is a four-year old that does not join the other children's games in the intervals between knitting. An unidentified person asks her what the matter is, and now we hear the gruesome story: Both parents were sick; a neighbour put her to sleep in her parents' bed – probably the only one in the house; she dreams about flying through heaven with her parents and then finding herself in a forest with large talking flowers that play with her, but when she wakes up in the morning, she realises that both her parents are dead. Now she waits for the neighbour to pick her up again – the other children are blissfully unaware of her situation.

Another example of 19th century delight in children's naiveté is "Lille Lise ved Brønden" [Little Lisa at the well] (XII 300), first published in April, 1830, in *Nyt Repertorium for Moerskabslæsning*. Another four-year old girl, Lise, stands at the well, where she, according to her mother, came from and from where she recently got a little brother. In the second and third stanzas she wonders whether or not to believe her big sister, who claims that the stork brings the children. But no, she prefers the well origin – the more so as now she can see a little girl just like her looking up from the bottom of the well (her reflexion) – if she only could get one instead of "min dumme Dukke her!" [my silly doll here]. So, the bulk of the text belongs to the third group, where a child is the speaker. Bodil Heister wrote music for this poem in the 20th century, surprisingly in a minor key.

TætvedHuset Brøndenstaar, lil-le Li-se til den gaar,
stir-rer tan-ke-fuld der-ned,

thi hun af sin Mo-der veed, at man her fra Brøndens Vand

These are period pieces, but also expressions of Andersen's sentimentality and his fondness of little girls as vessels of purity and simplicity, as we often find them in his tales. That is also the tenor of a little quatrain from 1854, "Under en ung afdød Piges Portrait" [Under the portrait of a girl who died young] (XII 295), nr. 55 of "Fem og tredsindstyve Smaavers" [65 miniatures]. In the depth of her eyes the poet sees a soul so pure, so full of love that there is no regret about her death "i Haabets unge Aar" [in the youth of hope] because she went "fra Hjertets Hjem ind i Guds Herlighed" [from the home of the heart right into God's glory] – a happy ending in Andersen's books.

Finally, I should mention the Christmas hymn "Barn Jesus i en Krybbe laae" [Baby Jesus was lying in a manger] (IX 63), first printed in the December part of *Aarets tolv Maaneder* [The twelve months of the year] in 1832; in the dramatised form he adapted in *Fire Aarstider* [Four seasons], Andersen has 'poor children in the street' singing it. The first stanza describes the Christ child in the manger, with an ox kissing its foot, and the second stanza celebrates what this means for mankind; it ends "Til Barnet vil vi træde ind / og blive Børn i Sjæl og Sind" [let us step in to meet the child and become children in soul and mind]. Again, a children's poem charmingly composed by Gebauer, later in a choir setting by Henrik Rung, by Gade 1859 in *Børnenes Jul* [The children's Christmas], and later for voice and piano accompaniment by Nebelong. Strangely enough, it only entered the Church's official hymn book in 2002, with Gade's melody.

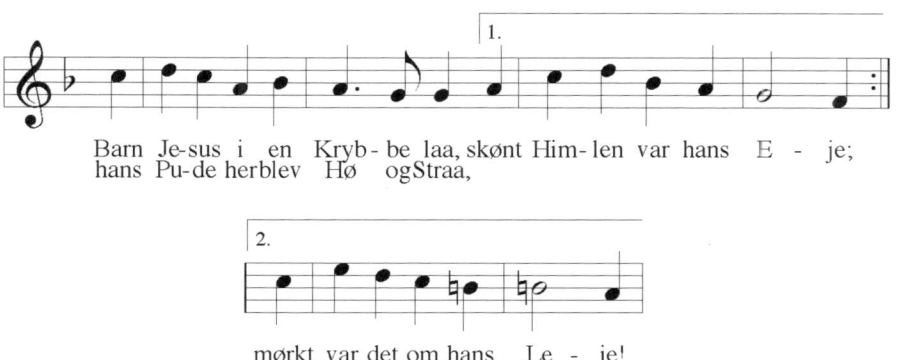

There is another part of *Aarets tolv Maaneder*, in the February section, which in the 1854 edition of his poetry appeared with the title "Herregaarden og Børnene" [The manor house and the children] (XI 143). It starts with a lengthy description of a manor house in winter and of its portrait gallery and then pictures two small children, a girl and a boy, in their bedroom, unable to sleep with excitement because the next day, they will for the first time visit a town or city. When the morning comes, they break into a song in a different metre, "Ud i Verden! rask afsted!" [into the wide world, off quickly] and it ends

"Verden er saa stor, saa stor! / Gud skee Lov, jeg lever!" [the world is so large, so large / Thank God that I'm alive!]. This simple poem, which belongs to our third group, the role poems for children, really throbs with Andersen's own excitement of travelling "nu paa Land og nu paa Sø" [now on land, now on water]. Then follows "Blomsterne under Sneen," where the flowers under the snow talk, then another short role poem for the children, "Børnene i Vognen" [The children in the carriage], where they notice that the dry leaves still sit on the trees in the middle of winter. This is explained with a legendary anecdote in the next section, "Løvet" [The foliage]. Then "Postkarlen" (the coachman] tells a local legend about how a heavy snowfall protected the cottage of a pious old man in war time. In the next poem, "Fuglene", the birds of the title talk to the travelling children, and the last word have the children themselves in "Børnene", greeting their arrival in the city, where they see a real cavalryman like the one their mother has drawn for them, and their excitement can be felt in the last two lines: "Her er Byen! søde Gud! / saadan seer vist Himlen ud!" [Here is the city! God almighty! that must be what heaven looks like!].

The second group is the one where the poet addresses a child. Many of Andersen's poems were occasional poems, in this case for children in families the poet knew well. The best-known of these is "Lille Viggo, vil Du ride Ranke?" [Little Viggo, will you ride on my knees?] (XII 191); it was published in October, 1832 in *Nyeste Repertorium for Moerskabslæsning*, when the boy thus addressed, Viggo Drewsen, whose mother was Ingeborg Collin, was just two years old. It is an eight-stanza poem, and much of what it says would have gone over the little boy's head – it is not 'realistic' in that sense; but it expresses what the poet sees and feels when he is with him. He promises to sing him to sleep and wonders whether Viggo once will sing when he, Andersen, is being put to eternal rest. This poem entered the Danish song repertoire with a melody by Paulli. When, nineteen years later, Andersen took Viggo along on a trip to Germany, he could tell people he met that his companion was the Viggo of "Lille Viggo …".

Dreng! Barn jeg er med dig i Sjæl og Tan-ke;

Viggo was a grandson of Andersen's protector Jonas Collin; Rigmor, in a poem thus entitled (XII 192), was a great-granddaughter, Rigmor Stampe, and she lived in Nysø, one of the manor houses the poet visited frequently; he was the girl's godfather. She was three at the time the poem was written, in 1853; it was published the following year. The girl is not described as a little angel but "som en Fugl, og saa ellevild, / et dansk lille Barn med Italiens Ild" [like a bird and so elfin-wild, a little Danish child with Italian fire]; she is only friendly occasionally and is called spoiled, jinxed, strong-willed ("forkjælede, trollede, villiefulde"). Both in rhythm and in language, the inspiration for this personal portrait is a similar poem by Christian Winther called "Min Skat" [My treasure] in his 1839 collection *Sang og Sagn* [song and legend]; Andersen's "Hvor nysselig, kysselig, Du, Kjælegrisen!" [How sweet and kissable, you pet] is a loan from Winther's "Hun er nysselig / og kysselig / paa Mund, Haand og Arm". Winther's song attracted at least four composers; I'm not aware of any musical settings of "Rigmor".

Turns of phrase from lullabies and children's songs characterise the last section of the melancholy autumn poem "October" of 1831, which was incorporated in *Aarets tolv Maaneder* in 1832, with an appropriate separate metre, beginning "Spillemand, spil paa Strænge" [Minstrel, play on your strings] (XII 155). The tenor of the poem is "Hvo kan savne længe / Barnets simple Sang?" [Who can go without a child's simple song for any length of time]; the minstrel is told to bring the childhood songs back to the listener. "Ride, ride Ranke" follows immediately after the lines quoted; in the second stanza, we get "Ro, [ro,] til Fiskeskjær" [row to the fishing ground], in the third "Klappe, klappe Kage" [pat-a-cake, pat-a-cake], in the fourth and last one "Visselul mit Hjerte" [Lullaby my heart]. It ends on a life-denying note: "Bedst i Graven Vuggen staaer ... Der ei Barnet græder" [The best place for the cradle is the grave ... there's no crying of children *there*]. This part was sometimes printed as a separate poem and had music written for it; from the 20th century I know simple settings by Ole Heyde and Bodil Heister.

In a role poem for a dead child's parents from the mid-1850s, "Ved et Barns Død" [At the death of a child] (XII 296), the child is addressed both as remembered in its lively sweetness and as a lifeless body; it must have died shortly before Christmas, since this is now for them a time for weeping rather than for anticipating a child's joy: "Vi pynte Dig ei grønne Træer, / vi mindes Dig – og græde" [We don't decorate green trees for you; we remember you, and we weep].

The composer Hartmann was a lifelong friend of Andersen's, and so was his son-in-law, Niels W. Gade. Sophie Gade had two small children, and for her to sing the poet wrote "Min egen stærke Dreng, min fine Pige …" [My very own strong boy, my delicate girl] (XII 376), a two-stanza expression of a mother's love. The second stanza starts "Igjennem Øinene til Hjertebunden / man seer, som man kan ind i Himlen see" [One can see through its eyes to the bottom of the heart, as one can see into the sky/heaven] – a thought Andersen repeatedly expressed when writing about children. Tragically, Sophie Gade died shortly afterwards, only 24 years old. The poem was only published after Andersen's death.

Another emotionally intense mother's lullaby is "Agnetes Vuggesang" from Andersen's poetic play *Agnete og Havmanden*, 1833 (XI 524); it has acquired an independent life of its own with music first by Gade, with a slow rocking rhythm,

then by Heise, with a more folksong-like even rhythm,

and, finally, by Fini Henriques. Agnete, the protagonist of a well-known ballad, has married a merman. In the song, she describes her baby's future life: riding on a seahorse, seeing the whales pass like clouds, and sun and moon way above the water's surface. Who will be its mother once her eyes are closed? At this stage she does not know that her desire to return to the human world will be the cause of both her own and her children's death.

Continuing with a song that belonged to a play but was included by Andersen in his Collected Poems, I'll mention Pantalone's "Mo'erlille sidder med Briller paa" [Little Mother sits with her glasses on] (XII 100) from *Ravnen* [The Raven], his 1829 adaptation of a Gozzi play of magic which, with Hartmann's music, was staged for the Queen's birthday in 1832. In this song, a fairytale about a valiant prince freeing a beautiful girl from captivity with the trolls is being told, but at the same time the telling is being staged. Not only Mo'erlille, the storyteller, is being described in the song, but also the listening children, and their reactions are anticipated with "Uh, uh!", "Hu, hu!", and "Hu, ha!", and the dancing and feasting at the wedding in the end is described in terms familiar to young children, e.g. "Der leves saa fiint, der leves saa flot / Med røde Roser og Æblecompot" [and there, they live it up in style with red roses and an apple dessert]. This was years before Andersen published his first fairytales; but it creates a situation that was going to be the afterworld's archeypical image of Andersen as the good-natured, lively, humorous entertainer of children.

A poem Andersen wrote in 1845 for *Maanedsskrift for Børn* [Children's Monthly] (XII 247) became common property because it is a variation on a game enjoyed by grown-ups and children in all times, touching different parts of the child's body and naming them, e.g. each individual finger. Andersen takes up and characterises six features of the head: "Pandebeen, Øiesteen, Næsetip, Mundelip, Hageflip" [Forehead, eye, nose, mouth, chin] and, finally, "Dikkedik", which goes with tickling the child's neck. Here, Andersen starts fairly seriously – reason and intelligence are behind the forehead, through the eyes you can see straight to the heart – but gets increasingly playful: the nose is a horse for spectacles, he snatches a kiss from the child's mouth, and on the chin and neck he looks for a "Lux", a little rascal, and catches him at last. A congenial melody by Gebauer helped this charming poem spreading.

Pan-de-ben!   Godt det gror!   Bag ved det For - stan-den bor. Den vil læ-se, den vil

læ-re, brin-ge dig i Agt og Æ - re,

In a poem entitled "Til den lille Marie" [To little Mary] (XII 417), published after his death, he addresses a girl not yet one year old and pretends that she and he, who is approaching the end of his life, are engaged; the contrast is stressed in "du yndige Barn, halvt Engel endnu! / Det bliver jeg snart, men Menneske Du", [you lovely child, still half an angel; I will soon be that, but you will be a person], and the poem apparently was accompanied with the gift of a book that should later remind her of him. I am not sure who the girl in question was; if it was Maria Hartmann, the poet's prophecy was not fulfilled, for she died at the age of five.

The last poem Andersen wrote before his death was also addressed to a child in his circle, Charlotte Melchior, born in 1871, a granddaughter of Moritz and Dorothea Melchior, who were among his closest patrons and friends. It is called "I Foraaret i Kjøge" [Spring in Køge] (XII 418) which is where Charlotte's parents lived. It starts "En lille Lærke qviddrende kom, / henover Kjøge den sang" [A little lark arrived twittering, it sang all the way over Køge]; a hen in a chicken-pen thinks this shows conceit, considering that she herself can "klukke og Triller slaae" [cluck and do trills], and moreover, she is "en af de Kjøge-Høns, / man kan lave Suppe paa" [one of the Køge hens used for making soup] – which is more than the lark could claim. So, here we have once more the conceited utilitarian Philistine, seen in humourous contrast with the songbird as the embodiment of the poet, the artist, the musician, whose realm is the whole world and who sees it from way above.

As the last poem addressed to a child I have to list a lullaby "Sov og drøm, du Engel blid" [Sleep and dream, you gentle angel], published in *Nyt Repertorium for Moerskabslæsning* 1831. But it is, as Andersen himself indicated, not an original but adapted from Bellman's ditty for his own son, "Lilla Charles, sof sött i frid" [Little Charles, sleep sweetly in peace] from 1787, which soon spread widely. That Andersen spelled Bellman with -*nn* showed that he was more familiar with German than Swedish at that time. He published it in his his collected poems of 1833[2] but dropped it later, though it survived in some anthologies.

In my last group, where Andersen speaks through a child's mouth, I have seven poems. This is not to be taken realistically, as 'child-speak'; the poet speaks his own adult language but seeks to express the viewpoint and the feelings of a child. The best known of these is also one of his earliest poems, "Det døende Barn" [The dying child] (XII 6), written when he was still suffering at school under the harsh Rektor Meisling. He gave it to a young German he met at Helsingør, Ludolph Schley, who translated and published it in a German newspaper; then it was printed, with both the German and the Danish texts, in *Kjøbenhavnsposten* in September, 1827. Holst took it up in his reader two years later, and it quickly spread with a melody written by Rudolph Bay;

Later musical settings were by Emil Hartmann and Fini Henriques; here the latter:

The idea probably came from a poem by Ludwig Uhland, "Das Ständchen", where a sick child claims it can hear sweet sounds. The mother says: "I can't hear anything, nobody is serenading you." The child answers: "It is not earthly music," and the poem concludes: "Mich rufen Engel mit Gesang / o Mutter, gute Nacht!" [singing angels are calling me; good night, dear mother]. In Andersen's poem, the child speaks throughout; it asks the mother not to cry, as her tears are burning its cheek. In the second stanza, it describes sweet music and an angel scattering flowers and wonders whether it will grow wings, too. In the third stanza it resumes its plea that the mother should not cry, and it concludes "O, jeg er saa træt! maa Øjet lukke – / Moder, se! ... nu kysser Englen mig!" [I am so tired and have to close my eyes; look, Mother, now the angel gives me a kiss]. Some of this will be echoed in the tale "Historien om en Moder" and was the sort of stuff a 19th century readership simply lapped up, full of family-bondedness, intense sentiment and the spiritual comfort provided by a beyond populated by angels. No wonder Andersen's Danish, German and English publishers gave him *Historien om en Moder* printed in fifteen languages for his 70th birthday.

A childish expectation to grow wings also occurs in the poem "Asylsang" [Orphanage or day-care centre song] (XII 368) written in 1838 and set to music by Bay the following year. The tone and the imagery were those of Ingemann's *Morgensange for Børn* of 1837 immortalised by Weyse's congenial melodies, especially "Gud ske Tak og Lov" where the children mention the 'asylum' in which they found a home. Andersen's dactylic poem starts "Hør, Spurven derude" [Hear the sparrow out there]; the sparrow tells the children to come out of the school room and play, which they are only too happy to do, and they wish they could follow the bird up into the tree. In the second stanza, they wonder about growing wings and speculate that "om vi er fromme, / kan de vel komme" [if we are pious/good, they might well grow], and the conclusion combines Andersen's earthly and heavenly travelling itches: "flyve langt der i Verden ud, / flyve høiere op end Skyen, / op til Himmelen og Gud" [fly way out into the world, fly up higher than the clouds, up to heaven and God]: again, a combination of childish naiveté and pious hope. In this context, I might mention two occasional pieces written for the benefit of these children's shelters. The first is "Sang ved Indvielsen af Frederik den Sjettes Asyl den 3die Juni 1842" [Song at the inauguration of Frederick VI's asylum on 3/6/1842] (XII 116), where the children to be housed there are directly addressed from the second stanza onward. I have not found any music for it; maybe Henrik Rung provided it, who, a few months before, had written music for the poem "Gurre" ("Hvor Nilen vander Ægypternes Jord"), performed at a concert for the benefit of this very institution. The second was written for a benefit performance in 1844 and is entitled "Udenfor Asylet" [Outside the asylum] (XII 232). It starts by quoting an earlier Ingemann poem about a down-and-out wandering minstrel, "Spillemand spiller paa Strænge", and describes, in the second stanza, the plight of poor children who would suffer bitterly if it were not for the properly heated asylum where, to their parents' relief, they are protected from the winter cold.

The next four poems are much later and have less tearfulness and piousness and more humour. In *Folkekalender for Danmark* 1857 [Almanach for Denmark 1857] there was an anonymous one-stanza poem called "Min Dukke" [My doll] where a girl is telling her two dolls, a "Frøken" [Lady] and a "Cavaler" [Cavalier] to dance. He is very elegant with hat and gloves, white trousers and a blue frock-coat, but he also has "Liigtorn paa den store Taa" [a corn on his big toe]. In November 1871, the poem, now called "Sangen til Dukkerne", appeared, extended to three stanzas and with a narrative frame, in *Illustreret Børneblad* (XV 225). In the second stanza, a doll from the year before, "Gamle Lisemo'er" [Old Mother Lisa], joins the party. She has new hair (of flax) and has been given a facelift ("Panden vasket er med Smør" [the forehead has been washed with butter]). In the third stanza follows the dance instruction proper, and the dolls are told how wholesome it all is ("neie, dreie, snurre rundt, / det er overmaade sundt!" [curtsying, turning, whirling around, it is all extremely healthy]) and are in the last line rewarded with "I er søde alle Tre!" [you are sweet, the three of you]. Here, the make-believe is consistent and successful. The narrative frame tells us that the girl is three years old and called Amalie that her aunt Malle disapproves of the song, and that a student who tutors her brothers has written it and taught Amalie, – again, the artist who, with his imagination and his simplicity of heart, relates to children but is reproved by grown-ups set in their ways and views. The illustrations showed Amalie dancing with her doll, the student dancing with Amalie and her dolls, and the disapproving aunt Malle. This poem was given musical wings by Fini Henriques in 1907.

"Drengen og Hundehvalpen" [the boy and the puppy-dog] (XII 415) appeared a year later in the same publication, with an illustration by Lorenz Frølich, the outstanding Danish book illustrator of the 19th century. Poems accompanied by a woodcut or lithograph often appeared in miscellaneous publications of the time; often the poem was written to fit an illustration, and this was probably the case in this little quatrain. The boy tells the puppy that "en velopdragen lille Hund / skal følge med og holde Mund" [a well-brought-up puppy is to follow and keep quiet] because "Vi lege, at vi kjøre nu, / og Kudsk er jeg og Sporvogn Du!" [we play at driving, and I'm the coachman and you're the streetcar]. Most boys, like Andersen himself, are fascinated by the latest means of transport, so it is no wonder that tramways enter into literature through a child's voice.

In 1873 the publication tried to extend its market and called itself *Nordisk illustreret Børneblad*. In the February 1875 issue, there was a suitable winter poem by Andersen, "Lille Svends Udtalelse om Veirliget" [Little Svend's pronouncement on the weather] (XII 399). It starts "Det er et løierligt Veir, vi har!" [What an odd weather we've got], and then goes on to describe how frost and thaw, snow and rain and clear weather follow each other in quick succession, old people fall on the icy streets, and he is off with his skates, obviously enjoying it all; "falder jeg – saa staaer jeg op igjen!" [if I fall, I'll get up again]. The Collected Poems, unfortunately, don't show the illustration that went with it.

The sixth poem of this group appeared a month later, in *Illustreret Tidende*, and is called "Et Barns Skriftemaal" [A child's confession] (XII 395). Here a boy, in a letter to his mother, gives an account of how he is doing at school in his different subjects: arithmetics, Danish, history, religion, geography. He does not much enjoy stuffing his head with all these things and wishes he could learn them by seeing the world instead: "Helst gad jeg være Storkefa'er, / han kan til Nilen drage, / og naar saa Alting seet han har, / Han komme kan tilbage" [If only I could be father stork, he can travel to the Nile, and when he has seen it all, he can return]. The poem is a recollection of Andersen's own suffering at school, now seen with a mature man's humour, and of his insatiable thirst for seeing the world. No wonder his favourite bird is here the symbol of his *Fernweh* as it is elsewhere in his work, notably in the wonderful poem already mentioned, "Hvor Nilen vander Ægypternes Jord". In our time, Ole Heyde has given "Et Barns Skriftemaal" a suitable simple melody, the relentless march of quavers expressing the feeling of being regimented, the minor key indicating how unpleasant it all was, yet not denying the latent humourousness of the situation as seen from a mature person's viewpoint.

Finally, I will mention a role poem for children in name rather than essence. It was printed in *Børne-Tidende* in January, 1866, and later incorporated in the travel account *Et Besøg i Portugal 1866* [A visit to Portugal in 1866] (VIII 553). It is a prayer in two stanzas, where God in the last line of the first one is addressed as "du Barnets store Ven" [you great friend of children]; before that, God is invoked as "eternal mystery", 'light for my intelligence', 'love and grace' and the source of all life. But the second stanza takes up the theme of Andersen's few other hymns, "Som Bladet der fra Træet falder" [As the leaf that falls from the tree] from 1853 and "Jeg har en Angst som aldrig før" [I feel an anguish as never before] from 1864, namely the terrifying thought of death and a prayer for God's assistance at that crucial moment. The speaker, plausibly the aging poet himself rather than a child, asks for his belief in God to be strengthened "i Angstens Stund" [in the moment of anguish] "og i den allersidste / kys mig med Fadermund" [and in the very last moment kiss me with a father's lips] – in that situation, even the grown-up person is a child again that needs a father's reinsurance and affection. The hymn melody suggested for it is one bestknown from Bach's St. Matthew's Passion, "O Haupt voll Blut und Wunden", in Denmark as the tune of another Gerhardt hymn, "Befal du dine Veje".

In Andersen's poems for and about children we meet the same range of moods as we do in the tales: the fancyful, the sentimental, the didactic, the religious, the clash between the trivial and the poetic, between innocence and experience. Increasingly, he moves from the clichés of his time to an unpredictable, puckish humour, which goes well with the way children react to a world which for them is still full of surprises.

Notes

1. Page references to *Samlede Skrifter*, Anden Udgave, 1876-80.
2. *Samlede Digte*, 46

Death and the Child

Johan de Mylius

Considering the fact that Hans Christian Andersen's fairy tales and stories from the first six years (1835-41) were by himself explicitly published as children's literature (*Eventyr, fortalte for Børn*, Fairy Tales, Told for Children) it is quite remarkable that most of these stories apparently aiming at amusement for the minors or even at bedtime reading deal with death as an important feature of the story or even find their climax in the death of the protagonist.

From 1835 Andersen published 6 volumes of *Fairy Tales, Told for Children*, comprising 19 stories. Out of that number of texts no less than 10 match the above-mentioned criteria. These stories are: "Little Ida's Flowers", "The Travelling Companion", "The Little Mermaid", "The Daisy", "The Steadfast Tin Soldier", "The Garden of Paradise", "The Storks", "Ole Lukøje", or "The Sandman", "The Rose-Elf" and the "Buck-Wheat". Death is also, but in a somewhat different way, a prominent feature of "The Tinder-Box", "Little Claus and Big Claus", and "The Wild Swans".

The contemporary reviews of the tales, in Denmark as well as abroad, did not find this heavy representation of death in any way objectionable in a context of children's literature. Only the soldier's unmotivated killing of the witch called for a few moralizing comments.[1]

Accordingly one may conclude that death as such was no taboo at Andersen's time. Literature, and even children's literature, was not meant to be silent about death. On the contrary it obviously had the mission to interpret death as an inevitable and integrated part of life. Only unmotivated killing conducted by the protagonist would, as was the case of the soldier in "The Tinder Box", provoke moralizing criticism.

Death as a theme or motif in Andersen's literary production is a very broad subject. In this paper I shall narrow the field of observation to a special feature, a motif of interest in connection with the general theme of this conference: Death as represented in a children's context.

As we all know, mortality among children was high in the centuries prior to the introduction of modern medicine and general hygiene. The death of a child was therefore in no way unusual and would not as such call for a theodicé or a justification of God. Parents losing a child would of course mourn deeply and need consolation, also religious consolation, but would not incline to turn into non-believers, being suddenly by this loss unable to find any meaning at all in life.

In poems as well as in fairy tales and stories – and even in some of his novels – Andersen has dealt with children in the context of death. Not only did his imagination again and again deal with this motif, but he was apparently fascinated by it.

The most well-known example, then and even today, is his poem "The Dying Child", written as early as 1826, when Andersen, only 21 years old, was still attending grammar school, at that time in Elsinore. Ludolph Schley, diplomat, merchant and translator, stayed in Elsinore that very same year, met Andersen, read the poem and translated it into German. Schley moved on to East-Prussia, and during the summer 1827 he published his translation in a newspaper in Libau. Andersen himself had the Danish original and the German translation published side by side on September 25, 1827 in A.P. Liunge's newspaper, *Kjøbenhavns-Posten* (The Copenhagen Post). In December 1827 the Danish original was printed in Johan Ludvig Heiberg's magazine *Kjøbenhavns flyvende Post* (The Flying Post of Copenhagen). A Swedish translation – again by Ludolph Schley – appeared January 1828 in *Scandinavisk Nytaarsgave for Aaret 1828* (Scandinavian New Year's Gift for the Year 1828). A Greenlandic translation made by a Danish missionary, Knud Kjer, appeared in *Kjøbenhavns-Posten* October 12, 1829. Andersen joked about it in a letter of June 15, 1830, to Edvard Collin, saying: "I have possibly won numerous Greenlandian hearts for my dying child".[2] Most amusing is the fact that on the occasion of Oehlenschläger's visit to Gothenburg in Sweden 1833, *Götheborgs Dagblad* (The Gothenburg Daily) on August 24 printed "The Dying Child" in a new Swedish translation and ascribed the poem to Oehlenschläger! The title was: "Det döende Barnet, efter Oehlenschläger" (The Dying Child, from Oehlenschläger).

No wonder that this poem, so instantly famous at home and abroad, can be found today on an American web site, there presented as "presumably by a Swedish author" and with a subtext saying: "Author unknown".[3] It has surpassed the fame of Andersen himself and lives a life of its own, completely independent of its author.

This American web site is launched by a mother who lost her child because it had caught meningitis. The local priest had given her the text for consolation, and it had meant so much to her in the process of mental healing that she would pass it on in this way to mothers in a similar situation.

Obviously "The Dying Child" as an immortal text worthy of mentioning in Harold Bloom's *The Western Canon* (1994)[4] has in its historical and present day reception a function of consolation for mothers losing a child.

But nothing indicates that this was a main purpose for young Andersen, when he conceived the poem in 1826.

Generally it is assumed that the poem was created out of Andersen's own despair considering his situation with the schoolmaster Simon Meisling, of whose household Andersen to his misfortune was a part.

But even this interpretation or rather explanation is less than plausible. Nothing in the poem indicates despair, at least not from the side of the child, the speaker, the ego of the poetic discourse. The poem illuminates the moment of death as a climax of intensity and light, far from the tears and the desperation of the mother, whose presence is only vaguely sensed through the child's monologue.

In a translation probably by Mary Howitt (published 1850) the poem goes like this in English, in traditional 4-lined verses in stead of Andersen's 8-liners, and therefore here in 6 stanzas instead of 3:

Mother, I'm tired, and I would fain be sleeping;
Let me repose upon thy bosom sick;
But promise me that thou wilt leave off weeping,
Because thy tears fall hot upon my cheek.

Here it is cold: the tempest raveth madly;
But in my dreams all is so wondrous bright;
I see the angel-children smiling gladly,
When from my weary eyes I shut out light.

Mother, one stands beside me now! and, listen!
Dost thou not hear the music's sweet accord?
See how his white wings beautifully glisten?
Surely those wings were given him by the Lord!
Green, gold, and red, are floating all around me;
They are the flowers the angel scattereth.

Should I have also wings while life has bound me?
Or, mother, are they given alone in death?

Why dost thou clasp me as if I were going?
Why dost thou press thy cheek so unto mine?
Thy cheek is hot, and yet thy tears are flowing!
I will, dear mother, will be always thine!

Do not sigh thus – it marreth my reposing;
But if thou weep, then I must weep with thee!
Ah, I am tired – my weary eyes are closing –
Look, mother, look! the angel kisseth me![5]

Instead of searching for biographical circumstances in order to explain the creation and the meaning of the text one should perhaps rather concentrate on the fact that Andersen's poem reveals a fascination with death, even an aesthetic fascination, a feature so characteristic of his lifelong dealing with the motif of death.

From that point of view one might find it more rewarding to search for a literary inspiration. And one would not have to search for long. That Andersen's poem might be conceived of as a parallel to Goethe's ballad "Erlkönig" has been pointed out before, but behind both another source should be considered, the German poet and author of the periodical, *Der Wandsbecker Bote*, Mathias Claudius (1740-1815).

A poem by Claudius is called "Der Tod und das Mädchen", known today perhaps only through Franz Schubert's "Lied" and his later string quartet titled "Der Tod und das Mädchen" (composed 1824-26). In the 20th century Schubert's string quartett inspired among others the Chilean exile-writer Ariel Dorfman to a stage-play, transformed into a film by Roman Polanski in 1994: *Death and the Maiden*.

Did Andersen know Claudius' poem, when he wrote "The Dying Child"? We don't know. He was familiar with Claudius and capable of quoting him, as can be seen from the opening chapter of his first travel book, *Shadow Pictures* (1831), where he describes a visit to the home town of the then deceased author, Wandsbeck.

Certainly Goethe must have known Claudius' poem, when he wrote "Erlkönig", because these two poems have a similar basic construction and idea: a dialogue between death and a child. I take it for granted that we all know Goethe's ballad, and I shall accordingly confine myself to quoting the probably not equally well-known poem by Claudius:

Das Mädchen:
Vorüber! Ach vorüber!
Geh wilder Knochenmann!
Ich bin noch jung, geh Lieber!
Und rühre mich nicht an,

Der Tod:
Gib deine Hand, du schön und zart Gebild!
Bin Freund, und komme nicht, zu strafen.
Sei Gutes Muts! ich bin nicht wild,
Sollst sanft in meinen Armen schlafen!

Not quite obscure, after all, is this poem, since the poem and Schubert's quartet together have inspired the Norwegian author Jan Fosse to a drama called "Dødsvariasjoner" (1992), staged in Germany under the title *Todesvariationen.*

The trick of Claudius' poem is the apparently friendly, soothing, even loving or sexual approach of Death to the terrified maiden. On one side this can be seen in connection with an expression used by Claudius in his *Wandsbecker Bote* (1775) concerning a traditional depiction of Death carrying a scythe: Freund Hein, Friend Death. On the other side the sexual undertone opens up for an interpretation in general terms of the male desire and the female anxiety aroused by the carnal approach. At least as these were seen traditionally in former centuries.

Returning to Andersen's poem, it is obviously different from both sources, Goethe's ballad and the poem by Claudius. Andersen's poem is literally speaking angelic, where the two others are diabolic. There is no dialogue in "The Dying Child" as there is in the others, no seduction and no horror or fear, neither on the side of the child, nor on the side of the reader.

But Andersen's poem is not just a sentimental, religious interpretation of the inevitable fact that a child might die, nor is it simply sugar-sweet Biedermeier or Victorianism.

More in the spirit of Biedermeier is a poem by the Lübecker poet Emmanuel Geibel (1815-84) with the same title as Andersen's poem, which may or may not be a coincidence. Geibel's "Das sterbende Kind" (*Gedichte* 1840), a short poem of two irregular stanzas, observes the moment of death from a position outside the situation, where life and death meet on a threshold:

> Wie doch so still dir am Herzen
> ruhet das Kind!
> Weiß nicht, wie Mutterschmerzen
> so herbe sind!
>
> Auf Stirn und Lippen und Wangen
> ist schon vergangen
> das süße Rot.
> Und dennoch heimlicherweise
> lächelt es leise.
> Leise küsset es der Tod!

Death and the child meet in a soft smile and a soft kiss. Key words are here "ruhet", "süße", "lächelt", "leise" (repeated).

Compared to both Geibel and to the previously mentioned German predecessors Andersen's poem "The Dying Child" has a different scope: Death is here conceived as a climax, an intense moment of light, a fulfilment, which leaves the grief of the mother behind, just like the tempest and the cold outside are surpassed and overcome by the all-embracing light and the kiss of the angel. The inner world, the vision has more reality than the seemingly factual world outside. To the inner eye Death is not just a friend, but a glorious reunion, the true meaning of life.

Elements from "The Dying Child" survive in a poem placed in chapter 13 of *Travel on Foot* (*Fodreise*, Cph. 1829, Andersen's official debut). Here Death invites the author to take a ride on his bus across the borderline of life and report to the readers from the land from which no wanderer has ever returned. Although tempted by the sensation of this proposal the author declines with thanks – he has another chapter of his book yet to write! But still Death makes him look around through St. Peter's glasses before taking a final decision, and there he catches the sight of a mother, "who died this night from an epidemic illness, and close to her sat her dear little boy, who followed her a few hours later. Full of longing she stretched her arms for him, still the sound of the child's pious consolation at her deathbed could be heard, where in the poor cabin he pressed his mother's hand with the flame of life in his eye and his heart".[6] And then comes the four-stanza poem, in which the child tries to console the mother and make her stop crying. Reality is more present and inevitable in this poem than in "The Dying Child", and since we know from the introduction that both mother and child are already dead, the attempt of the child to hold back the course of events is rendered in the ironic light of the disillusioned adult, only fascinated by the illusions of childhood, but not given to confuse them with reality.

After the poem the prose-text goes on like this:

> Thus was the consolation of the small one, until his shooting star as well shone in the nocturnal sky. O happy children's world with your joyful dreams – where the sky arches over us as the big, eternal Christmas-tree with all its sparkling candles, lit by the good God for rich and poor in his large crowd of children. But we grow older, we become more reasonable, then it is no more the sparkling Christmas-candles of Heaven; no, huge planets with – probably – pain and tears, misery and follies like it is on this earth.

The disillusioned approach to the combination of childhood and death is not an inherent feature of Andersen's treatment of the theme, but still the quotation from chapter 13 of *Travel on Foot* has to be considered, since it immediately leads our thoughts to a famous story written and published 1845: "The Little Match-Girl". Especially the picture of the heavenly Christmas-tree with its sparkling candles form a direct link from 1829 to 1845, from *Travel on Foot* to the death-scene of the match-seller.

The following year, 1830, Andersen was on a domestic travel to Jutland and Funen. In Jutland he only reached Viborg in Mid-Jutland and never saw the west coast. But since he had already read Heinrich Heine's "Nordseebilder" in his collection from 1827, *Buch der Lieder* (The Book of Songs), Andersen would compete with Heine in this field, also writing some poems about the North Sea – as seen from the west coast of Jutland. And so he did. One of these poems is called "Phantasie ved Vesterhavet" (Phantasy at the North Sea) – although it should rather be called "Phantasy about the North Sea"...

Close to the ending of this poem we find the following lines:

> – Nu fatter jeg først klart hvad Døden bringer
> Paa Cherub-Vinger!
> – Men døe? – ja det er underligt at tænke paa!
> Dog grumme lidt det Hele vi forstaae!

Det er saa stort og smukt hvad Døden skænker.
Ja, meget mer end nogen Digter tænker.
O, saae vi det kun klart med Aandens Blik,
Vi lige straks da ned i Graven gik.

(Now I clearly see, what Death brings
on his cherub's wings.
But die? Well, that is strange to consider.
So little do we understand it all.
What Death brings is so great and beautiful,
even more than any poet might imagine.
O, if only we were able to see it clearly with the spirit's eye,
we would immediately leap down into the grave).[7]

Andersen sent this poem together with some others from Jutland to his "maternal friend", the very religious Mrs. Signe Læssøe and asked for her opinion. In a letter of July 20, 1830, she answered, deeply concerned by Andersen's enthusiastic approach to death and advising him not to publish these lines of the poem. Andersen followed her advice and omitted them in the printed version in *Phantasier og Skizzer* (1831, Phantasies and Sketches). The Andersen-Center owns the original manuscript, from which the abovequoted lines have been added to the version printed in the edition of *Samlede digte* (Collected Poems) 2000/2005.

The main concern of "The Dying Child", describing the death of a child in affirmative terms, surfaces between 1829 and 1845 in two poems.

From 1836 is a small poem, discovered 1997, first published in a number of Danish newspapers and then printed in the above mentioned edition of *Collected Poems*, called "Til Frederiks Moder" ("To Frederik's Mother"). A boy of the poet Ingemann's acquaintance, and maybe also of Andersen's, Frederik de Klaumann, died in Sorø 1835 only 13 years old. Andersen's poem seems to be written immediately after his summer visit to Ingemann in Sorø, and is probably inspired not directly by the death of the child, but by a consoling poem written by Ingemann to the grieving mother. Presumably Ingemann has shown his poem to Andersen, and Andersen then has felt inspired to write a few poetical words on the same occasion.

Ingemann's poem has the title "Barnets Aand til Moderen" (The Child's Spirit to its Mother)[8] and is a long monologue of 8 stanzas spoken by the child from eternity to console the grieving mother, telling her that there is nothing to grieve for. Now, after the so-called death, true life is experienced by the child, who develops more and more: "Every moment I'm growing miraculously", it says in stanza 5.

Andersen's attempt to compete with Ingemann reveals itself as a much more traditional poem of consolation. In stanza 1 (out of three) Andersen writes: "Half a child yet and with the mind of a child/ he entered the joy of life".[9] And in the third stanza we read: "Now we know for certain/ the soul is immortal"[10] – meaning: since a soul, the dead child's soul, is now thinking of her, the mother, from beyond, we can know for a fact that there is an immortality, an eternal life after death.

Certainly not one of Andersen's best poems, and therefore fully understandable that he never printed it himself! But still a poem of a certain interest concerning our theme. Not as radical as Ingemann's poem, but in its view of life after death possibly inspired by a reading in Sorø of "The Child's Spirit to its Mother".

Another poem by Andersen, "Alfernes Blomster" (The Flowers of the Elves),[11] printed in *Portefeuillen for 1839*, but never reprinted by Andersen in any of his collections of poems, not even in the volumes 15 and 16 with poems (1854) in *Samlede Skrifter* (Andersen himself considered it a poem of low value, only written on request),[12] elaborates the idea of death and life after death as connected with happiness and not with grief. "The Flowers of the Elves" is a ballad. In the subtitle Andersen claims that it is a "Folkesagn", a folk tale, but it is not represented among J.M. Thiele's *Danske Folkesagn* (Danish Popular Legends).

The poem tells a story about a father and a mother losing a son and some years later also a daughter. Both were taken by the elves. The father is left alone, because also his wife dies. But one evening sitting outside his rural dwelling he sees in the dim moonlight a number of playful children among which his own two children bringing flowers to their mother's grave. He calls for his children and runs to the churchyard, but they are all gone. Only the flowers from the elves' land, mostly roses, are left on the grave.

The last stanza, then, is the voice of consolation from the hyacinths (hyacinths traditionally symbolized death, as we know it from "The Snow Queen"):

Fra Hyacinthens Klokker Trøsten klang:
"Der er saa stille og saa godt i Graven!"

> Og Roserne om Alfelandet sang:
> "Der dandse dine Børn i Blomsterhaven!
> Lad ikke Taaren væde meer din Kind,
> I Barnets Død er Solglands og ei Skygge.
> Det flyver fra sin Alfeverden ind
> Til Himlens Gud, til overjordisk Lykke!"
>
> (From the bells of the hyacinth the consolation sounded:
> "It is so quiet and magnificent in the grave!"
> And the roses sang about the elf-land:
> "There your children are dancing in the garden of flowers!
> Don't let the tear wet your cheek.
> In the death of the child there is sunshine and no shadow.
> It flies directly from its elf-world
> To God in Heaven, to celestial happiness").

This is the turning point of the poem, not so much because of the consolation itself, but because suddenly here the elves are not equalized with a deadly menace, but with childhood itself. The child dying passes from one elf-world into another. Consequently the death of a child is pure sunshine. There is no cause of grief!

This leads us to a brief survey of a number of Andersen-stories, most of them prominent titles in his production.

First of all "Ole Lukøie" (1841), or "The Sandman" or "Willie Winkie" in which the little boy, Hjalmar, in his last dream on Sunday night meets the dream-god's older brother, Death. Ole Lukøje says in Dulcken's version (in Dulcken's table of contents, and only there, the title is – quite meaninglessly – rendered as "Old Shut-Eye"):

> "I will show you my brother. His name, like mine, is Ole Luk-Oie, but he never comes to any one more than once; and he takes him, to whom he comes upon his horse, and tells him stories. He only knows two. One of these is so exceedingly beautiful that no one in the world can imagine it, and the other so horrible and dreadful that it cannot be described".
>
> And then Ole Luk-Oie lifted little Hjalmar up to the window, and said,
>
> "There you will see my brother, the other Ole Luk-Oie. They also call him Death! Do you see, he does not look so terrible as they make him in the picture-books, where he is only a skeleton. No, that is silver embroidery that he has on his coat; that is a

splendid husar's uniform; a mantle of black velvet flies behind him over the horse. See how he gallops along!"

And Hjalmar saw how this Ole Luk-Oie rode away, and took young people as well as old upon his horse. Some of them he put before him, and some behind; but he always asked first, "How stands it with the mark-book?" "Well", they all replied. "Yes, let me see it myself", he said. And then each one had to show him the book; and those who had "very well" and "remarkably well" written in their books, were placed in front of his horse, and a lovely story was told to them; while those who had "middling" or "tolerably well", had to sit up behind and hear a very terrible story indeed. They trembled and wept, and wanted to jump off the horse, but this they could not do, for they had all, as it were, grown fast to it.

"But Death is a most splendid Ole Luk-Oie", said Hjalmar. "I am not afraid of him!"

"Nor need you be", replied Ole Luk-Oie; "but see that you have a good mark-book!"[13]

There are obvious links in this description of Death and the relations between Hjalmar and Death back to Claudius and Goethe. The paradox in Andersen's text is that Hjalmar cheers the black rider, although he himself has a miserable writing in his copy-book, as we learn from "Monday"'s story, and in spite of the weeping children sitting behind Death on back of the big Ole Luk-Oie's horse. Biedermeier concepts like achievement and morality, "the mark-book", are introduced as the elements deciding bliss or misery. Acclaimed as they are by great-grandfather on the picture, previously very dissatisfied by Ole Lukøie confusing Hjalmar's ideas. He approves of the mark-book as a guideline to life and death – but the irony of the story is that Hjalmar has turned the picture against the wall. Then – what are great-grandfather's opinions really worth, when he cannot see what is going on?

A very popular story at least in the German speaking countries of Andersen's own time, famous also through numerous reproductions of Wilhelm von Kaulbach's illustration, "The Angel" (1843), is a post-mortem-story. An angel picks up a dead child and carries him to heaven, where he is given wings and joins the choir of praize.

Andersen introduces the story in generalizing terms like this – and for once I prefer Erik Haugaard's translation in the Penguin edition of *Complete Fairy Tales and Stories of Hans Andersen.*[14]

> "When a good child dies, an angel comes down from heaven and takes the dead child in his arms; then the angel spreads out his wings and flies with the child to visit all the places that the little one has loved: They pick a whole armful of flowers and bring them to God; in heaven, these flowers will bloom even more beautifully than they have on earth. God presses all the flowers to His heart; but the one that is dearest to Him, He gives a kiss, and then that flower can sing and join in the hosanna".
>
> This was what one of God's angels was telling to a dead child whom he was carrying up to heaven. The child heard it as though in a dream, while the angel flew with him above all the places where he had played and been happy [...].

The interesting thing about this story is, however, what happens during that flight from earth to heaven. That is the main part of the story, and there we find an Andersen not imagining heavenly joy, but faithful to his own experiences. Since the story in terms of genre is much more of a legend than of a fairy tale, it is remarkable that poverty, dirt and trash from the narrow streets of the big city are the environment from which the rise towards heaven takes its start.

Before carrying the dead child up to God the angel collects a withered and broken flower, lying in the street among the trash. On their way to heaven the angel tells the child the story of this flower, which once was the dearest and only joy of a sick boy. The boy died, and his flower was forgotten and finally thrown out of the window. And this sick boy is the angel.

Having told the story of the flower and the sick boy the angel says:

> "We shall take the poor dead flower along in our bouquet, for it has spread more happiness than the grandest flower in any royal garden".
>
> "But how do you know all this?" asked the child whom the angel was carrying up to heaven.
>
> "How do I know?" the angel said, and smiled. "I was myself that sick little boy who could not walk without crutches. Oh, I recognize my flower again!"
>
> The child opened his eyes as widely as he could and looked into the happy face of the angel. Just at that moment they flew into heaven, where all sorrows cease.[15]

Recognition – and the moment of "seeing" ("Schauen" in German), these are interconnected. Seeing is not only a physical thing, it is a sudden insight, a momentary but everlasting recognition, the moment of being face to face with God. The identity of the angel is revealed at a glance, and in that very moment they are in heaven.

Interesting also, how Heaven is organized. There God embraces the dead child and the flowers he and the angel have collected. A unification takes place, no one is excluded, all are joining the whole, also the poor and despised:

> God pressed all the flowers that they had given Him to His heart; but the dead wild flower He kissed and it gained a voice and could sing with the angels that flew around God, in ever widening circles out into infinity. All sang with equal bliss and fervour: those who had died when old and those who had come as children, and the little wild flower that had been thrown out into the trash in the dark and narrow lane.[16]

This is a picture close to so-called new-age pictorial imagination concerning eternity: Circles around circles widening into infinity, all centered around the divine, around God.

The dark and narrow lane, this place of social misery and despondency, reappears as the wintery cold and merciless setting for the last moments of a miserable life – in "The Little Match-Girl" (1845),[17] a story that takes its beginning in a street of some traffic and ends up in a corner between two houses, very much like the dark and narrow lane. This is how it starts:

> It was terribly cold. Snow was falling, and soon it would be quite dark; for it was the last day in the year – New Year's Eve. Along the street, in that same cold and dark, went a poor little girl in bare feet – well, yes, it's true, she had slippers on when she left home; but what was the good of that? They were great big slippers which her mother used to wear, so you can imagine the size of them; end they both came off when the little girl scurried across the road just as two carts went whizzing by at a fearful rate. One slipper was not to be found, and a boy ran off with the other, saying it would do for a cradle one day when he had children of his own.

The death of the little match-seller is presented in a double exposure: Seen from the outside there is darkness, hunger, poverty, misery and cold; seen from inside there is light, splendour and bliss in the rise towards Heaven. Body and soul, material and immaterial perspective:

> Never had Grannie looked so tall and beautiful. She took the little girl into her arms, and together they flew in joy and splendour, up, up, to where there was no cold, no hunger, no fear. They were with God.
> But in the cold early morning huddled between the two houses, sat the little girl with rosy cheeks and a smile on her lips, frozen to death on the last night of the old year. The New Year dawned on the little dead body leaning there with the matches, one lot of them nearly all used up. "She was trying to get warm", people said. Nobody knew what lovely things she had seen and in what glory she had gone with her old Grannie to the happiness of the New Year.[18]

This is the British Keigwin translation, published in Denmark in co-operation with the Hans Christian Andersen Museum in Odense. Erik Haugaard's Dano-American translation has the last paragraph slightly differently:

> And no one knew the sweet visions she had seen, or in what glory she and her grandmother had passed into a truly new year.[19]

Another Dano-American translation, that of Jean Hersholt, has this solution:

> No one imagined what beautiful things she had seen, and how happily she had gone with her old grandmother into the bright New Year.[20]

And Dulcken put it like this:

> No one imagined what a beautiful thing she had seen, and in what glory she had gone in with her grandmother to the New-Year's day.[21]

And finally, Madame de Chatelain:

> Nobody dreamed of the fine things she had seen, nor in what splendour she had entered upon the joys of the new year, together with her grandmother.[22]

Different translations, different interpretations,[23] the text by Erik Haugaard being more of an interpretation than a translation, but as it can be seen, even the expression "new year" can be rendered rather differently and thereby open a wide range of possibilities.

A vision it is, as Haugaard says, although without any literal background in Andersen's Danish text. And the point of the story is not merely the soothing perception of death as a joyful departure from the bitterness of life on earth, but the same point, as we have met in "The Dying Child": The moment of death is a climax, a moment of intensity surpassing any other possible experience, filled with light, a light descending from heaven, but at the same time growing out of the wish of the girl. A light more powerful than darkness and reality. The girl knows that her grandmother is only a vision and will be gone in the next moment, but still she begs her to take her with her – in spite of what she knows. One might here be tempted to introduce Søren Kierkegaard's concept of Faith as a parallel: Faith in spite of or even by virtue of the absurd.[24] But in Andersen's case still with a quite different note: not as a crucifixion of thought, of reflection, but being due to an experience exceeding what is generally accepted as reality.

The death of a child as seen by the adult, the parent, is the motif of "The Story of a Mother" (1847), as it was in Friedrich Rückert's "Kindertotenlieder" (written in the 1830's, published posthumously 1872 and set to music by Gustav Mahler 1905). Where Rückert's poems are desperate outbursts of a mourning parent – he himself had lost two children – Andersen has desperation balanced by a motherly love stronger than anything in the world, capable of any sacrifice whatsoever, and in the end stronger than death. The child is not really present in Andersen's text, which is in no way repeating "The Dying Child". It is a portrait of the mother, a myth more than a fairy tale. It is like carved in wood, naked and austere, far from Biedermeier sentimentality.

Here Death is not really terrifying. He is severe, but not without mercy and understanding. He is God's gardener and only fulfils his will. But still he permits the mother a choice.

The shocking point of the story is that the mother, given the possibility to have her child back, leaves it to Death to take it into "the unknown land". She might, if she were a female Søren Kierkegaard, have accepted the uncertainty of life, the jump into the bottomless ocean, having left it to God to carry her and her child. But facing the 50-50 possibility of a miserable life full of grief and suffering, she abandons her child. The key to this resignation is certainly not faith, but is to be found in the expression "the unknown land". God is invisible and cannot be reached. A mother's love can conquer Death, but it cannot live with the uncertainty of a choice for life.

A mother clinging to her dead child, but learning from the child to let go and choose the living instead of the dead, that is the theme of "The Child in the Grave" (1859) – a variation on the old theme, known from the medieval ballad, "Aage and Else", about the mourning of the living preventing the dead to pass on. The mother is drawn to the child's grave, where she is met by Death, a youthful figure like the big Ole Lukøie:

> She looked up, and near stood a man wrapped in a black cloak, with a hood drawn closely down over his face. But she glanced keenly up, and saw his face under his hood. It was stern, but yet awakened confidence, and his eyes beamed with the radiance of youth.[25]

She follows him into the realm of the dead and meets her child, who begs her to let go of him, so that he can fly up to God. And the child makes her listen to the living and understand her duties to them, see that they also have a need for her love and care. Then she can return to life, having been taught by the child in the grave.

Let us finally establish a tie over decades of Andersen's life and production and over this paper as well.

The last stanza of the poem "The Flowers of the Elves" (1839) had the lines

> I Barnets Død er Solglands og ei Skygge.
> Det flyver fra sin Alfeverden ind
> Til Himlens Gud, til overjordisk Lykke!

> (In the death of the child there is sunshine and no shadow.
> It flies directly from its elf-world
> To God in Heaven, to celestial happiness).

In his travel book, *A Visit to Portugal 1866* (published 1868), we find a poem with the first line "Er Du i Verden vide" (Are you in the wide world) with the comforting statement:

> Og der er ingen Død
> Og der er ingen Smerte;

Vort Jordlivs Stjerneskud
Er fra en Moders Hjerte
At flyve op til Gud.

(And there is no death,
and there is no pain;
the shooting star of our life is
flying from a mother's heart
up to God).[26]

Andersen made use of these lines on cartes-de-visite from the same period. He had a photo taken by G. Rosenkilde and had it reproduced on visiting cards. Beneath his portrait he then often wrote these words as a kind of personal confession:

Vort Jordlivs Stjerneskud
Er, fra en Moders Hjerte
At flyve op til Gud.
H.C. Andersen

(The shooting star of our life is
flying from a mother's heart
up to God).

The death of a child and the death of an author – both seem to find comfort in the assumption that there is no death. Life is a moment and so is death. They can both be a perceived as the brief lightning of a shooting star, just like the one, which contrary to all we know about the appearance of shooting stars was seen on New Year's Eve as a token of the nearby death of a little match-seller.

Notes

1. The Danish reviews are quoted or summarized and to some extent commented on (but not analysed) in Erling Nielsen: "Eventyrenes modtageleskritik" in *H.C. Andersens Eventyr*, published by Det danske Sprog- og Litteraturselskab, vol. VI, C.A. Reitzels Forlag, Copenhagen, 1990, pp. 121-230. For reviews of

the 1835 volumes see pp. 123-33. See also the web presentation of Andersen reviews at www.andersen.sdu.dk, subsection "Research" ("Forskning").
2. See H.C. Andersen: *Brevveksling med Edvard og Henriette Collin*, edited by C. Behrend and H. Topsøe-Jensen for Det danske Sprog- og Litteraturselskab, vol. I, Levin & Munksgaard, Copenhagen, 1933, p. 21.
3. See Henrik Lassen: "... from a Swedish tale by Andersen – ", "The Little Match Girl" in America and the topos of the dying child" in Per Krogh Hansen & Marianne Wolff Lundholdt (eds.): *When We Get to the End. Towards a narratology of the tales of Hans Christian Andersen*. University Press of Southern Denmark, Odense, 2005, pp. 305-80.
4. In his canon, Bloom regrettably had no mentioning of Andersen. A fact which did not prevent the city of Odense, Andersen's native town, from presenting Bloom with its honorary Andersen award 2005 for his alleged great Andersen achievements.
5. Henrik Lassen, Appendix, p. 344.
6. In the edition by Det danske Sprog- og Litteraturselskab (Danske Klassikere), edited by Johan de Mylius, Borgen Publishers, Copenhagen 1986, new edition 2003 (publ. 2004). Quotation translated by JdM..
7. The full text – in modern Danish spelling – can be found in H.C. Andersen: *Samlede digte* (ed. Johan de Mylius), Ascheoug, Copenhagen, 2000 and 2005, pp. 135-36. Quotation translated by JdM.
8. In Bernhard Sev. Ingemann's *Samlede Skrifter, Fjerde Afdelings ottende Bind, Romanzer, Sange og Eventyrdigte* (C.A. Reitzel, Copenhagen, second edition 1864, p. 87 f.).
9. "Halv Barn endnu med Barnets Sind/ Han gik til Livets Glæde ind".
10. "Nu staaer den Vished mere klar,/ Udødelighed Sjælen har".
11. "Alfernes Blomster", first printed in *H.C. Andersen. Digte der ikke kom med i eventyrdigterens "Samlede Skrifter"*, udvalgt og kommenteret af Jørgen Skjerk, Copenhagen. 2003, pp. 291-93.
12. As stated in letters of December 22 and 29, 1838 to Henriette Hanck (*H.C. Andersens brevveksling med Henriette Hanck*, ved Svend Larsen, Tredje Del, *Anderseniana* Vol. XI, p. 307 and 308, Copenhagen 1945).
13. Quoted (p. 111) from the reprint in *The Complete Illustrated Stories of Hans Christian Andersen*, translated by H.W. Dulcken, Ph.D., Chancellor Press, London, 1983 and later editions, as a facsimile edition of *Stories for the Household*, Routledge & Sons, London 1889.
14. A translation first published 1974, reprinted as a Penguin Book 1985. Quotation p. 200.
15. P. 202.
16. Ibid.
17. Quoted from Keigwin's UK translation (entitled "The Little Match-Seller") in *Hans Christian Andersen. Fairy Tales*, Vol. I, Hans Reitzels Forlag, Copenhagen, and Flensteds Forlag, Odense, 1986, p. 380.
18. Pp. 384-85.
19. Penguin p. 308.
20. *The Complete Andersen: All of the 168 Stories by Hans Christian Andersen [...] now freshly translated into english for this new edition by Jean Hersholt*, here in Vol. 6, "The Fairy Tales" (in contrast to volumes 3 and 4: "The Shorter

Tales"!), The Limited Editions Club, New York [no year of publication, original edition 1942-47], p. 249.
21. P. 359.
22. *Andersen's Tales and Fairy Stories*. New edition, London 1867, p. 304.
23. This listing might be continued into infinity. Let me just mention two recent translations, a US version by Diana Crone Frank and Jeffrey Frank (Boston and New York, 2003): "No one knew the beauty she had seen or in what glory she had gone with her old grandmother into the joy of the New Year" (p. 218), and another US version, that of Tiina Nunnally (Viking Penguin 2005): "No one knew what beauty she had seen, or with what radiance she and her old grandmother had passed into the joy of the New Year" (p. 249).
24. In Kierkegaard's *Frygt og Bæven* (*Fear and Trembling*), 1843.
25. Dulcken, p. 495.
26. In the original edition, *Samlede Skrifter af H.C. Andersen*, vol. 28, "Reiseskizzer og Pennetegninger", C.A. Reitzel, Copenhagen, 1868, pp. 158-59. A US-translation by Grace Thornton (The Bobbs-Merrill Company, Inc., Indianapolis / New York 1973 makes a nice American poem out of Andersen's poem, but says something very far away from the original text: "For Death and Pain are conquered/ And from the earthly strife,/ God draws His children to Him,/ To everlasting Life".

Literature

Johan de Mylius: *Forvandlingens pris. H.C. Andersen og hans eventyr* (The price of transformation. Hans Christian Andersen and his fairy tales), Høst & Søn, Copenhagen, 2004, second edition 2005.

The Language that Stayed at Home: Hans Christian Andersen's Ways with Words

Kirsten Malmkjær

Introduction

In this article, I introduce a project which is strictly work in progress, and in its early stages at that, although it looks back to work done previously, both my own and, of course, others'.

The project's provisional title is *The Language that Stayed at Home: Hans Christian Andersen's Ways with Words*. This title is inspired by Hjørnager Pedersen's remark (2004: 47) that while 'the simple, childlike and original Andersen did perhaps travel around the globe ... his art, in so far as it depended on language, did not always go with him'. In the past, I have explored some of the aspects of Andersen's language that translators into English have tended to leave behind, and also the reasons why they may have done so – deliberately, unknowingly, and sometimes for lack of invention. But looking at what translators do not re-create shows with particular clarity what was created in the first place and my plan now is to move on to a more general study of Hans Christian Andersen's linguistic dexterity or, as Kofoed (1967) calls it, his narrative artistry [*fortællekunst*].

Work on Andersen's Language

Of course, I am not the first to look at Andersen's language; nevertheless, as Hjørnager Pedersen (2004: 53) also says, linguistic and stylistic studies are 'a sadly neglected field of Andersen scholarship'. It is a field, furthermore, which was most thoroughly ploughed some time ago, so work can be difficult to get hold of, and it tends to be aimed at a Danish reading audience. So perhaps a study which would make findings from such work more widely available while also adding to them is timely.

Among existing work on Andersen's language (e.g. Rubow 1927, Jensen 1929, Kofoed 1967, Møllehave 1985, Brostrøm and Lund 1991), Skautrup (1953: 236-245) bears particularly directly on my own work on translations of the stories and tales. Skautrup provides a detailed discussion of how Andersen helped turn written Danish more towards the spoken language than it had been previously to create what he calls Andersen's central fairy tale language (*'centrale eventyrsprog'*); for example (approximate glosses mine):

FORMAL/WRITTEN LANGUAGE	*EVENTYR*/SPOKEN LANGUAGE
elske (*love*)	holde af (*be fond of*)
knælede ned (*knelt down*)	lagde sig ned paa Knæ (*got down on [his] knees*)
fuldblods Prindsesse (*thoroughbred princess*)	virkelig Prindsesse (*genuine princess*)
passere (*[come to] pass*)	komme (*come about*)
betragte (*regard*)	se (*look at*)
fyldestgørende (*sufficient*)	nok (*enough*)
den Indtrædende (*the entrant*)	han som traadte ind (*he who stepped in*)
Ankomsten af et Dagblad (*the arrival of a daily*)	Avisen der kom (*the newspaper which arrived*)
i Samtalens Løb (*during the course the conversation*)	imedens han talte (*while he was of speaking*)
en ung Theolog (*a young theologian*)	en student, der læste til at blive Præst (*a student who was studying to become a vicar*)
	for (explanatory conjunction)
	saadan en (pronominal adjective)
	saa (pre-modifying adverbial)
	Fatter (colloquial for 'Fader' (*'father'*))
	Mutter (colloquial for 'Moder' (*'mother'*))

He mentions a number of turns of phrase which Andersen learnt from the Collin household and the scarcity of words of foreign origin, before turning to what he calls Andersen's personal favourite words, including among many others, 'rigtig' and 'virkelig', adjectives which I have explored in Malmkjær (1995a and b) and which I will return to below in the context of Andersen's travel writing, the genre I have selected for the first stage of a comparison with the language in the stories and tales.

Choice of Travel Writing

There are several reasons for turning to the travel writing for a comparison with findings from the stories and tales.

First, the travel writing, along with the novels, seems to be generally accepted as the next most important of Andersen's genres after the stories and tales (Dal 2002a: 239). Secondly, and in addition, Rubow (1927: 98-101) maintains that it was during his travels that Andersen got to know the world and that his authorship matured, and that therefore, as far as Andersen's relationship with reality is concerned, the travel writing is the most interesting introduction to the stories and tales, even though the latter contain themes first introduced in the novels (1927: 98-101). I share Rubow's interest in Andersen's relationship with reality, but whereas Rubow seems oriented towards Andersen's psychological makeup, my interest is, literally speaking, semantic: I am interested in the relationship between language on the one hand and what and how it represents and creates on the other hand. In the current context, and given that interest, obviously the relationship between Andersen's fictional universe and his non-fictional universe is especially appealing – whatever level of grossness of simplification it is necessary to stoop to to maintain the necessary distinctions between language as creating and as representing fictional versus actual reality.

If I may be permitted these simplifications: It does not seem unreasonable to argue that the travel writing can be considered among Andersen's *least* fictional and the stories among his *most* fictional works for public consumption, so that we might expect to find optimal contrasts between these two genres, which would, in turn, set each genre in sharp relief against the other.

I report below on findings from Dal's (2002b) edition of the travel sketches 1826-1872 and the visit to Portugal in 1866. I have not examined *Billedbog uden Billeder*, which is in the same edition, because I consider it too fictional for my current purpose.

Obviously, not being fictional (in the simplified sense posited for the purposes of the current discussion) does not mean that a piece of writing cannot be literary, and I disagree with those who consider that

Et Besøg i Portugal 1866 ('A Visit to Portugal 1866') is not literary. For example, Grønbech (1971: 183; in Dal 2002: 278) says

> Bogen er uden literære pretentioner. At læse den er som at være sammen med en gammel ven der fortæller løst og fast om en rejse han nylig er vendt hjem fra. Man interesserer sig for den, fordi man holder af fortælleren, og fordi man måske gerne hører om fremmede lande.
>
> [The book is devoid of literary pretensions. Reading it feels like being with an old friend who is chatting away about a journey he has recently undertaken. It is fondness for the narrator, and perhaps for learning about foreign countries, that makes it interesting to listen.]

It may be that the work is not pretentious; it is, however, literary – at least, it displays literary characteristics and is in no sense an innocently constructed, chatty, narrative. Consider how Andersen frames an account of thirty three years of Portuguese history, over what in the Dal edition constitutes about two pages. The account is introduced as follows (Dal 2002b: 197; my translation):

> Som bekjendt er Kong *Fernando* Fader til den nu regerende Konge *Luis*. Paa min Hjemfart hen ad Quaien gjennem Gaderne ud til *Pinieros* var Tid nok til med Tankerne at følge de sidste tre og tredive Aars Historie i dette Land, der har prøvet saa mange Kampe, men nu synes at groe i Hvile og Velsignelse.
>
> [It is well known that King Fernando is the father of the current regent, King Luis. On my way home along the quay through the streets towards *Pinieros* there was plenty of time to think through the history of the last thirty three years in this country which has seen so many battles but now seems to be growing in peace and blessedness.]

After the historical account, we read again (Dal 2002b: 198; my translation):

> Dette er den korte historiske Skizze, der er at læse bedre andre Steder, men her er den lagt som min Tanketraad, idet jeg kom fra mit Besøg hos Kong *Fernando*.

[This is the brief historical sketch, which is available in better versions elsewhere, but here it is presented as the train of my thoughts as I was returning from my visit to King Fernando.]

This reminder that Andersen has been on a royal visit also serves to suggest again that the paragraphs in between it and the introduction to the historical account are Andersen's thoughts as he experienced them on his way home along the streets, whereas – assuming that he thought about the history of Portugal on his way home at all – what we read is in fact a carefully crafted account, created *a posteriori*. Clear literary techniques include free indirect thought, also listed by Skautrup (1953: 242) as characteristic of Andersen, as in the following passages (Dal 2002b: 198):

Flere fanger, som næste Dag skulde lide Døden, førtes ind i Capellet, hvor de i Præstens Selskab maatte tilbringe deres sidste Levenat; turde de haabe Frelse?

[A number of prisoners, due to be executed the following day, were led into the chapel, where they were to spend their final night in the company of the priest; dared they hope for salvation?]

The last clause – interrogative, in the past tense, and not likely to be met with a reply – is clearly the narrator's presentation of a question he imagines to have been in the prisoners' minds; it is not a genuine question of his own. In fact, the whole paragraph that this extract forms part of appears to be itself a report of what Andersen had been told about the sad era of Dom *Miguel*'s reign: 'Man har fortalt mig derom' ('I have been told about it') says Andersen (Dal 2002b: 197) before illustrating the cruelty of the era with examples of the sufferings of political prisoners.

A little later, as Andersen recounts the outcome of the battle between the liberal forces which supported Dom Pedro and the absolutists who supported Dom Miguel, we read (Dal 2002b: 198):

Seirens Udfald blev, at denne [Dom Miguel] maatte vige. Hvilken Jubel, Luften rystede af Sang og Glædesskrig. En Dame, som den Tid var Barn, fortalte mig, hvilket Indtryk hun i sin Forbauselse og Uvidenhed om det Hele fik ved at see dette lidenskabelige Røre.

[The victory was such that the latter [Dom Miguel] had to retreat. Such jubilation, the air shook with singing and cries of joy. A lady, who had been a child at that time, told me of the impression she formed of it all on seeing, in her astonishment and ignorance, this passionate commotion.]

Because Andersen presents the phrase 'Hvilken Jubel, Luften …' before he introduces the possible source of this thought, and because he in any case keeps it rather vague whether what we see is Andersen's representation of the lady's account of how she felt or whether it is Andersen's account of how he imagines it must have felt at the time, which we are party to as he strolls home after his royal visit – we are led to feel present *in medias res* both of the past events and of Andersen's thought processes. The account includes layer on layer of narration using multiple and ambiguous points of view.

So there is no doubt that the travel writing is carefully crafted and that it is, in that sense, literary in nature. It is to be expected, therefore, that Andersen is equally deliberate in his modes of expression in both genres.

Given that both genres are literary in the sense outlined above, and given that they differ in the relationships realized in them between language and what language is about (in terms of the simplification under which we can posit a distinction between a fictional and a non-fictional universe), we need to consider the micro-parameters for further comparison between them.

Relating the Travel Writing to the Stories and Tales

A number of writers, again including Rubow (1927: 202), have pointed to scenes from the travel writing which are later used in the stories, and one way of making my comparison would obviously be to compare such scenes. But although I am interested in how Andersen perceives the universe, my investigation is not primarily focused on what de Mylius (1981; 2005: 28ff and 30) calls 'mythologems', recurrent motifs in Andersen's oeuvre, such as the journey into the world, the wedding, death, and so on, and 'arche-situations' ('grundsituationer') such as dialogues, animations (of non-living things) and grave-side scenes. My focus is on the linguistic material used to represent, so my investigation will be structured in terms of categories commonly used to classify this material.

In my research on the language of Andersen's stories, I have looked at (i) the use of the adjectives *rigtig* and *virkelig* (Malmkjær 2003a); (ii) Andersen's use of pronouns to establish different kinds of relationship between characters, readers and narrator (Malmkjær 1996); (iii) techniques through which Andersen establishes empathy with characters, ranging from deitic shifts through intensifiers to indicators of indirect thought (Malmkjær 1999); and (iv) Andersen's construction, and his translator, H. W. Dulcken's careful deconstruction, of an undivided fictional universe (Malmkjær 2003b; 2004). Below, I shall briefly outline my findings from the stories and tales for the first two categories, though both await more solid, statistically sound measurements by electronic means. I will also briefly remark on the fourth category.

Andersen's Use of Pronouns to Establish Different Kinds of Relationship Between Characters, Readers and Narrator
(See also Rubow 1927: 170-171).

In the stories and tales, Andersen sometimes includes himself among the audience for a given story. For example (my emphasis; my translation of examples):

Nu skulle **vi** høre [now **we** shall hear] ("Lille Claus og Store Claus" ["Little Claus and Big Claus"] 1835)

At other times, he shifts from direct address:

I China veed **du** jo nok er Keiseren en Chineser [In China as **you** SINGULAR already know, the emperor is Chinese].

to another form of self-inclusion, made possible by the Danish general pronoun, 'man', which differs from its nearest English acquaintances, 'one' and 'you', in being unmarked for number – though it leans towards plural. In the first example below, which is from the introductory paragraph to the story, "Nattergalen" ["The nightingale"] (1844), the use of present tense suggests reference to both narrator and audience; in the second example, which is the first sentence of the narration proper, the use of past tense suggests that *man* refers to the people in the story time and place, but not to the narrator and audience. It is necessary to distance the latter from the former in order that narrator and audience can adopt a common satirical attitude to the majority of the story characters' inability to judge the merits of the genuine versus the artificial nightingale:

> Det er nu mange Aar siden, men just derfor er det værd at høre Historien, før **man** glemmer den! [It is now many years ago, but that is exactly why it is a good idea to hear the story before **we all** forget it].

> Keiserens Slot var saa kostbart, saa vanskeligt at røre ved, at **man** ordentligt maatte tage sig iagt [The emperor's castle was so precious, so difficult to touch, that **everyone** had to be very careful].

As these examples illustrate, Andersen tends to be present in the stories and tales as an implied presence (the addresser addressing the reader using 'du' ('you + SINGULAR) or a narrator self-included in a 'vi' ('we') or in a 'man' (PRONOUN OF GENERAL REFERENCE) in a present tense context). He uses the first person pronouns of explicit presence rarely if at all.

In the travel writing, each of the options just discussed is also found, though first person reference is, not surprisingly, very prominent. In the passage below, a certain logic can be perceived in the way in which Andersen first introduces himself and his reader(s) (interestingly enough initially in the third person, 'min Læser' ('my reader') and then immediately in the second person, 'Du' ('you') before switching to the inclusive 'vi' ('we')). When he turns to talk of his own memory, in contrast, he uses the exclusive 'jeg' ('I') (from "Reise fra Kjøbenhavn til Rhinen" ["Journey from Copenhagen to the Rhine"] 1833 (in Dal (ed.) 2002: 14-35), pp. 25-26; my emphasis; my translation):

> Da **min** Reisehistorie her er Sandhed og ikke Digtning, maa **min** Læser tilgive **mig** at **jeg** flyver noget stærkt afsted, sætter **mig** alt i Vognen igjen næste Morgen, thi det var Tilfældet, **min** Higen var efter Paris, det første store Ophold paa **min** Reise; dog skal **Du** med **mig** see noget mere af Cassel og Frankfurt, seile paa Rhinen, bestige Viinbjergene og se
>
>> "hvor Hyrden driver sine Faar og Oxer
>> Igjennem Borgens Sal hvor Græsset voxer,"

men nu maa **vi** reise fra Hanover, er **vi** først ved den franske Grændse, gaaer det endnu mere i Galop, uden Rast og Hvile, kun i Champagnie tør **vi** tømme et Bæger af den skummende Viin. – Nu smælder Pidsken! Hanover ligger bag ved **os**. – Ved *Thiedenwiese* rakte Heden **os** sin magre Haand til Afskeed og viiste **os** et noget bjergrigt Landskab, der meer og meer vandt i Skjønhed, Solen skinnede ogsaa saa varmt, til en styrtende Regn gjorte Ende paa **vor** Glæde, men **jeg** har i Erindringen endnu ...

As this account of **my** journey is truth and not invention, **my reader** must forgive **me my** somewhat hasty departure, placing **myself** in the carriage again as soon as the following morning, for that was the case, **my** longing was for Paris, the first major destination on **my** journey; nevertheless **you** will be with **me** to see something more of Cassel and Frankfurt, to sail on the Rhine, climb the vineyards and see

"where herdsmen drive their flocks of sheep and oxen
Between the castle walls where grass is growing,"

but now **we** must leave Hanover, once **we** reach the French border, progress is even faster, with no pause for rest, not until Champagnie will **we** empty a cup of the sparkling wine. – The whip is cracking! Hanover is behind **us**. – At *Thiedenwiese* the moor gave **us** its skinny hand in farewell, showing **us** a rather mountainous landscape which grew and grew in beauty, but then the sun did shine so warm, until a pouring rain put an end to **our** joy, but **I** can still recall ...

In contrast, once Andersen comes to rest in Cassel, he settles on the Danish tourism literature's pronoun of general reference (from *Reise fra Kjøbenhavn til Rhinen* 1833 (in Dal (ed.) 2002: 14-35), p. 27; my emphasis; my translation):

Her [på Frederikspladsen i Cassel] finder **man** Operahuset og den catolske Kirke, hvor **man** skiftevis forlyster med Musik ...

Here [on Friedrichplatz in Cassel] are the operahouse and the catholic church where musical entertainment varies with ...

These pronoun manipulations underline once again the literary nature of Andersen's travel writing. He is careful, always, to carry his reader with him – almost literally – at least in the recreation of the journey which narrator and reader come to share as the reader reads.

It is, however, in the use of the adjectives that the most interesting preliminary findings of my genre comparison occur.

The Use of the Adjectives 'Rigtig' and 'Virkelig'

In Malmkjær (2003a), I claim that Andersen uses the adjectives *rigtig* and *virkelig* to distinguish between phenomena that possess the essential properties of a type, of which they are therefore genuine tokens (*virkelig*); and phenomena which (perhaps merely) display inessential features commonly associated with the type (*rigtig*). The following are typical examples to illustrate this claim (adjectives in Danish; co-texts in my translation into English):

> From "The Swineherd" (1842):
> "Fie Papa!" she said, "it isn't artificial, it is *virkelig*!"

> From "The Nightingale" (1844):
> the virkelige nightingale sang in its own way, and the artificial bird was clockwork;

> From "The Shepherdess and the Chimney-Sweep" (1845):
> Have you ever seen a rigtig old wooden cupboard, quite black with age and carved with intricate patterns of leaves?

> From "The Puck at the Grocer's" (1853):
> There was a rigtig student, he lived in the attic and owned nothing; there was a rigtig grocer, he lived on the ground floor and owned the whole house

Obviously, in the first two examples, a nightingale that is 'virkelig' is being contrasted with one that is artificial; and in the last two examples, items that are being described as 'rigtig' are being identified by way of characteristics of their stereotypes, as opposed to by way of their essential features.

In the stories and tales, these adjectives occur regularly, whereas in the Dal (2002b) edition of the travel writing I have found just one occurrence of each. Both are from *Et Besøg i Portugal 1866* ('A Visit to Portugal 1866') and the contexts are the following:

> to rigtig danske Rødtjørne ('two rigtig Danish thorn trees') (Dal 2002b: 187)

> et virkeligt levende Menneske ('a virkeligt live human being') [as opposed to a wooden figure] (Dal 2002b: 199)

Et Besøg i Portugal 1866 ('A Visit to Portugal 1866') is known for its many references to how like Denmark Portugal is (Dal 2002b: 280). Nevertheless, to call two thorn trees growing in Portugal 'rigtig danske' ('really Danish') strongly suggests that the adjective is being used in precisely the sense "being like" and not in the sense "being". In the case of the example with VIRKELIG, the opposite holds: The sense is "being" as opposed to "being like". I could not be more pleased to find this: Here we are in a context where Andersen does not need to build a distinction in terms of fictionality within a setting that is already absolutely fictional, as he needs to do in the stories. The point of the travel writing is not at all to challenge the reader to discover, or to help the reader to see, often ahead of the characters in a story, what is genuine and what is not. In the travel writing, it is clear what is genuine and what just displays typical characteristics: The bushes display characteristics typical of such bushes growing in Denmark, but they are bushes growing in Portugal; the living person is genuine as opposed to the wooden figure it is being compared to. So here, a non-fictional context provides the sense that makes it natural for Andersen to use these two adjectives. I consider this to be strong support for my claim about his uses of the adjectives in the stories. The reason they are used so rarely in the travel writing is, I suppose, that there is little need for them in non-fiction.

Adjectives are of course particularly interesting in an investigation such as mine; they are, on the one hand, difficult to translate because languages seem to differ even more in the distinctions they draw between degrees of whatever kinds of quality adjectives denote than they do in the case of the much studied colour spectrum. On the other hand, it is clearly in large part by means of adjectives that narrators are able to describe and evaluate aspects of their worlds, fictional or otherwise, and my aim will be to look at Andersen's use of relatively *objectively* descriptive adjectives, as in 'jernbeslaaede, aabne Porte' ('iron-clad, open gates') (*Nürnberg* in Dal 2002b: 168) as well as more *subjectively* evaluative examples.

Creating an Undivided Fictional Universe

The creation of an undivided fictional universe, and its deconstruction in Dulcken's translations, is documented in some detail in Malmkjær (2003b and 2004).

Through his handling of relationships between humans, the divine, creatures in other states of being, and creatures of other ontological types, Andersen constructs a universe in the stories and tales which satisfies what de Mylius (1981: 20) describes as 'et helt elementært behov' ('an absolutely elementary need') which Andersen felt, namely 'længslen efter helhed. En trang hos ham til at ... erkende verdens fundamentale enhed' ('a longing for wholeness. A need within him to ... realize the fundamental oneness of the universe').

For example, Johannes, in "Reisekammeraten" ("The Travelling Companion") (1835) feels able to speak naturally with his dead father and he assumes that the latter can speak directly to God:

(Dal I, 68, 31-39; my translation):
Tidlig næste Morgen pakkede *Johannes* sin lille Byldt sammen, gjemte i sit Belte hele sin Arvepart, der var 50 Rdlr. og et Par Sølvskillinger, dermed vilde han vandre ud i Verden. Men først gik han hen paa Kirkegaarden til sin Faders Grav, læste sit "*Fader vor*", og sagde: "Farvel Du kjære Fader! Jeg vil altid være et godt Menneske, og saa tør Du nok bede den gode Gud, at det maa gaae mig godt!"

Early the next morning Johannes packed his little bundle together, hid in his belt his entire inheritance, which was 50 dollars and a couple of silver shillings, with that he intended to wander out into the world. But first he went to the churchyard to his father's grave, read his "*Lord's Prayer*", and said: "Goodbye my dear father! I will always be a good person, and then I'm sure you can pray to the good God that things will go well for me.

He considers God to be a kissable being:

(Dal I, 74, 33-35; my translation):
"Du gode vor Herre! Jeg kunde kysse Dig, fordi du er saa god mod os allesammen, og har givet os al den Deilighed, der er i Verden!"

'Our dear Lord! I could kiss you for being so good to us all and giving us all the splendour there is in the world.'

and he is pleased to pray to God at the same time as he is using other kinds of supernatural power granted by an embodied dead person, in order to lift a spell from a princess who assumes bird-form at night:

(Dal I, 84, 9-10; my translation):
Johannes bad fromt til vor Herre, og lod Vandet tredie Gang spille hen over Fuglen.

Johannes prayed piously to the Lord and let the water pour over the bird for the third time.

Consider, now, Dulcken's translations of the extracts above:

(Dulcken, 1866: 47):
Early next morning John packed his little bundle, and put in his belt his whole inheritance, which consisted of fifty dollars and a few silver shillings; with this he intended to wander out into the world. But first he went to the churchyard, to his father's grave, to say a prayer and to bid him farewell.

(Dulcken, 1866: 51):
"How kind has heaven been to us all, to give us all the splendour that is in this world!"

(Dulcken, 1866: 59):
John let the water close for the third time over the bird.

I should mention, that Dulcken is not adverse to the use of divine terminology under *any* circumstances: there are about as many instances in which divine vocabulary is translated as there are instances in which it is not translated (apart from instances where Andersen uses such vocabulary for swearing and in exclamations; such uses are never reproduced by Dulcken). However, the criterion for inclusion is that there should be no other forces involved and that a proper distance should be observed between God and humans, earth and Heaven, both physically and metaphorically. For example (from: "De vilde Svaner" ("The Wild Swans" 1838):

(Dal I, 128, 30-34; my translation):
Natten blev saa mørk; ikke en eneste lille Sanct Hansorm skinnede fra Mosset, bedrøvet lagde hun sig ned for at sove; da syntes hun at Trægrenene oven over hende gik til Side og *vor Herre* med milde Øine saae ned paa hende, og smaa Engle tittede frem over hans Hoved og under hans Arme.

The night grew so dark; not a single little glowworm shone from the moss, sad she lay down to sleep; then it seemed to her that the tree branches above her moved aside and our Lord with mild eyes looked down at her, and little angels peeped out above his head and under his arms.

(Dulcken, 1866: 562):
The night came on quite dark. Not a single glowworm now gleamed in the grass. Sorrowfully she lay down to sleep. Then it seemed to her as if the branches of the trees parted above her head, and mild eyes of angels looked down upon her from on high.

Dulcken's translation distances the dreaming girl physically further from the angels who observe her from 'on high' than the original's girl is from the Lord who looks at her from just where the branches of the tree are parting above her.

Metaphorically, the distance (in terms of familiarity, humanoid characteristics and formality of demeanour) between the divine participants in the original scene – the deity and the little angels who play around on his body – and the human participant is clearly less than in the translated scene which has the angels (alone) simply looking down.

Linguistically, these distances are reinforced by the absence from the translation of the name of the deity.

My findings on this parameter for the travel writing are preliminary in the extreme, though it is interesting to observe that Rubow (1927: 82) finds evidence for Andersen's desire to create an undivided universe in *Fodreisen* ("The Journey on Foot"). My hypothesis is that whereas in the stories the oneness is made partly through association between magic and religion, in the travel writing it will be done through an association between nature and invention, including art, and an association between these and the magical. This I think I can see some evidence of in statements such as: 'hvor Natur og Konst deiligt understøtte hinanden', 'how delightfully art and nature support each other' (Dal 2002b: 225), but also, again, in Andersen's use of adjectives. For example,

> fortryllende ('enchanting')
> hvor fortryllende deilig er dog Udsigten ('how enchantingly delightful is the view') (Dal 2002b, p. 8)
>
> Udsigten er ganske fortryllende ('the view is completely enchanting') (Dal 2002b, p. 12)
>
> forunderlig ('wonderous')
> forunderlige Blaahed ('wonderous blueness') (Dal 2002b, p. 44)
>
> vidunderlig ('wonderful')
> den vidunderlige Grotte ('the wonderful grotto') (Dal 2002b, p. 212)

So, I intend to go back to the adjectives where I began, and where I think that much remains to be learnt.

References

H.C. Andersens Eventyr. Kritisk udgivet efter de originale Eventyrhæfter med Varianter ved Erik Dal og Kommentar ved Erling Nielsen. I:1835-42, 1963; II: 1843-55, 1964. Copenhagen: Hans Reitzels Forlag.

Brostrøm, Torben and Jørn Lund 1991 *Flugten i Sproget: H. C. Andersens Udtryk* (The flight in language: Hans Christian Andersen's expressions). Copenhagen: Gyldendal.

Dal, Erik 2002a 'Efterskrift' (postscript). In *Rejseskitser 1826-1872 i: Billedbog uden Billeder; Et Besøg i Portugal* (ed. Erik Dal). Copenhagen: Det Danske Sprog- og Litteraturselskab (The Danish language and Literature Society), Borgen, pp. 239-284.

Dal, Erik 2002b *Rejseskitser 1826-1872: Billedbog uden Billeder, Et Besøg i Portugal* (ed. Erik Dal). Copenhagen: Det Danske Sprog- og Litteraturselskab (The Danish language and Literature Society), Borgen.

Dulcken, Henry William 1866 (tr) *Hans Christian Andersen's Stories for the Household*. London: Routledge. Re-issued as *The Complete Illustrated Works of Hans Christian Andersen*. London, Chancellor Press, 1983; 1994.

Grønbech, Bo 1971 *H. C. Andersen: Levnedsløb, digtning, personlighed*. Copenhagen: Nyt Nordisk Forlag.

Hjørnager Pedersen, Viggo 2004 *Ugly Ducklings? Studies in the English Translations of Hans Christian Andersen's Tales and Stories*. Odense: University Press of Southern Denmark.

Jensen, Anker 1929 *Studier over H. C. Andersens Sprog* (Studies of Hans Christian Andersen's language). Haderslev: Carl Nielsens Forlag.

Kofoed, Niels 1967 *Studier i H. C. Andersens Fortællekunst* (Studies in Hans Christian Andersen's art of narration). Copenhagen: Munksgaard.

Malmkjær, Kirsten 1993 'Who can make nice a better word than pretty?: Collocation, translation and psycholinguistics'. In M. Baker, G. Francis and E. Tognini-Bonelli (eds.) *Text and Technology: In Honour of John Sinclair*. Amsterdam and Philadelphia: John Benjamins Publishing Co., pp. 213-232.

Malmkjær, Kirsten 1995a 'Translating the real story'. In J.A. Payne (ed.) *Linguistic Approaches to Literature*. English Language Research, University of Birmingham, pp. 170-184.

Malmkjær, Kirsten 1995b 'What's in an adjective? Using cross-textual patterns of collocation in translating' *Norwich Papers in Languages, Literatures and Cultures* 3: 44-54.

Malmkjær, Kirsten 1996 'Who walked in the emperor's garden: The translation of pronouns in Hans Christian Andersen's introductory passages'. In G. Anderman and C. Banér (eds) *Proceedings of the Tenth Biennial Conference of the British Association of Scandinavian Studies*. The University of Surrey, Department of Linguistics and International Studies, pp. 77-86.

Malmkjær, Kirsten 1999 *Descriptive Linguistics and Translation Studies: Interface and Difference*. Platform Papers on Translation Studies 1. Utrecht: Platform Vertalen & Vertaalwetenschap.

Malmkjær, Kirsten 2003a 'On a pseudo-subversive use of corpora in translator training'. In Federico Zanettin, Silvia Bernardini and Dominic Stewart (eds) *Corpora in Translator Education*. Manchester: St. Jerome, pp. 119-134.

Malmkjær, Kirsten 2003b 'What happened to God and the angels: An Exercise in Translational Stylistics'. *Target* 15(1): 39-62.

Malmkjær, Kirsten 2004 'Translational Stylistics'. *Language and Literature* 13(1): 13-24.

Malmkjær, Kirsten and Murray Knowles 1991 'Key terms in H.C. Andersen's fairytales and their translations into English' *Babel: International Journal of Translation* 37 (4): 203-12.

Mylius, Johan de 1981 *Myte og Roman: H. C. Andersens romaner mellem romantik og realisme. En traditionshistorisk undersøgelse* (Myth and Novel: Hans Christian Andersen's novels between romanticism and realism. An examination in the history of traditions). Copenhagen: Gyldendal.

Mylius, Johan de 2005 *Forvandlingens Pris: H. C. Andersen og hans Eventyr* (The Price of Transformation: Hans Christian Andersen and his Fairy Tales) Copenhagen: Høst & Søn.

Møllehave, Johannes 1985 *H. C. Andersens salt: Om humoren I H. C. Andersens eventyr* (Hans Christian Andersen's salt: About the humour in Hans Christian Andersen's fairy tales). Copenhagen: Lindhardt og Ringhof.

Rubow, Paul 1927 *H. C. Andersens Eventyr: Forhistorien – Idé og Form, Sprog og Stil* (Hans Christian Andersen's fairy tales: The prelude – idea and form, language and style). Copenhagen: Levin and Munksgaards Forlag.

Skautrup, Peter 1953 *Det Danske Sprogs Historie: Tredie Bind, fra Holbergs Komedier til H. C. Andersens Eventyr.* Copenhagen: Gyldendalske Boghandel, Nordisk Forlag.

Romantic and Modern Metatexts: Commemorating Andersen and the Self-Referential Text

Marianne Stecher-Hansen

On the bicentenary of H.C. Andersen's birth, literary critics and scholars from around the world gathered in Odense to engage in a kind of academic commemoration of the great Danish poet. Commemoration is defined as "the act of honoring the memory of, or serving as a memorial to someone or something." An inscription on a tombstone or a poem honoring a deceased person is a commemoration. We may think of memorial stone or memorial statue. In Latin the term is *commemorare*. In Danish, one uses the terms, *at mindes* (to remember, to recollect, to commemorate), *mindeskrift* (memorial volume), *mindesmærke* (memorial, monument), *mindestøtte* (memorial column), and *mindetale* (memorial speech, eulogy). In the case of Andersen, we celebrate a writer who lived, but we have no living memory of that person. In actuality, we are engaged in a commemoration or the honoring of the memory of a "textual Andersen." The experience of reading or knowing Andersen by means of published texts about or by him. In fact, many of Andersen's texts are informed by a commemorative function. The idea of this paper is to investigate how Andersen formulates these textual commemorations of his own literary legacy.

We are all well aware that Andersen was deeply engaged during his lifetime in the project of crafting a narrative life-story, which would become a popular legacy worldwide. In this endeavor he was tremendously successful. Andersen wrote autobiographies, autobiographical novels, and allegorical tales that told "the fairytale" of his life. To this audience, I need not give examples of the discrepancies between his factual lived life and his idealized representations of it. It is not my project to investigate the patterns, omissions, or veracity in these representations of the nineteenth-century writer and celebrity. I propose to investigate the notion of a textual commemoration, and how Andersen applied a certain aesthetic – perhaps a modernist aesthetic – to his project of constructing textual commemorations of his literary legacy.

The idea which I suggest in my title, that elements of the modern or Modernism are to be found in some of Andersen's texts is not new. Readers of Andersen know of the stylistic experimentation, which the author conducted in the later years of his literary career. According to Jackie Wullschlager:

> The collections of 1858 and 1859 mark a new phase in Andersen's composition ... leaving behind the folk models of his youth and the grand classical archetypes of his middle years ... he reinvented the fairy tale as a modern, self-referential, experimental genre. He anticipated some of the ingredients of Modernism – the expression of meaning primarily through style, form and poetic image; fluidity of character and an awareness of the irrational working of the unconscious mind; a diminished importance of plot. (367)

While I do not think that Modernism has exclusive rights to 'the expression of meaning through style, form and poetic image,' I find Wullschlager's assertion that Andersen anticipated Modernism useful. More recently, Danish scholar Jens Andersen makes a bolder claim regarding H.C. Andersen's anticipation of Modernism by presenting his privileging of the child's experiential world as a direct precursor to early twentieth-century developments in psychology and aesthetics:

> Og som sådan blev H.C. Andersens eventyr en af modernismens vigtigste forudsætninger. Med sin insisteren på barnets rettigheder og muligheder foregreb den danske eventyrdigter ikke kun Sigmund Freuds psykoanalyse, men også de surrealistiske manifester fra 1920'erne (Jens Andersen, 376)

> [And, as such, the fairy tales of H.C. Andersen served as one of the most important foundations for modernism. With his insistence on the rights and potential of children, Andersen anticipated not only the psychoanalysis of Sigmund Freud but also the surrealist manifestos of the 1920s] (Nunnally, 240).

Over the past ten years a few of my predecessors at the International Hans Christian Andersen Conferences have presented evidence of early Modernism in Andersen's texts. The idea that Andersen employed a modernist or Baudelairean poetic vocabulary is explored by

Heinrich Detering in "The Phoenix Principle: Some Remarks on H.C. Andersen's Poetological Writings." By examining Andersen's programmatic writings on poetry, "Fugl Phønix" ("The Phoenix Bird"), "Poesiens Californien" ("The California of Poetry"), "Folkesangens Fugl" ("The Bird of Folk-song"), "Det nye Aarhundredes Musa" ("The Muse of the New Century"), and "Et Blad skrevet i Norge" ("A Paper Written in Norway"), Detering argues that these texts constitute an attempt to establish a new aesthetic or poetological concept situated between Romanticism and early Modernism. He concludes that, "Andersen's programmatic writings – inclined to radical modernist points of view and at the same time maintaining most conservative Romantic values (...) – these writings are situated on the threshold between late Romanticism and young Modernism, somewhere between Oehlenschläger and Wergeland, between Ørsted and Baudelaire" (Detering, 64). According to Detering, a 'phoenix principle' is at work in Andersen's programmatic writings on literary aesthetics.[1] These texts suggest that poetry, like the mythological Phoenix, will eventually be destroyed or consume itself in order to be resurrected from the ashes in a new form. Detering successfully demonstrates that these programmatic texts articulate a fairly consistent aesthetic credo based on a cyclical pattern of destruction and rebirth.

Scholarship has already clearly established that H.C. Andersen was acutely aware that the new industrialized and urban culture, which was emerging in the mid-nineteenth century, would require a new kind of poetry. He took to heart the dogma of natural scientist Hans Christian Ørsted, whose lectures published in the collection *Aanden i Naturen* (*The Soul in Nature*, 1849-50), expressed a dogma of scientific and cultural progress. In the essay "Naturvidenskabens Forhold til Digtekunsten" ("The Relationship of Natural Science to Poetry"), Ørsted is speaking directly to contemporary writers such as Andersen, when he argues that "Digterværket vil forfeile sin Virkning paa Mennesker med sand naturvidenskabelig Dannelse, naar det stiller det Overnaturlige paa en ret afstikkende Maade sammen med det Naturlige" (159) [Literary work will not produce the desired effect on people with genuine scientific understanding, when it combines the supernatural with the natural (i.e. scientific) in an incongruous manner]. Deeply inspired by Ørsted's ideas and fascinated with new technological discoveries and scientific advancements, Andersen attempted to incorporate the "wonders" of the new age into his literary fairytales. But it is often in these very "science fiction" tales that we see Andersen's naïve enthusiasm for the new age of technology mitigated by a strong ambivalence and ambiguity toward the developments of the future.² For example, tales such as "Om Aartusinder" (1851; "In a Thousand Years' Time"), are prophetic in a vision of a technologically advanced global civilization which is culturally and spiritually impoverished.

"Det nye Aarhundredes Musa" (1861; "The Muse of the New Century"), H.C. Andersen's poetic manifesto, depicting the arrival of the new muse of the modern age. Illustration by Vilhelm Pedersen.

Readers who doubt how seriously Andersen engaged in formulating a poetic credo for a future age should revisit his most allusive manifesto, "Det nye Aarhundredes Musa" (1861; "The Muse of the New Century"). The artistic manifesto imbedded in this text is veiled in an allegorical narrative about the infancy, youth and maturation of a new muse of poetry, born in "vor travle maskinbrusende Tid" (*Eventyr* 4:113) [our busy machine age]. The sonorous prophetic tone and Messianic language associated with the coming of the muse and the apocalyptic images of the concluding paragraph point to Andersen struggling with notions of a new aesthetic which rises out of the total destruction of the old. Blending Biblical imagery and Nordic mythology, the text anticipates the fall of the Wall of China, the Clash of Eastern and Western cultures, the demise of civilization, a Ragnarok and a new Gimle. In the final, curiously unforgettable and satirical image, we – that is the readers and the poets – become "os Orme" (4:117) [we the worms] who are killed and mutilated by the plough in order to create fertile new soil for the new generation. One could say that the idea of death, destruction, and rebirth is organically applied in this final image. As Johan de Mylius points out in his discussion of this final passage, it is the poet himself who greets the new century as he is cut down, ploughed under, and buried alive:

> Og digteren selv, der står og varsler det ny århundrede, skæres over, udslettes, for at det ny kan komme til. En hilsen fra en, der allerede er død eller levende begravet (264)

> [And the poet himself, who stands and forebodes the new century, is cut up and destroyed in order to make room for the new. A greeting from one, who is already dead or buried alive].

On the idea of Andersen as a transitional figure between the Romantic and the Modernist, Jacob Bøggild takes a somewhat different track. Building on earlier studies by Torben Brostrøm and Niels Kofoed, Bøggild explores not the Phoenix bird, but the "ruin" in Andersen's texts, an image which he calls one element of romantic "arabesque poetics." In "Ruinous Reflections: On H.C. Andersen's Ambiguous Position Between Romanticism and Modernism," Bøggild argues that the arabesque is a literary modality which "wiggles itself loose from its romantic origins and becomes an integral part of symbolist and modernist poetics" (76). His idea of a building in ruins which is crumbling away and gradually being reclaimed by nature has a certain likeness to the idea of destruction and resurrection of the Phoenix bird. Bøggild proposes that by tracing the development of this image in a series of texts chronologically, one can see the development of this arabesque modality, from the Romantic to the early modern.

The common thread in these essays by Detering and Bøggild is the idea of Andersen's literary texts anticipating literary developments of the next century. It is the conception of literary texts whose contributions are neither static, nor conventionally Romantic. The extent to which there exist specifically modernist elements in Andersen's work is a claim that the reader may continue to ponder. Modernism in arts and literature may be broadly defined as a movement during the century, 1850-1950, a period of unprecedented aesthetic experimentation. One might distinguish modernity in the historical sense (which begins with the Renaissance) from Modernism in the arts and letters. One could argue that aesthetic Modernism is a form of art characteristic of late modernity, a historical period in which social, economic, and cultural life in the Western world has been revolutionized or "modernized." Already in 1931 Edmund Wilson suggests in his introduction to *Axel's Castle* an aesthetic affinity between Romanticism and the modern movement: "Yet the movement of which in our own day we are witnessing the mature development is not merely a degeneration or an elaboration of Romanticism, but rather a counterpart to it, a second flood of the same tide" (2).

Drawing on some of these reflections on literary aesthetics which span late Romanticism and early Modernism, this investigation now turns its focus to Andersen's formulations of textual commemorations. Beginning with a discussion of the self-reflexive or metatextual elements of selected texts, I will focus on an element which is key to their commemorative function. Consider the idea of metafiction, a fiction that deals often playfully and self-referentially with the writing of fiction or fictional conventions. Metafiction – the modernist, experimental metanovel comes to mind here – problematizes the relationship between representation and the subject represented by referring back self-consciously to the writing process and the text itself. In the modern metanovel the reader experiences the protagonist (often depicted as a writer or diarist) reflecting on the act of writing the novel, which ostensibly is the text before us. The modern era abounds with metanovels often in diary form. In the Danish literary canon one could point to Kierkegaard's *Forførerens Dagbog* (1843; *The Seducer's Diary*) and forward to postwar existentialist novels such as Martin A. Hansen's *Løgneren* (1950; *The Liar*). By referring to the creative process, the narrative makes the reader aware of the problematic relationship of the lived experience to textual representation. The conventional mimetic notion of literature is disrupted. Fiction is being written about writing fiction.

To begin with a most light-hearted of Andersen's metatextual commemorations of the Self, let us consider a short text from his mid-career: "Flipperne" (1848; "The Collar"). Readers of Andersen remember this witty and ironic tale about the boastful and ultimately pathetic shirt collar. It is the story of the spunky, but dejected suitor who ends up in the rag-bin. The concluding paragraph of the tale reads:

> Og det blev de, alle Kludene bleve hvidt Papir, men Flipperne bleve netop til dette Stykke hvide Papir vi her see, hvorpaa Historien er trykt, og det var fordi at de pralede saa frygteligt bagefter af hvad der aldrig havde været; og det skal vi tænke paa, at vi ikke bære os ligesaadan ad, for vi kunne saamæn aldrig vide, om vi ikke ogsaa engang komme i Klude-Kassen og blive gjort til hvidt Papir og faae vor hele Historie trykt for paa, selv den allerhemmeligste og maa saa selv løbe om og fortælle den, ligesom Flipperne. (*Eventyr* 2: 167)

> [All the rags were turned into white paper, but the collar turned into this very piece of white paper that we're looking at now, the one on which this story is printed. That's because he boasted so terribly afterward about things that had never happened. That's something we should remember, so we don't behave the same way, because we never can tell whether we too might one day end up in the rag bin and be turned into white paper and have our whole story printed on it, even our innermost secrets, and then have to run around talking about them, just like the collar.] (*Fairy Tales*, 263)

The clever personification of inanimate objects, the self-deprecating and ironic humor of the narrator, the moralistic didactic tone of this conclusion, these are all quintessential elements of Andersen's tales. But most noteworthy in this context is the narrator and protagonist of the story (the collar itself) who ends up as a piece of paper upon which his own embarrassing story is printed, "Flipperne bleve netop til dette Stykke hvide Papir vi her see, hvorpaa Historien er trykt" [the collar turned into this very piece of white paper that we're looking at now, the one on which this story is printed]. The conclusion of the tale points not only to the private nature of the story, but also directly to the self-referential and tangible aspect of the text. This fiction is self-reflexive and metatextual in the most literal sense. Perhaps one should not argue that it be regarded as a kind of commemoration of

Andersen's literary legacy, but it is certainly an ironic commentary on the biography of a self-promoting celebrity. In writing "Flipperne" Andersen responded to the censorious Danish press, which had criticized him for boasting his way across England in 1847. Certainly, the tale is self-mocking, the author satirizing himself as a compulsive autobiographer. As a "commemoration," the text points directly to its own perpetuity as a published and printed piece of literature, which offers a representation of the author as a loveless bachelor, whose public status required that all the intimacies of his life story be "printed on a piece of paper."

In another text, "En Rose fra Homers Grav" ("A Rose from Homer's Grave"), first published as a chapter in the travel book, *En Digters Bazar* (1842; *A Poet's Bazaar*) and later in a slightly amended version in a collection of 1862, we can study closely how this particular self-referential aesthetic functions in a commemorative text.[3] By evoking ancient Greece, the birthplace of civilization, the grave of the immortal Greek poet – and by associating this setting with potent and favored Romantic symbols, the rose and the nightingale – Andersen's text announces ideas of literary longevity and also points to the material nature of textual production. The text functions as a textual commemoration of the author H.C. Andersen in the most direct sense, while it also hints at notions of death (organic decomposition in the grave of Homer) and at rebirth, those very elements that seem to form the basis of Andersen's poetic credo.

One can break down this short text into three layers of commemoration.[4] On the first level is the tale of the rose on Homer's Grave. The title of the tale and the text itself commemorate the great classical poet, Homer, the presumed author of the *Iliad* and the *Odyssey*. The reader is thus reminded that Homer gained literary immortality. A rose is the speaking subject of the text, representing poetry which springs out of the grave of Homer. The rose utters: "Iliadens Sanger blev Jord i denne Jord, hvorfra jeg spirer!" (*Eventyr* 4:44) [The poet of Iliad became earth in the earth from which I sprout!]. The rose (that is, Poetry) questions how she who is so sacred should only bloom for a poor nightingale. The nightingale then sings herself to death and is buried in Homer's grave.

The second level of commemoration in this text moves from Homer to Andersen. Interestingly, this action takes place in the dream of the rose. At night the rose folds its leaves tightly and dreams of "en Sanger fra Norden" (4:44) [a poet from the North] who arrives at the site of Homer's grave. The rose dreams that she is plucked and pressed between the pages of a book and taken as a memento by the young poet to "sit fjerne Fædreland" (4:44) [his distant Fatherland]. In this level of the text, Andersen the poet and his extraordinary journey to the Orient are commemorated. In this way, the author's literary legacy is associated with that of the great poet of antiquity. But, as in the first part of the story (with the death of the nightingale), there is a dark implication in the text. In a phantasmagorical appearance, the young poet plucks and steals the very rose of poetry from Homer's grave, with the result that: "Og Rosen visnede af Sorg og laae i den snevre Bog, som han aabnede i sit Hjem, og han sagde; 'her er en Rose fra Homers Grav.'" (4:44) [And the rose withered in sorrow and lay in the narrow book, which he opened in his home and said 'here is a rose from Homer's grave']. The rose's transformation from living organism to withered, textual artifact is a sorrowful metamorphosis.

"En Rose fra Homers Grav" (1842/1862; A Rose from Homer's Grave). In a tale commemorating H.C. Andersen's journey to the Near East, the rose plucked from Homer's grave becomes an artifact resting between the pages of the *Iliad*. Illustration by Vilhelm Pedersen.

The third and final level of commemoration in the text must be considered. The rose wakes up from the dream (the dream of being plucked or taken), the hot Asian sun rises, and the rose hears the footsteps of travellers. The rose's nightmare becomes a reality. The rose is plucked by a poet from the North in a passage, which is suggestive of the violation of virginity. The young poet breaks the rose off by the stem, and "trykkede et Kys paa dens friske Mund" (4:45) [presses a kiss on its fresh mouth] and takes it with him home to the land of fog and northern lights. Here in this third level of this highly self-reflexive text, the plucked rose is converted into a textual artifact. It lies pressed between the pages of a book (actually a volume of the Iliad) where, as a tangible artifact, it commemorates Homer's grave, Andersen's visit to that site, and the idea of the immortality of great literature.

One could stop here, and read this tale as a self-aggrandizing author's efforts to associate his own legacy with that of the ancient Greek poets. However, the reader notes yet another layer in this textual commemoration. The final lines of the text read: "Som en Mumie hviler nu Blomsterliget i hans *Iliade*, og som i Drømme hører den ham aabne Bogen og sige: 'Her er en Rose fra Homers Grav!'" (4:45) [Like a mummy the flower corpse now rests in his *Iliad,* and as in a dream it hears him open the book and say: 'Here is a rose from Homer's Grave!']. The rose of poetry is sadly desecrated in this final image; it is mummified, embalmed, a corpse of a flower confined to a book-coffin in a library of the foggy North. The narrative perspective of the tale is that of the rose (poetry), not of the young traveller. Here in the conclusion, in a kind of recurring nightmare, the rose hears the words spoken again and again over its bibliophilic grave, 'Her er en Rose fra Homers Grav!' ['Here is a rose from Homer's grave!']. The image is Gothic and eerie, reminiscent even of the horror tales of American poet Edgar Allan Poe. It is a darkly pessimistic commentary on the process of converting life into art, the symbol of the dead and decaying rose echoing the aesthetic sensibilities of the late Romantic period.

One might ask whether the text might be read as a disturbing allegory of poetic representation. The organic rose, a symbol of poetry sprung from the ancient Greek poet's grave and plucked by the young Romantic poet travelling in the exotic Orient, is transformed in the final passage into a textual artifact (a dried flower), pressed into a volume of poetry. It functions like text printed on a page. It is a tangible artifact of what once was. One could argue that there is some kind of aesthetic principle at work here in Andersen's text. Similar to the crumbling "ruins" being reclaimed by nature, or similar to the Phoenix bird who consumes herself in order to rise anew from the ashes, the rose is destroyed – sacrificed or deflowered, if you will – in order to produce a text about it. The fate of the rose plucked from Homer's grave – like the collar ("Flipperne") which becomes the paper upon which its story is printed, is ultimately one of alienation. Andersen's text when read closely is neither nostalgic nor sentimental, but is a story which is both Romantic and Modernist in the most profound sense. It addresses the question of how poetic idioms (even those indebted to classical literature) are converted and transformed into new literary art forms; this process, Andersen suggests, requires a radical desecration of old forms in order to create new fictions. In the case of "En Rose fra Homers Grav," this de-composition (like the soil in Homer's grave) is sorrowful and painful. In the end the text does not tell a story of the immortality of poetry. The text implies that the destruction and death of a poetic discourse is worthy of mourning, worthy of a commemoration.

"Den stumme Bog" (1863: "The Silent Album") by H.C. Andersen, a short tale about death and the transitoriness of poetic discourse, symbolized by a collection of pressed flowers. Illustration by Vilhelm Pedersen.

In closing I might also point to another text in which images of flowers (memories) and texts (books) are conflated, although to a somewhat different effect. It is the text entitled "Den stumme Bog" (1863), which is translated as "The Silent Album" (1974) by Erik Christian Haugaard. A better translation of the title would be "The Mute Book" (The book which does not speak). This text opens with a description of a corpse lying in an open coffin. Under the head of the deceased, the old student from Upsala, is placed,

> en stor, tyk Bog, hvis Blade hvert var et heelt Ark graat Papir, og mellem hvert laae, gjemt og glemt, visne Blomster, et heelt Herbarium ... Til hver Blomst knyttede sig et Capitel af hans Liv. (*Eventyr* 4:57)

[a large, thick book, whose pages were a large sheet of grey paper, and between each one lay, preserved and forgotten, withered flowers, an entire herbarium ... To each flower was tied a chapter in his life.]

This short tale turns on the idea of the pressed flowers as tangible signs which tell the stories of the rich "chapters" in the life of the deceased. The tragic implication of the tale is that, with the passing of the man these signs (the pressed flowers) can no longer be read. The tale speaks to the transitoriness of life and of the texts, which represent it. The artifact or textual sign, without its proper reader or audience, may quickly lose its significance for the next generation. It is "gjemt" (saved), but also soon "glemt" (forgotten). This final textual commemoration expresses a dark and very modern pessimism about the longevity of poetic discourse and about the author's literary legacy.

Works Cited

Andersen, H.C. *Eventyr*. 7 vols. Eds. Erik Dal, Erling Nielsen and Flemming Hovmann. Copenhagen: DSL/Reitzel, 1963-90.

Andersen, Jens. *Andersen: En biografi*. 2 vols. Copenhagen: Gyldendal, 2003. Trans. Tiina Nunnally. *Hans Christian Andersen: A New Life*. New York/Woodstock/London: Overlook Duckworth, 2005.

Bøggild, Jacob. "Ruinous Reflections: On H.C. Andersen's Ambiguous Position Between Romanticism and Modernism." *H.C. Andersen: Old Problems and New Readings*. Ed. Steven P. Sondrup. Odense: University of Southern Denmark Press, 2004. 75-96.

Detering, Heinrich. "The Phoenix Principle. Some Remarks on H.C. Andersen's Poetological Writings." *Hans Christian Andersen: A Poet in Time*. Eds. Johan de Mylius et al. Odense: Odense University Press, 1999. 51-65.

Haugaard, Erik Christian, trans. "The Silent Album." *The Complete Fairy Tales and Stories*. By Hans Christian Andersen. New York: Doubleday, 1974. 381-382.

Mylius, Johan de. *Forvandlingens pris: H.C. Andersen og hans eventyr*. Copenhagen: Høst & Søn, 2004.

Nunnally, Tiina, trans. "The Collar." *Fairy Tales*. By H.C. Andersen. Ed. Jackie Wullschlager. New York: Viking, 2004. 261-263.

Wilson, Edmund. *Axel's Castle: A Study in the Imaginative Literature of 1870-1930*. New York: Charles Scribner's Sons, 1969.

Wullschlager, Jackie. *H.C. Andersen: The Life of a Storyteller*. Chicago: University of Chicago Press, 2002 (Original edition: The Penguin Press, London, 2000.

Ørsted, H.C. "Naturvidenskabens Forhold til Digtekunsten." *Aanden i Naturen*. Fourth Edition. Copenhagen: Vintens Forlag. 1978. 155-175.

Notes

1. The myth of the Phoenix describes an Arabian bird, said to make a nest of spices, sing a melodious dirge, flap its wings to set fire to the pile, consume itself in the ashes, but then arise with new life to repeat the former one. The 'phoenix cycle' is the period between transformations of the phoenix, generally supposed to be five hundred years.
2. For further discussion of this topic, see Stecher-Hansen, "Science Fiction in the Age of Romanticism: Hans Christian Andersen's Futuristic Tales." *Selecta* 14 (1993): 74-77.
3. English translations of the quotations from "En Rose fra Homers Grav" and "Den stumme Bog" are by the author of the article, not by Erik Christian Haugaard.
4. This analysis of "En Rose fra Homers Grav" is inspired by an idea in Mark Hebsgaard's unpublished lecture, "From Time Immemorial to Immortality: Callimachus, Hans Christian Andersen and Literary Perpetuity," delivered at the Second International Hans Christian Andersen Conference, Odense, 1996.

"Out of a Swan's Egg": Metamorphosis in Hans Christian Andersen's Tales and in *The Fairy Tale of My Life*

Maria-Sabina Draga Alexandru

> It does not matter in the least being born in a duckyard,
> if only you come out of a swan's egg.
> (H.C. Andersen, "The Ugly Duckling")
>
> Now I am ready to tell you how bodies are changed
> Into different bodies.
> (Ovid, *Metamorphoses*, trans. Ted Hughes)

Metamorphosis – a common pattern in fairy tales – is, in classical mythology, a change in the body. It is a change for the worse when it happens as a result of God's/the gods' revenge on someone as punishment for hybris, or for the better, following initiation through suffering and purification. In Andersen's fairy tales both patterns occur. They have an educational function within the world of children's values: one can become what one wants to be if one has the power to imagine oneself as such. In *The Fairy Tale of My Life* these values are used as guidemarks along Andersen's path throughout his life as various experiences change him from "the ugly duckling" into the swan. Travelling and performance – changing location and disguise – contribute to various temporary and permanent forms of metamorphosis in the writer's identity formation.

This paper will study the concept of metamorphosis in Andersen's writing in a double perspective. One dimension will be mythical, as proposed by Ovid and Marina Warner. The other will be contemporary, in an attempt to reposition Andersen's view of metamorphosis within the frame of nomadic understandings of the self as proposed by Deleuze and Guattari on the one hand and Rosi Braidotti on the other. I would like to suggest that from today's perspective, increasingly informed by the experience of globalisation, where time and space are becoming more compact, Andersen's own metamorphosis through travelling (or "flying") can be reread as a foreshadowing of the contemporary model of the citizen of the world.

My paper is divided into four sections – "Storytelling", "Performance", "Travelling" and "Metamorphosis". This division is merely a practical and methodological one. Actually, the last three sections are also about storytelling, about the ways in which the respective concepts interact to make Andersen's storytelling what it is.

Storytelling

Andersen is to us, first and foremost, an author of beautiful fairy tales. Elias Bredsdorff, one of Andersen's major biographers, describes his early perceptions of the author as situated between reality and legend in the following terms:

> The first time I realized that Hans Christian Andersen was a person who had really lived, and was not just the title of a wonderful book of fairy tales, was when my grandmother, having read me one of Andersen's tales, told me how she had once met him, even danced with him at a party when he was an old man and she a young girl of seventeen.[1]

It is a well-known fact in Andersen's life that at one point the real man was replaced by his own literary persona. As he started publishing, he came to be known as H. C. Andersen rather than by either of his full Christian names. Moreover, this overlap of legend and history signals the condition of the literary fairy tale, where a folk genre is used creatively by an author, but at the same time it projects its legendary aura onto the author.

The fairy tale is primarily known as a genre for children. But it is also a genre which attracts romantic imagination through its potential for transgressing the world of the real. The fairy tale became a literary genre through the works of Charles Perrault and the Brothers Grimm, but really took off as a creative genre in its own right in Andersen's writing. Change – or metamorphosis – is very common in fairy tales and there is nothing surprising about it. In Andersen's tales – which are not just for children – characters travel and are changed in the process of travelling (as, one can argue, Andersen changed himself). Some of these characters start poor and become rich through the generosity of their hearts ("The Travelling Companion") or through tricks ("The Tinderbox"). Others travel in search of true love, which is seldom attainable; however, they reach something else instead (the promise of an eternal soul in "The Little Mermaid" or union with the beloved in the afterworld of death in "The Steadfast Tin Soldier"). Death, the ultimate expression of the intensity of living, can also be a change for the better, as it provides escape from a life of need and suffering ("The Little Match Girl").

Andersen's tales propose an extraordinary scenario of transgressing boundaries by exploring the tough real world and ultimately changing it – through love, death or simply "flying" away ("The Little Mermaid", "The Ugly Duckling"). Transgression implies emerging from a troubled consciousness which, having experienced sorrow and despair, sublimated them into storytelling. For Andersen, storytelling, through its exploration of performance and travelling, is a way of refashioning the self in its aiming towards the desired metamorphosis of the ugly duckling into the beautiful swan. This is why his definitive autobiography, *The Fairy Tale of My Life*, carefully filters all the real events of his life through fairy tale. The beginning is very well known:

> My life is a lovely story, happy and full of incident. If, when I was a little boy, and went forth into the world poor and friendless, a good fairy had met me and said, "Choose now thy own course through life, and the object for which thou wilt strive, and then, according to the development of thy mind, and as reason requires, I will guide and defend thee to its attainment", my fate could not, even then, have been directed more happily, more prudently or better. The history of my life will say to the world what it says to me, – There is a loving God, who directs all things for the best.[2]

Andersen's life certainly was full of incidents and, in this sense, provided good material for storytelling (which is exactly how the author consciously designed it to be). It also had a certain purpose to it, to which Andersen liked to attach a religious connotation. But – as his Diaries and other first hand evidence would show – the happiness he mentions was not easily granted. Andersen, however, was very careful to always project his life as happy and to convince himself that it was so. To that effect, he even altered some events and character descriptions to fit this image he so carefully tried to build. In *The Fairy Tale of My Life*, for example, he portrayed his parents as a very happy and loving couple, even though evidence has it that they were in fact seriously mismatched.[3] It was part of Andersen's project of rising from rags to riches, of turning from the marginalised "ugly duckling" into the swan that became emblematic for Denmark,[4] to alter his real life truth and make it match his purposes. As such, it was not so much a fairy or God who traced the smooth path of Andersen's extraordinary life; it was rather Andersen himself, the God in the world of his stories, who expanded his authorial function to the re-writing of his own life as if it had been a fairy tale. Throughout the journey of his life he consistently did his best to leave his modest origins behind and to reach status through the power of his genius.

Andersen's tales outline character evolution through an initiation journey – travelling – during which characters experiment with various possible alternative images or try on different masks – performance – and thus reach an improved and significantly different state of the self – metamorphosis. The same concepts – performance, travelling, and metamorphosis – work in very similar ways in *The Fairy Tale of My Life* as the ingredients through which Andersen refashions his own life and ultimately himself. I shall look at these three concepts in turn.

Performance

As Andersen's various biographers point out, the Danish author was always concerned with his image. Portraits made throughout his life show him in carefully aestheticised poses which would have been worthy of any of the people he was so keen to mix with – the social and cultural elites of his time. Fascinated with the theatre from the very beginning, he left Odense (where he no longer wanted to live with his recently remarried mother) to go to Copenhagen and become an actor (therefore someone who is professionally trained to become someone else). He consistently tried to build himself as what he wanted to be. Acting is the job meant to produce make-believe par excellence; but beyond the boundaries of the stage it can provide very useful strategies for dealing with serious real life issues. These, at first sight, may look like escape strategies, but can become active part of a process of self-education and self-reinvention. This is exactly what Andersen wanted, as he was not exactly proud of his humble origins and was confident that, as a literary genius, he had a few things to say to the world. He succeeded by becoming a writer of fairy tales whose commitment to storytelling goes as far as telling the story of his life as a fairy tale. In his travels, he transgresses the sorrow of realistic detail towards a personal metamorphosis into his own idealised princely hypostasis. All this is possible in the fairy tale world. The way to do it is first suggested by careful observation of the techniques and internal logic of performance.

Andersen's love affair with the theatre began very early on. He was deeply impressed by the Royal Theatre's Production of *Cendrillon* at Odense Theatre in 1818, which became a model from his "rags-to-riches" life-scenario that must have inspired "The Ugly Duckling". When he left Odense he was going to Copenhagen to become an actor. Even though his acting was never exactly successful, he started to write for the stage and some of his plays were very well received by the audience. Andersen's involvement in the world of the stage was a long and complex one and it was not restricted to his actual plays. Beyond the world of the stage strictly speaking, there is an important degree of romantic theatricality in Andersen's understanding of identity and character both in his life and his tales. The old motif of the world as a stage appeals to the romantic imagination with an increased sensitivity as seen through the lens of Sanskrit philosophy,[5] for which Romanticism has a great attraction. The romantic conflict between essence and appearance projects as a conflict between masking and unmasking in Andersen's tales. It is here that performance techniques become relevant to a desired metamorphosis pattern. The shedding of the mask – the revealing of the protagonist's true essence, set free through suffering – is always a highly spectacular moment. "The Princess and the Pea" is a concise study of the triumph of essence over appearance, similar, in that respect, to "The Ugly Duckling". In both tales we learn about an essence which is initially concealed, but which does not fail to reveal itself when the right time comes. As she refuses to kill her beloved prince at the expense of her own life, the Little Mermaid reveals the kindness of her soul, hence she is truly deserving of her soul's immortality. Her love sets her free from the witch's spell and makes her worthy of becoming a daughter of the air with the prospect of gaining an immortal soul. A similar moment of unmasking takes place in "The Wild Swans" the moment the spell is broken and Elisa, having saved her brothers from the spell, is free to proclaim her innocence.

The romantic motif of the shadow is a complex variation on the theme of the mask (the appearance which covers the essence and the misleading interplay between the two) in "The Travelling Companion". Here the ghost of the dead man whose corpse poor Johannes looks after at the expense of all his modest fortune becomes an accompanying protector figure who leads the protagonist on his way to success. In Andersen's world, completely selfless sacrifice always pays double. At the end of the story there is a dramatic moment of unmasking as the companion reveals his true nature and, having fulfilled his mission on earth, disappears to rejoin the world of shadows. In "The Shadow", the same motif is given concrete expression as the initially playful exchange of roles between the philosopher and his shadow gains real consistency. It is significant that the protagonist is a philosopher, therefore someone whose existence is so completely restricted to the world of his ideas that it is no surprise such ideas become tangibly true.

In his study of initiation patterns, Andersen is interested in the dialectic relationship between change in appearance and real change, which affects the essence. What happens to his characters during their initiation journeys is very much a matter of the interaction between essence and appearance. Mirrors – which reflect the appearance, but sometimes become potent enough to reveal at least part of the essence – are crucial in this act of unmasking. In "The Ugly Duckling" the world watches the gradual metamorphosis – again at the price of suffering – of the ugly duckling into the beautiful swan. But to the duckling himself the shedding of the mask only becomes known when he sees his reflected image in the mirror as he has been invited by the other swans to join them. To him, the moment of unmasking is a moment of recognition by his peers, as it was to Andersen, even though in reality a deeper transformation has taken place:

"I shall fly over to them, those royal birds! And they can hack me to death because I, who am so ugly, dare to approach them. What difference does it make? It is better to be killed by them than to be bitten by the other ducks, and pecked by the hens, and kicked by the girl who tends the henyard; or to suffer through the winter."
And he lighted on the water and swam towards the magnificent swans. When they saw him they ruffled their feathers and started to swim in his direction. They were coming to meet him.
"Kill me", whispered the poor creature, and bent his head humbly while he waited for death. But what was that he saw in the water? It was his own reflection; and he was no longer an awkward, clumsy, grey bird, so ungainly and so ugly. He was a swan![6]

A mirror and its capacity to reflect wholeness or the lack of it in an inverted way – thus successfully hiding the essence under misleading appearances – plays a central part in "The Snow Queen", where Andersen produces a personal version of the genesis of the fight between good and evil. The devilish mirror broken into millions of splinters acts as an attempt of evil appearance to become essence – an attempt of the devil to turn performance (temporary change) into metamorphosis (permanent change), to adapt the world to his design:

> When a sliver like that entered someone's eye it stayed there; and the person, forever after, would see the world distorted, and only be able to see the faults, and not the virtues, of everyone around him, since even the tiniest fragment contained all the evil qualities of the whole mirror. If a splinter should enter someone's heart – oh that was the most terrible of all! – that heart would turn to ice.[7]

As in "The Little Mermaid" and "The Wild Swans", it is through the power of love (which is always a matter of essence) that the ice melts and the balance of good and evil is restored.

An important version of theatricality in Andersen's work is theatre disguised for children – puppet theatre. References to puppet theatres – like the one made by Andersen's father for his son in order to stimulate the power of his imagination – are made in the tales either explicitly or implicitly, in the guise of a whole world of inanimate objects endowed with a life of their own, Andersen's own animistic universe which humans cannot comprehend. Little insignificant objects – sometimes but not always with an anthropomorphic appearance, such as toys – assume human qualities, including feelings and a morality of their own, as in "The Steadfast Tin Soldier" or "The Darning Needle". This is precisely the function of puppet theatres: to allow objects to mimic the real world and to comment allegorically on its virtues and vices. The puppet theatre which comes to life in "The Travelling Companion" through the power of the magic salve is – like the travelling companion himself – a metaphor of the power of love and kindness to fight death and change it into life. "The Darning Needle" is an allegory of the consequences of vanity which cannot go unpunished. Beyond such explicit moral studies, however, the most important function of object and animal fables is their capacity to fill up with life. Inanimate matter can move and feel, as suggested by the many ballerinas – dance arrested in graceful poses – in Andersen's paper cuttings. Not all matter comes to life, though; in "A Steadfast

Tin Soldier", the one-legged soldier, marginalised by his handicap, lives through a whole adventure, whilst the paper ballerina he is in love with never lives other than as the object of the soldier's passion. Passion is the condition to achieve human life and a human soul (as in "The Little Mermaid"). Man-made things can come to life if they have enough passion. It is passion rather than a "natural" origin that the man-made nightingale lacks as compared to the real one ("The Nightingale").

Objects coming to life or toys having a life of their own blur the boundaries between the real world of living people and a world of fairy tale where objects and beings are not that different. However, objects are sometimes confined to their inanimate status which they cannot overcome, as is the case in "The Nightingale". Performance which cannot affect the essence and is thus arrested on the level of appearance is the subject matter of "The Emperor's New Clothes", which denounces vanity as the sin of mistaking appearance for the essence.

As a storyteller constantly interested in improving his technique, Andersen identifies with various role-models. Two of the most important ones come from *The Arabian Nights*, one of Andersen's earliest readings, as it was on his father's bookshelf together with the Bible and Holberg's plays. A play which deeply influenced Andersen's storytelling not just thematically, but also technically and on the conceptual level is Oehlenschläger's *Aladdin*. Aladdin – who thus comes to Andersen both through reading and through performance – is a particular type of fairy tale character who obtains the key to the other-wordly mystery as soon as he owns the magic lamp. Aladdin is explored as a model for Andersen's own characters – for instance in "The Tinderbox" or in "The Flying Trunk", but also as an alter ego of himself. He is the storyteller who wants to possess the key to the magic world of fairy tales where everything is possible. The storytelling act provides a way to transcend the contingent. The symbolism of storytelling as life-preserving and life-giving is also importantly related to the figure of Scheherazade. As she tells stories in order to seduce the King and thus save her life, Scheherazade's storytelling is a world-changing act through transcendence of the struggle for power that dominates the world into a space of better values. While listening to her, Shahryar changes from the ruthless villain into a loving husband. As he learns how to love, he also learns to see things in a wider perspective and thus to be more tolerant. Scheherazade uses storytelling to reach a purpose and in that she prefigures the romantic taste for literary, creative storytelling – a journey rather than a source of entertainment. She is the embodiment of storytelling for survival. But survival is not just physical, it is also moral; in this respect she is importantly a figure of transcendence and change for the better.

Andersen used performance in order to transcend the condition he was born into. He studied himself and the world, and himself in interaction with the world, and constantly struggled to overcome, through education and through the power of his genius, the social determinations of his background. He succeeded by continuously refashioning himself as he travelled around Europe in a way which would normally have been impossible in nineteenth-century Denmark. Travelling and performance are both concerned with changing the self by confronting it with the *other*. They become intrinsically connected as travelling turns into an act of knowledge. I shall look into this more closely in my following section.

Travelling

Travelling fascinated the Romantic imagination. European Romanticism coincides with a time when exotic European and non-European spaces are increasingly explored. The encounter with alternative spaces reveals a way of transgressing the boundaries of one's self, of escaping terrestrial limitations. As the experience of space multiplies, spaces are projected differently through the filter of imagination. The Romantic traveller, however, is not a happy one. The broken-hearted hero whose chaotic soul hides some secret sorrow, addiction or sin and who runs away from himself in the hope of leaving that sorrow behind is a typical Romantic presence (of which Lord Byron, the great performer of the Romantic poetic pose, is a very good example). Andersen launches himself into travelling in an impulse to move physically away from his original poor background, but also out of his thirst for knowledge, his desire to learn new things that will make him a more accomplished intellectual. For Andersen, travelling is a deeply intellectual experience, so intense that it is perceived as lifegiving. Moreover, as he confesses in *The Fairy Tale of My Life*, travelling is a catalyst that activates the potential material hidden within the poet's self, waiting to be brought to light for the benefit of himself and his audience:

> Travelling operates like an invigorating bath to the mind – like a Medea-draught which always makes one young again. I feel once more an impulse for it – not in order to seek material, as a critic fancied and said, in speaking of my "Bazaar"; there exists a treasury of material in my own inner self, and this life is too short to mature this young existence; but there needs refreshment of spirit in order to convey it vigorously and maturely to paper, and travelling is to me, as I have said, this invigorating bath, from which I return as it were stronger and stronger.[8]

As he interacts with various places along his trajectories, Andersen is very perceptive of their own personalities. He learns from them and filters them through his sensibility, so that local colour is not just a matter of different appearances. In *The Fairy Tale of My Life*, places are depicted not just in terms of what they look like, but with personalities of their own. Copenhagen, the first "great city" he encounters, fascinates him with its "noise and tumult" (p. 25). A lot of attention is given to Italy, seen as the perfect example of nature and art going together. In contrast, Germany is a serious place where professional interest replaces aesthetic contemplation. In Germany Andersen meets the great poets of his time, but he is also greatly disappointed. In Berlin (p. 243), his encounter with Jacob Grimm, who has not heard of him, is deeply embarrassing to the Danish writer and deeply hurts his ego. Berlin is at that point projected as a rather hostile city, by contrast to the friendliness and inspirational warmth of places like Rome and Naples.

Places are rated by the intensity with which one experiences them – hence by the degree to which they contribute to the inner life of Andersen's self. Whilst Italy is associated with art experienced to the full, France is perceived in terms of the contrast between the almost religious greatness of its fame and negative personal experience:

> People say that the South of France is a portion of Paradise; under the present circumstances it seemed to me a portion of hell with all its heat.[9]

Cities are placed in a hierarchy of their own. London is a "city of politeness", even though its tumult is greater than Copenhagen's. As compared to Rome, one of Andersen's favourites up to that point, "a macrocosm, a bas-relief of the day" (p. 295), London is the "city of cities":

> London, the city of cities! Yes, I felt immediately that it was so, and I learnt to know it from day to day afterward. Here is Paris with a mightier power; here is the life of Naples but not its bustle. Omnibus after omnibus passes – they say there are four thousand – teams, carts, cabs, hansoms, and elegant carriages are rattling, training, rolling, and driving away, as if they were going from one important event in the city to another. And this tide is always moving! Always! When all those people we now see in such activity are in their graves, the same hurried activity will still continue here, the same waves of omnibuses, cabs, cars: the men walking with signs before and behind, signs on poles, signs on coaches, with advertisements of balloons, Bushmen, Vauxhall, panoramas, and Jenny Lind.[10]

The emotional element related to the presence of Jenny Lind, with whom Andersen was in love at the time, invests the space with a personal dimension.

Travelling in Andersen's writing outlines an evolution in his perspectives on identity in relation to place (e.g. national identity) from cultural in-betweenness (romantic travelling as escape/exile from oneself) to nomadism (a state of freedom from spatial limitations). If exile marks a split in identity, nomadism represents one step further, where the self, no longer connected to place, is freed from limitations and can dwell in imaginary spaces of one's own. Andersen was very objective and unprejudiced towards the spaces he encountered, which were for him opportunities to become richer intellectually. He travelled very much for his time and related to all the places with equal, unprejudiced interest. In his travels, he both asserted his Danishness and transgressed it in becoming a citizen of Europe.

Gilles Deleuze and Félix Guattari differentiate the nomad from the migrant in the following terms:

> The nomad is not at all the same as the migrant; for the migrant goes principally from one point to another, even if the second point is uncertain, unforeseen, or not well localized. But the nomad goes from point to point only as a consequence and as a factual necessity; in principle, points for him are relays along a trajectory.[11]

The prevalence of trajectory over fixed points on it in Deleuze and Guattari's view cannot be reduced to an opposition between stasis and movement, but, rather, comes down to a different understanding of space:

> (...) there is a significant difference between the spaces: sedentary space is striated, by walls, enclosures, and roads between enclosures, while nomad space is smooth, marked only by "traits" that are effaced and displaced with the trajectory. (...) The nomad distributes himself in a smooth space; he occupies, inhabits, holds that space; that is his territorial principle. It is therefore false to define the nomad by movement. Toynbee is profoundly right to suggest that the nomad is on the contrary *he who does not move*. Whereas the migrant leaves behind a milieu that has become amorphous or hostile, the nomad is one who does not depart, does not want to depart, who clings to the smooth space left by the receding forest, where the steppe or the desert advances, and who invents nomadism as a response to this challenge. Of course, the nomad moves, but while seated, and he is only seated while moving (the Bedouin galloping, knees on the saddle, sitting on the soles of his upturned feet, "a feat of balance"). (...) (It is therefore not surprising that reference has been made to spiritual voyages effected without relative movement, but in intensity, in one place: these are part of nomadism.)[12]

Andersen's interest in travel as such – in the trajectory – is definitely greater than his interest in the places he visits (the points on the trajectory). There is in him an urge to go, to enrich himself by experiencing places but never really relocating to any of them. In being "he who does not move", Deleuze and Guattari's nomad carries, in a sense, his home with him on the journey. He annihilates the binary set of dichotomies according to which place is necessarily defined as "here" and "there". His journey is internal in that it contains in a horizontal simultaneity all the past moments at which the nomad has been in various places along his trajectory. The map of the points covered in his journey is perpetually changing, it is a figuration, a living map,[13] situated in a perpetual state of temporariness defined by movement. Movement and change, progress rather than stasis, is what interested Andersen. Just as his plays, I want to argue, are not his most representative approaches to performance (but his fiction is), his travel books are not his most important thoughts on the meaning of travel. Both performance and travel are means of refashioning himself and his characters. They are Andersen's tools for identity study towards an ideal attainable through metamorphosis.

Metamorphosis

Biographers and critics of Andersen have outlined his imaginary pattern of ascent from "rags to riches" in various ways. Various interpretations of his dream of leaving his poor origins behind and rebuilding himself as someone worthy of the company of poets, kings and princes have varied from interpretations which come close to his own casting of his life as a fairy tale (Monica Stirling) to criticisms of his lack of a class consciousness (Elias Bredsdorff, Jack Zipes) to literal accounts of a royal origin, even though based on "scant" evidence (Alison Prince).[14] In *A Fairy Tale of My Life*, Andersen often errs on the side of fictionalising his life to the detriment of factual truthfulness. In the end, what matters is less fact – which has always fared poorly in Romantic imagination – but the capacity to give substance to an extraordinary dream of greatness which, in Andersen's tales, can come true. The metamorphosis of the ugly duckling into the beautiful swan is the true product of an act of imagination which refashions the shoemaker's son into a prince of European letters.

Some of Andersen's tales are about transgressing the boundaries between "species". In "The Ugly Duckling", transgression by virtue of natural laws is reinterpreted as transgression through merit. "The Little Mermaid" and "The Wild Swans" are variations on the theme of sacrifice and physical pain as a price for the desired metamorphosis, for the heroine's will to transgress. The theatrical unmasking of her true nature must reveal itself unexplained to the onlookers. As Elisa sheds the forced mask of witchcraft, the stake where she is supposed to be burnt metamorphoses into a rosebush which stands proof of her innocence and her brothers regain their human appearance. The Little Mermaid undergoes two metamorphoses: into a human being – a condition accompanied by the pain which characterises human life on earth – and into a daughter of the air – when the pain is lifted, but transcendence is still a promise rather than a certainty. Nothing, Andersen maintains, can be achieved without paying the price.

All the stories to which I have referred in my section on performance use performance as a transitory stage towards a desired metamorphosis, which is achieved during a journey. The Little Mermaid travels to the witch to give her voice in exchange for her metamorphosis into a human being. Then she travels to the shore and leaves the sea behind, she thinks, for ever. She is under the impression that she is a migrant to human territory and that her journey is only one way. She is wrong, but, even though her plan fails, she is given a second chance because she has proved she deserves it. The Ugly Duckling also travels: he runs away from persecution, he "earns" his status through suffering and, in the end, metamorphosis into a swan brings him more travelling. Travelling is good, it is an ideal state of grace, as opposed to stasis (being stuck in a hen's yard, where one's potential for the better is stifled). "The Travelling Companion", "The Tinderbox", "The Wild Swans" and many others are stories about metamorphosis through travelling.

What is metamorphosis? What did it mean originally, what did it mean to Andersen, and what does it mean to us?

In European culture, the word "metamorphosis" is inevitably related to Ovid, for whom it represents the principle of organic vitality in nature, as well as the pulse in the body of art:

> All things are always changing.
> But nothing dies. The spirit comes and goes.
> Is housed wherever it wills, shifts residence
> From beasts to men, from men to beasts, but always
> It keeps on leaving. (…)[15]

We should point out here that Andersen also sees nature and art as supporting each other, for instance in his descriptions of Italy, Spain and Portugal, but also in *A Poet's Bazaar*, where the Orient is imagined as a source of challenging alternatives to European art and artistic perceptions of nature. Ovid is an important reference as he points out that metamorphosis takes place in the body: it is, therefore, a change in the essence, not just in appearance (as performance is). With Andersen, it is metamorphosis – change of the self for the better – that is sought through travelling, even though, as I have tried to show, performance is a temporary stage – a rehearsal – of this change in the essence.

Starting from Ovid's definition of metamorphosis and his illustration of the universe as inherently metamorphic ("All things are always changing / But nothing dies"), Marina Warner builds a theory of metamorphosis as an underlying pattern in "all fairy tales, myths and their literary progeny" – therefore in all stories engaged in a process of transcending the real towards liminal "other worlds", characterised by unstable, shape-shifting personae and plots. As the title of Warner's book suggests – *Fantastic Metamorphosis, Other Worlds: Ways of Telling the Self* – metamorphoses take place when characters encounter other worlds and are importantly about identity formation. Warner stresses the fact that metamorphosis always takes place in cross-cultural zones, therefore it is tightly connected to travelling. As people come in touch with different cultural backgrounds, they borrow features from them and change in order to adapt. Therefore it is no surprise that fairy tales were first written down in Mediterranean ports, widely circulated areas, full of people continuously exposed to different cultural backgrounds. Metamorphosis, as it is connected to travel and identity construction in relation to it (to nomadism), is also emblematic for Andersen.

As they were transmitted through time, Ovid's *Metamorphoses* – written before his exile from Rome – came, interestingly enough, to be associated with his reinvention of himself at Tomis, the place of his exile. Posterity has been tempted to read him as a poet who transcends exilic trauma through the motif of metamorphosis. As such, he also transcends spatial limitations into a world of poetic imagination where all decisions were his. Like Ovid, Andersen – exiled from power through his low birth – reinvented himself through art and travelling. In their transcendence of space, both are nomadic rather than exilic selves.

More recent studies of nomadism, such as Rosi Braidotti's, relate it to an option which she positions "at the top of the agenda for the new millennium", when people change location much more often than they used to: "the point is not who we are, but rather what, at last, we want to become, how to represent mutations, changes and transformation, rather than Being in the classical sense".[16] Such metamorphic views of the self shift the emphasis from identity, or Being, to becoming. Braidotti relates this to a way of life characteristic of the new millennium, when connections to place are no longer possible, because people are continuously on the move from one state to another and even from one status to another.

There is a danger to err on the side of projecting our own readings and meanings onto Andersen's writing. But it is part of the destiny of literature – and even more of fairy tales – to be subject to continuous reinterpretations by new audiences. Andersen's relevance to our time, as much as to his, is an important consequence of his genius. If we read his passion for travelling and his continuous reinvention of himself in interaction with other cultures he encounters, we can perceive him as a version *avant-la-lettre* of today's nomadic citizen of the world, whose sense of self is no longer dependent on space, but redefines spaces in relation to himself, as part of his own inner being.

Notes

1. Elias Bredsdorff, *Hans Christian Andersen: The Story of His Life 1805-75*, London: Phaidon, 1975, p. 7.
2. Hans Christian Andersen, *The Fairy Tale of My Life: An Autobiography*, New York: Cooper Square Press, 2000, p. 1.
3. Jackie Wullschlager signals the differences between H.C. Andersen's parents in rather neutral terms: "Andersen described his parents romantically: his father as 'a man of a richly gifted and truly poetical mind', and his mother as 'ignorant of life and of the world'. In fact, theirs was an unlikely match between two different but well-meaning people; each had come through a hard childhood and wanted something better for their son, but their opposing outlooks quickly put a strain on the marriage" (Hans Christian Andersen: *The Life of a Storyteller*, London: Allen Lane, The Penguin Press, 2000, p. 8). Alison Prince goes much further than that in suggesting it was actually a paid match, meant to cover up for one of King Christian VIII's illicit affairs: "The known facts are scant but fundamental. On 2 April 1805 or a day or two earlier, at Broholm Castle on Funen, owned by the French count, Hofjaegermester Frederik Severin, a baby boy was born to the young countess Elise of Ahlefeldt-Lauernvig, daughter of a general who later rose to be Field Marshal of the Danish army. The child's father was Prince Christian Frederik, then nineteen years old, son of King Frederik V. Such a scandal could not be allowed to touch this Crown Prince of Denmark who would rule as Christian VIII, and so the child was whisked away by Severin's wife and given to her maid, Anne Marie Andersen, to be brought up as her own son. Anne Marie, who rather conveniently could not read or write, was not a woman to insist on any formalities. She had just three months previously married a young shoemaker, possibly as part of a paid arrangement." (Alison Prince, *Hans Christian Andersen: The Fan Dancer*, London: Allison & Busby 1998, p. 11). This view, however, is widely disapproved. Prince herself quotes Johan de Mylius' conviction that this hypothesis on Andersen's princely origins is "fiction minus fact" (p. 13).
4. Denmark is pictured as a nest where "have been and will be hatched swans whose fame will never die" in Andersen's allegorical tale entitled "The Swan's Nest" (Hans Christian Andersen, *The Complete Fairy Tales and Stories*, translated from the Danish by Erik Christian Haugaard, London: Victor Gollancz, 1977, p. 408). The swan metaphor has been used by critics and biographers to refer to Andersen himself, mostly as a result of an identification with the protagonist of "The Ugly Duckling" (Monica Stirling's

biography, for example, is entitled *The Wild Swan: The Life and Times of Hans Christian Andersen*, London: Collins, 1965).
5. According to Sanskrit philosophy the world is *maya* (illusion) and *lila* (the play of the gods). Hence the theatricality of all Hindu ritual to the point that "what a Hindu does is more important than what a Hindu believes" (Gavin Flood, *An Introduction to Hinduism*, Cambridge: Cambridge University Press, 1996. p. 12).
6. "The Ugly Duckling", in Hans Christian Andersen, *The Complete Fairy Tales and Stories*, translated by Erik Christian Haugaard, London: Victor Gollancz, 1977, p. 224.
7. "The Snow Queen", ibid., p. 235.
8. H. C. Andersen, *The Fairy Tale of My Life*, ed. cit., p. 235.
9. Ibid., p. 269.
10. Ibid., p. 292.
11. Gilles Deleuze and Félix Guattari, *A Thousand Plateaus: Capitalism and Schizophrenia,* trans. Brian Massumi, London: Athlone, 1988, p. 382.
12. Idem.
13. Rosi Braidotti, *Prologue to Metamorphoses*, ed. cit., p. 3.
14. See note 3 on Alison Prince's biography.
15. Ovid, *The Metamorphoses*, Book XV, verses 165-68, http://classics.mit.edu/Ovid/metam.html
16. Rosi Braidotti, op. cit., p. 2.

Bibliography

Andersen, Hans Christian, *The Complete Fairy Tales and Stories,* trans. Erik Christian Haugaard, London: Victor Gollancz, 1977.

– *A Visit to Portugal 1866*, trans. Grace Thornton, London: Peter Owen, 1972.

– *A Visit to Spain and North Africa 1862*, trans. Grace Thornton, London: Peter Owen, 1975.

– *A Poet's Bazaar: A Journey to Greece, Turkey & up the Danube* (1842), trans. Grace Thornton, New York: Michael Kesend, 1988.

– *The Complete Andersen*, trans. Jean Hersholt, The Limited Editions Club, New York 1949.

– *The Fairy Tale of My Life: An Autobiography* (1871), New York: Cooper Square Press, 2000.

The Arabian Nights: Tales from A Thousand and One Nights, trans. Sir Richard F. Burton, New York: The Modern Library, 2001.

Braidotti, Rosi, *Metamorphoses: Towards a Materialist Theory of Becoming*, Cambridge: Polity, 2002.

Bredsdorff, Elias, *Hans Christian Andersen: The Story of His Life and Work 1805-75*, London: Phaidon, 1975.

– *Hans Christian Andersen: An Introduction to His Life and Works*, Copenhagen: Hans Reitzels Forlag, 1987.

Deleuze, Gilles and Félix Guattari, *A Thousand Plateaus: Capitalism and Schizophrenia*, trans. Brian Massumi, London: Athlone, 1988.

Flood, Gavin, *An Introduction to Hinduism*, Cambridge: Cambridge University Press, 1996.

Irwin, Robert, *The Arabian Nights: A Companion*, Allen Lane, The Penguin Press, London: Penguin, 1994.

Ovid, *The Metamorphoses*, trans. Sir Samuel Garth, John Dryden et al, http://classics.mit.edu/Ovid/metam.html, posted 2000, accessed August 2005.

Prince, Alison, *Hans Christian Andersen: The Fan Dancer*, London: Allison and Busby, 1998.

Stirling, Monica, *The Wild Swan: The Life and Times of Hans Christian Andersen*, London: Collins, 1965.

Warner, Marina, *Fantastic Metamorphoses, Other Worlds: Ways of Telling the Self*, Oxford: Oxford University Press, 2002.

Wullschlager, Jackie, *Hans Christian Andersen: The Life of a Storyteller*, Allen Lane: The Penguin Press, London: Penguin, 2000.

Chronotope of Hans Christian Andersen's Fairy Tales and Stories

Andrey Korovin

It is not an exaggeration to say that the literary fairy tale ("eventyr") as a genre was definitively formed by H.C. Andersen. While he did not create the genre, he wrote the most original examples of this new literary form, and he single-handedly established the literary fairy tale as separate from folklore and as a distinct genre of short prose. The problem for analysis is that Andersen not only created the genre of the literary fairy tale, he also destroyed it when he created another new genre form – "historie" (story, tale). "Historie" is genetically connected to the fairy tale but has a number of essential differences from it, the main one being specific "genre polyphony", meaning that "historie" can adopt the genre features of many other literary forms – as a fairy tale, a Christmas story, a novel, a ballad, a short story, a novella, etc. At the same time, "historie" is opposed to all these genres. "Historie" is a term that is not used extensively by many scholars as it is normal to use the name "eventyr" (fairy tale) for all of Andersen's tales. But the fact is that his late texts definitely are not fairy tales. Because Andersen's later tales have been included in the fairy tale genre, then, a certain instability has arisen in the genre definition. The causes of this similar instability can be found in the specifics of space and time of the literary fairy tale. Mikhail Bakhtin used the term chronotope to show the syncretism of space and time in a literary text in his work, *Forms of Time and Chronotope in the Novel*. The chronotope seems to be one of the most important characteristics of a text.

It is necessary to distinguish the chronotope of a folklore fairy tale from that of a literary fairy tale. A folklore fairy tale has a conservative form, which has a simple chronotope with a non-specific time and place. Events are initially presented as unreal – fantastic – and in this way they take place in some "parabolic system of coordinates" where time exists only as the categories "before" and "after". There is a syncretism of space, which depends on the movement of the plot and hero and displays itself only as a point in reference to events within that same folklore fairy tale. Also one of the important features of folklore genres is the simplicity of this space; there are no different worlds and spaces. Even if a hero enters another universe (the underground world, a magic wood, etc.), this other world is not a separate reality. This new space exists according to the same set of rules as the space from which the hero has come, and there are the traditional oppositions: at home and abroad, known and unknown. So it is possible to conclude that the chronotope of a fairy tale is closed and linear. Heroes move in time and space but they do not come out of this fantastic reality. Also, all the adventures of the heroes are regarded as usual and normal. Events that we might regard as "supernatural" or "magic" are not perceived as extraordinary or mystical in the folklore fairy tale.

The literary fairy tale inherits many aspects of this system; in the poetics of the fairy tale, there is another set of natural laws, so that what is normal for a literary fairy tale is unusual in our reality. Some of Andersen's fairy tales are good examples of this. The chronotope is still simple, but in some of his texts we can see this principle changing. In such tales as "The Angel" and "The Little Match Girl" religious themes penetrate into the inner world of the fairy tale. Religious motives are alien for fairy tale poetics, which represent a fantastic world where everything is possible, but nobody believes in it. But religious and mystical motives disrupt this system. The logic of the fairy tale is broken – no longer is there a traditional chronotope with one syncretic world. The main reason for the penetration of the religious element into fairy tale poetics is the influence of romantic aesthetics with its idea of the dual world, the opposition between the real world, with its common rules, and the world of ideas (religion), where these rules do not apply. There is a conflict between the logic of reality and the logic of other levels of existence. This other existence in Romanticism is represented as a world of dreams, imagination and fantasy. Objectivity is replaced by subjectivity, because the concept of the microcosm is of paramount significance in Romanticism.

The epoch of Romanticism shows an increasing interest in folklore, and romantics started to collect folk tales and publish them. The best-known example of this activity is the Brothers Grimm's "Children and Family Fairy Tales". These fairy tales follow the fairy tale chronotope very closely. Although the Brothers Grimm, in their aspiration to reconstruct a certain initial form of national fairy tale actually destroyed the original folklore form, at the same time, they contributed greatly to the poetics of the literary fairy tale. The categorical attribute of the genre of the literary fairy tale became a specific, closed, linear chronotope, transferred to the literary text from folklore.

The fairy tale as a literary form, admitting unlimited freedom of creative imagination, became very popular. The romantics started to develop this genre very actively and actually they followed three different traditions in this genre: literary, folk and original romantic, based on the idea of the dual world. The literary and folk traditions are in a subordinated position in relation to the original romantic. Literary fairy tales were too pretentious for romantic poets. Folk tales were very attractive for Romantics, who tried to find in them their national roots. But the folk tale genre was not a suitable embodiment of romantic ideas; it had a simple form and linear chronotope. Romanticism actually created not a literary fairy tale, but a fantastic novella where the mystical component is very important, in a way alien for fairy tale poetics. The literary fairy tale should have the syncretism of the inner space of a text, the linear chronotope, which is more like a folk tale. The presence of the duality of the world is a collateral element for the poetics of a fairy tale and its ebbing connects with the destruction of a genre.

H.C. Andersen was the first writer to combine all of the existing fairy tale traditions. In doing so, he created a new literary form which is now considered to be the classical literary fairy tale. His first experimentation with the genre of fairy tale was the collection "Fairy Tales Told for Children" ("Eventyr, fortalte for Børn") published in 1835-41; it was mostly an adaptation of folk plots and images: "The Tinderbox" ("Fyrtøiet"), "The Wild Swans" ("De vilde Svaner") etc. But at that time he also wrote original tales like "The Little Mermaid" ("Den lille Havfrue") and "The Goloshes of Fortune" ("Lykkens Kalosker"), which indicate the influence of romantic esthetics. But the new collection "New Fairy Tales" ("Nye Eventyr") issued in 1843-48 is absolutely original and includes tales which are typical for Andersen's poetics: "Ole Lukoie, the Dream-God" ("Ole Lukøie") "The Shadow" ("Skyggen") etc. There are no disagreements in definition of the genre – the author uses a word "eventyr" (fairy tale) in the titles of his books. The main feature of these fairy tales is the duality of the world, but it's not as explicit as in the Romantic fantastic novella. The fairy tale "Shadow" is very typical for that period, where the fairy tale element is very strong, the chronotope is simple, the space is syncretic and the mystical component is reduced. But already in tales from that period it is possible to see that Andersen aspired to fill the simple literary form of the fairy tale with complex philosophical and religious ideas, so even at the time of its inception, the genre fairy tale showed signs of instability and flexibility.

In the 1850s, the chronotope of Andersen's texts became complicated; the duality of the world was displayed more and more. But Andersen did not return to the romantic novella; he created a special genre – "historie", which could be translated as "story" or "tale." The first small volume with the title "Historier" (Stories) was issued in 1852. The traditional fantastic form of the fairy tale with the dominance of the plot as a central feature, was transformed in texts included in this collection: "The History of the Year" ("Aarets Historie"), "The World's Finest Rose" ("Verdens deiligste Rose"), "A Picture from the Ramparts" ("Et Billede fra Castelsvolden") and others. Andersen wrote "historier" for 20 years; they are more or less large narratives included in the collections published in separate issues in 1852 – 1855 and in 1858 – 1872. After 1858 the names of the volumes were "New Fairy Tales and Stories" (*Nye Eventyr og Historier*).

Andersen wrote: "'The story' (Historien) – the name, which as I think can be the most suitable in our language for my fairy tales according with their form and their genesis. Common language uses this word for the simple story and for the freest imagination. A fable, a tale and a novella are determined by children, peasants, common people only with one short name – a story." Small narratives, which Andersen started to name "Historier", are very different; their forms and contents are not similar, but all of them have a specific chronotope and a feature of genre universality. Andersen's story is a very complex form, which could have features of other genres, so it is possible to see a specific genre syncretism as a main genre definition of "historie".

The genre "historie" is one of the small narrative genres ("kortprosa") and if we speak about its originality it is necessary to define its place in the genre system, its relations to other literary and folklore genres, to investigate its sources. It is clear that Andersen's story is generically connected with his fairy tales written in the years 1835-41. The beginning of the evolution of stories lies in some fairy tales, which did not have a simple chronotope like "The Bell" ("Klokken"), "The Old Street Lantern" ("Den gamle Gadeløgte"), "The Story of a Mother" ("Historien om en Moder"), etc. One problem is distinguishing such stories from fairy tales, since the fairy tales of 1835-41 have features of stories and the later stories borrow many elements from the earlier fairy tales. Andersen combined two traditions in fairy tale poetics: folk tales and philosophical romantic novellas, and created his own fairy tale. But we claim that Romantic short narratives were more fantastic novellas, and combination of these two forms finally destroyed the fairy tale as a simple form and created a new one – the story. There is not too much philosophy in Andersen's fairy tales of the 1830s; the author tries to follow the folk tradition, where there is no concept of the duality of the world and the linear chronotope. Some fairy tales of the 1840s have a more complex internal structure because Andersen tries to bring Romantic ideas and symbolism to the fairy tale tradition; plots and adventures exist only in a philosophical context. This is especially visible in the fairy tale "The Nightingale" ("Nattergalen"), where the main focus is on a typical romantic problem: the relationship between art and life, the romantic opposition between natural and artificial. This text does, however, retain the closed and linear chronotope which is normal in fairy tale poetics.

In the 1850s Andersen tried to create a new universe where reality existed side-by-side with fairy tale fantastic and Romantic ideas. This combination was not possible within the limits of the fairy tale chronotope. Andersen had to change the traditional form to bring real life and philosophy into his texts. Therefore, he used the form of the romantic fantastic novella with its duality of the world, but brought in real characters and situations. There are two separate but strongly connected worlds, the real and the fantastic (mystical), and reality depends on the supernatural world. The connection between these two worlds is a symbol that is displayed in the crossing between the worlds. But Andersen is not a typically romantic writer, because for Andersen, real life is more interesting and important than the fantastic world. Fantastic elements help to understand the situation, ideas and philosophical elements are in parity with the elements of the plot and intrigue. Narration in Andersen's stories has a foreground, real life, and symbolic background, which consists of another world.

This world is dual and divided like the world in Romanticism but it no longer creates myths about the world, its myths are about human life. The real world and all its concreteness are present in Andersen's stories. This Danish writer was an ingenious interpreter of life, whose stories did not merely create a poetic image of this life but captured the essence of this life in all its variety. One criterion for differentiating between Andersen's fairy tales and his stories could be to ask whether the fantastic dominates as a main structural element. In fairy tales, the most important aspect of the text is the value of wonder. In his stories the fantastic images and situations are only present to lend a special color to the text, and support for the basic idea of the narrative. The story is mostly based on a certain vision of reality, and supernatural elements may equally well be present or not in any given story. For example, the supernatural is a very important component of the composition in "The Ice Maiden" ("Iisjomfruen", 1861) but it is absent in "The Poultry-Maid Grethe's Family" ("Hønse-Grethes Familie", 1870). Thus, the fantastic element cannot function as a defining aspect of this genre as a literary form.

Fairy tale poetics assumes the strong opposition of good and evil. These two forces are in permanent struggle that determines all peripeteias. This simple antithesis is not essential in Andersen's stories any more; the author aspires to represent life in its infinite variety. The fantastic and symbols only help to make this representation more complete. Because they belong to the supernatural existence, they show the duality of the universe.

Ultimately Andersen rejects the traditional fairy tale form and puts his heroes in the real world, but the borders of this world are expanded to include the spiritual world, the world which could not be seen or felt by the author and readers. The author brings the supernatural world and reality closer to each other and shows the deep interrelation of all the described events. The complexity of composition and the indissolubility of an internal space in stories are basic features of Andersen's texts in the period 1850-70. There are two levels, the fantastic and the real, combined in these stories, just as in fairy tales. But this combination is different than in fairy tales where they are not opposed and exist in one closed space; in stories they are divided by a boundary between them.

Andersen always used the traditional Romantic concept of the duality of the universe, but this concept changed between 1835 and 1841 and in 1850-70. In the early fairy tales it is simple: the hero has features of a real person, but he is not a concrete individual; he is able to manage with unusual, fantastic circumstances, but he does not see them as unusual because his world does not have the same limits as our reality. It is possible to see this in such fairy tales as "The Tinderbox" ("Fyrtøiet"), "The Travelling Companion" ("Reisekammeraten"), "Little Claus and Big Claus" ("Lille Claus og store Claus"), etc.

The duality of the universe in the fairy tales written in the 1840s is displayed in two levels of a narration: one level is for children, another for adults. The appearance of this second adult level of understanding in the text shows already a more complex type of duality.

The fairy tale as a genre is oriented first of all to a children's audience, and Andersen wrote fairy tales like "The Nightingale" ("Nattergalen") "The Snow Queen" ("Sneedronningen"), "The Shadow" ("Skyggen"), up to the middle of the 1840s. But in the 1850s Andersen's text become very deep and philosophical; there is a symbolical level instead of a child's level. Symbols are very important for the composition of a story and they are the basic structural elements of the text in such stories as "The Wind Tells about Valdemar Daae and His Daughters" ("Vinden fortæller om Valdemar Daae og hans Døttre"), "The Silent Book" ("Den stumme Bog"), "The Bottle Neck" ("Flaskehalsen"), etc.

It seems to me that a productive way to establish criteria for the genre "historie" is to distinguish not only between Andersen's stories and fairy tales, but also novellas, because the novella as a literary genre influenced the "historie" in the same measure as the fairy tale. I have mentioned above the differences between fairy tales and Romantic novellas. Actually the novella and the fairy tale are two centers for the development of "historie". The novella is a widespread genre, which has many constructive features, the main one being brevity, and it is one of the genres of short prose like fairy tales and stories. Andersen's stories have many features, which are inherent also in novellas but not usual for fairy tales. There are more or less realistic characters in stories similar to novels and novellas but fairy tale heroes are more archetypes than individuals. Personages in stories live in the real world, but we know that a plot from Boccaccio's novella was adapted by the fairy tale poetics in "The Elf of the Rose" ("Rosenalfen", 1841).

The well-known novelistic plot has received a fantastic frame (this technique is used by Andersen for some of his stories too): the elf and his world is more common and usual than extraordinary events in the "big" human world in which he takes part: the brother kills his sister's lover, and she puts his head in a flowerpot. It is the absorption of a non-fantastic motive by a fantastic one. The novelistic content is subordinated to the fairy tale poetics. It is necessary to create a closed, unified internal world. "Historie" has a completely other chronotope: there are also two parallel worlds, fantastic and real, but the first one is not equal to the second one, it plays absolutely another role: to create the Romantic duality of the universe. Circumstances in a story can be quite common but just not be perceived as usual, that is inherent for fairy tales. Andersen makes everyday life very poetic, novelizes it: the most ordinary events are perceived as exclusive, subnormal, it is possible to see in "A Great Grief" ("Hjertesorg", 1853) – a story about a small girl who could not see a dog's grave. It is a sign of the destruction of the traditional novelistic opposition between extraordinary and common. Andersen wrote: "Our life, an external world and our internal – everything is a number of wonders, but we have got used to them too much, that we call these phenomena common."

The novel as a genre had some influence on Andersen's stories. Andersen wrote six novels in total and has undoubtedly used his experience as a novelist to create texts of stories. From 1850-70 Andersen created a number of texts which could be called mini-novels: "A Story from the Dunes" ("En Historie fra Klitterne"), "The Wind Tells of Valdemar Daae and His Daughters" ("Vinden fortæller om Valdemar Daae og hans Døttre"), "The Poultry-Maid Grethe's Family" ("Hønse-Grethes Familie"), etc. They have many features of the novel as a genre: "the chronotope of the way" (M. Bakhtin's term) as a main sign of novel poetics, a broad panorama of life, the individual hero etc. But the central structural component in them is the episode; the narration is built as a combination of episodes. Novel poetics is more descriptive and the role of individual episodes is less important in the narration as a whole.

The internal worlds of Andersen's stories become more complex than those of fairy tales when some elements of folklore and clerical genres are included in it, whether it be legends, ballads, religious fables or other types of texts. This has the effect of making a story more poetic but also makes the chronotope more open; the inner space and time receives intertextual parallels. For example, the text of one medieval ballad about Marsk Stig in the story "The Wind Tells of Valdemar Daae and His Daughters" is to show all tragic circumstances as fated, inevitable, strongly connected and dependent upon the past. The past, the present and the future are equally objective and real, like the near and far in space. The future is materialized and becomes real in the present because it is only a repetition of some events which took place in the past. Old texts confirm this inevitability: Valdemar Daae's family must die like the family of Marsk Stig in the ancient ballad. There are two times, two textual realities, which create a special open chronotope which is common in Andersen's stories.

"The Marsh King's Daughter" ("Dyndkongens Datter", 1858) is a significant Andersen text with a very complex composite chronotope. The plot and the system of personages of this story are connected with fairy tales written in the 1830-40s. In the beginning of the story, the story-teller is a stork. This is very similar to fairy tale poetics, where main animals, birds, plants and forces of nature can be heroes. The images of storks exist in Andersen's earlier texts, for example in "Storks" (1839). The system of images of many stories in the 1850-70s also includes such types of personages but they have a completely different role: they are very often symbols connecting two worlds or story-tellers. Andersen destroys traditional fairy tale fantastic poetics because he brings in real historical events and a concrete chronotope, using historical allusions. In such a story we can see indications of the place and the time of action, and find certain philosophical contents, which correspond to genre features of a story.

The image of Helga is the center of the composition of this story; all of the basic ideas of narration are focused on her image. Helga has two embodiments: a toad and a beautiful girl. She was born to the Marsh King and is also an Egyptian princess, she is native to the supernatural world, and finds her true soul under the influence of Christianity. Even when Helga comes back to Egypt, where she finds harmony and her existence is not divided any more, the light of Christianity does not leave her; the Danish word "hellig", which means "sacred" or "saint", has the same root as the name Helga. She is a symbol of the eternal good, and her image is connected with a lotus flower, which is also a symbol of cleanliness, and sanctity comes to be a symbol of rescue, both physical, for the Egyptian King, and spiritual, for Helga, that is similar in traditional symbolical value to the symbolism of a rose and a lily in Christianity.

Helga is one of these strong, romantic persons who are common as heroes in Andersen's tales from that time – Marie Grubbe, Valdemar Daae etc. It is common for such heroes not to be simple and to have opposing features of character within themselves, but in this image, two different aspects of a human being, evil and good, are locked in struggle, and only Christian religion can help to win this battle for the human soul. Andersen chooses the time of the struggle between Paganism and Christianity for his narration to focus on Christian values as eternal. Two essential symbols of this story are the marsh and the sun. The marsh personifies forces of evil, night, sorcery, and darkness capturing the light. The sun corresponds to the light of Christianity and symbolizes the triumph of good over evil.

Andersen's stories have two levels: real life and the world of legends and myths. The time of the vikings is evident in this story. The ancient beliefs in the Scandinavian gods are still alive; it is possible to feel the atmosphere of that time, which is reproduced very realistically. The writer tries to reconstruct the historical epoch when the legend about the wonderful transformation of a toad into a beautyful girl was born, because believing in miracles is natural for the Middle Ages, when miracles and reality co-existed. The Medieval type of mentality was very attractive in the epoch of Romanticism. For Andersen as a romantic poet the world is arranged integrally, there are no absolute distinctions between one part of life and another, between imagination and everyday life – they create the universe together. The bridge between legendary and real levels of narration is found in the images of the storks. They bring an ironical element into the story, but at the same time they are surrounded with an atmosphere of myth and secrecy. They live both in Egypt and in Denmark; the stork-papa has high ideas but the stork-mamma is petty bourgeois and ordinary. This opposition of philistinism and spirituality is very important not only for Andersen but for Romanticism as well.

The stork as the storyteller is a link between two worlds: Egypt and Denmark. Egypt is the legendary, fantastic world that exists in contrast to everyday Denmark. In the Egyptian system of coordinates, time is arranged according to the principles of "after – before", but is not definite. Denmark is located in real space and time, and there is basically nothing supernatural or unusual there.

Time in Denmark is well determined. Andersen describes Scandinavian olden days in a very realistic and picturesque way. He creates an atmosphere of the Vikings' pagan life in just a few words, showing himself to be a master of a short form. "A great cask of mead was drawn into the hall, piles of wood blazed, cattle were slain and served up, that they might feast in reality, the priest who offered the sacrifice sprinkled the devoted parishioners with the warm blood; the fire crackled, and the smoke rolled along beneath the roof; the soot fell upon them from the beams; but they were used to all these things. Guests were invited, and received handsome presents. All wrongs and unfaithfulness were forgotten. They drank deeply, and threw in each other's faces the bones that were left, which was looked upon as a sign of good feeling amongst them." Andersen was influenced by Walter Scott's method in the creation of a historical and local color, which should help the reader feel the historical epoch in all its originality. He does not want to idealize the Pagan time, unlike other Danish Romantic poets such as A.G. Oehlenschläger and N.F.S. Grundtvig, who aspired to present the Viking age as a Golden age for the North. But he has taken some of Grundtvig's ideas and as a result the viking's wife identifies the young Christian priest as Baldur – the Scandinavian god of good and light.

The epoch of vikings is the past in absolute measurement but in the internal time of narration it is the present, which takes place in opposition to the future – the epoch of Christianity, which is the absolute present. Christianity replaces Paganism, taking from it everything good and kind, but rejecting everything dark and malicious. Christian religion helps the Marsh King's Daughter to find her real form: everything brutal and awful leaves her, the toad disappears, and a pure Christian soul unites with the body of the beautiful Nordic girl.

It is very important for Andersen to claim the ideals of good and the validity which are brought by Christianity – the main force replacing the time of myths and gods in the North. The dream of the viking's wife confirms it. The doomsday of Scandinavian mythology – ragnarok – is coming. The old world is falling down, the last awful hour is near: "but she knew that a new heaven and a new earth would arise, and that corn-fields would wave where now the lake rolled over desolate sands, and the ineffable God reigns. Then she saw rising from the region of the dead, Baldur the gentle, the loving, and as the viking's wife gazed upon him, she recognized his countenance. It was the captive Christian priest."

The world of the Pagan North faces the world of Christianity. Andersen uses the principle of allusion to Scandinavian Mythology, putting in the text of the story some lines from "The Poetic Edda", the scald sings on the feast: "Gold and possessions will flee away, Friends and foes must die one day; Every man on earth must die, But a famous name will never die." It marks the end of an epoch, which will be replaced by Christianity. And if the time of the vikings is an undetermined abstract past, the coming era of Christianity and the modern epoch is concrete, has a linear chronotope. There is an indication of time, the 9th century, when St. Ansgarius christened pagans in Denmark and constructed the first church and the first school. The internal world of the story is supplemented and extended through the use of various cultural elements in their unity.

This story is typical for Andersen in the years 1850-60 and has all the features of Andersen's new genre "historie": a complex chronotope, based on the combination of historical time, an abstract fairy tale time and cyclic mythological time and two different worlds in opposition: reality and the supernatural fantastic world. This story exemplifies the polyphony of the "historie" genre. It is possible to see elements of different genres: the attributes of the fairy tale such as the fantastic, animals as heroes, etc.; the romantic novella with its dual worlds and ideologies, everyday realism, and historical determinism; and clerical genres with Christian mysticism and edifications. There are, moreover, other literary allusions which make the text more complex. "The Marsh King's Daughter" demonstrates the final collapse of the fairy tale form in Andersen's poetics. When Andersen combined the various traditions he created an entirely new type of text. These later texts are not fairy tales at all, but indeed represent the complete destruction of the fairy tale genre as a simple form and replaced it with the new, complex "historie".

The Shepherdess and the Chimney Sweep

Martin Lotz

Introduction

I think I have to introduce myself, as it seems I'm the only medical man in this honoured company of literary people. Actually I'm a psychiatrist specialising in non-psychotic disorders. Furthermore, I have trained as a classical Freudian psychoanalyst, and I have been working as such for about 30 years. In 1988 I published a book on Andersen *Eventyrbroen, psykoanalytiske essays om H.C. Andersen.* I also made a contribution to the First International Conference (1990), and shall be referring to these texts in the following. Some of my fundamental observations and ideas, also shared by other scholars have been heavily challenged in the years since 1988, which is the reason that I venture to give a rebuttal today. My position in line with that of Hjalmar Helweg (1927) was that Andersen in his adult life was predominantly heterosexual in his choice of love objects. Recently, in two comprehensive biographies Andersen is consistently described as a homosexual (Jackie Wullschlager 2002, Jens Andersen 2003). In addition to these two biographies several articles and smaller books have been published based on the same idea (Wilhelm von Rosen 1982, Heinrich Detering 1991, Dag Heede 2005). These works present a major challenge to the scientific research on the psychology of Andersen (see Lotz 2004).

In the following I shall discuss this challenge and try to reach a more precise characterization of some central themes in Andersen's psychology including his handling of sexual desires. I have chosen one segment out of the huge material before us. The segment spans the period from January 1844 until April 1845, and it contains one biographical event: Andersen's involvement in the first months of 1844 in the love story of the two young people, Jonna Drewsen and Henrik Stampe, and one of the classic stories: "The Shepherdess and the Chimney Sweep" written in the spring of 1845.

In my discussion I shall try to show you that

1) the claim of homosexuality is not built on solid grounds. However, it cannot be dismissed completely.
2) The scientific information on homo- and heterosexuality does not seem to have been up to date.
3) Andersen's heterosexuality cannot be dismissed.
4) The love affair between Jonna Drewsen, Henrik Stampe and Andersen needs to be reviewed.
5) The psychoanalytical analysis of "The Shepherdess and the Chimney Sweep" can be taken a step further than I did in 1988.
6) In the end I shall try to summarize by giving a suggestion of a central psychological theme which is valid both for the artist Andersen and for the private man.

The Shepherdess and the Chimney Sweep

In the story "The Shepherdess and the Chimney Sweep" we find four figures.

A couple of porcelain figures, two young people, are standing on a shelf under a mirror. They are together with a figure three times their size, a China nodding-doll also made of porcelain. A fourth figure, a satyr, is carved out of dark wood and is to be found on the front of a cupboard standing opposite, the shelf. The Satyr has made a proposal to the Shepherdess and she has turned him down. The old China man claims to be the grandfather of the Shepherdess and he has nodded to the Satyr. The Shepherdess is scared and asks the Chimney Sweep to run away with her. The two young people take flight up through the chimney. As they reach the top the Shepherdess again is scared and the couple returns to the shelf under the mirror. The only change is that the China man had made an effort to follow them, had fallen off the table and had broken into three pieces. Later on the family has him riveted together, but he cannot nod anymore.

I would like to mention some of the most important sources of inspiration for this story:

1) March 15, 1845 Andersen had a chimney fire and he wrote in his almanac: "Fire in the chimney flue. Shepherdess and the Chimney Sweep".

2) March 15 was also the birthday of a close friend of Andersen, Henrik Stampe. Just one year earlier, Andersen had been heavily involved in Henrik's love story. Henrik, aged 24, had fallen in love with the 16-year-old Jonna Drewsen. Henrik was of noble birth and the only heir to a barony. His mother, the Baroness, was still alive and Andersen had been a frequent guest at her manor. Jonna Drewsen was a commoner but still from upper society. She was a grandchild in the Collin family, where Andersen since his youth had been considered more or less a member of the family. Andersen had known Jonna from the time of her birth and they had always been fond of each other. Now the young couple wanted to become engaged, Andersen played courier, carrying love letters between them, and he pleaded for them with the Baroness. But she refused, due to the fact that Jonna was a commoner. Henrik, Jonna and Andersen could be seen as sources of inspiration to the three figures, the Chimney Sweep, the Shepherdess and the big, old china man. The Satyr seems to be a symbol of dangerous sexual impulses (Brix 1935).

3) I have previously also made another comment (Lotz 1988). In Denmark a new more democratic constitution was under debate. Jonna Drewsen had a father whose brother was a close friend of old Jonas Collin. This uncle was a left wing politician, and shortly before he had been an active participant in a preparatory

meeting for a new constitution. At that meeting he had spoken out courageously against the nobility. If nothing was done to improve the conditions of the peasants, he had said, "the china will go to pieces".

4) E.T.A. Hoffmann's story "The Nutcracker" was loved by Andersen. We recognize the Biedermeier interior where the toys come alive, and where the hero and heroine take flight up through the sleeve of a fur coat.

Interpretation A

At the most superficial level then the story tells us that the safest place in the world for a young loving couple is at home close to the fireplace. Here no one (like the satyr) will hurt you and you will be protected by beneficent forces. The distribution of sexual roles is unambiguous. Symbols of male and female gender are used with refinement and precision. The cost of this secure arrangement is postponement of sexuality.

Biographical Notes

The reason that I have chosen the segment 1844/45 is that according to the defenders of the homosexuality line, this is one of the highpoints of Andersen's disclosure of his homosexuality. In his letters to both of the two young people Andersen expressed himself with a number of loving and amorous phrases.

Both biographers elaborate on the relations between Andersen and the young couple. Both believe that Andersen was in love with Henrik but not (or much less) with Jonna. Both quote amorous remarks in the letters from Andersen to Henrik such as the following (winter 1843/44):

> My beloved Henrik! It is strange that I am writing to you, as I any moment actually can be together with you, talk to you, shake your hand, but – at least I do express myself more freely in writing. There one is less bound by a thousand small things for which to give consideration, as when you are face to face, even with you!! – I have often heard people say about the English that they have spleen. The only thing I know about that disease is that it is an oddity, but still a melancholy in which they often take their own

life! (Jens Andersen, vol. I, p. 472; Wullschlager, p. 235. my transl.).

At the same time the two authors minimize or leave out any sort of amorous remarks to Jonna, such as the following written on January 1, 1844 (Lotz 1988, p. 205; Stampe 1918. p. 110):

> My thoughts embrace you and your heart the best so heartfelt, so faithfully, I cannot explain it to myself! Never before have I known a feeling like this – – – "My own, my beloved Jonna!"

Wullschlager (p. 236) heads straight for a simple explanation of the episode. She is preoccupied with a note Andersen made in the almanac on March 4: "Henrik caressed me" (in Danish: "Henrik kjælede for mig."). Although the Danish expression is most probably used here in its old sense, meaning "being tender and showing care or perhaps caressing someone" (*Ordbog over det danske sprog*, 1929), Wullschlager is convinced that Andersen was a homosexual, and she takes the note as a proof that the relationship developed in a physical way. Wullschlager thinks it is evident that Henrik Stampe was one of Andersen's homosexual lovers. As we have here got a striking example of Wullschlager's argumentation, I shall restore the remark to its original context.

Already a few months earlier, Andersen had used the same phrase in his almanac (January 13. 1844). It goes like this

> Saturday 13. At Næboe's – – heard the reading of Lipmann. Something in the eye, Henrik caressed me

Then a month later the notes go like this:

> 29.2. Not very well!
> 1.3. Depressed over Jonna
> 2.3. Letter from Jonna
> 3.3. Dinner at Stampe's. Not in the mood.
> 4.3. This morning a card from Henrik. Thank you for your dishonesty! – My temper; the whole thing explained by his jealousy. Visit from general Guldberg; was with H, he was later together with me, he caressed me, I was sick and irritable. Thoughts about going crazy. Dinner at Pätau. – The evening with Thieles+

The notes quoted here do not seem to be compatible with a longed for sexual satisfaction. Instead of being in the seventh heaven Andersen was sick, irritable and hypochondriac. I, for one do not find the interpretation made by Wullschlager the least credible (Lotz, 2004).

It appears from diaries and letters that Andersen in this period was often in a sad, depressed mood. On January 21 when Henrik was visiting Andersen, Andersen worked on the aforementioned amorous letter to Jonna. Henrik noticed the depressed mood of his friend. He grabbed the pen and wrote some lines into the letter after Andersen had written "*my own, my beloved Jonna*". Henrik's lines were

> I'm so very fond of And. Tonight he is immensely amiable, although not very happy

My guess is that Andersen was closer to tears than to exhilaration. I think the caressing is better understood as showing affection or perhaps even a consolatory caressing of Andersen's hand rather than an erotic caressing of his penis.

Wullschlager and Jens Andersen think that Henrik was jealous, because his beloved Andersen was intimate with Jonna. However it seems even more probable that Henrik was jealous because his fiancée, Jonna, was so intimate with Andersen. Now again on the March 2 she had written a private letter to him. Both biographers make the point that Andersen five months later (June 28, 1844) in his travel diary from Germany wrote about the two young people:

> The engagement declared last week. It's a lie!

Both underline the words "It's a lie" and take it as proof that Andersen was jealous toward the "faithless" Henrik. Actually it may not be easy to see what else it could be; but the fact is that Andersen always reacted in this way, when he heard of any engagement. Years earlier (1832) he had made this clear to a friend (JA, vol. I, p. 264). The quotation is;

> Everybody gets engaged. Eduard Collin is happy with his Jette; I'm seeing the family quite often and am presented with the happiness of the lovers – It is foolish of me, but I cannot help it, every time I hear that some people are getting engaged, I get grumpy. Although the Lord knows I have not at all been infatuated with any of the people that have up to now been expedited."

The expression now loses its specific meaning and it cannot be used with any weight in 1844. It was just an old habit of Andersen's expressing sorrow that he himself never got engaged.

I have detailed and scrutinized these few examples to show that even during this short, but to the homosexuality argument most important period the biographical authors distort evidence; they exaggerate the homosexuality of Andersen and neglect his heterosexuality. I think they steamroller through the material led by their own prejudice rather than by an open-minded attitude.

Psychoanalytic Information

At this point I want to make a digression. The last 50 years have brought us supplementary knowledge about homosexuality and heterosexuality, and I shall try shortly to resume some points of special importance in our context.

1) Psychogenesis

The classical psychoanalytical theory on the psychogenesis of homosexuality is still valid. In early development the homosexual boy has felt attracted to the negative Oedipus complex perhaps because he has had trouble in working through the positive Oedipal complex, perhaps also for other reasons.

The negative Oedipus complex is the designation of a period of a child's development, a period when he wishes to have full possession over his same-sex-parent, while simultaneously imagining himself to be identical to the other-sex-parent. This means that a boy unconsciously wishes to have sexual intercourse with the father and bear his children like the mother has done. (Regression to the negative Oedipus complex means a homosexual disposition, and if this continues into adulthood, homosexuality may offer a quite strong and durable solution to his tensions. It may give him sexual satisfaction, and through the sexual encounter moreover cover his narcissistic requirements of identifications with the beloved and admired father-figure.)

2) Bisexuality

In some cases homosexuality can be prevalent during a lifetime; but in many other cases it may come and go alternating with heterosexuality (Mackintosh 1994, Socarides 1968). In such mixed forms one or the other tendency may predominate, but sometimes an even balance is found. I shall return to discuss this point later. Against this background it is doubtful whether one can characterise a man as a homosexual unless he is completely dedicated to this specific form of sexuality. You can say that a man sometimes indulges in homosexual feelings, fantasies or even in actual practice. It is however not necessarily justified to characterise as homosexual, someone, who as a young man has had some homosexual episodes while being heterosexual for the rest of his life. Andersen masturbated regularly, and he wrote about loving feelings for both women and men. To state a more definite belonging to one or the other category while neglecting the alternative seems inappropriate.

3) Zeitgeist

In 1969 Thorkil Vanggaard, the Danish psychoanalyst and sexologist, said: "From the end of the 18th and the beginning of the 19th century – the sensitive period – we have inumerable descriptions in history and in literature of intensely emotional relations between men. In these relationships hot feelings are often ventured, and kisses and embraces are exchanged." Vanggaard thought that the homosexuality in all men can have more or less favourable conditions in different historical periods.

Two male idols of the time (they were also idols for Andersen) may be mentioned, Byron and Goethe. In his youth Goethe was hesitant towards closeness to women and he had his sexual debut quite late (Eissler 1962). Byron on the other hand was probably sexually experienced with both men and women as a young man, and was called "mad, bad and dangerous to know" (Brent 1974). Both postponed marriage, which would have incurred responsibility.

Was Andersen a Homosexual?

Nobody can doubt that Andersen fell in love with men. It seems undeniable that he had such homosexual potentials. I wrote: "There can been no doubt that Andersen's psychology was more marked by preoedipal structures than that of most people. And as far as homosexuality is concerned, it was less inhibited and more prominent than what is common today." (Lotz 1988, p. 317)

It seems to me that the new "homo-sex" writers all make themselves advocates of one simple solution to the problem. Both Jackie Wullschlager, Jens Andersen and Dag Heede assert that they are not sure about the details of Andersen's love life, or whether Andersen was predominantly homosexual or not. However, at the same time they all act as if uncertainty was never in their minds. As far as heterosexuality is concerned, they consider Andersen as a counterfeit, even an impostor.[1]

They collect all related items in the enormous posthumous material and they cannot imagine anything but being forced to choose side: either he was homosexual or he was heterosexual. The result of their efforts does leave the impression of a homosexual man. However, it seems to me that his homosexuality is still only one side of the man, and our problem is that a number of things speak strongly in favour of his heterosexuality.

My main hypothesis has up till now been that Andersen was predominantly heterosexual, but that by the circumstances of his life he was forced to seek compensation. One such compensatory endeavour was to seek relief in platonic homosexual friendships. However, today I do find it questionable to ask for a definite yes or no concerning the person. His supposedly lifelong abstinence and masturbatory practice also contribute to making the question difficult or even impossible.

Was Andersen a Heterosexual?

My main arguments for accentuating the heterosexuality hypothesis are the following:

1) The Crisis in Italy

I find it very convincing that Andersen while in Italy received a letter that changed his life. The letter (dated December 18, 1833, arrived January 6, 1834) came from Edvard Collin and contained the most personal, direct and forceful confrontation with Andersen's regressive tendencies – and among them his sentimental homosexual appeal. I am convinced that Andersen was deeply shaken by the letter. He felt hurt and angry. His emerging rage against Edvard helped him feel more free and independent and to review his self-image. Once and for all he gave up his infantile dependency on the Collin family.

Immediately following this, he was challenged intensively, sensually and aggressively by sexual temptations in Rome and Naples. Psychologically he changed, matured and obtained more back-bone, as he came into better contact with the strength of his own feelings. In some of these moments, I surmise, he must have felt that the weak, feminine part of him was not his true self. His feeling of his own identity came out strengthened, – he was a man who in full consciousness was able to declare that he would not give in to any sexual temptation but remain independent as an artist.

He began writing the novel *The Improvisatore* and shortly after his return to Denmark, he wrote his first fairy tales ("The Tinderbox" and "Little Claus and Big Claus"). These works brought him fame. "The Tinderbox" probably takes the prize as the most universally loved text for children ever written. These works were inspired by what he found in Italy, his angry rebelliousness and new-found male self-esteem. Georg Brandes said that aggression propped up and strengthened the figures in these first fairy tales to their advantage (1919, p. 86).[2]

2) Jenny Lind

Some years later, in 1843, Andersen fell in love with Jenny Lind. His love was deeply felt and his inspiration blossomed. The result of this inspiration was some of his masterpieces: "The Ugly Duckling" and "The Nightingale".

Through the entire Jenny Lind period a number of the classic fairy tales followed until the definitive disappointment, when Jenny turned him down in Weimar 1846. The reaction to this disaster was the story "The Shadow", and from this point he wrote almost nothing that is still read today. I do not think this development can be understood, if you do not realize the importance of Jenny Lind. No male ever inspired Andersen to such achievements.

3) Andersen, an Honest and Open Sort of Person

Andersen, I think, was open-minded and honest with himself and his feelings.[3] If necessary, Andersen could easily have hidden his personal life-story from the audience. He might have destroyed his letters and his diaries and have omitted his autobiographies. But he did not.[4] As a matter of fact he did not conceal either his infatuations with men or women, but he never seems to have been in doubt that his love for women held first priority. You will need strong arguments to go against this. You will have to operate with the idea of a lifelong shamming.

In the new biographies Andersen's relation to Edvard Collin has been called a lifelong infatuation. Perhaps it was for a period, but the strength and duration of the feeling has been greatly exaggerated. At times he did consider himself half a woman, having a soft, feminine side. I suggest, he now and then used this knowledge of his feminine feelings not as a serious proposal to Edvard Collin, but jokingly to provoke his rigid, inflexible friend. On August 28, 1835, for instance, he wrote to Edvard that he was like "a lovely woman from Calabria with a fiery flash in her dark eyes" (in Danish: opflammende Blik). Eleven years later, in a theatre play, *Hr. Rasmussen* the protagonist in the first scene proclaims that he has fallen in love. He is asked, "Who is she?" and he answers "it is not a she, it is a man" (Andersen 1854; my translation). It seems Andersen tried to be indelicate in a funny way trying to imitate a French Boulevard-comedy. The Collin family laughed, and the stern critic Heiberg laughed, so it went ahead as a performance at the Royal Theatre. However, the audience regrettably could not see the fun. Neither can the homo-wave-critics of today. They all take it dead seriously: Look, he was gay!

Discussion

In Italy Andersen had become a less inhibited and less restricted sort of person, both in his aggressions and in his impulses towards women. He also seems to have been highly tempted to approach women sexually, but even if heterosexuality had become more accessible to him, it was still sprinkled with difficulties. On the other hand, while his chances of a homosexual platonic love-relation to a man also had become less restricted, his ability to displace and sublimate his sexual longings had also improved, and this ability was the winner in the long run.

If Andersen had not been strong enough to control his sexual impulses, he would have been forced to make some heavy compromises. A Danish woman should certainly be very much in love to marry this ugly, egocentric, vulnerable and economically rather poor and dependant man, a man that all his life was the target of ridicule (even Jenny Lind laughed at him behind his back; (Lotz 1988, p. 366). To Andersen, having a marital partner could mean the same disaster for his social and mental position, as the situation he had feared so desperately that his mother should leave Odense in order to latch onto him.

Of course it was not only for social reasons that Andersen feared sexual engagement in a woman. There were also very important unconscious reasons. He suffered from unconscious guilt-feeling towards his father and ambivalence towards his mother. He also feared the loss of narcissistic identity (especially his social ambitions and extreme self assurance as an artist). In childhood withdrawal into narcissistic day-dreaming had been an easy way out, but during his youth he developed a hard-earned, more realistic identity, won through many wounds and many tears in the house of the Collins. His youth as a foster child in the Collin family did help him to feel secure in an advanced and self-idealising environment. But his new identity was connected to a strong dependency and a fear of falling back or being pulled back into the swamp.

The Shepherdess and the Chimney Sweep
Interpretation B

If you interpret the story and the inspirational sources behind it, just like you interpret a dream in psychoanalysis, you may get an idea of what the story meant to the author. As I saw it in 1988, Andersen had fallen more or less in love with the young girl and sublimated both his love for her and his anger towards the old Baroness by writing the story. The story also had a hidden critique of the stiffness of society.

The narcissistic nobility could not move beyond their class, the risk being a break-down. The same was true on an individual basis, being narcissistic meant feeling admirable and perfect but also vulnerable and suffering from a permanent loss of vitality. To tell the story served the same purpose for the author as the rivet did for the china man. The rivet restored the self to wholeness, but hindered sexuality. By turning around the proportions of the three figures, the big china doll became the smallest. The china doll then represented another aspect of the poet, i.e. a child of the young couple, undetermined as for gender while the phallus was projected to the satyr.

Interpretation C

Somewhat impressed by the weight of the homosexual figures, found by recent authors, I feel like trying to extend the interpretation beyond the focus of heterosexual pre-oedipal phallic narcissism. It may be worthwhile putting more emphasis on a double love affair [5].

If we accept that Andersen was equally infatuated by Henrik and by Jonna, it becomes evident why Andersen invested excited feelings in them both: He did not want to interrupt anything, but to go along with and be part of their experiences. The interpretation that he was like a child, who wanted to be with his two beloved parents, comes again in focus. Travelling up the chimney can now be seen as a primal scene, i.e. a parental intercourse. The child is left out and it appears that an involvement in the parent's affair maybe tempting but also risky (cf. Lotz 1993).

Discussion

We are dealing here with one of the large enigmatic areas which is provoking and scaring for all children. The parents have an erotic solidarity, which is quite incomprehensible to the child. The child knows it, feels it and is excited about it, but it cannot participate in it. It is important for the child to be able to deal with the situation, as it might otherwise give in to its own destructiveness towards the couple. The problem is that he feels deeply dependant upon the idealized couple, whom he both loves and envies. To leave the still-life position seems risky. However, the moment the child matures and acknowledges and tolerates that his parents do have a real and procreative, sexual interaction, the child no longer is so tempted to interfere, but becomes instead a much more independent observer (Britton 1989).

Hollowness and fragility of narcissistic figures comes around, if they are based on pathological narcissism. This means that such hardened, brilliant, but hollow and fragile selves are reactions to threats to a fragile identity newly established in infancy, and they constitute defences against a breakdown.

In the case of Andersen, his childhood narcissism was largely based on reality (real achievements and real admiration) rather than on hurt day-dreaming. This means that he did not manifest fragility, but on the contrary showed himself to be effective and stable even under the upheavals he went through. As an artist he always had a keen eye for narcissism and was a brilliant observer of all its complications.

It seems that in a number of his fairy tales Andersen shows us the two themes, narcissism and object-love, changing in a dynamic way. If there are troubles in the sphere of love-life, he leads us on an excursion into the sphere of narcissism, where the problems may find some sort of solution, the duckling becomes a swan in a park, the tin soldier becomes a whole tin-heart, the mermaid becomes a daughter of the air, and the china doll becomes riveted. The same pattern holds true for the person Andersen in his private life. Whenever he was dejected or hurt, he resorted to his inner life and to his never disappointing muse. He was then both man and woman and his stories were his beautiful children. They brought him fame and solace, and he was immensely proud of them. But they did not restore his life to the sort of completeness he wished for, and from the summits of his fame, he constantly longed for the closeness, the intimacy and the fulfilment of ordinary life.

Loose Ends

The end of the story is not in complete harmony. Porcelain can be riveted, but it cannot grow together like a natural wound. The broken china doll is an element of disharmony that challenges the reader's imagination (Segal 1952). The child is reassured on a deep level concerning its fear of going to pieces. But how can it get on, grow and mature? How can the primitive idealized conception of the perfect but infertile parents be changed to an idea of a living family with a procreative parental couple?

To a child in harmonious development the triangle: father, mother and child, is not a self-mirroring still-life, but a living being-together, where the differences in gender and in generations are respected as stabilising and well functioning structures. It is only here that new children can be conceived and be born.

Andersen met Jenny Lind and fell madly in love at the end of 1843. The following year, 1844, his writings started with the fairy tale "The Hill of the Elves" (Elverhøj), a cheerful story of a wedding, and it ended with a theatre play *The Flower of Happiness (Lykkens Blomst),* where you are presented with a small family with a newborn child. "The Shepherdess and the Chimney-Sweep" belongs to this period. Here someone is threatened by splitting and collapse, but fortunately all involved parties can return to their proper places on the shelf beneath the mirror. The problems are solved at one level, but remain unresolved on another.

Resume and Conclusion

The crucial point in Andersen's psychology does not seem to be the problems with his choice of sexuality. The point is that he was psychologically centred on an unstable point between the world of narcissism (here are all the stiff idealized creatures, often pin-pointed with sublime humour) and the world of love (where you will find life and death in all variations, hate, love, conflicts and the fun and risks of daily living).

Both as an artist and as a private person Andersen stuck to this intermediate position. It gave him the freedom to play on the inner scene with the narcissistic figures, while at the same time he made us love all the everyday unimportant people and all the small creatures, who are striving to express their selves and by means of love and aggression try to gain their shares in a sometimes scary world.

However, he was also limited in his performance, and he could not transgress his own limits. Just as he had to harden his soft feelings, when he had a crush on someone close to him, he was in his art often forced to kill the lovers just before their goal came within reach.

References

Andersen, H.C. 1933. *H.C. Andersens brevveksling med Edvard og Henriette Collin.* Ed.: C. Behrend og H. Topsøe-Jensen. Vol. 1. Levin og Munksgaard, Cph.

Andersen, H. C. 1935. *Eventyr og Historier.* Gyldendalske Boghandel, Cph. (With commentaries by Hans Brix.)

Andersen, H.C. 1845. *Hr. Rasmussen.* Nielsen og Lydiche, Cph. 1923. (With preface by J.L. Heiberg.)

Andersen, J. 2003. *Andersen. En Biografi.* Vols. 1-2. Gyldendal, Cph.

Bollas, C. 1987. *The Shadow of the Object. Psychoanalysis of the Unthought Unknown.* FAB, London.

Brandes, G. 1919. "H.C. Andersen som Eventyrdigter", in: *Samlede Skrifter.* Danmark. Vol. II, 2nd ed. Gyldendalske Boghandel, Cph.

Brent, P. 1974. "Lord Byron" Weidenfeld and Nicholson, London.

Brix, H. 1935. "Kommentar" in: H.C. Andersen. *Eventyr og Historier,* Gyldendal, Cph. Vol. 2, p. 391.

Britton, R. 1989: "The Missing Link". in R. Britton, a.o. (eds.) *The Oedipus Complex Today.* Karnac Books, London.

Detering, H. 1991. *Åndelige Amfibier: Homoerotisk camouflage i H.C. Andersens forfatterskab.* Odense Universitetsforlag, Odense.

Eissler, K. R. 1961 *Leonardo da Vinci.* Hogarth Press, London.

Fenichel, O. 1946. *The Psychoanalytic Theory of Neurosis.* Routledge and Kegan Paul, London

Heede, Dag. 2005. *Hjertebrødre. Krigen om H.C. Andersens seksualitet.* Syddansk Universitetsforlag, Odense.

Helweg, Hj. 1927. *H.C. Andersen. En psykiatrisk Studie,* 2nd ed. 1954. H. Hagerup, Cph.

Hoffmann, E.T.A. 1816. *Nøddeknækkeren.* Danish ed. 1985. Apostrof, Cph.

Lotz, M. 1989. *Eventyrbroen. Psykoanalytiske Essays om H.C. Andersen.* Gyldendal, Cph.

Lotz, M. 1993. Den farlige kløft mellem kønnene", in: J. de Mylius et al. *Andersen og Verden.* Odense Universitetsforlag, Odense.

Lotz M. 2004. "The new biographies and the probability of Andersen being homoseksual". www.hca2005.com/Life+_+Work/Scholars/Discussions/ca30/forumid/45/ threadid/50

MacIntosh, H. 1994. "Attitudes and Experiences of Psychoanalysts in Analyzing Homosexual Patients", *Journal of the American Psychoanalytical Association,* Vol. 42, pp. 1183-1205.

Rosen, Wilhelm von. 1982. "Venskabets mysterier" *Anderseniana,* 3. rk. Vol. 3, pp. 157-214.

Shengold, L. S. 1988. *Halo in the Sky. Observations on Anality and Defense.* Guildford Press, London.

Socarides, C. 1968. *The Overt Homosexual* Grune and Stratton, N.Y.

Stampe, Rigmor. 1918. *H.C. Andersen og hans nærmeste Omgang.* Aschehoug & Co, Cph.

Vanggaard, T. 1969. *Phallos.* Gyldendal, Cph.

Wullschlager, Jackie. 2002. *Hans Christian Andersen. The Life of a Storyteller.* Penguin, N.Y.

Notes

1. Could it possibly be a self-deception, when Andersen wrote about his love to Jenny and to other women in his diaries, letters and in the autobiographies?
   Could it then also be self-deception when in his novel *To be or not to be* he made a portrait of him and Jenny through Niels Bryde and his Esther. Here he used the following words: "How Esther was lovely. How melodically had not her farewell sounded! Niels Bryde forgot himself in her. Love, how great is your power! The air was so light and refreshing. There was silence and calm around him, but in his inner being a purifying flame was shining. It was clear to him that he loved Esther, she was his first, his only love, – ".
2. What happened resembles what can happen when a talented patient meets a clever psychotherapist. Repressions are lifted, primitive superego-content is weakened, and id-impulses break through to the enrichment of the whole character. In Andersen's case, he won sexuality – which he had to suppress –, he won aggressiveness that he personally profited so much from and as may be the best, he won an almost ruthless sense of humour. Consideration to the people close to him no longer inhibited his ability – or rather genius – in using any small or big event in his writings.
3. In our field of discussion some arguments go that one feeling covers up for other, especially: heterosexual interest for a woman covers up for homosexual feelings for a man. I take it as examples of dualistic thinking. There are two possibilities and if homosexuality is not there all the time, it may be covered up by heterosexuality. However there are some mistakes here. One is that there are only these two alternatives; the other mistake is that it should be easy to decide which one covers which one. That homosexuality quite often seems to cover heterosexuality does not dawn upon them. Some find that even Andersen's childishness is abused by traditional authors as a cover for homosexuality (Jens Andersen, Vol. 2, p. 355; Dag Heede, p. 45). Actually, he was called immature and a child all his life and even by Jenny Lind. A third mistake is that what is covered is the truth while the cover up is only some make-up. Psychic life is not quite so uncomplicated and there is no guarantee that he hidden things are more true than the so-called cover up.
4. As a psychoanalyst you might get the feeling that he had some contra-phobic traits. Homosexuality is not the best idea in this regard. Rather he still repressed the primitiveness of his rebellious anger and his bitterness (Lotz 1989). As a person he became a contra phobic character (Fenichel 1946). In stead of still being aggressive, he was unusually nice and submissive.

5. It seems there is an alternative to the dichotomy homosexuality/heterosexuality. A sexuality that may spread further to the narcissistic, autoerotic area. If we return to the situation as it looks from this angle, Andersen fell in love with a man, Henrik, and with a woman, Jonna, and with the trio where all three were participating: "O yes, we all love each other, the two of you maybe a little more between you, but I have not been forgotten." *(*Stampe 1918, translation by ML*)*. The trio may alternatively be seen as a derivation of one single body that is split into three parts. It is the Chinese, who broke into three. The single body can further be described as child's body: sex is not developed; it may be like a mermaid, a snowman, a one-legged tin soldier. Confronted with adult sexuality it may melt down, or break into pieces. (Bollas 1987, pp. 82-99).

Hans Christian Andersen Tourist?
An Investigation of Etymology, Social History and Ideology

Hans Christian Andersen

Andersen travelled a great deal in his life, in particular in Europe, so much that we now think of him as one of the great travellers of his own lifetime. But important changes were taking place in the Europe of his time. Some were political and had to do with the formation of new European states, such as the new Germany, and this kind of change had an effect on Andersen's travel habits. Others were to do with technology, something which interested Andersen greatly.

Yet others again involved politics and new social trends, namely those that affected *travel* in general. The moment in time when Andersen lived and travelled is also the moment in history when modern tourism comes into being. Indeed, Andersen's own activities as a traveller exemplify the transition between *travel* as the preserve of the few and the (relatively) wealthy and *tourism*, as a modern leisure activity for the many. This allows us to use him and his travelling career as an exemplar and as an illustration of a general activity: travel and tourism.

However, and this is more important in the context of this paper: it also allows us to assess Andersen specifically as a traveller.

This paper investigates the intersection between biography, fiction and language. It is concerned with Hans Christian Andersen, the world-famous, even the world's famous, author of fairy tales and so much else.

The aim here is to "*classify*" Andersen as a traveller / tourist. Based on the assumption that this double description ("traveller / tourist") – also implies a *qualitative* distinction (being a traveller is more "worthy" or "dignified" than being a "tourist"), an attempt will be made to see whether these concepts are, indeed, in conflict and whether by calling Andersen a "tourist" one is somehow betraying Andersen's true nature as a "great nineteenth century traveller".

A true attempt at a general typology is not being made. In literary studies, modern typologies have their roots in literary genres, whose antecedents go back several millennia. On the other hand, in the relatively young discipline of tourism studies, typologies are naturally a fairly new phenomenon.

The nature of these typologies depends on the purpose for which they are developed. There are, broadly speaking, two approaches to the study of tourism. Firstly, tourism can be seen as a *field of economic activity*: an industry or an area of business. It is quite normal to devise typologies which help those involved in running the industry distinguish between different kinds of tourist as customer, with different needs and different behaviours. This kind of typology is related to the discipline of market segmentation, as developed in modern marketing, and it is based on characteristics that reveal what kind of accommodation, transport etc. that particular groups of tourists use.

In the context of this present paper, tourism is considered in the second way: as a sociological / historical / anthropological phenomenon, where tourism is not merely an area of business but a *field of human / social activity*, where those involved are engaged not just in travel to, and residence in, destinations, but where they are also fulfilling personal goals and adding experience to their lives as they engage in tourism.

The attempt to create tourism typologies in the latter sense can be traced back to the work carried out in the 1970s and 1980s by the sociologist Erik Cohen (1972, 1974, 1979, 1984 and 1988), partly referring to work carried out in history (Boorstin, 1964), sociology (Mac Cannell, 1976) and anthropology (Turner, 1973). Characteristically, Cohen is creating a typology of tourists only: the dichotomy of *travellers* and *tourists* is not considered relevant in the 21st century.

But in the 19th century, the situation is still one where tourism is coming into being and where a behavioural classification between traveller and tourist is still realistic. This is where this paper is situated.

A Point of Departure

That Andersen travelled is, of course, beyond dispute: he is, indeed, *famous* as a traveller. He was constantly on the move in his adult life, travelling first in Denmark and then, from 1831 to 1873, in Europe, with forays into Asia Minor (1841) and North Africa (Morocco in 1862). He saw most of what a tourist was meant to look out for in his own time and a great deal more, as this increasingly experienced man of the world developed his social and professional network and had access to parts of the countryside and cities that other people did not even attempt to find.

Some might argue that Andersen's entire life is best understood through the *metaphor* of a journey: here is a man who, once he had embarked on his adult life by leaving the city where he was born, Odense, in 1819, was forever restlessly on the move in the pursuit of his career (or, sometimes, on the run from his merciless critics in Denmark). With Andersen, restlessness and rootlessness seem to be two sides of the same issue. Although he would always pay homage to his beloved fatherland, and prove his love by returning to it, he also constantly turned his back on it in pursuit of other foreign "loves." His personal story is not that of his own little mermaid: *his* pursuit of happiness does not end in isolation and death. And yet, nor is his story that of a man achieving stability and permanence. Andersen lives in a state of constant *in*stability, never relaxing into bourgeois "hygge": he is constantly driven on by his need to create and perform, to meet and satisfy new audiences.

That travel and career were the same to Andersen is borne out by his production of travel books: As is the case with Andersen's literary production, the quality is uneven but it spans a range other travel writers would envy, from the not very inspired (such as his book on Portugal) to the uniquely talented and experimental.

Andersen is also an increasingly experienced practical traveller, who amasses enough experience to allow him to guide others on their tours: Europe becomes his territory, where he moves with confidence.

Are "Tourists" and "Travellers" Different?

"What," one needs to ask, "is the supposed difference between 'travellers' and 'tourists'"? Until the 19th century, travel was a comparatively rare thing. You did not travel without some kind of purpose: after all, travel was not only difficult, it could also be dangerous. The difference between "travel" and "tourism" can be located in two factors: the *rarity* of travel before the middle of the 19th century, as opposed to the increased normality of travel after that point in time; and the purposeful nature of travel before the middle of the 19th century, contrasting with the increased status of travel as a "leisure activity" after that point.

Traditional travel might be work-related, including participation in military campaigns, it might be educational, it might even be in the nature of actual exploration. It was not usually related to anything which would be recognized as leisure, as "holiday", since that concept did not exist until the late 19th century.[1]

It is therefore useful to look at how the concept of travel develops in the 19th century, and it is proposed that this is done by looking at the etymology, history and ideology of travel and tourism.

Tourism – the History

From an "ideological" point of view, tourism has a bad name. To many people, perhaps in particular those who have seen modern mass tourism develop into a branch of the entertainment industry since the early 1960s, tourism means package tourism, tourism directed by tour organizers and their staff, tourism of the "three S's": Sun, Sea and Sand, liberally sprinkled with cheap alcohol and sex.

This is, of course, a cliché, but like all clichés it also has an eleent of truth in it. It is this "truth", this image of modern tourism as unbridled pleasure that has put the more serious traveller off the concept of tourism, creating a degree of snobbery against those who travel primarily for relaxation, and given tourists a reputation as, perhaps, uncivilized, uneducated participants in what the serious traveller might see as a quest for knowledge and insight. That, too, is, of course, a cliché and it is becoming increasingly difficult to maintain the qualitative differentiation. Travel for discovery is almost impossible on our thoroughly-known planet, travel for excitement and education is an option open to anybody who can find that kind of offer in the travel agency's catalogues and book the journey.

In that context, you can both understand the resistance among some travellers to being called a tourist *and* the resistance to calling Hans Christian Andersen a tourist, but also the difficulty in distinguishing the two.

This is particularly so because the concept of tourism in the modern sense has been so *long* in developing. It is not a 20th century concept but a 19th century one, with roots going back several centuries. What is, of course, undeniable is that modern *mass* tourism is a post-World War Two phenomenon. Andersen could not have been a part of this.

But tourism as a leisure activity – being a tourist in your spare time, away from your workplace, achieving your personal goals – can be said to start in England when King George III starts visiting Weymouth in Dorset on a regular basis, on holiday, from 1789. Obviously royal holidays are by their nature exclusive and the behaviour of royalty not typical of any kind of ordinary people, but George III initiates what will become seaside resort holidays, in the first instance based on health: on sea-bathing. Early tourism is thus associated with the beach, albeit not as found in the "sun-sea-and-sand" formula, and we know that Andersen himself was partial to sea-bathing, for pleasure if not for his health.

So, even if modern tourism has what is *partly* a sullied image, it does not follow that this image automatically rubs off on anybody who is a tourist. In terms of the "ideology" of tourism, what is really happening is that modern travellers are making what we would now call "life-style decisions" about the way they spend their leisure time. They are concerned that their choice of holiday should reflect their personal image. It becomes important for the person who, say, likes to travel independently, without an itinerary or company, perhaps carrying only a rucksack for luggage and a copy of the relevant *Rough Guide*, to be seen as an "anti-tourist" or a "non-tourist." The backpack traveller, carrying his alternative tourist guide in his pocket, will perhaps look down on the "tourist" as one who travels on a package tour and who prefers the security of travelling with fellow-countrymen on a carefully managed and guided tour with no real danger or uncertainty.

But it is not likely that these two kind of traveller / tourism definitions are truly distinct. The backpack tourist may look for greater "authenticity" and more "genuine encounters" with local people and local cultures. In reality, the backpack tourist is not likely to find herself in places where truly genuine encounters with local unspoilt culture can happen. Most areas have now become part of the tourism industry and are intentionally seeking to formalize the encounter with tourists into one that is economically (and, perhaps, also socially and culturally) beneficial to the host population and to the development of a professional tourist industry. Really authentic encounters with original peoples are potentially dangerous and often not allowed since such encounters could harm the original peoples; or the kind of region that is not already overrun by other tourists may be one that is inaccessible for political reasons, such as has been the case for Algeria and still is the case for Chechnya.

If Andersen needs to be categorised in this context as a tourist or traveller, then probably he is more like a "backpack" tourist early in his travelling career, seeking out and finding more or less authentic and genuine encounters with the local populace, but these are often members of the budding European travel and tourism industry (they run hostelries or own the carriages Andersen travels in) or they are native members of the middle classes whom Andersen seeks out or who try to get into contact with him.

Modern tourism proper starts in the 19th century and it is created with the introduction of modern transport technology: the steam engine, used in ships and trains. With that new technology comes the development of predictable, timetabled, fast, convenient and increasingly affordable travel and the creation of new networks of large, modern hotels. As we know from Andersen's diaries and travel books, he is no "Luddite". At no point does he reject these new developments or pretend to insist on the "advantages" of old-fashioned slow travel by horse and carriage or by sailing ship, and his approach to choosing hotels is conditioned more by financial concerns that by a denial of the advantages of comfort. Andersen does not seek out the discomfort of primitive travel although he comes from an age when you had to be able to accept discomfort when you had to.[2]

Tourism – the Ideology

Modern tourism and the package tour are usually linked together, not least by the critics of modern tourism. The man normally credited with the "invention" of the package tour is Thomas Cook (1808-92). On 5th July 1841, he organized a "package", an excursion, the prize covering the rail fare and food, for people wanting to travel from Leicester to Loughborough to attend a Temperance meeting. This established a particular form of travel, which Andersen never took part in, where group travel, guided tours, at an inclusive rate, offers travellers the opportunity travel in groups to visit ever more exotic locations without having to organize the itinerary themselves.

Thomas Cook formed a company devoted to organizing excursions and during the Great Exhibition of 1851 he was responsible for arranging transport for 165,000 visitors to the exhibition. He later – in 1865 – added the reservation of accommodation to the services he offered, published guidebooks and created hotel coupons (1867), and banking and currency exchange were added in 1879. You could book your trip to destinations in the UK or abroad, through the offices of Thomas Cook & Sons (as the firm was known from 1871). Thus, in the 19th century, we see the development of the tour organizer and the travel agency as we know it today, offering much the same services as today.

Whether or not the package / guided tour deserves the reputation it has acquired – I would suggest that it does not – Thomas Cook can not be held responsible for its reputation as a travel form for travellers with no sense of independence or adventure:

"... as early as 1865 over 95 per cent of those visiting Switzerland with a ticket issued by Cook travelled independently, though initially about two thirds had joined one of his parties. Cook's voucher system and the guidebooks were specifically geared to individual travellers."[3]

On hindsight, this seems entirely reasonable. Thomas Cook was recruiting new customers for the new world of leisure travel but it seems that they were aspiring to the status of being individual travellers, like the Grand Tourists who had laid the foundations for tourism. Andersen had no need to partake of this: he was already fully "trained" as a Grand Tourist.

Modern mass tourism, like new 19th century tourism, came about through several developments. One was the increase in the number of people who were able to travel. After World War Two, as unemployment disappeared, disposable income increased and the fear (very real to many people until the 1960s) of foreign travel faded away, the market for foreign travel increased and the gap that appeared in the market was *not* filled with more customers for traditional, sub-Grand Tourism but with sun-sea-and-sand tourism. The need for this kind of holiday was very real in a world where many people still spent their working lives carrying out hard routine labour in factories. It was made available to large numbers of people through the development of the equivalent of the steam locomotive in the 19th century. The jet passenger aircraft, on charter flights, flew thousands of expectant holiday-makers to destinations on the coasts of the Mediterranean, where guaranteed sunshine, cheap wine and the promise of one or two weeks in temporary luxury offered the complete alternative to one's working life.

The people who went on these holidays would not have the "cultural capital" of the middle classes, including its habit of independent travel, often with an element of intentional self-betterment. These new tourists went for pleasure – it is assumed – and perhaps attracted the somewhat snobbish criticism of those who felt that travel purely for pleasure was an inferior type of travel. Perhaps one needs to avoid any comparison between "serious" traditional, educational travel and this new kind of mass tourism. Travel for pleasure, even to the Costa del Sol, the coast of Turkey or even to Bali may have more in common with a Sunday picnic than with education. No doubt Andersen would have been able to distinguish. Whether he would have looked down on modern mass tourism is impossible to say, since there is no way we can ask him.

But we are allowed to speculate a little and bearing in mind that Andersen was usually positive towards modern technology and to entrepreneurialism, he would probably have approved of the efforts of two twentieth century Danes to develop modern package tourism. The Reverend *Eilif Krogager* (1910-92) (with his company, Tjæreborg[4]) and the psychologist *Simon Spies* (1921-84) (who owned and managed Spies Rejser) shared the Danish charter market in the 1960s and 1970s and were pioneers in modern European charter tourism. Andersen might have avoided this kind of travel but would have understood the urge to develop large-scale Danish enterprises.

Tourism – the Etymology

Andersen's own travel habits have several sources and if we try to investigate the etymology of the tourist phenomenon, this is where we reach the greatest certainty.

Tourism has its origins in a "classical" form of European travel: the Grand Tour. The word "classical" is over-used these days: anything can be a classic, from a new Hollywood movie to a Cola drink. But in the case of travel, the word can be used with some justification about the Grand Tour.

The Grand Tour has its origin in 16th century England, where it was developed as a means of educating young aristocrats for their future positions as land-owners and holders of practical and political power. The Grand Tour would take the young man on a trek across Renaissance Europe, mostly following a set route and stopping at predetermined destinations. The ultimate goal Italy, in whose great cities the young man could be brought into direct contact with the classical European (Roman and to a lesser extent Greek) culture which was seen as the intellectual foundations of contemporary English, British, European culture at the time.

As European neo-classicism set the tone in European art and literature in 17th and 18th Europe, a tone borrowed from or based on Roman and Greek examples, the Grand Tour developed into a pan-European form of aristocratic educational travel, where the traveller might prepare by studying the classical authors in the original languages and where the young student was accompanied by a personal tutor tasked with supporting his learning and keeping him away from the temptations which threatened the young man's morality and health.

By the 19th century, Goethe had defined this form of travel as the modern "Bildungsreise" – an educational / formative journey, which is what the Grand Tour was – and not only artists but also travelling journeymen and enterprising members of the growing middle class were finding their way onto the Grand Tour network. It is as one of the artistic members of the Grand Tour we find Andersen joining the world of travel, as he seeks to better himself through contact with a great European artistic tradition. Andersen does not simply go on a Grand Tour, following a pre-set itinerary. At the time when he starts his European journeys, in 1831, "his" Europe is already much wider and much more easily accessible than it would have been to the early Grand Tourists. There is an increasing number of major destinations to travel to and a complex aesthetic network of European cultural personalities for Andersen to seek out and visit. But the basic framework for travel at the time is that of the Grand Tour, with Italy as the ultimate goal.

The very *word* "tourism" emerges in the English language – from where it spreads into other languages – in the early nineteenth century, in 1811, as an indication of how central British travellers are to the development of modern tourism. Berghoff and Korte (2002) point to the fact that Goethe, in his Faust II (1831), refers specifically to the omnipresence of British travellers on the European Continent, with that famous question "Sind Briten hier?" ("are there any Britons here?"), followed by what is a description of the British as early, inveterate cultural tourists:[5]

Sphinx
Wir hauchen unsre Geistertöne,
Und ihr verkörpert sie alsdann.
Jetzt nenne dich, bis wir dich weiter kennen.

Mephistopheles
Mit vielen Namen glaubt man mich zu nennen –

Sind Briten hier? Sie reisen sonst so viel,
Schlachtfeldern nachzuspüren, Wasserfällen,
Gestürzten Mauern, klassisch dumpfen Stellen;
Das wäre hier für sie ein würdig Ziel.
Sie zeugten auch: Im alten Bühnenspiel
Sah man mich dort als Old Iniquity.

Sphinx
Wie kam man drauf?

Mephistopheles
Ich weiß es selbst nicht wie.[6]

We find the word applied in the context of the ever-growing tourist Europe in an advertisement from 1846:

> TOURISTS are informed that "THE CRITIC," the largest Literary Journal in Europe, published every SATURDAY, price 4*d*., or 5*d*. stamped, devotes a department under the title of "The Tourist," to all kinds of information useful to Tourists, and to which they are invited to contribute their experiences of Routes, Hotels, Conveyances, Charges, Sights, and such like, addressed to the EDITOR, CRITIC OFFICE, 29 Essex Street, the Strand.[7]

This advertisement clearly appeals to individual travellers, of the kind who might, in our own time, send their personal recommendations to such travel guides as the *Rough Guides*. More significantly, it is appealing to the growing post-Grand Tour market of travellers who use printed guides to find their way around a wider range of European destinations, the Europe of H.C. Andersen, the traveller, whose range went beyond Europe itself. Modern tourism may be an English or British phenomenon, and the British tourist is evident in Andersen's own travel writings. But the activity of modern tourism is spreading well beyond Britain and the British in Andersen's own time.

Towards a Conclusion

Gathering together some of the threads of the debate about Andersen as a tourist, we might thus say that *historically* "tourism", at Andersen's time is developing into the modern form we now recognize, but that it is not quite "there"; that *ideologically* the word "tourism" is tainted by its negative association with mass tourism (or guided tourism or package tourism) but that this negative association is partly predicated on snobbery and a misunderstanding of what tourism is; and that etymologically the word itself is coming into existence in a modern meaning before Andersen's own travel career has begun.

The contemporary 20th and 21st century distinction between "travel" and "tourism", where the former is given greater intellectual validity than the latter, does not really hold. It persists, among those who prefer to see themselves as "travellers", as a label indicating that the traveller is engaged in a more independent, adventurous, authenticity-seeking, exploratory activity. In that respect, it certainly applies to Andersen the early traveller, whose journeys were more difficult, dangerous and unusual than travel is now. Perhaps we would also call it more "rewarding" as a personal experience. But seen in the context of Andersen's own age, Andersen himself simply travelled as you had to in those days. He himself was not making a "lifestyle-choice" between travel and tourism or between comfortable and uncomfortable travel. He travelled in the only way available at the time, to somebody of this means and with his background. Less comfortable travel would have meant travel on foot and, perhaps, nights spent in hospitable farmers' haylofts.

Hans Christian Andersen – Traveller

Andersen's career as a traveller arguably begins on September 4th 1819, when he sets out on his life's journey from Odense, arriving in Copenhagen on 5th September 1819. We have several descriptions, from his period at school, of how he travels on foot to Copenhagen. He undertakes a summer journey to Sjælland and Funen from 30th June to 21st August 1829, which we can see as an early example of Andersen as a traveller proper, visiting new (and also some known) people and places and describing the experience. Between 16th May and 24th June 1831 he makes his first trip abroad, to the Harz Mountains in Germany. This is the first of a number of characteristic Andersen journeys, carried out, ostensibly, for their mind-broadening, educational effect, by a writer noting everything busily in his notebook, for use in later publications. Andersen the traveller is also always Andersen the professional writer, intellectual and celebrity. We rarely if ever meet Andersen purely on holiday, between 1831 and the end of his travelling career in 1873, when he travels outside Denmark for the last time, visiting Germany and Switzerland between 14th April and 28th July.

Hans Christian Andersen – Travel Writer

One type of result of his travels is a series of travel books, some of which are among Andersen's finest works. If one discounts his literary experiment from 1829, *A Journey on Foot from the Holmen Canal to the Easternmost Point of Amager Island in the Years 1828-29*[8], which can be seen as an early experiment in the travel book genre, his debut as a travel book author is his *Shadowy Images of the Harz Mountains* (1834), where he plays both with the travel book genre and with his own role as a traveller. His *A Poet's Bazaar* (1842), based on his journey through Europe, across to Greece and Turkey and back through Central Europe, is his literary masterpiece in this genre and is also a landmark in European travel literature, taking the reader to places rarely visited by the ordinary traveller. *In Sweden*, from the same year (1851) has great power as a literary experiment, taking the genre well beyond pure geographical and anthropological description, whereas *In Spain* (1863) and *A Visit to Portugal* (1866) are less rewarding aesthetically but do offer vicarious travel experiences to relatively unknown parts, namely Northern Africa (in the former case) and to Portugal which was fairly unknown to travellers in the 19th century. *A Visit to Portugal* has retained its currency as a valid description of Portugal well into the 20th century.

Hans Christian Andersen – Tourist

So, do we meet Andersen the traveller or Andersen the tourist in these books? In truth, we meet neither, at least not primarily: we meet Andersen the travel writer, showing us the world as seen, uniquely, through his eyes and his creative imagination.

However, this does not invalidate the question of whether Andersen is a "traveller" or a "tourist". As 21st century tourists, and students of both Andersen and of tourism, we can claim that modern tourism consists of the following major constituents:

transportation

accommodation and hospitality (lodgings and food)
destinations and attractions
services (travel organisers, guides, guide books)

We know Andersen the traveller through his diaries, correspondence, published travel books (and several novels and fairy tales also contain relevant references) and through the testimony of others who travelled with him. What we see there is a development in Andersen's own travel practice that is determined by developments in several of those constituents in the 19th century. *Transportation* develops, in particular through the development of the modern railways, opening up Europe to travellers in a way it had never been before and to an extent that would only be equaled by modern jet-liner transport in the 20th century. In terms of *accommodation*, we see Andersen making use of a full range of accommodation types, but it is clear that modern hotels with modern conveniences are available to him in the late 19th century. The range of both destinations and attractions which Andersen (and other travellers) can reach in the 19th century is steadily growing, as the number of travellers grows and as the destination industry itself grows. Finally, although there is little (if any) evidence of Andersen carrying a Baedeker with him on his travels, a comparative study of 19th century travel guides and Andersen's own travel descriptions and notes suggest that he shared the knowledge available in the guidebooks and that perhaps he even got the knowledge from them.[9]

Hans Christian Andersen – Literary Tourism

Perhaps we cannot easily say that Andersen is a tourist in the modern sense, if we see him solely in the context of his own time. The distinction is not really made in the 19th century. But tourism, as that great social, cultural and economic area of concern in our own century, came into being in Andersen's time and we see him making full use of its advances. In that respect it is easy to see him developing into a tourist in his own time and we may legitimately include him in our studies of modern tourism, as well as making tourism a sideline in our study of Hans Christian Andersen the world writer.

Andersen himself has become a source of tourism in his own right. His birthplace (or the building we are almost certain is his birthplace) and the town of *Odense* are places of Andersen pilgrimage, in the same way that Stratford upon Avon is a place for Shakespeare pilgrims, and in the Andersen year of 2005 Odense (like much of the rest of Denmark) is using Andersen's Bicentenary for the development of events tourism on a large scale. *Copenhagen* offers a self-guided tour around the places Andersen knew and is associated with in the Danish capital and the region of *Skælskør* on Sealand, where Andersen spent much of his time, has developed Andersen-tourism as its own speciality over a number of years. Andersen now lends his name to holidays such as GoToday.com's "Hans Christian Andersen Getaway". *Rome* has commemorative plaques on buildings visited or lived in by Andersen (e.g. Caffé Greco) and *Vienna* will soon see its own, similar memorial to Andersen, so that Andersen tourists can identify localities associated with his life and works. There are now books following in the footsteps of Andersen, allowing the modern tourist to follow Andersen's journeys, such as Michael Booth's *Just as Well I'm Leaving*; *Around Europe with Hans Christian Andersen* or Helge V. Qvistorff's *Resa i Sverige med H.C. Andersen*. And, of course, if would be relatively straightforward to visit locations which Andersen incorporates in his own works.[10]

Andersen is not only a tourist and an illustration of the development of tourism in Europe and beyond generally. He is himself strong evidence of the comprehensive nature of *literary tourism*, that kind of tourism which is based on the interest in authors and their works and which attracts tourists to locations associated with the lives and works of authors, including museums devoted to them. There is a strong argument for claiming that such tourism is, in fact, not merely part of the socio-economic activity of tourism but is, in fact, an aspect of the appreciation of literary works. Under the concept covered by the word "appreciation" one would include the literary and biographical study of the author and his works, and visits to literary tourist attractions become a part of the practical study of the authors and their works.

So, with Andersen covering a wide range of aspects of modern tourism – its early history and its contemporary manifestations – the road is open for further detailed exploration of "Hans Christian Andersen Tourist".

Literature

Andersen, H.C. (2002; written 1829), "Dagbog paa en Sommer-Udflugt 1829" in Dal (2002).

Andersen, H.C. (2003, first published 1829), *Fodreise fra Holmens Canal til Østpynten af Amager i Aarene 1828 og 1829* (Copenhagen: Det danske Sprog- og Litteraturselskab).

Andersen, H.C. (2003; first published 1851), *I Sverrig*, ed. Mogens Brøndsted (Copenhagen: Det danske Sprog- og Litteraturselskab).

Andersen, H.C. (1988; first published 1842), *A Poet's Bazaar. A Journey to Greece, Turkey and Up the Danube* (excerpts; tr. Grace Thornton) (New York: Michael Kesend Publishing).

Andersen, H.C. (1986; first published 1831), *Skyggebilleder af en Reise til Harzen, det sachsiske Schweitz etc. etc., i Sommeren 1831* (Copenhagen: Det danske Sprog- og Litteraturselskab).

Andersen, H.C. (1972; first published 1868), *A Visit to Portugal 1866*, tr. Grace Thornton (London: Peter Owen).

Andersen, H.C. (1875; first published1863), *A Visit to Spain and North Africa, 1862*, tr. Grace Thornton (London: Peter Owen).

Andersen, Hans Christian (2005 paper, Edinburgh University; due for publication by 2007), "Ways to the World: Travelling With Andersen Through Published Sources."

Andersen, Hans Christian (1999), "The Author at the Museum" in Mylius, J. de, Jørgensen, Aa., and Hjørnager Petersen, V. (1999), *Hans Christian Andersen: A Poet in Time. Papers from the Second International Hans Christian Andersen Conference ... 1996* (Odense: The Hans Christian Andersen Center / Odense University Press)

Andersen, Hans Christian (2004 paper, UCL; in press, due for publication 2007), "Hans Christian Andersen: Raising Expectations, Managing Perceptions" in *The Discovery of Nineteenth-Century Scandinavia* (Norwich: Norvik Press)

Andersen, Hans Christian (2005 paper, Vienna University), "Andersen Into Europe – Conqueror, Connoisseur or Consumer? An Interpretation of Hans Christian Andersen's Approach to Travel in the 19th Century."

Berghoff, H. (2002), "From Privilege to Commodity", in Berghoff et al. (2002), pp. 159-179.

Berghoff, H., and Korte, B. (2002), "Britain and the Making of Modern Tourism" in Berghoff et al. (2002), pp. 1-20.

Berghoff, H., Korte, B., Schneider, R., and Harvie., C. (2002), *The Making of Modern Tourism: The Cultural History of the British Experience, 1600-2000* (Basingstoke: Palgrave).

Boorstin, D.J. (1964), *The Image: A Guide to Pseudo-Event in America* (New York: Harper).

Booth, Michael (2005), *Just as Well I'm Leaving; Around Europe with Hans Christian Andersen* (London: Jonathan Cape).

Cohen, E. (1972), "Towards a Sociology of International Tourism". *Social Research*, 39, pp.164-82.

Cohen, E. (1974), "Who is a Tourist? A Conceptual Classification." *Sociological Review*, 22/4, pp. 527-55.

Cohen, E. (1979), "A Phenomenology of Tourist Experiences." *Sociology*, pp. 179-201.

Cohen, Erik (1984), "The Sociology of Tourism: Approaches, Issues, and Findings." *Annual Review of Sociology*, Vol. X, pp. 373-92.

Cohen, Erik (1988), "Traditions in the Qualitative Sociology of Tourism," *Annals of Tourism Research*, vol. XV, p. 29-46.

Dal, E. (2002), *H.C. Andersen: Rejseskitser* (Copenhagen: Det danske Sprog og Litteraturselskab).

Goethe, Johann Wolfgang v. (1831), *Faust II* on Project Gutenberg DE *(http://gutenberg.spiegel.de/goethe/faust2/2faus001.htm)*

Handesten, Lars (2005), *Rejsekammerater. En rejse i Europa med H.C. Andersen* (Copenhagen: Gyldendal).

Inglis, Fred (2000), *The Delicious History of the Holiday* (London: Routledge).

Lerena A.H., López, M.J.A. (June, 2004), *Typology of Tourists in Spain. An Operational Analysis: The case of tourists whose main destination is the Autonomous Community of Euskadi* (7th International Forum on Tourism Statistics) Stockholm, Sweden.

MacCannell, D. (1976), *The Tourist: A New Theory of the Leisure Class* (London: MacMillan).

Morrell, J. (1998), *Miss Jemima's Swiss Journal: The First Conducted Tour of Switzerland* (first published 1863), (London: Routledge / Thoemmes Press).

Murray, John (1846), *A Handbook for Travellers in Switzerland, and the Alps of Savoy and Piedmont* (London: John Murray).

Qvistorff, Helge V. (1996), *Resa i Sverige med H.C. Andersen* ("Travelling in Sweden with Hans Christian Andersen," not currently available in English) (Skørping: Jysk Lokalhistorisk Forlag).

Turner, V. (1973), The Center Out There: Pilgrim's Goal. *History of Religions,* No. 12, pp. 191-230.

Urry, J. (1990), *The Tourist Gaze*. (London: Sage).

Wivel, Henrik (2006), *Det jordiske paradis: Med H.C. Andersen på rejse i Portugal* (Copenhagen: Gyldendal).

Yiorgos, A., Leivadi, S. and Yiannakis, A. (eds.) (1996), *The Sociology of Tourism: Theoretical and Empirical Investigations* (London: Routledge).

Notes

1. It is worth reminding oneself that the concept of leisure travel is so new in some places that it is being developed at the time of writing, as happens currently in the People's Republic of China.
2. Andersen travelled by train for the first time on 10th November 1840, when he caught the train from Magdeburg to Leipzig, a line that had opened only a short time before, in 1839-40. The first Danish railway, from Copenhagen to Roskilde, opened in 1847. Steam-driven ships were already getting common in Andersen's early life. Robert Fulton's pioneering steam boat The Clermont sailed in America in 1807 and from 1819. The Caledonia sailed the first Danish route from Copenhagen to Kiel.
3. Berghoff (2002), p. 173.
4. Tjæreborg is now part of the British firm MyTravel.
5. Berghoff and Korte (2002), p. 2.
6. Goethe (1831), *Faust II*, Act I Scene iv
7. Murray, John (1846), *A Handbook for Travellers in Switzerland, and the Alps of Savoy and Piedmont*
8. It *can* be seen as a "proto-travel book". Please see Andersen (2004).
9. Andersen (2005).
10. As an indication of how this might be done, please see Andersen (1999), "Andersen and the Museum."

Hans Christian Andersen Was No Hypochondriac, He Was Ill

Annelies van Hees

The Danish psychiatrist Hjalmar Helweg looked into Andersen's complaints as early as 1927 and concluded from reading in his diaries, mostly for the years of his Grand Tour in 1833 and 1834 that he most certainly was ill. "Without knowledge of Andersen's everlasting struggle with illness and weakness his singular personality is incomprehensible."[1]

Helweg is convinced that Andersen's weakness is an inheritance from his father's side of the family, this father being of weak health and of a disappointed nature.[2] His father again is described in terms of madness, walking through Odense in peculiar outfits, talking to himself.

Andersen's melancholia is, according to Helweg, the most conspicuous sign of his being ill. His conclusion is that Andersen is a psychopath, a diagnosis less offending in the early twentieth century than it would be nowadays. Martin Lotz recognised an oedipal problem in Andersen and in his thorough reading of the tales he concludes that Andersen's problem was an enlarged ego-ideal. The ego-ideal that Andersen tried to comply to, was not really his own, but his father's: what the father had not reached in life the son should do.[3] This seems logic in the light of Andersen's wish to always please father-figures like Jonas Collin and many others.

Janine Chasseguet-Smirgel concluded from a reading of "The Nightingale" that Andersen suffered from a "false self."[4] That too seems reasonable, seen in the light of other tales like "The Shadow". But Andersen also seems to have a problem with his female identification, thus having trouble with an uncertain sexual identity.

His behaviour and his mood swings caused Helweg to diagnose him as a psychopath, a diagnosis that today would rather take the form of "narcissistic" or "borderline personality". The problem is, however, that all these diagnoses, probable as they might seem, never can be true altogether. The narcissistic stage, the pre-oedipal stage, where the sexual problem belongs, and the oedipal stage that Lotz speaks of, are consecutive stages in the human psychological development. Now, if one is stuck in one stage, e.g. the narcissistic phase of development, it is quite improbable to be stuck in the next two stages as well. One either has a narcissistic problem, a pre-oedipal problem or an oedipal problem, but not all at the same time.

I believe that Andersen's sufferings, both physical and psychic, are of a purely biochemical nature, due to a disease that he suffered from all his life. I am well aware of the risks present when a literary scholar moves into the medical field. On the other hand, however, since the patient has been long dead, all his symptoms, described in his diaries and by other written evidence, have now turned into texts. And texts can be interpreted, with or without some help from other sciences, like the psychoanalysis mentioned above, or medicine, used in the example below.

In his diaries that he kept for so many years, though mostly when travelling, we find the everlasting complaints about his health problems. There are the well known problems with his teeth that even found way into his tales. But apart from those, there is a consistency in his complaints that looks like a pattern. There are thousands of complaints; hardly a day goes by without some suffering and when he has a good day, he is careful to mention this and his happiness about it: "felt really well today", "unusually well".

In the ten volumes of the Danish edition of his diaries we find an average of 300 complaints per volume, which amounts to 3000 in all. However, since he only kept a diary when travelling, which he did roughly speaking half of his life, this number should be doubled. This means that of the 37 years (1833-1870) that are recorded, he does not feel well about 6000 times, which means nearly every other day. Which must make him either a hypochondriac or a very sick man. I opt for the last. Let us see why.

His usual complaints are:

- Fatigue, weariness, lassitude (træt, ugidelig, føler mig meget mat, uendelig træt, ikke Kræfter til at naa hen til Barberen).
- Unwellness (ikke vel, ikke ganske vel, ikke i Stand, ikke ganske i Velbefindende, følte mig ikke rask, jeg var lidende, angrebet, en Fornemmelse af ikke at være vel, var legemlig og aandelig syg).

- Abdominal pain (Mavepine, Maven ikke vel, Maveonde, idelig Kneb i Maven, Maven daarlig, ondt i Maven, Maven smertefuld, min Mave ængster mig).
- Abdominal discomfort (min Mave underlig, min Mave igjen urolig, Maven ikke ganske god).
- Diarrhoea (Diarrhe, tynd Mave, Maven i Uorden, nerveus Mave, fik stærk Diaré).
- Obstruction (Ingen Udgang).
- Abscesses (Byld, Byld i Enden, Byld paa Tandkødet, Byld i Halsen, Philipens paa Brystet).
- Throatache (ondt i Halsen, Halssmerte, Halsbetændelse, var meget syg i Kind og Hals, Rheumatiske Smerter i Mund og Hals).
- Weakness (slap, mat, var ved at segne, ikke i Stand til at bevæge mig, til at røre mig af Stedet, jeg vaklede og var nær ved at besvime).
- Dizziness (svimmel, svindel, bange for at falde, turde ikke komme ned).
- Anxiety (en underlig Angst, ængstelig, uforklarlig Angst, Pasangst, Rejseangst, Pengeangst, alle Angster fyldte mig, Angest med min Kuffert).
- Febrility (febril, Feber i Blodet).
- Fear of death (bange for at dø).
- Deathwish (ønskede jeg laa i min Grav, var jeg dog død, idelig Tanke om at det er mine sidste Levedage).
- Insomnia (sov slet, sov slet ikke, sov uroligt, ikke faldet i Søvn, sov ikke hele Natten for voldsom Smerte).
- Irritability (irritabel, gal, lynende gal, ærgerlig, blev meget heftig, krænket).
- Mood swings (ikke i Humeur, urimeligt tungt Humeur, afficeret, i en ilde Stemning, jeg var i denne selvpinende Stilling der er dræbende, gnaven, havde Ulyst, var ikke elastisk i Sindet, ilde stemt, i tungt Humeur, en skrækkelig nerveus Sygelighed, følt mig i mindre godt Humeur).
- Muscle complaints (tung i Benene, kunne daarligt gaa, slap, kunne ikke bevæge mig af Stedet, det var en Qval at komme ned).
- Melancholia (i en Veemod gik jeg til Ro, kom i Krampegraad, opløst i Graad).
- Colds (forkølet, Snue, stærkt forkjølet med Snue).
- Eye complaints (øm i Øiet, mit Øie angreebet).

- Headaches (Ondt i Hoved og i Lemmerne, Hovedpine, mit Hoved bankede).
- Hemerrhoids (Hæmoridal-Blod, Hæmoroider).
- Cold Shudders (men jeg har Kulde, forunderlig kold i Livet, skrantede og frøs).
- Rheumatism (Rheumatiske Smerter i Bryst og Mave, øm i Lemmerne).
- Nocturnal Sweats (i den frygteligste Sveed, laae i febril Sveed, hele Natten igjen i voldsom Sveed).

According to the testimonies of his contemporaries, Andersen looked pale and thin. Some express their concern for him, the ladies of the houses he stayed in, took good care of him: most obvious are all the drops they gave him, as well as compresses and poultices. His life-long physician, Theodor Collin, was of the opinion that he should try and have a regular sexual life, and to this end did send him to prostitutes, to which he sometimes complied, but without, as it seems, more results than talk, admiration or pity on Andersen's side. Lately, Andersen's heterosexuality has been questioned[5]. The obvious result of these investigations are that he was interested in both men and women, but by no means the authors want to pinpoint him to either homo-, hetero- or bisexuality. His writings show that Andersen clearly had a female identification, which explains his somewhat unclear sexual identity and the difficulty to decide in either direction.[6]

But none of this, however, can explain the multitude of physical and psychological complaints he obviously suffered from. One understands the diagnosis of hypochondria that people during his lifetime and until this very day pinpoint on him. When complaints are so various and so prolonged, without an obvious diagnosis, there is no explanation left but hypochondria.

In my opinion Andersen suffered from a disease that to this very day is difficult to diagnose, even for doctors, since the complaints are so varied. Medical tests in these cases tend to give so-called flat results, by which is meant: results that are undecisive either way. The average time for a correct diagnosis is today fifteen years and many patients stay undiagnosed and miserable all their life.

The disease, let us call it CD for the moment, was already known by the ancient Greeks; in the first Century A. D. Aretaeus the Cappadocian described several clinical features of the disease.[7] After him we had to wait eighteen hundred years for a new description that included the name CD by Gee in 1888. The symptoms were described, although no cure was found until the Dutch doctor Willem Karel Dicke in 1950 in his thesis showed the improvement of the patient on a diet.[8]

CD is an immunological disease of the small intestine with lots of consequences and symptoms. The clinical picture the patients present shows complaints as varied as follows:

Fatigue, weariness, lassitude
Abdominal pain
Abdominal discomfort
Abscesses
Sore tongue
Bone pain
Skin lesions
Palpitations
Diarrhoea
Obstruction
Muscle weakness
Weight loss
Vit. D-deficiency producing the characteristic waddling gait
Anemia
A-vitaminosis
Intoxitation
Shortage of glycogene in the liver
Glossitis, stomatitis
Aphtous ulceration of the mouth
Oedema
Paraesthesia
Bouts of depression
Melancholia
Epileptiform fits
Muscle wasting
Sensory loss
Bleeding, due to the vitamin K-dependent clotting feature
Osteoporosis
Liver disease
Cold shudders
Joint complaints
Headaches
Insomnia
Irritability

Mood swings
Anxiety

Of these thirty-something symptoms of CD H.C. Andersen suffered from 28, that we know of. In this light it is highly probable that H.C. Andersen suffered from CD.

His deathwish, although he mentions it several times, never went as far as a suicide-attempt or even a consideration of suicide as a possibility. The deathwish is recognised in many CD-patients. John S. Morris describes, how in his Bristol-sample of 70 patients one committed suicide, while 3 others tried to do so, an average of six percent, which by far surpasses an average rate.[9] The deathwish in CD-patients, however, is not so much due to a tendency to suicide, as to a wish to be free from the misery they feel. Andersen expresses this wish clearly in a diary entry for november 12th 1860: "jeg er forstemt, ønsker at døe og dog at leve, har ikke Lyst til at være her i Hjemmet og veed dog at jeg ikke føler mig lykkelig ude."[10]

M.G. Carta describes psychological effects in CD-patients: "A study of 36 adult CD-patients from Cagliari and 144 healthy controls show significantly elevated risks for major depressive disorders, dysthymic disorders, adjustment disorders and panic disorders."[11] According to Morris half of the patients in the Bristol-sample suffered from a pyroxine deficiency, which explains the severe depression he found in 10% of his patients. The vitamine E-deficiency explains the profound muscle weakness. The paraestesia found in 30% of the sample is due to hypocalcaemia, hypomagnesaemia and anaemia, the last factor also causing the pale skin colour found in CD-patients.

In a more recent study, Ciacci and Navarone compared 92 CD-patients with 100 normal Control patients and 48 hepatitis patients. Their conclusion was: "Depressive symptoms are a feature of CD; they are present to a similar extent in patients with childhood- and adulthood-diagnosed CD."[12]

CD or Coeliac Disease is a chronic immunological disease of the small intestine; the only treatment available is a diet with no gluten. To call the disease "gluten allergy", however, as often is the case in Denmark, is to simplify things, since it is no allergy at all. It is a hereditary, chronic disease with, when untreated, serious consequences, such as: osteoporosis, diabetes and malignancy, besides serious neurological and psychic complaints, going as far as schizophrenia or psychotic episodes.

Assuming H.C. Andersen suffered from this disease, which is highly likely in the light of the abundance of symptoms that fit the picture, even his death of liver cancer fits the clinical picture:

> "An increased incidence of autoimmune conditions including thyroid dysfunction, insulin dependent diabetes mellitus and chronic liver disease has been found among patients with Coeliac Disease. (...) Already in 1967 it was pointed out that the patient in whom malignancy is most likely to develop is a male over 50 years of age with longstanding Coeliac Disease."[13]

A certain genetic constellation is common among Coeliac patients, since "80% have the HLA-B8 antigen compared with 20% of the normal population. (...) the HLA-D3 antigen is present in almost 90% of patients with Coeliac disease."[14]

If this is true and H.C. Andersen really suffered from Coeliac Disease (which of course is now impossible to verify by the usual tests, apart from an eventual DNA-test), what then are the consequences? The first one is of course that he must never again be accused of hypochondria, since he was really very ill. Secondly, that he deserves our admiration for his facing the physical difficulties and making the most of his life, with all the discomfort that his disease caused him and the additional discomfort travelling brought about in the first half of the 19th century. And lastly, that he deserves our compassion.

Notes

1. Hjalmar Helweg, *H.C. Andersen. En psykiatrisk Studie,* H. Hagerups Forlag, København 1927, p. 11: "Uden kendskab til Andersens bestandige kamp med sygdom og svaghed er hans besynderlige personlighed uforstaaelig." – Hans Brix, *H.C. Andersen og hans Æventyr,* København 1906, p. x: "Han led af et yderst skrøbeligt Nervesystem; det viste sig ved en Dirren og Vibreren om det saa var i hans Øjenlaag; og af en ulidelig Mathed, der plagede ham hele Livet igennem, en Svækkelses- og Svagheds Fornemmelse, der, naar Sindsbevægelse kom til, kunde gøre ham det omtrent umuligt at slæbe sig frem; han var af en pirrelig Sensibilitet, der gjorde ham til en opfindsom Selvplager, vedligeholdt en aldrig hvilende Mistro hos ham overfor de ligevægtige og lod ham analysere hvert ubekymret Ord; ... hans Sygdom berøvede hans Sind Evnen til at være paa Højde med en stor ydre Begivenhed; han knækkede over i saadanne Øjeblikke ...

2. Helweg 1927, p. 13.
3. Martin Lotz, *Eventyrbroen. Psykoanalytiske essays om H.C. Andersen*, Gyldendal; København 1988, pp. 30 ff.
4. Janine Chasseguet-Smirgel, "Le rossignol de l'empereur de Chine. Essai psychoanalytique sur le 'faux'." In her. *Pour une psychanalyse de l'art et de la créativité*, Paris, Payot 1971, pp. 183-215.
5. See Jackie Wullschläger, *Hans Christian Andersen. The Life of a Storyteller*. The Penguin Press, London 2000, and Dag Heede, *Hjertebrødre. Krigen om H.C. Andersens seksualitet*, Syddansk Universitetsforlag, Odense 2005.
6. Cf. Annelies van Hees, "Venskabspagten eller to køn er intet køn", part of her: "Incest in de letterkunde" in Michel Thijs (red.), *Trauma en taboe. Psychoanalytische beschouwingen over incest*, Garant, Leuven 1995, pp. 117-40.
7. H. Stenstam, *Clinical Studies in Coeliac Disease. With special references to Complications*, Studentlitteratur, Lund 1985, p. 9.
8. Willem Karel Dicke, *Coeliakie. Een onderzoek naar de nadelige invloed van sommige graansoorten op de lijder aan coeliakie*, Utrecht 1950.
9. J.S. Morris, "Neurological Disorders and Adult Coeliac Disease", *Tijdschrift voor Gastroenterologie*, Vol. 15, 1972, pp. 107-15.
10. *H.C. Andersens Dagbøger 1825-1875*. Vol. IV, G.E.C. Gad, København 1974, pp. 459-60.
11. Mauro Giovanni Carta a.o. "Recurrent brief Depression in Coeliac Disease", in *Journal of Psychosomatic Research*. Vol. 55, 2003; (6) pp. 573-74.
12. C. Ciacci and A. Navarone, "Depressive Symptoms in Adult Coeliac Disease" in: *Scandinavian Journal of Gastroenterologyi*. Vol. 33, 1998, pp. 247-50.
13. Stenstam 1985, p. 18.
14. Stenstam 1985, p. 20.

Hans Christian Andersen's View of the Orient and His Dealing with Otherness

Nina Hintz

In Hans Christian Andersen's travel book *A Poet's Bazaar (En Digters Bazar)*, published in 1842, where Andersen describes his journey through half of Europe, Greece, Turkey and the Balkans in 1840/41, we read about the Turks: "Turks are the most good-hearted and honorable people in the world."[1]

I was rather astonished by his positive, modernistic, open-minded opinion. Even today, when Turkey's membership of the European Union is discussed, negative associations towards the Turks preponderate. Certainly only few will call them "the most good-hearted and honorable people in the world". That was not different in 1842.

Before Andersen's view of the Orient and his dealing with the stranger is analysed, I will address the issue in its historical context and explain why the Oriental subject was so popular in Europe and what ideas of the Orient the European travel reports put across.

Andersen's view of the Orient will be exemplified through the depiction of the Turks and Constantinople, which was at that time a common subject of travel narratives.

Historical Context and General Opinion of the East

Europe was undergoing fundamental transitions: social order and everyday life were changed by industrialization; the idea of freedom and democratization was unfolding all over. Greece had just won its war of independence against Turkish supremacy, supported by all of Europe. Although in the mid 1800s, the infamous cruelty of the Turkish empire should long be forgotten, the bad reputation of the Turks as "terrible, overly aggressive, fanatical Barbarians" was still carved firmly into contemporary consciousness and a vivid, common stereotype in literature.

England, France and the Russian Empire battled for imperialism and struggled for supremacy in the Middle East. After Napoleon's campaign to Egypt, an Oriental wave flew over Europe and influenced the fine arts, music, literature as well as architecture and everyday-life (for example fashion and furniture).

"On s'occupe beaucoup plus de l'Orient qu'on ne l'a jamais fait. L'Orient est devenu une sorte de préoccupation générale," wrote the French Victor Hugo 1829 in his introduction to *Les Orientales*.[2] "Exotic" had become synonymous with "oriental". Therefore there was a boom of travel and Orient-depictions and the journeys to the exotic Orient became "en vogue" among artists and writers.

Despite this fashion and the literary image of the East as a wonderland, the general attitude towards the country and its people was rather negative. The opinion consolidated to a negative hetero-stereotype, by which the European dominators' culture justified their superiority in civilizational, moral, technical, religious or economic aspects and legitimized an im- or explicit intervention in the autonomy of the foreign culture, to the supposed benefit of that same culture.

I will illustrate this by two travel reports of Constantinople: *Orientalische Briefe* (Oriental Letters) from 1842 by the German Countess Ida von Hahn-Hahn, belonging to the most famous writers of the German "Vormärz", and *Brogede Rejsebilleder* (Colorful Travel Pictures) by Elisabeth Jerichau-Baumann. This painter with residence in Denmark was a friend of Andersen's. As most of the travel narratives, these books were dominated by the dichotomy Occident (education, progress, enlightenment, Christianity) and Orient (backwardness, disorder, primitiveness, Islam).[3]

Jerichau-Baumann experienced the contrast between East and West as follows:

> It was strange to see this monster of our industrial age [the locomotive] invading the land of the fairy tales. I'll never forget the contrast I felt, when I saw the Turkish railway-workers in their used, motley clothes digging into the earth to set the track for the railway. These men, whose foreheads were clearly painted with the sign of barbarism, those men paved the way for industrialization and enlightenment.[4]

Similar to Hahn-Hahn, Jerichau-Baumann sees Constantinople primarily as a disgustingly dirty city where infrastructure, logistics, hygienic and urbanistic standards are primitive and medieval. They blame it upon Islam, its old-fashioned regime and the Oriental mentality.

"The disorder, confusion and neglect shaping the cityscape are characteristic of the inner conditions of this country," resumed Hahn-Hahn.[5] The backwardness, which overlaps the local color of the expected wonderland disgusted both women. "Good-bye illusion! This is not a pixies' city, but a dirty city," wrote Hahn-Hahn.[6]

Moreover both feel uncomfortable and cheated. They cannot stand or handle the Turkish mentality: According to Jerichau-Baumann, the Turks' most prominent characteristics are laziness, dullness, corrupttion, begging, oriental curiosity and general inferiority. Hahn-Hahn calls them "human steamboilers", or even "slow, stupid and degenerate", then she adds: "The barbarian must have beauty, otherwise he is unbearable."[7] Remember that all characteristics are negative – so is the diction!

Both review the other culture by the rules of their own background, their pre-fabricated images and their pre-knowledge. They cannot engage with the other culture and counteract it by distance and by feeling their European superiority. Their lack of comprehension turns into judgement and becomes, in Hahn-Hahn's case, even racist and defaming. For them the Orient is an uncivilized, deficient culture.

Andersen's View of the Orient

Andersen's representation of Constantinople has a different prevailing mood and offers another gateway to the country. He meets the foreign culture with the required amazement,[8] openness and almost euphoric enthusiasm. Andersen's Orient is a wonderful, friendly world much akin to the 1001 nights of Arabian tales. He experiences Turkey as teeming with great colors, mysterious smells, exotic fruits, animals and people as well as beautiful buildings. He describes Constantinople as a beautiful, unique city, "a Venice built of Fantasy,"[9] whose multi-ethnic society excites him.

> one is overwhelmed with the sight, the splendor and the tumult. It's a bee-hive one enters, but every bee is a Persian, an Armenian, an Egyptian, a Greek. Orient and Occident hold a great market here. Such a throng, such a variety of costume, and such a diversity of goods for sale is seen nowhere else.[10]

Andersen also treats common stereotypes: for example heavily armed Turks. But they wear their weapons first of all for image reasons: "Pomp and glamour are very important for the Turks," he explains. Second of all their grueling looking daggers prove to be a combined inkwell and quill which enable the Turks to compose poems whereever they are. So, according to Andersen's experiences, poetry and feeling for art are more in Turkish nature than fighting, violence and fanaticism. Here he refers to the current, European stereotypes of the Turks which he describes so well in the Greece chapter "The Pact of Friendship".[11] Generally, Andersen often refers to old cliches, which he dispels as wrong stereotypes and reinterprets by giving them an completely different (new) sence, i.e. as above where the cruel, violent Turk becomes docile poetry. In Andersen's eyes, the "violent, cruel Turks" are part of the past and are no longer suitable for the Turks of this period.

> Some years ago, it was a custom that the heads of all those who were executed in the yard of Seraglio should be thrown out into this place for the dogs; now there was nothing of the kind.[12]

Finally, Andersen subtly critizises the Danish society by his description of the Turks and the Orient. In contrast to the Danish "Andegaard" the Turkish social life is based on respect, sympathy and tolerance. Everyone seems to be welcome and allowed to be himself. Consequently, Andersen presents the Turkish society as an ideal of humanity and tolerance.

Also culture, be it poetry, storytelling, theatre or music, is highly esteemed and poets and storytellers enjoy high prestige – once more a high contrast to Denmark, as Andersen knows it.

Strikingly Andersen constructed the Turkish society as a positive counterpart to the Danish one, especially concerning aspects Andersen disliked in Denmark.

Contrary to other travellers, the Turkish mentality does not cause him any problems: Also before his journey, in his Oriental dramas *Mulatten* (The Mulatto) and *Maurerpigen* (The Moor's Girl) the Orientals feature by their virtues like wisdom, hospitality, humanity, pride, and nobleness. The easygoing Turkish lifestyle is his ideal. In letters, he repeated several times the wish: "I wish I were a Turk." When an old Turk said to him he deserved to be a Turk, he felt pleased. A compliment, which Hahn-Hahn would have considered an offense.

Andersen describes the Turks in *A Poet's Bazaar* as full of "savoir vivre", enjoying life with all comfort and according to the motto "life is pleasure". There is plenty of time for all. There is time for all the important things: family, poetry, coffeehouse entertainment, smoking, soulful and bodily pleasures, even light use of narcotics. Their life seems to be happy and paradisiac. "Amongst the graves under the black cypresses, the old man [a Turk] thinks of life – and life is enjoyment!"[13]

As regards the content, *A Poet's Bazaar* does not differ from other depictions of Constantinople. Andersen also picks up the typical elements as the erotic and exotic Orient of *1001 Arabian Nights*, sights – as for example the Hagia Sophia, the slave market, the Seraglio, the bazaar –, folk and country, everyday life as well as the common cliches and stereotypes. So why does Andersen's report differ so much from other representations?

Andersen's Intentionally Positivized Presentation of the Orient

In my opinion, Andersen pursues a specific aim by his travel book: his intention is to build up a positive, glamorous view of the Orient!

The basic differences are: 1) The continuous positive representation: even negative aspects of Constantinople are positivized by narrative strategies and techniques and by the aesthetic program "poetifying the truth" – a combination of realistic and fictive storytelling, which I call "two-phases-technique". 2) The narrator's position. 3) The approach to and handling of the unknown, which is almost non-existing with other writers.

My thesis results inter alia from the existential importance Andersen attached to the journey. His reactions to a possible failure of the travel arise from physical signs (serious illness, headache, nausea, stomach pain) as well as from psychic signs (deep desperation, anxiety neuroses, outbursts of fury).

Even though he suffered from anxiety, neuroses and phobias already on harmless travels through Denmark, he took the risk (i.a. danger for life) and the huge stresses and strains which a journey to the Orient included. Much more was at stake than only getting material for his travel book, which he might have written without going abroad, as did Victor Hugo and Johann Wolfgang Goethe.[14]

Another point is the fact that Andersen actually does not experience the Orient as positively as he pretends – a fact on which his diary, letters and even *A Poet's Bazaar* shed light. Often he comprehends the Orient as scary and alienating. The loud, disorderly everyday life and the lack of hygiene overwhelm him and make him sick. These feelings and experiences are factored out in *A Poet's Bazaar,* or at least understated or swamped out by narrative techniques and strategies.

The Dance of the Dervishes however exceeds his limits and becomes a boundary phenomenon.[15] No wonder as, in pietistic, protestant Denmark, the worship was celebrated calmly, devoutly, without music or dance. Therefore, the bawdy, wild dances, the trance, the fanaticism, the loud unmelodious music and especially the unpredictability of the event disgusted him so much that he had to leave earlier, trembling and close to a nervous break-down. Anyway, instead of giving up, Andersen returned to see the show once more. This learning and working process is typical for his dealing with a phenomenon he cannot handle.

Narrative Strategies and Techniques

Instead of presenting his Dervish experience on the narrative level as frightening as he felt it, Andersen describes three Dervish episodes reflecting a gradual change of approach from complete refusal and horror to tolerant, although reserved acceptance.

The first experience is another traveller's report of the monster-like Dervishes in Tiflis. So Andersen had bad expectations, when he went to see his first Dervish Dance in Scutari. There, his bad expectations were fulfilled, he could not stand the ceremony and had to leave. But the last episode, his second try at Pera's convent, was a success. Andersen managed to see the system behind the ceremony. He still did not feel comfortable, but he could accept the event and found a way to handle it. He was not frightened any longer.

> This dance lasted a whole hour; but there was nothing horrifying in it. It might almost be called graceful; one had only to forget that they were men, to believe that they were puppets.[16]

By starting with the worst example, he brings the experiences to a good end at last. Furthermore by putting those ceremonies in perspective, comparing them to ceremonies from other countries and cities, the reader gets the impression that the Dervishes' Dance in Constantinople is less wild and horrifying than similar phenomena elsewhere.

If negative aspects of folk or country cannot be denied, they are casually and factually added in a depiction, so that the reader does not realize them as negative. Examples are the butchery at the waterside, or the raw sewage in the middle of the street, hidden in an exciting description of the bazaar.

> We can see directly into the workshop of the shoemaker and carpenter, we fancy that we go right through the kitchen and bakehouse, there is such a cooking, and baking, such a steam and odor from the ovens and chimneys in the open houses. [...] Large pieces of sail-cloth, or old carpets, are drawn across the street from shop to shop, like a roof. The pavement is very bad, and the gutter is in the middle of the street.[17]

As we have seen from the dagger example, Andersen picks up common stereotypes, turns them around, so that they finally get either a new meaning or prove to be false.

While Hahn-Hahn and Jerichau-Baumann blame the Turkish oarsmen of being sharks or double dealers (as they were according to other travel books), Andersen shows them as intrinsically honest:

> I offered the oarsman a silver coin, the value of which I was not really as yet aware of. He shook his head, took from his pocket a quite small coin, showed it to me and assured me that he could not take any higher payment. So honest are the Turks! And every day during my stay here I had more and more proof of this.[18]

Another method is the humorous and charming narration of facts which Andersen must have noticed as negative as, e.g., the long waiting time at Mohammed's birthday:[19]

> The procession was to commence at nine o'clock; but it was almost twelve before it pleased the Sultan to set out from the Seraglio. – The sun burnt with the warmth of summer: One cup of coffee after the other was drunk. The scaffolding fell down two or three times, and all the Turkish women rolled in a heap together.[20]

Neither the long waiting time nor the primitive, dangerous construction of the grand-stands are commented critically, but the event is reported humorously instead.

The best example of "putting something into a positive light" is offered by the slave-market description. Throughout Europe freedom ideals were spelled out and slavery was banned in Denmark in 1803. There simply was no way that Andersen could turn the institution of slavery into a harmless phenomenon nor in any way justify what he experienced with his very eyes. Instead of erasing this experience, he chooses the two-phase technique, the synthesis of romantic and realistic narration:

First phase: authentic representative description of place and people:

> We come to a place surrounded by wooden buildings, forming an open gallery; [...] are small chambers where traders stow their goods, – and these goods are human beings – black and white female slaves.
>
> We are now in the square; the sun shines, straw mats are spread out under the green trees, and there sit and lie Asia's daughters. A young mother gives the breast to her child, and they will separate these two.[21]

The picture Andersen draws is nearly idyllic, the atmosphere is nice and calm.

Second phase: Taking the point of departure in factual events, he constructs a story thereby passing from realistic to fictional level.

By starting a fictive dialogue with a potential buyer, he cleverly finds a way to change the subject, by depicting the Oriental beauty, the Houri. Here he uses the "principle of the strangers' voice". To describe the beauty, he quotes a Turkish poem about the Houri technique. Afterwards he ends his report of the slave market with the words "but we shall do best to ride away from Ibn Katib and Constantinople's slave market."[22]

Instead of giving a realistic, critical description of the slave market, he "sings an ode" to Oriental beauty at the fictive narrative level – also something nice and romantic. Moreover he also changes to another obligatory subject of an Orient depiction: the erotic Orient. By this strategy he avoids a statement as to the negative subject of slavery. Again he takes refuge in poetry when reality is uncomfortable and negative.

The Narrator's Position[23]

Instead of commenting from a superior, dominant colonialist's point of view, Andersen is sympathetic to the strange country and is full of admiration and respect for the old culture and history of Asia, which represents for him the site of the ancient world, the cradle of European culture and Christendom. In his opinion Europe stood to benefit from the Orient in several ways through the ages and not vice versa. Being there, in the land of fairytale and poetry, makes him feel having been ordained a poet. He staged the transgression to the other continent as a rebirth and return to the origin of poetry.

His pictures of the different ethnicities and nations are moderate or positive. None of them is characterized or judged in a negative way. Cultural peculiarities are presented with sympathy, tolerance and humour, whereas he anyway shows his preferences: Andersen was for example rather sceptic towards the Greek, who were quite popular in phil-Hellenistic Europe, and favored the Turks: "I know them too little to judge, but I do not love this race; the Turks on the other hand pleased me much more; they were honorable and good-natured."[24] Again, he presents his opinion kindly and diplomatically.

He also takes over the point of view of the Turks and the host country, so he calls the Europeans "strangers" or "foreigners" and not vice versa, such as Hahn-Hahn and Jerichau-Baumann do. Moreover he voices the Orientals to explain their culture themselves in the form of poems, sagas, fictive dialogues or anecdotes (principle of the strangers' voice). Thereby Andersen's depiction differs from other travellers' uni-dimensional attitudes.

In a letter to Signe Læssøe, Vienna June 20, 1841, Andersen stresses his intention of giving a "true picture" of the Orient.[25] In my opinion, this must be understood as follows: Andersen's focus is not on a comparison with Denmark or other countries, but on an ethnographic depiction of the traditional Orient in its local color and nativeness, before the fall of the Ottoman Empire and European infiltration. Therefore he ignores all aspects of the modern Orient – facts about the political, social and economic situation – as well as the European infiltration, what he was heavily criticized for. But for him these facts are irrelevant for his cultural-historical, ethnographic depiction.

Andersen's Dealing with the Other/Otherness

As mentioned before, Andersen's attitude towards the Orient was kind and respectful. He realizes the Orient as a discrete culture with its customs and rules and accepts it in its strangeness, with which he tries to engage.

Andersen propagates the right way to meet the other culture: to adapt oneself to a country's customs and practice and to respect them and other human beings. I will show it by two examples:

> My Russian travelling companion had offered our Moor only a few Pence for his walk with us and the fellow would not accept so little. I saw how much the sum was and thought too that it should be increased. The Russian said no and opened the door [...]. I wanted to give him more money, but the Russian placed himself between us, gave the waiters a nod, and they pushed the malcontent outside. And that, for them, was the end of the story. Immediately afterwards I went into the streets where I expected to find the Moor [...]. I proffered about three times as much as he had been offered, giving him to understand that it came from me. He would accept Nothing.[26]

Andersen condemns the repressive, discriminating behavior of the Russian and tries to make up for it.

The other episode is about the monastery of the Dervishes, where you have to take your shoes off to enter. One of his group ignored that by putting slippers on his shoes, which the Turks took as disrespect. But Andersen behaved in a different and better way:

> My companion took a pair of Moroccan leather slippers out of his pocket, put them on over his boots and went in like that, but the Turks looked angrily at him muttered to each other.
>
> I had straps sewn to my trouser legs so it was difficult to take my boots off, but since one should always follow the customs of the country or keep out, I quickly took a knife to cut the straps and walked, like the Turks, in my stocking feet. An old man with a turban clapped me on the shoulder, nodded gently and said something

which my interpreter translated for me: I was a good man who respected the religion and deserved to be a Turk! "God give you Light" was his last word.[27]

Andersen's behavior was appreciated by the Turks who on their part treated Andersen with respect and sympathy.

In general, Andersen's approach towards the others can be described as follows. In the beginning, he is passive and neutral, the description is objective and does not show previous knowledge.[28] Then he is observing and analyzing from a distance, which he realizes at the textual level by narrative techniques such as "panorama view" and "the bird's eye view". Finally he is "understanding by taking part": though it is a hard learning and working process, he actually deals with the unknown. He illustrates some scenes of interaction as funny and harmonic events, driven by all kinds of communication – signs, mimics and gestures, foreign languages or interpreters. So the others' lifestyle becomes less scary and dangerous.

> I offered some fruits to the young Turk who was telling the story and he thanked me with a friendly look [...]. He seized his pen, tore a sheet of paper from his notebook and wrote – while he nodded and smiled at me. Then he handed me the paper with a verse in Turkish written on it. I thanked him for the verse and he asked me to write a few words in my language. I wrote a little Danish verse for him, and it was passed around and turned up and down just as I had done with the Turkish poem.[29]

By this, Andersen presents the Turks as equal. The way the young Turk is treating the strange poem is the same as his own.

By reciprocal exchange and dialogues the cultural interaction becomes a dynamic model. Concerning the remaining unknown, he transforms it into well-known, or at least, acceptable strangeness or "objectifies" it, in order to ease the cultural opposites.

When these methods fail, he hides his discomfort and bad feelings in another way. For example he changes from the realistic to the romantic/fictive level (as we have seen at the slave market). Or he uses a stylistic register (birthday event) or refers to something well-known from his own culture, for example French theatre in town and of course, the European colony, so that the foreign country resembles more and more his own culture and homeland. Again, we get a proof of the importance of the narrative techniques, which alone makes the maintenance of the positive image possible.

Andersen demonstrates cross-cultural exchange and communication as inspiring and broadening one's horizon. By his positive presentation, he also wants to increase the knowledge of other nations and cultures as well as international understanding. His vision of literature as propagator of a cosmopolitan world outlook and international understanding is close to the concept of "Weltliteratur" – world literature.[30]

Conclusion

In most travel books of the 19th century the Orient is seen from an imperialistic and Euro-centric point of view and accordingly described as a primitive, deficient culture, which does not live up to the romantically, misty-eyed expectation of wonderland. Though *A Poet's Bazaar* presents a designed, intentionally positivized view of the Orient, which only can be realized by the complex narrative techniques and the poetical program of "poetifying the truth", Turkey is brought out as equal to Europe and as a partially superior, separate culture because of its impact on the development of European culture in the past. Furthermore it becomes the positive counterpart distinguished by intact values, tolerance, humanity and feeling for arts. Values which were lost in the imperialistic and industrialized Europe.

As often before, Andersen sides with the weaker ones. His intention is not only giving a description of the stranger and his culture, but to make them understood. He wants to verify the one-sided image of the Turks by his "true picture", to obtain comprehension and recognition for this culture and to abolish strangeness and prejudices. This can be seen as criticism of the narrow-minded, Danish and European society and as a pleading for international understanding in times of nationalization. With the depiction of the happy, positive Turks, he might be trying to make the Danes rethink their own way of life and motivate them to watch beyond their own noses.

Other differences to other depictions of the Orient are Andersen's cultural and not at all imperialistic approach, his modern handling as well as active dealing with the stranger and the unknown which he regards with favour. Cultural interaction becomes a reciprocal dynamic model.

Bibliography

Andersen, Hans Christian: *En Digters Bazar*. København 1842.

A Poet's Bazaar. Translated by Charles Beckwith. London 1846.

A Poet's Bazaar. New York 1988.

En Digters Bazar. Text edited by Finn Gredel Jensen. Post-script by Lars Handesten. København: Det danske Sprog- og Litteraturselskab/Borgen 2006.

Maurerpigen: *original Tragedie i fem Akter*. København 1840.

Mulatten: *originalt romantisk Drama i fem Akter*. København 1878.

"Ja ich bin ein seltsames Wesen" Tagebücher. 1825-1875. 1-2. Göttingen: Wallstein Verlag 2000.

Bille, C.St.A. & Nicolaj Bøgh [eds.]: *Breve fra H.C. Andersen*. København: Aschehoug 2000.

Brenner, Peter J. [ed.]: *Der Reisebericht. Die Entwicklung einer Gattung in der deutschen Literatur*. Frankfurt a.M. 1989.

Detering, Heinrich: "Dänemark und Deutschland einander gegenüber – Kosmopolitismus, Bikulturalität und Patriotismus bei H.C. Andersen". In: Heinrich Detering, Anne-Bitt Gerecke, Johan de Mylius [eds.]: *Dänisch-deutsche Doppelgänger. Transnationale und bikulturelle Literatur zwischen Barock und Moderne*. Göttingen: Wallstein Verlag 2001, pp. 174-95.

Dreyer, Kirsten: *H.C. Andersens brevveksling med Signe Læssøe og hendes kreds: En dokumentarisk fremstilling*. København: Museum Tusculanums Forlag 2005.

Greenblatt, Stephen: *Marvelous Possessions*. Chicago 1991.

Hahn-Hahn, Ida von: *Orientalische Briefe*. Berlin 1842 and http://gutenberg.spiegel.de/hahnhahn/orientbr/orientbr.htm

Handesten, Lars: *Rejsekammerater. En rejse i Europa med H.C. Andersen*. København: Gyldendal 2005. Pp. 165-95.

Hugo, Victor: *Les Orientales*. Paris 1829 and 1952.

Jerichau-Baumann, Elisabeth: *Brogede Rejsebilleder*. København: Forlagsbureauet 1881.

Stemmler, Susanne: *Topographien des Blicks. Eine Phänomenologie literarischer Orientalismen des 19. Jahrhunderts in Frankreich*. Bielefeld: Transcript Verlag 2004.

Sundermeier, Theo: *Den Fremden verstehen. Eine praktische Hermeneutik*. Göttingen: Vandenhoeck & Ruprecht 1996.

Topsøe-Jensen, H: *H.C. Andersen og Henriette Wulff. En Brevveksling*. Odense: Flensted 1959.

Notes

1. *A Poet's Bazaar.* New York 1988, p. 99.
2. "Everybody was more interested in and occupied with the Orient than ever before. The East had become a kind of general preoccupation." Quoted from Victor Hugo: *Les Orientales.* Paris 1829. Preface, p. 13.
3. Both these authors had a pre-knowledge and images of different, overlapping, and self-contradicted associations (imaginative, erotic, antique Orient etc.), they wanted to get confirmed. Their basic view of the orient was already a self-contradiction: the deficient culture on one hand and the land of fairy-tales on the other hand!
4. Jerichau-Baumann, p. 7; 9.
5. Hahn-Hahn: *Orientalische Briefe.* http://gutenberg.spiegel.de/hahnhahn/orientbr/ orien12.htm
6. Andersen picks up the point of disillusion of the literary Orient depiction. He describes an episode in the Harbour of Syra, where he met an angry Russian, who was calling all romantic travel writers bounders and their depiction nothing but lies. "They are all bounders those writers and Lamartines!"
7. Hahn-Hahn: *Orientalische Briefe.* http://gutenberg.spiegel.de/hahnhahn/orientbr/orien06.htm
8. Greenblatt's principle of amazement as one of the most important conditions for alterity.
9. *A Poet's Bazaar*, p. 98.
10. *A Poet's Bazaar*, p. 104.
11. *A Poet's Bazaar*, pp. 72-79.
12. *A Poet's Bazaar,* p. 251.
13. *A Poet's Bazaar*, p. 245.
14. Hugo: *Les Orientales*, and Goethe: *West-Östlicher Diwan.*
15. Boundary phenomenon: an experience which exceeds a person's tolerance and limits at such a rate that the person has to turn away from it horrified.
16. *A Poet's Bazaar*, p. 242.
17. *A Poet's Bazaar*, pp. 228f.
18. *A Poet's Bazaar,* p. 99.
19. Andersen hated tardiness and to wait. Once, when he was invited to dinner at Elisabeth Jerichau-Baumann's house, he left in a rage, because dinner was not ready on time, and he ignored the painter for a period.
20. *A Poet's Bazaar*, p. 251.
21. *A Poet's Bazaar*, p. 231.
22. *A Poet's Bazaar*, p. 232.
23. The narrator and the author are identical in *A Poet's Bazaar*, so we can estimate the narrator's position for Andersen's personal opinion. Furthermore, the narrator's position and the dealing with the stranger are closely connected.
24. Quoted from "The Court in Athens".
25. Nicolaj Bøgh, pp. 438-43.
26. *A Poet's Bazaar*, p. 32.
27. *A Poet's Bazaar*, p. 114.

28. This behavior is called "époque" in Husserl's "Transcendental phenomenology".
29. *A Poet's Bazaar*, pp. 93-94.
30. The term "Weltliteratur" was etablished by Herder, Goethe, Mme de Staël and Lessing.

Children and Moods in Hans Christian Andersen's Travel Books

Lars Bo Jensen

Dealing with Andersen, it is not very simple to draw a line between children's literature and adult literature. Søren Baggesen[1] has pointed out that only very few of Andersen's tales are actually children's literature, if one defines children's literature as literature about children for children. Among the well-known fairy tales only "Little Ida's Flowers", "Ole Lukøie" and "The Little Match Girl" are children's literature according to this definition – according to Baggesen, who is mainly concerned with the well-known tales. Other tales by Andersen are really about adult themes such as death, love or e.g. choosing a partner for marriage. Baggesen speaks of the "double articulation in Andersen's fairy tales". This refers to the fact that the adult core of the tales, which adults all over the world read aloud to children, is narrated in a way that amuses children. This suitability for children is, according to Baggesen, achieved by making things in the fairy tales seem familiar – that is, imitating the traits of the bourgeois homes in which the primary audience lived.

Baggesen has called attention to a certain discrepancy between surface and essence in Andersen's tales, and he states that even when children sometimes are main characters, they are not really children – for example Thumbelina and Kay and Gerda in "The Snow Queen". These children do not grow (up), and they are involved in stories about adult issues.

Recollecting Baggesen's interesting points and a certain episode in the story about "The Metal Pig", a story that forms part of the travel book *A Poet's Bazaar*,[2] I conceived that it might be interesting to take a closer look at how children's presence is described in Andersen's travel books. What moods[3] are connected with children? I shall return to the episode from "The Metal Pig".

I have been reading Andersen's five travel books, *Skyggebilleder*, 1831 (*Rambles in the Harz Mountains*), *En Digters Bazar*, 1842 (*A Poet's Bazaar*), *I Sverrig*, 1851 (*In Sweden*), *I Spanien*, 1863 (*In Spain*), and *Et Besøg i Portugal 1866*, 1868 (*A Visit to Portugal*

1866), and I have been focusing on occurrences of children. How is the motif 'child' or 'children' deployed?

The travel books, Andersen wrote, do not claim to be told to children, and they are not. Indeed, it is expectedly a genre for adults, that is to say, it is not children's literature, but simply literature. However, children are often present in the travel books. Of course, you might say, because he would be expected to see some children on his journeys. And so he did. The ways these children are represented, and especially the contexts they are put in by Andersen, are often rather peculiar, though – and maybe not suitable for children, as we shall see. Instead of cozy, calm, funny or foolish situations and moods, children are in most cases connected with poverty, death or sexuality.

The depicted children are usually ignorant of the contexts they are put in. Indeed, most children in the travel books are glad, unconcerned and innocent. It is in the eyes of the either melancholic or aroused traveller, children become signs of something else, referring mostly to either death or sexuality, and from time to time to poverty and thus a socio-political context.

I shall now move on to the burden of evidence, representing some distinguishing examples of children's appearances in each of the five travel books.

Rambles in the Harz Mountains

In *Rambles* children are usually present only with a sort of stage property, representing an innocence that contrasts darker parts of the shadow pictures, be it surroundings, other people or the narrator, and, especially, in what one may name "the context of life history": Children occur as beings, who shall be transformed by time. They too will age and eventually die. Sometimes the perspective is the opposite: children remind adult or old people (and the reader) that they were once children. In general death is the horizon of the motif "child" in *Rambles*. This fits neatly with the philosophy of travel, which is expressed in the preface of the book and repeated, though in a much darker tune, in the beginning of chapter eight: transitoriness reigns everything. Everything flows, and this may be expressed as: everything travels, "even the dead in their silent graves course with the earth around the sun. Yes, – 'to travel!' – it is a strange fancy with the whole universe."[4] To travel is to live – and to die.

I shall quote only one typical example of how this philosophical context and the often bitter, melancholic tone sets its mark on the child motif:

> We went past a pleasant little house, with red-painted wood-work and vines growing up the walls: there sat a little sun-burnt boy, with silvery-white hair, practising on an old violin. Perhaps that little fellow will one day be a great virtuoso, astonish the world with his playing, be admired and honoured, whilst a secret worm gnaws all the green leaves off his life's tree.[5]

A Poet's Bazaar

A Poet's Bazaar is in several ways quite different from *Rambles*, and this applies also to the use of the child motif. The difference shows already in the first occurrence of a child. Children are not merely a picturesque and symbolic motif in this travelogue, but have become[6] interesting in themselves. Andersen is being shown around at the King's castle in Nürnberg by the castle's bailiff,[7] whose son is with them. Andersen feels more like hearing the boy tell, or rather to behold the (hi)story of the castle with the child's eyes of imagination:

> I'd like to sit with the little fellow under the linden in the narrow castle yard and together with him see, what the legend tells about Eppelin, the wild knight of Gailingen.[8]

A more significant and general difference between the *Bazaar* and *Rambles* is that the perspective of the child motif in the former is not life and death, but adolescence, the transition from childhood to sexual maturity.

The erotic element appears in several passages, e.g. in "The Metal Pig", a story, in which Andersen tells about Florence. The boy beholds the two Venuses in the Uffizi Palace:

> The little fellow hadn't yet said a word; he was half frightened, half delighted. They entered a long gallery, which he knew well, for he had been there before. The walls were covered with pictures, and the statues and busts all stood in a light as bright as if it were day; but the most splendid sight of all was when the door to one of the adjoining rooms opened. Yes, the splendor here the little

> boy remembered, but tonight everything was especially magnificent.
>
> Here stood the statue of a nude woman, as beautiful as only nature and the greatest marble sculptor could make her; she moved her lovely limbs, dolphins sprang to life at her feet, and immortality shone from her eyes. She is known to the world as the *Venus de' Medici*. Marble statues of superb men were grouped around her; one of them, the Grinder, was sharpening his sword; the next group was the Wrestling Gladiators. The sword was whetted, and the athletes wrestled for the goddess of beauty.
>
> The boy was dazzled by the magnificence; the walls were radiant with color, and everything there had life and movement. The picture of Venus, the earthly Venus, impassioned and glowing life, as Titian saw her, shone in redoubled splendor. Near her were the portraits of two lovely women, reclining on soft cushions, with beautiful, unveiled limbs, heaving bosoms, and luxuriant locks falling over rounded shoulders, while their dark eyes betrayed passionate thoughts.[9]

Truly an erotic mood, in which the innocent boy seems rather misplaced. It is more likely the erotic fire of the traveller and (possibly) of the adult reader, this scene is really about.

There are more examples of the connection of children and sexuality in the *Bazaar*: In "The Bond of Friendship",[2] the little girl, Anastasia, suddenly has become "a beautiful, fullgrown girl, and I was a strong youth" – says the young man, who eventually marries her. She used to be his little step sister.

In chapter five of The Orient part of the *Bazaar* there is a little Turkish girl on the ship. In Andersen's imagination she is transformed into "a grown maiden, beautiful as she was now as a child and glowing like the sun which had left its rays in her dark eyes". The girl, Zuleika, has an elder sister at the age of six, so she is quite young. I shall not put forward the thesis that Andersen was a pedophile,[10] but it is remarkable, how his thoughts in the company of even very little girls almost always are about love and the girls' transformation into young maidens, suitable for marriage.

In Sweden

In Sweden is not very interesting in the context of this paper. In this travelogue the past is a deep, into which the narration repeatedly descends and ascends from again. Thus, at the level of composition, the past in *In Sweden* is a parallel to the numerous caves, mines, ravines and valleys in *Rambles*. *Rambles* and *In Sweden* are similar in several ways. Children in *In Sweden* are, as most sites and landscapes in the book, seemingly not quite enough in themselves, but must be depicted more fully through their history. Also, in *In Sweden* several children are connected with death, as in *Rambles*. Maybe the similar use of the child motif in these two travel books is related to their overall less sensuous and more symbolic character, compared to *A Poet's Bazaar* and *In Spain*, which both have the erotic instead of death at the basis of the moods connected with child motifs.

In Spain

Compared to the earlier travel books, sites in *In Spain* are only to a small extent described by legends and history. Instead one gets the impression of detailed and straightforward descriptions of locations and situations.

The most conspicuous feature of the descriptions of children in this travelogue is the eroticism. There are many erotically attuned descriptions of Spanish girls, particularly of the many "Andalusian eyes". *In Spain* is characterized by the traveller's lustful walking among strangers, the fleeting meetings with dark eyes – what Henning Bech calls cruising and defines as a fundamental phenomenon of the city, connected with and creating a sexualized mood. In the chapter on Malaga, Andersen wrote:

> I had to go down on to the Alameda and join the throng, to admire the beautiful women with their dark flashing eyes, who so gracefully fluttered their black, bespangled fans (...).[11]

Shortly after is a poem, which I have had to translate myself:

> No one knows me, I know no one,
> As in a new age I wander about;
> One of the Seven Sleepers I seem to be here
> The place and the people, everything is new to me.

> Oh, what pleasure! Just as the straw I will
> Drift down the stream, turn around;
> I wish I dared it, the straw dares it,
> Kiss every flower on the swelling stream!

This is what it is about – moving in the crowd, enjoying looks that attract and excite. The chance of erotic encounters.

There is another quote, which has also carefully been left out in Grace Thornton's translation from 1975, which I have been quoting from. The passage has been censored.[12] This, of course, confirms my impression that it is rather improper reading. I have translated it myself:

> We went into the sutler's house, actually in order to see beautiful eyes; they were here. The daughter, a sixteen years old girl, was a real beauty, hair and eyes sparkling black, the teeth fresh and white (...) The young girl brought us swelling grapes; how beautiful she was, slender and floating! The eyes spoke, the mouth didn't need to; those eyes were enough to pervade an entire poem with light and fire, so you would burn yourself on it.[13]

To make clear that the eroticism in *In Spain* also applies to girls, who are really not young maidens at the threshold of maturity, which a sixteen year old girl may be said to be, certainly in those days, I will refer to chapter ten, in which it says about some girls in a theatre: "The ladies eleven years old, but fullgrown (in Danish 'fuldkommen udviklede' – maybe it should be translated as 'fully matured'). This episode has also been left out of Thornton's translation! In chapter nine, Granada, the travelling poet meets a girl in a dark avenue at night: "a child – but here under the Spanish sun she would be called a lovely young bride". This is present in Thornton's translation.

A Visit to Portugal 1866

A Visit to Portugal 1866 contains quite wonderful passages, but does not add much new, when it comes to ways of presenting the child motif or analyzing the range of moods in Andersen's travelogues.

The Portugal book mentions for the most part children in memories, either people's personal memories about childhood episodes, or Portuguese stories about children. In general these memories and stories about children are horrible – they are about death and fear.

Thus, in this paper's perspective this travel book is most similar to *Rambles in the Harz Mountains* and *In Sweden*.

Conclusion: Two Main Types of Moods

Generally children are misused as motifs in Andersen's travel books, for purposes that belong to the world of adults, namely eroticism and death. Speaking in terms of moods, these themes are connected with arousement and melancholy respectively. This conclusion is similar to what Søren Baggesen once said about the fairy tales: They are in fact mainly for adults, only the surface is for children.

When it comes to the relation between death and children, I want to make it clear that I do not refer to the death of children, but merely to sceneries or passages, where children are present in a discourse about aging and death, such as it is the case in for example the story "A View from Vartou's Window".[14]

Children are rarely just children in the travel books. They are described as children in their own right in a few cases in *In Spain*, which overall contains the most uncomplicated and objective descriptions, but in general children are symbols referring to something else, and this is always a part of life history: the past or the future. The moments or transformations in life which particularly occupied Andersen in relation to children, are adolescence and death. The former is always viewed in a sexual or erotic light, and it always involves girls or women.[15] It is the future maiden, the flower bud that is beheld – at safe distance.[16] Especially *In Spain* is full of such moments and pictures of girls. In particular the meetings of eyes are in the centre: the eyes of the traveller and the Andalusian, black, burning eyes. The traveller's eyes may fall elsewhere, but it is the eyes and the tempting (charming, kissable, expressive) mouths of the girls, which arouse him.[17]

There is a simple correlation between the perspectives, I have sketched, and the moods that are connected with children: Girls are very often linked with an erotic or sexualized and elevated mood. It is not dirty, but neither is it solely devout. Andersen is not only concerned with spiritual beauty, as one might imagine, but also with the bodily, as we have seen. Children placed in the context of death, on the other hand, are related to more depressed, gloomy and mixed moods.

Literature

Andersen, Hans Christian: *Rambles in the Romantic Regions of the Harz Mountains, Saxon Switzerland, &c.* Translated from the Danish original, *Skyggebilleder* (1831), by Charles Beckwith. London, 1848.

Andersen, Hans Christian: *A Poet's Bazaar*. Translated from the Danish original, *En Digters Bazar* (1842), by Grace Thornton. New York, 1988.

Andersen, Hans Christian: *I Sverrig*, in H.C. Andersen: *Romaner og Rejseskildringer,* vol. 7. Copenhagen: DSL / Gyldendal, 1944.

Andersen, Hans Christian: *In Spain*. Translated from the Danish original, *I Spanien* (1863), by Grace Thornton. London, 1975.

Andersen, Hans Christian: *Et Besøg i Portugal 1866*, in H.C. Andersen: *Rejseskitser*. København: DSL / Borgen 2002.

Baggesen, Søren (1993): "Dobbeltartikulationen i H.C. Andersens eventyr" ('The Double Articulation in Andersen's Fairy Tales'), in Johan de Mylius et al. (eds.): *Andersen og Verden / Andersen and the World. Papers from the First International Hans Christian Andersen Conference 25 to 31 August 1991*. Odense: Odense University Press 1993, pp. 15-29. Online at: http://www.andersen.sdu.dk/forskning/konference/tekst.html?id=9685

Bech, Henning (1998): "A Dung Beetle in Distress: Hans Christian Andersen Meets Karl Maria Kertbeny, Geneva, 1860. Some Notes on the Archaeology of Homosexuality and the Importance of Tuning", in *Journal of Homosexuality*, vol. 35: 3-4 [= Jan Löfström (ed.): *Scandinavian Homosexualities. Essays on Gay and Lesbian Studies*], 1998, p. 139-61.

Notes

1. Baggesen 1993.
2. "The Metal Pig" ("Metalsvinet"), "The Bond of Friendship" ("Venskabs-Pagten") and "A Rose from Homer's Grave" ("En Rose fra Homers Grav") were originally parts of the travel book *A Poet's Bazaar*, 1842, and were issued as independent stories for the first time on 15 December 1862, in the fairy tale collection *Eventyr og Historier. Første Bind*, 1862.
3. Henning Bech, a Danish sociologist concerned with the moods of modernity and late modernity, has argued (in Bech 1998) that the word "tuning" ought to be used instead of "mood" when describing this subject matter in English, because "mood" refers to something merely psychological, the sentiments of the individual, whereas "tuning" refers to something more, namely also the surroundings of the individual. Moods are inevitably connected with locations, because moods do not only come from within. The word "tuning" may remind us about the complexity of the subject matter: that it is beyond, but not apart from, the individual. From now on I shall nevertheless refer to "moods", because I do not intend to make associations to tuning of engines or antennas.

Henning Bech also sometimes speaks of moods, even though he has argued otherwise.
4. Quoted from *Rambles in the Romantic Regions of the Harz Mountains, Saxon Switzerland, &c.*, translated from the Danish original, *Skyggebilleder* (1831), by Charles Beckwith, London 1848.
5. *Rambles,* chapter 12, p. 217
6. Assuming a sort of progress or evolution in the course of the oeuvre. This assumption is very common indeed in literary history. It may be an illusion, though. An author's works do not neccessarily get better during the oeuvre, even though they may vary in different respects. In the case of Andersen's travel books, viewed from this paper's angle, there are two main types of travel books: the erotic and the "morbid". The former takes place in the warm South (Italy, Turkey), the latter in the cold North (Sweden, Germany). The "cold" travelogues are more reflected and have a more symbolic character, whereas the "warm" ones seem to find the beauty of the travel's sites and people interesting enough in themselves. Oddly, the Portugal book belongs to the "cold" ones concerned with death. Portugal's resemblances with the North is a recurring motif in that book, which is an interesting mix of the two sketched types.
7. In Danish: slotsfoged.
8. My own translation. I have been referring to Grace Thornton's translation of *A Poet's Bazaar*, New York 1988, which is not complete. Most of the chapters on Germany have been left out.
9. Quoted from Jean Hersholt's translation of "Metalsvinet" in *The Complete Andersen*, New York 1949, vol. 1, p. 21-22
10. Some among the audience, who heard this paper presented at the conference, objected, saying that "he was not a pedophile", "not a pervert", and so on. Some argued that one should not apply today's norms on Andersen, who lived in another time. I fully agree. I did not say "perverse" at any time, and "pedophile" only when rejecting such a conclusion beforehand. People jumped to "perversion" themselves, but this is not fair to the paper nor to Andersen.
11. Alameda means poplar avenue. Andersen consistently refers to promenades in Spain with this word. The quote is from Grace Thornton's translation, London 1975, p. 70.
12. Certain "improper" passages have been left out. Thornton hasn't translated the poems of *In Spain*, and that is, of course, not a matter of censoring. Mrs. Anne S. Bushby has translated the poems – and done it quite well – in her translation, *In Spain*, 1864.
13. This part has been left out of Thornton's *In Spain* right after "We went into the sutler's house" on p. 88.
14. A quote from Jean Hersholt's translation, "A View From Vartou's Window", 1949: "The poor children, how gaily they play! What bright eyes and what red cheeks! But they have neither shoes nor stockings. And they are dancing and playing on the green rampart, on that very spot where, as the old story goes, the ground always sank in until an innocent child was lured with flowers and toys into its open grave, which was walled up even while the child played. Then the ramparts were firm and were soon covered with a garment of beautiful green turf. But the children have never heard that old legend, or else

they would hear the poor little one still weeping beneath the mound, and the dew on the grass would seem to them the pearls of her tears." The tradition about the child that was buried alive under the rampart of Copenhagen, is old folklore. According to J.M. Thiele's *Danmarks Folkesagn* (1843-60), 1968, vol. 1, p. 125, on "Københavns Volde", it is a well-known characteristic in many traditions to make a sacrifice by burying something or someone alive, in order to make buildings stand forever. Usually the sacrifice is an animal, but here it is a child that is being decoyed into this cruel fate. In Andersen's lyrical picture of the old woman in Vartou, which was an institution for the elderly, founded by King Christian IV in 1607, Andersen employs the dark legend to create a strong tension between the thoughtlessness of the playing, joyful children and the dark, melancholic tale about the old woman.

15. As opposed to boys and men, cf. the discussion about the sexuality and desires of Andersen and of his fictional characters in, among others, Wilhelm von Rosen: *Månens kulør. Studier i dansk bøssehistorie 1628-1912*, Rhodos, Copenhagen 1993; Heinrich Detering, *Das offene Geheimnis. Zur literarischen Produktivität eines Tabus von Winckelmann bis zu Thomas Mann*, Wallstein Verlag, Göttingen 1994; Jackie Wullschlager, *Hans Christian Andersen. The Life of a Storyteller*, Penguin Press, London 2000; Jens Andersen, *Andersen. En biografi*, Gyldendal, Copenhagen 2003; Dag Heede: *Hjertebrødre. Krigen om H.C. Andersens seksualitet*, Syddansk Universitetsforlag, Odense 2005.

16. This distance – the silent yearning, the glances, merely beholding the objects of desire – is a common feature in Andersen's stories. Cf. among others the steadfast tin soldier and the snow man. They don't touch, they look.

17. But yet not *faces*. The focus is on the eyes and/or the mouth, isolated from what surrounds them.

Hans Christian Andersen between Rootedness and Modernity, with Special Reference to His Fairy Tale "The Dryad"

Aage Jørgensen

In the very heart of Jutland, on the Gudenå river, lies the provincial town Silkeborg. It came into existence around a paper factory established in the 1840's by Michael Drewsen, nephew of A.L. Drewsen, who was married to Ingeborg, a daughter of Jonas Collin, Hans Christian Andersen's benefactor. Andersen visited the place several times and took lodgings with the enterprising factory owner in his beautifully situated house. In 1853, after one of these visits, he reflected in an essay entitled "Silkeborg"[1] on the mid Jutland Wirtschaftswunder, where the river created good conditions and even formed a waterway down to the Randers fjord harbour.

Andersen's essay inscribes the industrial adventure into a context of nature and history as well. It moves, as pointed out by Johan de Mylius, "through a landscape penetrated by dim legends and by romantic 'woodland loneliness' towards its absolute opposite: the factory – and the attempt to mediate between nature and modern 'culture': the Drewsen garden".[2]

In Andersen's account the grand landscape of this Jutland region is, as a matter of fact, seen as marked by 'Waldeinsamkeit':

> Only few Danes know Denmark's most beautiful inland region, and still fewer belonging to the huge, sensible, usefulness-appreciating world are aware of the powers of the Gudenå river, which were wasted for centuries. The use and development of the material powers also bear spiritual treasures with them, and are the branches on which future spiritual fruit will grow. In this part of the country, at the deep river, Culture has plowed its field and sown its rich seed.

What Drewsen accomplished, was a victory of the human spirit, in relation to which the powers of nature were instrumental. In exactly the same way that the famous physicist Hans Christian Ørsted's accomplishment in the natural sciences was a triumph of the spirit. The paper factory and the activity it gave rise to, the formation of the city, is seen in this light, as a result of courage, skill, power, perseverance. "Blessedness was everywhere." This is, of course, a positive and culturally optimistic statement. Granted, but it was by way of "the monotonous music of the factory wheel" that Drewsen conjured it all up.

The essay does not question Drewsen's activity. It emphasizes, on the contrary that "it is a pleasure to enter into this huge, lively greenhouse", the factory with its life and bustle. Here there is no conflictual clash of interest, human and mechanical activity do not produce any threat to "solitude and wonderful silence", – "the entire landscape with town, forests and lakes is shining wonderfully in the red evening sun".[3]

*

The title figure of the fairy tale "Great-Grandfather" (1870) is "such a kind and intelligent old man".[4] When he tells about the sedate solidarity of the old days, the childish narrator is fascinated by all the beautiful things of the past: the liberation of the peasants, the abolition of slavery, etc. The great-grandfather, however, cannot get a proper foothold in the modern days with their nervous madness ("now everything has to move so fast – at a gallop – and values have been turned upside down"). But he consoles himself by thinking that Our Lord will "lead and direct it". This is exactly what happens in the tale, – that Our Lord turns out to be obliging.

He does so by rescuing Frederik, the narrator's older brother, from drowning, as his ship is wrecked at the western coast of Jutland on his return from a business trip to America; he brings with him a beautiful woman, whom he had met and married over there. Frederik is the prophet of modernity in the family. When he tells about "the latest scientific advancement, which are the strange and wonderful part of our times", great-grandfather is listening "with eyes wide open", but also with ethical scruples: "Human beings are getting cleverer, but not better!" And further on: "They use their knowledge to invent the most horrible ways of destroying one another."

However, human beings also invent equipment to be used, when for instance a rescue boat cannot get through. A rocket carries a rope to the wrecked ship, and when contact has been established, a kind of rescue-basket is used for the rest. Frederik and his young bride are saved in this way. And the great-grandfather, who by way of another modern invention, that of photography, has already been fascinated by the face of Frederik's bride, – feels thankful and grants a major sum of money to a monument for Hans Christian Ørsted, whose discovery in 1820 of electromagnetism had tremendous impact on technological development, as well as on Hans Christian Andersen's thinking about it, – and on the attitude of the great-grandfather, in so far as he finally pays tribute to progress. However, the fairy tale does not deny his ethical objection, nor does it question Frederik's counter-argument that wars as necessary blood-lettings of national bodies will end sooner, if military power is increased.

*

Between the two texts mentioned above, "The Dryad" is situated, a fairy tale written by Andersen after his visit to the World Exhibition in Paris 1867.[5] His relatively detailed remarks on the text disclose what attracted him to the exhibition. He felt "delighted" and "overwhelmed", and the view of the exhibition buildings was "marvelous and amazing". He felt inclined to depict "this splendour". A fellow-countryman gave it to be understood that this was a task for a Dickens, but Andersen felt that he, too, might have the necessary talent. The specific idea came to him as he saw an old chestnut tree at the square in front of his hotel being replaced by a young tree. The Dryad, i.e. the nymph attached to the tree, waved to him.[6]

But what does such a natural creature do in the metropolis and at its World Exhibition? Why does she long so irresistibly for the big city, civilisation and modern technology? Why does she not stay where she comes from, in her village out there in the French landscape? Indeed, the history of the Dryad is a tragic one, she has to die after some days and nights in the metropolitan surroundings and in the unbearable scent of gas typical of big cities. This is the price to be paid for the desire for intense life on the conditions of modern times.

The narrator refers to these modern times as "the age in which fairy tales come true", toward the end even as "our own wonderful times, the age when fairy tales come true". This sounds right in a fairy tale devoted to an event intended to amuse the audience by conjuring up the blessings of progress.

Dryaden. Et Eventyr fra Udstillingstiden i Paris 1867. Published 5 December 1868, reprinted 15 December. Cover illustration by Pietro Krohn. Dedication on p. 5 to the poet J.M. Thiele. A note on p. 60 in the second printing indicates that translations into English and French "are under way". *The Wood-Nymph* was published in London in 1870, translated by Augusta Plesner and Alice Milbank (58 pp., 3 illustrations). The first translation of the Parisian fairy tale into French was made by P.G. Chesnais in *Contes d'Andersen*, vol. 4, Paris 1943, pp. 144-64.

"The age of the fairy tale" is also "the age of progress, and progress is a blessing". This is, at least, "the opinion of a human being", but not the opinion of the rats, which below in the sewers suffer from modern cleanliness and wish they were back in "the age of the tallow candle", which was "a romantic period, as the human beings call it". The "wonderful old days" of their great-grandparents were "delightful", with plagues and other pleasures for rats, – just as the medieval time of King Hans was in "The Magic Galoshes".[7]

But of course it is not in the sewer system that the "wonder of the world" is to be found. This wonder the Dryad travels to Paris to see. Before following her, let us glimpse some of those blessings of rural life, which she disdains. Out there she was connected with a young chestnut tree placed near an old oak tree, in the shadow of which the old village priest often told the children about "great deeds done in bygone days, about men and women whose names are still mentioned with reverence".[8] At this place and in this nature the Dryad feels happy, even though she has to be content with a more limited horizon than the birds, which "might see all around, in every direction, far beyond the horizon of the Dryad"; they are, in short, privileged. This feeling of limitation turns into a longing, as a poor and lovely girl comes into the tale and sets off for Paris in spite of what the priest says: "It will be your ruin!" A few years later she returns as a distinguished lady: "It became your ruin, poor Marie!" In her state of innocence the Dryad is not able to understand that Marie has obtained her distinction by way of prostitution. The Dryad is attracted even more by the city lights, which in the evenings are seen in the distance. From that direction one night a thunder-cloud approaches, and a bolt of lightening strikes the oak tree and splits it, – "the trunk was cloven in two, as if it had wanted to embrace the messenger of light". From another fairy tale – "The Old Oak Tree's Last Dream" – we know that Andersen assigns a great unfurling of life-energy to the moment of death.[9]

From now on the Dryad is occupied with her own observations. As railroad traffic is intensified because people flock to the city, her enchantment also intensifies. And rumours spread about the World Exhibition, which the visitors understand in different ways. To some it is a magnificent sunflower that radiates all kinds of knowledge, to others it is a marvellous lotus, whose life cycle is summarized in this way: "it shot forth in spring and will be full grown in its magnificence come summer; but by fall it will be gone, neither leaves nor root will be left."

On the whole the rumours assure us of the magnificence of the World Exhibition. Normally the Field of Mars, i.e. the soldier's drill ground, looks like "a large sandy expanse without a blade of grass, as though it had been cut out of the Sahara Desert, where Fata Morgana shows strange castles of air and hanging gardens". But the buildings that now shoot up in record time, are still much more magnificent and wonderful, because they are "reality produced by human skill". Rumours compare them to Aladdin's castle, but in a contemporary version. All in all there is no end to the splendor of the World Exhibition or to its power to fascinate and attract people. Nonetheless the reader may feel unhappy about the entire description. The comparison with the lotus has a poetic scent, but does it not also indicate infertility, rootlessness, a sudden ecstatic blossoming, before everything dissipates and becomes nothing? And how much does the assurance mean that the buildings are more real than the strange desert mirages? After all their foundations are in the sand. And even the castle of Aladdin required some kind of defence. And what about the reference to the myth of the Tower of Babel? Is the narrator (or the author) garnishing what rumour brings to the ears of the Dryad, with hints to the attentive reader?

The Dryad's longing develops into "purpose in living", but the fulfilment, which is foretold by a gigantic luminous figure "speaking softly and yet as penetratingly as the trumpet that will sound on Judgement Day", is far from unconditional. The Dryad will be admitted to "the magic city" (the same expression that was used in connection with Marie), her longing and craving will increase, she will abandon her "nature", i.e. the tree, but her life will decrease to "half that of a mayfly: one single night". The figure also repeats the priest's words to Marie: "Poor Dryad, it will be your ruin!" In this way a link is created to urban sexuality and a link is broken to religion, as will be shown.

The chestnut tree is moved to Paris in order to replace a tree strangled by "scent of gas, smell of food and the foul, polluted air of the city". The narrator who from his hotel balcony observes the placing of the tree, makes the words of the old priest his own: "Poor Dryad!" But the Dryad is happy, even though the poster-covered houses prevent her from seeing the sights, and even though the multitudes of the daytime depress her, while in the evening she feels a breath of fresh air from her native soil: "a mild sweet breeze". However, a few days and nights later the Dryad knows her "little dead corner" so well that (as foreseen by the mighty luminous figure) she asks for having "the life of years" replaced by "half of the mayfly's life", i.e. for being allowed to leave her tree and mingle with human beings and experience human happiness. What she expresses is a carpe diem: "There is a life I can sense; and that I must grasp. I must be alive among the living, be part of the human world, and fly like the birds. I would give up the years of boredom – the everyday life that wears you away slowly, till you disappear like a fog on the meadow – for one night of being alive." Her wish comes true, but not without a ritual reference to Marie. As the Dryad has been freed from her jail and sits underneath "the gas-lit leaves of the tree", the narrator offers his comparison: "young and beautiful as poor Marie, of whom it had been said: 'The great town will be your undoing!'"

Wood-Nymph in Its Chestnut Tree. Drawing by Lorenz Frølich (1820-1908), *Nye Eventyr og Historier*, vol. 3, 1874, p. 63. In *Samlede eventyr og historier. Illustreret af danske kunstnere 1837-1974*, vol. 5, 1975, pp. 185-206, the illustrations were made by the French artist Ludmilla Balfour (born 1952). Moreover the excellent illustrations by the Russian artist Oskar Klever (1887-1975) are available in a Danish edition: *Eventyr*, ed. by Johan de Mylius, 1991, pp. 203-27. – *The Complete Andersen*, translated by Jean Hersholt, New York 1949, Blue Section, pp. 165-84, contains illustrations by Fritz Kredel.

This is the real fall of the Dryad. As she is sitting under her tree, but now separated from it, the narrator sees her leaning against "the door of her house; but she had locked it and thrown the key away". She has lost identity – to leave her tree is, as already mentioned, to leave her (inner) nature. True, she moves around among human beings, but without being recognized, and capriciously inconsistent, always on her way to somewhere else, chasing what is marvellous. She is compared to a glittering lotus that is "torn away from its roots".

Now comes a grand tour of Paris by night. She sees the boulevard and crosses it at the risk of her life; with Marie in her thoughts she approaches the Madeleine church, where distinguished ladies call attention to themselves in expensive fashionable clothes as they kneel in prayer or confess their secret sins. By way of experiment the Dryad identifies with these veiled women, "maybe each of them was a child of longing as she was?" But this is not a place for her, "here she breathed not fresh air but incense".

After this follows the visit in "the depths of the earth", i.e. in the sewer system of Paris. A man of the crowd waiting in front of the stairs mentions it as "the real wonder of our time", and so the Dryad must believe that she has arrived at the entrance to the World Exhibition.

The next station on the route is a place of entertainment called "Mabille", a kind of garden with an open-air dance floor and "small, silent bowers" – and: "Music tickled the ear, charmed and captivated the listener, making his blood rush more quickly", – that is a place for sensual lust, the unsuspecting young women remind her and us about Marie. The Dryad is whirled into the dance, which is characterized as "wild as a bacchanal", – and she "felt herself being devoured by her own lust for life, as though she were in an opium dream".

But just as her partner whispers words to her, unintelligible to her (as to the narrator, but not to the reader), she is carried away by a breeze and further on to what the text again calls the mirage of the Field of Mars, i.e. the World Exhibition. There she descends into the depths once again, in so far as she suddenly finds herself in a diving bell made of glass on the bottom of an aquarium belonging to the man-made exhibition complex. Everything here is managed by machinery, in the same way as the world observed by Johannes V. Jensen at another World Exhibition, the one of 1900. But while Jensen sees behind the machinery "the originator of it all, the human being",[10] it should be noted that Andersen mentions it as "Master Bloodless", in the very same way as he did in his travelogue *In Sweden*, in its sombre description of how modern technology makes itself a master of man.[11] The diving bell arrangement gives the narrator an opportunity to depict the human world from a point of view belonging to fish. In this way he fulfils a promise to the reader that the Dryad may see those fish that the swallow told her about when she was still connected to her tree out there in the village. But it is unfolded so long-windedly, as a self-contained little satire that one might be tempted to question its role in the tale from an aesthetic point of view.

When back in fresh air, the Dryad at long last experiences the World Exhibition. "She drank in the entire view with the lust of her eyes", while "memories from home, from the country" – including a recollection of Marie – mingle with feverish restlessness and tiredness, because her life is slipping away. She asks the running water that springs "from the depth of the earth and has everlasting life", to refresh her, but it replies that it does not "spring from our eternal mother", it "rushes because a machine wills it".[12] She asks the grass for freshness, but it replies that it dies when picked. She asks the wind to kiss her once more, but is assured that "all this will be gone" and become dust before the year is over. And finally she falls in front of a little church, from which music issues from the organ. It is as if she perceives the rustling of the old oak tree and hears the old priest tell about "what God's creation *might* give as a present to future times, and *had* to give in order to win everlasting life for itself". But the organ not only proclaims the blessing of continuous life, it also pronounces the sentence: "Your longing, your desire, tore you from the place that God had given you; that was your tragedy, poor Dryad!"

In this way the devilish pact is fulfilled. If you commit an offence against what you have been given by God, you have to accept your verdict and punishment. The sun rises, the Dryad is hit by its first beam and bursts like a soap bubble. At the same time the young transplanted chestnut tree dies, hurt by the uprooting when it was moved, but hurt also by the urban scent of gas.

The meaning of the text is complicated. Is it a fairy tale about the marvellous present age? Is the World Exhibition a positive reply to a romantic time when plagues smouldered in the metropolitan underground and threatened the lives of the closely packed population? What is the point of view of the narrator, who has arrived in town without "witchcraft", and who observes and experiences the entire story, from the arrival of the tree to its withering? And who after his report on the rural prehistory in the countryside even passes judgement over the project of moving the tree: "We, who tell about it, stood on the balcony, we looked down into the square. We saw the messenger of spring that had come from the country where the air is sweet and fresh, and we said, as the old priest would have, 'Poor Dryad!'"

The press gilded binding of the Low edition.

Augusta Plesner (1817-85) collaborated with Alice Milbank on the English translation of "Dryaden." It appeared in *Aunt Judy's Magazine* (under the title "The Dryad") and subsequently in *Fairy Tales and Sketches* (1870) – and again the same year in a special printing by the publisher Sampson Low (under the title "The Wood-Nymph"). See Viggo Hjørnager Pedersen, *Ugly Ducklings? Studies in the English Translations of Hans Christian Andersen's Tales and Stories*, 2004, pp. 220-25. – Here the three anonymous illustrations of the Low edition are shown.

Why does this narrator assure us that the present age is the age of fairy tales, at the very same time that his narration argues overwhelmingly that the present age is doomed and self-destructive? And why does the curse and the self-destruction so strikingly relate itself to sexuality and godlessness? Is the fairy tale perhaps an ironic dismantling of the authority possessed by the two decisive assertions about the marvel of modern times because of their position, – at the very beginning and the very end of the tale?

The Dryad isn't in itself a modern phenomenon, she belongs to the mythology of nature and is connected to her tree, and this is what we call her "nature". This rootedness represents, of course, some sort of limitation, but this should be positively understood. The tree is related to its part of the countryside, and this part is her native soil, it is connected to history and to great deeds, and thus it becomes an expression of connectedness to tradition, to a context that may explain why the local children feel devotion when the priest talks. The mere fact that the Dryad in this specific case separates from her tree, indicates a decisive and fundamental split in the relation of the present age to nature and origin, a threatening rootlessness.

On the other hand the modern city is associated with moral ruin, sinful depravation, unbounded lust and prostitution: Marie with the red flower in her dark hair, who travels to Paris and comes back as a distinguished lady who is able to manage her beautiful team of horses – and with "a smartened-up small jockey" on the back of her fine carriage.

It is evident that "The Dryad" also deals with the theme of everything's being perishable, familiar throughout Andersen's writings. After the fall of the oak tree the Dryad says it herself: "Everything passes [...]. Passes as the clouds pass by in the sky: pass and never return." She says so, however, just after we have been told that a painter will portray the oak tree "as a lasting memory". And the radiant figure that draws up the conditions of liberation for the Dryad, does it too, while stressing the relation between Dryad and tree: "your life will be snuffed out, the leaves of the tree will wither and die, and never come back."[13]

*

The contrasting in "The Dryad" of countryside and big city is a variation over another theme, which is also unfolded several times in

Andersen's writings, usually in a much more general way, such as in the paradigmatic fairy tale "The Bell" (1845).[14] The point of departure for this story is the contrasting of a town characterized by noise and distraction with a landscape that gives room for reflection. The decisive borderline, however, does not run along the town gate, but at the edge of a forest behind the tent of a confectioner who is visited every Sunday by townsmen eager to feel that they are "in the green" (i.e., in contact with nature and surrounded by natural scenery). As a matter of fact most of the newly confirmed youngsters also stop there, as evidence that they do not have the human qualifications required by Andersen. To those few that cross the borderline into unknown territory, the forest that is fascinating and dangerous as well, the elimination process continues. As is well known only the king's son and the poor boy reach the slope in front of the sea and hear the ringing of the bell "in the midst of nature's and poetry's great cathedral". It is like an echo of Adam Oehlenschläger's famous poem "The Golden Horns", in which the requirement is also formulated in such a way that most are unable to fulfill it: "The few who know / The gift we bestow / [...] / Surely they hear / Again thy clear / 'Let there be Light!'".[15] The fairy tale has almost no concern with the bourgeois life which the two boys leave behind them, i.e. with ordinary life on worldly conditions. It may be added that the definition of the town as the place of distraction is rather vague and without reference to any kind of "modern" development. The town is so to speak defined negatively in relation to the countryside – or, to be more precise, in relation to the forest and the sea, if the text is to be taken at face value. The petit-bourgeois way of life as well as universal commercialization reach, as pointed out, all the way to the edge of the forest.

Hans Christian Andersen diagnosed the shallowness of modernity – and all the dullness and materialism it implies – in "In a Thousand Year's Time" (1852),[16] a satiric-pessimistic tale about how "America's young generation" manages to pick up the entire syllabus of classical European culture in only eight days. In any case they manage to visit all the holy places of this culture that nonetheless remains indifferent to them.

"Om Aartusinder", originally appearing in *Fædrelandet* on 26 January 1852, was reprinted in *Historier. Anden Samling* (1853), and also with two drawings by Vilhelm Pedersen in *Historier* (1855). Although as is well known, Andersen lets "America's young inhabitants" cross the ocean "on the wings of steam", one drawing shows balloons, while on the other one we see a more sophisticated, Jules Verne type airship (cf. "air steamer", used once in the text). – "Have balloons been discovered?" asks the fourth brother in "De Vises Sten" (1858). They have not, but in this text that makes no difference at all, since the father, the philosopher, possesses special powers. The brother gets his balloon but after the trip forgets to moor it: "where it went, there was no way to know, but that makes no difference, since it wasn't yet invented." It would be by the brothers Montgolfier in 1782. – Also in "Flaskehalsen" (1858) a balloon voyage is depicted, and it is inspired by the flights of the Swede, Victor Granberg, in Copenhagen in 1857, including the failed attempt which gave rise to the saying, "Den går ikke, Granberg!" (roughly equivalent to "No way, Jose!").

Despite the title, this has long ago become reality incarnate. And Andersen has become included in that part of the syllabus, to which the airborne visitors have set one day aside: "One day in Scandinavia, Ørsted's and Linnaeus's fatherland, and Norway, the land of ancient heroes and young Norwegians." In this context Ørsted represents the "useful" natural science, which created the conditions for the technical development that Andersen so desperately wanted to believe in and to see in a perspective of Enlightenment. But by retaining the idea that there was "spirit" behind it all.[17] At this point he did in fact often experience a profound doubt.

Literature

– *H.C. Andersens Eventyr*. Critical edition based on the original fairy tale booklets with variant notes by Erik Dal and commentary by Erling Nielsen and Flemming Hovmann. Vols. 1-7. København, 1963-90. (Vols. 1-5, 1963-67; vols. 6-7, 1990.)

– *The Complete Fairy Tales and Stories*. Translated by Erik Christian Haugaard. London/Garden City 1974. Pp. 934-53 ("The Wood Nymph") and p. 1092 (notes by Andersen). [Abbreviated in the notes: ECH.]

– Detering, Heinrich & Heike Depenbrock, "Der Tod der Dryade und die Geburt der Neuen Muse". In: Kurt Braunmüller & Mogens Brøndsted (eds.), *Deutsch-nordische Begegnungen. 9. Arbeitstagung der Skandinavisten des deutschen Sprachgebiets 1989 in Svendborg*. Odense, 1991. Pp. 366-90.

– Detering, Heinrich, "Andersen dans les 'Passages parisiens'. 'La Dryade' entre Baudelaire, Rilke et Benjamin". *Études Germaniques*, Vol. 58, 2003, pp. 711-33. (*Numéro spécial sur Hans Christian Andersen, offert en hommage à Regis Boyer.*)

– Fechner-Smarsly, Thomas, "Elektrifiziertes Schauen oder: Von der Beleuchtung zur Belichtung. Hans Christian Andersens Märchen 'Dryaden'". *Skandinavistik*, Vol. 26, 1996, pp. 83-101.

– Kragh, Helge, "H.C. Andersen, Ørsted og Naturvidenskaben". *Gamma. Tidsskrift for Fysik*, No. 139, 2005, pp. 12-20.

– Mylius, Johan de, "Problemer omkring H.C. Andersens realisme. En skitse". In: Jørgen Breitenstein, et al., *H.C. Andersen og hans kunst i nyt lys*. Odense, 1976. Pp. 105-31, esp. pp. 126-31.

– Mylius, Johan de, *Forvandlingens pris. H.C. Andersen og hans eventyr*. København, 2004. 385 pp. (On "Dryaden" pp. 254-59.)

– Nielsen, Birger Frank, *H.C. Andersen Bibliografi. Digterens danske Værker 1822-1875*. København, 1942. 462 pp. [Abbreviated in the notes: BFN.]

Notes

1. "Silkeborg", *Folkekalender for Danmark 1854*, 1853, pp. 97-106 (BFN 637). Reprinted in: *Samlede Skrifter*, 2nd ed., vol. 6, 1877, pp. 273-83. Here quoted from: *'Hr. Digter Andersen'. Liv, Digtning, Meninger*, ed. by Johan de Mylius, 1995, pp. 239-47.
2. *'Hr. Digter Andersen'*, presentation of the text pp. 238-39; quotation from p. 239.
3. In the introductory remarks Johan de Mylius finds a "remarkable pessimism" in this essay. But the expressions called for to strengthen his argumentation belong to specific contexts. "The spirit of oblivion" refers to what is lost in times so remote that "neither written text nor oral legend relates about it", and "the desolate land" characterizes the present experience, not necessarily conflicting with the faintly discerned future when the railroad will open the area for tourists from all over the world wanting to see "the marvels of this part of the country". – In the poem "Jutland" (1860) the invitation is: "Come! Ere many years are born, / here'll be fields of standing corn". (*Syv Digte / Seven Poems*, transl. by R.P. Keigwin, 1955, p. 11.)
4. "Great-Grandfather" (BFN 1002), *H.C. Andersens Eventyr*, vol. 5, pp. 136-40; ECH, pp. 987-91.
5. *Dryaden. Et Eventyr fra Udstillingstiden i Paris 1867*, 1868; 60 pp. (BFN 978.) Reprinted in: *Nye Eventyr og Historier*, vol. 3 [= *Eventyr og Historier*, vol. 5], 1874, pp. 63-98. Also reprinted in: *H.C. Andersens Eventyr*, vol. 5, pp. 69-90. (Cf. vol. 6, pp. 213-16 [Erling Nielsen on reception criticism], and vol. 7, pp. 334-38 [commentary by Flemming Hovmann].) English translations: (1) *The Wood-Nymph*, by A.M. and Augusta Plesner, London 1870; (2) *The Complete Andersen*, by Jean Hersholt, New York 1949, Blue Section, pp. 165-84; (3) *The Complete Fairy Tales and Stories*, by Erik Christian Haugaard, London/Garden City 1974, pp. 934-53.
6. Andersen's notes on "The Dryad" date from 1874. Reprinted in: *H.C. Andersens Eventyr*, vol. 6, pp. 26-27. (On Andersen's stay in Paris September 7-21, 1867 and his visit to the World Exhibition, see *H.C. Andersens Dagbøger 1825-1875*, vol. 7, 1972, pp. 343-51.)
7. In the fairy tale "The Magic Galoshes" (1838; BFN 321; *H.C. Andersens Eventyr*, vol. 1, pp. 211-38; ECH, pp. 82-107) councilman Knap defends the traditional romantic point of view that the Middle Ages were happier than the modern age, which on the contrary Hans Christian Ørsted had celebrated in a treatise published in 1835. When Knap leaves the party, he gets hold of the wrong galoshes, and consequently his wish to be transported to the time of King Hans is fulfilled. However, this experience turns out to be rather shocking.
8. The landscape is "lovely", and so is the human activity within it, – but "much more lovely" are the narratives of historical men and women (Joan of Arc, Charlotte Corday, Henry IV, Napoleon, etc.) told by the priest.
9. Cf. Johan de Mylius, *Forvandlingens pris*, 2004, esp. pp. 320ff.
10. Johannes V. Jensen, *Den gotiske Renaissance*, 1901, chapter "Maskinerne"; quotation from 2nd ed., 2000, p. 129.

11. H.C. Andersen, *I Sverrig*, ed. by Mogens Brøndsted, 2003, pp. 14-15. The expression "Bloodless", coined by Adolph Törneros, is here used about the steam engines of the Motala ironworks. – In the final hymn to "the age of discovery" it says that "the California of Poetry is in the natural sciences". And in "The Muse of the New Century" (1861) we are once again told, and this time in a tone of conjuration that "Master Bloodless and his busy helpers, who may seem to be the mighty rulers of our age, are just servants" to the muse that "with the innocence of the child, the enthusiasm of the young girl and the composure and knowledge of the married woman will raise the wonderful lamp of poetry".
12. Cf. Johan de Mylius, *Forvandlingens pris*, p. 258. The expression "I do not spring from our eternal mother" is explained in this text as a biblical allusion (John 4,14).
13. As is well known, Hans Christian Andersen dwelled throughout his life on the theme of mortality, both of human beings and of poetry. On November 24, 1870 he wrote the following entry in his diary: "I will soon be forgotten and cast aside by a coming generation". And he added, with a quotation from "The Fir Tree": "It's over! It's all over! And that's how it is with all stories!" As far as poetry is concerned, in "Auntie Toothache" we learn: "Often things go into the paper barrel that shouldn't." Towards the end of the original version this is sharpened to: "Everything goes into the barrel!" Nonetheless, before he died the student must have polished the text that was saved from the paper barrel by the grocer's apprentice, – and that wound up in Hans Christian Andersen's final collection of fairy tales. In the same way as the protagonist of "The Pixy and the Grocer" saves the wonderful book of poetry, while the house burns. The Dryad perishes, but "The Dryad" endures. The written word defies mortality, it continues to find new readers and interpreters. In this sense one could say that poetry defeats modernity or absorbs it. Unless one dare believe that the text, at the same time as it lets the Dryad perish, points to a divine salvation for her in the world beyond ("the unknown land", as Andersen puts it in the final passage of "The Story of a Mother").
14. "The Bell" (BFN 474), *H.C. Andersens Eventyr*, vol. 2, pp. 204-08; ECH, pp. 275-79.
15. Quoted from R.S. Hillyer's translation in *A Book of Danish Verse*, ed. by Oluf Friis, 1922, pp. 14-21. The original Danish text (in Oehlenschläger's *Digte*, 1803) has: "For de sieldne Faae / som vor Gave forstaae, [...] For *dem* lyder atter vort Bliv!".
16. "In a Thousand Year's Time" (BFN 599), *H.C. Andersens Eventyr*, vol. 2, pp. 259-60.
17. Cf. the fairy tale "Two Brothers" (1859; BFN 799; *H.C. Andersens Eventyr*, vol. 5, pp. 20-21; ECH, pp. 694-95), which is a celebration of the famous physician and his almost equally famous younger brother, the jurist Anders Sandøe Ørsted. – By the way, "Little Hans Christian" shared a preoccupation with balloons with "Big Hans Christian", who in 1836 published the poetic cycle *Luftskibet* (*The Airship*). Cf. Ane Grum-Schwensen, "H.C. Ørsted and the Art of Poetry, or: The Airship – 'Truth, Goodness and Beauty'", in Mogens Bencard (ed.), *Intersections. Art and Science in the Golden Age*, 2000, pp. 60-73.

Shadow Pictures – Truth or Tale

Lone Funch Kofoed

Hans Christian Andersen was a very young man when he went on his first journey abroad in 1831. His geographic destination was Dresden in Germany, which at that time was the centre of romantic art. Whilst travelling, Andersen kept a diary, and when he arrived home in Denmark, he wrote the travelogue *Shadow Pictures from a Journey to the Harz Mountains, Saxon Switzerland etc. etc. Summer of 1831* (hereinafter *Shadow Pictures*).[1] This paper is about the travelogue and its playful mixture of truth and tale.

Shadow Pictures consists largely of descriptions of the dramatic beauty of the scenery in the mountains and the valleys of Germany; it praises nature at its most marvellous. It is Andersen's first depiction of places other than his home country. He had never before witnessed mountains, and his descriptions are full of excitement and eagerness. But the travelogue is more than a romantic praise of nature. Andersen challenges his readers to go with him to a place where reality and fantasy are blended into a shadowy picture – where the story of the journey is the main thread, but where the thoughts and memories, dreams and fantasies of the poet play an important role in the narrator's experience of the journey as well as the reader's experience of the travelogue.

The Question of Narrative Origin

For decades literary theorists have been divided on one question: Does a given narration descend from or represent a series of essential events, and can this line of events be reconstructed?[2] That is, can we desiccate a story and put the different parts of it together again to form the chronological line of events and thoughts in the way they really were, in order to see and fully understand what is the raw material of the narration?

On the subject of Andersen's travelogues this question has challenged literary critics to investigate Andersen's many diaries and personal letters in the hunt for some "evidence" of what actually happened when Andersen was travelling. How much of what he has written in his travelogues did he actually experience and how much did he make up? Trying to separate the truth from the tale, so to speak, may give us a better idea of how the imagination and poetic talent of great authors become materialized. It may even teach us ways of transforming experience into art. However, this is not the aim of my study, although I am very much interested in the truth.

My interest in this paper lies in Andersen's stylistic method as it functions in this early travelogue. With examples from the text I will illustrate the technical decisions Andersen has made in writing this travelogue in order to make us, his readers, receive the story as a documentary description of an authentic journey – in other words: as the truth. I will examine Andersen's storytelling focusing on the narrator's role in painting a picture of a true story, and I will show how the narrator in different ways deceives his own good intentions.

One of my students made a rather accurate remark in class one day, concerning the element of truth in Andersen's work. He said that of all Andersen's fairy tales, his favourite was "The Ugly Duckling", and the reason for this was that he thought the tale was very realistic. It may sound like a contradiction that a fairy tale be called realistic, since by definition a fairy tale is a supernatural and utterly fictional genre. But the student explained himself like this. It happens all the time in real life that somebody is being bullied because they are different. The situation is well-known.

So the realism of the fairy tale of "The Ugly Duckling" lies in the fact that it draws upon an event that most of us have experienced ourselves in one way or another. We recognise the situation and we relate to the feelings of the ugly duckling.

The tale of the duckling turning into a swan is a brilliant example of Andersen's remarkable ability to see the universal aspects in everyday events and transform these events into metaphors – or in the case of the tales into allegories. In his travelogues he used that ability with similar fervour. In 1831 Andersen represented and depicted places that to most of his readers at the time were unknown or at least unseen, and he put into use his ability to familiarize events and feelings. That ability is one of the cornerstones of what is called storytelling.

Storytelling

Andersen's storytelling is famous. Many times he has been portrayed in storytelling postures – holding a book, reading aloud – for instance in the sculptures in Central Park in New York and the Town Square in Copenhagen, to mention but a few. His narration draws upon a long tradition of oral storytelling. Of course a great deal of Andersen's audience all over the world actually consists of listeners and not readers: because they are children who are being read to, who are being told a story.

The oral tradition of Andersen's literary game reveals itself in his continuous use of a narrator. Whether he is writing for children or aiming specifically at an adult audience, as with the travelogues, he never stops using the narrator as mediator of the story. The work before us here and now is no exception.

As a literary game, storytelling must be placed in between fiction and information. The informational narration is characterized by a mode where the narrator tries to depict things correctly. In contrast hereto, fictional narration withdraws the narrator as a mediator from the text and distributes the narrative to the acting agents. It tries to establish a non-contact between the narrator and the reader, and often the narrator will "hide inside" one of the characters, and see his side of the story and only that.

In storytelling the case is nearly the exact opposite: here the contact and interaction between narrator and reader is explicit and the defining element of the mode.[3] In this respect the travelogue *Shadow Pictures* meets the narrative criteria of storytelling, by installing a strong and potent narrator, who from the beginning establishes an explicit and direct contact with his reader.

The Switch to Present Tense

Like most narrators, the narrator in *Shadow Pictures* tells his story mainly in the past tense, a summary of the type "it was a dark and stormy night". The past tense allows the narrator to reconstruct or reintegrate the story's raw material in whatever way he sees fit because he needs not consider the immediate line of events – everything has already happened and so it can wait. The narrator using the past tense can place descriptions of inner thoughts, dreams, or even flashbacks accordingly.

Sometimes for effect Andersen's narrator switches to the present tense. The change suggests that we are actually there, that this is happening here and now. In the case of a travelogue, of course, the places Andersen visits, and his narrator tells about, do actually exist. Therefore it is very natural for the narrator to switch to the present tense, whenever he wants to tell about the places, which of course are still there, as opposed to the events that have already taken place.

These switches to the present tense often serve to explain and familiarize the experience, containing for instance a comparison to Denmark, or a generalization of the event to an abstract level, always founded in a concrete and genuine wondering. For example, when the narrator is in a grotto in Goslar, he wonders how the life of the men working inside the mountain is different from the sailor life at sea. Everyday the workers go to the same place inside the same mountain, while the sailor's life is always changing due to weather and new harbours. The concrete example depicts and familiarizes the abstract thought to the readers.[4]

But the switches to present tense also have a different function in relation to the narrator. Ironically the paragraphs in the present tense actually hold back the story and create a kind of commentary for the narrator. Moreover, they provide the readers with a certain time for thought – like arias in an opera. For instance, Andersen has inserted small poems in the text. Most of the poems introduce narrators of their own, named on their titles: "The Traveller," "The Spider," "The Choir," "The Lover," or "The Blind Mother." These poems work as intermezzos or bridges to new sequences, while at the same time they add new characters and viewpoints to the story.

But just as often these intermezzos allow the narrator to come out in the open and take a stand. Several times the narrator takes a stand on aesthetic art, which he has experienced, such as dance, music, literature and above all theatre plays. The travelling narrator goes to the theatre in every town that has one, and in the German city of Braunschweig, he sees a play that he truly dislikes. To comfort himself after the horrible experience, the narrator starts telling himself a fairy tale.

The tale is about a king, who believed in everything he ever heard – much like a child does. He could not imagine anything to be a lie. Being very sad about his inability to mistrust the stories he hears, he declares to the public that his beautiful daughter, the princess, will marry whoever can tell him something he cannot believe. Of course, a prince arrives and tells the king about his mother's garden in which the cabbage is so big that a full regiment of soldiers can stand beneath one leaf. And the king says words to the effect of "That is very possible, the power of Nature is great." This pattern repeats itself and in his lifetime the King never hears anything he would consider a lie. After death he wanders the earth as a ghost, unable to find peace because of his childish belief in the stories, he hears.

Finally it is the poet, the narrator of our story, who relieves the old King of his misery. The poet tells the king about the play he has just seen at the theatre in Braunschweig, about how the play depicted human nature, and after the poet has finished the king says: "Dear poet, what you have just told me is truly a lie – no human beings could ever react like that. Now I can rest in peace."[5] The lie consists of the unnatural, the unrealistic and therefore – in Andersen's opinion – aesthetically unworthy piece of dramatic poetry, which he witnessed in Braunschweig. In the following, I shall elaborate on Andersen's concern with the aesthetics of representation as it appears in *Shadow Pictures*.

The True Depiction – a Shadow Picture

The meaning of this short but central fairy tale and its placement in the travelogue has to do with the overall theme of the truth in two different aspects.

Firstly, the tale reconfirms the everlasting importance of the poet, since he plays the part of the saviour in the tale. The climax of the travelogue as such is Andersen's meeting with the great German romantic poet Ludwig Tieck in Dresden, and one could argue that this meeting is the main purpose of Andersen's journey. But one also finds traces of the concern with the aesthetic challenges of the writer within the textual lines of the travelogue, and it is here that the element of truth comes into the picture. In the very beginning of the text, the narrator claims that before he went on his travel, he imagined that he would write the travelogue as a play – a travel drama, with music, and it could have been unique, one of a kind. But as he went away, so did all his original ideas, and he realized that what he wanted to do was "to give it, the way it was given to me."[6] In other words: With this text Andersen, the romantic poet, is trying to capture the sensation which he experienced, and as he experienced it. Or at least so he claims.

Because, just as the narrator claims to be telling the truth he regrets the artists' lack of true representational skills. At one point he states: A painter cannot replicate the colours, how could the writer?[7] The concern with the writer's abilities compared to those of other artists runs like a red thread throughout the book. Even though the writer has talent, skill and imagination the representation of nature – or of anything real, one might add – can only be a mere shadow picture of the real thing. The title of the book is a further statement of that philosophy.

Maybe now is a good time to consider what the concept of shadow pictures actually implies. The word refers to the pictures that are made when you hang up white cloth on a wall and make figures with your hands or with objects. It is not the backside of something, but a shadow that is actually something else than the thing it stems from.

So, when Andersen is creating shadow pictures, he is transforming his experience, his sensation, into something else than what it originally was; he is transforming it into a story. His skills as a writer manifest themselves in the reintegration of the events of his journey into a constructed story consisting of fairy tales, poems, and prose, which brings me to the second aspect concerning the element of truth in the fairy tale about the king and the poet.

The Blending of Story and Tale

I am sure you noticed how the two stories – the fairy tale and the travelling story – mixed and overlapped each other, much like a dream, where events from your day combine with pure imaginary elements. The poet telling the fairy tale plays a role in the same fairy tale. This technique of blending what is so obviously fiction with the main story of the travelogue is a reminiscence of how the writer works. Fantasy and reality are joined together by the writing of the poet and what emerges is something in between.

Likewise, at one stage in the text the narrator expresses regret that a couple of co-travellers from Hamburg are getting off the carriage, which he is travelling by, before he has got to know them. "I could have used them in my story", he says. "They would have fitted perfectly in the third chapter. How sad it is for a writer, when his characters disappear between his fingers."[8]

In literary terms such remarks are called meta-remarks, because the narrator is referring to his own writing, and thereby pointing to the fact that the text in front of the reader is a construction. In as much as the narrator is concerned with his own writing and story, the narrator goes beyond his own story, so to speak, and refers to something that seems to be outside of it. A storytelling narrator can of course do that without causing any stylistic problems because the storyteller is constitutional of the story. That is, without the storyteller there would not be a story.

Still, meta-remarks of this type tend to have a certain shock effect for the readers, since they illustrate a crack in the illusion that the story is the truth – that the story was already there before we read it. The meta-remarks create that hole in the story through which we catch a glimpse of the directing, the making of the set design and the special effects. The meta-remarks surprise us, as if we were not aware that the story is fiction. Or rather, they surprise us, because we don't want to be aware that the story is not the documented reality, we believe it is, while we are reading it. Just like the old king in the fairy tale, we don't want to accept the lie.

Conclusion

Concluding the aspects of this paper, Andersen's storytelling in *Shadow Pictures* is somewhat dubious.

The travelogue has by definition an element of realism. Like the biography, it always has a documentary storyline. The journey has really taken place, the life has been lived – the artistic liberty lies in the description of it.

And Andersen takes a lot of liberties. His use of storytelling techniques, like installing a strong narrator of the travelogue, adds to the story's sense of realism, but as I have shown it also adds to its sense of falseness. Even when the narrator is claiming to tell something real, it is probably still a combination of realism and fiction. The travelogue should be grasped in no other way.

I have tried to show how Andersen's narrator jumps out of his narration, to speak on his own account in intermezzos formed as poems and fairy tales. I wanted to draw attention to the way the narrator blends the genres, and for example how he plays a part in the fairy tale about the old king, and how in meta-remarks the narrator interferes in the story, thereby letting it be seen that the text is a construction. In plain words: Andersen spends a lot of time and effort constructing a story that seems true and real and at the end of the day he discloses his own construction principles – like going behind the scenes in a theatre.

Perspective

To put this into perspective, let me finish with a quick glance at history. Around the middle of the 19th century, the idea of an omnipotent narrator making all the decisions and running the entire show was going out of fashion. Artists started looking for more mimetic modes of narrating. Telling stories through the institution of a narrator such as Andersen did, was considered old-fashioned and boring. Instead to "show" not to "tell" was in vogue.[9] The limited point of view became the new thing, where the narrator would hide inside one of the characters and present everything from that character's point of view. Andersen's narrator never hides, but he very often takes the cover of a poet, who has a great deal in common with Andersen himself and that can lead us to believe every word he says.

If we were to desiccate the story, if we were to separate the story of the travelogue from all the rest of it, so that the chronology fits, we would destroy the story. In that case we would not have a storyteller, and we would not have one of Andersen's travelogues. The personal experience, the subjective depiction, the added value – the lie, if you will – is what makes the story worth reading.

Bibliography

Andersen, H.C.: *Skyggebilleder af en Reise til Harzen, det sachsiske Schweitz etc. etc. i Sommeren 1831*, ed. by Johan de Mylius, Copenhagen: Det danske Sprog- og Litteraturselskab, 1986. (New edition, 2003).

Andersen, H.C.: *Skyggebilleder af en Reise til Harzen, det sachsiske Schweitz etc. etc. i Sommeren 1831*, ed. by H. Topsøe-Jensen, Copenhagen: Nordlundes Bogtrykkeri, 1968. (Ill.by Henrik Bloch; postscript ppp. 185-213).

Benjamin, Walter: "Fortælleren", in: P. Madsen (ed.) *Fortælleren og andre essays*. København, Gyldendal 1996.

Houe, Poul: "Ude er hjemme. Om H.C. Andersens 'Et besøg i Portugal 1866'", *Danske Studier*, 1988, 115-32.

Skalin, Lars-Åke: "'Out of the Real Grows the Most Wonderful Tale': Extra- and Intrafictional Levels in H. C. Andersen's Storytelling", Paper from H.C. Andersen Symposium, Center for Narratologiske Studier, University of Southern Denmark, 15-17 August 2003 (www.humaniora.sdu.dk/narratologi).

Svendsen, Erik: "Hans Christian Andersen – An Untimely Journalist", in: *A Poet in Time. Papers from the Second International Hans Christian Andersen Conference 29 July to 2 August 1996,* ed by Johan de Mylius, Aage Jørgensen and Viggo Hjørnager Pedersen, The Hans Christian Andersen Center, Odense University, Odense University Press, 1999

Wallace, Martin: "Narrative Structure: A Comparison of Methods", in: *Recent Theories of Narrative*, Ithaca: Cornell University Press, 1986, pp. 107-29.

Wallace, Martin: "Points of View on Point of View", in: *Recent Theories of Narrative*, Ithaca: Cornell University Press, 1986, pp. 130-51.

Winsatt, W.K.: The Intentional Fallacy, *The Verbal Icon*, (The University of Kentucky Press, 1954)

Notes

1. I am using the Danish title of the book in my own translation because I find the notion of *shadow pictures* important in the context of my paper. The official English title of the book is, however, *Rambles in the Romantic Regions of the Hartz Mountains, Saxon Switzerland, etc.* London 1847.
2. Wallace: "Narrative Structure" pp. 107.
3. Skalin, Lars-Åke (cf. bibliography).
4. Andersen, p. 44.
5. Andersen, pp. 33-35. The quote is my summary of the passage
6. Andersen, pp. 10.
7. Andersen, pp. 49.
8. Andersen, pp. 24-25. The quote is my summary of the passage.
9. In essence film making provided the opportunity to show, not tell, without limiting the scope of temporality of the story. As literature, film can create flash-backs and visions of the future, without it seeming very unrealistic and disrupting as long monologues in theatres sometimes do.

Encyclopaedic "Portraits" of Hans Christian Andersen in Contemporary Polish Encyclopaedias and Lexicons

Zbigniew Baran

Introduction

Writing this paper, I should like to answer these questions: What is the significance of Hans Christian Andersen in contemporary Poland at the beginning of the 21st century? and: What can Polish people learn about Andersen when reading Polish encyclopaedias and lexicons edited in the last 25 years in Poland? A review of fifty encyclopaedic and lexicographic entries has given me general information about those matters.

Three kinds of encyclopaedias and lexicons have appeared during the last 25 years in Poland: encyclopaedias and lexicons for pupils, universal encyclopaedias and lexicons for "everyone", and professional encyclopaedias and lexicons addressed especially to experts.

Hans Christian Andersen in Polish Encyclopaedias and Lexicons for Pupils

The school-encyclopaedias (or the school-lexicons) as well as textbooks are important teaching aids for Polish pupils. The encyclopaedic knowledge is unquestionable. Therefore, I should like to discuss the problem: What has been written on the life and literary works of Andersen by Polish authors of encyclopaedic and lexicographic entries for Polish pupils within the last 25 years?

In these entries, Hans Christian Andersen is presented as "a Danish writer" (see: [3], p. 15; [16], p. 49; [30], p. 20; [31], p. 10; [32], p. 23; [37], p. 19; [41], p. 256; [42], p. 13; [43], p. 13; [44], p. 8; [48], p. 33, [49], p. 8), "a Danish writer of fairy tales, novelist and dramatist" ([15], p. 37), or "a Danish novelist, poet and dramatist" ([36], p. 7;

[41], p. 256; [45], p. 5), as "a writer of fairy tales" ([49], p. 8), and as "an author of poetical collections (volumes), theatrical plays and travel-books" ([3], p. 16; [48], p. 33).

Andersen is also presented as "an author of *Eventyr* [*Fairy Tales*]" ([37], p. 19) and as "an author of *Eventyr* [*Fairy Tales*], novels, stories, theatrical plays and (literary) autobiography *Mit Livs Eventyr* [*The Fairy Tale of My Life*]" ([31], s. 10). In very few entries is he presented nobly as "the creator of fairy tales" ([48], p. 33), "the creator of literary fairy tales" ([30], p. 20) and "the creator of poetic fairy tales" ([16], p. 49) or as "the creator of 'the world of literary fairy tales'" ([37], p. 20). The encyclopaedic entries inform us that the fame of Andersen rests on his fairy tales ([3], p. 16; [16], p. 49; [30], p. 20; [32], p. 23; [36], p. 7; [41], p. 256; [45], p. 5; [49], p. 8), or on his writing of fairy tales ([42], p. 13; [43], p. 13). One of the encyclopaedic entries informs the reader that "he was the creator of modern Danish literary language" (see: [44], p. 8).

We may find a little more knowledge of Andersen's life and literary works in some school-encyclopaedias and school-lexicons: Hans Christian Andersen [was born on 2 April 1805 in Odense – and died on 4 August 1875 in København, Copenhagen] "was the son of a shoemaker and a washer-woman" ([41], p. 256). "He learnt in the college in Slagelse" ([31], p. 11) and "[he] studied at the Copenhagen University" ([31], p. 11). Andersen "was a highly sensitive, imaginative and egocentric man" ([3], pp. 15, 16). "He had a passionate love for books (for literature) and theatre" ([48], p. 33). "His life was dominated by an incessant existential anxiety and feelings of loneliness" ([3], p. 16).

The entry in *Encyklopedia szkolna: Literatura i nauka o języku* informs the reader that "Andersen, the author of Danish Romanticism, was related to Danish poetic realism" ([3], p. 16).

Andersen "published his first literary volume of stories in 1822" ([41], p. 256; [42], p. 13; [43], p. 13; [44], p. 8; see also: [31], p. 11). "A play *Miłość na wieży Mikołaja* [*Kjærlighed paa Nicolai Taarn / Love in St. Nicolas Church Tower*] (1829) was the first drama by Andersen" ([41], p. 256; [42], p. 13; [43], p. 13; [44], p. 8). [He] "wrote about 30 (thirty) plays for the theatre" ([41], p. 256; [42], p. 13; [43], p. 13; [44], p. 8). "In 1835, the first volume (collection) of his *Eventyr, fortalte for Børn* [*Fairy Tales, Told for Children*] was published" ([31], p. 11; see also: [32], p. 23; [41], p. 256; [42], p. 13; [43], p. 13; [44], p. 8). "The volumes of his *Fairy Tales* had been published until 1872" ([31], p. 11). "His *Fairy Tales and Stories* were published *every year* (!) between 1835 and 1872" ([**41**], p. 256; [**42**], p. 13; [**43**], p. 13; [**44**], p. 8).

The writer "travelled extensively throughout Europe" ([**48**], p. 33; see also: [**3**], p. 16; [**31**], p. 11; [**41**], p. 256). [He] "met famous men of his days. He visited the brothers Jacob and Wilhelm Grimm and Charles Dickens" ([**48**], p. 33).

The entry in *Encyklopedia szkolna: Literatura i nauka o języku* informs us that

> Andersen's novel *Improwizator* [*Improvisatoren / The Improvisatore* (1835)] that is full of autobiographical material, was a real literary success. [Andersen] wrote also two other novels: *Tylko grajek* [*Kun en Spillemand / Only a Fiddler*] (1837) and *Piotr Szczęściarz* [*Lykke-Peer / Lucky Peer*] (1870), and his literary autobiography *Baśń mojego życia* [*Mit Livs Eventyr / The Fairy Tale of My Life*] (1855) ([**3**], p. 16).

The entry in *Encyklopedia szkolna* informs us that

> Andersen was the author of novels: *Improwizator* [*Improvisatoren / The Improvisatore*], *O.T., Tylko grajek* [*Kun en Spillemand / Only a Fiddler*] and *Piotr Szczęściarz* [*Lykke-Peer / Lucky Peer*], and drama-play *Miłość na wieży Mikołaja* [*Kjærlighed paa Nicolaj Taarn / Love in St. Nicolas Church Tower*] ([**15**], p. 37).

Joanna Kułakowska-Lis has mentioned Andersen's travel-book *Bazar poety* (*En Digters Bazar / A Poet's Bazaar*, 1842) in her entry ([**37**], p. 19) in *Encyklopedia szkolna: Język polski. Gimnazjum*.

Hans Christian Andersen in Polish Universal Encyclopaedias and Lexicons for "Everyone" and in Polish Internet-encyclopaedias

Now, I should like to discuss the question: What has been written on the life and literary works of Andersen by Polish authors of encyclopaedic (lexicographic) entries in universal encyclopaedias and lexicons for "everyone", published during the last 25 years in Poland, and in Polish online-encyclopaedias?

In these entries, Hans Christian Andersen is presented as "a Danish writer" ([4]; [6], vol. I, p. 386; [7]; [8], vol. I, p. 73; [11], p. 32; [13], p. 103; [14], vol. I, p.103; [17], p. 37; [18], p. 55; [19], vol. II, p. 17; [20], p. 42; [21], vol. I, p. 157; [22], vol. I, p. 243; [23], p. 57; [27], vol. I, p. 293), "a Danish writer and the author of *Eventyr* [*Fairy Tales*]" ([9], vol. I, p. 134; [10], p. 33; see also: [26], vol. I, p. 141), "a Danish writer of fairy tales" ([28], p. 121), "a Danish writer of fairy tales and novelist" ([5]) and "a Danish writer of fairy tales and novelist of Romanticism" ([12], vol. I, p. 127). In some entries, he is presented as "a master of world literature for children" ([8], vol. I, p. 73; [9], vol. I, p. 134; [11], p. 32; [17], p. 37; [18], p. 55; [23], p. 57) and as "the most famous writer of fairy tales in the history of world literature" ([20], p. 42).

He is also presented as "an author of *Eventyr* [*Fairy Tales*]" ([19], vol. II, p. 17), or as

an author of *Eventyr* [*Fairy Tales*] and some novels *Improwizator* [*Improvisatoren / The Improvisatore*], *O.T.*, *Tylko grajek* [*Kun en Spillemand / Only a Fiddler*], *Baśń mojego życia* [*Mit Livs Eventyr / The Fairy Tale of My Life*], *Piotr Szczęściarz* [*Lykke-Peer / Lucky Peer*], *Książka obrazkowa bez obrazków* [*Billedbog uden Billeder / Picture-Book without Pictures*] and an opera with the national theme *Mała Kirsten* [*Liden Kirsten / Little Kirsten*] ([12], vol. I, p. 127).

The encyclopaedic entries stress that "the fame of Andersen rests on his fairy tales" ([6], vol. I, p. 386; [7]; [13], p. 103; [14], vol. I, p. 103; [21], vol. I, p. 157; see also: [22], vol. I, p. 243).

We may also find some information about the Danish poet and writer of fairy tales in these entries [for example: He was "the child of a poor family" ([5]). The entries inform us that Andersen "was related to [Danish] poetic realism" ([6], vol. I, p. 386; [7]; [21], vol. I, p. 157; [22], vol. I, p. 243). "Andersen's collection of poems [*Digte, Poems* (1830)] was his first literary work" ([6], vol. I, p. 386; [7]; [13], p. 103; [22], vol. I, p. 243; [27], vol. I, p. 293). "In 1835, the first volume (collection) of his fairy tales [*Eventyr, fortalte for Børn* / [*Fairy Tales, Told for Children*] was published" (see: [5]). "The volumes of his "*Fairy Tales*" were edited between 1835 and 1872" ([5]).

The entries in encyclopaedias and lexicons mention Andersen's novels: *Fodreise fra Holmens Kanal* ..., (*A Journey on Foot from Holmen's Canal* ... (1829) [imitation of the style of German

Romantic writer Ernst Theodor Amadeus Hoffmann] as his first important literary work ([**27**], vol. I, p. 293), *Improwizator* (*Improvisatoren, The Improvisatore*, 1835) ([**5**]; [**6**], vol. I, p. 386; [**7**]; [**13**], p. 103; [**17**], p. 37; [**21**], vol. I, p. 157; [**22**], vol. I, p. 243; [**26**], vol. I, p. 141; [**27**], vol. I, p. 293), *O.T.* (1836) ([**5**]), *Tylko grajek* (*Kun en Spillemand / Only a Fiddler*, 1837) ([**5**]; [**27**], vol. I, p. 293), *Książka z obrazkami bez obrazków* (*Billedbog udder Billeder / Picture-Book without Pictures*, 1840) ([**5**] and [**27**], vol. I, p. 293), *Dwie baronówny* (*De to Baronesser / The Two Baronesses*, 1848) ([**5**]) and *Piotr Szczęściarz* (*Lykke-Peer / Lucky Peer*, 1870) ([**5**]; [**27**], vol. I, p. 293), his literary autobiography *Baśń mojego życia* (*Mit Livs Eventyr / The Fairy Tale of My Life*, 1855) ([**5**]; [**27**], vol. I, p. 293), Andersen's play *Mulatten / The Mulatto* (1840) ([**27**], vol. I, p. 293), his volumes of fairy tales: *Baśnie, opowiedziane dla dzieci* (*Eventyr, fortalte for Børn / Fairy Tales, Told for Children*, 1835) ([**6**], vol. I, p. 386; [**7**]; [**13**], p. 103; [**14**], vol. I, p. 103; [**21**], vol. I, p. 157; [**22**], vol. I, p. 243; [**27**], vol. I, p. 293; [**28**], vol. I, p. 121), *Baśnie* (*Eventyr / Fairy Tales*, 1837) ([**27**], vol. I, p. 293), *Nowe baśnie i opowieści* (*Nye Eventyr og Historier / New Fairy Tales and Stories*, 1858-1872) ([**5**]; [**27**], vol. I, p. 293), his travel-book *Bazar poety* (*En Digters Bazar / A Poet's Bazaar*, 1842) and a libretto of national opera *Mała Kirsten* (*Liden Kirsten / Little Kirsten*, 1846) ([**5**]).

One of the authors has written that "Andersen was a votary of philosophy with 'humanistic values'" (see: [**26**], vol. I, p. 141).

Maria Krysztofiak wrote an entry "Andersen Hans Christian" for *Wielka Encyklopedia PWN* [**38**, vol. II, p. 28]. In that entry, we may read:

> Hans Christian Andersen [was born on the 2nd of April, 1805, in Odense – and died on the 4th of August, 1875, in Kopenhaga / København, Copenhagen], Danish writer.
>
> In childhood, he produced stories in a little toy-theatre that he built himself. As a boy of fourteen, he went to Kopenhaga (København, Copenhagen) in vain hopes of winning fame as an actor or a singer. He received help from his benefactor – J[onas] Collin, one of the directors of the Royal Theatre. He also received the royal travelling grant that allowed him to travel to Italy, 1833–34. He travelled in Germany, France, and also in Spain, Britain, Greece, Turkey and Sweden.
>
> He was one of the authors of Danish Romanticism, and he was related to [Danish] poetic realism.

His first book, a fantastic volume *Fodreise fra Holmens Canal til Østpynten af Amager / A Journey on Foot from Holmen's Canal to the East Point of Amager* (1829) was recognized as his first important literary work.

In 1835, Andersen's novel *Improwizator* (*Improvisatoren / The Improvisatore*), with elements of autobiography, was published. (...) The plot of the novel is full of descriptions of the Italian landscapes. The novel *O.T.* (1836) with the main character Otto Thostrup who is born in Odense Tugthus (Odense jail / prison) is full of autobiographical material. Also his novel *Tylko grajek* (*Kun en Spillemand / Only a Fiddler*, 1837) is autobiographical. (...) S[øren] A[abye] Kierkegaard ironically attacked that book.

In the 1830s Andersen started publishing his books of tales." ([**38**]).

Hans Christian Andersen in Polish Professional Encyclopaedias and Lexicons

A review of Polish professional encyclopaedias and lexicons, addressed especially to experts, has given some new information about Hans Christian Andersen.

Polish readers who are interested in literature may discover information about Andersen in seven encyclopaedic entries in the encyclopaedias and lexicons "of literature" edited during the last 25 years in Poland.

Łucja Ryll has written the biografical entry "Andersen Hans Christian" for *Nowy słownik literatury dla dzieci i młodzieży* [1984] ([**39**]). She has presented Andersen as "a Danish writer". The day of Andersen's death is incorrect: the 4th of July [!], 1875, in that biographical entry. The author of this entry has repeated the common knowledge.

Nevertheless, she has described Andersen's life and literary activity adding some new information. We may read about Hans Christian's grandmother "[who] introduced him to the world of tales and stories" ([**39**], p. 20). Ryll mentions that "Andersen was a lover of physics and natural science" ([**39**], p. 20).

The first literary efforts of Andersen were printed under the pseudonym of Villiam (William) Christian Walter. (...) Among his friends were Bertel Thorvaldsen, Adam Gottlob Oehlenschläger, Johan Ludvig Heiberg, Jenny Lind, Bjørnstjerne Bjørnson, brothers

Jacob and Wilhelm Grimm, Charles Dickens, Hans Christian Ørsted, and Søren Aabye Kierkegaard. (...), ([**39**], p. 20).

Łucja Ryll has stressed that "Andersen was the creator of modern Danish literary language and a master of literary fairy tale as a literary genre" ([**39**], p. 20).

Stefan H. Kaszyński has written the biographical entry "Andersen Hans Christian" [presenting "one of the most famous Danish writers"] (see: [**46**], p. 25 for *Słownik pisarzy skandynawskich* [1991]). We may find some new information in that entry.

The reader is informed that Andersen's acquaintance with literary works of the German Romantic writer Ernst Theodor Amadeus Hoffmann and Danish Romantic writer Adam Gottlob Oehlenschläger is evident in his first book, a fantastic volume *Fodreise fra Holmens Canal til Østpynten af Amager / A Journey on Foot from Holmen's Canal to the East Point of Amager* (1829) ([**46**], p. 23).

The famous Copenhagen writers judged Andersen's juvenilia very kindly. J[ohan] L[udvig] Heiberg printed his literary juvenilia in "Kjøbenhavns flyvende Post". A[dam] G[ottlob] Oehlenschläger and [Bernhard Severin] Ingemann helped him to receive the royal travelling grant for his journey to Italy ([**46**], p. 23).

In 1835, Andersen's novel *Improwizator* (*Improvisatoren / The Improvisatore*) was published. (...) That novel (Entwicklungsroman) reminds us of the novel *Corinne ou l'Italie* of Madame de Staël ([**46**], p. 23).

[Søren Aabye] Kierkegaard ironically attacked Andersen's novel *Tylko grajek* (*Kun en Spillemand / Only a Fiddler*) in his work *Af en endnu Levendes Papirer* ([**46**], p. 24).

Stefan H. Kaszyński has presented Andersen's *Eventyr / Fairy Tales* and their artistic value in forty four lines of his entry ([**46**], p. 24).

Stanisław Frycie in the entry "Andersen Hans Christian" [in *Leksykon literatury dla dzieci i młodzieży*, 1999] has presented Andersen as "a Danish writer" ([**47**]). The day of Andersen's death is incorrect: the 4th of July [!], 1875, in that biographical entry.
Frycie informs the readers that

> Andersen was the son of a shoemaker and a washer-woman. His grandmother introduced him to the world of tales and stories. He

received the royal grant that allowed him to go to school and study at the university ([**47**], p. 9).

He travelled in France, Switzerland, Sweden, Greece, Turkey, Holland, Belgium, Germany, England, Scotland, Spain, Portugal, and Norway. During his stay in Germany, he visited brothers J[acob] and W[ilhelm] Grimm. Among his friends were B[jørnstjerne] Bjørnson, an eminent Norwegian writer, Ch[arles] Dickens, an English novelist, and B[ertel] Thorvaldsen, well-known Danish sculptor ([**47**], p. 9).

The author of the analysed entry has repeated the common knowledge about literary works of Andersen (see: [**47**], p. 9).

Also Grzegorz Leszczyński in the entry "Andersen Hans Christian" [in *Słownik literatury dziecięcej i młodzieżowej* [2002] has presented Andersen as "a Danish writer" ([**34**]). The Warsaw historian of Polish literature for children has repeated common knowledge about literary works of Andersen (see: [**34**], pp. 16, 17). Among new biographical information, Leszczyński has mentioned that "a prison and a mental hospital were near Andersen's house in his childhood" ([**34**], pp. 16). He has also written that "there are two museums dedicated to Andersen in Odense" ([**34**], pp. 16, 17).

Andersen is presented as "a Danish writer and one of the authors of Danish Romanticism, who was related to poetic realism" in a short entry of encyclopaedic dictionary *Pisarze świata* ([**24**], p. 32; [**25**], p. 32). He is also presented as "a Danish writer of fairy tales and novelist" in a short entry of another encyclopaedic dictionary of world literature ([**29**], pp. 17, 18).

Wanda Achremowiczowa is an author of the valuable entry "Andersen Hans Christian" in *Encyklopedia katolicka* [1985] ([**1**]), and Antoni Bednarek has written the entry "Andersen Hans Christian" for *Religia: Encyklopedia PWN* [vol. I, 2001] ([**33**]). There is common knowledge about Andersen's life and his literary works in those two entries.

Jacek Wojtysiak has mentioned the great Danish Romantic writer and the creator of literary fairy tales in the entry "Kierkegaard Søren Aabye" in *Słownik filozofii* [2004]. Wojtysiak has written that "Andersen's literary fairy tales were a source of philosophical reflexion for Kierkegaard" (see: [**35**], p. 327).

I would also like to remind you of only one of the encyclopaedic entries edited earlier [in 1979] in Poland [in *Encyklopedia muzyczna PWN*: *Część biograficzna*] [1979] ([**40**]). It is an especially valuable entry. Mieczysław Tomaszewski, the author of that entry ["Andersen Hans"] ([**40**, vol. I, pp. 46, 47]) has presented Andersen as "a Danish poet, an author of *"Eventyr"* / *"Fairy Tales"*), and a master of world literature for children". Tomaszewski has informed the reader that

> Andersen described his life in his memoirs *Mit Livs Eventyr* [1855] and these literary memoirs are a source of information about Andersen's keen interest in music. The Danish writer was a lover of Richard Wagner's operas, Ferenc Liszt's compositions and Jenny Lind's singing ([**40**, vol. I, p. 46).

Tomaszewski has also described musical qualities in Andersen's literary works (nightingale songs, swan song, ringing of bells, organ music, mother's singing and rustling of the wind) ([**40**, vol. I, p. 46).

The author of that entry has informed us that literary fairy tale of Hans Christian Andersen often inspired Polish and world composers. Among those inspirations were: the opera *Dziewica lodowców / Dziewica lodów* (*Iisjomfruen / The Ice Maiden*) composed by Adolf Gużewski in 1907, the opera with a ballet *Syrena* (*Den lille Havfrue / The Little Mermaid*) composed by Witold Maliszewski [in 1927] and with a libretto by Ludomir Michał Rogowski, a ballet-pantomime *Nagi książę / The Nude Prince* which was inspired by the fairy tale *Keiserens nye Klæder / The Emperor's New Clothes*) by Romuald Twardowski in 1959 (or 1960) and a musical *Cień* (*Skyggen / The Shadow*) composed by Maciej Małecki and with a libretto by Wojciech Młynarski.

Summarizing this short review of the encyclopaedic entries on Andersen in Polish encyclopaedias and lexicons edited in the last 25 years in Poland, I would like to point out that they are an example of unsatisfactory knowledge about one of the greatest Danish Romantic writers and the creator of literary fairy tales. It is probably the result of ignorance of Danish and Scandinavian literature in contemporary Poland.

Only the entries of Wanda Achremowiczowa in *Encyklopedia katolicka* [1985] ([**1**]), Stefan H. Kaszyński in *Słownik pisarzy skandynawskich* [1991] ([**46**]), and Maria Krysztofiak in *Wielka Encyklopedia PWN* [2001] [**38**] present Hans Christian Andersen satisfactorily.

The remaining entries are too general and superficial, and not detailed enough for an average reader of Andersen.

In contemporary Poland, Hans Christian Andersen is known exclusively as a Danish fairy tale writer.

Bibliography

[1] Achremowiczowa, Wanda, 'Andersen Hans Christian' in: *Encyklopedia katolicka*, pod red. F. Gryglewicza, R. Łukaszyka, Z. Sułowskiego, vol. I, Lublin, Towarzystwo Naukowe Katolickiego Uniwersytetu Lubelskiego, 1985 [dodruk].
[2] ad [= Domosławska, Agnieszka], 'Baśń' in: *Encyklopedia szkolna: Język polski. Gimnazjum*, Kraków, Wydawnictwo "Zielona Sowa", 2003.
[3] 'Andersen' in: *Encyklopedia szkolna: Literatura i nauka o języku*, Warszawa, Wydawnictwa Szkolne i Pedagogiczne, 1995.
[4] 'Andersen Hans Christian' [*Encyklopedia*] in: http://encyklopedia.wp.pl/
[5] 'Andersen Hans Christian' [*Encyklopedia*] in: http://portalwiedzy.onet.pl/
[6] 'Andersen Hans Christian' in: *Encyklopedia Gazety Wyborczej*, vol. I, Kraków, Mediasat Poland / Mediasat Group S.A. / Warszawa, Wydawnictwo Naukowe PWN S.A. / Warszawa, Agora S.A., [2005].
[7] 'Andersen Hans Christian' "*Encyklopedia PWN*" in: *http://encyklopedia.pwn.pl/*
[8] 'Andersen Hans Christian' in: *Encyklopedia PWN w trzech tomach*, red.: D. Kalisiewicz, A. Krupa, vol. I, Warszawa, Wydawnictwo Naukowe PWN S.A., 1999.
[9] 'Andersen [Hans Christian]' in: *Encyklopedia popularna PWN*, vol. I, Warszawa, Wydawnictwo Naukowe PWN, 1997.
[10] 'Andersen Hans Christian' in: *Encyklopedia popularna PWN*, wyd. 28. uzupełnione i uaktualnione, red. B. Petrozolin-Skowrońska, A. Karwowski, Warszawa, Wydawnictwo Naukowe PWN S.A., 1998.
[11] 'Andersen Hans Christian' in: *Encyklopedia popularna PWN*, Warszawa, Wydawnictwo Naukowe PWN S.A., 1999.
[12] 'Andersen Hans Christian' in: *Encyklopedia powszechna* [8-tomowa], vol. I, Kraków, Wydawnictwo "Ryszard Kluszczyński", 2002.
[13] 'Andersen Hans Christian' in: *Encyklopedia powszechna PWN*, wyd. II, Warszawa, Państwowe Wydawnictwo Naukowe, 1983.
[14] 'Andersen Hans Christian' in: *Encyklopedia powszechna PWN*, [4-tomowa], vol. I, wyd. III, Warszawa, Państwowe Wydawnictwo Naukowe, 1983.
[15] 'Andersen Hans Christian' in: *Encyklopedia szkolna*, [Wrocław], Wydawnictwo "Europa", 2004.
[16] 'Andersen Hans Christian' in: *Encyklopedia ucznia: Gimnazjum*, pod red. E. Banaszkiewicz-Zygmunt, Warszawa, Wydawnictwo Naukowe PWN S.A., 2002.
[17] 'Andersen Hans Christian' in: *Ilustrowana encyklopedia PWN*, Warszawa, Wydawnictwo Naukowe PWN S.A., 2004.
[18] 'Andersen Hans Christian' in: *Leksykon PWN*, Warszawa, Wydawnictwo Naukowe PWN S.A., 2004.

[19] 'Andersen Hans Christian' in: *Leksykon uniwersalny. A – Ż*, opracowali: D. i W. Masłowscy, vol. II, Kęty, Wydawnictwo "Antyk", 2000.

[20] 'Andersen Hans Christian' in: *Nowa encyklopedia powszechna. A – Z*, wyd. II. uaktualnione, Kraków, Wydawnictwo "Zielona Sowa", 2004.

[21] 'Andersen Hans Christian' in: *Nowa encyklopedia powszechna PWN*, [6-tomowa], vol. I, Warszawa, Wydawnictwo Naukowe PWN, 1995.

[22] 'Andersen Hans Christian' in: *Nowa encyklopedia powszechna PWN*, vol. I, Warszawa, Wydawnictwo Naukowe PWN S.A., 2004.

[23] 'Andersen Hans Christian' in: *Nowy leksykon PWN*, Warszawa, Wydawnictwo Naukowe PWN S.A., 1998.

[24] 'Andersen Hans Christian' in: *Pisarze świata: Słownik encyklopedyczny*, Warszawa, Wydawnictwo Naukowe PWN S.A., 1998.

[25] 'Andersen Hans Christian' in: *Pisarze świata: Słownik encyklopedyczny*, Warszawa, Wydawnictwo Naukowe PWN S.A., 1999.

[26] 'Andersen Hans Christian' in: *Popularna encyklopedia powszechna*, vol. I, Kraków, Oficyna Wydawnicza "Fogra", 1994; see also: "*WIEM – Wielka Internetowa Encyklopedia Multimedialna*" in the Internet version: http:// wiem.onet.pl/

[27] 'Andersen Hans Christian' in: *Popularna encyklopedia powszechna*, vol. I, Kraków, Oficyna Wydawnicza "Fogra" / Warszawa, Grupa Wydawnicza Bertelsmann Media, 2001.

[28] 'Andersen Hans Christian' in: *Popularna encyklopedia powszechna*, vol. I, Kraków, Wydawnictwo "Pinnex", 1994; see also: "*Encyklopedia Internautica*" in the Internet version: http://encyklopedia.interia.pl/

[29] 'Andersen Hans Christian' in: *Słownik encyklopedyczny: Literatura powszechna*, autorzy: A. Cisak, M. Żbik, Wrocław, Wydawnictwo "Europa", 2000.

[30] 'Andersen Hans Christian' in: *Słownik encyklopedyczny wiedzy szkolnej*, oprac. zespół pod kier. J. Tomaszewskiego, Warszawa, Oficyna Wydawnicza "Graf – Punkt", 2003.

[31] 'Andersen Hans Christian' in: *Słownik lektur dla gimnazjum*, pod red. H. Sułka, wyd. II rozszerz., Kraków, Wydawnictwo "Zielona Sowa", 2004.

[32] 'Andersen Hans Christian' in: *Szkolny słownik biograficzny*, pod red. F. Kiryka i A. Jureczki, Kraków, Wydawnictwo Edukacyjne, 1996.

[33] Bednarek, Antoni, 'Andersen Hans Christian' in: *Religia: Encyklopedia PWN*, red. nauk.: VOL. Gadacz, B. Milerski, vol. I, Warszawa, Wydawnictwo Naukowe PWN S.A., 2001.

[34] GL [= Leszczyński, Grzegorz], 'Andersen Hans Christian' in: *Słownik literatury dziecięcej i młodzieżowej*, pod red. B. Tylickiej i G. Leszczyńskiego, Wrocław, Zakład Narodowy im. Ossolińskich – Wydawnictwo, 2002.

[35] J. Wt. [= Wojtysiak, Jacek], 'Kierkegaard Søren Aabye' in: *Słownik filozofii*, pod red. J. Hartmana, Kraków, Wydawnictwo "Zielona Sowa", 2004.

[36] Januszewski, Tomasz, 'Andersen Hans Christian' in: Januszewski, Tomasz: *Słownik pisarzy i lektur dla szkół podstawowych*, Warszawa, Oficyna Wydawnicza "Delta W-Z", br. r. w. [po / after 1989].

[37] jkl [= Kułakowska-Lis, Joanna], 'Andersen Hans Christian' in: *Encyklopedia szkolna: Język polski. Gimnazjum*, Kraków, Wydawnictwo "Zielona Sowa", 2003.

[38] Krysztofiak, Maria, 'Andersen Hans Christian' in: *Wielka encyklopedia PWN*, vol. II, Warszawa, Wydawnictwo Naukowe PWN S. A., 2001.

[39] ŁR [= Ryll, Łucja], 'Andersen Hans Christian' in: *Nowy słownik literatury dla dzieci i młodzieży: Pisarze – Książki – Serie – Ilustratorzy – Nagrody – Przegląd bibliograficzny*, red. nauk.: K. Kuliczkowska, B. Tylicka, Warszawa, Państwowe Wydawnictwo "Wiedza Powszechna", 1984.

[40] M. Tom. [= Tomaszewski, Mieczysław], 'Andersen Hans' in: *Encyklopedia muzyczna PWN: Część biograficzna*, red.: E. Dziębowska, vol. I, Kraków, Polskie Wydawnictwo Muzyczne, 1979.

[41] Miłkowski, Tomasz, 'Andersen Hans Christian' in: Miłkowski, Tomasz: *Leksykon dzieł i tematów literatury powszechnej*, Warszawa, „Książka i Wiedza", 2002.

[42] Miłkowski, Tomasz, Termer, Janusz, 'Andersen Hans Christian' in: Miłkowski, Tomasz, Termer, Janusz: *Leksykon lektur szkolnych*, wyd. III rozszerz. i uzupełn., Warszawa, Wydawnictwo "Graf – Punkt ®", 1993.

[43] Miłkowski, Tomasz, Termer, Janusz, 'Andersen Hans Christian' in: Miłkowski, Tomasz, Termer, Janusz: *Leksykon lektur szkolnych*, wyd. IV rozszerz. i uzupełn., Warszawa, Wydawnictwo "Graf – Punkt ®", 1996.

[44] Miłkowski, Tomasz, Termer, Janusz, 'Andersen Hans Christian' in: Miłkowski, Tomasz, Termer, Janusz: *Leksykon lektur szkolnych dla gimnazjum*, Warszawa, Oficyna Wydawnicza "Graf – Punkt", 2000.

[45] Poznański, Jacek, 'Andersen Hans Christian' in: Poznański, Jacek: *Słownik lektur dla szkół podstawowych*, Warszawa, Wydawnictwo "Skrypt", 1995.

[46] S.H.K. [= Kaszyński, Stefan H], 'Andersen Hans Christian' in: *Słownik pisarzy skandynawskich*, pod red. Z. Ciesielskiego, Warszawa, Państwowe Wydawnictwo "Wiedza Powszechna", 1991 (see: [38]).

[47] SF [= Frycie, Stanisław], 'Andersen Hans Christian' in: Frycie, Stanisław, Ziółkowska-Sobecka, Marta: *Leksykon literatury dla dzieci i młodzieży*, Piotrków Trybunalski, Wydawnictwo Filii Kieleckiej WSP w Piotrkowie Trybunalskim, 1999.

[48] Tylicka, Barbara, 'Hans Christian Andersen' in: Tylicka, Barbara: *Bohaterowie naszych książek. Przewodnik po literaturze dla dzieci i młodzieży*, Łódź, Wydawnictwo "Literatura", 1999.

[49] Ursel, Marian, 'Andersen Hans Christian' in: Ursel, Marian, *Leksykon literatury polskiej [dla uczniów i nauczycieli]: Romantyzm*, Wrocław, Wydawnictwo Dolnośląskie, 2004.

The Motif of Mermaid in Baltic Literatures (Karlis Skalbe, Maironis, Leons Briedis, Aspazija, Kazys Puida, Violeta Palčinskaitė)

Silvestras Gaižiūnas

In his works, Hans Christian Andersen used many nomading subjects. Among them we find Ahasfer, Faust, the little mermaid and others, who have inspired many writers before and after Hans Christian Andersen.

How did the subject of the mermaid and Hans Christian Andersen's fairy tale "The Little Mermaid" influence the literature traditions of Baltic writers?

It is interesting that underwater worlds arise in chrestomatic works of Baltic romanticists and neo-romanticists. In Lithuanian literature from this point of view the best known poem is *Eglė – the Queen of Grass-snakes* (*Eglė – žalčių karalienė*) by S. Neris, where the protagonist, the grass-snake Žilvinas, lives in an underwater world and his bride comes from the real world. This constellation also appears in the Latvian drama, written by Aspazija "The Bride of the Grass-snake". In the Latvian epos, written by A. Pumpurs, "*Lačplesis*" the protagonist Lačplesis is searching for his bride in the castle, which is situated at the bottom of the lake. In this castle, the memory of the nation is preserved. In the novel of Latvian neo-romanticist J. Poruks *The Flushing of Druviena Lake* the motif is the collision between mermaids living at the bottom of the lake and people digging the channel. Through this conflict J. Poruks exposed the conflict between culture, civilization and nature; civilization – the source of troubles, having nothing in common with moral values; the destroyed life of the mermaids destroys the life of people as well.

The subject of "The Little Mermaid" in Baltic – Lithuanian and Latvian – literary and cultural traditions occupies a special place. This fairy tale by Hans Christian Andersen was translated into Latvian 7 times, and some Lithuanian and Latvian writers created new works on the basis of this fairy tale, the Latvian composer Martiņš Brauns together with choreographer Agris Danilevičs based on this Hans Christian Andersen fairy tale staged a water-ballet, the composer A. Kukuvass and the poet L. Briedis – a rock opera.

The reflections of the subject "The Little Mermaid" in Baltic literatures are hardly discernible from nomading legends about mermaids, which are widely spread in Baltic countries.

In 1913, two works appeared in Baltic literatures, in which the legend of the Mermaid was used – in Latvian literature the fairy tale of Karlis Skalbe *Mermaid* (*Jūras varava*) and in Lithuanian literature the melodrama of Kazys Puida "the Mermaid". They belong to different genres.

In the "Mermaid" by Karlis Skalbe (1874-1945) the Mermaid does not rescue the prince, but the other way round – a young wanderer helps a Mermaid to return from deromantized surroundings to her natural element – the depth of the sea. It's natural, that differently from Hans Christian Andersen's tale, where the action takes its beginning in an underwater world, Skalbe's subject of "the Mermaid" reflects sea-shore and earth life. The male hero is the saviour, not the Mermaid, – the fairy tale describes his way from the country to the town and from the town to the bottom of the sea. This development is a process of initiation, a school of life. His direction is opposite to that of the little Mermaid, heading for the kingdom of God, the hero approaches the Mermaid's kingdom. James Massengale has described the catholic conception of the Mermaid's salvation in Hans Christian Andersen's story[1]; K. Skalbe is closer to a pantheistic view concerning the development of his protagonist. Meaning that not only the Mermaid, but her savior as well are connected with the water element and with nature. Karlis Skalbe treating the mythologema of the Mermaid at the beginning of the 20th century, accentuates as such the conflict between idealism and materialism/the pragmatic world. As such this conflict is specific for Baltic new-romanticism. There are still Mermaids as in Hans Christian Andersen's world, but now she becomes a prisoner – fishermen take her prisoner in their nets, and she is exhibited at the fish market for the crowd to gaze at.

The market becomes the main place of action in the fairy tale of Skalbe. The market is the meeting place between the Mermaid and the young wanderer. The mermaid coming from the bottom of the sea, the young hero of K. Skalbe – from the Latvian countryside. He enters Rīga, fascinated by the Mermaid vision. With him he has the book of songs, given to him by his mother. This book symbolizes the wanderers connection with his motherland and his soul. In the episode of selling the book K. Skalbe exposes the view of the world concerning spiritual values: what his master buys is not the songs, but the golden cover of the book, not spirituality, but materialism.

The little Mermaid by Hans Christian Andersen is inspired by Christian values, about which she knows from her grandmother. She leaves the bottom of the sea because of her immortal soul, but she cannot find this soul in the earthly world. The little Mermaid is the victim of romantic idealism. Accordingly, she is finally resurrected into the realm of "the daughters of the air", a purely spiritual world.

In K. Skalbe's fairy tale the mermaid is the victim of a vulgar view of romantic symbolism (fishermen catching her in their nets, beating her with oars). Skalbe's mermaid is transferred into material value, just like the book of songs of the wanderer, who was searching for the Mermaid.

Both mermaids – the little mermaid by Hans Christian Andersen and the mermaid by K. Skalbe emphasize the gap between dreams and earthly reality, between transcendence and empiric reality.

In Hans Christian Andersen's fairy tale the little mermaid is attracted by the human world as the possible place of reaching the immortality of the soul, whereas in Skalbe's tale, the mermaid escapes from the human world to save her essence and natural fascination.

The hero of K. Skalbe becomes the mermaid's guard. In this episode, the idea of the myth's de-romantization is most brightly expressed: the protagonist dreaming about the Mermaid in the amber castle of the ocean, but finding her at the market: "During the night he was the guard of the Mermaid and was sleeping on the sack of straws. And when rambling through darkness the moonlight touched the slits of untidy knocked plank ends with golden fingers, the man with sorrow remembered the old legend about the amber castle at the bottom of the sea, in which lived the mermaid. So what was the amber castle?"[2]

Richard Wagner says: "Only in the depth can you find the truth". The depth in K. Skalbe's fairy tale arises as a counterversion of the market: the market stripping all in a vulgar manner, but in the depth the amber castle hiding the ideal. In the market the mermaid loses her voice, but she can speak in the deep. So the value system of K. Skalbe's tale is mono-semantic: the mermaid does not rise to the surface, for fear of being caught in the fishermen's nets – to be brought to the fishmarket, and the fishermen of the new world are not searching for mermaids.

In contrast to Hans Christian Andersen, K. Skalbe localizes the place of action and the portraits of heroes: The wanderer, searching for the mermaid is a typical Latvian "searcher for happiness" at the end of the 19th and the beginning of the 20th centuries. Skalbe underlined the local colours: the river Daugava, the market of Riga city, the sculpture of St. Cristophore, the mountains of Kangari.

K. Skalbe, continuing the tradition of romanticism, in his tale actualizes one of the main motifs in romantic literature – *the nostalgia of the soul* (Sehnsucht). K. Skalbe's mermaid embodies the same as the Blue flower by Novalis or the Blue bird by Maeterlinck. The wanderer, searching for the mermaid, escapes from home, as a protest against the traditional way of life, against "the soul's emprisonment". Several of K. Skalbe's heroes are guided by the motto: *the instant life is as extensive as the whole world*. They are inspired by distant and mysterious lands. The Mermaid is ideal, but also inviting to enter the wide world. In relation to K. Skalbe's hero the mermaid is like a "spiritus movens", not allowing him to be at peace.

In K. Puida's drama *The Mermaid* (*Undinė*) (1913) as in K. Skalbe's fairy tale the motif of the mermaid is used as methaphoric parallel, underlining the action and the love story of two main heroes. The main hero Jonas Garšva is wandering between home and distant exotic lands. When his parents from far-away Russia want to return to their motherland, Lithuanian Garšva must choose between patriotic feelings and feelings for the Russian girl Irma. Even in the portrait of Irma we can see allusions to the mermaid. Like the mermaid, Irma has her origin in nature, here the *Siberian snows*; in contrast to Hans Christian Andersen's little mermaid, desiring an immortal soul, Irma can give her soul to her lover and lead him into the wide spaces of the world; but these Mermaids are similar in that both of them follow the prince to his homeland ("from sorrow nostalgic I arrive to You, not You to me"). In K. Puida's drama there is a melodramatic interpretation of the mermaid and her prince; the motif of the mermaid casting light into the wandering of the main hero between his homeland and the world.

Comparing K. Puida's drama and K. Skalbe's fairy tale, we notice one main difference: in the drama of the Lithuanian writer, the mermaid is not with the sea as in Skalbe's or Andersen's fairy tales, but with the opposite element – with earth and lands far from the sea.

One of the most popular themes in 20th century Lithuanian art is the legend of Jūratė and Kastytis.

The legend about the love of Jūratė and Kąstytis was spread in the western part of Lithuania. It's very interesting that this legend as one of the brightest examples in Lithuanian folklore was been told to Danish readers in 1895 by the famous Danish ethnologist Åge Meyer-Benedictsen in his book *Lithuania. The Awakening of a Nation*. So Danish readers even at the end of the 19th century could compare "The Little Mermaid" by Hans Christian Andersen with the Lithuanian legend, where the main hero Jūratė is the queen of the seas, living in the amber palace at the bottom of the sea. Jūratė tempts the dark-haired fisherman Kastytis. The love between the goddess and the mortal fisherman makes Perkūnas angry, so he chains the fisherman to the amber palace[3].

The brightest variant of the mermaid subject in Lithuanian literature is the ballad by the romanticist Maironis *Jūratė and Kastytis* (*Jūratė ir Kastytis*) (1920). This ballad is created by the poet-priest, but his mermaid is not connected with Christian ideas, but with the Lithuanian mythological world (Jūratė is protected by Perkūnas). In the ballad Jūratė also embodies the element of the sea: the love of Kastytis for Jūratė expressing the desire of a son of the earth to flow into the element of the sea. This desire is generally applicable to Maironis' creation. Harmony is not available because Jūratė belongs to strictly divine order, and she is punished by her father Perkūnas, who destroyed the amber castle.

Andersen's little mermaid turns to the human world to obtain the possibility of having an immortal soul, but Jūratė by Maironis is immortal herself, because she belongs to the divine world. For the little Mermaid, loving a man may be the possibility to obtain immortality, but Jūratė in Maironis' ballad, falling in love with a son of the earth, is condemned to eternal pain and eternal sobbing. Her pain is symbolized by the waves of the sea and the lagoon. Whereas in Hans Christian Andersen's tale the depth of the sea is idyllic, and earthly troubles begin by entering the dry land.

This ballad is created on the basis of the canon of national romanticism and that means that the love story between the mermaid Jūratė and the fisherman Kastytis is linked to the manifestations of the problematics of national romanticism and national spirit. As a national romanticist Maironis is not only interested in the love drama between Jūratė and Kastytis, but also in the consequences of this drama in the life of the nation: amber given by the waves of the Baltic sea, is the remains of the castle by Jūratė, and every Lithuanian woman, who adorns herself with amber, reminds us of the mermaid Jūratė.

Among many mythological heroes in the creation of the Latvian neo-romanticist Aspazija we find Mermaids and related heroines. In her poem *Ūdenīte* (*The Little Mermaid*) the meeting between two related souls – the little mermaid and an ordinary girl – is described. The little mermaid on the sea-shore is found not by the prince, but by the troubled girl. In the poem showing external contrasts between the mermaid and the girl (the mermaid is clothed in a silver wave, the girl dressed in grey clothes, the mermaid has the green sea as her native town, the life of the girl is like her grey cloth). The poem is written in the form of an application to the Mermaid, as a supplication to the girl. The little mermaid in Aspazija's poem symbolizes freedom and peace, she is like an ideal, making the future bright for the girl, turned out of her grey life, as a hope of liberation for troubles:

Oh my nice girl Mermaid,
Oh, the sister whom I found in my way!

In the context of the poetics of neo-romanticism, it is interesting to compare "The Mermaid" to the poem by Aspazija *The Daughter of the Sun* (*Saules meita*) (1894). The main hero in the poem is the daughter of the Sun, and like Andersen's little Mermaid she is the victim of love for a man. Both of them leave their home, their mysterious spaces: the little Mermaid arriving in the human world from the depth of the sea, and the daughter of the sun – from divine space, from the residence of gods. For both of them a connection with earthly life means the loss of their home, their essence. In the poem by Aspazija, Perkūnas warns the daughter of the sun: on the earth she must wear earthly clothes and would never been allowed to find the way to her heavenly home. In Hans Christian Andersen's tale the grandmother tells the little mermaid: "You will never be allowed to return through water to your sisters in your father's castle". The little mermaid and the daughters of the sun are rescued by the spirits of the air: the daughter of the sun, disappointed in the son of the earth, wants to kill herself, but she is raised by "light, rose clouds"; similarly the little mermaid rising higher, is also accompanied by the air spirits, striving for immortality.

In modern Lithuanian literature the motifs of Hans Christian Andersen are often transformed by Violeta Palčinskaitė. She wrote the play about Andersen –*The Rose of Christian Andersen* (*Kristiano Anerseno Rožė*) and the cycle of poems *Remember Hans Christian* (*Prisiminkim Hansa Kristiana*). In the poem of this cycle "The Little

Mermaid", the mermaid symbolizes the soul yearning for people and sailing to a harbour, thus underlining the bilateral relation between the mermaid and a man: the man is the object of her nostalgia, and she is the child of man's creativity.

The poem *The Little Mermaid (Nāriņa)* by Latvian Leonas Briedis is the libretto for a rock opera, so it hardly seems to be an original interpretation of Andersen's tale. In the poem there is a figure, not taken from Andersen's "The Little Mermaid", a cockle-shell. Her voice narrates and comments the events. The Mermaid of L. Briedis at the end of his poem does not think about revenge, she is hiding her sorrow, not vindicating her offence, but instead talking about luck and joy. The poet underlines the ephemerality of the mermaid, her unbroken relation with the depth of the sea.

Comparing the interpretations of the little mermaid and the subject of the mermaid in Lithuanian and Latvian literatures, we notice one common tendency – this subject was mostly taken up by neo-romanticists, searching for archetyphical and mythical images. We notice an essential difference between Lithuanian and Latvian concepts: The Latvian mermaids (works by Skalbe, Aspazija, Briedis) are more closely connected with Andersen's tale, the Lithuanian writers (Puida, Maironis) seem to base their creations on the Lithuanian legend about the mermaid. Besides that, in Latvian culture there are more musical interpretations of the mermaid motif.

Notes

1. Massengale, James. "The Miracle and a Miracle in the Life of a Mermaid. – Hans Christian Andersen." *A Poet in Time*. Odense University Press, 1999, s. 566.
2. Skalbe, Kārlis. *Pasakas*. Rīga, "Zvaigzne ABC" s. 116.
3. Meyer Benedictsen, Åge. Lithuania. *The Awakening of a Nation. A Study of the Past and Present of the Lithuanian people.* – Copenhagen, 1924.

Hans Christian Andersen and Evgeny Shwartz – Means of Reinterpretation

Elizaveta Isaeva

It is well known that Hans Christian Andersen's works greatly influenced the further development of the fairy tale genre. The present paper intends to examine this influence in the plays of the Russian dramatist Evgeny Swartz, who reinterpreted Andersen's plots and characters in relation to the social realities of the 20th century.

Let me give a small introduction to the biography of Evgeny Shwartz, who is a very famous playwright in our country, but is less known abroad.

Evgeny Shwartz was born in 1896 into a mixed Russian-Jewish family – this is an explanation of his name, which is not originally Russian. His parents belonged to the Russian liberal minded intelligentia, a fact that determined Shwartz's philosophy during his entire life. After his university studies had been disrupted by the October revolution, he joined a small amateur theatre company as an actor (he was a successful one), and also it led him towards playwriting.

He had his debut as a playwright in 1928 in Leningrad's theatre for children, and although the theme of this play *Underwood* had no links with fairy tales inventory, his treatment of the plot showed that his vision of life was that of a fairy-teller. So, as fairy tales have a very strong genre memory (according to the notion of M. Bakhtin), his approaches to classic Andersen-works were predictable. The first one – in 1933 – was connected with the proposal of the young stage director Nicolas Akimov to write a play, based on a few of Andersen's stories – "The Swine Herd", "The Emperor's New Clothes", "The Princess on the Pea". Shwartz combined and partly modified these plots.

Firstly, the play's main character, the Swine Herd, was not a prince, but a true swine herd, and as the Princess has fallen in love with him her mother-queen forced her to marry the Emperor. Thus the weavers actually were not swindlers in the common moral sense: aiming to free the Princess, the Swine Herd and his friend pretended to be weavers and cheated the Emperor. It was interpreted like tricks of the jesters and finally ended with a wedding. Love, which is the supreme value, prevails.

This first reframing of Andersen's plots was satiric: Shwartz used the traditional fairy tale inventory and the characters of the perfectly known author as a kind of Aesop language. Such kind of interpretation was caused by the epoch, that Shwartz described – it was the initial period of Stalin's and Hitler's rule. Andersen's plot was strongly associated with the psychology of deceit and Shwartz made use of this pattern, so in his play the opposition between essence and appearance unfolded the hypocrisy of the regime, which perverted values and created a kind of false reality. The cheated Emperor had been presented as a type of dictator, both silly and cruel. So it was no wonder that the play was banned by the Soviet censorship because of the obvious allusions to Stalin. It was staged only in 1961 by the newly founded theatre of the young and liberally minded actors – "Sovremennik" ("Contemporary"). They also had chosen the title – "The Naked Emperor". This production greatly influenced the public opinion, reviewing the past, the Stalin period in the history of the country. But these events took place after Shwartz's death in 1958 – he never saw his creation on stage.

So Shwartz's next approach to Andersen in 1938 was connected with the children oriented play, based on "The Snow Queen". It should be mentioned, that after the revolution special theatres for the children had been created, which did not exist before. Children's literature was also in focus. The leader of these trends was the poet and translator Samuil Marshak. Being en enthusiast for children's literature, he united a number of young writers, Shwartz among them, in children's magazines, publishing houses and theatres. This period became the "golden age" of children's literature in the country, gathering the activities in this field. In the adoption for children "The Snow Queen", one of the most sophisticated of Andersen's stories, was simplified.

First of all, Christian motives had been excluded – not because of the dramatist's own will. It should be said, that Shwartz himself was a believer. But even in the previous Russian (Soviet) translations of Andersen's stories the Christian ideas had been weakened because of the atheistic regime. Only now the new translations without any cuts are to be published – in order to commemorate the bicentenary.

So in Shwartz's version of "The Snow Queen" we can see a strong tendency to emphasise the strength of eternal ethic values as an equivalent of Christian morals.

Gerda follows them, this is why she prevails. This was the way the dramatist improved the idea of the psychological nature of the fantastic, which he called "the usual wonder" – the wonder that comes from human courage, fidelity and love.

Then, the playwright involved in the plot the newly created character – the fairy-teller himself. He takes part in the action, helps Gerda or warns her, when some misfortunes are coming. By all means, he had to resemble Hans Christian and at the same time Shwartz expressed his thoughts through this character, which partly served the didactic purpose.

The third approach to Andersen was also connected with Nicolas Akimov. He proclaimed later, that the play Shwartz wrote has become as significant for his theatre as *The Seagull* by Anton Chekhov for the Moscow Art theatre.

The dramatist wrote this play during 1939, when the social landscape was gloomy. It was the peak of Stalin's repressions, when some of Shwartz's friends, who belonged to the avantgarde trends in the twenties, had already perished or had been arrested. He himself was also expecting this fatal knock at the door at night. The Second World War began this same year, so it was no wonder, that Nicolas Akimov attracted Shwartz's attention to Andersen's story "The Shadow", which was also inspired by folktales and the novel by the German romantic writer Adelbert von Chamisso.

Shwartz transformed the plot deeply. Certainly, some changes were determined by conditions of the theatre – firstly, in terms of chronotope. The action takes less than three weeks and the setting doesn't change. Secondly, the playwright added the characters, creating a kind of group portrait of the city aiming to make its social diagnosis.

Then the author signaled by means of a series of indices that his play was a reconsideration of traditional motives and archetypes. The main hero, the Scientist, comes to the city, which is both ordinary and magic, the place where fairy tales come true. He says that he lives in the hotel in the same room where his friend, Hans Christian Andersen, lived. His name is Christian Theodor, which is also significant, resembling the names of Andersen and Hoffmann – the author, who widely used the motif of doubles. The other characters (for example, the Doctor) remind him of the story of the shadow and its tragic ending. Using the names of Andersen and Chamisso, discussing the story behind the play, et cetera, makes the relationship with reality much more complex. The universe of the play is detached both from fairy tales (as they are coming true) and from reality (as they still are fairy tales). The characters consider the plot a new fairy tale they are composing themselves. So the fairy tale/reality opposition is weakened, we see the interplay between them, and it paves the way for another level of social observation. The playwright pointed out the surrounding realities, painting a picture of contemporary life. The main collision is determined by essence/appearance and true/false oppositions, which lead to the general opposition between good and evil.

Thus in Shwartz's version the duplication and the further replacement of the human being by his shadow are presented as the overt dramatic conflict between antagonists: the Scientist symbolizes the creative power of life, the Shadow – the Philistine philosophy. This conflict is reflected in the love triangle, the rivalry for the heart of the beautiful princess, so her infidelity to Christian Theodor, who was her bridegroom, becomes a manifestation of his defeat.

We may also look at the other doubles in the play, for example the Doctor. Christian Theodor is only going to make the choice, which the Doctor has already done, accepting the rules of the game. The next example is the double of the Princess, the simple girl Anunciata, who truly loved the Scientist. Such doubling involves the motif of the ethic choice – for all the characters. According to tradition the Shadow refers to the essential archetype of the Double. But unlike Andersen, the problem of authenticity – who is the shadow or who is the true human being – is of no importance. The inhabitants of this magic-ordinary kingdom are not concerned about the cognition of truth. They prefer the Shadow, because mediocrity is much more acceptable for them, than the romanticism of the Scientist. Thus, Shwartz asserted that the Philistine ideology of the kind could be – and actually was – a background for any kind of tyranny or, in terms of the 20th century – dictatorship. This was his conception of the social incarnation of evil.

But this was only one part of the picture. The deeper level reflected the substantial opposition of good and evil.

The ending in Andersen's "The Shadow" is one of his most pessimistic endings. In Shwartz's play it is a different story altogether. He doubled the ending. The first one marks the defeat of the hero, who has been executed, while the Shadow was going to marry the Princess. But it was only the temporary victory of evil over good as after the execution of Christian Theodor the Shadow, which was a double being and repeated the owner's movements, has also lost the head. Then the kind of magic resurrection followed.

This denouement is meaningful. It confirms the substantial primacy of Good. Evil is only a double, so it is destined to fail. "You can spoil our work, you can annihilate our work, but the world continues living due to us – those who work" – that's one of the final phrases of the Scientist before he leaves this kingdom of shadows. There is no need to prove the idea that the author was not so simple-hearted and did not intend to punish evil immediately, according to the conventional fairy tale. Shwartz reflected the tragic paradox: although Good is always crucified, mankind still survives due to it. This was Shwartz's message. Thus we have to maintain that the subject matter in his plays was contemporary life, described in terms and from the point of view of a fairy tale, its ethics (involving eternal values) and aesthetics.

The eternal values prevail in his drama. Although the heroes are not victorious, they never renounce them even under the pressure of social circumstances.

Aesthetically Shwartz continued and developed Andersen's traditions in terms of innovations in the field of fairy tales, first of all – in the field of psychological principles. Numerous studies have examined Andersen's profound psychology, which was unknown to the simple black and white classification of the folktale. Being a contemporary of the great realistic literature, Andersen introduced the principles of psychologically motivated behavior, of determination in his stories. Shwartz followed these principles in the portrayal of his characters, and as he progressed, the characters in his works became more and more complicated and even contradictory. In his first approach to Andersen, in the play *The Naked Emperor* it was still obvious who was a villain and who was a hero. But in *The Shadow* he already escaped from inherently good or bad characters. Their behavior became deeply determinated. In relation to that the Princess was described in terms of a duality of her profound qualities and her inherently given social manifestations. This is why she could be affected by the Shadow and become a victim of false illusions.

Even the fairy tale references had been used in order to create the previous off-stage biography of the characters, increasing by this the area of psychological motivation. For example, taking this into account we can examine such character as Julia, a popular singer, who, having fallen in love with Christian Theodor, has betrayed him because of her career. She reminds us of the girl who trod on a loaf so as not to soil her pretty shoes.

Thus the main collision in Shwartz's plays is placed not only outside, but inside, it is related to the inner life of the characters, first of all of the hero, who has to choose his way and to avoid a temptation. Therefore, the conflict he is passing through, is an inner one and the ending could be open, as in *The Shadow*, where the Shadow disappears "to meet me again and again" as Christian Theodor proclaims.

We can conclude that the author is moving towards a certain degree of realism. And this degree could be regarded as the edge of the fairy tale genre conventions. Could we assume that the further development of these principles could break not only the established fairy tale canons, but overstep the genre's borders? Shwartz's works signaled such a tendency. We can see that in the 20th century the writers were searching other means of expression in this field: for example, they created a universe of a fairy tale as a universe of childhood, which symbolized the paradise lost. For example, we can see such patterns in the works of P.L. Travers, A.A. Milne, and J.M. Barrie.

As to Shwartz, his plays could be considered fairy tales in a certain stage of the genre's development. On the other hand they belong to a segment of so-called intellectual drama (or problem play) of the 20th century, represented by such authors as Bernard Shaw, Bertold Brecht, and Jean Anouilh, who were close to reinterpretations of traditional forms, characters and inventory. The difference is, that their ideas were mostly connected with mythological landscape, while those of Shwartz were of fairy tales, firstly and mostly connected with Andersen.

Literature

Hans Christian Andersen. *Fairy Tales and Stories*. Moscow: Axmo, 2005.

Evgeny Shwartz. *Plays*. Leningrad: Sovetsky pisatel, 1972.

Bakhtin, M. *The Aesthetics Problems of Dostoevsky*. Moscow: Sovetsky pisatel, 1966.

Propp,V. *The Morphology of the Folktale*. Moscow: Nauka, 1969.

Propp,V. *We knew Evgeny Shwartz*. Leningrad – Moscow: Iskusstvo, 1966

Hans Christian Andersen in Puppet Theatre

Rossitsa Minovska-Devedzhieva

During the last eight years I've been the administrative and artistic director of the Puppet theatre in the city of Rousse, Bulgaria. My fascination for Andersen's fairy tales and my desire to learn as much as possible about his life and work have led me to this Conference. I think what is common for us all is our admiration for Andersen's creative talent. Our participation in this unique international forum is a way to manifest our deepest respect for this incredibly talented personality – a personality, obviously chosen by Destiny to unite people, to cultivate generations of children around the world, leading them into eternal moral notions such as Good & Evil, Faith, Love, Mercy, Compassion... – and continuing to do that successfully long after having left this world. Actually, it seems he never has.

Being surrounded by scholars and researchers, I hope to provoke your interest by telling you about how Hans Christian Andersen is situated in contemporary Bulgarian art for children; and, more precisely – in puppet theatre art. I am grateful to have spent two decades as a puppet theatre director, as this now gives me the opportunity to share my personal experience on the interpretation of Andersen's tales through the means of puppet theatre – as well as my observations on their effect on the children's audience.

Puppet Theatre Art in Bulgaria

Unlike in most West European countries, puppet theatre art has a long-standing tradition in Bulgaria. There are some 20 puppet theatre companies in the country (whose population is less than 8 million), and they enjoy the support of both the Ministry of Culture and the municipal administrations. Our theatre, which was among the first to receive the status of "state" puppet theatre, celebrates its 45th anniversary in a few months.

Over the years, the National Academy of Theatre and Cinema Art in Sofia has produced a lot of puppet actors, directors and scenographers. So, that's where I come from.

What Does Puppet Theatre Art Give to Children?

Playing is the most specific feature of childhood. Playing is also a basic element in theatre art. In puppet theatre, the basic means of expression is the puppet. Actors make it play various roles. In addition to being a means of aesthetic influence, the puppet is a major element in a stage solution; it exceeds the value of a theatre symbol and turns into a real personality – one very close to the children's psychology.

Puppet theatre art occupies a special place in the spiritual formation of a child's personality. It represents a symbiotic mix of music, visual arts, dance, pantomime and theatre, and is an ideal opportunity for a child to experience his first encounter with all these arts. Puppet theatre is an art which is alive. Children perceive the action on stage with all their senses – and consume it in the very moment in which it is happening. In addition, while doing that, a child is not alone: he can co-experience with his older companion, as well as compare his reactions with the rest of the audience, which is a process of sociallisation.

The effect of puppet art on children represents a very powerful blend of excitement and entertainment, an indicator of life values, a precious aid in forming a child's value system by distinguishing between Good and Evil. Besides, it gives insight into the magic of art in general. Given all this, puppet art is an extremely beneficial – and virtually irreplaceable – factor for provoking and shaping the way children think and act.

Puppet Theatre and the Best Models of Literature for Children

Puppet theatre art is recognized as one of the most popular ways to acquaint children with world drama and literature standards, both classical and modern. It's the perfect place to obtain knowledge of children's literature. This is why I believe a puppet theatre repertoire must be built very carefully, and based on high standards. In fact, we puppet theatre professionals participate in building a child's view of the world, together with his parents and teachers – which is a task of high responsibility.

Andersen wrote: "For me, a fairy tale is all poetry, and those who master it need to be able to include in it tragedy, comedy, naive simplicity and humour; there are many things that work in their favour: the lyrical touch, the typical way children say things, and the language, with which Nature is described."

A child can not only sense all this, reading (or listening to) Andersen's fairy tales; a child can co-experience it, watching those magic stories on the puppet theatre stage. It is true that each theatre play carries the vision of its creators; however, the spectator has the opportunity to rethink, to interpret things through his individual views and experience, and to reveal implicit meanings.

Why are Andersen's fairy tales so overwhelmingly successful with young readers all around the world? He himself gives the clue in a letter sent to Ingeman in 1835: "I wrote them just as I would have told them to a child."

Place and Role of Hans Christian Andersen in Bulgarian School Education

Andersen has been known to Bulgarian children since the end of the 19th century. I myself keep in the family library a 1942 and a 1946 edition of Andersen's fairy tales - presents to my mother and father when they were young. Andersen is one of the favourite childrens' authors in Bulgaria, and takes a special place in elementary school education. Studying "The Ugly Duckling", "The Little Match Girl", "The Nightingale" and "The Princess on the Pea" is included in the obligatory tuition programme for the first four school-years, approved by the Ministry of Education. When children come to the theatre to see an Andersen fairy tale on stage, they have already read the most popular ones and it is easy for them to follow the performance.

As for preschool education, Andersen is always a precious guest in tuition programmes. Children listen and try to reveal the meaning in his tales, then often do improvised dramatisations or make drawings, taking the tale as a general theme. I have brought some, to bring to your attention. They show us how children imagine Andersen's world. Some of them were done by pupils from elementary schools after watching a puppet theatre show, and reflect the children's perception not only of what they feel and think, but also of what they have seen. These are pictures with "theatre" elements – you can see spotlights, puppets, scenery sets, props, even ideas for posters. We often make exhibitions of such drawings in the theatre's entrance area, or use them to decorate the performance hall.

Hans Christian Andersen and Puppet Theatre

It is known that, as a child, Andersen had his home puppet theatre and, already adolescent, he continued to play with marionettes, to sew clothes for them, to write drama and play shows. In fact it was his father who stimulated and encouraged his interest for literature and theatre and influenced his intellectual development.

Hans Christian Andersen in the Repertoire of the Rousse Puppet Theatre

In Bulgaria we don't have the tradition of public storytelling; a similar practice exists only in kindergartens where children still cannot read. By putting fairy tales on stage, we allow children not only to perceive the content of a tale (as through reading) but to see the tale live. Frankly, I don't think there is a puppet theatre in Bulgaria that lacks an Andersen title in its repertoire. Taking the Rousse Puppet Theatre as an example – in the past its stage has seen "The Snow Queen", "The Little Match Girl", "Thumbelina", and "The Emperor's New Clothes". I remember two of these performances. "The Little Match Girl" was put on stage with small marionettes, some 30 centimetres high. It let children feel sympathy towards the heroine – so tiny, so pretty, and so unhappy. "The Emperor's New Clothes" was a synthesis of puppet and live acting. The King was a real actor who stood out strikingly amidst the puppet characters and thus the impact of his presence was a lot stronger.

Currently our programme includes "The Ugly Duckling" and "The Princess on the Pea", (cf. photos on next page). On the basis of an inquiry among the audience, we are planning to add "Thumbelina" and "The Steadfast Tin Soldier" in the near future.

A Few Personal Notes Based on My Work as a Puppet Theatre Director

During the last twenty years I have directed about 40 performances. A particular interest for me lies in the works of Charles Perrault, Tove Jansson, P.L. Travers, as well as of contemporary Bulgarian and European writers and playwrights. I have good practice, too, in staging educational performances, conceived upon essential themes from a child's everyday life, like road traffic rules, dental care, basic geometry etc.

While working on a literary source, I always do my best to reveal and stay true to the substance of the author's message. My main purpose is to allow the little theatre audience to get in touch with the genuine literary original. It is no secret that the most famous storytellers – like Andersen – are being adapted and re-narrated in various modifications which often deviate too much from the source. Of course, this is being done in search of artistic value; still, I believe that staying true to the source is the better way when it refers to a story that belongs to world classics.

I would now like to share with you my observations on how Andersen's fairy tales influence children's thoughts and emotions. In order to research this, in 2004, I initiated an inquiry on the subject, which ended up with interviews of 229 children aged 8 to 13.

Only twice so far have I endeavoured to interpret Andersen in puppet theatre – staging "The Ugly Duckling" (in 1998) and "The Steadfast Tin Soldier" (in 2001). I am, however, already working on another Andersen project, "Thumbelina", which is due to be realized in a year or two.

I am not a supporter of the popular art direction practice, to use an author's text for the purpose of backing up your own thesis which is not a main thesis in the original work (or even doesn't exist there at all). This is why – in "The Ugly Duckling", for instance – I have used the most important parts of the original text as a link between the separate scenes. The key to my stage interpretation is a group of travelling merchants selling wicker baskets, who narrate the story using improvised puppets made from the objects they sell. It is fascinating for a child to discover how simple everyday objects can turn into wonderful puppets. In his eyes, the famous fairy tale lives in flesh and blood, through the miraculous world of theatre art.

I ought to mention that there is one very important prerequisite for the success of a dramatization: to build dialogue where it does not exist. A dialogue true to the author's idea, contributing to the overall effect of the performance, and revealing the characters' personalities and the motives for their actions. While working on "The Ugly Duckling", for instance, it was an important task for me to reveal – in the dialogue – the reasons why the inhabitants of the duck-yard reject the Ugly Duckling. I had to communicate my understanding – the understanding of an adult with fairly long life experience – through the dialogue between the characters; later, while directing the actors' play, I had to build the characters in a way that would help children to perceive that dialogue unequivocally.

One of the questions in the inquiry received answers that showed that I had succeeded. The question was: "Did the Ugly Duckling do right when it left the duck-yard?" The children answered:

"Yes! He did not feel isolated any more."
"Yes! He ran away from the pain, hoping that someone else would accept him, without humiliating him."
"Yes! In order to find friends and live with less trouble."

Only one child expressed doubt: "Not exactly! Everyone he knows is there. Maybe they would have got used to him. But maybe they also would have envied him when he became a swan."

Creating his fairy tales, Andersen founded a new art form. As far as I know, "The Steadfast Tin Soldier" was the first fairy tale in which Andersen gave life to inanimate objects. Like in tales with animals, the behaviour of the characters is a reflection of human behaviour. This is one of the specific features of puppet theatre stylistics. It is something that children adore. So it's only natural for them to see this story in the puppet theatre performance hall. Basically, it's a love story. But the theme is not unknown to children. So they follow the development of the story on stage with growing attention. And although the end of the story is sad, children applaud, because they co-experienced the dramatic unfolding of events, and were touched by the power of Love.

How Children Perceive Performances Based on Andersen's Fairy Tales

Children usually identify themselves with the leading puppet's personality. Its influence on the audience is at maximum when the personality is also a child. The main character is the one who would find him/herself in a fairy situation; the one who would need to overcome various obstacles and go through trials in order to reach recognition, the one who is a carrier of an important philosophical message.

The young spectators follow the action, experience different kinds of emotions, estimate relationships, events and values. They live through the situations together with the play character – and learn, and grow wiser.

The following reactions can be repeatedly observed:

- dead silence: happens regardless of whether the audience is mixed (e.g. kindergarten and school audience together) and regardless of the audience's age – this means that the children's attention is attracted by what is happening on stage ("The Ugly Duckling");
- quiet comments and questioning the accompanying adults, seeking to make sure that nothing bad will happen to the main character ("The Ugly Duckling");
- loud, mocking comments referring to the Princesses and the Queen ("The Princess on the Pea");
- exclamations of admiration for the puppets of the Prince and the Princess ("The Princess on the Pea");
- vocal expression of personal attitude towards a character: "Because you are ugly and stupid!" (to a Princess in "The Princess on the Pea"); "Go away from here!" (to the Dog in "The Ugly Duckling");
- answering to a character self-questioning him/herself ("The Ugly Duckling": "Am I ugly?" – audience: "You're not!");
- clapping hands with the songs (for instance, the song of the Princesses in "The Princess on the Pea"); this does not happen during performances of "The Ugly Duckling", because children are tensely following the actions of the main character; and because the song he is singing is sad;
- adults laugh spontaneously, while watching the futile attempts of the Princesses to capture the Prince's heart – the puppets are large and grotesque ("The Princess on the Pea");

Here is yet another reaction which is not typical for other puppet performances: when the young swan flies together with the other two swans, the audience starts to applaud. This is a sign that the spectators' feeling for justice is satisfied. It is also an expression of being contented that the Ugly Duckling survived the period of heavy trials and, fighting, managed to find his deserved place. He is happy, at last. In that moment it happens that some of the adults cry, too.

Every Sunday we give performances for parents and children. Usually the children's age is between 2½ and 11 years. There are whole families that come to watch one and the same performance several times. One of the shows where I have observed this happen, is "The Ugly Duckling". After the show is over, children want to see and touch the puppets, especially their favourite – the Duckling. The youngest ones cry for him, because they cannot accept his transformation into a swan. Actors and parents help them understand that this was in fact a baby-swan, quite different from the baby-ducks. And when he grew up, a natural change took place, for his best (he became handsome).

Shaping my director's solution, I have decided to put the moral of the story into the Swan's words:

The Ugly Duckling (after seeing his reflection in the water): "But how is this possible? I was ugly, wasn't I?"

The Swans: "Were you?"

The Ugly Duckling: "Yes. Everyone told me so."

The Swans: "Poor you! Ugliness for some is beauty for others. That's all..."

My observations have shown that the fairy tales mentioned above easily reach both children and adults (of course, in different ways), when presented from the puppet theatre stage. While entertaining themselves, children continuously learn about life, and adults have the opportunity to think over some basic problems, to remember moral values, to look back upon the times of childhood and sometimes – unexpectedly – feel like children again.

The performance of "The Ugly Duckling" ends with the fairy tale's original final sentence: "... a good heart doesn't know pride." I find a proof of the beneficial influence of the performance on the little spectators also in the following answers (again, to questions from the inquiry): "If you were a writer yourself, how would you have continued the story?" Of course, most children think that "it is not necessary to continue it, it is complete enough", but one finds also answers like these:

- "I would have continued it because the young swan should teach his children not to pay attention to the criticisms of other birds, and not to be ashamed by the way they look."
- "He has to teach them (his children) to become tolerant."

Why the Ugly Duckling wins the children's sympathies, is clear from the answers of this question: "Which character did you like best, and why?" The children unanimously point out the Ugly Duckling. Because:

- "He is good-natured, and has a loving heart."
- "He doesn't blame the others for offending him."
- "He suffers most of all."
- "He evokes compassion."
- "He doesn't get haughty when he becomes a beautiful swan."

Another likeable character is the Peasant, because "he saves the Ugly Duckling".

Altogether, based on my long-time observations of children's reactions during a puppet theatre performance, I can certainly conclude that children do understand the general idea of a literary work, as well as the main message of a performance.

Here are some more interesting answers from the abovementioned inquiry. "What did you understand from what you saw in theatre?"

- "We shouldn't be ashamed of our appearance, because everyone is different in their own way."
- "The most important thing is the soul."
- "One should not lose hope."
- "It is important that you like yourself, not that others like you."
- "Even if you have lost something, you have to look forward – for life is ahead!"

It goes without saying that music has an extremely important place in a puppet theatre performance. Children define its role like this: "expresses the feelings of the characters", "makes the situation stronger", "creates the necessary atmosphere".

Children Create Andersen's World

A month ago, during a summer workshop in our theatre, I gave a task to a group of children aged 8-13, to try to create a scenography solution for "Thumbelina". Although the tale was familiar to them, we read it again together and discussed it. Then we tried to conceive how we could present the different places of action. The children did quite some cutting-and-pasting, constructing, drawing, glueing, modeling ... They matched materials and colours, adapting them to the specifics of the characters. We will continue in the autumn, after the school-year begins. I have brought here pictures of some elements of what they produced within two days session.

The results of this workshop have convinced me once again that not only can children recreate in drawings their impressions from a given puppet play, but they can also work on their own, based on a familiar story interpreted in a new direction.

Andersen in the Future

In the beginning of 1845 Andersen wrote to Henriette Hanck: "Now I am starting to write "Magic Tales for Children". I want to win the future generation, do you understand that?" Well, he did it. He succeeded in an enchanting way to win childrens' hearts and love.

I'm sure Andersen will live forever. Because of the continuity between parents and children; because of the fantastic world he has created; because of the immortal themes that he treats in his works, and that are so important for a child's upbringing. And mainly because of everyone's need of beauty and compassion in human relations – the beauty and compassion that one can find in Andersen's fairy tales.

Those who have been touched by Andersen's works keep the feeling as long as they live. He successfully managed to achieve his intention: tell a variety of stories to children, having in mind that their parents will read them and, no doubt, will understand what they are all about.

Being asked: "If Hans Christian Andersen could appear here now, what would you ask him?", the majority of children wanted to tell him how much they like his stories. There were also other answers – like:

- "Thank you!"
- "I'd ask him how he feels in the 21st century!"
- "I'd ask him what he thinks about today's children."
- "How he estimates the work of modern writers."
- "When will your next fairy tale come out?"

Conclusion

Andersen wrote: "... There goes the saying: 'Take a white pin in your mouth and you will become invisible!' – but that must be some special pin, the one that The Lord gave us. I was lucky to have one of these, and I am able to dig out clear-ringing gold – the best one, the one that shines in children's eyes, that rings in children's voices and in the voices of Mom and Dad, too. They keep reading the stories, and me, I stand in the middle of the room together with them, but I am invisible, because I have that white pin in my mouth; as soon as I feel they enjoy the stories I've told, then yes, I say too: 'Luck may lie in a pin'."

Indeed, two centuries after his birth, the spirit of this great writer is still alive, and his deeply humane wisdom has never ceased to touch children's hearts. The magic of puppet theatre art is a powerful mediator in the process, for the puppet stage is a place where miracles really happen. And as long as there will be children, the love for Andersen will never die and the puppet theatre will be one of the harbours for his fairy imagination.

Life and Death in "The Little Mermaid": Three Contemporary Adaptations of Hans Christian Andersen's Fairy Tale

Elisabeth Oxfeldt

What constitutes a happy end? When it comes to contemporary Andersen-adaptations, it is not surprising that today, Andersen's romanticist metaphysics based on part Christian, part neoplatonic ideals are rewritten or simply omitted.

In this paper I shall pursue the question of how Andersen's dualistic tale of life and death in "The Little Mermaid" is renegotiated in three turn-of-the-21st-century animation films from three different continents. Disney's "Little Mermaid" will serve as a point of departure, after which I will consider an Australian version of the tale produced by Burbank Animation Studios in Sydney in 2000.[1] I will end my study with the Nordic co-produced "Fairytaler" series, carrying the "Hans Christian Andersen 2005" sign of support and approval.[2]

Disney's Material Girl

Disney's version from 1989 is the most aestheticist of the three. It is a lavish production that often interrupts its epic development with gags, comic interludes and the musical performances that earned the film two Oscars. As Roberta Trites has pointed out, contentwise, the movie can be considered *pre*-modern in its sexism (Trites, 145).[3] And, as Finn Hauberg Mortensen writes, formally the movie can be considered *post*-modern in its fragmentary style (Mortensen, 158).

Let's look at the theme first: Disney's main character, Ariel, swims around with a shopping bag collecting human objects and then displays these in a subterranean cave. Like Andersen's mermaid, she yearns for the world above. But there is a difference: Andersen's maid longs for the sensual aspects of nature while Ariel wants material goods: "Look at this stuff – isn't it neat?" she begins her song of longing, culminating in "I want more!" Ariel is a material girl longing for a material world, and the filmmakers seem to admit to her vanity by placing an hourglass prominently at the treasure cave's entrance.[4] After Ariel has seen Prince Eric the first time, noting that "he's very handsome, isn't he," she returns to her song, now including Prince Eric among her objects of desire.

Andersen's mermaid also desires a man, but her desire is marked as ideal rather than phenomenological. Pointing to the mermaid's spiritual and sexual awakening is her garden's centerpiece: a marble statue of a young man she later recognizes as the prince. In accordance with romanticist neoplatonic philosophy, the statue and the human being are placed in a hierarchy: the ideal (the marble) is absolutely superior to the phenomenological (the human).[5] So, although the mermaid falls in love with the human prince, her ultimate longing is of a platonic kind. What she wants is an eternal soul, and the prince ends up serving as a means to a higher end.

Medial Self-reflection

Disney cleverly turns the neoplatonic hierarchy of original and copy around. Prince-Eric-in-the-flesh is the original and ideal, while Prince-Eric-in-stone is as a gaudy copy – a statue he receives of himself for his birthday. The vulgar copy ends up in Ariel's treasure-trove where Ariel can play at being with the prince. She wraps herself around the statue in a state of daydreaming, then cries when her father, Triton, blasts it into pieces.

If we look at the statue of the prince as a self-reflective gesture – as a sign of the film-makers' reflecting over their own film – we see that the movie both denigrates and delights in the notion of the vulgar copy. It presents it as ridiculous, but also as potentially dangerous. The movie, we might say, turns on the idea of the fake. While the statue of Eric is one example of this type of self-reflection, Ursula, the sea-witch, is the main carrier of medial self-reflection.

Compared to the sea-witch in Andersen's tale, Ursula is given a prominent, active role in the Disney version. As Laura Sells has pointed out in her feminist reading, Ursula is "unlike any other Disney villain" (Sells, 182). Feminists have read Ursula as a classical Medusa figure pointing to Disney's patriarchal ideologies. On a more positive note she has also been read as a gender-bending, cross-dressing drag queen who teaches Ariel that gender is performance (Sells, 183).[6] In the following, though, I will read Ursula metapoetically as a reflection not on gender, but on art and artfulness. Ursula represents imitation, magic, duplicity and transformation, and in the film she stands forth as Disney's figure of identification – as a figure of self-figuration.

As feminists have pointed out, Disney turns the sea-witch into a power-hungry "castrating bitch" (Sells, 181), enticing Ariel with an evil pact. In exchange for her beautiful voice, Ursula turns her into the human being she wants to be and gives her three days to attain Prince Eric's love. If Ariel does not succeed, she will turn back into a mermaid and belong to Ursula. Ursula's ultimate ploy in preventing "the kiss of true love" is her possession and assumption of Ariel's voice. Appropriating this voice, she poses as Prince Eric's "dream girl" and casts a spell over him.

The Theme of the Appropriated Voice

The motif of the authentic voice placed in the wrong body is entirely absent from Andersen's tale. Yet, as it appears in Disney's film, it may be read as an allegory of adaptation and appropriation. In an article about Disney from 1995, Jack Zipes accuses the Disney animation of having stolen the voice of the literary fairy tale (Zipes, 32).[7]

Still, in *The Little Mermaid*, the theme of the appropriated voice is ambivalent. If Ariel's voice is taken to represent Andersen's original tale, and Ursula represents Disney, we see on the one hand, the delightfully camp, beguiling, shape-changing charm of the imposter. Ursula is magical, causes transformations and provides her share of entertainment. On the other hand, Ursula is an unreliable medium of imitation, and all nature's forces combine to return the voice to its original owner. In the final, apocalyptic scene, Eric slays Ursula, Triton regains his ocean kingdom, and all Ursula's magic is undone. Ursula has played a huge role in the adaptation, leaving a great impression, but ultimately the film also seems to question the power of a camp adaptation to kill off its predecessor.

Overtly, the film is not about poetics, but about growing up. As Finn Hauberg Mortensen maintains, Disney has privatized the metaphysical conflict and resolution of Andersen's tale by transferring it to the family realm (Mortensen, 155; cf. Bendix, 289). Ariel's rebellious teenage behavior brings about a father-daughter conflict resolved at the end, when Triton recognizes that Ariel "really does love"

Eric, and that "children got to be free to live their own life." Drawing on all its tracks to reassure its viewers this *is* a happy end, the movie culminates with loud, cheerful music and imagery including rainbows, sparkles and as reassuring as the rest: the Disney logo.[8]

Disney for Children

As Torben Weinreich points out in his dissertation on adaptation strategies in children's fiction, the fairy-tale in its oral form is a genre common to people of all ages (Weinreich, 14). As soon as the tales are written down, however, they are adapted. There is for instance no doubt that Hans Christian Andersen consciously adapted his tales with regards to both children and adults.

As animation films, the tales are once more adapted for what is considered family audiences, taking into consideration a child's abilities and interests. Contentwise, many scholars on – and writers of – children's fiction operate with what they consider a criterion of appropriateness (Weinreich, 16). Several theorists insist that fiction aimed at children must provide the child with a sense of purpose, security, life-optimism and self-confidence.

According to a thematic criterion of appropriateness, children today would be poorly served by a tale in which it appears that a young girl who is ultimately willing to sacrifice herself for the person she loves, is rewarded with death. The child seeing the prince live happily ever after with another woman while the mermaid turns into a spirit of the air having to prove herself for an additional 300 years, may be left feeling discouraged rather than encouraged.

Andersen's ending, however, does not only pose problems on a thematic but also on a formal level. According to some experts on children's fiction, a story aimed at a child needs a single-stranded plot, and too many side-plots and digressions might confuse them (Weinreich, 17-19). Andersen's surprise ending of the mermaid entering a realm of air-maids may be confusing even to the adult reader. So in the end, omitting the daughter-of-the-air ending seems a matter of both ideological and formal adaptation. Disney's adaptation comes across as aimed at the child because it emphasizes an individual's ability to work at, and succeed in attaining something, because it follows a single plot line, and because it focuses on the relationship between children and adults.

Anti-aesthetic Ideals from "Down Under"

While Disney adapts and modernizes Andersen's idealism by turning it into materialism, the Australian Burbank Animation Studio sticks with Andersen's double story. It does so, though, by converting neo-platonic ideals into an environmental issue. In the year 2000 the concern with the eternal, in other words, is projected onto what will hopefully be an everlasting planet rather than immortal individual human beings. Instead of wishing for a prince and an eternal soul, the Australian Miranda longs for a prince and a clean ocean. In this low-budget animation film, the step towards preservation is taken not only on the level of content, but also on the level of form.

While Disney's *Little Mermaid* barely mentions Hans Christian Andersen in the closing credits, the Burbank Animation series presents itself as a "Fairy Tale Classic," recounting the tale of "the master story teller": Hans Christian Andersen (Anderson, on the DVD-cover). While Andersen is given full credit for a highly rewritten story, Disney – serving as the other source of inspiration – is not mentioned. The Burbank version nevertheless is highly reliant on Disney's aesthetics, narrative techniques and overall fame. In terms of a female aesthetic, the mermaids are hyper-realistic Barbie figures. If anything, the Australian mermaids are a bit "fuller" than Disney's – with broad hips and bosoms about to burst through their tops. Miranda, in the shape of a human being for instance, wears a dress that makes her look like a cross between Snow White and a Saint Pauli Girl. She, herself, seems somewhat bothered by this, occasionally trying to avert attention by holding her hands up in front of her chest.

As to narrative technique, the structure of the opening scene is just like Disney's. The Burbank version, too, begins with a voice-over accompanying the image of a seagull providing a bird's-eye view of the setting. After having presented the human world, the voice-over accompanying the gull presents "The Merfolk Kingdom". Miranda, we find out, "was just a few days from her ascension" which "would change her life so completely [...] that ever after she would be known as The Little Mermaid – the most famous mermaid of all." Thus, the Australian version admits to this being a tale already told and cleverly uses the fame Disney has granted the story to recount it in the style of a historical documentary.

On the plot-level, the distinguishing feature of the Burbank version is its *coup de* pedagogy, turning a spiritual concern with life after death into an environmental concern. Human remnants falling into the sea are not treasures at all – they are pollution. The ocean should not be used as a dumping site, and Miranda decides to apply her beautiful voice to an awareness campaign. She will sing about her beautiful kingdom and "shame" the humans above.

Miranda's anti-pollution song is the film's only original song – played over and over again as a *leitmotif*. The first time we hear it, a boat full of garbage cans appears on the ocean with a sailor singing: "What shall we do with the garbage, sailor." Lo and behold, they throw it into the ocean, and this is where Miranda steps forward and sings her song:

> People of the human world
> Please hear my song to you.
> A mermaid cannot swim through the sea
> That's brown instead of blue
> In the ocean deep
> All the creatures weep

We then see a big fish crying. To keep the theme consistent, pollution also turns into the cause of Prince William's near-drowning accident. Instead of a storm causing the shipwreck, it is brought about by the merfolk king's whale that has just had garbage dumped on his head. With brown gunk dripping down his face, the upset whale swims to the surface and wrecks Prince William's ship. William's body whirls towards the bottom of the sea, and Miranda saves him, brings him to land and kisses him in an effort of mouth-to-mouth resuscitation.

Unlike the Disney film, the Burbank version sets out to provide its viewers with a sense of security, avoiding what the Swedish specialist on children's literature Göte Klingberg calls "unexpected experiences of horror" (Weinreich, 21).[9] This means that the witch cannot be too evil. Like Andersen's witch, she is not actively out to get the mermaid – the mermaid comes to her. And unlike Andersen's witch, her realm is not slimy and morbid. Visually the only scary thing about this purple sea-witch is her warty nose and saggy breasts.

In terms of the plot, the deal struck between the witch and the mermaid is softened. Nobody is going to die. Miranda simply has to deposit her voice for a year in order to be a human. The same softening of the plot and the visual imagery applies to the second pact. When the sisters sacrifice their long hair, it is not for a knife that the mermaid can plunge into the prince's heart, but for Miranda's voice.

The witch lets her have her voice back just long enough to sort out the prince's confusion. Again, the visuals are gentle. Rather than being bald – in a manner evoking thoughts of punishment, concentration camps or sickness – the sisters emerge with chic haircuts as if they had just stepped out from a salon.

This prim and proper film ends with a scene on the ocean. Both families are joined aboard a boat, and the human King David promises there will be no more pollution, and the anti-pollution song is played one more time. Prince William and Miranda close their eyes and perk their lips for a kiss, but just as they get close, Miranda's little otter friend shows up between the two of them, receiving a kiss on each cheek.

The film certainly lives up to the demand for children's fiction to convey optimism and security. Relating to the childish otter, the child has no reason to feel excluded. While Andersen's original tale, in certain passages, borders on the sadistic in its treatment of the implied child reader, this adaptation cuddles and reassures the child of his or her central position.[10] Through the character of Miranda, the child is encouraged to be proud of his or her background and stand up for him- or herself. What Pil Dahlerup has referred to as Andersen's mermaid's masochistic, romanticist and Christian passivity is converted into self-assertive action and communication (Dahlerup, 156). By turning even the sea-witch benign, all nature is presented as good, and the child is given a purpose through the role it can play with regards to environmentalism – both as an environmentally conscious being and as one who, like Miranda, spreads environmental awareness.

In terms of understanding the cultural context, the film's translating romanticist metaphysics into modern environmentalism can be seen as a sign of our times – of what Ulrich Beck has called a second, or late, modernity.[11] Thus, the Disney and Burbank films reflect two very different aspects characterizing the end of the 20th century. Disney, on the one hand, represents a sense of liberating, materialistic, postmodern aestheticism, heeding no boundaries, while the Burbank version, on the other, represents a sense of late modern environmental risk, resulting from the lack of boundaries brought about in an increasingly globalized world.

A Modified Literary Adaptation From the North

I do not have time to go into as much detail with the Nordic "Fairytaler" adaptation from 2004. It is, however, the one of the three films that sticks most closely to the plot, tone and moral of Andersen's text. Still, it is clearly marked as an adaptation aimed at children, and ultimately carries a message of social equality.

Aesthetically, the "Fairytaler" version seems to be more inspired by stereotypical Japanese rather than American animation aesthetics, leaving the little mermaid more stylized, infantilized and desexualized than the other versions.[12] The background pictures are more muted, and using fewer distinct boundaries and flat color realms, the fluid aesthetic may be viewed as supporting the series' social message of fluid mobility and human equality across class boundaries.

In terms of plot, the physical violence pertaining to the witch pacts is left intact – only the imagery surrounding the witch and her realm are softened. In the "Fairytaler" film, the little mermaid is also rewarded with a surprise daughter-of-the-air ending. Yet, much effort is put into reassuring viewers that this indeed makes her happy. First, she returns to her sisters, saying: "Tell them [father and grandmother] not to be sad. I'm amongst friends, and everything is fine." Second, being a daughter of the air is presented as a final, ideal state rather than as one more purgatory. Thus, the tale reaches a point of final closure. Third, Disney-like visual and audial support is added to reinforce the notion of a happy end. Fourth, the Andersen-narrator of the frame tale delivers the final moral: "Her spirit lives on still in every kind deed done by children the world over." Thus, the child viewer is given a purpose in life, is encouraged to behave well, while the idea that he or she might in any way be – or do – evil is suppressed (unlike in Andersen's menacing tagged-on ending).

Formally, the plot is streamlined and a very important change pertaining to the message of social equality occurs in the prince's drowning accident. As the storm breaks out, causing his ship to wreck, he sacrifices his own life – not to save his dog, as in Disney's version – but to save the life of a common sailor.

Finally, we may note that the notion of material hierarchies is negated in the depiction of the mermaid's statue. Rather than being made of durable marble, signifying the ideal and eternal, it is made of a stone, dissolving and peeling off in big flakes – as subject to the hands of time as other materials.

Conclusion

I have compared three different contemporary adaptations of Hans Christian Andersen's "The Little Mermaid" in order to show how seemingly outdated romanticist themes of life and death are adapted in contemporary animation films. The American Disney version, the Australian Burbank version and the Nordic "Fairytaler" series illustrate how this adaptation may occur in a postmodern, late modern or simply modern manner.

As I hope to have shown, all three animation films make accommodations for the child viewer. The Disney version does so in particular by focusing on parent-child relations and by flooding its audience with the icons of a happy end. The Burbank version is child-friendly in its attempt to avoid "unexpected experiences of horror", presenting all beings as rather benign, and providing its viewers with a clear purpose in life. Finally, the "Fairytaler" version relies on a tactic of streamlining, subordinating narrative digressions to the main plot. In addition it stresses its end as happy through the little mermaid's and the frame-tale narrator's explicit reassurances.

In sum, Andersen's "The Little Mermaid" seemingly lends itself well to the creative processes of modern adaptations, not *despite,* but rather *because of* its strangely incoherent, dual and open-ended plot. It is precisely the tale's gaps and multi-level narrative that invite timely additions, omissions and substitutions, allowing the story to remain ever-relevant. [13]

Literature

Barlby, Finn (ed.), *Det flydende spejl. Analyser af H.C. Andersens "Den lille Havfrue"*. København: Dråben, 1995.

Beck, Ulrich, *Risikogesellschaft. Auf dem Weg in eine andere Moderne*. Frankfurt am Main: Suhrkamp, 1986.

Bendix, Regina, "Seashell Bra and Happy End. Disney's Transformations of 'The Little Mermaid'". *Fabula. Zeitschrift für Erzählforschung*, 34, 1993: 280-90.

Dahlerup, Pil (ed.), "Splash! Six Views of 'The Little Mermaid'". *Scandinavian Studies*, 63, 1991: 141-63.

Furniss, Maureen, *Art in Motion. Animation Aesthetics,* London: John Libbey, 1998.

Lauridsen, Palle Schantz, "Den ustabile tekst. Om 'Den lille Havfrue' og 'The Little Mermaid'". In: Peter Allingham, Per Aage Brandt & Bent Rosenbaum (eds.), *Set fra sidste punktum. Tekst og udsigelse i et semiotisk perspektiv*. København: Borgen, 2002: 191-211.

Mortensen, Finn Hauberg, "Disneyfication – den lille oversøiske havfrue". In: Anne Scott Sørensen et al. (eds.), *At se teksten. Essays om tekst og billede*. Odense: Odense Universitetsforlag, 1993: 145-58.

O'Brien, Pamela Colby, "The Happiest Films on Earth. A Textual and Contextual Analysis of Walt Disney's 'Cinderella' and 'The Little Mermaid'". *Women's Studies in Communication*, 19, 1996: 155-83.

Oxfeldt, Elisabeth, "Life and Death in 'The Little Mermaid': Three Contemporary Adaptations of Hans Christian Andersen's Fairy Tale". *Animation Journal*, 2006 (forthcoming).

Sanders, Karin, *Konturer. Skulptur- og dødsbilleder fra guldalderlitteraturen*, København: Museum Tusculanums Forlag, 1997.

Schickel, Richard, *The Disney Version. The Life, Times, Art and Commerce of Walt Disney*. New York: Simon and Schuster, 1968.

Sells, Laura, "'Where Do the Mermaids Stand?' Voice and Body in 'The Little Mermaid'". In: Elizabeth Bell et al. (eds.), *From Mouse to Mermaid. The Politics of Film, Gender, and Culture*. Bloomington: Indiana University Press, 1995: 175-92.

Trites, Roberta, "Disney's Sub/Version of Andersen's 'The Little Mermaid'". *Journal of Popular Film and Television*, 4, 1991: 145-52.

Weinreich, Torben, *Askepots sko. Børnelitteratur og litteraturpædagogik 1965-90*. København: Danmarks Lærerhøjskole, 1992.

White, Susan, "Split Skins. Female Agency and Bodily Mutilation in 'The Little Mermaid'". In: Jim Collins et al. (eds.), *Film Theory Goes to the Movies*. New York: Routledge, 1993: 182-95 and 284-88.

Zipes, Jack, "Breaking the Disney Spell". In: Elizabeth Bell et al. (eds.), *From Mouse to Mermaid. The Politics of Film, Gender and Culture*. Bloomington: Indiana University Press, 1995: 21-42.

Notes

1. According to their website, the Burbank Animation Studios Pty. Ltd., located in Sydney, Australia, produced 13 animated telefeatures incl. Hans Christian Andersen's "Thumbelina" and "The Emperor's Clothes" between 1991 and 1994. After 1995 they were commissioned by Anchor Bay Entertainment Inc., located in Troy, Michigan, USA, to produce an additional 12 50-minute telefeatures, including "The Little Mermaid" (1997/98). The version I have is a 41-minute DVD distributed by WHAMO Entertainment 2000. See www.burbankanimation.com.au/profile.html.
2. On the occasion of Hans Christian Andersen's bicentennial in 2005, Egmont Imagination, A. Film and Magma Films produced a series of 12 DVDs containing a total of 30 Hans Christian Andersen fairy-tale animation adaptations.

The series, called *The Fairytaler,* was released in the fall of 2004. Intended for a Nordic audience, it contains language tracks in Danish, Norwegian, English, Swedish and Finnish. The original adaptations are written in English and subsequently translated into the other languages mentioned. Jørgen Lerdam is the series' director. It is distributed by Nordisk Film A/S. See www.fairytaler.com. I will henceforth refer to it as the Nordic version/adaptation.

3. According to Trites, Disney's changes result in characters, images, and conflicts that rob women of integrity, making the movie even more sexist than the original story (Trites, 145).
4. Laura Sells, by contrast, reads the song positively as being about an ambitious adolescent girl – "an upwardly mobile mermaid", singing "of access, autonomy and mobility", yearning "for subjecthood and for the ability to participate in public (human) life" (Sells, 179).
5. In the nineteenth century, marble was the object seen to capture the ethereal and ideal (Sanders, 21).
6. While I agree with Sells' description of Ursula, I do not necessarily buy her argument that Ursula has been Ariels *teacher,* and that Ariel has *learned* gender "as a performed construct". Sells' is a feel-good post-feminist analysis opting to view Ariel as a positive role model who, by the end of the movie, has gained access to a male, public sphere, while regaining her voice/subjecthood. The fact that Ursula has kept and used the voice leads Sells to conclude that the future Ariel in some way will replace Ursula as a balanced female Ursula-Ariel figure. This is, of course, possible, but seems somewhat optimistic and speculative.
7. Cf. Schickel, 227.
8. Throughout, the animated film has reveled in gags and comic relief accompanying the main plot. Visually both land and sea world repeatedly turn into big Las Vegas shows with various objects and creatures engaging in singing and synchronized dancing. The crayfish Sebastian is the comic relief figure *par excellence* especially as he is chased by the French chef wanting to stuff, boil and serve him on a platter. Verbally, the movie is full of puns establishing parallels between the human and merfolk worlds: Being a guppy corresponds to being a chicken, Ursula takes matters "into her own tentacles," Ariel wonders if Flounder is "getting cold fins". As Pil Dahlerup has pointed out, the main rhetorical figure in Andersen's text is the simili establishing connections between the two worlds (Dahlerup, 159). In addition, claims Dahlerup, the story functions as one big simili (Dahlerup, 162).
9. "Oväntade skräckupplevelser" (quoted in Weinreich, 21).
10. Pil Dahlerup discusses the logic of sadism in connection with Andersen's tale, pointing out that phrases such as [...] 'day by day, she [the mermaid] became dearer to the Prince; he cared for her as one can care about a good, dear child, but to make her his queen never even occurred to him' ('Dag for Dag blev hun Prindsen kjærere, han holdt af hende, som man kan holde af et godt, kjært Barn, men at gjøre hende til sin Dronning, faldt ham slet ikke ind') divulge an aggressive attitude of the prince and the narrator towards the mermaid and the child reader (Dahlerup, 160-61; cf. White, 190-91).
11. This is a reference to Ulrich Beck's terminology and his view of the "reflexive modern" characterizing a skeptical attitude – towards the end of the twentieth

century – towards a first modernity's sense of optimism vis-a-vis industrialization and development. An important aspect of our globalized world is, according to Beck, a sense of increased risk and an ecological crisis. See Ulrich Beck, *Risikogesellschaft. Auf dem Weg in eine andere Moderne* (Frankfurt am Main: Suhrkamp, 1986); Danish translation, 1997.

12. She looks less human than in either of the other two adaptations, portrayed, for instance, with webbed hands. Aside from that, she stands out among her sisters as the blonde, blue-eyed one. These characteristics seem to be attributed to a combination of innocence and (inner) beauty.

13. This paper is a shortened version of an article appearing in *Animation Journal*, vol. 14, 2006.

"Everything in the Picture Book Was Alive": Hans Christian Andersen's Strategy of Textual Animation in His Fairy Tales and the Interactive Child Reader

Jacqueline Reid-Walsh

In "The Wild Swans" (1838) the heroine has been reduced to living in a forest. She dreams a compensatory dream about her former life as a princess when she possessed a "picture book that cost half of a kingdom". Now this priceless picture book has become even rarer for "everything in the picture-book was alive. The birds sang, and the people came out of the book, and spoke to Elise and to her brothers. When she turned over a page they skipped back into their places again, so that there should be no confusion among the pictures." (*Fairy Tales* 68.)

In this quote the inclusion of multimedia effects of sound, sight, motion and the interaction of the child with the book evoke an impression of a miniature theatrical performance, or even prefigure techniques of film animation or computer game play. As elsewhere in his fairy tales, Andersen creates a "picture book without pictures" with the significant addition of movement. As well, his animated beings have some sentience: as performers they pay attention to the textual limits of the page as if it were a textual stage or platform and they may relate directly to the child reader/viewer.

In this paper I have two main aims: my first is to explore the idea that Andersen is evoking a technique of "textual animation" that conveys his knowledge of and pleasure in popular performance transposed onto the textual platform of words on a page. Andersen was very knowledgeable about the visual and performance culture of the period since as a child he played with mechanical changing pictures, a toy theatre and dolls, was both a spectator and a writer of popular theatre throughout his life, and as an adult he created drawings and paper cuts of the stage and performers.[1] He drew upon this knowledge in composing his fairy tales. I believe that by examining passages concerning toy theatres and paper cutouts we can gain insight into how Andersen transposed his competence in these areas of play, performance and art into his writing technique. My second aim is to explore the active role of the child reader as the initiator of the textual performance through turning the pages of the book and as the visualizer of the textual animation. My theoretical impetus in exploring this aspect of Andersen's technique is derived from some observations of the cultural critic Walter Benjamin.

Danish toy theatre of wood and glass *circa* 1840, 28 x 40 cm. National Museum of Copenhagen. In Baldwin, illus. no. 61, p. 100.

Andersen and Toy Theatres

As a child in the early 19th century Hans Christian Andersen played with a home made toy theatre with his dolls enacting plays based loosely on some of the drama he had seen or read but largely improvising from his imagination, using theatre bills, for example, as prompts (Andersen 11, Baldwin 101, Wullschlager 20). Although the Andersen family could not have afforded to buy a toy theatre, during this period there appears to have been no commercially produced toy theatres in Denmark. Wealthy families imported German toy theatre structures and sheets (Baldwin 101-102). Andersen's toy theatre has not survived but the physical structure of the toy theatres could range from being a rough performance space cut out of a box to a wooden reproduction of an actual theatre with an arch, curtain, space for the wings, a stage that may be grooved, traps and so on.

Around 1830 paper sheets for the toy theatre began to be reproduced and these included figures of actors, background and wing scenery, props as well as a truncated script of an actual play. The paper sheets were all to be cut out and the figures were then mounted on a material that enabled them to stand up and to be manipulated by some means. Indeed, the challenge of toy theatre play generally was the difficulty of moving these paper figures about, as Robert Louis Stevenson remarks in his article "A Penny Plain and Twopence Coloured" (1884).

Later in life Andersen included toy theatres in several of his fairy tales and in some of his paper cuts. Examining two passages where toy theatres appear shows how and where the toy theatres were set up, who the audience might be, and significantly for toy theatre historians how the paper actors were manipulated on stage and the attendant difficulties. In "The Shepherdess and the Chimney Sweep" (1845) Andersen uses his knowledge of toy theatre play partly to establish the personality of the female protagonist. The shepherdess takes temporary refuge in an open drawer where a toy theatre play with its limitations is in process:

> Here lay three or four packs of cards, which were not complete, and a little puppet show, which was set up as well as it was possible to do. A play was being performed, and all the ladies, Diamonds, as well as Hearts, Clubs, and Spades, sat in the front row, and fanned themselves with the tulips they held in their hands, and behind them stood the knaves. The play was about two persons

who could not have each other. At this the Shepherdess wept, for it was her own history. "I cannot bear it longer" she said.

Seeing the play as a microcosm of her life impels her to act, for she then leaves to pursue her brief adventure. (*Fairy Tales* 133).

In "The Money-Box" (1855) there is long description of a performance that includes the mechanics of the paper actors' movements and the varying attitudes of the spectators. The detailed audience reception is nicely graduated spatially according to rank and self-importance in a parody of live theatre audience itself (as seen in "Aunty"). Interestingly, an excerpt of this quote is used in a book on the history of toy theatre to describe the mechanics of stage movement in Danish toy theatres prior to 1880:

> The little toy theatre was therefore put up in such a way that the money-pig could look directly into it. Some wanted to begin with a comedy, and afterwards to have a tea party and a discussion for mental improvement, but they commenced with the latter first. The rocking-horse spoke of training and races; the wagon of railways and steam power, for these subjects belonged to each of their professions, and it was right they should talk of them. The clock talked politics – "tick, tick;" he professed to know what was the time of day, but there was a whisper that he did not go correctly. The bamboo cane stood by, looking stiff and proud: he was vain of his brass ferrule and silver top, and on the sofa lay two worked cushions, pretty but stupid. When the play at the little theatre began, the rest sat and looked on; they were requested to applaud and stamp, or crack, when they felt gratified with what they saw. But the riding-whip said he never cracked for old people, only for the young who were not yet married. "I crack for everybody," said the cracker.
>
> "Yes, and a fine noise you make," thought the audience, as the play went on.
>
> It was not worth much, but it was very well played, and all the characters turned their painted sides to the audience, for they were made only to be seen on one side. The acting was wonderful, except that sometimes they came out beyond the lamps, because the wires were a little too long. The doll, whose neck had been darned, was so excited that the place in her neck burst, and the money-pig declared he must do something for one of the players, as they had all pleased him so much. So he made up his mind to remember one

of them in his will, as the one to be buried with him in the family vault, whenever that event should happen. They all enjoyed the comedy so much, that they gave up all thoughts of the tea party, and only carried out their idea of intellectual amusement, which they called playing at men and women; and there was nothing wrong about it, for it was only play. All the while, each one thought most of himself, or of what the money-pig could be thinking. *http://hca.gilead.org.il/moneybox.html*

In each passage the degree and type of animation is carefully graduated according to the material substance of the figures. The physical theatre has been set up, the paper figures and scenery cut out properly, glued on wood, and attached to wires. The paper toy actors are self propelling for there is no sense of anyone pulling the wires to make them move. They have a limited sentience since they know to show their painted side to the audience but their essence remains that of paper figures with only one side drawn on and the other blank. In this way the toy theatre may come alive and play itself, but it does not become anthropomorphic and exceed the limits of toy theatre action. In each passage it is only the protagonists (who are three dimensional objects) who have a rounded character and a consciousness, limited as it may be. Significantly, Andersen describes the theatres with plays in progress. They are not playthings deposited on a shelf but their purpose is enacted for the child reader as well as for the protagonists of the tales. I believe these scenes of miniature theatre in progress form part of his technique of textual animation.

Andersen and Paper Cuts

Andersen was a skilled artist producing landscape sketches, collages and paper cuts throughout his life. Although many of the same images from the stories would appear in his paper cuts, such as dancers, swans, ballerinas, castles, theatres and so on, they were not used to illustrate his published tales nor his narrated tales (Brust 14). As Andersen stated in a letter to a young friend, his paper cuts exist in a visual realm parallel to the textual fairy tales: "From Andersen's scissors / Fairy tales instantly spring" (cited by Jens Andersen 2). His technique was to recount an improvised fairy tale while he cut out paper freehand with his scissors. Andersen understood the qualities of paper as a medium for he wrote on it, drew on it and used it in his paper art (Jens Andersen 11.) This sense of the plasticity of the medium seems to be present in his presentation of paper cuts in fairy tales such as "Little Ida's Flowers" (1835), "The Tin Soldier" (1838) and "The Court Cards" (1869). In these tales where Andersen presents both the subjects of his paper-cut art and transposes some of the qualities of paper art into words, he also provides some insight into his animation technique.

In "Little Ida's Flowers" (1835) the student, who is an autobiographical representation of Andersen himself, is a favourite with the young girl because he "knew the most wonderful stories, and he cut out the funniest pictures – hearts, with little ladies in them who dance, flowers, and big castles with doors that opened." (*Fairy Tales* 49)

Paper cut of ballerinas/ tightrope dancers in theatre. Image from the website of the Royal Library, Copenhagen (*http://www.kb.dk/elib/mss/hcaklip/portman/P280.jpg*)

This fictional account accords with accounts of members of Andersen's contemporary audience. For example at Holsteinborg manor Andersen made many paper cuts for daughters of the family. Later in life, the eldest recounted, "He always cut with an enormous pair of paper scissors, and I simply couldn't understand how he could cut such pretty, delicate things with his big hands and this enormous pair of scissors." (cited in Jens Andersen 7). She continues "When I was a child I was delighted when he cut out chains of little dolls in white paper that I could stand on the table and blow so they moved forward (cited in Brust 54; Jens Andersen 7).

Both a castle and a dancing doll are featured in the fairy tale "The Tin Soldier" (1838). The two-dimensionality of the paper-cut doll is transposed into her flat characterization that is in sharp contrast with the rounded delineation of the tin soldier with his consciousness and emotions (albeit within the limits of his material construction.) To emphasize the significance of his perspective, the reader's initial view of the castle is focalized through the tin soldier's eyes:

> The toy that struck the eye most was a lovely castle of cardboard. Through the little windows one could see straight into the rooms. Outside the castle some little trees stood around a little looking glass, which made believe it was a lake. Wax swans swam on this lake, and were mirrored in it. This was all very lovely but the loveliest thing of all was a little lady, who stood at the open door of the castle. She was also cut out in paper but she had a dress of the clearest gauze, and a little narrow blue ribbon over her shoulders, that looked like a scarf, and in the middle of this ribbon was a shining spangle as big as her whole face.
>
> The little lady stretched out both her arms, for she was a dancer; and then she lifted one leg so high that the tin soldier couldn't see it at all, and thought that, like himself, she had only one leg. (*Fairy Tales* 125-26.)

Here, the paper figure has a more restricted animation than the toy theatre actors, and no self awareness of her art. She does not move beyond possessing the ability to strike her ballet pose, one that is difficult to achieve and impossible for a living individual to maintain. Her only motion is passive when she is wafted by a breeze into the fire and is consumed.

Unlike the paper actors on the toy stage, and the illustrations in Elise's picture book which are more mobile and have different degrees of sentience, the paper ballerina does not seem to have any consciousness. She is almost entirely an object of desire constructed by the tin soldier due to his limited vantage point. The characterization of the paper figures (they are flat or stock characters) in a fictional sphere does not exceed the physical constraints of their material construction. In terms of the artistic design of objects this is called real affordance.[2] In these tales there seems to be a graduated scale of consciousness in the depictions of the paper toys similar to the graduated response of the toy and furniture audience to the toy theatre performance as described in "The Money Box". This seems to be linked to their ability to move. The buildings such as the toy theatre or castle are inanimate, the flat paper doll may be able to stand up on one toe and be blown about easily (as in Andersen's paper cuts) but she cannot move herself. By comparison, the paper actors on the toy stage and the figures in the picture pop-up book have the ability to move consciously within the physical limits of their design. Yet only the three dimensional objects have mobility, self-consciousness and agency although limited by their physical and psychic natures.

"The Court Cards" (1869) was published after Andersen's death and features a full scale paper castle with animated playing cards and a little boy owner. This tale describes fictively the large scale nursery projects that Andersen would occasionally attempt for his young friends (Jens Andersen 6).

> How many beautiful things may be cut out of and pasted on paper! Thus a castle was cut out and pasted, so large that it filled a whole table, and it was painted as if it were built of red stones. It had a shining copper roof, it had towers and a draw-bridge, water in the canals just like plate glass, for it was plate-glass, and in the highest tower stood a wooden watchman. He had a trumpet, but he did not blow it.
>
> The whole belonged to a little boy, whose name was William. He raised the draw-bridge himself and let it down again, made his tin soldiers march over it, opened the castle gate and looked into the large and elegant drawing-room, where all the court cards of a pack – Hearts, Diamonds, Clubs, and Spades – hung in frames on the walls, like pictures in real drawing rooms. The kings held each a scepter, and wore crowns; the queens wore veils flowing down over their shoulders, and in their hands they held a flower or a fan; the knaves had halberds and nodding plumes.

> One evening the little boy peeped through the open castle gate, to catch a glimpse of the court cards in the drawing room, and it seemed to him that the kings saluted him with their scepters, that the Queen of Spades swung the golden tulip which she held in her hand, that the Queen of Hearts lifted her fan, and that all four queens graciously recognized him. He drew a little nearer, in order to see better, and that made him hit his head against the castle so that it shook. Then all the four knaves of Hearts, Diamonds, Clubs, and Spades, raised their halberds, to warn him that he must not try to get in that way. (*http://hca.gilead.org.il/inkling/court_cards.html*)

The little boy, urged on by the paper card knaves, plays with fire which results in disaster for the paper artifact. As a twist on the conventional didactic tale, not only does the boy survive but also the narrator does not blame him for the accident.

Andersen's Technique of Textual Animation and the Interactive Child Reader/Viewer

The account of another child listener, Rigmor Bendix, Andersen's god daughter, suggests his method of paper cutting: "While Andersen was talking he would fold a piece of paper, let the scissors run about in curves, then unfold the paper, and there the figures were" (cited in Brust 13-14). Frequently he would stop to add new longitudinal or transverse axis on the paper, break the symmetry of the folds, and provoke new angles and perspectives. As Jens Andersen states, his method of paper cutting seemed to correspond to his devices of oral and written storytelling, for he would start "editing" "in a filmic sense" and adjust the chronology or the composition by bringing in new angles, scenes and characters (4). Later Jens Andersen discusses another type of paper art, the collages in picture-books for children that were composed of varied materials such as cut-out fragments of tickets, bills, ads, label, stamps, surplus from a paper cut, a short poem and so on. He considers this "expressionist idiom" to be a precursor of the collage art of Dadaism and the surrealism of the 1920's (9).[3]

I think both of these aspects, the filmic sense of working with a plastic medium and the expressionist idiom which could be seen as a precursor of Dadaism, are present in Andersen's technique of textual animation in his fairy tales. By drawing on the movement inherent in the play realm of the toy theatre and in the plastic medium of the paper cut Andersen inserted a sense of motion into his representations of toy figures, both three dimensional and two dimensional, that cannot simply be accounted for as anthropomorphism. Rather the technique seems to be a visual description of an effect of pre-cinema animation constructed from a combination of these two areas of artistic production.

Collage of dancing men with little boy from *Christine's Picture Book*. Image from the website of the Royal Library, Copenhagen (*http://img.kb. dk/hca/manus/stampe/stampe091.jpg*)

Keeping these ideas in mind, let us return to the initial quote from "The Wild Swans" about Elise's picture book that comes alive. To the child the characters seem to emerge suddenly from the pages of the book, move towards her, speak to her and then pop back again. The combination of the appeal to different senses evokes a tactile quality. This textual animation effect recalls the description of Walter Benjamin comparing Dadaist art to techniques of early film. In *The work of art in the age of mechanical reproduction* (1936) Benjamin states,

> [Dadaist art] hit the spectator like a bullet, it happened to him, thus acquiring a tactile quality. It promoted a demand for the film, the distracting element of which is also primarily tactile, being based on changes of place and focus which periodically assail the spectator. Let us compare the screen on which a film unfolds with the canvas of a painting. The painting invites the spectator to contemplation; before it the spectator can abandon himself to his associations. Before the movie frame he cannot do so. No sooner has his eye grasped a scene than it is already changed. It cannot be arrested ... The spectator's process of association in view of these images is indeed interrupted by their constant, sudden change. This constitutes the shock effect of the film ... (XIV; 238).

Significantly, the child's reaction to the shock of the surprising movement is delight. A notable difference between a film spectator or even a theatre spectator (whose role is reactive and critical) and the picture book reader is the degree of agency of the reader. While Andersen states the role of the child in curtailing the animation by turning over the page, it is equally apparent that by opening the page the child has set this animation in motion. In Andersen the motion not only seems to move out towards the mental spectator but to flip back, analogous perhaps to a pop-up book or a flap book. The reader's role then becomes one of agent and onlooker. She controls the action by turning the pages and then has the pleasure of watching and listening to the characters in the theatre of her mind.[4]

In another early essay Benjamin quotes the above passage about the picture book that comes alive in order to criticize Andersen's style and then to introduce his own ideas about how children read picture books, presenting them in terms of direction, as opposite to that of Andersen. He goes on to state,

> Pretty and unfocused, like so much that Andersen wrote, this little invention misses the crucial point by a hair's breadth. The objects do not come to meet the picturing child from the pages of the book; instead, the gazing child enters into those pages, becoming suffused, like a cloud, with the riotous colors of the world of pictures. Sitting before his painted book, he makes the Taoist vision of perfection come true: he overcomes the illusory barrier of the book's surface and passes through coloured textures and brightly painted partitions to enter a stage on which fairy tales spring to life. ... The child stands in the centre of a masquerade and joins in, while reading ...

Next, Benjamin uses a similar theatrical metaphor to discuss how children read and compose fairy tales. "When children think up stories, they are like theater-producers who refuse to be bound by 'sense'" ... "This is how children write their stories, but also how they read them." "A Glimpse in to the world of Children's Books" (1927, pp. 435-36).

Unlike Benjamin, I do not believe that Andersen was unfocused; rather Benjamin is perhaps responding to Andersen's complex technique of graduated textual animation. While even the smallest figure appears to have some potential for movement, there seems to be a scale of animation through the partly sentient and then onto the fully rounded characters. Neither are Andersen's and Benjamin's ideas of the reading process in opposition to one another. Both stress the active role of the child reader and the impact on the child but they are emphasizing different aspects of the flow of the reading process. Andersen stresses a two directional flow, while Benjamin is stressing the movement of the reader into the text. Both rely on theatrical images and metaphors.

In another tale Andersen uses an image similar to that of Benjamin with respect to the child listener/dreamer passing through the imaginary barrier of the surface of the text. In "Ole Shut-Eye" the passage is literal, for Ole Shut-Eye not only animates a landscape picture for Hjalmar but places the little boy in the picture:

> Ole Shut-Eye touched the painting with his magic gun, and the birds began to sing, the branches of the trees stirred, and the clouds began to move across it; one could see their shadows glide over the landscape.

> Now Old Shut-Eye lifted little Hjalmar up to the frame, and put the boy's feet into the picture, just in the high grass ... He ran to the water, and seated himself in a little boat which lay there. It was painted red and white, the sails gleamed like silver, and six swans, each with a gold circlet round its neck, and a bright blue star on its forehead, drew the boat past the great wood, where the trees tell of robbers and witches, and the flowers tell of the graceful little elves, and of what the butterflies have told them. (*Fairy Tales* 530-31.)

Here, as with Elise's picture book, the figures of the landscape are not only imbued with motion but also speak and interact with Hjalmar. As he joins the play or masquerade the effect is of an immersive experience with the significant proviso that the reading child controls the turn of the page.[5] In "Ole Shut Eye" the mode of transport that allows the dreaming boy to view the action as a spectator located on the stage recalls that used in Tchaikovsky's ballet "The Nutcracker" based on the E.T.A. Hoffmann tale. Here, similarly, the child watches the ballet from a vantage point on the stage and is transported in an exquisite vehicle. This would suggest that the state of reception of the child reader/viewer is complex and various. The child may be so close to the action that he or she is on the periphery of the stage or as in Elise's case is the instigator of the action. Despite their proximity though, the child reader/viewers are not actors in the drama but privileged spectators of an imagined performance.

Bibliography

Andersen, Hans Christian. *The Fairy Tale of My Life*. London: Paddington Press, 1975.

Fairy Tales. Afterword by Clifton Fadiman. Toronto: London: Collier-Macmillan, 1970.

Fairy tales and Stories. Transl. by H.P. Paul (1972) http://hca.gilead.org.il/

and Adolph Drewsen *Christine's Billedbog. Christine's Picture Book* (1859). Introduction by Erik Dal. Facsimile. London: Kingfisher, 1984. Copenhagen: Royal Library, http://www.kb.dk/elib/mss/stampe/index-en.htm, accessed September 21, 2005).

Andersen, Jens. "Scissor Writing." Transl. by David Hohnen. Det Kongelige Bibliotek 2002. http://www.kb.dk/elib/mss/hcaklip/intro-en.htm (accessed July 18, 2005).

Benjamin, Walter. *Illuminations*. Ed. by Hannah Arendt. New York: Schocken, 1969.

Selected Writings, vol 1. *1913-1926.* Ed. by Marcus Bullock and Michael W. Jennings. Cambridge Mass.: Harvard UP, 1996.

Bredsdorff, Elias. *Hans Christian Andersen the Story of his Life and Works 1805-1875.* New York: Scribner, 1975.

Brust, Beth Wagner. *The Amazing Paper Cuttings of Hans Christian Andersen.* New York: Ticknore & Fields, 1994.

de Mylius, Johan. *H.C. Andersen Papirklip/Paper Cuts.* (1992). Copenhagen: Aschehoug, 2005.

Marker, Frederick J. *Hans Christian Andersen and the Romantic Theatre. A Study of stage practices in the prenaturalistic Scandinavian theatre.* Toronto: University of Toronto Press, 1971.

Stevenson, Robert Louis. "A Penny Plain and Twopence Coloured." *The Magazine of Art* April 1884. Rpt. In *Memories and Portraits.* New York: Charles Scribner's Sons: 1917, 198-211.

Wullschlager, Jackie. *Hans Christian Andersen: The Life of a Storyteller.* London: Penguin, 2001.

Notes

1. Please see the discussions in Bredsdorff, Brust, de Mylius and Marker.
2. Affordance is a design term, now used especially in new media. Affordance is categorized as real and perceived. Don Norman states,
   In graphical design, one is really talking about conventions, or what I called logical and cultural "constraints" in POET. Physical constraints are closely related to real affordances: Thus, it is not possible to move the cursor outside the screen: this is a physical constraint. Logical constraints use reasoning to determine the alternatives. Thus, if we ask the user to click on 5 locations and only 4 are immediately visible; the person knows, logically, that there is still location left.
   Cultural constraints are learned conventions that are shared by a cultural group. The fact that the graphic on the right hand side of a display is a "scroll bar" and that one should move the cursor to it, hold down a mouse button, and "drag" it downward in order to see objects located below the current visible set (thus causing the image itself to appear to move upwards) – all this is a cultural, learned convention. The choice of action is arbitrary: there is nothing inherent in the devices or design that requires the system to act in this way. *http://www.jnd.org/dn.mss affordances-and-design.html* accessed July 18, 2005.
3. The verse accompanying this collage is as follows:
   Andersen got / That blot.
   Into a piece of grown-up art
   Comes a boy with a little cart.
   Andersen snipsits.

Plate 91, Hans Christian Andersen and Adolph Drewsen, *Christine's Billedbog. Christine's Picture Book* (1859). Introduction by Erik Dal. Facsimile. London: Kingfisher, 1984.

4. Benjamin's description is unidirectional and could be compared to attending a theatrical performance such as a pantomime where the mixture of different modes of dance, music, drama, speech, mime and scene changes created an ever changing spectacle for the audience. The sudden transformations that occur one after the other never permit the spectator to abandon him or herself to the contemplation of a scene but create a sequence of pleasurable shocks. In flap books based on the harlequinade sections of pantomime, called harlequinades, this large scale, multimodal, participatory event is transposed to a small paper platform. The act of reading/viewing a harlequinade may achieve the effect of a miniaturized theatrical experience due to the emphasis on speed by the narrator and due to the tactile pleasure of turning the flaps to discover what lies underneath. This participatory experience is moderated by the critical spectator role created for the reader for similar to attending a pantomime the reader/viewer is invited to give critical comments on the textual performance of the characters. At the same time, the reader/viewer is placed in a position of an enabler of the plot, perhaps similar to that of a stagehand whose engagement was crucial to the success of the tricks and the safety of the performer. The unusual level of engagement with the flap book suggests the role of collaborator analogous to the many who mounted the pantomime performances. This level of involvement gives the reader/viewer an insider's perspective on the narrative. It is this multiple active role that places the reader/viewer in a position of control with respect to the telling of the narrative.

5. The immersive effect also recalls techniques that are used in contemporary digital animation on the large screen such as in the "Toy Story" films where the point of view draws the viewer into the action almost as an actor. In various ways computer games draw the child user into the action on the screen so the child seems to participate not only through the visual point of view, but through a multimodal appeal, the appeal to the sense of agency though using the mouse, and identification with the figures through creating an avatar or as in the *Sims* through creating characters in a domestic environment.

It is important to note that both Hjalmar and Elise are asleep. By presenting the animation within a dream sequence Andersen may be suggesting that the mode of reception when reading the words and mentally viewing the images is one akin to watching phantasmagoria in magic lantern projections. (OED). This is the subject of another fairy tale, "The Old Street Lamp" where the lamp, unknown to his owners, has the ability to "cover these white walls with the most gorgeous tapestry, to change them into noble forests, and all that they can possibly wish." (*Fairy Tales* 234.)

Translations of Hans Christian Andersen in Latvian and Lithuanian (1990-2005)

Arūnas Bliūdžius

Differences between Latvian and Lithuanian translations of H.C. Andersen have existed during all periods, and translations from the new Independence Period (1990-2005) is no exception. As to previous periods we noticed that Latvian editions of H.C. Andersen mostly included tales translated from Danish, whereas Lithuanian editions mainly included tales republished from earlier editions translated mostly from German and Russian.

The new Independence Period for the Baltic states brought some changes in the situation of H.C. Andersen translations and publications:

1 *language* – most Latvian translations are totally new because they are made from the original Danish text, and half of the Lithuanian translations are republished in spite of their not so modern language and authenticity; only translations from Danish are new;
2 *translators* – Latvia has few translators, but almost all of them translate from Danish; Lithuania has more translators, but practically only one translates from Danish; furthermore half of the Lithuanian translators are not specialized on H.C. Andersen, and their interpretations of tales are too controversial;
3 *illustrators* – in both countries (Latvia and Lithuania) illustrators are mostly foreigners and not concentrated on H.C. Andersen;
4 *prefaces* – Lithuanians make prefaces and comments to H.C. Andersen tales and present the compiler of the book, more often than Latvians do;
5 *number of tales* – before the Independence, Latvians translated almost all H.C. Andersen tales, whereas Lithuanians translated only a little more than half of the tales. Latvians furthermore "renovated" old translations from German by translating them from Danish, whereas Lithuanians continued to publish not so good translations; even new translations are rarely done from the original language, but from other European languages;

6 *number of editions* – if in previous periods the number of H.C. Andersen editions in Latvian and Lithuanian has been similar (32 and 28), then during the last 15 years the number of Lithuanian editions has increased much more than the number of Latvian (31 and 11), but, of course, quantity doesn't mean quality because most tales by H.C. Andersen in Lithuanian are translated from different languages, whereas Latvian translations are mostly made from Danish;

7 *separate editions* – Lithuanians more than Latvians like separate editions of tales and selected works of 2-3 volumes, and only Lithuanians published two books by H.C. Andersen with motives for children's painting;

8 *H.C. Andersen tales in other books* – only Lithuanians published books of selected tales of major authors in which several tales by H.C. Andersen are included as part of those books;

9 *unuseful editions* – Lithuanians make more unuseful editions than Latvians do, by publishing the same not original translations of the same well-known H.C. Andersen tales instead of doing some new translation; this is still the biggest problem of Lithuanian Andersen publishing;

10 *author rights* – this problem is much bigger for Lithuanians than for Latvians, because in many Lithuanian editions the publication on which the translation is based is not at all given credit, nay the main author H.C. Andersen is not mentioned at all.

Translations from Danish 1990-2005

Four books by Andersen were translated from Danish into Latvian during this period.

The most outstanding translator from Danish to Latvian, Peters Jankavs, published the 1st volume of H.C. Andersen tales in 1997, Riga, Atena (65 tales; with illustrations by Danish Vilhelm Pedersen and Lorenz Frølich; and preface by the owner of "Atena", Karsten Lomholt).

The same translator, Peters Jankavs, also prepared another book of Andersen translations – "Tales about Flowers" – published in 2000, Riga, Alberts XII (16 tales with illustrations by Latvian Modris Adumanis).

In 2004 two books were translated from Danish – separate edition of "The Princess and the Pea" (Riga, Zvaigzne ABC, translator Gita

Andersone, illustrator Gundega Muzikante) and "The Most Beautiful Tales", with five fairy tales: "The Ugly Duckling", "The Little Mermaid", "The Emperor's New Clothes", "The Snow Queen", and "The Little Match Girl" (Riga, Egmont Latvija, translator Sandra Rutmane, illustrator Andzejs Fonfara).

Four books by Andersen and one translation in a magazine from Danish into Lithuanian appeared during this period. Almost all translations are made by one translator, Liudas Remeika. The first book is "Twelve from the Post Carriage" which contains twelve tales and extracts from Andersen's diaries, letters and other works concerning Christmas (Vilnius, UAB Alumnus, 2002, illustrators Vilhelm Pedersen and Lorenz Frølich). The second book translated by Liudas Remeika contains "The Little Match Girl" (Vilnius, Nieko Rimto, 2004, illustrator Kęstutis Kasparavičius).

The other two books are translations of separate tales – "The Steadfast Tin Soldier" translated by Vaida Tupčiauskaitė (Vilnius, Egmont Lietuva, 1997, illustrator Vif Dissing) and "The Snow Queen" translated by Laura Blaževičiūtė (Vilnius, A. Remeikos Publishing House, 2000, illustrator Lina Eitmantytė-Valužienė). Furthermore, "Holger Danske" was published in 1995 in *Rubinaitis*, a magazine for children's literature.

Editions of Separate Tales by H.C. Andersen in 1990-2005

"Thumbelina" was published in Latvian two times (1998 and 2002, Riga, with full colour illustrations), and in Lithuanian three times (1999 and 2000, Vilnius, with full colour illustrations, and 2001, Vilnius).

"The Tinder Box" was published in Latvian one time (2003, Riga, with full colour illustrations).

"The Princess and the Pea" was published in Latvian one time (2004, Riga, with full colour illustrations).

"The Snow Queen" was published in Latvian one time (2001, Riga, with full colour illustrations) and in Lithuanian six (!) times (1998 Vilnius, 1999 Kaunas, 2000 Vilnius, 2001 Vilnius, 2002 Kaunas, 2002 Vilnius, all with full colour illustrations except the Kaunas edition 2002).

"The Snow Man" was published in Lithuanian once (1991, Vilnius, with full colour illustrations).

"The Emperor's New Clothes" was published in Lithuanian twice (1992 and 1997, Vilnius, with full colour illustrations).

"The Steadfast Tin Soldier" was published in Lithuanian once (1997, Vilnius, with full colour illustrations).

"The Little Match Girl" was published in Lithuanian once (2005, Vilnius, with full colour illustrations).

"The Swineheard" was published in Lithuanian once (2000, Vilnius, with full colour illustrations).

"The Ugly Duckling" was published in Lithuanian once (1996, Vilnius, with full colour illustrations).

Five tales ("The Ugly Duckling", "The Steadfast Tin Soldier", "The Wild Swans", "The Emperor's New Clothes" and "The Little Mermaid") were published as separate volumes of "My Small Luggage" in Latvian (1997, Riga) and in Lithuanian (1997, Vilnius) with full colour illustrations.

Stocktaking 1990-2005

11 editions of H.C. Andersen were published in Latvian and 31 editions of H.C. Andersen were published in Lithuanian.

From 11 Latvian editions there were:
    5 selected volumes;
    5 separate tales;
    1 collection of 5 books.

From 31 Lithuanian editions there were:
    7 selected volumes;
    1 with 3 volumes;
    17 separate tales;
    1 collection of 5 books.

In 5 books H.C. Andersen tales are only part of the contents.

All the 11 Latvian editions of H.C. Andersen were published in Riga; of 31 Lithuanian editions, 25 were published in Vilnius, and 5 in Kaunas.

Of 11 Latvian editions 2 had prefaces, of 31 Lithuanian editions 12 had prefaces.

All 11 Latvian editions are illustrated in colour, of 31 Lithuanian editions 25 are illustrated in colour, whereas 5 are with black/white illustrations and 1 without illustrations.

Latvians translated almost all of H.C. Andersen's tales, Lithuanians translated about 2/3 of them.

The most popular tales by H.C. Andersen in Latvian during this period are: "Thumbelina", "The Emperor's New Clothes" and "The Ugly Duckling" (each – 5 editions). The most popular tales of H.C. Andersen in Lithuanian during this period are: "The Snow Queen" (13 (!) editions); "The Emperor's New Clothes" (10 editions); "The Ugly Duckling" (9 editions").

Of 11 Latvian editions 5 were translated from Russian, 1 from German, 1 from English, and 4 from Danish. Of 31 Lithuanian editions 12 were translated from German, 6 from English, 2 from Russian, 2 from Italian, 1 from French, 1 from Polish, and 5 from Danish; 2 books were meant for colouring.

Bibliography of Latvian Translations of H.C. Andersen

Hansa Kristiana Andersena dargumu kratuvite. [5 pasaku gram.] Karala jaunais terps. Maza nara. Meža gulbji. Neglitais zilens. Nelokamais alvas zaldatinš. No anglu val. tulk. M. Rūmniece. Riga.: SIA "Gulbis", 1997. – 29 pp.: il.

Pasakas Hanss Kristians Andersens. No danu val. tulk. P. Jankavs; il. V. Pedersens un L. Frelihs; atdzej. K. Skujenieks. – Riga: Atena, 1997. – 466 [1] pp.: il., portr.

Andersens H.C. Ikstite. Tulk. A.Bauga; il. S. Skopa. Riga: Zvaigzne ABC, 1998.– 29 [2] pp.: il.

Hansa Kristiana Andersena Pasakas. Atstast. N. Bakstere; latv. val. Atstast. Laura; il. Keitija Šatlverta. Riga: Egmont Latvija, 1999. – 96 pp.: il.

Pasakas par ziediem/ Hans Kristians Andersens; ar makslinieku klusa dabas gleznam. Riga: Alberts XII 2000. – 124, [1] pp.: il.

Sniega karaliene: pec Hansa Kristiana Andersena pasakas motiviem. Il. V. Jerko. Riga: Eve, 2001. – 30 [2] pp.: il.

Ikstite: pec Hansa Kristiana Andersena pasakas motiviem. Il. V. Solncevs. Riga: Eve, 2002. – [16] pp.: il. (Pasaku tinite)

Skiltavas: pec Hansa Kristiana Andersena pasakas motiviem. Il. V. Solncevs. Riga: Eve, 2003. – [16] pp.: il. (Pasaku tinite)

Pasakas. Il. V. Medvedevs. – Riga: Zvaigzne ABC 2003. – 200 [3] pp.: [14] pp.: il.

Andersens H.C. Princese uz zirna: [pasaka ar uzdevuviem]. Maksl. G. Muzikante; uzd. sast. G. Andersone. Riga: Zvaigzne ABC, 2004. – [23] pp.: il.

Visskaistakas pasakas. Teksts: A. Sojka; tulk. S. Rutmane; il. A. Fonfara. Riga: Egmont Latvija, 2004. – 96, [1] pp.: il.

Bibliography of Lithuanian Translations of H.C. Andersen

Andersenas, H.C. Sniego senis. Iš vok. klb. vertė J. Balčikonis; il. A. Žvilius. Vilnius: Vyturys, 1991. – 15 pp.: il.

Andersenas, H.C. Nauji karaliaus drabužiai: pasaka. Il. V. Hansenas. Vilnius: Egmont Lithuania Ltd., 1992. – 41 pp. Įsk.virš.: il.

Pasakos. Vertė J. Balčikonis. Kaunas: Caritas, 1992. – 270, [1] pp.: il.

Gražiausios Anderseno pasakos. Iš vok. klb. vertė J. Balčikonis; il. E. Jakubčionytė; pasakas parinko ir red. R. Keturakis. Kaunas: Vaiga, 1995. – 191 [1] pp.: il. – 2-as leid.

Andersenas, H.C. "Holgeris Danas". Iš danų klb. Vertė L. Remeika. Rubinaitis. 1995. Nr. 1(2). Pp. 21-23.

Andersenas, H.C. Bjaurusis ančiukas. Atpasak T. Četrauskas; il. B. Beyerholm. Vilnius: Egmont Lietuva, 1996. – [40] pp.: il.

Andersenas, H.C. Nauji karaliaus drabužiai. Vertė J. Balčikonis. Il. Chr. W. Hansen. Vilnius: Egmont Lietuva 1997. – [40] pp.: il.

Andersenas, H.C. Alavinis kareivėlis: pasaka. Iš danų klb. Vertė V. Tupčiauskaitė; il. V. Dissing. Vilnius: Egmont Lietuva, 1997. – [41] pp. įsk.virš.: il.

Andersenas, H.C. [Mano mažoji skrynelė: 5 knygos dėžutėje]. Bjaurusis ančiukas. Drąsusis cino kareivėlis. Laukinės gulbės. Nauji karaliaus rūbai. Undinėlė. Iš anglų klb. Vertė R. Staneliūnaitė; parengė A. Guigaitė. Vilnius: Trys Nykštukai, 1997. – 29 pp.: il.

Gražiausios Anderseno pasakos. Iš vok. klb. Vertė J. Balčikonis; dail. D. Dapkutė; sudarė V. Vaitkūnas. Kaunas: Vaiga, 1997-99. –

    D.1. – 1997. – 190 [1] pp.: il.

    D.2. – 1998. – 191 [1] pp.: il.

    D.3. – 1999. – 191 [1] pp.: il.

Andersenas, H.C. Sniego karalienė: septynių pasakų istorija. Vertė J. Balčikonis; dail. E. Mikalauskas. Vilnius: Vaga, 1998. – 51, [3] pp.: il.

Coliukė: pasaka. Perpasak. O. Petkevičiūtė; dail. C. Busquet. Vilnius: Mažoji Rosma, 1999. – [8] pp.: il.

Sniego karalienė: pasaka. Il., atpasak. ir tekstą adapt. P. Viržintaitė. Kaunas: Nizamas, 1999. – [17] pp. įsk. virš.: il.

Pasakos. Liet atpasak. D. Sirijos Giraitė; il. C. Shuttleworth. Vilnius: Egmont Lietuva, 1999. – 96 pp.: il.

Andersenas, H.C. Coliukė: pasaka. Iš vok. klb. vertė J. Balčikonis; il. V. Šatunovas. Vilnius: Alma Litera, 2000. – 24 [11] pp.: il.

Andersenas, H.C. Kiauliaganys. Liet. tekstas L. Petkevičiūtės, pieš. R. Maminskaitės. Vilnius: Trys Nykštukai, 2000. – 44 pp.: il. (Močiutės Šnekutės sakymai sekimai)

Andersenas, H.C. Sniego karalienė: septynių pasakų istorija. Iš danų klb.vertė L. Blaževičiūtė; dail. L. Eitmantytė-Valužienė. Vilnius: A. Remeikos l-kla, 2000. – [38] pp.: il.

Rinktinės pasakos vaikams. Vilnius: Rosma, 2001. – 2d.

D.1. Coliukė.

D.2. Bjaurusis ančiukas.

Coliukė: H.C. Anderseno pasakos motyvais karpyta knygelė. Il. V. Dubrova. Vilnius: Naujoji Rosma, 2001. – [12] pp.: il.

Pasakos. Iš vok. klb. vertė J.Balčikonis; il. T. Markevičius. Vilnius: Alma Litera, 2001. – D.1. – 220 [3] pp.: il.

Vakaro pasakaitės. Iš italų kalbos vertė L. Gudynienė. Vilnius: Rosma, 2001. – [230] pp.: il. – Tame tarpe: Stebuklingas skiltuvas; il. P. Cataneo. Bjaurusis ančiukas; il. Kennedy.

Andersenas, H.C. Sniego karalienė: pasaka. Iš anglų klb.vertė D. Barisauskaitė; dail. V. Jerko. Vilnius: Naujoji Rosma, 2001. – 30, [2] pp.: il.

Sniego karalienė: perskaityk ir nuspalvink. Perpasak. ir il. H. Matulionytė. Kaunas: IĮ "Jumena", 2002. – 16, [1] pp., įsk.virš.: il.

Dvylika iš pašto karietos: žiemos pasakos: dienoraščio, laiškų, autobiografijų fragmentai. Iš danų klb.vertė ir sudarė L. Remeika; il. V. Pedersen, L. Frølich. Vilnius: UAB "Alumnus", 2002. – 238, [2] pp.: il.

Negirdėtos Anderseno pasakos. Iš anglų klb. vertė I. Matusevičiūtė. Kaunas: Vaiga, 2002. – 134, [2] pp.: il.

Andersenas, H.C. Sniego karalienė: pasaka. Iš anglų klb.vertė D. Barisauskaitė; dail. V. Jerko. Vilnius: Naujoji Rosma, 2002. – 30, [2] pp.: il.

Geriausių pasakų didžioji knyga. Vert. iš rusų klb. Kaunas: Vaiga, 2003. – 283, [5] pp.: il. – Tame tarpe: Coliukė; Karalaitė ant žirnio; Nauji karaliaus drabužiai; Narsus alavinis kareivėlis; Laukinės gulbės.

Gražiausios pasaulio pasakos mažiesiems. Iš lenkų klb. vertė R. Dičiuvienė; il. P. Salamacha. Vilnius: UAB "Mūsų knyga", 2003. – 190. [3] pp.: il. – Tame tarpe: Bjaurusis ančiukas; Mergaitė ir degtukai; Sniego karalienė; Undinėlė; Nauji karaliaus drabužiai.

Wolf, Tony. Mano gražiausios pasakos. Il. T.Wolf; pasakėles rašė A. Casalis; sumanė A. Dami; iš italų klb.vertė A. Gudaitis. Vilnius: Alma Litera, 2004. – Tame tarpe: Karalaitė ant žirnio.

Pasakos. Liet. tekstas L. Petkevičiūtės; il. H. Matulionytės, A. Čapskytės. Vilnius: Aktėja, 2004. – 336 pp.: il.

Andersenas, H.C. Mergaitė su degtukais: pasaka. Iš danų klb. vertė L. Remeika; il. K. Kasparavičius. Vilnius: Nieko rimto, 2005. – [32] pp.: il.

Like Roses to a Cow?
Hans Christian Andersen in English Translations

Lise Bostrup

According to Viggo Hjørnager Pedersen[1] and Elias Bredsdorff,[2] two scholars who have made research into the Andersen translations, we have more than 34 different translations of Hans Christian Andersen's tales into English. Since the publication of Viggo Hjørnager Pedersen's study, two more translations have been published: one by Tiina Nunnally and one by Diane Crone Frank and Jeffrey Frank.

In his study *Hans Christian Andersen and England,* Bredsdorff concludes:

> The result of this investigation of the English translations of Andersen's tales ... is rather sad. Among the eleven translators, whose work has been examined above not one has proved able to offer a really congenial English version.

Bredsdorff has a collection of very funny and sometimes most unfortunate translation mistakes from the Andersen translations. One translator translates the expression "den bløde jord" with "the bloody earth"; another mixes up the Danish word for "butterflies", "sommerfugle" with "summer birds"; and a third translator mistakes "Hyp, alle mine heste" for "Hip, hip, hurray!"

How Bad are the Old Translations?

The above mistakes are indeed fatal, but today all these funny mistakes can only be found in libraries. The old translations[3] are not read any more, so it seems to me a bit unfair to legitimize the new translations by referring to translations which have not been reprinted for decades.

Classical Hans Christian Andersen Collections and Modern Translations

The big, cheap editions from Chancellor Press,[4] Wordsworth,[5] and Avenel Books,[6] are all based on an old translation by Sir Henry William Dulcken. Dulcken lived in England from 1832 to 1894. His mother was German and his father British, and he himself was bilingual. Dulcken's translations are today free of rights, and they have been published in millions of copies in all English-speaking countries.

Elias Bredsdorff describes Dulcken's Andersen translation like this:

> It is very likely that Dr. Dulcken has translated Andersen from Danish, and he must have had good command of the Danish language. Possibly, he also used good German translations. There are very few misunderstandings, and it is obvious that Dr. Dulcken paid great attention to follow Andersen's text as closely as possible. Unfortunately, he did it to such an extent that the translation often becomes clumsy and awkward. (Bredsdorff, p. 515)

Dulcken's translations were published for the first time from 1864 to 1889.[7]

A British translator called Mrs. H.B. Paull was, like Dulcken, a translator of German literature into English. In her *Hans Andersen's Fairy Tales, A New Translation by Mrs. Paull, With a Special Adaptation and Arrangement for Young People*, published in 1867, she has changed the order of the tales so "that those intended for juvenile readers appear in the earlier pages".[8]

Bredsdorff says later that Dulcken placed notes in the text, and that Mrs. Paull copied them:

> As far as her "special adaptation" is concerned, it partly consists of notes that she adds with explanations of the text. Some of these are transferred from Dr. Dulcken's edition in slightly changed form. (Bredsdorf, p. 515)

Viggo Hjørnager Pedersen is not so sure that Dulcken actually used the Danish original:

> It is impossible to say whether Dulcken in fact used Andersen's original text. But there is no evidence that he did. On the other hand, he clearly used the Leipzig edition for a number of the early tales, and this is very close to Danish, good German editions might well have been his only source. (Hjørnager p. 170)

After this, it would be interesting to find out whether the old British translator Dulcken and Paull in fact used the original Danish text of the fairy tale or not.

Hans Christian Andersen and the German Language

To Hans Christian Andersen, German was the most important foreign language. In his *Mit Livs Eventyr,* he describes how as a child in Odense, he saw theatre pieces in German, and he adapted the language that he had heard in the theatre. In her *Den gyldne trekant, H.C. Andersens gennembrud i Tyskland 1831-1850*[9], Ivy York Möller-Christensen described how Andersen copied the works of the great German writers in his notebooks.

Andersen saw Germany as the first step on his way to international success. In 1831, he wrote to the German poet Adelbert Chamisso, whom he had met while travelling in Germany:

> Denmark is a bit out-of-the-way, so that its poets will remain totally unknown if they are unable to make some spiritual emigrations to the neighbour countries.

Andersen's German is not perfect,[10] but he is without any doubt capable of communicating with Chamisso in German. Andersen was very often in Germany, and he also had many German friends.

Hans Christian Andersen was himself active as a translator. According to Frank Hugus[11] he translated four pieces from German into Danish.[12] One of them, *En Landsbyhistorie*, was played at Casino in Copenhagen 1855, with great success, and Andersen's translation was published by Reitzel the same year.

When Andersen's first works were published in German, he was very displeased with the translations, and especially with respect to the fairy tales he found that he was misunderstood. Together with the Danish publisher Carl B. Lorck, who lived in the German city of Leipzig, he started planning an original German edition of his collected works. For this edition, Andersen wrote a pr-text, a so called "Prospectus".

> In the last years, a great part of my works has been published in Germany. The more heartily these have been received and the milder the critique has been in its judgement, the more embarrassing the big lacks and the important misunderstandings in most translations have touched me. A strong desire arose in me to prepare an edition of my collected works which, as far as possible, could appear as an original. (Lorck, p. 66[13])

Andersen here clearly states that the edition published by Lorck has a special status as Andersen's own original work. This fact corresponds with the contract made between the two of them. It says:

> Mr. Andersen sees to a revision of this translation and provides it with the necessary corrections and remarks. (Lorck, p. 26[14])

In the numerous letters from Hans Christian Andersen to Lorck that the Museum in Odense has published, it is possible to follow the big correction process.

It is clear that Andersen felt quite capable in German and he corrects with a lot of energy. One part of the translation is made by a woman named W. Caroline Christiani, but Andersen is not very pleased with it:

> this [Christiani's] translation is so totally unsuccessful that I could almost half rewrite it myself. (16.2.1848)

He corrected and partly rewrote the translation by Hans Reuscher, which had already been published by the publishing house Simion:

> The booklet with Reuscher's translations is enclosed, carefully read through and corrected and with the necessary notes added. (4.2.1847)

To Andersen the roles were given: He was the writer, and as a writer he worked with a publisher. Under them work several translators; sometimes Andersen did not remember their names, and sometimes – like here – he could not spell their names correctly:

> Reutscher translates badly, with Böttcher I have had to correct his German and found holes in it, places he has skipped, for there was nothing which you might find reason to delete.

The writer is free and can change the text if he wants to, and the publisher can make suggestions in order to adapt the work to the cultural climate in the new country – but the translator is some kind of worker who is paid to translate exactly the text he is given. Hans Christian Andersen demanded – with a concept from modern translation theory – formal equivalence.[15]

The works, which were rewised by Hans Christian Andersen and Lorck in cooperation, were printed with the inscription: "Deutsche, vom Verfasser besorgte Originalausgabe" ("original German version made by the writer himself").[16]

This inscription had three functions:

> first, Andersen pointed out that this translation was the one and only German translation and that other translations did not really matter;

> second, this sentence would give him the right to receive royalty from the publisher. Andersen lived before the time of the first copyright convention,[17] and many of the first translations of Andersen's works were made without any payment or even contact with the author.

As the cooperation between Lorck and Andersen stopped in 1868, Andersen pointed out that the sentence "vom Verfasser besorgte Originalausgabe" was not to be used any more:

> Would you then ask him not to print "German original version made by the writer himself" but just: The Dryade is a fairy tale from the exhibition days in Paris by H.C. Andersen (or *after* H.C. Andersen).[18]

One of the reasons why Andersen took so much care about this translation was that he wanted to use it as an entrance card to the world. In many letters, Hans Christian Andersen asked Lorck to send copies of his works in German – not only to German friends, but also to people in Holland, France and England. For Andersen this translation really mattered.

"Skyggen"

For this article, I have chosen the fairy tale "Skyggen" (1846-47; "The Shadow") as an example because it contains a lot of challenges for translators.

In "Skyggen", Andersen writes about a man coming from the North to a country in southern Europe. One evening, he sits on his balcony and watches his shadow, and just for a joke he asks the shadow to go inside the flat on the other side of the street and take a look. The next morning, the sun is burning and he can't see his shadow any more. He thinks it has gone and tries to get it back, but the shadow seems to be lost. Luckily, little by little a new shadow starts growing, and on the way back to the North, the new shadow gets as big and mighty as the old one.

Then one day the old shadow returns in the shape of a very polite, noble foreigner. The man asks the shadow what he saw in the house on the other side of the street, and the shadow explains that it was the court of poetry. In the meantime the shadow has earned a fortune by looking into people's bedrooms and blackmailing them, and he invites his former master to a spa (a health resort). Here they meet a young princess who falls in love with the shadow, and when the man threatens to disclose the shadow's real identity, the shadow makes the princess order his execution.

The Second Hans Christian Andersen Original?

"Skyggen" was already as a manuscript sent to the publisher Carl B. Lorck in Leipzig together with two other fairy tales. In a letter to Lorck from the first of March 1847, Andersen commented on "Skyggen":

> The last ["Skyggen"] might be one of my most successful fairy tales and the few who have heard my reading of it, place it next to The Ugly Duckling and The Snow Queen. Do not forget, dear friend that this change, or addition [the addition of the three fairy tales] should be mentioned in the preface to the fairy tales, and let me then know immediately when you are *printing* these so that I can make Reitzel[19] happy. I would like to have a small booklet with the three published together as a little green in the spring at home.[20]

Hans Christian Andersen's plan originally was that the three fairy tales should appear at the same time in Copenhagen and Leipzig in order to give both of them the status of an original.[21] For this reason, he had asked the Danish publisher Reitzel not to print the Danish version before the German translation was ready to be printed. "Skyggen" was published by Reitzel April 3, 1847, and later that year, the authorized Lorck-version appeared in volume 15 of *Gesammelte Werke.* Then in 1848 another translation, by Julius Reuscher, appeared (*Neue Märchen*, Verlag M. Simion, Berlin).

In Denmark, "Skyggen" was published by Reitzel in April 1847, and the first German edition was published as a pirate copy in 1848 with the title *Neue Märchen* in Reuscher's translation by the publisher M. Simion in Berlin.[22]

The Danish and the German Original Texts

The Danish text of the fairy tale "Skyggen" consists of 4453 words; while the Lorck-version is 219 words longer. Andersen's authorized German version is not just a translation, it is an adaptation.

In the Danish version, Andersen lets the princess consider her situation at the Kurhotel:

> Men jeg tager ikke bort, for nu bliver her morsomt; den Fremmede synes jeg overordenligt om. Bare hans Skjæg ikke voxer, for saa reiser han!

This was translated almost word for word by Reuscher in the Simion edtion, 1848:

> Aber ich reise nicht ab, denn jetzt wird es hier **amüsant**; der Fremde gefällt mir. Wenn nur sein Bart nicht wachsen möchte, denn sonst reist er ab!

But in the Lorck-version, 1847 it says differently:

> Aber ich reise noch nicht von hier fort, denn jetzt wird es erst **amüsant**; der Fremde **Prinz – denn ein Prinz muß es sein** – gefällt mir außerordentlich gut. Wenn nur sein Bart nicht wächst, denn dann reist er wieder ab!

It is possible that Hans Christian Andersen's German friends had told him that the fact that a princess would marry a commoner might be such a provocation in the German speaking countries of that time that the balance might be spoiled.

At the end of the fairy tale, we find another highly significant addition to Andersen's German original:

"Stakkels Skygge!" sagde Prindsessen, "han er meget ulykkelig; det er en sand Velgjerning at frie ham fra den Smule Liv han har, og naar jeg rigtig tænker over det, saa troer jeg det bliver nødvendigt at det bliver gjort af med ham i al Stilhed!"

Reuscher translated quite accurately:

"Der arme Schatten!" sagte die Prinzessin. "Er ist sehr unglücklich; es ist eine wahre Wohltat, ihn von dem bißchen Leben, was er hat, zu befreien, und wenn ich recht darüber nachdenke, so glaube ich, es wird nothwendig sein, daß man es in aller Stille mit ihm abmacht."

The Lorck-version had a political explanation:

"Der arme Schatten!" rief die Prinzessin. "Er ist sehr unglücklich; es wäre eine wahre Wohltat, ihn von **seinem Leben** zu befreien, und wenn ich recht darüber nachdenke, **wie in unserer Zeit das Volk nur allzu bereit ist, die Partie des Geringern gegen die Höheren zu nehmen, da** scheint es mir nötig zu sein, dass man ihn in aller Stille beiseite schaffe."

According to Andersen's letters, he would never have allowed a translator to make such an important addition to his text, but maybe in order to make the text clearer, he nevertheless accepted this addition in the authorized German version.

Two British Translations

To me, it seems very interesting that precisely these two additions to the fairy tale are to be found in the two most popular British translations of the fairy tale.

Men jeg tager ikke bort, for nu bliver her morsomt; den Fremmede synes jeg overordenligt om. Bare hans Skjæg ikke voxer, for saa reiser han!

Sir Henry Dulcken translated:

But I'm not going away from here yet, for it begins to be amusing. **The foreign Prince – for he must be a Prince** – pleases me remarkably well. I only hope his beard won't grow, for if it does he'll go away.

The princess' consideration about the foreigner being a prince is here directly taken over by Dulcken.

At the end of the tale, we find another addition. In the Danish original, the princess felt sorry for the learned man:

"Stakkels Skygge!" sagde Prindsessen, "han er meget ulykkelig; det er en sand Velgjerning at frie ham fra den Smule Liv han har, og naar jeg rigtig tænker over det, saa troer jeg det bliver nødvendigt at det bliver gjort af med ham i al Stilhed!"

Dulcken has the Lorck-addition:

"Poor shadow!" cried the Princess; "he's very unfortunate. It would really be a good action to deliver him from his little bit of life. And when I think **how prone the people are, now-a-days, to take the part of the low class against the high**, it seems to me quite necessary to put him quietly out of the way."

Dulcken is not alone in taking oveer this addition.

Mrs. Paull[23] is close to Dulcken. First, she let the princess think about the shadow as a prince:

"**This foreign prince – for he must be a prince** – pleases me above all things. I only hope his beard won't grow, or he will leave at once."

Then she takes over the idea about the classes:

"Poor shadow!" said the princess; "it is very unfortunate for him; it would really be a good deed to free him from his frail existence; and, indeed, when **I think how often people take the part of the**

lower class against the higher, in these days, it would be policy to put him out of the way quietly."

Bredsdorff and Hjørnager Pedersen claim that the similarities between the two translations by Paull and Dulcken are caused by Mrs. Paull copying Dulckens text.

> As suggested by Bredsdorff (1954:555), Mrs. Paull's text is based on Dulcken's. He also believes that she used Andersen's own text, but that is not necessarily so. Nevertheless, she obviously drew on more than one text. (Hjørnager, p. 187)

To me it seems much more likely that both translators have taken the Andersen-Lorck text as a model for their translation; and as far as the fairy tale "Skyggen" is concerned, it is not possible to find a single addition from the two which cannot be traced to the German translation published by Lorck. Both Dulcken and Mrs. Paull were experienced translators of German literature, and Mrs. Paull also translated Grimm's Tales.[24] It is obvious that the two British translators were excellent in German, but it has never been proved that either of them were able to understand the Danish language. This fact makes it reasonable to conclude that the classic British translations that have been on the market for about 150 years were not translated from Danish, but from German.

Roses or Muscats

Another fact which makes it very likely that Dulcken and Paull both translated from the Lorck version is the use of the expression "Roser for en Ko":

The learned man – the main character in Andersen's tale – is very frustrated and Hans Christian Andersen describes it like this in the Danish text:

> hvad han talte om det Sande og det Gode og det Skjønne, det var for de Fleste ligesom Roser for en Ko!

Reuscher again translated very close to the Danish original:

> was er über das Wahre und das Gute und das Schöne sagte, das war für die Meisten gerade wie die Rosen für eine Kuh!

But Andersen apparently accepted a change of his own expressions, so Lorck has it differently:

> was er von dem Wahren, dem Guten und dem Schönen sprach: das war den meisten, **was die Muskatnuß** der Kuh.

> [what he told about the true, the good and the beautiful: that was to most as **nutmeg** to a cow.]

Dulcken followed:

> what he said of the true and the good and the beautiful was as little valued by most people **as a nutmeg would be by a cow**.

Mrs. Paull also translated the German expression, but she was more free and changed the order of "the true, the good and the beautiful":

> what he said about the good, the beautiful, and the true, was of as much value to most people as a nutmeg would be to a cow.

Again it seems to me as very likely that both Dulcken and Mrs. Paull worked not from the Danish original, but from the Lorck-translation.

From the letters written by Hans Christian Andersen to Lorck, it is clear that Lorck often criticized Andersen for not being clear enough. Maybe this is why the German version contains more explanations than the Danish one. Here is an example:

> Der blev saa levende oppe og nede. Skomagere og Skræddere, alle Folk fløttede ud paa Gaden

> dann war es lebhaft unten und oben; unten **setzten sich** Schuster und Schneider, **worunter man alle Leute versteht** – auf die Straße hinaus.

Dulcken followed:

> then it became lively above and below; the tinkers and tailors – **by which we mean all kinds of people** – sat below in the street.

The Lorck-version also sometimes deleted details:

der blev Liig begravede med Psalmesang, **Gadedrengene skjød med Troldkjællinger**, og Kirkeklokkerne ringede

Leichen wurden begraben mit Gesang: die Kirchenglocken läuteten

Dulcken followed:

dead people were buried with solemn songs; the church bells rang

Andersen also sometimes accepted an adaptation of the style to the new context:

"Hvorledes saae der ud i de inderste Sale?" spurgte den lærde Mand. "Var der som i den friske Skov? Var der som i en hellig Kirke? Vare Salene som den stjerneklare Himmel, naar man staaer paa de høie Bjerge?"

"Wie sah es **denn** in den inneren **Gemächern** aus?" fragte der gelehrte Mann. "War es dort wie in dem **kühlen Haine**? War es dort wie in einem heiligen **Tempel**? Waren **die Gemächer** wie der sternenhelle Himmel, wenn man auf den hohen Bergen steht?"

To change the expressions *friske skov* (fresh forest) into *kühlen Hain* (cool grave) and *kirke* (church) into *Tempel* (temple) – I think – is related to the vocabulary used in the German romantic period, which Andersen knew very well from his many German poet friends.
Again, the British translator Dulcken followed the German version:

"How did things look in the inner room?" asked the learned man. "Was it there as in **a cool grave**? Was it there like as in a holy **temple**? Were the chambers like a starry sky, when one stands on the high mountain?"

Summing-up

In order to sum up the Andersen-Lorck adaptation of the fairy tale "Skyggen" to German culture, we see a difference between demand of formal equivalence from the translators and the freedom to add, delete and change elements in his own works, apparently accepted in the authorized Lorck-version. Probably, Andersen himself intends to create a dynamic equivalence, which makes his tales as tailored to the new countries as they were in Denmark.

It is interesting to see that the popular English translation of Hans Christian Andersen's fairy tales still depends on the adaptations of Andersen's German version of the fairy tales, whereas the researchers have forgotten Andersen's German way to the English readers.

Translation Problems for the Old British Translators

As we have seen, Dulcken and Mrs. Paull follow the original German Andersen-Lorck text closely, – but in some cases, the English differs from German which creates difficulties for the British translators.

In "Skyggen" the mode of address plays a very central role. In the beginning of the text, the man addresses his shadow as "du", and when the shadow comes to visit the man the first time, the conversation is asymmetric. The shadow addresses the man in the formal manner as "De", and the man uses "du".

> "sid ned, gamle Ven og fortæl mig bare lidt om hvorledes det er gaaet til, og hvad **Du** saae ovre hos Gjenboens, der i de varme Lande" –
>
> "Ja, det skal jeg fortælle **Dem**," sagde Skyggen og satte sig ned, "men saa maa **De** ogsaa love mig, at **De** aldrig til Nogen her i Byen, hvor **De** endogsaa træffer mig, siger at jeg har været **Deres** Skygge! jeg har isinde at forlove mig; jeg kan føde mere end een Familie!"

In the Lorck edition, this is translated into German without any problems:

> "Setze **dich** nieder, alter Freund, und erzähle mir doch ein wenig, wie das zugegangen ist und was **du** dort in den warmen Ländern, in dem uns gegenüberliegenden Hause sahst!"
>
> "Ja, das will ich **Ihnen** erzählen", sagte der Schatten und setzte sich, "aber dann müssen **Sie** mir versprechen, daß **Sie** niemals ir-

gend jemand hier in der Stadt, wo **Sie** mich auch antreffen sollten, es sagen wollen, daß ich **Ihr** Schatten gewesen bin!"

As the conversation develops, the shadow protests against the conversation form, and the man accepts the suggestion to address each other at the same level:

"og jeg skal fortælle Dem det, men, – det er slet ingen Stolthed af mig, men – som Fri og med de Kundskaber jeg har, ikke at tale om min gode Stilling, mine fortræffelige Omstændigheder, – saa ønskede jeg gjerne at de vilde sige De til mig!"
"Om Forladelse!" sagde den lærde Mand, "det er gammel Vane, som sidder fast! – De har fuldkommen Ret! og jeg skal huske det! men nu fortæller De mig Alt hvad De saae!"

Again, the German version is very close to the Danish original:

"Und das will ich Ihnen erzählen, aber – es ist wahrlich nicht Stolz von meiner Seite – als freier Mann und bei den Kenntnissen, die ich besitze, abgerechnet meine gute Stellung und meine ausgezeichneten Vermögensverhältnissen, wünschte ich doch, dass **Sie** "Sie" zu mir sagen möchten."
"Bitte um Verzeihung, " sagte der gelehrte Mann; "Das "**du**" ist eine alte Gewohnheit, und solche legt man schwer ab. **Sie** haben vollkommen recht, und ich will daran denken. Aber nun erzählen **Sie** mir alles, was **Sie** sahen."

After this the man and his shadow address each other with "De"/ "Sie" for a while, but then the man suggests a more informal conversation form:

"da vi nu saaledes ere blevne Reisekammerater, som vi er det og vi tillige ere voxne op fra Barndommen sammen, skulle vi saa ikke drikke Duus, det er dog mere fortroligt!"

The Danish expression "at drikke dus" has no direct, formal equivalent in German, but the Andersen-Lorck translation again chooses the dynamic equivalence and uses the German expression "Brüderschaft trinken", which refers to a German tradition.

> "Da wir nun auf solche Weise Reisekameraden geworden und zugleich von Kindesbeinen an miteinander aufgewachsen sind, wollen wir da nicht **Brüderschaft trinken**? Das Du klingt doch vertraulicher!"

This is an important point in the fairy tale. The shadow does not want the man to use the informal way of address – but he is willing to use the informal way of addressing the man. In this way, the original asymmetric way of addressing each other is changed totally, and it shows clearly the change in the power relations between the man and the shadow. After this point, the shadow is the master of the two.

The change between the informal and the formal modes of address works well in Danish as well as in German, but it was difficult for the translator to find an equivalent way of expressing this in English.

Dulcken tried with the informal *thou* and the formal *you*. He lets the shadow ask the man:

"And what didst **thou** see then?"

The man protests:

"I wish **you** would say **you** to me."

Dulcken was, however, not consistent in this matter. He did not form sentences with *thou,* and as regards "Brüderschaft trinken", he gave up finding an adequate solution and added a note:

> "As we have in this way become travelling companions, and have also from childhood's days grown up with one another, shall we not drink brotherhood? That sounds more confidential. [...]
> You see that this is a feeling, not pride. I cannot let you say "**thou**"[1] to me; but I will gladly say "thou" to you; and thus **your** wish will be at any rate partly fulfilled.
> [1] On the Continent, people who have drunk "brotherhood" address each other as "thou", in preference to the more ceremonious "you"."

Dulcken's solution is not optimal, but Mrs. Paull's is not better:

> One day the master said to the shadow, "We have grown up together from our childhood, and now that we have become travel-

ling companions, shall we not drink to our good fellowship, and say **thee** and **thou** to each other?

Mrs. Paull avoided the note, but the expression to "say thee and thou to each other" does not function well.

Hans Christian Andersen Translations Today

All the modern translators translate from the original Danish version of Hans Christian Andersen's tales – maybe with a glance at the former translations.

The Danish born Hollywood-actor Jean Hersholt[25] is the first to find a pragmatic way of solving the "De/du"-problem. He wanted his translations to function as a work that all American children might understand with no help of footnotes or parental explanations and he used the English expression "old friend" for symmetry, "first names" and the English way of showing distance by using "Sir".

The shadow's protest is changed from

"saa ønskede jeg gjerne at **De** vilde sige **De** til mig!"

to

"I do wish you wouldn't call me **your old friend**."

And the learned man answers the shadow:

"You are perfectly right, my dear **sir**, and I'll remember it. But now, my dear **sir**, tell me of all that you saw."

Later he uses the firm "first name" to indicate the familiar way of speaking:

"As we are now fellow-travellers and have grown up together, shall we not call each other by our **first names,** the way good companions should? It is much more intimate."

And the shadow answers:

"I cannot let you call me by my first name, but I shall be glad to call you by yours, as a compromise. So thereafter the shadow called his one-time master by his **first name**."

Jean Hersholt's way of changing the focus from the original text and emphasizing that the fairy tale should be used in direct readings to American children without any kind of footnotes or explanations worked brilliantly. Hersholt's translations were a great success and won many important American friends, for example Walt Disney, who first made a version of "Den grimme Ælling" that inspired him to create his famous Donald Duck, and later made "Den lille Havfrue" famous all over the world.

No matter how successful Jean Hersholt's translations were, they did not totally match the linguistic ideals of translation which appears to have been essential to the British translator Richard Prescott Keigwin,[26] who worked very closely together with the Danish professor and Andersen expert Elias Bredsdorff. Keigwin and Bredsdorff's translation puts a special emphasis on bringing all of the details in Andersen's work correctly over into English.

Keigwin and Bredsdorff go a bit further in their pragmatic translation. They give up looking for specific words to solve the "du"/ "De"-problem and use expressions of content.

> "I should be much obliged if you would address me **with rather more respect**."
>
> Seeing that we now travel together as equals like this and that we also grew up from childhood together, oughtn't we to pledge ourselves in a **toast of friendship? It would be so much more sociable**.
>
> So, although I can't allow you to **be familiar** with me, I am quite willing to meet you halfway and myself to be familiar with you."
>
> It really is a big steep, thought the learned man that I have to call him '**Sir**', while he can call me what he likes. Still, he had to put up with it."

In 1964, Keigwin was awarded the Hans Christian Andersen medal by the Andersen Society. His tales are published by the Danish publishers Høst og Søn,[27] and this translation is recommended by and sold at the Hans Christian Andersen Museum in Odense.

Reginald Spink was a British journalist living in Denmark. His *Hans Christian Andersen Fairy Tales*,[28] has been printed in a very beautiful edition and is today sold as a souvenir by the Royal Danish Library.

Reginald Spink is very close to Keigwin, but he chooses the term "Christian name" instead of "first name". The term "Christian name" might not be appropriate here. Hans Christian Andersen describes the shadow as an evil creature and leaves it to the readers to associate him with the devil or not.

Sven H. Rossel is a Danish scholar of literature who has lived for many years in America. In cooperation with Patricia Conroy, a professor of Scandinavian Studies at the University of Washington, he published *Tales and Stories by Hans Christian Andersen* in 1980.[29]

Patricia Conroy and Sven H. Rossel follow the others – and avoid the term "Christian name":

> "I do wish you would call me by **my last name**."
>
> "Since we're now travelling companions, and we've likewise grown up together from childhood, why shouldn't we use each other's **first names**? It sounds so much more **familiar**."
>
> "I get exactly the same feeling when I hear you **use my first name**. I feel as if I were pressed down to the ground – reduced to my former position with you. You see, it's a question of feeling, not pride. I can't let you use my first name with me, but I could easily call you by yours, so half of your wish will be fulfilled."
>
> "And so the shadow called its former master by **his first name**."

Erik Christian Haugaard[30] is a bilingual Danish-American children's book writer, and his *The Complete Fairy Tales and Stories* is – as we shall see – a very free recreation of Andersen's work. Haugaard's translation has been published again by the Danish publishing house Gyldendal to mark the bicentennial of Andersen's birth.

Tiina Nunnally[31] is an American translator of Danish litterature. Her *Hans Christian Andersen Fairy Tales* was published by Penguin Books in 2004.

Also Tiina Nunnally takes over the use of "Sir" and elaborates on the idea of using names, so that the shadow also gets a last name:

> "I would appreciate if you would address me **in the formal manner**!"
>
> "Now that we've become travelling companions, as we have, and since we've also grown up together since childhood, shouldn't

we **drink a toast** and call each other by our **first names**? That would be much more friendly?"

"Things have certainly gone too far," the learned man thought, "when I have to use his **last name** while he calls me by my **first.** But he had to put up with it."

Finally, the American publishing house Granta Books, published a new version of Andersen's tales in 2004, also translated from Danish: *The Stories of Hans Christian Andersen,* translated by Diana Crone Frank and Jeffrey Frank.[32] Jeffrey Frank is an American author of three novels, and Diana Crone Frank is his Danish-born wife. Their translation was published in the United States and England to mark the bicentenary of Andersen's birth.

Also the two new translations by Frank and Frank and Tiina Nunnally use the "sir solution", but Frank and Frank seem unsure, whether "sir" is appropriate today:

"I'd really appreciate it if you would address me formally, as '**sir**' or '**mister**' [...] "shouldn't we stop being so formal? After all, it's friendlier not to keep saying '**sir**'".
"I can't let you call me by my **first name**, but I'll be happy to use yours – then we are halfway there."

In this case, the pragmatic translation of "du"/"De" seems to work much better than the older word for word translations.

Modern Individualism

It is obvious that the situation of the translators has changed since Andersen's days. At that time, a translator did not always get his name on the books, and he had to translate exactly what the author had written. Today the names of the translators are sometimes even on the front page of the book – and the publishing houses mark the new Andersen translations by printing the names of the translators.

The translators are much more free and much more individual today. A simple counting of the number of words used in the translation of "Skyggen" shows that some of the translators add quite a few new words.

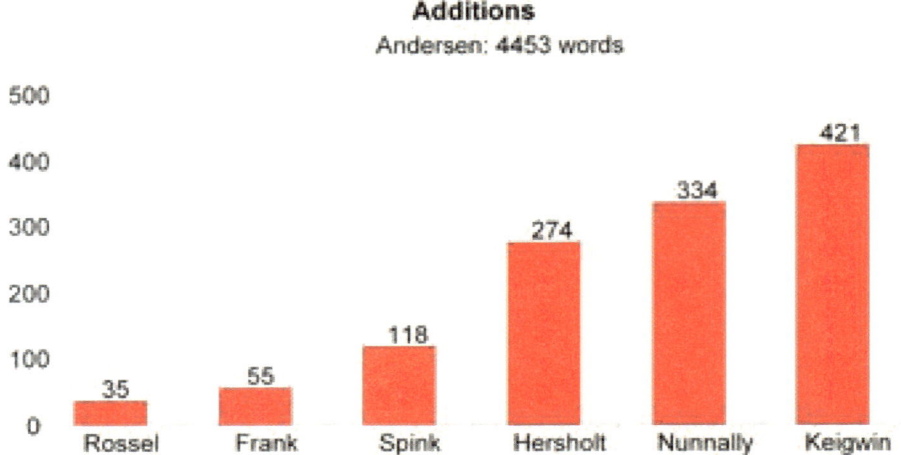

The translators Rossel/Conroy and Frank/Frank are quite close to the number of words in the original text, whereas Tiina Nunnally and Keigwin add about 8-10 percent more words to the original text.

An example of this is the expression "Roser for en Ko" in Andersen's original Danish text.

All the modern translators translate directly from the Danish text, but they tend to elaborate on the expression:

> what he said about truth, beauty, and goodness was as **appealing** to most people **as roses would be to a cow**. (Frank)
> what he said about the true and the good and the beautiful that was as for most people **like casting roses at the feet of a cow**. (Rossel)

> what he had to say about truth, goodness, and the beauty was to most people **like offering roses to a cow**! (Spink)

> what he had to say about the good, the true, and the beautiful, **appealed** to most people about as much **as roses appeal to a cow**. (Hersholt)

> what he said about the true and the good and the beautiful, was for most people **like tossing roses to a cow**. (Nunnally)

> his ideas about the true and the good and the beautiful were to most people **about as attractive as roses to a cow**. (Keigwin)

The variation is relatively big – the translators seem to try to make Andersen's text clearer – and none of them choose the simple way of translating "som Roser for en Ko" by "like roses to a cow", which would be quite as acceptable in English as in Danish.

Ambiguity

In "Skyggen", Hans Christian Andersen creates a lot of ambiguity. Is it true that the shadow can change into a man? Does the princess really marry the shadow? Does the man actually die?

To compound this ambiguity, Andersen uses the words "virkelig" eight times, "rigtig" seven times and "sand" four times.

In the German version, Andersen translates the Danish word "virkelig" as "wirklich", and Dulcken follows literally. Let us look at four examples.

In the first one, the word "virkeligt" is used by the man concerning the heat in Italy:

"det var **virkeligt** ikke til at holde ud!"
"es war **wirklich** unerträglich!" (Lorck)
"it was **really** unbearable!" (Dulcken)

The translators Keigwin, Rossel and Frank also follow:

"it was **really** more that one could stand." (Keigwin)
"It was **really** unbearable!" (Rossel)
"It was **really** unbearable!" (Frank)

But Hersholt, Spink and Nunnally choose other solutions:

"– unbearably!" (Hersholt)
"It was **simply** unbearable!" (Spink)
"It was **truly quite** unbearable!" (Nunnally)

In my second example, "virkelig" is used to state that the shadow has disappeared:

"jeg har jo ingen Skygge! saa er den **virkelig** gaaet i Aftes"
"So ist er also **wirklich** gestern abend fortgegangen" (Lorck)

Again Dulcken follows:

"So it **really** went away yesterday evening" (Dulcken)

And so does the big group of modern translators:

"So it **really** did go away last night" (Hersholt)
"Then it **really** did go off last night" (Keigwin)
"So, it **really** must have gone yesterday evening" (Rossel)
"So it **really** must have gone over there last night" (Nunnally)

But two of them, Spink and Frank, differ:

"Then it did go last night, and it hasn't returned." (Spink)
"So it **actually** did leave me last night and didn't come back." (Frank)

In the third example, Andersen uses "virkelig" in a quotation of what people say to the man:

"De seer **virkelig** ud ligesom en Skygge!" sagde Folk til ham
"Sie sehen **wirklich** aus wie ein Schatten!" sagten die Leute zu ihm (Lorck)

Again, Dulcken literally follows Andersen:

"You **really** look like a shadow" (Dulcken)

And so does Hersholt and Frank:

"You **really** look like a shadow," (Hersholt)
"You **really** look like a shadow," (Frank)

But Spink, Keigwin and Nunnally find other solutions:

"You look **just** like a shadow!" (Spink)
"Why, to look at, you're **no more than** a shadow!" (Keigwin)
"You look like a shadow **of yourself**," (Nunnally)

And Rossel deletes it:

"You look like a shadow!" (Rossel)

In my last example, Andersen lets the princess use the word "virkelig" when she is considering whether she had recovered from her sickness, which was that she was able to see much too clearly:

> "Hvad?" tænkte Prindsessen, "skulde jeg **virkelig** være kommet mig!"
> "Wie?" **sagte** die Prinzessin, "sollte ich mich **wirklich** erholt haben?" (Lorck)

Dulcken, Keigwin, Spink, Frank and Hersholt follow:

> "How!" said the Princess; "can I **really** have been cured?" (Dulcken)
> "Heavens!" thought the Princess. "Have I **really** been cured?" (Keigwin)
> "What?" said the princess. "Can I **really** have recovered?" (Spink)
> "**Really?** the princess thought. Am I **really** cured?" (Frank)
> "My!" the Princess thought. "Can I **really** be cured?" (Hersholt)

But Rossel and Nunnally seek other solutions:

> "What?" thought the princess. "Am I **actually** recovered?" (Rossel)
> "What?" thought the princess. "Is it **true** that I've **actually** recovered?" (Nunnally)

It is obvious that Andersen with the repeated use of "virkelig", ironically underlines the aspect of unreality in the text. Of course, it would have been possible in Danish to use synonym expressions like *i virkeligheden, faktisk* or *rigtigt,* but Andersen chooses in the Danish text, as well as in the German translation corrected by himself to repeat the words "virkelig" ("wirklich"). The old translator Dulcken interprets the word literally as "really" every time and obtains the same effect as Andersen, but three out of four times the modern translators Tiina Nunnally and Reginald Spink prefer the dynamic equivalence and use synonym expressions, even if it was actually possible to translate directly. All the modern translators use the concept of dynamic equivalence, but as we see in this example this concept moves the emphasis from the author's original text towards the individual feelings of the translator. If the translator has not understood Andersen's intention by repeating the word "virkelig", this stylistic feature is simply lost in the translations.

Political Correctness

At Andersen's time, people from different continents were considered exotic. In 1843, Copenhagen opened the amusement park Tivoli, which Andersen visited quite often. The most popular attractions were animals like elephants, lions, tigers, jackals and wolves in cages. Twice, parades with people from Arabic and African regions were organized.

The Nubean Caravan in 1878

In several fairy tales, Andersen uses the fascination of people from different continents, and also "Skyggen" has an element of this fascination. In the beginning of the tale, Andersen wrote:

> **I de hede Lande, der** kan rigtignok Solen brænde! Folk blive ganske mahognibrune; ja i de allerhedeste Lande **brændes de til Negre**

> **In the hot countries** the sun burns very strongly; there the people become quite mahogany brown, and in the very hottest countries they are **even burned into negroes**. (Dulcken)

> **In very hot climates**, where the heat of the sun has great power, people are usually as brown as mahogany; and in the hottest countries they **are negroes, with black skins**. (Paull)

Today, the word "negro" is a problem, and Andersen's deliberately naive joke is simply deleted:

> In the hot countries the sun really burns. People get as brown as mahogany, and in the hottest countries they **get burned black.** (Frank)

> In the hot countries the sun is certainly scorching! People turn as brown as mahogany. Why, in the hottest countries of all **they're even baked black.** (Nunnally)

The Danish-born translator Erik Haugaard, almost takes over the role of the author:

> **On the shores of the Mediterranean** the sun really **knows** how to shine. It is so powerful that it tans the people a mahogany brown; and the young scholar who came from the north, **where all the people are as white as bakers' apprentices, soon learned to regard his old friend with suspicion**.

Status of the Translations of Andersen Today

The tendency to adapt Andersen's tales to the political climate today, fits well the ideal of the dynamic equivalence of the translation, but might seem to be contradictory when Diane Crone Frank and Jeffrey Frank have a note from the famous American showman Garrison Keillor on their front page:

> This is the **real Andersen**, restored to life.

In their foreword, they express their project:

> In translating Andersen, we aimed to be **faithful** to the Danish text and his distinctly colloquial voice, **which was often lost in the Victorian language of earlier versions**.

Tiina Nunnally is even more critical in her "Translator's Note":

> I was introduced to the stories of Hans Christian Andersen long before I learned Danish and discovered **how poorly** the previous English translations have represented his work.

As I have shown in this paper, these "poor" translations are not so poor – but they are based on the German original, and not on the Danish. They tend to translate Andersen according to the idea of formal equivalence whereas the modern translators prefer the dynamic equivalence and tend to be very free – maybe even too free – in their individual way of interpreting Andersen's words and phrases. The modern translators do not like the Victorian way of changing Andersen – but their own way of acting politically correct is also a way of adapting that is worth discussing.

Literature

H.C. Andersen's Märchen. Aus dem Dänischen übertragen von Julius Reuscher. Mit Federzeichnungen von Theodor Hosemann. Berlin: M. Simion, 1848, 1851

Gesammelte Märchen von H.C. Andersen. Deutsche vom Verfasser besorgte Original-Ausgabe, Verlag von L. Wiedemann 1948

Aus Herz und Welt von H.C. Andersen. Deutsche vom Verfasser besorgte Original-Ausgabe, Verlag von L. Wiedemann, 1860

Andersen: *Sämtliche Märchen.* Herausgegeben und eingeleitet von Leopold Magon, Dietrich'sche Verlagsbuchhandlung zu Leipzig, 1953.

H.W. Dulcken: *Fairy Tales and Stories by Hans Christian Andersen.* Routledge, 1864-89; Wordsworth, 1997, Chancellor, 2002

Mrs. Henry B. Paull: *Hans Christian Andersen's Fairy Tales.* 1869

The Modern American and British Translators

Jean Hersholt (1886-1956) was a Danish actor living in Hollywood. He made a lot of readings of Hans Christian Andersen's tales and for this purpose he made a new translation directly from Danish, but also with an eye in the previous translations – but he put a special emphasis on the oral style of the tales. He wanted the tales to be successful on stage. And he had a lot of success and he was the one to make the American actor Danny Kaye (Wonderful, wonderful, Copenhagen) and Walt Disney (Walt Disney first made a small film on The Ugly Duckling, and then he got so interested in this little duck that he invented his own Donald Duck) interested in Andersen's tales.

Jean Hersholt's translations are chosen as the English translation of the collected fairy tales on the homepage of The Hans Christian Andersen Centre in Odense.

Jean Hersholt: *The Complete Andersen,* Heritage Press, 1942-47, CWR Publishing 2005.

Richard Prescott Keigwin (1883-1972) was a British translator who worked very closely with the Danish professor and Andersen-expert Elias Bredsdorff. Keigwin and Bredsdorff's translation has a special emphasis on bringing all details in Andersen's work correctly over into English. In 1964, Keigwin got the Hans Christian Andersen medal by the Danish Andersen-society. Keigwin's translations are recommended and sold at the Hans Christian Andersen Museum in Odense.

K.P. Keigwin: *Hans Christian Andersen 80 Fairy Tales,* 1950, Høst & Søn, 2004.

Reginald Spink was a British journalist living in Denmark. His translations have been printed in a very beautiful edition and is today sold as a souvenir by the Royal Danish Library. Spink has also published a book about Andersen: *Hans Christian Andersen and His World,* Thames and Hudson, 1972.

Reginald Spink: *Hans Christian Andersen Fairy Tales,* Everyman's Library, Knopf, 1960, 1992.

Patricia Conroy and Sven H. Rossel are two translators with academic background. Patricia Conroy is professor at the Department of Scandinavian Studies, University of Washington, and Sven H. Rossel is professor of Scandinavian Studies in Vienna.

Patricia Conroy and Sven H. Rossel: *Tales and Stories by H.C. Andersen*, University of Washington Press, Seattle and London 1980.

Erik Christian Haugaard is a bilingual Danish-American children's-book writer, and his translations were first published in America, 1974. Erik Christian Haugaard's translation has been published again with illustrattions by a Danish illustrator by the Danish publishing house Gyldendal to mark the bicentenary of Hans Christian Andersen's birth.

Erik Christian Haugaard: *The Complete Fairy Tales and Stories,* Doubleday 1974, and Gyldendal 2005.

Tiina Nunnally is an American translator of Danish literature. Her translations of Andersen's tales were first published in America 2004 and in England 2005. *Hans Christian Andersen Fairy Tales*, was published by Penguin Books, 2004, 2005.

Tiina Nunnally: *Hans Christian Andersen Fairy Tales*, Penguin Books, 2004, 2005.

Diana Crone and Jeffrey Frank are a Danish-American couple. He is a writer, and his wife grew up in Denmark. Together they have made a collection of fairy tales to mark the bicentenary of Hans Christian Andersen's birth.

Diana Crone Frank and Jeffrey Frank: *The Stories of Hans Christian Andersen*, Granta Books 2004.

Notes

1. Viggo Hjørnager Pedersen: *Ugly Ducklings? Studies in the English Translations of Hans Christian Andersen's Tales and Stories*, 2004.
2. Elias Bredsdorff: *Hans Christian Andersen and England*, 1954.
3. Translations by Charles Boner, Caroline Peachey, Meta Taylor, Charles Beckwith Lohmeier, Madame de Chatelain, Anne S. Bushby, Alfred Wehnert, Augusta Plesner, Carl Sievers, A. Gardiner, H. Oscar Sommer, R. Nisbet Bain, W. Angeldorff, Mrs. Edgar Lucas, H.L. Bækstad, W.A. and J.K. Craigie, M.R. James and Paul Leyssac.
4. *The Complete Illustrated Stories of Hans Christian Andersen*, Chancellor Press.
5. Hans Christian Andersen, *The Complete Fairy Tales*, illustrated throughout, from Wordsworth.
6. *The Complete Hans Christian Andersen Fairy Tales*, from Avenel Books.
7. Viggo Hjørnager Pedersen, p. 166.
8. Here from Viggo Hjørnager Pedersen, p. 185.
9. Ivy York Möller-Christensen in her *Den gyldne trekant. H.C. Andersens gennembrud i Tyskland 1831-1850* writes: "Og når drengen spillede komedie med sine dukker, foregik det på et morsomt kaudervælsk, der var en efterligning af det sprog, han havde hørt på teatret. Dette kuriøse tidlige møde med tysk kultur blev fulgt op af en levende interesse hos den unge mand for det, der rørte sig i nabolandets litteratur. I skoletiden læste han Heinrich Heine og E.T.A. Hoffmann. Disse to digtere gik ham – sammen med Walter Scott – formelig 'i Blodet'. Hans poesibog fra Slagelse- og Helsingør-tiden viser, at over to tredjedele af afskrifterne stammer fra tyske digtere som Goethe, Schiller, Jean Paul, Wieland, Tieck, Gellert og Lessing – og selvfølgelig Heine og Hoffmann." (p. 57)
10. The use of the Danish translation "se sig i stand til" with "sich im Stande sehen" instead of "sich in der Lage sehen" is not optimal.
11. Frank Hugus: "H.C. Andersen Adapts Eugéne Scribe for the Danish Stage", in *H.C. Andersen. Old Problems and New Readings*, The Hans Christian Andersen Center, the University Press of Southern Denmark, 2004.
12. *Der Diamant des Geisterkönigs* by Ferdinand Raimund (1849), *Der Sonnwendhof* by Simon Mosenthal (1855) and *Der Rothmantel* by August von Kotzebue (1964).
13. H. Topsøe-Jensen: *H.C. Andersens Breve til Carl B. Lorck*, Odense Bys Museer, 1969, p. 26
14. § 2 in the contract.
15. Eugene A. Nida: *Toward a Science of Translating*, Leiden: E.J. Brill, 1964.
16. Andersen was very serious about this text. As Lorck 1855 dropped the publishing house and T. Wiedemann, one of his employees, took over, Andersen wrote to him: "Vil De dernæst bede ham om at der paa Bogen ikke sættes, 'af Forfatteren besørget Udgave', men at der staar ligefrem: Dryaden et Eventyr fra Udstillingstiden i Paris af H.C. Andersen (eller efter H.C. Andersen)."
17. The first international agreement on copyright, the so-called Berner Convention, was established 1886 and accepted by Denmark as late as 1903.

18. From a letter to Lorck 2.12.1868.
19. C.A. Reitzel is Andersen's Danish publisher.
20. *H.C. Andersens Breve til Carl B. Lorck*, ved H. Topsøe-Jensen, udgivet af Odense Bys Museer, 1969, pp. 86-87.
21. This also has a background in the German copyright at that time.
22. The book was published without printing year, and according to Ivy York Möller-Christensen there has been some discussion whether the book was printed 1848 or 1849.
23. Dulcken's and Paull's translations are the most sold Andersen translations in the USA and England, e.g. by Chancellor Press (1984, 2001), Worthworth (1997), and Avenel Books (1984).
24. Mrs. Paull's translation of Grimm's Tales was published 1872.
25. Jean Hersholt, see p. 27.
26. Reginald Keigwin, see p. 28.
27. Latest edition 2004.
28. Reginald Spink: *Hans Christian Andersen Fairy Tales*. Everyman's Library, Knopf, 1960, 1992.
29. Patricia L. Conroy & Sven H. Rossel: *Tales and Stories by Hans Christian Andersen*, University of Washington Press, 1980, 2004.
30. Hans Christian Andersen: *The Complete Fairy Tales and Stories*, Doubleday, 1974, and Gyldendal, 2005.
31. Tiina Nunnally: *Hans Christian Andersen Fairy Tales*, Penguin Books, 2004.
32. Diana Crone Frank and Jeffrey Frank: *The Stories of Hans Christian Andersen*, Granta Books, 2004.

Hans Christian Andersen and His First Romanian Translators

Anca Dumitrescu

The world-known Danish writer H.C. Andersen is mainly famous for his stories and fairy tales addressing children, but also other age groups who get enchanted by their freshness, wisdom, and power to amuse. Full of fantasy and colour these literary works are based on Danish or universal folk themes, much enriched by H.C. Andersen, or they are entirely created by their author so skilful in giving life to the most unexpected objects and plants, such as: the fir tree, the pen and the inkstand, the pea, the flax, tin soldiers, the snowman. This great Danish magician was also very gifted at endowing with human traits certain birds and animals (e.g. the ugly duckling, the swans, the snail) or insects (the butterfly).

Few years after having been printed in Denmark, Andersen's fairy tales got translated in Germany (in many editions), in England (4 volumes of fairy tales in 1846), in the USA (1846/1847), in France (2 volumes in 1848 and 3 volumes in 1853), etc. Unfortunately, in Romania, Andersen's work started to become known rather late and it hasn't been completely translated yet.

Our poet Gheorghe Asachi from Moldova made the first translation from H.C. Andersen's work using a French version. It was the poem "The March Violet" that happened to be issued in October 1841, the year when this outstanding Danish writer could see the Wallachian people and landscape during his trip on the Danube in Southern Romania. This first translated poem was printed in bilingual (French-Romanian) text in the review *Le graneur moldo-valaque (Spicuitorul moldo-român)* published in the Iași town. The translator didn't mention the author's name, but only the fact that this poem was "traduit du danois" (translated from Danish). Later on, G. Asachi included the Romanian version of Andersen's poem in the second edition of his volume *A Collection of Poems,* published in Iași, in 1854, without pointing out that this was a translation. Such a thing was rather usual during that epoque.

Only 33 years later on 15th September 1874 (according to our bibliographical information[1]) in Bucharest, in the final issue of the little known ephemeral literary publication, called "Collectiune Litteraria" ("Literary Collection") the first Romanian translation of a fairy tale written by H.C. Andersen was issued. It was the very popular fairy tale "The Emperor's New Clothes". Probably this anonymous translation was based on the German version, as the Romanian title was "Hainele cele noi ale Marelui Duce" – ("The Great Duke's New Clothes").

Our historical comparative research has to outline the post-1874 period as being better for the access of Andersen's work into the Romanian space, because the literary and daily press started eagerly to publish translations of the Danish writer's fairy tales from the French versions in old Romania from German versions in Transylvania. Examples of such reviews and newspapers are: *Femeia romana* ("The Romanian Woman"), Bucharest, 1878; *Revista literara si politica* ("The Literary and Political Review"), Bucharest, 1885; *Biblioteca nouă romană* (The New Romanian Library), Brasov, 1882; *Familia* ("The Family"), Budapest, 1875; etc. In these publications occurred a variety of Andersen's fairy tales and stories: "The Story of a Mother", "The Fir Tree", "The Hardy Tin Soldier", etc. Some of these translations were signed by important representatives of Romanian culture at the end of the 19th century: Moses Gaster (excerpts from *Picture Book Without Pictures*), Zamfir C. Arbore ("The Christmas Tree" issued in his own review *Amicul copiilor* ("The Children's Friend") in 1893), and Lazar P. Petrini ("The Story of a Mother" and "The Wild Swans").

In The New Romanian Library, the bi-monthly literary review led by Theohar Alexi in 1882, were issued the first biographical remarks about H.C. Andersen followed by the translation into Romanian of his story "The Steadfast Tin Soldier" ("Soldățelul de plumb").

We also have to mention that in 1886 in Sibiu No. 22, in *Tribuna* ("The Tribune") edited by the novelist Ioan Slavici "Scăpărătoarea" ("The Tinder-Box") by Andersen was published representing chronologically the first volume (in fact a 14-page booklet) printed in the Romanian language. Two similar booklets came up in 1887 in the collection *Biblioteca Scolarilor* ("The School Children's Library") founded in Brasov by N. I. Ciurcu (in No. 17 "O familie fericită" ("A Happy Family") was translated by a primary school teacher Ion Popivici and in No. 18 "Bunica evlavioasă" ("The Pious Grandmother") was translated by Ion Popescu, another primary school teacher.

The last part of this paper is focused on Dumitru Stăncescu, who in the 19th century made the most important quantitative and qualitative contribution to providing the Romanian readers with a significant range of Andersen's fairy tales and stories, so skilfully translated that even today, after more than one century, they can compete with other more recent Romanian translations of the respective fairy tales and stories.

Dumitru Stăncescu (1867–99) was a prolific publisher and translator as well as a fine novelist. He started his career 17 years old in 1883, publishing in Alexandru Macedonski's review *Liberatorul* ("The Liberator") his "True Stories" inspired by Romania's war for independence in 1877-78. Then, he collaborated with many reviews and journals of his time being highly appreciated for the valuable collections of folklore fairy tales considered the best in that epoch[2], after the ones by Petre Ispirescu (1830-87).[3]

His first volume of *Basme populare româneşti (Romanian Folk Fairy tales)* was published in 1885, with a foreword by Moses Gaster who warmly welcomed these "genuine, clear Romanian fairy tales" brought to light for the public at large by the young ambitious translator so much concerned with Romania's folklore values and old traditions.

In 1890 D. Stăncescu was in Liege (Belgium) to get his Doctor's Degree in Political and Administrative Sciences. Then he took the chance to go to Paris to listen to Prof. Emile Picot's lecture about the Romanian folk fairy tales (collected and translated into French by D. Stăncescu) delivered during his course of Romanian language at the School of Oriental Languages in Paris.

In 1892 D. Stăncescu published at Haimann Printing House in Bucharest his main volume of folk fairy tales entitled *Basme culese din gura poporului* ("Fairy Tales Collected from People's Mouth"). This was eulogically introduced to the readers by the Romanian historian Nicolae Iorga in The Time Journal. The other 3 volumes of folklore collections printed in 1893: *Cerbul de aur si alte povesti pentru copii*, ilustratii de pictorul Jiquidi ("The Golden Deer and Other Fairy Tales for Children", illustrated by the painter Jiquidi); *Alte povesti culese din popor* ("Other Fairy Tales Collected from People"); *Snoave* ("Folk Jokes") proved D. Stăncescu's steady commitment as a folklorist. It was no wonder that when this gifted translator approached H.C. Andersen's fairy tales, he was delighted and eagerly started to translate part of them into Romanian.

In 1894 he became the literary Director of Biblioteca pentru toti (The Library for All), being responsible for preparing and coordinating the issue of a new book collection. The first publication in this collection was a great success: the first volume with a series of stories and fairy tales by H.C. Andersen translated from French into Romanian by Dumitru Stăncescu[4] who addressed the readers in the foreword: "I haven't known until now that anything had been translated into Romanian from the creation of this author whose fame is universal and whose fairy tales have been translated into all languages. We launch the Book Collection "The Library for All" with Andersen, being sure that we can bring pleasure and favour to all Romanian readers in whose bookcases this Danish writer's volumes will be in the front row".

As all the 5000 copies of this newly-printed book were sold out in the summer of 1895, in the autumn of the same year, Carol Muller Publishing House had to print a new edition stylistically improved by Dumitru Stăncescu, again in 5000 copies. The Danish author's portrait was included in this second edition.

This hardworking young translator from foreign literatures was especially successful with children's stories and fairy tales, where he felt at his ease, having also a rich experience in writing collections of Romanian folk fairy tales, so full of fantasy and colour. We have to point out here Stăncescu's good initiative of including in the first volume a number of Andersen's fairy tales printed in Romanian exactly two decades after the Danish storyteller's death. Together with the enchanting fairy tale "Micuța Sirenă" ("The Little Mermaid"), one of those stories which Andersen himself was very fond of, the translator selected "Ib și Cristina" ("Ib and Christine"), a story with realistic details, taking place in a typically Danish landscape where fantastic elements are significant. Then also the nice story of "Bradul" ("The Fir Tree") with many moral points, which are, however, so cleverly suggested as to be quite unobtrusive, as well as "Condeiul și călimara" ("The Pen and the Inkstand").

A particularly difficult translation practice for Dumitru Stăncescu was the very much translated – at the end of that century – *Billedbog uden Billeder* (*Carte de chipuri fără chipuri*[5]) with its special charm and many incidences in the culture of Scandinavia, Germany and other parts of the world. The book was entirely translated from German by this gifted young Romanian in 1896 when he was 30 years. The access to the German version was facilitated by the mysterious Miss. X.Z. with whom he signed the respective translation and whose name we probably shall never know. On this book cover there was only the Jubilee number: *O sută (One Hundred)* that indicated the position of the book in Carol Muller Printing House Catalogue.

A third volume published at Librăria pentru toți (The Library for All) in 1895 was an anthology of various texts edited by the Literary Director Stăncescu with a view to offer it to the readers for Christmas days. This book included valuable literary pieces for children, as the Romanian version of Andersen's "Fetița cu chibrituri" ("The Little Match Girl") or "Iarna" ("Winter"), which is a lovely poem by our poet Vasile Alecsandri, "Despre pomul Crăciunului" ("About Christmas Three") written by the Romanian story teller Petre Ispirescu, and also other Christmas stories for adults.

Against the 19th century background Dumitru Stăncescu proved to be a very a good publisher and a prolific translator, without being a great writer. Despite his short life span of only 33 years (1866-99) he made the most numerous and best translations from foreign literatures in the second half of the 19th century. He approached different literary works written by well-known European writers. The climax of Stăncescu's activity in this respect was the series of translations in the collection Library for All, between 1895-98. In 4 years he managed to publish 22 volumes of successful translations valid until today.

Besides the foreign writers more or less known in Romania of his time, D. Stăncescu seemed to have developed a special calling for H.C. Andersen's fairy tales and stories. As the author of several collections of Romanian folk fairy tales and the first publisher of the 5 volumes: *Complete Works* by Ion Creangă (1837-90) that was Romania's national story-teller, this enthusiastic young scholar who could travel and study in Europe, managed to explore and understand the realm of the Danish author's fairy tales. He was the one who published the first volumes of translations from H.C. Andersen's work, which remained vivid and well appreciated after more than a century. Stăncescu's interest in the Danish writer's life and literary activity was reflected also in the relevant and detailed manner of writing in Romanian the first chronological table on H.C. Andersen. It was published in 1895 at the end of his first volume of translations from this outstanding Danish storyteller's work.

For more than 130 years, generations and generations of Romanian children sailing on imagination's seas together with this famous writer admired the brave tin soldier's deeds, watched full of emotion the little Gerda's trip through the snow kingdom, and enjoyed themselves for the revival of the 11 princes turned into swans. The children became sad hearing the little mermaid's sufferings, or they burst into tears at the little match girl's death.

Later on as adults, the Romanians get enchanted by the richness of images and descriptions, by the poetry, fantasy and realism of these fairy tales, and above all by the moving, deeply humane message conveyed in time and space worldwide.[6]

Notes

1 The Bibliography of the Romanian Literature Links with the Foreign Literatures in Periodicals between 1859-1918, Vol. I, Academia Printing House, Bucharest, 1988.
2. Dumitru Stăncescu, Romanian Folk Fairy Tales, Literary Review, Bucharest 1885; Fairy Tales Collected from People's Mouth, Haimann Printing House, Bucharest, 1892; The Golden Deer and Other Fairy tales for Children, Bucharest, 1893; Other Fairy tales Collected from People, Bucharest, 1893; Folk Jokes, Bucharest, 1893; Sitting by the Fireside, Folk Jokes and Fairy Tales, Carol Muller Printing House, Bucharest, 1895; Christmas Fairy tales (Selection and Translation by Dumitru Stăncescu), Carol Muller Printing House, Bucharest, 1895.
3. Petre Ispirescu, Fairy tales, The Romanian Peasant, Iași, 1862; Legends or the Romanians' Fairy Tales, Iași, 1872; Folk Jokes or Folk Stories, Iași, 1873; Romanian Fairy tales and French Fairy tales, Bucharest, 1877; The Legends or The Fairy tales of Romanians Collected from the People, Bucharest, 1882; Games and Toys for Children (Children's Folklore), Bucharest, 1885.
4. Andersen, Selected Fairy tales, translation by Dumitru Stăncescu, Carol Muller Printing House, Bucharest, summer 1892; Second Edition with the Author's portrait, autumn 1895.
5. Andersen, Carte de Chipuri fără Chipuri, translation by Miss X.Z. and Dumitru Stăncescu, Carol Muller Printing House, Bucharest, 1896.
6. See also: Dorothea Sasu-Timerman and Sv. Juel Møller, *Bidrag til H.C. Andersen Bibliografi*. vol. 4: *Værker af H.C. Andersen oversat til rumænsk*. Det kongelige Bibliotek, København 1972. 59 pp.

"Prenez garde aux enfants!" – Swedish Versions and Varieties of Hans Christian Andersen's Eventyr

Ivo Holmqvist

When a Swedish translation of some of Hans Christian Andersen's tales appeared in 1838, he was much pleased, as evident from an exuberant letter in December of that year to his confidante Henriette Hanck: "I Sverrig er udkommet en original Børnebog: "Lekkameraden", og tænk Dem, det er en Oversættelse af mine Eventyr"/ A first edition of a children's book has been published in Sweden: The Play Pal, and can you imagine: it is a translation of my tales! He obviously appreciated these versions by J.W. Liffman, headmaster in the city of Gävle north of Stockholm who printed them in his magazine *Lekkamraten* which had started appearing in that year, and which continued for five years. A good dozen years later, a slightly more blasé Andersen was less happy with translations being made between as closely related languages as Danish and Swedish, as seen in an 1851 letter to his Stockholm publisher Albert Bonnier who had asked for a postscript: "ønsker De et par Slutnings Ord, da skulle disse følge, dog maa jeg ogsaa deri sige, hvad jeg her ovenfor har sagt at jeg helst ønsker at Bøger ikke oversættes, mellem os Naboer." / If you would like a few concluding words, I will supply them, but then I have to state what I have said above, that I rather wouldn't have books translated between neighbours.

Fredrika Bremer, his novelist colleague and his close friend until her death in 1865, was of the opinion that Hans Christian Andersen's style ("De fint nuancerade egenheterna som finnas dels i språket dels i författarens sätt och lynne" / The finely nuanced peculiarities to be found both in the language, and in the author's manners and spirit) was untranslatable, basically: too much was lost when his tales were rendered into another language – his writing ought to be read in its original Danish. Reciprocal interscandinavian language understanding has had its many ups and downs. In Andersen's lifetime, the student guilds on either side of Öresund formed close links and met regularly ("studentskandinavismen"), only to collapse when confronted with the 1864 political realities of the German attack on South Jutland. The Second World War saw a second wave of brotherly and sisterly interscandinavian sentiments, but the post-war efforts to launch a specifically Nordic TV-channel came to nothing. It is to be hoped that the 21st century bridge across the Sound, Öresundsbron, will result in a third and more lasting era of a heightened language awareness between closely related nations, and a wide-spread general knowledge of Swedish in Denmark and Danish in Sweden. But translations will still be needed.

On the surface, Andersen's 1852 tale "Det er ganske vist!" ("It's Perfectly True!") is a simple story, seemingly offering few difficulties for the translator. But as will be demonstrated below, some instances in it have proven stumbling blocks for interpreters both into Swedish and into other languages. To a certain degree, these difficulties seem to arise from the fact that this is a story in which Andersen shows his double talk, his mastering the "double articulation" when addressing himself simultaneously to young readers (and listeners) and to adults. Especially outside Scandinavia, this has not always been appreciated, and thus the view of Andersen has had its limits, with critics reducing him to a writer solely for children.[1]

*

A whole range of successful – and less so – translators have rendered Hans Christian Andersen into Swedish over the years, from Liffman in 1838 until recent attempts in the 2005 jubilee year.[2] Some ten of them will be mentioned here, briefly. In 1852, an anonymous translator published *Sex nya sagor* by Andersen, one of them "Det är mycket säkert!" Another translator, the radical journalist Karl Henrik Rydberg (1820-1902) – not related to the more well-known Viktor Rydberg – was a dramatist, a columnist in *Aftonbladet* and *Dagens Nyheter*, and like Liffman a publisher of magazines in which Andersen's texts appeared. Karl Johan Backmann, five years his junior, died at not quite fifty years of age but had by then proven himself an able translator.[3] At the time of his death, his manuscript of Andersen's *Sagor och berättelser* was not quite finished. Six additional tales, added when the book was published in 1877, were translated by a young and enterprising man of letters who also took on American writers like Mark Twain and Bret Harte in his stride: August Strindberg (1849-1912).[4] Hugo Gyllander (1868-1955) was a poet and spiritualist, fondly remembered for his translations of fairy tales (Charles Perrault, the Brothers Grimm, Andersen) and of his many adaptations of world literature masterpieces – more often than not truncated – for children, published in his extremely successful series Barnbiblioteket Saga. As demonstrated below, his versions often show a clear pedagogic intent which is not always to be found in the original. Fredrik Böök (1883-1961) was for many years the leading critic in Sweden as well as an eminent literary scholar, and the author of a life of Andersen (1938, 1955; translated by George C. Schoolfield in 1962). His 1939 version of almost all of Andersen's tales tried to fill a gap: an up-to-date rendering into colloquial Swedish was missing, he asserted:

> Den som har gjort försöket att läsa sagorna för barn kan vitsorda att behovet verkligen finns. Inte därför att de tidigare översättningarna varit dåliga. Det finns förträffliga; men det finns ingen som återger levande svenskt talspråk.[5]

> Everyone who has tried to read the tales aloud to children knows that such a need exists. Not because the earlier translations were bad. There are some excellent ones; but none renders them in lively spoken Swedish.

His translation, in many ways admirable, was by its insistence on topical colloquialisms destined to wear badly with age. Einar Nerman (1888-1983), a well-known illustrator in an elegantly idiosyncratic art deco-style and the originator of the most widely reproduced of all Swedish art-works with a curious link to Andersen, the Solstickan box of matches,[6] translated and illustrated a handful of Andersen's tales, as did the prolific and eminently versatile Britt G. Hallqvist (1914-97) who found an easy match in Andersen. She met with more of a challenge when swedifying Shakespeare or T.S. Eliot's *Old Possum's Book of Practical Cats* (*De knepiga katternas bok*, 1949) – in which she showed her mastery of rhyme and meter. Three 20th century Swedish writers, finally, have translated the complete Hans Christian Andersen Eventyr cycle: Erik Asklund (1908-80) who made his debut as one of the 1930s vitalists and whose subsequent writings mainly centred on his native Stockholm; Åke Holmberg (1907-91) who was a brilliant stylist, as witnessed by his much-loved series on Ture Sventon, privatdetektiv (a mildly satirical take-off on Sherlock

Holmes), and Bengt Anderberg (b. 1920), poet, novelist (his *Kain* caused an uproar in 1948, on moral or rather immoral grounds), and columnist whose many years in Danish exile on the island of Bornholm helped him solve many of Andersen's linguistic intricacies.

*

"Det er ganske vist!", ("It's Perfectly True") written in the winter of 1852 and published in April of that year, varies a story well-known from Saxo's *Gesta Danorum*, Lafontaine's *Fables*, and English, French and German 16th and 17th century collections of anecdotes, and is reminiscent of Carsten Hauch's drama *Den hjemkomne Sømand*.[7] The originality of Andersen's tale thus does not lie in the story line, but in how it is told. The article on Andersen in *Nordisk Familjebok*, for many years the authoritative Swedish encyklopedia, underlines his originality, without neglecting his adherence to tradition:

> Men som sagoberättare erövrade han ett eget rike, där han står o-upphunnen. Han utvecklade här en egendomlig diktart i ett lika egendomligt språk, som uppstått ur barnens och allmogens tal. Icke sällan nyttjar A. något gammalt sagomotiv, tillhörande den märkvärdiga sagoskatt, vilken tyckes vara gemensam för hela den indoeuropeiska rasen, emedan samma sagor återfunnits från Hindostan [sic] till Island. Men A:s inbillningsförmåga ägde just den ursprunglighet i uppfattning och den poetiska naivitet, som i folkens barndom givit upphov åt dessa sagor. Därigenom blev det honom möjligt att i samma anda röra sig självskapande och fritt, icke endast till formen, utan även till innehållet. Hela människolivet med dess glädje och sorg, dess storhet och litenhet återspeglas i denna, i god mening, barnsliga fantasivärld, åt vilken alla tider och länder lämnat sceneri och färger, där allt lever och talar.[8]

But as a teller of fairy tales he conquered his own empire, where he is outstanding. Here he developed a peculiar way of writing in an equally peculiar language, with its roots in child and peasant language. Quite often A. makes use of an old fairy tale motif from the marvellous story treasure which seems to be a common inheritance for the Indoeuropean race, as the same tales have been found from Hindostan to Iceland. But A's imagination had just that original perception and that poetical naivety which in the youth of nations gave rise to these tales. Thus he was able to move freely and creatively in the same spirit, both in form and content. Human life in its entirety, with its happiness and sorrow, its grandure and pettiness, is reflected in this childish (in a positive sense) fantasy world which borrows scenery and colours from all times and nations, and in which everything is alive and speaking.

*

Vilhelm Pedersen's illustration to "Det er ganske vist!" shows a well-heeled man and an elegantly attired lady gossiping, with two witnesses whose curiosity clearly is aroused by what they happen to overhear. "Gossip" is also the title of one of Norman Rockwell's well-known covers for *The Saturday Evening Post*. It could well serve as an illustration of Hans Christian Andersen's "It's Perfectly True!" (the author himself was not always assured that illustrations were needed, at least not by other hands than his own). Rockwell shows a line of fifteen people, along which a rumour is spread fast, and distorted, as evident when the last person who is also the one who started the gossip hears what is complete news to her. She is as scandalized as are all the others – but the piece of gossip she finally hears obviously is far from the one she sent into the world. By the looks of the persons, the message is both enjoyable and spicy, but also well within the bounds of decorum – otherwise the picture could not have been used as cover for a magazine intended for a large middle class American readership, in support of strong and stable moral values.

Rockwell has a keen eye on how news is spread by word of mouth (halfway through the chain of gossipers, modern technique is made use of, via the telephone): the news is cast far and wide. It is quite apparent that sensationalism is part of the allure of news, in Rockwell's painting, in modern journalism, and in Andersen's tale. Hans Christian Andersen tells the same story in his concentrated tale, almost as efficiently and economically as in Norman Rockwell's illustration. "It is perfectly true!" can be read as a blue-print of how urban legends are constructed and spread: the sensational tidbits of a dreadful event, always in another part of town, is traded on by someone who has not seen it but who has it from an absolutely reliable and trustworthy source.

And thus the news is spread, from each pair of ears to the next with certain embellishments and distortions, snowballing on towards ever greater inaccuracy. Andersen's tale is also one of good manners in middle-class society, of how to behave properly, but it has an intriguing ambiguity: it warns of what will happen if you deviate from societal norms and if you break the firm regulations of respectability: shame and disgrace follow. It has the immediacy of spoken language, with a colloquial narrative voice – which makes it hard to translate even into closely related languages, of which more later – and it starts in medias res, when the rumour has already travelled far and wide. The first few lines are part of the narrative framework which is then resumed at the very end, with its mock morale.

The irony is obvious in the teller's voice (if we assume that we listen to Hans Christian Andersen) and his ironical stance towards society – the hen "lagde sine reglementerede Æg"; "hun var en respectabel Høne"/ "laid her eggs when they were due"; "she was a respectable hen, etc. "It's Perfectly true!" is a tantalizing catch phrase: we know already from the outset of the story that it has developed into something blatantly untrue. The tale is not just a comment on how sensationalism originates and propagates, the mechanisms on which the yellow press and tabloids thrive. It is also a comment on innocence and experience, and a mildy satirical observation of the workings of hypocrisy in a bourgeois society.

*

In his *The Art of Translation* 1957 (new and enlarged edition 1968), Theodore Savory gives a set of opposites, helpful to anyone interested in the process of literary translations. According to him, a translation must give the words of the original, or: give the ideas of the original; it should read like a translation, or: like an original work; it should read as a contemporary of the original, or: as a contemporary of the translator. It should not add to or omit from the original, or: sometimes add to or omit from the original. Illustration of all aspects can be found in the different Swedish versions of Andersen's tales.[9] In a close textual analysis of some Swedish translations of "The Emperor's New Clothes", Hans Holmberg has shown "the difficulty of grasping Andersen's special qualities as a writer, even in translations between closely related Scandinavian languages. His imagery can also be rendered more or less Andersenesque by the translators ..."[10]

And after these preliminaries, the text itself, in which even the opening line may cause some minor problems for the translator. The adjective in "Det er en frygtelig Historie!"/ "It is a horrible story" is rendered as "faslig" (1852, anon.), "förskräcklig" (1876-77, C.H. Rydberg), "ryslig" (c. 1900, Hugo Gyllander) and "förfärlig" (1939, Fredrik Böök), with different connotations and stylistic values (the same word – and the same variety among translators – can be found in the early story about "The Princess on the Pea": "En Aften blev det da et frygteligt Veir ...").

Three sentences in particular will cause some concern for the translators. The first one reads slightly odd in the original. In a clever way, it pinpoints the values of disregarding some news, if you want your peace of mind undisturbed: "Hun hørte og hun hørte ikke, som man jo skal i denne Verden, for at leve i sin gode Rolighed." Jean Hersholt translates this in a straightforward way: "She had heard and had not heard, as one should do in this world, if one wishes to live in peace." The German of L. Tronier Funder is more verbose but possibly also more elegant: "Es hörte halb, halb hörte es nicht, wie man es ja in dieser Welt handhaben soll, um seine Gemütsruhe zu bewahren." In a Dutch rendering, the passage reads more or less as a proverb: "Ze luisterde en ze luisterde niet, zoals dat hoort in dese wereld als je rustig wilt leven." A slightly abbreviated Norwegian version misses much of the satirical point of how to keep one's equanimity in respectable society. It is more diluted than Andersen's original: "Litt hörte hun, og litt hörte hun ikke, slik som det jo pleier å være her i verden."[11]

Of the six Swedish translations under discussion, at least one is overstating the case in its efforts to be as pedagogically unequivocal as possible. Gyllander's version is close to a mistranslation, perhaps due to a slight misapprehension of the passage: "Hon hörde – men hon hörde inte på det sätt man bör höra för att kunna leva i lugn och ro här på jorden (by italicizing, Gyllander also puts an unneccessary stress on one word in the opening sentence: "Det var en ryslig historia! Sa en höna borta i en utkant av staden, där händelsen *inte* hade tilldragit sig"). The point he misses is that the ideal way of listening is quite often to turn a deaf ear to what is being said. Bengt Anderberg, in 1982, solved the problem in his idiomatic Swedish rendering: "Hon hörde och hon lät bli att höra, som man ju bör göra här i världen för att leva i lugn och ro," which is almost identical with Åke Holmberg's "Hon hörde och hon hörde inte, som man ju bör här i världen för att få leva i fred" (the Danish "skal" is of course stronger than the Swedish "bör"). Böök had varied much the same phrase in 1939: "Hon hörde och hon hörde inte, som man ju ska göra här i världen för att få leva i lugn och ro."

Of greater interest is how translators have tackled a second passage in Andersen's tale, the one which I have used as the title of this paper: "'Prenez garde aux enfants!' sagde Ugle-Fader, 'det er ikke noget for Børnene'". It is maybe the best of all the many examples that can be found of Hans Christian Andersen's almost uncannily perfect double talk, his "dobbelte artikulation",[12] of which the Stockholm critic Hellen Lindgren was aware in his 1900 pamphlet on Andersen:

Och dock är det märkvärdigt nog hos honom ingen oförmåga att liksom se ut över sig själv och se ned på sin egen barnslighet och narraktigheten i sin egen barnsliga natur. Han är därför den underbara blandning av det reflekterande och impulsiva, som gör de största diktarnas storhet – förmågan att vara på en gång barn och man, omedveten och medveten.[13]

And yet, strangely enough, he is able – as it were – to look beyond himself and down on his own naivety and the foolishness of his own childish nature. He is thus that wonderful mixture of the self-reflective and the impulsive which is typical of the greatness of the greatest writers – the ability to be at the same time a child and a man, spontaneous and thoughtful.

Andersen had, without the slightest trace of condescension, the not very common ability to direct himself to two age groups simultaneously: to a circle of young listeners, and to adults. His sentence is also a bit of a challenge for the translators, unless they leave the French words untouched. For obvious censorial reasons, the father Owl resorts to this foreign phrase, while at the same time it also hints that he belongs to the proper, well-educated class in society.

The German and the Dutch renderings keep the French catchword, and so do four out of five Swedish ones. Jean Hersholt, in his American version, tries to solve the problem by replacing a French proverb with an English one: "'Little pitchers have long ears', said the father owl. 'Children shouldn't hear such talk'". A Norwegian version misses much of the point when it replaces a refined phrase, intentionally incomprehensible to young ears, with something which they can understand well enough and which whets their appetite for innuendos of immorality even further: "Hysj da, hysj da, sa uglefar, du må ikke si sånt når barna sitter og hörer på!" Hugo Gyllander, in his schoolmasterly way, emendates the original in a way which must have caused young listeners to want to know what the French phrase really meant, and why it was used: "Prenez garde aux enfants! Sa ugglefar på franska. Det där är inte något för barnen att höra!" The bland anonymous 1852 translation misses the point altogether: "Tänk på barnen! Sade uggle-pappa; det är icke något för dem att höra på!" In Regis Boyer's 1992 French translation of Andersen's Tales, "Prenez gardes aux enfants" is rendered in French, just with a note explaining that the phrase is also in French in the original. Accordingly all of Boyer's readers will immediately understand something which some of them should not, as intended by both the father owl, and by Andersen himself.

The emphasis of the conclusion ("Og det kom i Avisen og det blev trykt og det er ganske vist: en lille Fjeder kan nok blive til fem Høns!"/ and it appeared in the paper and was printed and it is perfectly true: one small feather can certainly become five hens) is also varied by the different Swedish translators. The anonymous 1852 translator: "Och det kom i tidningarne och det blev tryckt och det är mycket säkert, att *af en liten fjäder kan det till slut bliva fem höns!*" This is how C. H. Rydberg sums up the story: "Och det kom i bladet och det blev tryckt och det är riktigt sannt [sic]: *En liten fjäder kan nog förvandlas till fem höns*. And thus Hugo Gyllander: "Och den kom verkligen i tidningen. Där stod den tryckt – och det är riktigt sant: *En enda liten fjäder kan verkligen bli fem hönor*." Fredrik Böök abstains from any italics: "Och det kom i tidningen och det blev tryckt och det är alldeles säkert: av en liten fjäder kan det nog bli fem höns!"

*

Fredrik Böök held Hans Christian Andersen in high esteem. In closing, his appreciation of how Andersen left most authors far behind may be cited:

> Han lämnade dem i skuggan. Hans sagor äro Danmarks största insats i världslitteraturen, och det finns överhuvud ingen diktare, som förvärvat en friskare och sannare odödlighet än hans. Hans

plats är vid sidan av Homeros, Cervantes, Dante, Shakespeare och Goethe[14]

He overshadowed them. His tales are Denmark's greatest contribution to world literature, and there is on the whole no author who has attained a livelier or truer immortality than his. His place is beside Homer, Cervantes, Dante, Shakespeare and Goethe.

Notes

Quotations are translated by Ivo Holmquist.
1. "Især I udlandet – uden for Skandinavien – har man aldrig rigtigt kunnet slippe den opfattelse, at Andersens eventyr 'kun' er for børn" (Especially abroad – outside Scandinavia – they have not really been able to leave the opinion behind that Andersen's Tales were for children "only". Johan de Mylius, *Forvandlingens pris. H.C. Andersen og hans eventyr,* 2004, p. 11).
2. For early translations into Swedish, cf. Harald Åström, *H.C. Andersens genombrott i Sverige. Översättningarna och kritiken 1828-1852* (1972), for the later ones, cf Ivo Holmqvist and Aage Jørgensen, "H.C. Andersen, Sverige och svenskarna – en selektiv bibliografi", in: *H.C. Andersens underbara resor i Sverige,* red. Ivo Holmqvist (2005), pp. 207-38.
3. "B. Var en synnerlig flittig och skicklig översättare, som lämnat omsorgsfulla tolkningar av en mängd moderna utländska skriftställare, såsom H.C. Andersen, Bulwer, Dickens, Paul Heyse, Fritz Reuter och Thackeray" (B. was an extremely prolific and skillful translator who has left us careful renderings of many modern foreign writers, like Hans Christian Andersen, Bulwer, Dickens, Paul Heyse, Fritz Reuter and Thackeray. *Nordisk Familiebok,* vol. II, 1904, col. 605).
4. On Strindberg and Andersen, cf Margareta Westman, "När Strindberg översatte HC Andersen", in: *Från språk till språk. Sjutton uppsatser om litterär översättning,* ed. Gunnel Engwall and Regina af Geijerstam, 1983, and *H.C. Andersens underbara resor i Sverige,* pp. 248-50
5. Quoted by Svante Nordin in his essay on "H.C. Andersen och Fredrik Böök", in *H.C. Andersens underbara resor i Sverige,* pp. 165-71.
6. On Nerman and Andersen, cf. Anders Palm's essay "Tommelise, Tummetott och tändstickspojken. Androgyna eventyrligheter", in: *H.C. Andersens underbara resor i Sverige,* pp. 25-58.
7. As listed in the ADL (Arkiv for Dansk Litteratur) commentary on the net, which also maintains that a Turkish novel may have played a part.
8. E. Ebg (E. Eberling, librarian at the Danish Parliament), in *Nordisk Familjebok,* vol. I, 1904, col. 939.
9. Similar translation principles and practices are discussed at length by Martin Sutton in his *The Sin-Complex. A Critical Study of English Versions of the Grimms' Kinder- und Hausmärchen in the Nineteenth Century,* 1996.

10. Cf. Hans Holmbergs essay on "Kejsarens bedrägliga kläder" in *H.C. Andersens underbara resor i Sverige*, pp. 173-82, which also makes some interesting political points on how Andersen's translators used the story as a vehicle for attacks on the conservative establishment around King Karl XIV Johan in the 1840s.
11. All examples can be found on the H.C. Andersen Centret-website.
12. Cf. Johan de Mylius' discussion of this concept, in *Forvandlingens pris*, p. 26, and its reference to a similar one by Søren Baggesen, in *Andersen og verden*, 1993.
13. Quoted in *H.C. Andersens underbara resor i Sverige*, p. 247.
14. Fredrik Böök, *H.C. Andersen. En levnadsteckning* (1938), p. 262f.

The Identity and Integrity of the Slovene Andersen in the Post-WW2 Period: Translation as the Right of Passage

Silvana Orel-Kos

By Way of Introduction: "Look in the passport!" said the man. "I am myself!"

The line from H.C. Andersen's "Twelve by the Mail" in Jean Hersholt's translation[1] aptly serves as an introduction to the present article, which will be addressing some recurrent issues in the history of translation studies, focussing on the three milestones on the passage between the source and target literary systems: the author's original work, the translator's strategies, and the target culture's norms and reception. The first issue deals with the question of the identity versus identities of the author's work in translation: does the translated text relate to the notion of equivalence with the original or does it bear a mere interpretational resemblance with it? The second issue suggested by the title is the notion of integrity, whose double meaning is applicable to translation: the work's integrity as an expression of the translator's professional integrity. Which translation strategies can/should a translator undertake in order to produce an 'integral' integral translation?[2] The third issue addresses the manifold impact of the target culture on the translational process and, naturally, the product: translation is not just a 'rite' of passage from one literary system to another, it can also exemplify the 'right' of passage into a social system with a different set of ethic and aesthetic values.

To illustrate the three issues at work, we shall look at some of the translations of H.C. Andersen's fairy tales made by the Slovene translator Rudolf Kresal during the post-World-War-Two period, when Slovenia was part of the Socialist Federal Republic of Yugoslavia. What kind of passport was required to make it possible for H.C. Andersen to cross the border of the socialist Slovenia in the early 1950's: was he still himself?

Periods in the Slovene Translation of H.C. Andersen's Fairy Tales

So far 112 H.C. Andersen's fairy tales and stories[3] have been published as (supposedly) integral translations in the Slovene language, the first Slovene rendering of H.C. Andersen's fairy tales was, however, two anonymous adaptations published in a youth periodical in 1850. The history of H.C. Andersen's fairy tales in Slovene translation can be divided into the following periods:

- the first translational period: from 1850 to H.C. Andersen's death in 1875,
- the second translational period: from 1875 until the end of WW2 in 1945,
- the third translational period: from 1945 until Slovenia's cessation from the Socialist Federal Republic of Yugoslavia in 1991, ie. the post-WW2 period,
- the fourth translational period: from Slovenia's independence in 1991 onwards.

The first translational period differs from the others in that its end point is marked by the death of the great Dane rather than the end of a specific historical period synonymous with the end of a particular social and political system in force on the Slovene territory during the indicated periods of time. The translational periods are characterized by specific translational approaches and strategies.

The first translational period spans the time during which the translators were theoretically able to contact the author, and their Slovene translations appeared while the author was still alive. It is also interesting in view of the great variety of translation approaches to Andersen's fairy tales; it was marked by two adaptations, the first integral translation and the first collection of fairy tales. The first adaptation was anonymous to serve as a moralistic story,[4] while the other was written and used by Fran Levstik, author and translator, to illustrate his own critical literary views.[5] The first Slovene translation that could be considered an attempt at an integral translation of an Andersen fairy tale was "The Story of the Year", appearing in 1858 and translated by the Slovene author and natural scientist Fran Erjavec, who was also the translator of the first Slovene collection of ten Andersen fairy tales, published in 1863.

The second translational period saw the appearance of four collections of fairy tales, with the last one, translated by Miklavž Kuret and published in 1944, being the first collection of fairy tales in Slovene translation that even today can pass for integral translations. The first and second translational periods are marked by characteristic translation shifts. The 19th-century translations show the religious and moralistic-*cum*-educational Andersen, which is reflected in both the choice of texts and the textual additions as well as deletions to highlight Andersen's, and, above all, the editor's or the translator's, stance on the moral and religious education of God-fearing young readers. The translator's integrity was established by the target culture, translations were a means of propagating the ideas and ideals approved by the target culture.

Throughout the first half of the 20th century there was a tendency away from the expressly religious and moralistic Andersen towards the classic and entertaining Andersen, which, again, was reflected at the microtextual level: the 1923 translator Utva [Ljudmila Prunk] and the 1940 translator M.K. [Mirko Košir] are noted for their overall tendencies towards explication. They applied translation strategies which resulted in more idiomatic and expressive literary style: was that the reason they chose to remain rather anonymous? Another general feature common to the translations from the first two translational periods is that the Danish poet only goes by his surname Andersen; it was first in the introduction of the 1944 publication that the domesticated version of his first names, 'Janez Kristijan', was printed. This attitude towards H.C. Andersen's authorship implies that H.C. Andersen's fairy tales have often, also during the third translational period, been interpreted and understood merely as 'Andersen fairy tales', ie. as a special fairy-tale literary form.

The third translational period was dominated by the translator Rudolf Kresal and several reprints of 36 fairy tales out of his 91 translations.[6] Only during the 1980's did the same publisher, Slovenia's leading publishing house, ask two translators to provide new renditions of three fairy tales that were translated by Kresal in the 1950's: "The Flying Trunk", "The Little Mermaid" and "The Swineherd".

The present, fourth translational period began in 1991 when Slovenia became independent, introducing a parliamentary political system and market economy. The same period is also marked by a keen academic interest in translation studies. These three circumstances have necessarily influenced Andersen translation activity. On the one hand, the leading Slovene publishing house has published 50 fairy tales (in two volumes, 1998 and 2005) in rendering by Orel-Kos from the Danish originals. The chosen fairy tales show the editor's wish to present the many-sided H.C. Andersen, including the classic, the religious, the moralistic and the entertaining Andersen. On the other hand, minor publishing houses have struggled to survive the cut and thrust of the ruthless market economy by publishing lavishly illustrated co-prints[7] furnished with Kresal's translations or new translations of abridged or adapted mediating (mostly English) texts, for example, the 'politically correct' and toned down rendition of "The Wild Swans",[8] in which the illustrator is said to own the copyright in the illustrations, yet there is no mention that H.C. Andersen's text has been tampered with.

The post-WW2 Translational Period Until 1991

The third translational period differs from the other three periods in that it coincides with a social and political system radically different from that of H.C. Andersen's time. It starts after World War Two, when Slovenia was recognized as part of the Socialist Federal Republic of Yugoslavia, which was well-known for its unique social and political system, Tito's socialism. Tito's variant of the socialist system would present itself as a democratic one in comparison with *both* the exploitative capitalist systems in the West and the radically socialist, so-called communist systems in the East: *we,* 'the children of socialism', were led to believe that we were the lucky dwellers of the best of possible worlds.

This regime, however, was not (particularly) conductive to religious matters, especially not within the framework of the education of young children. These were seen as future propagators of the atheist society of workers who were encouraged to believe that they were (smart enough to be) not only factory workers but also factory runners. Yet religion was not and could not be totally ousted from people's lives: it was regarded as an activity practised by backward elderly people, mostly living on the countryside. It will be shown that the seemingly democratic socialist period marked an introduction of a fairly non-democratic translational policy. This almost half-a-century-long manipulation of young people through translation of children's literature is becoming evident only with re-translations and scholarly intertextual studies.

1950, which is exactly one hundred years after the first anonymous introduction of H.C. Andersen's fairy tales into the Slovene literary system, saw the beginning of a very prolific decade in the Slovene translation of H.C. Andersen's fairy tales. The translations were done by the Slovene translator, journalist and author Rudolf Kresal, who, incidentally, was born and died exactly 100 years after Hans Christian Andersen. With 81 different titles Rudolf Kresal is the most productive Slovene translator of H.C. Andersen's fairy tales ever. His translations from the 1950's dominated the bookshelves and young readers' minds for almost fifty years.

In the following we shall present the findings emerging from intertextual studies of the translation strategies Kresal used in the translations he undertook for two Slovene publishing houses in the early 1950's. In 1950 and 1953 he translated via German as many as 78 fairy tales, and in 1954 another three fairy tales for a different publisher. In 1955, when the 150th anniversary of H.C. Andersen's birth was celebrated, the first publisher issued an Andersen anthology of 30 classic fairy tales. In 1967, when the International Children's Book Day was introduced, the first publisher expanded his anthology of Andersen's fairy tales by another six titles. This edition adorned with illustrations by a renowned Slovene artist was reprinted three times until 1984 and can still be found in people's homes and libraries.

Kresal's Second-hand Translation Strategies

As stated in some of his translations, Kresal did not translate directly from Danish but "via German". On the basis of intertextual studies, it has been noted that he relied on several mediating translations. Since he did not translate directly from Danish, we may assume that his translation strategies actually mirrored those applied by the other translators, as can be observed in the following passage from "Twelve by the Mail", which abounds in departures from the original Andersen: there are more concrete images with more specific meanings and additions of words and phrases. The same translation strategies are used in the Slovene translation, which shows that when translating "Twelve by the Mail", Kresal indeed relied on this particular German translation.[9] The departures are indicated by the underlined items, the slots with added German words or phrases are marked by the /+Germ/ sign in the Danish original:

Danish:
Nu kom den Sidste /+Germ/, den gamle Mo'erlille /+Germ/ med Ildpotten; hun frøs, men hendes Øine straalede som to klare Stjerner. Hun bar en Urtepotte /+Germ/ med et lille Grantræ /+Germ/. "Det vil jeg pleie og det vil jeg passe, saa at det /+Germ/ bliver stort til Juleaften, naaer fra Gulvet lige op til Loftet, og groer med tændte Lys, forgyldte Æbler og Udklipninger. Ildpotten varmer som en Kakkelovn, jeg tager Eventyr-Bogen op af Lommen og læser høit, saa at alle Børnene i Stuen blive stille, men Dukkerne paa Træet blive levende og den lille Engel af Voks, øverst oppe i Træet, ryster med Knittergulds-Vingerne, flyver fra den grønne Top og kysser Smaa og Store inde i Stuen, ja de fattige Børn med, som staae udenfor /+Germ/ og synge Julesangen om Stjernen over Bethlehem!" (Andersen 1966: 74)[10]

German:
Endlich kam der letzte Reisende zum Vorschein, das alte Mütterchen Dezember mit der Feuerkiepe; die Alte fror, aber ihre Augen strahlten wie zwei helle Sterne. Sie trug einen Blumentopf auf dem Arme, in dem ein kleiner Tannenbaum eingepflanzt war. "Den Baum will ich hegen und pflegen, damit er gedeihe und groß werde bis zum Weihnachtsabend, vom Fußboden bis an die Decke reiche und emporschieße mit flammenden Lichtern, goldenen Äpfeln und ausgeschnittenen Figürchen. Die Feuerkiepe wärmt wie ein Ofen; ich hole das Märchenbuch aus der Tasche und lese laut aus ihm vor, daß alle Kinder im Zimmer still, die Figürchen an dem Baume aber lebendig werden und der kleine Engel von Wachs auf der äußersten Spitze die Flittergoldflügel ausbreitet, herabfliegt vom grünen Sitze und klein und groß im Zimmer küßt, ja, auch die armen Kinder küßt, die draußen auf dem Flure und auf der Straße stehen und das Weihnachtslied von dem Bethlehemsgestirne singen."[11]

Slovene:
Nazadnje je izstopil zadnji potnik, stara mamica December z žerjavnico. Starko je zeblo, a oči so ji sijale kakor dve svetli zvezdi. V roki je imela lonec za cvetlice, vanj pa je bila vsajena majhna jelka. "Drevesce bom gojila in negovala, da bo uspevalo in da bo veliko do božičnega večera, tako veliko, da bo od tal do stropa segalo in da zaživi vse bleščeče se od gorečih svečic, pozlačenih jabolk in izrezljanih podobic. Žerjavnica nas bo grela kakor pečica.

Iz žepa bom vzela knjigo pravljic in iz nje glasno brala, da bodo v izbi vsi otroci potihnili, <u>podobice</u> na drevesu pa bodo oživele in voščeni angelček prav na vrhu drevesca <u>bo razprostrl</u> zlate peruti in splaval z zelenega vršička in vse otročiče in odrasle v sobi poljubil, pa tudi tiste tam zunaj, <u>ki stoje pred vrati in na cesti</u> in prepevajo pesem o tihi sreči in daljni zvezdi." (Andersen 1950: 32)

Comparing the Slovene translation with the German version it may be noted that Kresal followed closely the substitute for the Danish original, and in this sense produced an integral translation of the mediating version. Consequently, the Slovene translation also tends towards various forms of explication, a translation approach quite typical of the first half of the 20th century, characterized by the use of synonyms with more specific meanings as well as additions at the phrase and sentence levels.

Kresal's First-hand Translation Strategies

The professional integrity of Kresal's work was illustrated by the intertextual comparison with a mediating translation. The latter, however, may not reflect the identity of the original, and this is the price readers of indirect translations have to pay.

Yet the main purpose of this article is to illustrate the Slovene translator's 'genuine' translation strategies, and these did not as much modify H.C. Andersen's literary style as the author's religious outlook on life. H.C. Andersen's faith in God and absorption in Christianity were an essential part of H.C. Andersen's identity and the identity of his work: they were a very intense motivation for writing and an extensive source of motifs. As already stated, the religious element in H.C. Andersen's fairy tales was a convenient source of education notably in the 19th-century translations in Slovenia. What happened to H.C. Andersen's fairy tales in the post-war period, to the fairy tales with religious titles, plots, themes, motifs, imagery, lexemes?

The above passages can now be reused to illustrate Kresal's own translation strategies in his dealings with religious elements. There are two religious references in the last sentence, ie. "the little wax angel" and "the Christmas carol about the star of Bethlehem". In Slovene translation, the mention of the little wax angel is retained, the Christmas carol, however, is transformed into 'the song of silent happiness and a/the faraway star'. Was the translator inconsistent in his target-culture-norm-oriented translation strategies? Analyzing the functions of the two references, we realize that they perform two different functions: the angel is just a decoration, whereas the Christmas carol about Nativity is a sentimental, subversive means of enemy propaganda.

A number of contexts have been found in which angels are not merely decorative but celestial beings, for example in "The Snow Queen", "The Wild Swans", "The Nightingale", and "Ole Lukoie". In "The Snow Queen", for instance, the reference to angels and God is replaced by a phrase which depicts the children just as lively children, rather than mischievous children instigated by the Devil in the mirror:

> Then they wanted to fly up to heaven itself, <u>to scoff at the angels, and our Lord</u>.[12]

Back-translation from Slovene:

> Then they wanted to fly into the sky, <u>just for the goofy fun of it</u>.[13]

Angels are a recurrent religious motif in "The Snow Queen", functioning as a means of stylistic iteration and, more importantly, as an expression of consolation to the children:

> [...] and all the dreams came flying back again. They looked like <u>angels</u>, [...][14]

Back-translation from Slovene:

> All the dreams came flying back again into the bedroom, they flew back in the form of <u>elves and dwarves</u>, [...][15]

The angels and God in "The Wild Swans" are transformed into stars:

> Then it seemed to her that the branches parted overhead and the Lord looked kindly down upon her, and little angels peeped out from above His head and behind Him.[16]

Back-translation from Slovene:

> Now it seemed to her that the branches parted overhead and that all the stars in the dark blue sky bowed to her.[17]

Studying the intertextual relationships in Kresal's translation of Andersen's fairy tales we find that 'stars' and 'elves' or 'dwarves' are commonplace translation equivalents for supreme divine or celestial beings. It can be inferred from these translation shifts that Kresal applied the translation strategies inspired or required by the target culture, rather than the source text. In this way, Kresal made it possible for Andersen's fairy tales to enter the literary system, to become acceptable and functional within a socialist society. What shall we call such translation shifts: ideological censorship, "manipulation of the source text",[18] a fulfilled skopos,[19] instances of dynamic equivalence?[20] It depends on the angle of our analysis. From the point-of-view of the then target culture Kresal's decisions seemed only natural: religious concepts had no place, were considered as non-existent in the minds of young readers, and the opposite would run counter to the education envisaged and practised by the regime. The most natural and harmless substitutes appeared to be natural phenomena or, as befitting the fairy-tale genre, mythological creatures. Or simply 'no-one-will-notice' deletions. Skopos-based translations are functional if/as long as there is no protest from the parties involved (cf. Reiss/Vermeer 1984: 99). In the case of Kresal's translations it was only after the new 1998 translation directly from Danish that there was a protest by an angry (mature) reader, who in the 1970's as a child would read Andersen in Kresal's translation. In her letter published in the religious weekly *Družina,* the author exemplified the acts of manipulation and discussed them as a source of emotional child abuse and erroneous interpretation of a literary text:

> That is why I felt cheated, since, as a child, I adored these fairy tales, yet because of the suppressed notions I misinterpreted them. I was indignant at the way society strove to conceal God from the children; some of us would associate this word only with something funny, something that stupid and illiterate people believed in. Such education has horribly affected my generation.[21]

This leads to the conclusion that the level of democracy is proportionate to the level of freedom of thought and speech. Disregarding the skopos of Kresal's translations, the translation shifts resulted in different interpretations of the fairy tales, of the characters and Andersen the author. They created new, if not false, identities for them.

Author proposes, translator disposes.

We have already exemplified some issues regarding the translation of religious concepts in the post-World-War-Two translation of H.C. Andersen's fairy tales. The translator Rudolf Kresal used different translation strategies, depending on the ideological relevance and the narrative/textual function of the religious references. These can be grouped into four categories ranging from the core concepts of Christianity and the main character's involvement in religion, over the religious practices and artefacts that were tolerated during the 1950's, to the religious references with purely linguistic functions to which the regime did not seem to have any objections.

1. At the top of the detested religious concepts were the essential, but arcane and very intimate ideas of Christianity: first and foremost, God, presented by H.C. Andersen as the Creator or the uppermost authority, secondly, concepts of the immortal soul, the afterlife and heaven,[22] as well as divine creatures such as angels, as was illustrated above. In Kresal's translation the reference to God was deleted or, typically, transformed into some natural phenomenon, as exemplified by "The Daisy" and "The Little Match Girl" respectively:

> "Oh, I must die! I must leave the warm sunshine, and the fresh green, and all the splendor that God has created!"[23]

Back-translation from Slovene:

> Oh, I must die, leave the warm sunshine, the fresh green, all this splendour /deletion/![24]

> [...] and up there was neither cold, nor hunger, nor fear – they were with God.[25]

Back-translation from Slovene:

> The little girl no longer felt any cold, hunger or fear – she and her granny were among the shining stars of the New Year tree.[26]

2. Another very important aspect was the main character's personal involvement in religion: giving expression to her or his faith in God, especially when the character is depicted during the act of saying her or his prayers, singing and reciting hymns or songs and poems with religious content (especially when the texts are provided). This anti-

Christian attitude is shown throughout Elisa's story in the Slovene translation of "The Wild Swans". The following passage illustrates the deletion of and substitution for the concept of God, which at the same time causes a macrotextual shift in the textual world, and, moreover, in Elisa's character:

> She thought of her brothers, and she thought of the good Lord, who she knew would not forsake her. He lets the wild crab apples grow to feed the hungry, and he led her footsteps to a tree with its branches bent down by the weight of their fruit.[27]

Back-translation from Slovene:

> She thought of her brothers, who, she believed, had not forgotten her. /deletion/ Then she saw a wild apple tree with its branches bent down by the weight of their fruit.[28]

Not seeking help with God, Elisa is shown as not having any affinity for the sublime. Her mental world is not as complex as is in the original. In the Slovene translation she merely registers what is happening around her, she is endowed with a rather simple, if not simpleton, mentality: first she thinks of her brothers and then she sees a wild apple tree, under which she will be having lunch. In the 1950's translation, Elisa is bereft of her faith, she prefers to rely on her own ingenuity and perseverance, thus becoming a very modern super girl.[29] She is not allowed to declare her beliefs, because as the main character she is perceived as a model child that a young reader is likely to identify with.

3. The often tolerated religious references consist of standard, official, observable ideas, practices and artefacts. We find here religious activities, such as attending the service, singing hymns (without the lyrics being given, of course), religious holidays, quotations from the Bible, as, for example, in "Twelve by the Mail": "In the sweat of thy face shalt thou eat bread [...] That is written in the Bible."[30] This category also includes the mention of Church representatives and religious places, churches, church towers.

The ambivalent attitude to religious holidays can be illustrated from two fairy tales "Twelve by the Mail" and "The Old Oak Tree's Last Dream". In the already discussed "Twelve by the Mail", the religious holiday "Christmas Eve", as well as the quotation from the

Bible and the decorative angel, show no ideological bias in the Slovene translation. On the account of similar cases we may presume this is the reason why this fairy tale has not been reprinted ever since the first edition in 1950.

In "The Old Oak Tree's Last Dream", however, "a Christmas fairy tale" is rendered as "a winter fairy tale" and 'Christmas Eve' as 'New Year's Eve'. The lyrics of H.A. Brorson's hymn have been deleted and the hymn scenes deleted and paraphrased as follows:

[...] the hymn sung on the ship, sung in thanksgiving for the joy of Christmas, for the bliss of the human soul's salvation through Christ, for the gift of eternal life:

Sing loud, sweet angel, on Christmas morn.
Hallelujah! Christ the Saviour is born.
In joy receive His blessing.
Hallelujah! Hallelujah! [31]

Back-translation from Slovene:

Thus sounded the old hymn, and everyone aboard the ship felt himself lifted heavenward by the hymn, and by prayer, even as the old tree had lifted itself in its last, most beautiful dream that Christmas Eve.[32]

Over it [the tree] resounded from the ship the sounds of a song of New Year joy. And everyone aboard the ship felt himself lifted /deletion/, even as the tree had felt itself lifted in its most beautiful dream on New Year's Eve.[33]

Having suffered consistent ideological neutralisation and cultural assimilation, this fairy tale was rendered acceptable to the target culture, and thus it became one of the 36 anthology fairy tales.

4. The last category of religious references consists of metaphorically used references to religion, such as idioms taken from the Bible and set exclamations ('Gud!', 'Herre Gud!', 'Gud bevar' os!'). The metaphorically used religious references are interesting since they need not be rendered as religious references, yet they predominantly were, because they did not present a threat to the regime. A subcategory showing Andersen's stylistic use of religious concepts can be exem-

plified by adjectival and adverbial uses of the word 'velsignet' ('blessed'), which, even today remains difficult to translate literally in a number of contexts, as it produces unusual collocations.

In addition, the above categories must be considered in the light of narrative relevance criteria: what role does a religious reference play in a fairy tale? The mention of religious concepts in the title or a religious theme dominating the greater part of the fabula would prevent certain Andersen fairy tales from entering the Slovene literary system during the third translational period. The editorial policy of the 1950's would disregard fairy tales such as "The Angel", "The Garden of Paradise", "The Red Shoes", and "The Girl who Trod on the Loaf", which had all – save for the "The Red Shoes" – been rendered into Slovene at least once during the first two translational periods.

Another telling feature of the 1950's editorial policy can be observed in the 1955 and 1967 collections of H.C. Andersen's (classic) fairy tales, in which the editors had to cut the number of Kresal's translations from 78 to 30 and to 36 respectively. The decisive criterion was not particularly intricate: disregarded were the majority of fairy tales that included some standard religious references listed in the above section, such as the mention of religious holidays or going to church, as was the case with, for example, quite well known tales, such as "Great Claus and Little Claus", "The Fir Tree", "The Story of the Year" and "Twelve by the Mail". Included were the fairy tales in which the mention of religious holidays had already been subject to 'cultural assimilation' during the 1950's, for example, "The Little Match Girl" and "The Old Oak Tree's Last Dream".

Conclusion

The article tried to show how the Slovene translations done by Rudolf Kresal in the early fifties and reprinted throughout the socialist era conferred on H.C. Andersen's fairy tales different interpretations and identities, an identity that deeply religious Andersen would not readily identify with, but it enabled him to cross the border and survive in the Slovene literary system during that particular period. The ideological censorship was performed in two principal areas: the first one being the core of Christian credo and the second the narrative relevance. Particularly alien appeared to be the ontological concept of God as the Creator and the belief in the afterlife and the immortal soul, as well as the main character's ardent faith in God, since it was probably feared that the young socialist reader would be led to identify with the 'abhorrent' ideas of Christianity.

Kresal's translation strategies involved ideological neutralisation through the substitution of natural and mythological concepts, cultural assimilation through the substitution of, for example, target culture holidays and, simply, by deletion at different levels: from the phrase level up to the editorial exclusion of whole fairy tales. In this way, an important facet in the identity of H.C. Andersen the author was either blurred or ignored.

Should one criticize Rudolf Kresal for his translation deeds? Certainly not, from the point-of-view of the then regime. Kresal and the editorial board at the leading Slovene publishing house pursued a specific translational policy that tried (or was forced?) to meet the needs and demands of the then political and, quite tellingly, educational systems. One could, of course, sneer at the fact that Kresal showed some professional integrity in mentioning he was translating from a mediating language, yet there was no mention of the translation strategies he used on top. To be honest, this ethical act would not have been permitted by the regime. What *does* deserve strong criticism, though, is the fact that his 'politically correct' translations have been reused so many times, even though the gradual political changes would have allowed the use of more democratic translation strategies. Because of economic interest, even now, during the present translational period, in 2002, a minor Slovene publisher reused Kresal's "Little Match Girl", where in the final scene the granny and the little girl are depicted stuck among the shining stars, instead of being with God.

References

Andersen, Hans Christian (1966). *H.C. Andersens Eventyr.* Vol. IV. Ed. by Erik Dal. Copenhagen: Hans Reitzel.

Andersen, Hans Christian (1950). *Pravljice.* (Translated, edited and introduced by Rudolf Kresal.) Ljubljana: Mladinska knjiga.

Andersen, Hans Christian (1975). *Andersenove pravljice.* (Translated by Rudolf Kresal.) 2nd edition. Ljubljana: Mladinska knjiga.

Andersen, Hans Christian (1997). *Divji labodi.* (Translated by Andreja Blažič.) Tržič: Učila.

Dollerup, Cay and Silvana Orel-Kos (2001). "Co-printing: Translation without Boundaries". In: Hebenstreit, Gernot (ed.), *Grenzen erfahren – sichtbar machen – überschreiten. Festschrift für Erich Prunč zum 60. Geburtstag.* Frankfurt am Main, Berlin, Bern, Bruxelles, New York, Oxford, Wien: Lang, pp. 285-300.

Hermans, Theo (ed.) (1985). *The Manipulation of Literature. Studies in Literary Translation.* London: Croom Helm.

Kobe, Marijana (2001). "Andersenova pravljica kot moralična zgledna zgodba". In: Martina Ožbot (ed.): *Prevajanje Prešerna – prevajanje pravljic. Translation of Prešeren – Translation of Fairy Tales. (26. zbornik Društva slovenskih književnih prevajalcev.)* Ljubljana: Društvo slovenskih književnih prevajalcev, pp. 265-68.

Leuven-Zwart, Kitty M. van (1989). "Translation and Original. Similarities and Dissimilarities. I." *Target* 1:2, pp. 151-81.

Nida, Eugene A. (1964). *Toward a Science of Translating. With Special Reference to Principles and Procedures Involved in Bible Translating.* Leiden: Brill.

Orel-Kos, Silvana (2001, a) "Zgodnji slovenski prevodi Andersenovih pravljic". In: Martina Ožbot (ed.): *Prevajanje Prešerna – prevajanje pravljic. Translation of Prešeren – Translation of Fairy Tales. (26. zbornik Društva slovenskih književnih prevajalcev.)* Ljubljana: Društvo slovenskih književnih prevajalcev, pp. 269-88.

Orel-Kos, Silvana (2001, b) "Let divjih labodov med nebesi in peklom. (Pravljica *Divji labodi* H.C. Andersena v slovenskih prevodih.)" In: Martina Ožbot (ed.): *Prevajanje Prešerna – prevajanje pravljic. Translation of Prešeren – Translation of Fairy Tales. (26. zbornik Društva slovenskih književnih prevajalcev.)* Ljubljana: Društvo slovenskih književnih prevajalcev, pp. 289-309.

Reiss, Katharina and Hans, J. Vermeer (1984) *Grundlagen einer allgemeinen Translationstheorie.* Tübingen: Niemeyer.

Notes

1. On-line: http://www.andersen.sdu.dk/vaerk/hersholt/TwelveByTheMail_e.html.
2. A translation is integral when it contains no additions or deletions transcending the sentence level. (Leuven-Zwart 1989: 154.)
3. Henceforth, the term fairy tale will be used to refer to both H.C. Andersen's fairy tales and stories.
4. The two adapted fairy tales with moralistic and religious supplements were entitled "New Clothes" and "The Little Nightingale". See Kobe 2001.
5. See Orel-Kos 2001 a.
6. Since Rudolf Kresal's translation strategies are the topic of this article, his translations will be considered in more detail in the following sections.
7. See Dollerup/Orel-Kos 2001.
8. The reference is made to the picture book Andersen (1997).
9. On the strength of the information gathered from the site stated underneath, the German translator may well have been (Charlotte) Tronier Funder, who is supposed to have translated H.C. Andersen's fairy tales before 1935. (On-line: gutenberg.spiegel.de/andersen/maerchen0htmldir.htm, and www.fortaellinger.frac.dk/#043.

10. Here and henceforth underlined by Orel-Kos.
    The passage in English translation by Jean Hersholt:
    Now came the last passenger, a little old mother, with her firepot. She was cold, but her eyes sparkled like two bright stars. She carried a flowerpot with a little fir tree growing in it.
    "I shall guard and nurse this tree, so that it may grow large by Christmas Eve and reach from the ground right up to the ceiling, and be covered with lighted candles, golden apples, and little cut-out paper decorations. This fire-kettle warms like a stove. I take the storybook from my pocket and read aloud, so that all the children in the room become quiet. But the dolls on the tree come to life, and the little wax angel on top of the tree shakes its golden tinsel wings, flies down from the green top, and kisses in the room, yes, the poor children, too, who stand outside and sing the Christmas carol about the star of Bethlehem." (On-line: http://www.andersen.sdu.dk/vaerk/hersholt/ TwelveByThe Mail_e.html.) – Unless otherwise stated, English translations are by Jean Hersholt.
11. See note 9.
12. On-line: http://www.andersen.sdu.dk/vaerk/hersholt/TheSnowQueen_e.html.
13. Nato so hoteli zleteti proti nebu, zgolj zaradi norčij. (Andersen 1975: 5.)
    Here and henceforth my English translations for Kresal's translations are used.
14. On-line: http://www.andersen.sdu.dk/vaerk/hersholt/TheSnowQueen_e.html.
15. V spalnico so priletele spet vse sanje, priletele so v podobi samih vil in palčkov /.../ (Andersen 1975: 24.)
16. On-line: http://www.andersen.sdu.dk/vaerk/hersholt/TheWildSwans_e.html.
17. Zdajci se ji je zazdelo, da se veje nad njo razmikajo in da se vse zvezde na temno modrem nebu sklanjajo k njej. (Andersen 1975: 226.)
18. The school of manipulation investigates target-culture context and norms, which are supposed to govern translation activity: "From the point of view of the target literature, all translation implies a degree of manipulation of the source text for a certain purpose." (Hermans 1985: 9.)
19. Introduced by Vermeer (and Reiss) within the framework of skopos theory, the term *skopos*, which is the Greek for 'aim', 'purpose', refers to the function or purpose of the target text: "Die Dominante aller Translation ist deren Zweck." (Reiss/Vermeer 1984: 96.)
20. A translation of dynamic equivalence aims at complete naturalness of expression, and tries to relate the receptor to modes of behavior relevant within the context of his own culture; it does not insist that he understand the cultural patterns of the source-language context in order to comprehend the message. (Nida 1964: 159.)
21. Zaradi tega sem se počutila ogoljufana, saj sem kot otrok te pravljice oboževala in sem jih potemtakem, zaradi zamolčanih pojmov, narobe razumela. Ogorčena sem bila nad tem, kako se je družba trudila, da otroci ne bi mogli odkriti Boga; nekateri smo to besedo poznali samo kot nekaj smešnega; nekaj, v kar verjamejo neumni in nepismeni. Takšna vzgoja je pustila strašne posledice moji generaciji. (Nataša Lorenzutti. "Nezaslišano potvarjanje." *Družina,* 12 January 2003.)
22. The concepts of the afterlife and heaven were shunned, the Devil and Hell, however, were retained.

23. On-line: http://www.andersen.sdu.dk/vaerk/hersholt/TheDaisy_e.html.
24. "Ah, umreti moram, se posloviti od toplega sončnega sija, od svežega zelenja, od vse te krasote!" (Andersen 1975: 45.)
25. On-line: http://www.andersen.sdu.dk/vaerk/hersholt/TheLittleMatchGirl_e.html.
26. Deklica ni več čutila ne mraza ne lakote ne strahu – z babico je bila med sijočimi zvezdami novoletne jelke. (Andersen 1975: 128.)
27. On-line: http://www.andersen.sdu.dk/vaerk/hersholt/TheWildSwans_e.html.
28. Mislila je na svoje brate, ki je gotovo niso pozabili. Potem je ugledala divjo jablano, katere veje so se upogibale pod obilnimi plodovi. (Andersen 1975: 226.)
29. Orel-Kos (2001) has done an analysis of the different identities that the heroine Elisa assumes in eight Slovene translations of "The Wild Swans".
30. On-line: http://www.andersen.sdu.dk/vaerk/hersholt/TwelveByTheMail_e.html.
31. On-line: http://www.andersen.sdu.dk/vaerk/hersholt/TheOldOakTreesLast-Dream_e.html.
32. Ibid.
33. Tale nagrobni govor, kratek, toda dobro mišljen, je prejelo drevo, ki je ležalo stegnjeno na snežni odeji ob morski obali. Čezenj pa so z ladje zveneli glasovi pesmi o novoletnem veselju. In sleherni na ladji se je čutil dvignjenega, prav kakor se je čutilo drevo dvignjeno v svojih najlepših sanjah v novoletni noči. (Andersen 1975: 42.)

Hans Christian Andersen's Fairy Tales for Estonian Readers

Mare Müürsepp

The aim of the paper is to give an overview of publication of Andersen's fairy tales in Estonian. The tendencies in translations and publications will be analyzed and the most significant translators and illustrators will be introduced.

Four issues are treated in the paper:

1. Addressee of Andersen's fairy tales published in Estonian.
2. Cultural background of different translation traditions.
3. Translators of Andersen's works.
4. Some examples of illustrations of Andersen motifs.

Addressee of Andersen's Fairy Tales Published in Estonian

The question about Andersen readers is often discussed: are the fairy tales told and written for the child or for the adult audience, or for both, according to how Andersen himself through the titles of his collections did or did not indicate the group of readers intended, or as the researchers and critics consider the problem important.

The possible addressee of Andersen's fairy tales will be treated here accepting the formal type of publications. Many earlier translations of fairy tales were published in periodicals, intended for adult and not especially for children as readers. So the first translation of fairy tales in Estonian was the story "Sukanõel" ("Stoppenaalen") by Lydia Koidula, published 1866 in the newspaper *Eesti Postimees* (Estonian Postman) in a column for stories and novels. Two books were published by T. Kerr 1876, *Vigane Hans* ("Krøblingen") and *Üks tüdruk, kes leiva peale astus ja tema elukäik surma* (*"Pigen som traadte paa Brødet"*), and the subtitle of the first mentioned books is "The Christmas story for old and young people", so the dual readership is mentioned there.

In the years 1887-90, many of Andersen's fairy tales were published in newspapers, calendars and almanacs, not addressed to children, like *Meelejahutaja* (Entertainer), *Maarahva Kasuline Kalender* (Useful Calendar for Country People), and others.

In the beginning of the 20th century children's periodicals were founded, e.g. *Lasteleht* (Children's Magazine), and then Andersen's works were published there, unambiguously addressing children.

At the same time the tradition of the collections was developing. The first collection 1877 was titled as *H.C. Andersen's Fairy Tales. Part I*, but it had no sequel, obviously the publisher had no success with this book. The collection included fairy tales like "Pöial-Leene" ("Tommelise"), "See on terve tõsi" ("Det er ganske vist"), "Kuninga uued riided" ("Keiserens nye Klæder"), and "Veike mereneid" ("Den lille Havfrue").

The foreword to this collection written by the translator Wilhelm Friedrich Eichhorn was the first publication in Estonian introducing Andersen's life and work, and also mentioning the dual address of Andersen's fairy tales. There the idea is expressed by Eichhorn that these fairy tales are loved by the children and by childlike adults.

Twenty years later the more successful collections were published beginning from 1897. Translated by Liina Grossschmidt 5 tales were published in the book *Andersen's Fairy Tales. Funny Allegories for Education and Amusement*. Then 11 tales were published in 1906 as the enlarged volume of the collection, reprinted in 1908, being also the first illustrated publication of Andersen's works.

In the beginning of the 20th century collections were composed and published in series intended especially for young readers, like 14 fairy tales translated in 1913 by Anna Haava in the series "Nooresoo kirjavara" (Youth Library), and 2 tales translated by Madis Küla-Nurmik in the series "Laste jututuba" (Children's Column). The largest selection, 25 fairy tales, was translated by Hugo Raudsepp in 1928 in a series of school and youth literature. Although the form of these publications pointed to the child and young reader as the addressee of Andersen's fairy tales, the forewords and the comments in critical articles treated the ambivalence of his texts.

Both translators, A. Haava and H. Raudsepp, made it clear that Andersen was writing for children as well as adults. Anna Haava wrote: "The connection with true life and everyday reality will never break in Andersen's fairy tales; it is as if we are like walking together with a highly gifted poet on the road of life, we look and see the world through the mental prism of his poetry, and the human love and reconcilable humour is bucking up all over, the golden gossamer of idealism is winging over all, and we have an inexplicable inkling of the light from a higher world." (Teder 1996, 512.)

There have been certain problems of understanding and accepting Andersen's works and their translations by the critics. The translation by Anna Haava was criticized because of the use of modern language. Nevertheless, today the most widespread opinion is that Anna Haava as the best known lyric poetess of that period, a sensible and romantic writer, was very close to the spirit of Andersen's tales. She was the first translator of the tales "The Ugly Duckling", "The Steadfast Tin Soldier", and "The Wild Swans".

Of course it is difficult to say, whether or not the rebukes were caused by the style of translation or by the unique tone of Andersen's narration itself. The Estonian readers were used to Grimm's fairy tales and to sentimental stories mostly influenced by German literature. From another side there was a tendency to modernization of Estonian original literature in the waves of new art movements, and the works of new literary groups were often not accepted by the contemporary common reader. Anna Haava's translation of H.C. Andersen may have seemed somewhat too innovative.

So the publishing of Andersen's fairy tales was not a simple task for the publisher. Just as the first planned series beginning 1877 stopped after the first volume, the 1913 collection had no sequel either, and fairy tales translated already by A. Haava for the 2nd part (or even for the 3rd) were published only in periodicals.

The books published in the 20th century were obviously addressed to children. Only the biggest collection (in 1987 volume 1 and in 1996 volume 2, including the entire body of all 156 fairy tales, translated by Henrik Sepamaa) seems to be intended for the adult reader by its design, both by the size of letters and the style of illustrations.

To sum up – the history of translation demonstrates the understanding of Andersen's fairy tales as ambivalent texts, not only as texts belonging to children's literature.

Cultural Background of Different Translation Traditions

In the 19th century before the national awakening movement, the German language was used in Estonian educated families both in reading/ writing and in everyday communication. So the reading of Andersen's works in German and translating from German was self-evident. The first translator, Lydia Koidula (1843-86), the founder of Estonian national poetry, remembered in her letters how Andersen's "The Fir Tree" was read in her family in 1850 and this was quite an experience. Other fairy tales by Andersen tales were mentioned in her letters.

The tradition of German translation of H.C. Andersen's works was strongly criticized in 1914 by Estonian folklorist Mattias Johann Eisen. The only true way, he said, is to translate the author from the original text.

The first translator from Danish was young Agnes Antik, who was Danish by origin, and after marrying the Estonian bibliographer Richard Antik learned Estonian at a level that enabled her to translate Andersen's works. The collections of her translations, all together 24 fairy tales, were published in 1933-34 and 1937.

After World War II, in the beginning of the Soviet period the publishing of fairy tales generally was very active – obviously also because of the lack of contemporary literature. Also Andersen's fairy tales were published in many separate publications. There were books without the translator's name: It was forbidden to use Agnes Antik's name, because in 1944, she emigrated to Denmark. There have also been cases where her translations were retold and changed a little bit, and signed by another name.

In 1950 the publishers were ordered to translate the books written in smaller languages only from Russian versions. Some of these translations are very good, like "Thumbelina" by Hardi Tiidus, translated from the Russian translation of Anna Gansen [= Hansen]. Published many times, this is one of the most popular fairy tales in Estonian (printed 1956, 1976 and later – more than 140 000 copies!).

Of course, all translations of Andersen's works during the Soviet regime had to accept the atheistic ideal of education: all sentences, words, details, mentioning religious motifs were cut out.

In the 1960s in the atmosphere of the general liberalization, Henrik Sepaaa began to review the translation from Danish. His first translations of Andersen's fairy tales appeared in 1964, and then he decided to translate all Andersen's fairy tales. The first collection *The Little Mermaid* was printed in 1987, then in 1990 H. Sepamaa died, and three colleagues, Arvo Alas, Arnold Ravel and Anu Saluäär finished his work. The second collection *The Snowdrop* was published in 1996.

Translators of Andersen's Works

A remarkable fact has to be mentioned: many persons translating Andersen's fairy tales into Estonian are not generally known as translators, but rather as writers, poets, critics, or researchers. Comparing the personalities of translators of H.C. Andersen's works and of translators of other very famous authors, translated many times in different periods, like the brothers Grimm or W. Shakespeare, the difference mentioned below would be significant.

Obviously, the motifs to translate Andersen's works have been multifarious. The so-called national nightingale, the herald of Estonian literature Lydia Koidula (1843-86) (the pen name Koidula may be translated as the Symbol of Dawn, cf. Puhvel 1999) would like to introduce the fairy tales enjoyed in her childhood and their author, not published in Estonian as yet. In 1866, she translated the tale "Stoppenaalen" to publish it in *Estonian Postman*, edited by her father Johann Woldemar Jansen. Lydia Koidula was working together with her father to help him in writing and publishing.

Anna Haava (1864-1957), best known today as a lyric poet, also translated many other classics (works by Shakespeare, Schiller, Goethe) for the series of young readers. Her translation of Andersen's fairy tales is accepted as a special literary event by historians of Estonian literature. "it seems that the greatest author of love poetry in the end of 19th century in Estonian literature felt at home in Andersen's fairy tale world." (Jaaksoo 1998) Anna Haava offered new translations of "Thumbelina", "The Princess on the Pea", "The Emperor's New Clothes", "The Tinderbox", and "The Little Mermaid", and introduced the fairy tales not known for Estonian readers at that time.

Hugo Raudsepp (1883-1952) wrote a number of very popular dramas and comedies, but was active as a critic and researcher as well. Why did he begin to translate Andersen? Maybe because of his interest in the theatre and the satirical tone? Anyway, Raudsepp has written forewords also for other translators, to introduce the works and their background. The nature of Andersen's fairy tales was treated in his foreword, where his original characters and duality of naive and philosophical approach were pointed out. Hugo Raudsepp about Andersen's style: "He was highly symbolic, emotionally affecting, wantonly grotesque, and full of humour and gentle derision. He had a rare gift of giving life to everything he would touch, there are no spiritless things in his fairy tales; the stone, the flower, the animal has a human voice, not losing its own character at the same time. Andersen's fairy tales have been seen by children's eyes, but there is wisdom behind the fictitious naivety." (Jaaksoo 1998, 12.)

Friedebert Tuglas (1886-1971) was a multi-gifted developer of literature. He wrote novellas, novels, short stories and poems, also criticism, organized the activities of the Estonian writers' organizations both in the beginning of the 20th century and in the 1940s as well as later on. He is accepted as an initiator of the

20th century in Estonian prose because of his innovatory works. At the time of Stalin's repression writing was forbidden for him. Then he translated Andersen's works using the pen name A. Kabral.

Lea Nurkse (1904-60) was lecturing on children's literature in education courses for school teachers, and she translated Andersen accepting the children's abilities in language and thinking. She also performed Andersen's fairy tales like other classics in broadcasts for children by Estonian Radio. Her son Eno Raud grew up under these influences and turned into a children's writer, accepted as one of the best in Estonian children's literature. He often used motifs similar to living toys with true human character in Andersen's fairy tales, he wrote about the potato masher, vacuum cleaner, about cars and other things endowed with human characteristics, so the impact of Andersen's works might be seen in Eno Raud's fairy tales.

Henrik Sepamaa (1905-90) was the best known translator from Scandinavian. Ibsen, Hamsun, Laxness, Andersen Nexø, and Strindberg are examples of authors translated by Sepamaa. In 1964 he got the idea to translate all Andersen's fairy tales, and this great work was finished in 1996 by three younger translators. Sepamaa's translation is considered to be the one that is closest to Andersen's original text.

Illustration of Andersen's Fairy Tales.

The first illustrated collection of H.C. Andersen's fairy tales in Estonian was printed 1908, and the source of the woodcuts was a German publication. The tradition of original Estonian illustrations is essentially shorter than the history of translation of Andersen's works in Estonian.

The female effort is remarkable concerning illustrations of Andersen's fairy tales, as it is in the field of translation. The best female artist of the first part on the 20th century Karin Luts (1904-93) illustrated Andersen in 1937 in many books. K. Luts studied art not only in Estonia, but also in Paris and Rome. In 1937 she was awarded a gold medal in the World Exhibition in Paris for her tapestry. The collection of Andersen's fairy tales 1937 translated by Agnes Antik and illustrated by Karin Luts is accepted as the best collection of the first half of the 20th century.

The most widely distributed publication of Andersen in Estonian is *Thumbelina* illustrated by Siima Shkop (born 1920). Shkop was working at the publishing house "Valgus" (Light) and illustrated a lot of popular fairy tales and children's books. "Thumbelina" illustrated by Shkop has for many generations been one of the most beautiful books of all. (See the digital collections of the Estonian National library: www.nlib.ee)

Surprisingly, preparing the Andersen's bicentennial the illustrations of Viktor Aleksejev were found in the archives of The National Library. V. Aleksejev was born in Tartu 1902, studied art in Voronezh, Leipzig and Dresden. There are three H.C. Andersen's works published with his illustrations. The series on motifs of the Apostle John's Apocalypse is recognized as the most important work by V. Aleksejev. He created the miniatures to Andersen's "Thumbelina" in 1942-44, but due to the war time they were not used in print. In 1944 Aleksejev was arrested, and 1945 he died. Friends of his family have given the pictures to the archive of the National Library. Only now, 2005, they were "discovered" and published. (The illustrations by Alekejev are also available in the digital collection, www.nlib.ee).

Because of the variety and emotionality of Andersen's style and also according to the popularity of his works in Estonian the artists here are highly interested in creating illustrations based on his motifs. The publishing of illustrated books is not simple in a population so small as the Estonian. So it is very important that the artists would find some other opportunities to draw and paint Andersen motifs. In April 2005, an exhibition of original illustrations was opened in The National Library.

The newest art project was organized by the weekly newspaper Estonian Express' art editor Harry Liivrand. He asked 9 famous Estonian artists to illustrate "The Steadfast Tin Soldier", to present the whole fairy tale with examples of different illustrators' works in the weekly (instead of all usual rubrics and columns). Also, the comments of the illustrators on their works and generally on Andersen's fairy tales were published there. (See www.ekspress.ee)

Translation of H.C. Andersen – Comparing Estonia, Latvia and Lithuania

The comparison here is completing a paper by Arunas Bliudzius (1999). The first translation in Estonia appeared 7 years later than in Latvia, but they are both conneced with the general cultural wave of the 1850-60s, called the period of national awakening both in Estonia and Latvia.

As A. Bliudzius has pointed out, there are differences in language of the sources used for the translation of Andersen's fairy tales. If Latvian translations are mostly from German and Danish, and Russian publications were used in the Soviet period, so the Estonian translation tradition seems to be analogical to the Latvian tradition.

Concerning the aims of publication of H.C. Andersen's works Bliudzius noted that Latvian translations primarily had the religious intention to change the children's minds and their view of Bible reading, wheras Lithuanian translators had a more practical purpose, orientated mostly toward adults. As mentioned before, many Estonian translations had presented the ambivalence of Andersen's works, both their dual address and the variety of "goals" (if it would be possible to discern one function from another concerning Andersen's multifarious emotionally stimulating, stylistically complicated texts at all), evident from the subtitles and appearing in comments in forewords about the educational and amusing qualities of Andersen's fairy tales.

The tendencies in Andersen translation have depended on different cultural, political, religious and economic factors. For example now, in the beginning of the 21st century, having a good tradition in Estonian culture of translating Andersen from the Danish original, some publishers prefer to publish the books (picture books with Andersen's fairy tales) in Estonian, using Italian or Spanish productions as the sources.

Andersen's Influence on Estonian Children's Literature

How did the knowledge of Andersen's fairy tales influence the writing of Estonian children's authors? The connection between translator Lea Nurkse and her son, the very popular writer Eno Raud, has been mentioned above.

As we know about the Estonian readership for Andersen's German publications in his lifetime, we may suppose also the impact of his works already from the middle of the 19th century. The motif of a child's death, treated by Johan de Mylius (2005), may be discovered also in the poetry of Andersen's first Estonian translator Lydia Koidula. Even one of her most popular texts, "My Fatherland", used long time as the non-official hymn of the Estonian people, includes the idea of sweet and happy death of the child. If the homeland is in the role of the Father (Fatherland) and the lyric "I" is a child, there would be no pain involved in dying under the protection of the Fatherland, sent by the singing of his birds and flourishing of his flowers.

Many of Andersen's fairy tales reflect his interest in science and scientific observation of nature. There is the possibility that one of the leaders of Estonian national awakening, the publisher of newspapers and author of textbooks Carl Robert Jakobson was also in contact with Andersen's works. A number of his short stories about nature in the collection "The Reader for the School" (1867-76, 3 volumes) express the spirit known from Andersen's stories and fairy tales about nature, giving human qualities to plants, water and other phenomena.

According to the results of the research by Helle Laanpere, who analysed answers by nearly 900 children and teenagers in a children's library, "The Ugly Duckling" is the most popular fairy tale among Estonian young readers. Also the motif of Andersen's "Ugly Duckling" (reading it, thinking about it) is the motif many times used in contemporary Estonian children's literature, as in the best known Bildungsroman "Kadri" (written by Silvia Rannamaa in 1959, cf. Laanpere 2005.)

Obviously the question about similarities between writers demands a detailed comparison and analysis of the secondary sources – letters, diaries, critical articles. Certainly an issue worthy of further research.

Literature

Bliudzius, A. 1999. The Translations of H.C. Andersen into Latvian and Lithuanian Languages (Comparative Aspects). In: *Hans Christian Andersen. A Poet in Time*. Ed. by Johan de Mylius et al., Odense University Press, Odense, 1999, pp. 323-35.

Digital collection of illustrations of Estonian National Library: http://www.nlib.ee/html/digi/rmt_ill/autorid

Jaaksoo, A. 1998. "Iga haritud rahva keeles" – Nukits 1998. Tallinn: Eesti Lastekirjanduse Teabekeskus. /"In the language of each educated nation"/

Laanpere, H. 2005. *Andersenist, emotsioonidega. Ettekanne konverentsil "Hans Christian Andersen 200: Meie elu muinasjutud"* Tallinna Ülikoolis 22. sept. 2005.

Mylius, Johan de. 2005. "Death and the Child." Plenary lecture on the IV International Hans Christian Andersen Conference – Between Children's Literature and Adult Literature.

Puhvel, M. 1999. *Symbol of Dawn. The Life and Times of the 19th Century Estonian Poet Lydia Koidula*. Tartu University Press.

Teder, E. 1996. Hans Christian Andersen ja Eesti. Rmt Lumikelluke /Hans Christian Andersen and Estonia. Epilogue in H.C. Andersen. The Snowdrop. Fairy tales and stories./ Tallinn: Eesti Raamat.

Vankumatu tinasõdur. (The Steadfast Tin Soldier.) www.ekspress.ee/ITF/EE/EE Foto.nsf/$All/FEFF86632ACFF393C225702F0040B762/$file/tinasodur.pdf

For Adults Only

Yoichi Nagashima

Ever since the 1880s, when some of H.C. Andersen's *eventyr* were first introduced to Japanese readers, his name has primarily been remembered as an author of fairy tales for children. In the beginning his works were retold through English, French, and German translations, often manipulated and adjusted to Japanese circumstances. Still they were so popular that no few *eventyr* were adapted and rewritten as Japanese tales. Even his novel *Improvisatoren*, translated from the German version by Mori Ôgai, one of the most prominent writers in modern Japan, was Japanized in such a way that the translated version has been much more celebrated than H.C. Andersen's original.

H.C. Andersen's works have always been known in Japan, but Japanese readers have had very little knowledge of the author himself and of the background of his literary production.[1] One could say that his 'fictive' autobiographies have been more or less believed to be real or at least highly probable. Under these circumstances the works of H.C. Andersen have been 'consumed' in Japan as they have delighted the reader. A solid image of H.C. Andersen as a pleasant storytelling uncle has thus been constructed.

Some scholars have not been ignorant of the phenomenon and have tried hard to break the distorted image of the Danish poet, but the attempts have remained unsuccessful.

Ôhata Suekichi translated H.C. Andersen's *eventyr* directly from the Danish original and he included explanatory postscripts, where he elaborated on the links between H.C. Andersen's life and his tales. Ôhata's translations are fine though old-fashioned, but unsatisfactory, because they are first and foremost made for children.

Suzuki Tetsurô, a competent translator of H.C. Andersen's works, succeeded in publishing Japanese versions of the novels and travelogues of H.C. Andersen. He was very promising as a refreshing and reliable translator of H.C. Andersen's tales into Japanese, but he died without finishing his lifework.

On the occasion of the 200th anniversary of H.C. Andersen's birth, I have taken the liberty of making a new translation of his *eventyr* especially designed for adult readers, thus challenging the existing image of H.C. Andersen in Japan as well as expanding and deepening the world of his *eventyr* for Japanese readers.

When talking about translation of H.C. Andersen's *eventyr* into Japanese, one must be aware of some of the idiosyncrasies of the Japanese language.

First of all there are clear distinctions between the languages of male/female, adult/child and so on; there are also different levels of honorific forms between senior/junior etc. expressing respect or humbleness.

Similar phenomena are to be found in other languages, too, like the well-known distinction between 'De' and 'du' in Danish, but the Japanese can say a sentence like: "Would you please open the door?" in a specifically masculine, feminine, or childish way, in most cases without even using pronouns.

In any communication in Japanese, you cannot speak properly to anybody without mapping out your own position as a speaker in relation to the surroundings. You have to decide and make clear who you are, and to whom you are speaking. A translator should do this, too.

One of the crucial tasks of a translator of H.C. Andersen into Japanese is to choose the voice of narrator with reference to the imagined readers and to define the readers themselves. Unfortunately, almost all translators of H.C. Andersen's *eventyr* have hitherto chosen the voice of narrator who talks exclusively to children, by using a language familiar to them.

Not only in the style of the language, or choice of vocabulary, but also graphically, you can recognize whether a given translation is made for children or not, namely by the type and numbers of the *kanji* characters used, the Chinese characters in the Japanese usage. The Japanese language has two sets of alphabet-like syllables, called *kana* – *hiragana* and *katakana*. In a Japanese text *kanji* characters are mixed with *kana*/characters, thus making the text readable as a genuine Japanese text.

During their six years at elementary school children are expected to learn 881 *kanji*, a certain number of which are taught progressively each year, and in junior high schools, before starting at high school, they should have learned 1850 *kanji* in all. Furthermore, you need to recognize approx. 3000 *kanji* characters in order to be able to read newspapers.

Thus one can use the numbers and types of *kanji* in a Japanese text as an indicator of the level of difficulty and readability of the text. In texts for children, certain words are written in *kana* alone without using *kanji*, according to how many *kanji* the school children have been taught.

Besides, printed types are bigger in texts for children, and some *kanji* are provided with reading, called *furigana*, written in small types of *kana* and placed on the right side of the *kanji*, or above the *kanji* when they are written horizontally, as shown below for the word *dôwa*, fairy tale.

どうわ
童話

All these indicators are erased from my new translation of H.C. Andersen's *eventyr*.[2] They are purposely translated as literary works for general readers, using *kanji* frequently without providing them with *furigana*. In such a way my texts signify graphically that they are not written for children.

My new translation has been published in four volumes, each of which contains my comments. They are written exclusively for adult readers. This alone was considered so innovative and provocative that all the major newspapers in Japan have introduced my publication for their readers.

Until 2005 no distinction was made between '*eventyr for børn*', '*eventyr*' and '*historier*' in Japan. All of them have been translated and understood as 'fairy tales' or 'tales for children' – '*eventyr for børn*', *dôwa* in Japanese, told by a kind and polite narrator exclusively for children, no matter what the subject is.

In the previous Japanese versions, the multilayered stories of the original '*eventyr og historier*' have been simplified and made banal, even changed into Disney-like fantasies. Only the surface stories are retold, and some stories are transformed drastically according to the readers' supposed expectation. In one version of "Historien om en Moder" for example, the dead boy comes to life again, after the mother has prayed sincerely to the God of Death. This is no longer an act of interpretation but a manipulation, or one could say a cultural translation made in a country without a Christian background.

Drawing by John Shelley from Yoichi Nagashima's new translation into Japanese, Hyoronsha publisher,.

One of the main purposes of my new translation is to disclose the discretely composed undercurrent in the text – the subtext of H.C. Andersen's works. In so doing I have tried to give the general readers in Japan an opportunity to understand the suppressed sexuality of H.C. Andersen, the vanity of a single man, the price of solitude and the absurdity of life, which in fact are actual themes of today. I have given the adult readers in Japan stylistically neutral texts of H.C. Andersen's works in a Japanese rendering, which are to be read as 'allegories' and not as more or less manipulated fairy tales exclusively for children.

The themes of the four volumes I have published are the following:

Absurdity – *Skyggen*
Eros – *Sneemanden, Thepotten, Sommerfuglen, Loppen og Professoren*
Life and death – *Historien om en Moder, Grantræet*
Love – *Den lille Havfrue*

The Japanese are very fond of H.C. Andersen's *eventyr*, but, up til now, they have only been able to read the somewhat spoiled and filtered versions for children. Certainly they have loved them and created their preferred image of H.C. Andersen.

Many of the readers of my translation for adult readers are shocked to discover the naked H.C. Andersen, the author in the flesh, in the subtexts of his *eventyr*. They have discovered the breadth and the depth in his allegorical works of a pre-Freudian world of sexuality, which hitherto has been concealed, because they have been considered inadequate for children.

Other readers have reacted against my translation by saying: "It's not Andersen!"

Like the princess in "Svinedrengen", they prefer the artificial rose of H.C. Andersen to the real poet.

Notes

1. See Yoici Nagashima: "De første H.C. Andersen-oversættelser i Japan", in: *Anderseniana*, 3. rk., bd. 3, [1978-81] Odense 1982, pp. 255-274, and "Hans Christian Andersen remade in Japan: Mori Ogai's translation of *Improvisatoren*", in: Johan de Mylius et al. (eds.): *Hans Christian Andersen: A Poet in Time*, Odense University Press, Odense 1999, pp. 397-406.
2. *Anata no shiranai Andersen* (H.C. Andersen you don't know), a new translation of H.C. Andersen's *eventyr* into Japanese with illustrations by John Shelley (Hyoronsha, Tokyo):
Vol. 1 *Kage* (Skyggen), December 2004, 68 p., ISBN 4-566-02176-9 CO397.
Vol. 2 *Yukidaruma* (Sneemamnden), January 2005, 68 p., ISBN 4-566-02177-7 CO397 [Thepotten, Sommerfuglen, Loppen og Professoren].
Vol. 3 *Hahaoya* (Historien om en Moder), March 2005, 68 p., ISBN 4-566-02178-5 CO397 [Grantræet].
Vol.4 *Ningyohime* (Den lille Havfrue), April 2005, 72 p., ISBN 4-566-02179-3 CO397.

"Out in the World, Thoughts Come"

Viggo Hjørnager Pedersen

In the conclusion of my dissertation *Ugly Ducklings?* (2004) I suggested as a possible field for further investigations of Andersen translations "Studies of idiomaticity in translated texts. A working hypothesis would be that if translated texts are generally less highly regarded than their originals, a reason could be that they are less idiomatic [...]."

As a beginning, I have now looked at idioms and half-idioms in a number of tales, and compared them with Dulcken's late 19th-century translation, and in some cases also with some more recent translations. My results so far confirm my suspicion that one of the great stumbling blocks for translators – and certainly for Dulcken – is interference from the source language(s), in this case Danish and/or German.[1]

One of the main ideas in Theo Hermans' epoch-making *Manipulation of Literature* (1985) was that one should describe translations, not evaluate them. This coincided with a general tendency in academic studies of literature at the time to move from criticism to "theory" – perhaps an understandable response to the exposure during a century or more to the more or less spontaneous overflow of the gut reaction of an endless number of more or less distinguished scholars.

However, in a situation where the market is constantly and increasingly being flooded with literary material, it has always seemed to me a natural and necessary part of the work of literary scholars to voice their opinion about the texts they have studied. Without going back to the times of Georg Brandes, when it was said that if you had read his *Hovedstrømninger* you need not bother to read the books discussed there, it is still a fact that nobody can form a personal opinion of all the books that are published, and that you often have to rely on the opinion of people who have studied the books you do not have the time to read – nor the inclination, if the expert's opinion is negative.

This is why in my discussion of English Andersen translations I have always tried to evaluate the texts as well as to describe them, and this is why I have come back to a question which was more or less outlawed by the Descriptivists of the 1980's and 1990's – why it is that a translation of a great literary work nine times out of ten strikes bilingual readers as being inferior to the original.

I have no intention of opening a general debate on that topic here, and I agree with the Descriptivists that one should look at translations such as they are rather than grumble because they are not much better. But in the following, I shall point to a couple of features that contribute to the situation such as it is, but which nevertheless do not seem to me to have received the attention they deserve in translation studies, i.e. the difficulty of matching idioms and wordplay on the one hand, and, perhaps even more importantly, the unperceived interference in the target language (TL) of constructions that are alien to it, even though no obvious linguistic rules seem to have been violated.

Preliminaries

Just for the record, there are of course also other and more basic problems than those outlined above that interfere with the rendition of Andersen's message. There are not many actual mistakes in Dr. Dulcken's Andersen – far fewer than in Caroline Peachey's, for instance – but there are some, and some of them tend to interfere negatively with their context. Examples like

> Pral var det og Pral blev det og saa gik jeg i Vasken!
> There was nothing but bragging among them, and therefore <u>I went away.</u> (The Darning Needle)²

> "See <u>nu blev det forfremmet!</u>" sagde Stoppenaalen,
> "<u>So, he is disposed of,</u>" observed the Darning-Needle.

> deres eget Hoved
> a peculiar head (The Darning Needle)

– are merely wrong translations, even though in most cases the translation loses an interesting aspect found in the original, such as the fact that the Darning Needle is thinking of social advancement all the time; but when in "Jack the Dullard" the princess talks of "hanekyllinger" (cockerels), "young pullets" is not a very smart translation, as pullet primarily refers to the female bird, so that the satiric reference to the wooers is lost:

> Det er fordi min Fader i Dag steger <u>Hanekyllinger</u>!
> my father is going to roast <u>young pullets</u> to-day. (Jack the Dullard)

Likewise with the following example:

> "Imorgen skal vi koge Suppe paa jer!" sagde *Hjalmar* og saa vaagnede han, (Ole Lukøie)
> ... we shall make <u>songs</u> of you

Hjalmar is angry with the hens, which is why he wants to make soup with them. The English translation loses the point of the original, but is probably an attempt to avoid the idea of eating some of the characters of the narrative – if it is not simply based on a misreading of the manuscript.

However, some examples are distinctly odd, so that it is not only by comparing with the Danish that you discover that something is wrong – the TL text in itself does not feel quite satisfactory:

> ... Griffelen gjorde Commers <u>paa Tavlen</u>;
> The pencil amused itself <u>on the table</u> (Tin Soldier)

Similar mistakes are found in other translations.

Reduction also occurs:

> dybe Grave, hvori voxte <u>Duunhammere,</u> Siv og Rør.
> a deep moat, in which grew reeds and grass (Everything in its Right Place)

One word, presumably unknown to the translator, has been left out. Not a great problem, perhaps, but if it happens often, it impoverishes the text.

> Brødrene det er <u>Stads-Karle</u>!
> Your brothers are <u>very different fellows</u> from you. (Jack the Dullard)

"Out in the World, Thoughts Come"   377

As can be seen from the treatment in ODS of the variant form, 'stadsekarl', the word was originally used of a person dressed in his very best to lead a procession. The derived sense of the Danish noun, meaning 'kernekarl' = 'good man', is idiomatic, smacking of provincial lower or lower middle class. The English, on the other hand, is quite neutral.

> Pludder der er kastet lige op af Grøften
> that is nothing but clay out of the ditch

Disregarding homonyms (pludder = babble), most Danes only know the word 'pludder' from this one context out of "Jack the Dullard", even if it is also used by Blicher and a few others. At any rate, this is clearly Andersen's attempt at spelling the Funen word for mud, 'plore', standard Danish 'pløre', and thus seems to be one of the dialect forms that have survived Andersen's educators and correctors. The English, apart from being lexically wrong, is colourless.

> "Krask!" sagde Æggeskallen, der gik et Vognmandslæs over den.
> "Crack!" went the egg-shell, for a hand-barrow went over her.
> (The Darning Needle)

Exactly why the wagon-load has been reduced to a wheelbarrow is difficult to tell; but the impact is not quite the same as that of the original.

> "Saa skal I have Kinderpulver!" sagde *Ole Lukøie.*
> "Then you must take medicine," said Ole Luk-Oie.

Here the Danish is specific, the English general.

Deletion

> ... og saa bleve de Porcelæns Folk sammen og de velsignede Bedstefaders Klinke og holdt af hinanden til de gik i Stykker.
> And so the porcelain people remained together, and loved one another until they broke. (The Shepherdess and the Chimney-Sweep)

The American editors of Glyn Jones' collection of tales also had difficulties with the word 'rivet' which should have been used here, and suggested replacing it with a 'screw' (see Jones 1993); in the end, they like Dulcken simply left it out.

Wordplay and Allusion

From the very beginning, and increasingly with time, as he grew more experienced as an artist, Andersen loved puns and allusions. Thus at the end of his first tale, "The Tinder-box" we read that "Hundene sad med til Bords og gjorde store Øine."[3] and in later stories there are usually several instances of verbal wit or presuppositions that are not necessarily shared by a TL audience.

The difficulty is illustrated in Erik Haugaard's translation of the following passage from "The Storm Shakes the Shield":

> Der fløi et Skilt med en afridset tør Klipfisk lige hen over Døren, hvor der boede en Mand, som skrev en Avis. Det var en flau Spøg af Stormvinden, den huskede nok ikke, at en Avisskriver aldeles ikke er at spøge med, han er Konge i sin egen Avis og i sin egen Mening.

> The wind carried a sign with a dried codfish on it to the door of a newspaper editor. I think that was a very poor joke. <u>In the first place it is only in Denmark that a codfish is a sign for stupidity;</u> and the storm should know of the great power of the press, which makes an editor king on his own newspaper and in his own opinion.

Haugaard, here as elsewhere, wants to explain what he does not think that the TL audience will understand. Whether the dried fish carries the same connotations as 'torsk' (cod) is a different question, however.

Sometimes Andersen uses words spoken by animals to imitate their voice. 'Bra', says the raven in "Elverhøi"; but if it does so in English also, we do not get the double meaning of assent and the sound a raven makes. (Cf. Hjørnager Pedersen (2004: 269).)

Allusion

One problematical aspect of translation is that texts may allude to other texts or to phenomena that are well known to the source language but not to the target language audience. "A String of Pearls" offers several examples of this:

> Nu komme vi til *Sigersted* ved Ringsted By; Aaleiet er lavt; det gule Korn voxer, hvor *Hagbarths* Baad lagde an, ikke langt fra *Signes* Jomfrubuur. <u>Hvo kjender ikke Sagnet om *Hagbarth*</u>, der hang i Egen og *Signelils* Buur stod i Lue, Sagnet om den stærke Kjærlighed.

> Now we reach Sigersted, near the town of Ringsted. The bed of the river is low here; yellow corn waves over the spot where Hagbarth's boat lay at anchor, not far from Signe's maiden bower. <u>Who does not know the legend of Hagbarth</u>, who was hanged on the oak tree while the bower of Signe burst into flames? Who can forget that legend of immortal love? (Jean Hersholt)

The point is that whereas most of Andersen's Danish readers knew the said legend, the English readers did not.

The section on Korsør alludes to the poet Baggesen, but never mentions his name! In this case, Hersholt supplies the missing information:

> ... Korsör, birthplace of Baggesen, master of words and wit!

Descriptive Synonyms

Phenomena such as proper names often have descriptive synonyms, like the Danish for the North Sea, "Vestervov-vov," rendered by some translators as "The Western Bow-wow", which, however, is not idiomatic. A similar example can be found in the nicknames of the fingers in "Stoppenaalen", where again the English translations are not idiomatic:

> de vare fem Brødre, <u>alle fødte "Fingre"</u>, de holdt sig ranke op til hverandre, skjøndt af forskjellig Længde; den yderste af dem: *Tommeltot,* var kort og tyk, han gik udenfor Geledet, og saa havde

han kun eet Knæk i Ryggen, han kunde kun bukke een Gang, men han sagde: at blev han hugget af et Menneske, saa var hele det Menneske spoleret for Krigstjeneste. *Slikpot* kom i Sødt og Suurt, pegede paa Sol og Maane, og det var ham, der klemte, naar de skrev; *Langemand* saae de andre over Hovedet; *Guldbrand* gik med Guldring om Maven og lille *Peer Spillemand* bestilte ikke noget og deraf var han stolt. Pral var det og Pral blev det og saa gik jeg i Vasken!

There were five brothers, all of the finger family. They kept very proudly together, though they were of different lengths: the outermost, the thumbling, was short and fat; he walked out in front of the ranks and only had one joint in his back, and could only make a single bow, but he said that if he were hacked off from a man, that man was useless for service in war. Dainty-mouth, the second finger, thrust himself into sweet and sour, pointed to sun and moon, and gave the impression when they wrote. Longman, the third, looked at all the others over his shoulder. Goldborder, the fourth, went about with a golden belt round his waist; and little Playman did nothing at all, and was proud of it.

Puns

Under the heading of wordplay should of course also be discussed puns proper. However, as this has already been done by de Mylius (1993) and Jakobsen (2000), I shall here merely refer briefly to their findings.

De Mylius in his article makes the point that puns translate well into German, but not into English and French.

Jakobsen, commenting on the solutions of three translators, considers that Keigwin is rather good at this, followed by Haugaard, but that none of the translators match the original. This is probably one of the reasons why their texts seem less attractive than the original.

Just one example:

De veed ikke hvad der stikker under dem! jeg stikker, jeg sidder her.
They don't know what is under them! I'm here, I remain firmly here. (The Darning Needle)

Modes of Address, Conjunctions and Prepositions, Exclamations

In Hans Christian Andersen's Danish, and well into the 20th century, it was customary to address people in the third person, to mark social distance. Underlings would be addressed by 'hun' or 'han' (he or she), people to whom respect was thought to be due by their title. This obviously is not the case in English, but the Danish usage (which is also found in German) is often transferred into English, especially by Dulcken.

> "Det er kjønne Børn, <u>Moder</u> har!" sagde den gamle And ...
> "Those are pretty children that <u>the mother</u> has there," said the old Duck (The Ugly Duckling)

> "Gud, skal <u>Frøkenen</u> selv have Uleilighed!" sagde *Hjalmar* ...
> "Will <u>the young lady</u> really take so much trouble?" cried Hjalmar. (Ole Luk-Oie)

The second of the above examples also illustrates the fact that Danish exclamations involving the name of God are often avoided in translation – cf. Hjørnager Pedersen (2004: 336)

Especially in reported speech 'ja' (yes) is often used to mark a connection. In English, 'well' may often be used with a similar function, but 'yes' is distinctly odd:

> "Hearts!" repeated the Portuguese, "yes, that we have, almost as much as in Portugal." (In the Duck-yard)

> The next day – yes, it will be best that we pass over the next day. (The Old Street Lamp).

> If I were only in the warm room, among all the pomp and splendour! And then? Yes, then something even better will come, ... (The Fir Tree)

Adverbs of Place in Combination

In my book *Ugly Ducklings* (2004: 328ff) I describe the very Danish combination of adverbs of place with prepositional phrases. This is rare in English, but frequent in translations, especially Dulcken's, who grew so fond of this construction that he introduced it even when it was not in the original as in the below example.

> udefra komme ogsaa Tanker (The Windmill)
> Out in the world, thoughts come (The Windmill)

Cf. also:

> Ude paa Landet var der en gammel Gaard
> Far in the interior of the country lay an old baronial hall (Jack the Dullard)

> Langt ude i Havet er Vandet saa blaat, som Bladene paa den deiligste Kornblomst ...
> Far out in the sea the water is as blue as the petals of the most beautiful corn-flower ... (The Little Mermaid)

Collocations: Idioms and Pseudo-idioms

Under this heading I shall treat both idioms and what I have called pseudo-idioms (Hjørnager Pedersen: 1997). Idioms, though not necessarily of a totally fixed form, are easily recognized and should normally not be transferred verbatim into TL, though in translated fiction I have found examples like "han kunne charmere fugle ned fra træerne" ("he could charm birds off the trees").

Such examples are ludicrous and easy to spot as mistakes. But often an idiom is just translated more or less verbatim without much harm being done, only it does not function as an idiom in TL:

> "Det brænder Altsammen!" sagde hun. "Det brænder i lys Lue!"
> "It's all on fire!" she answered. "It's burning with a bright flame!"
> (The Porter's Son)

> Dagen efter talte man ikke om den Begivenhed, derfor har man den Talemaade "at stikke Piben ind!"

> The day afterwards not a word was said about this marvellous event; and thence has come the expression, "pocketing the flute". (Everything in its Right Place)

Apart from the fact that "pipe" or "whistle" is probably a better translation than "flute" here, the problem is that one does not have the expression "pocketing the flute" in English – unlike its Danish original, this phrase is not idiomatic.

In other cases the translator will substitute an authentic TL idiom for the source language idiom that is not found in the target language. In Danish, you can be "fuld som en allike" (drunk as a jackdaw), in English, "drunk as a lord", and unless there is reference to the exact form of the idiom in the context, such a substitution works alright. But not always:

> det kunde nok knage i En at bære dette, endsige bære to Vaabenmærker, og det knagede i *Generalinden*, naar hun strunk og stadselig kjørte til Hofbal.

> A man might well have a bee in his bonnet, when he had such a coat of arms to carry as that, let alone having to carry two; and the General's wife had a bee in hers when she drove to the Court ball, as stiff and as proud as you please. (The Porter's Son)

The English is certainly very idiomatic, but it does not render the stiffness implied by the original.

Much more insidious, however, are constructions which are not easily recognized as faulty TL, but which are just extremely unlikely in texts originally written in TL. Elsewhere, I have drawn attention to the auctorial observation about the decapitated witch in "The Tinder Box" "There she lay" (several translators). Der laae hun.

Dulcken, not to mention Peachey, are full of such constructions which in my opinion are largely to blame for the comparatively bad reputation of these translators. Here are a number of examples from "The Porter's Son". Translations are by Dulcken.

> ... Tegninger, og dem havde han mange af; de kom ligesom ud af Blyanten og Fingrene.

he had a great number of drawings. <u>They seemed to shoot out of his pencil and out of his fingers'-ends</u>.

This is not at all bad – but Andersen is, as it were, more organic than Dulcken.

> de havde to Vaabener paa deres Vogn; eet for hver af dem; Fruen havde det paa hvert sit Stykke Tøi, ude og inde, paa sin Natkappe og sin Natsæk; hendes, det ene, var et kostbart Vaaben, kjøbt af hendes Fader for <u>blanke Dalere</u>, for han var ikke født med det, hun ikke heller, <u>hun var kommen for tidlig</u>, syv Aar før Vaabenet;

They had two coats of arms on their carriage, a coat of arms for each of them; and the gracious lady had had this coat of arms embroidered on both sides of every bit of linen she had, and even on her nightcap and her dressing-bag. One of the coats of arms, the one that belonged to her, was a very dear one; it had been bought for <u>hard cash</u> by her father, for he had not been born with it, nor had she; <u>she had come into the world too early, seven years before the coat of arms</u>,

Again a good translation, but is "hard cash" really the same as "blanke dalere"? And the Danish "hun var kommen for tidlig" carries a perfidious additional sense of illegitimacy – of a child not conceived in wedlock – which is not quite so obviously conveyed by the English translation.

> kom han i Selskab, var det, som om han kom ridende ind paa sin høie Hest, og Ordener havde han paa, saa mange, at det var ubegribeligt, …

When he came to a party, he looked somehow as if he were riding into the room upon his high horse; and he had orders, too, such a number that no one would have believed it;

Nonce-formations that Read Like Idioms:

Andersen has a facility for coining memorable phrases and expressions which feel like idioms, though they are not – at least they were not before his time. The translations are normally less convincing. Here are a couple of examples from "Jack the Dullard":

> "Duer ikke!" sagde Kongedatteren. "Væk!"
> "He is of no use!" said the Princess. "Away with him!"

> "Hvad be – hvad?" sagde han, og alle Skriverne skrev Hvad be – hvad!
> "Duer ikke!" sagde Kongedatteren. "Væk!"

> "What – what were you – were you pleased to ob-" stammered he- – and all the clerks wrote down, "pleased to ob-"
> "He is of no use!" said the Princess. "Away with him!"

> "Det var fiint gjort!" sagde Kongedatteren, "det kunde jeg ikke have gjort! men jeg skal nok lære det!" –
> "That was very cleverly done," observed the Princess. "I could not have done that; but I shall learn in time."

Collective Impact

To get an overview of the factors involved in the problems I have tried to investigate here, I have split the translation problems up into several categories. But when you read a story, it is the total impact that counts. Let me conclude with a whole paragraph from "Everything in its Right Place", where several of the features discussed above may be observed together:

> <u>Velsignet og godt</u> var der paa den gamle Gaard, <u>Moder</u> stod selv for det Indvendige og Fader for det Udvendige; det var ligesom Velsignelsen vældede frem, og hvor Velstand er, der kommer Velstand til Huse. Den gamle Gaard blev pudset og malet, <u>Gravene</u> rensede og Frugttræer plantede; venligt og godt saae der ud og Stuegulvet var blankt som et <u>Spækkebræt</u>. I den store Sal sad om Vinteraftnerne <u>Madamen</u> med alle sine Piger og spandt Uldent og Linnet; <u>og hver Søndagaften læstes der høit af Bibelen, og det af Justitsraaden selv, for han blev Justitsraad, Hosekræmmeren, men det var først paa hans meget gamle Dage. Børnene voxte til, – der kom Børn, – og alle bleve de vel oplærte, men de havde jo ikke lige gode Hoveder, saadan som det er i enhver Familie.</u>

> It was a good thing now to be in the old mansion. <u>The mother managed the domestic affairs, and the father superintended the estate and it seemed as if blessings were streaming down. Where rectitude enters in, prosperity is sure to follow</u>. The old house was cleaned and painted, the <u>ditches</u> were cleared and fruit trees planted. Everything wore a bright cheerful look, and the floors were as polished as a <u>draught board</u>. In the long winter evenings <u>the lady</u> sat at the spinning-wheel with her maids, <u>and every Sunday evening there was a reading from the Bible by the Councillor of Justice himself – this title the dealer had gained, though it was only in his old age. The children grew up – for children had come – and they received the best education, though all had not equal abilities, as we find indeed in all families.</u>

Apart from little inaccuracies – such as "the ditches" for "gravene" (the moats), the rhythm and whole way of presentation of the narrative is very different in the last part of the paragraph, from "og hver Søndagaften ...". The Danish is full of little ironical afterthoughts: "Børnene voxte til – der kom Børn, –" where the English tries to be more logical: " – for children had come –"; and yet the English construction breaks down a little when the "Councillor of Justice" is to be explained, whereas the Danish sentence is perfectly natural and easy. We note in passing that a typical Andersen comparison "blankt som et Spækkebræt" (as well polished as a chopping board) is modified to "polished as a draught board." One cannot really have chopping boards introduced in polite society! But this of course tends to defeat the point of the whole passage: The pedlar and the goosegirl remain themselves in spite of their new dignity, in contrast to their descendants, who are apt to give themselves airs.

Conclusion

Readers may find that we have strayed a little from a strict application of the concept of idiomaticity in the above. My point, however, is that all the features mentioned here are relevant for the easy reception and for the enjoyment of the tales. It is indeed necessary for thoughts to come into the head of the translator when a great writer is to be taken abroad. However, some of the problems discussed are insoluble, and as I hope the above has demonstrated, Dulcken and the other translators quoted here normally do their best; only the wit and poetry of Andersen does suffer in most English translations.

Bibliography

Andersen, H.C. *Eventyr og Historier I-VII*. Ed. by Erik Dal and Erling Nielsen. Copenhagen: Hans Reitzel, 1963-90.

Andersen, H.C. *The Complete Illustrated Stories of Hans Christian Andersen*. London: Chancellor Press, 1983.

Andersen, H.C. *The Complete Fairy Tales and Stories*. Translated by E.C. Haugaard, 1974. Harmondsworth: Penguin, 1985.

Bredsdorff, Elias. *H.C. Andersen og England*. Copenhagen, Rosenkilde og Bagger, 1954.

Hjørnager Pedersen, Viggo. "Ugly Ducklings? Reflections on some English Versions of Hans Andersen's "Den grimme Ælling"". *Translation Theory in Scandinavia. Proceedings from SSOTT III*. Eds. Patrick Nigel Chaffey, Antin Fogner Rydning and Solveig Schult Ulriksen. Oslo, 1990. Pp. 229-42.

Hjørnager Pedersen, Viggo. "Description and Criticism: Some Approaches to the English Translations of Hans Christian Andersen." *Text Typology and Translation*. Ed. Anna Trosberg. Amsterdam, Philadelphia: John Benjamins Publishing Company, 1997. Pp. 99-115.

Hjørnager Pedersen, Viggo. *Ugly Ducklings? Studies in the English Translations of Hans Christian Andersen's Tales and Stories*. Odense: University Press of Southern Denmark, 2004. (Doctoral Thesis, 'disputats', 389 pp.)

Jacobsen, F. *H.C. Andersens ordspil i original og engelsk oversættelse. DAO 9*. Copenhagen: Center for Translation Studies, 2000.

Jones, W. Glyn. "Hvad har de dog gjort ved Andersen – en historie til skræk og advarsel." *DAO* 4. Eds. Viggo Hjørnager Pedersen and Birgit Nedergaard Larsen. Copenhagen: Centre for Translation Studies, 1993. Pp. 67-80.

Mylius, Johan de. "Ordspil i H.C. Andersens eventyr". *Om at oversætte H.C. Andersen. DAO 4*. Eds. Viggo Hjørnager Pedersen and Birgit Nedergaard Larsen. Copenhagen: Centre for Translation Studies 1993. Pp. 28-42.

ODS = Ordbog over det danske Sprog (1919), Copenhagen, 1975.

Notes

1. It is not clear what is the original of Dulcken's text. He certainly used the German Leipzig edition, but may also have referred to the original Danish. See discussion in Hjørnager Pedersen (2004).

2. Unless otherwise stated, the translation used in this article is Ducklen's (Andersen 1983).
3. "Hundene sad med til Bords og gjorde store Øine" is often rendered "and the dogs sat with them at the table, their eyes wide with astonishment", or "staring about them with their big eyes". This is not adequate, as the Danish phrase combines wonder with humour, but it is nevertheless the standard solution. Dulcken improves this to "the three dogs sat at the table too, and opened their eyes wider than ever at all they saw". Conversely, James's "sat at table and made great eyes" is hardly an improvement. The best solution is probably Spink's "the dogs sat at table with the rest and were all eyes", because this translation in fact uses an idiom: however, it is much easier to translate this phrase as many other idioms into German: "die Hunde saßen mit zu Tisch und machten Große Augen" (Storrer-Madelung).

Dynamism in Perception of Hans Christian Andersen in Saint Petersburg, one of the most Andersenous Cities of the World

Boris Zharov

The constantly changing world reflects various sides of Hans Christian Andersen's creativity. This also applies to understanding how Hans Christian Andersen was perceived in Russia. Russia showed an interest in him as early as the 1830s. The priority among the Russian cities belongs to Saint Petersburg, which was called by the Russian poet Alexander Pushkin "the window towards Europe" not by chance.

During the first presentation of Hans Christian Andersen Russian readers got acquainted with his works in foreign languages. Translations appeared later, and they were not done from Danish, mostly they were done from German.

One of the first works appreciated by Russian readers was the novel *The Improvisatore* translated from German. The Russian historian and philologist Jakob Grot, working in the University of Helsinki as a History professor, recommended the novel to the magazine *Sovremennik*. His sister Roza Grot translated – or to be more exact adapted – this novel. In 1844 her translation appeared as a magazine version and then as a separate edition. The novel was not really successful, as it was noted by reviewer Pjotr Pletnjov, who wrote that the novel "was not created for common people, but for the selected few". Russian readers perceived *The Improvisatore* as a romantic novel, which appeared "too late". The reviewers wrote: 'We wanted to see our contemporary whoever he was."[1] The last remark is quite typical. It shows that the novel was perceived not as a work in remote time and space, but as an inseparable part of contemporary literature.

Later Hans Christian Andersen's fairy tales attracted the greatest interest. Readers got acquainted with the fairy tales either in foreign languages or in Russian translations. And they became popular pretty soon. The reviewer Nikolaj Dobroljubov, who read the fairy tales in the 1850s called them "nice, funny, touching" and recommended them for children. In his opinion the most successful fairy tales were satirical ones such as "The Emperor's New Clothes" and "The Princess on the Pea". The reviewer Nikolaj Černyševskij put Hans Christian Andersen in the range of the best Danish writers.[2]

The first collection of Andersen's fairy tales in St. Petersburg was published in 1869, i.e. in Andersen's lifetime. It included 14 fairy tales translated from German. In the introduction it was said: "Nothing can be compared with them in the extreme power of imagination, freshness of images and charm of story telling."[3] This collection of fairy tales had a great success and was noted by critics especially in the magazine *Sovremennik*: "For the first time the Russian public will be able to get acquainted with the works of the wonderful and unique storyteller, to get acquainted with this original literature form non-existing in Russian literature... The fairy tales are fresh and poetical."[4]

It is interesting to note that the critic Vladimir Stasov argued with this point of view: the reviewers "were probably not able to appreciate the significance of Hans Christian Andersen as a whole. They felt only his poetry and high artistic value and managed to see that a serious idea reigns *almost always* in his fairy tales. They did not know that 'the idea' was predominant *everywhere*."[5]

Due to the great success of this collection a new edition appeared. It led to an interesting correspondence. The translators Maria Trubnikova and Nadežda Stasova sent a letter to Hans Christian Andersen, and he wrote to them in response. Hans Christian Andersen's letter became well-known in Russia, but remained unknown in Denmark, and the letter of the translators, published in Denmark, couldn't find its way to the Russian reader for a long time.[6]

The above mentioned collection helped Russian readers to learn about the existence of fairy tales by Hans Christian Andersen. But a real turning point which led to his everlasting glory came when two translators Peter Hansen (in Russia Pjotr Gotfridovič Ganzen, 1846-1930) and Anna Hansen (Anna Vasil'jevna Ganzen, 1869-1942) started translating directly from Danish and published separate fairy tales and a collection of works by Hans Christian Andersen.[7]

These translations are not only a part of foreign literature which a Russian reader can get acquainted with if he wants. It is a really existing element of the Russian language culture. The contribution of these two translators to Russian culture is greater than the contribution of some writers using their native language in their work.

During numerous conferences and meetings which were held in St. Petersburg in 2005 in connection with 200th birthday of Hans Christian Andersen I heard the words: "Hans Christian Andersen is not a foreign, but a Russian writer." That is how many generations of Russian readers perceive Hans Christian Andersen.

Peter Hansen was born in Copenhagen and planned to be an actor (like Hans Christian Andersen who as a boy moved to Copenhagen with ambitions of becoming a star). He was taken to the Royal Theatre and worked there for 6 years. But the expected success did not come. He didn't know that his major achievements in life would be connected with literature. Peter Hansen knew Hans Christian Andersen personally, they corresponded, and he is mentioned in the diaries of Hans Christian Andersen.

In 1871 Peter Hansen gave up his theatrical ambitions and made up his mind to change his life. He got a job which at that time was demanded and fashionable – a telegrapher. The Great Scandinavian Telegraph Company (Storno) recruited telegraphers to work in China and to the telegraph line along the Trans Siberian Railway. Peter Hansen decided to work in China. But travelling through Siberia he decided to stay in Omsk and persuaded his colleague to go to China instead of him. This is a family tradition kept by his descendants in St. Petersburg.

He lived in Siberia for 10 years. During long cold nights he thoroughly learnt Russian. He made notes, translated different texts, fragments from literary works. Once he read the novel by Ivan Goncharov *A Common Story*. He liked the novel immensely and started translating it into Danish just for himself. When finished he decided to send the novel to Danish publishers. It was immediately published and had a great success in Denmark.

The first translating success inspired Peter Hansen, and several translations of Russian authors into Danish appeared. Later on he translated Danish writers into Russian. In 1881 a telegraphy school was opened in St. Petersburg, and Peter Hansen moved to the capital of Russia and started teaching there. In 1888 he married Anna Vasil'jeva, who was gifted in literature and who soon shared the translating activity of her husband.

Due of the Revolution, Peter Hansen returned to Denmark in 1917 and never came back to Russia. In spite of the fact that the fairy tales had been translated by both of them, under the Soviet regime it was not always allowed to mention his name as a translator. Anna Hansen went to see her husband in Denmark several times, but not for long.

She received new literary works from him and carried on the translating activity. She was a very active member of "The Writers' Union", which sprang into existence at that time. Anna Hansen remained in Leningrad during the blockade of the Second World War. In the time of starvation and cold she thought about conservation of the books in her family library and allowed her relatives to burn only the back of them. She died in the spring of 1942.

During the two centuries there were many translators of Russian literature into Danish and Peter Hansen was only one of them. But it is quite another thing when we deal with translating from Danish and other Scandinavian languages into Russian. These two translators worked together from 1890 to 1917, i.e. for 28 years, quite a lot of time. But if we start counting from 1877, when Peter Hansen began to translate, and finish by the fall of 1941, when Anna Hansen stopped working, we have more than 60 years. This fact is quite unique. Moreover they translated from the original language, while in the 19th century it was quite normal to use an intermediate language, and as a rule it was German in the case of Scandinavian languages. And the quality of their translating was very high.

Many thousands of pages by different authors were translated, from numerous languages, mostly originating from areas quite close to the north-western part of Russia. Thereby the Russian readers not only got access to several good writers, these translators opened Scandinavia for Russia, like America was discovered and opened for Europe a long time ago. Reading Russia knew both ancient Scandinavian literature and writers of the 19th century, but it was greatly interested in the mental world of those who lived nearby and was extremely close to it in time – the end of the 19th and the beginning of the 20th century. The translators introduced a number of works which were not only *read* by Russians, but became an inseparable part of their cultural world.

People who do not deal with literary translation think that it is quite easy. But this is not true. The diligence of Peter and Anna Hansen is wonderful. When the husband left home for work the wife took his place at the table and worked with new translations. When the husband came home, it was his turn to translate and the wife did her home chores. And they could dedicate much more time to their work while spending the summer in their summer cottage. This extreme diligence became part and parcel of the life of their children.

There are kept memories how these translators worked with Hans Christian Andersen's fairy tales. When the first version of some fairy tale was done they gathered the children. The fairy tale was read aloud slowly, meanwhile attention was drawn to the reaction of the small listeners. If something was misunderstood or the reaction was not natural, corrections were made and a new checking took place. Everything should sound quite natural.

It is not surprising that Hans Christian Andersen's fairy tales translated by Peter and Anna Hansen are now being published in millions of copies practically unchanged, and it distinguishes them from many others that were quite good some time ago, but sound old-fashioned nowadays.

Alongside with editing separate works by Hans Christian Andersen the translators accomplished something quite unique: they published a collection of Hans Christian Andersen's works in four volumes.[8] The edition was appreciated as the best one in the world. Later they published a full collection of Henrik Ibsen's work in eight volumes and published their own magazine called 'Fiords: Danish, Norwegian and Swedish writers in translation by Anna and Peter Hansen'. No less than 13 volumes appeared.

Besides translating, Peter Hansen wrote some works of his own, which made Russian readers familiar with different sides of life in Scandinavian countries. He corresponded with Russian writers and spent a few days in Jasnaja Poljana with Leo Tolstoy. Interesting memories about this visit have been preserved.

Nevertheless, if one appreciates the activity of these remarkable personalities, the contribution of Anna and Peter Hansen by translating Scandinavian literature into Russian should be singled out for special mention.

A special interest in the life and work of these translators was generated in 2005 during the preparation for the Hans Christian Andersen jubilee. Anna Hansen was born in a small town of Kasimov located nearly 300 km to the south-east of Moscow. In April children libraries in Kasimov and Riazan organized in Kasimov a wonderful holiday devoted to Hans Christian Andersen and Anna Hansen for kids and grown-ups. A scientific conference was included into the frame of the holiday.

Being inspired by the success of this event the organizers, among them St. Petersburg State University, decided to establish *Hansen Centre,* devoted to both of the translators, and to hold *Hansen conferences* with participation of Russian children's writers and translators working with Scandinavian languages annually in April. The organizers are ready to receive the guests from Scandinavia in their home in case of financial difficulties.

Peter and Anna Hansen had six children. Marianna Hansen-Koževnikova (1889-1974), their daughter, took the way of her famous parents. She translated books. But still more important is that she became the first teacher of Danish in the history of education in Russia. She started teaching at the Philological Faculty of the University of Leningrad (St. Petersburg) and worked there for 16 years. Teaching was pretty hard. Texts typed by the teacher herself, compiled from books from Hansen family's library were the only material for students. There were no Danish-Russian or Russian-Danish dictionaries, grammar books, readers, and no Danish newspapers. But the first book read by the students in Danish was the biography of Hans Christian Andersen. They also read a lot of his works. About 30 students were taught, many of them connected their lives with Scandinavian countries as did the author of these lines.

The Hansen dynasty is developing. A well-known translator Inna Streblova is a grand-daughter of Marianna Hansen-Koževnikova. She graduated from the Danish department of the University and translated a lot of books from all Scandinavian languages, German and English. The grand-son Pjotr Koževnikov is a writer.

The translations of Hans Christian Andersen's works made by Anna and Peter Hansen served as a foundation of all further publications in the Russian language, as well as the ones in numerous languages of the people who lived in Russia and some other countries. As a result many millions of copies appeared during the following 120 years.

The 1920-30s was a period of great popularity of fairy tales by Hans Christian Andersen. But we should take into account that under the Soviet regime all literary works, including fairy tales, passed through censorship. The fragments colored by religion were shaded and sometimes even rewritten. I have two examples. In the fairy tale "The Sandman" the pages about death, sadness and God were changed in many editions. "The Nightingale" stopped to be published after The People's Republic of Chine was founded in 1949.

But the year of 1955, the previous Hans Christian Andersen jubilee year, made him one of the most famous writers in our country. It was the so-called "Thaw", the time of the first reforms in political and social life in Russia after the Stalin regime. The human virtues were put at the top. The fairy tales of Hans Christian Andersen were published in great numbers.

The next peak of interest took place at the time of crucial reforms at the beginning of the 1990s. The old ideological platform was ruined, but the new one wasn't yet developed. Hans Christian Andersen's works became greatly demanded again.

In making books for children, the artists' work is of great importance. St. Petersburg's artists illustrated Hans Christian Andersen's fairy tales; their number is great. The Traugot family is really worth mentioning. Georgij Traugot was the first who started illustrating Hans Christian Andersen's fairy tales. When his two sons grew up, they joined him. And from that time on, appeared the initial letters of the three artists before their family name. When their father died his sons became famous. Each of them has his own manner and artistic interests. But when they illustrate Hans Christian Andersen's works they use the initial letters of all the three.

Special attention should be drawn to the theatre artist Oskar Klever (1887-1975) who painted in oil and water-colour. He loved Hans Christian Andersen's books greatly. During 60 years he created more than 100 water-colour illustrations which looked absolutely unlike the previously published ones. If one looks at them it is quite clear that Hans Christian Andersen is a tragic writer who worked for grown-ups. Having lost all hope to be published in his own country the artist presented part of his water-colours to the Hans Christian Andersen Museum in Odense in 1969. Now they are published and known to a wide range of people.

Hans Christian Andersen's books are printed in a great number of copies. Anyone can buy them in any shop or borrow them in any library. Besides one can get acquainted with his fairy tales in other ways. They can be easily performed on the stage.

St. Petersburg was always the city of theatres. During the 20th century one could see many performances based on Hans Christian Andersen's fairy tales. The peak of theatrical interest in Hans Christian Andersen's work falls in the middle of the 1990s. At this time there were shown 32 performances in the city: 28 on professional stages, and four in theatres with a constant cast of students and professional instructors. As for the genres there were: 14 dramas (with fragments of music), seven operas, four ballets, and seven puppet shows. It is worth mentioning that theatres in St. Petersburg have a repertoire status, i.e. several different performances are made at the same time.

Such a great amount of performances based on Hans Christian Andersen's works allows us to draw two conclusions. First, there is no writer whether alive or dead, whether writing for children or for grown-ups to be compared with Hans Christian Andersen – concerning his work used as a plot for performances. Hans Christian Andersen is the most theatrical writer. Secondly, there is no city in Russia or in any other country where Hans Christian Andersen's work generated such an enormous interest. From this point of view St. Petersburg is the most Andersenous city in the world. It is quite natural that fairy tales are not staged as they are in books. It is a well-known fact that even Shakespeare's plays are staged with some changes – to say nothing of the use of prose instead of blankverse. Moreover every producer has not only the right but the duty to stage the performance in the given period, for the given viewer on the certain day.

One of the most famous Russian producers and theatre artists Nikolaj Akimov created a performance based on the play *The Shadow* by Jevgenij Švarc in the Comedy Theatre. The theatrical effects, extraordinary scenery in particular, were considered as the gold fund of the Russian theatre. The play *The Snow Queen* by Jevgenij Švarc is very often staged in the city and in the country. St. Petersburg saw it in the stage version of Nina Reikhštein, who is a fairy tale lover. The earliest play by Jevgenij Švarc based on Hans Christian Andersen's *The Emperor's New Clothes* was in the Fontanka-Youth Theatre at the beginning of its theatrical career. It is a real surprise that the talent of the old writer who lived in a different world and had different artistic values helps modern theatres to find their own way. His thoughts and characters are so extraordinary that they help the actors to find extraordinary means of interpretation.

The most interesting operas are *The Emperor's New Clothes* (music by Tikhon Khrennikov), *The Snow Queen* (music by Sergej Banevič), *The Nightingale* (music by Igor Stravinskij).

There were 14 fairy tales by Hans Christian Andersen in the repertoire of St. Petersburg's theatres. The most popular is *The Swineherd*. This short, but informative fairy tale tells not only about love and sufferings of the loving heart, but also about art and its power to identify true and false. The others are *The Snow Queen*, *The Emperor's New Clothes*, *The Tinder-Box*, *Thumbelina*, *The Shadow* and at last but not least *The Little Mermaid*. This list reflects the main core in the fairy tales of Hans Christian Andersen known practically all over the world.

Speaking about the films we should mention Russian films produced by The Lenfilm-studio – "The Snow Queen" and "The Very Old Fairy Tale" ("The Tinder-Box") by the famous producer Nadežda Kaševerova.

In the 20th century a scientific study of Hans Christian Andersen's works in Russia takes its start. St. Petersburg scholar Ljudmila Braude made a great input to Russian "Anderseniana". She published a great number of research works as well as translations during the past years. In 1996, 2000 and 2005 there were organized three scholarly Hans Christian Andersen-conferences by St. Petersburg State University.[9]

Nowadays every bookshop has a lot of fairy tales by Hans Christian Andersen of different sizes and shapes. Librarians also note their great popularity. In every home where Hans Christian Andersen's fairy tales are read, in every theatre where they are staged, grateful hearts of both grown-ups and children beat in unison with the heart of the great Danish poet.

Notes

1. Šarypkin, Dmitrij, *Skandinavskaja literatura v Rossii*. Leningrad, 1980. Pp. 243-45.
2. Braude, Ljudmila, "Khans Kristian Andersen v Rossii". In: Andersen, Hans Kristian, *Skazki, rasskazannyje detjam; Novyje skazki*. Moskva, 1980. P. 323.
3. *Polnoje sobranije skazok Andersena*. Sankt Peterburg, 1863. P. 4.
4. *Sovremennik*, 1864. 9, pp. 96-101.
5. Stasov, V., *Nadežda Vasil'jevna Stasova*. Sankt Peterburg, 1899. P. 132.
6. Braude, Ljudmila. *Op. cit.* Pp. 327-28.
7. About A. & P. Hansen in Russian: Braude, Ljudmila. *Op. cit.* Pp. 328-32; Zharov, Boris, "Perevodčeskij podvig A. i P. Ganzenov". *Skandinavskije čtenija 2000*. Sankt Peterburg, 2002. Pp. 545-51; Streblova, Inna, "Ganzen", *Tri veka Sankt-Peterburga. Enciklopedia v 3 tomakh*. Tom 2. 19 vek. Kniga 2. Sankt Peterburg, 2003. Pp. 26-28; *Ona naučila Andersena govorit' po-russki: Anna Vasil'jevna Ganzen (1869-1942)*. Rjazan', 2005.
8. *Sobranije sočinenij Gansa Khristiana Andersena v perevodakh A. i P. Ganzen v 4 tomakh*. Sankt Peterburg, 1894-95. Vols. 1-4.
9. *H.C. Andersen i Rusland: Bidrag til et symposium på Skt. Petersborgs Universitet 17. maj 1996*. Ed. by Aage Jørgensen, Boris S. Sjarov and Michael Jakobsen. Aarhus, 1997.

Hans Christian Andersen's Fairy Tales – Children's Literature?

Anette Øster

Introduction

In Denmark Hans Christian Andersen is regarded as a writer who wrote not only for children, but also for adults. However, in English-speaking countries he is mostly considered a children's writer. In contrast the debate in Denmark among researchers in Hans Christian Andersen's oeuvre is how far he wrote for children at all. Without wishing to delve any deeper into this issue, I don't think, however, there can be any doubt that Andersen did write for children and that his fairy tales have had enormous significance for the development of Danish children's literature and still have.

In this article I would like to show how it has come about that Andersen is seen as a children's writer abroad while in Denmark we discuss whether children were his primary audience. My intention is to demonstrate how Andersen's writing directs itself more to the child reader in English than it does in Danish, and how the fairy tales in translation are intrinsically much closer to traditional folk tales. It is my contention that the differences between the Danish source text and the English target text are not only a result of differing views of the child, but also of divergent understandings of genre.

Did H.C. Andersen Write for Children?

Andersen's fairy tales were, until 1842, given the sub-title "Told for Children" and several fairy tales were first published in one of the many children's magazines of the time, even after 1842. *Klokken* [The Bell], considered by many an adult story, first appeared in *Maanedsskrift for Børn* (*2. hæfte*) [Children's Monthly, 2nd issue] in 1845. In a letter to B.S. Ingemann, on February 10, 1835, Andersen himself stated that the fairy tales were for children:

> Dernæst har jeg begyndt paa nogle: "Eventyr, fortalte for Børn", og jeg troer de lykkes mig. Jeg har givet et Par af de Eventyr jeg selv som Lille var lykkelig ved, og som jeg ikke troer ere kjendte; jeg har ganske skrevet dem saaledes som jeg selv vilde fortælle et Barn dem.
>
> [Furthermore, I have started some new "Fairy Tales, Told for Children" and I think they are successful. I have taken a couple of the fairy tales that I enjoyed when I was a child and that I do not think are well known; I have written them in the way I myself would tell them to a child.]

Andersen himself had no doubt that he was writing for children, but he was also very conscious of the adult audience. In another letter to B.S. Ingemann he wrote in 1843:

> Nu fortæller jeg af mit eget Bryst, griber en Idee for den Ældre og fortæller saa for de smaa, medens jeg husker paa, at Fader og Moder tidt lytte til, og dem maa man give lidt for Tanken'
>
> [Now I tell stories of my own, I take an idea for adults and use it with little ones, always remembering that Mother and Father often listen in and you have to give them something to think about].

Thus, Andersen was well aware of what we refer to as "dual address" in modern children's literature and it is this duality that is often missing in translations which will be shown in my analysis below. According to the Danish scholar, Viggo Hjørnager Pedersen, the English reading public classified Andersen's fairy tales solely as children's literature and therefore refused to accept the duality of Andersen's writing.

> [...] fordi den engelsksprogede offentlighed som hovedregel nægtede at acceptere det dobbelte sigte, han [H.C. Andersen] havde med sine eventyr. I Danmark havde forfatteren tilkendegivet, at teksterne var både for børn og voksne. [...]. I England blev hans fortællinger derimod meget hurtigt af de allerfleste rubriceret som ren børnelitteratur, hvilke gjorde tolerancen over for ting, der skønnes anstødelige i indholdet endnu mindre, end den ellers ville have været. (Hjørnager Pedersen 2005, p. 15)

[...] because the English-speaking readership in general refused to accept the duality of his [H.C. Andersen's] writing. In Denmark the writer had made it clear that his fairy tales were for both children and adults. [...] By contrast, in England his stories were very soon classified by most readers as pure children's literature, which made the tolerance for matters of potentially objectionable content even lower than would otherwise have been the case.

Nevertheless, not all Andersen's writing was for children; he also wrote stories, novels, travelogues, and much more with an adult audience in mind.

One of the arguments used against the assertion that Andersen wrote for children was that his writing was too multi-layered and that the stories were too complex for children. I see this argument as part of the debate about the nature of children's literature and the extent to which it is pedagogy/education and/or literature. Children's literature has often been judged as having less literary worth than adult literature, but research has shown that literary genres and literary devices are not only features of adult literature; children's literature also has a variety of genres and literary devices which are adapted for children. As my examples will demonstrate later, it is often the irony, the dual layers of interpretation and the dual address which have been removed in the translations, possibly suggesting that the translators also considered that the stories were too complex. To me, this translation strategy is an indication that the translators were not only mindful of the child reader, but also of a particular expectation of genre while the fairy tale as we know it from the Brothers Grimm's collection of folk tales are more simple in their composition than Andersen's fairy tales.

Fairy Tales Versus Folk Tales

We know that seven of Andersen's fairy tales were originally folk tales. The folk tale as a starting point was not children's literature, but when it was written down it found its way to children's bedsides and since then it has been considered a part of children's literature. As Andersen, particularly in his earliest writing, took the folk tale as his point of departure, the obvious move would be to compare the two forms. However, Knud Wentzel, a Danish researcher, writes the following about such comparisons:

Men selve denne sammenligning er meningsløs eller sker på forkerte præmisser. For fællesskabet mellem folkeeventyret og H.C. Andersens eventyr rækker ikke ret langt. Genrefællesskabet er temmelig udvortes; det bedrager. Der er tale om dybt forskellige fortællekulturer.

[But these comparisons are meaningless or are carried out under false premises. The similarities between the folk tale and Andersen's fairy tales don't take you very far. The similarities of genre are only on the outside; they are deceptive. In fact, they are radically different narrative cultures.] (Wentzel 2004, p. 19)

The reason why I still choose to include a comparison in my analysis of the translations of Andersen's fairy tales is that Andersen was inspired by the folk tale and that the translations of his fairy tales are closer to the folk tale in terms of the statement they make. Andersen took the folk tale as his starting point, but he distanced himself from it by making the stories literary. By this I do not mean to say that he took a critical distance, I merely mean that they are two quite different genres. In the translations we are often confronted with a very neutral style without much detail or many literary or even oral devices, a style that we know from folk tales. The explanation for Andersen's international popularity may then be that he has been placed in the folk tale tradition alongside with the Brothers Grimm, and Asbjørnsen and Moe. Thus, while we in Denmark consider Andersen to be a great literary figure who not only expanded the repertoire of the fairy tale and many people's understanding of genre, but also enriched literary language, in an international context he is only known as a great writer of fairy tales primarily for Children.

The literary tale has a named writer and is part of written culture, unlike the folk tale. The origins of the folk tale are unknown and it belongs to oral culture. The folk tale has a simple 'home – out – home' structure, it is formulaic and the descriptions of characters are flat and tend to be based on opposites, such as rich versus poor, beautiful versus ugly, wise versus stupid. The folk tale concentrates on the plot, leaving out details since only the elements which have direct significance are described. The hero is at one with his actions and characters act similarly in similar situations. Characters are known by their functions, such as the smith, the step-sister or the king. The secondary characters are important in terms of the development of the main protagonist and there are seldom parallel sub-plots. This stands in stark contrast to Andersen's fairy tales, which are particularly well-known for the quantity of detail, the subtle delineation of characters, sub-plots and tiny additions with no direct link to the plot. Characters in folk tales are simple and unambiguous, while Andersen's are rounded and are given the scope to develop instead of appearing merely as extras. Andersen's characters are individualised. Minor characters are described and given their own personal traits. The folk tale is a picture of general human life while Andersen's stories are based on reality. His stories are rooted in fresh observations; they are not re-creations of the past. Unlike, for example, two collectors of folklore, Sven Grundtvig and Evald Tang Kristensen, Andersen had no ambitions to add to folklore. He took his lead from the folk tale and made use of whatever he could. This is what Andersen wrote about folk tales in the prologue to a collection of stories published in 1837:

Paa min Maade har jeg fortalt dem, tilladt mig enhver Forandring, jeg fandt passende, ladet Phantasien opfriske de i Billederne afblegede Farver.

[I have told them in my own way, I have taken the liberty to change anything I thought fit, I have allowed my imagination to brighten up faded colours]

In a comparison between Andersen's fairy tales and their source, the most obvious difference is the length. Andersen's fairy tales tend to be twice as long. The heroes of Andersen's stories are frequently unusual people, while those of the folk tale are entirely normal young people who follow their instincts. Andersen's characters do not follow the formulae and behaviour patterns of the folk tale. Furthermore, Andersen's relationship to time is also quite different. There is detailed reference to time in Andersen's stories while in folk tales there are very few real time markers. Another very clear difference is the level of individualisation, which is very apparent in the literary tale, but absent in the folk tale. In the story "Hvad Fatter gjør, det er altid det Rigtige" ["What the Old Man Does is Always Right"] there is a clear reference to the reader. The story begins:

Nu skal jeg fortælle Dig en historie, som jeg har hørt, da jeg var lille ...

[Now I'm going to tell you a story which I heard when I was young ...] (Andersen 2003, vol. 2, p. 352).

By way of comparison the corresponding folk tale, "Vil du ikke købe, så kan vi jo bytte" [If you do not Want to Buy, We can Always Barter] opens with "Der boede en husmand ved Øksenhede, tæt ved Sæbygård." [A small farmer lived by Øksenhede, close to Sæbygård] (Kofod 1989, p.96). In Andersen's stories there is a relationship between the narrator and the reader (the child), and the reader is encouraged to empathise. In the folk tale, however, there is a distance between the narrator and what is being narrated, and the narrator and the reader. There is no unnecessary description; only what is absolutely necessary for the plot is described. Thus, the folk tale lacks Andersen's idyll, his romanticisation, the wealth of detail and the particular literary devices he uses. The folk tale is more faithful in the introduction to what is being told than Andersen's fairy tales, which, amongst other things, idealise poverty.

It is a fact that many of the English translations of Andersen's writing do not have the kind of detail, the irony or verbal expression which is so typical of Andersen. They have not captured his ability to play with language, his idiom. In my opinion, this is because the stories have been adapted to a child readership and a very precise expectation of the style of the genre. Hjørnager Pedersen writes:

Det er, som om H.C. Andersens fortælling føres tilbage til det fælles underlag af folkelig fortællekunst, der ligger til grund for den.

[It is as if H.C. Andersen's writing has been reduced to the underlying common features of folk storytelling which is its basis] (Hjørnager Pedersen 2005, p. 109).

This is particularly clear in shortened and re-told versions of the stories, but it can also be seen in the translations, which are neither shortened nor re-told.

Examples

In Erik Christian Haugaard's translation of "The Little Match Girl" there is a greater distance from the plot than in the source text. In the descriptive language the role of imagination is distanced. For example: "[...] det var et underligt Lys! Den lille Pige *syntes* hun sad foran en stor Jernkakkelovn med blanke Messingkugler" [there was a strange light! The little girl thought she was sitting in front of a big iron stove with brass knobs] (Andersen 2003, p. 436; my emphasis, AØ). This becomes in Haugaard's translation: "How strange! It *seemed* that the match *had become* a big iron stove with brass fixtures." (Andersen 1983, p. 104; my emphasis, AØ). Haugaard's translation gives an explicit interpretation of the image of how it seems to the girl that she is sitting in front of an iron stove in the source text. The notion of dreaming is tied to the match in the translation and the exclamation "how strange" indicates that it is not an entirely normal experience.

The same is true in the following example where the unreality of the image is emphasised in the translation by translating "med" into "although": "Gaasen sprang fra Fadet, vraltede hen af Gulvet *med* Gaffel og Kniv i Ryggen" [The goose jumped from the dish, waddled along the floor with a knife and fork in its back] (Andersen 2003, p. 436; my emphasis, AØ) became "[...] the goose – *although* a fork and knife were stuck in its back – had jumped off the table and was waddling towards her." (Andersen 1983, p. 104; my emphasis, AØ).

In Haugaard's translation of "[...] og hun strøg ihast den hele Rest Svovlstikker, der var i Bundtet, hun vilde ret holde paa Mormoer" [and she hastily struck the rest of the matches left at the bottom, she just wanted to hold onto her grandmother] (Andersen 2003, p. 436) the suggestiveness of the language has been removed and the image is interpreted and concrete: "Quickly, she lighted all the matches she had left in her hand, so that her grandmother could not leave." (Andersen 1983, p. 104).

Also, in "The Little Mermaid" Haugaard mediates between the text and the reader: "[...] thi deres Bedstemoder fortalte dem ikke nok, der var saa meget de maatte have Besked om" [... for their grandmother did not tell them enough, there was so much they wanted to know] (Andersen 2003, pp. 155-156) "For the old grandmother could not satisfy their curiosity" (Andersen 1983, p. 151). Here it is made explicit that it was the girls' curiosity the grandmother was unable to satisfy. In the Danish source text the sense of "der var saa meget de maatte have Besked om" is open to interpretation. This particular translation of "The Little Mermaid" is less poetic than the Danish original. It has been linguistically simplified and the evocativeness of the descriptive language is removed. The underlying mystique is absent in the English version.

Of other examples of the way in which the translation has been manipulated to address the child, I should mention "The Nightingale", also taken from Erik Haugaard's 1974 translation. In "The Nightingale" "prægtigste" [most magnificent] was rendered as "most beautiful" and "kostbart" [precious] "most costly to build". In "The Swineherd" the song of the bird, in the original text, is described as: "og saa havde han en Nattergal, der kunne synge, som om alle deilige Melodier sad i dens lille Strube" [and he had a nightingale that could sing as if all the wonderful melodies resided in its little throat] (Andersen 2003, p. 258). while the translation adds explicit detail: "ever composed" and "so beautiful was its song". Thus: "The prince also owned a nightingale which sang as though all the melodies *ever composed* lived in its throat – *so beautiful was its song.*" (Andersen 1983, p. 32, my emphasis, AØ).

As a last example of the way in which the translation addresses the child I would like to mention the end of "The Swineherd" where, in Haugaard's translation, it is the narrator who has the last word, thus emphasising the point of the fairy tale. "Og så gik han ind i sit Kongerige og lukkede Døren i for hende, saa kunde hun rigtignok synge: / 'Ach, Du lieber Augustin, / Alles ist væk, væk, væk!'" [And so he went into his kingdom and closed the door behind her, then she really could sing: 'Ach, du lieber Augustin, Alles ist weg, weg, weg.'] (Andersen 2003, p. 261). This is translated as "The prince entered his own kingdom and locked the door behind him; and there the princess could stand and sing: / 'Ach, du lieber Augustin, / Alles ist gone, gone, gone.' / *For, indeed, everything was 'all gone!'*" (Andersen 1983, p. 37, my emphasis, AØ).

The ironic distance, so typical of many of Andersen's fairy tales and particularly prominent in "The Swineherd", is absent from most English translations. What happens to the princess in this story is comical as she is described as a smug and very naive young woman; however, in Haugaard's translation it is tragic-comic.

The missing ironic dimension in English translations may be partly due to the fact that irony can be difficult for children to decode and thus the dual references have been removed, and partly that folk tales rarely use irony. Furthermore, irony is difficult to translate.

Where it can be quite clearly seen that the implicit child reader in the target text is different from that of the source text, there has been some adaptation to the folk tale taking place and it can be noticed in the more neutral descriptions and the reduced amount of detail.

Conclusions

My intention has been to show how Hans Christian Andersen's fairy tales, as translated into English, differ in a number of ways from the Danish original. This has not necessarily meant that he is less popular in the target culture, but that he has been attributed other values and therefore his position in literature is different.

Among the translations of Andersen's fairy tales, where there are more paragraphs and sentences are shorter, there are several examples of a lack of appreciation of Andersen's linguistic creativity. There are many examples of omissions, changes and additions. What is implicit tends to be made explicit and there is throughout a layer of mediation in the English translation which does not exist in the Danish original.

Andersen's Danish fairy tales differ from the folk tale in that there is a high degree of information and detail. The narrator is more present and there is room for stage directions and comments. This dimension tends not to be apparent in the English translations. Information which has no direct influence on the action is frequently omitted in the translations. Although Andersen's stories are full of literary devices, the translations end up being a lot closer to the simple, neutral style of the folk tale without any superfluous description. Andersen was able to express ironic distance and mockery, inner calm and intimacy with language, which is a quality that translators rarely emulate, although this may also be a translation ploy on the basis that children do not understand irony. The end result is that Andersen's stories in English do not have the dual level which they have in Danish.

However, the fact that English translations of Andersen's stories are somewhat simplified has not stood in the way of Andersen's enduring popularity.

Primary literature

Andersen, H.C.: *Andersen. H.C. Andersens samlede værker. Eventyr og Historier I*, ved Klaus P. Mortensen, Gyldendal 2003.

Andersen, Hans Christian: *Hans Andersen – His Classic Fairy Tales*, translated by Erik Haugaard, Victor Gollancz Limited [1976] 1983.

Andersen, Hans Christian: *The Little Match Girl*, Grosset & Dunlap 1944.

Dolch, Edward W., Marguerite P. Dolch and Buelah F. Jackson: *The Fir Tree*, The Garrard Press 1963 (retold from H.C. Andersen's fairy tale).

Secondary literature

Andersen, H.C.: *H.C. Andersens eventyr*. Kritisk udgave efter de originale Eventyrhæfter med varianter / ved Erik Dal og kommentar ved Erling Nielsen, Hans Reitzel, 1963-1990, bd. 6 (Bemærkninger m.m., tekstkritik. modtagelseskritik).

Bredsdorff, Elias: *H.C. Andersen og England*, Rosenkilde og Baggers Forlag 1954.

Brostrøm, Torben and Jørn Lund: *Flugten i sproget – H.C. Andersens udtryk*, Gyldendal 1991.

Hjørnager Pedersen, Viggo: *Ugly Ducklings? – Studies in the English Translations of Hans Christian Andersen's Tales and Stories*, University Press of Southern Denmark, 2004.

Hjørnager Pedersen, Viggo: "H.C. Andersen og Victoria: Engelske attenhundredetals oversættelser", in: *Sprogforum*, nr. 33, 2005, s. 14-19

Kofod, Else Marie: *De vilde svaner og andre folkeeventyr. Sidestykker til syv af H.C. Andersens eventyr*, Foreningen af Danmarks Folkeminders Skrifter bind 86, 1989.

Lundquist, Lita: *Oversættelse. Problemer og strategier, set i tekstlingvistisk og pragmatisk perspektiv*, Samfundslitteratur 1994.

Mortensen, Klaus P.: "H.C. Andersens eventyr og historier", in: *Andersen. H.C. Andersens samlede værker. Eventyr og Historier I*, ved Klaus P. Mortensen, Gyldendal 2003, pp. 14-45.

Møller, Poul Martin: "Om at fortælle Børn Eventyr", i Weinreich, Torben (red.): *Lyst og Lærdom*, Høst & Søn 1996, pp. 22-25.

Nikolajeva, Maria: "Till otrohetens försvar. Om att svika texten till förmån för barnläsaren", in: *Barnboken*, årg. 27, nr. 1 2004, pp. 23-32.

Oehlenschläger, Adam: "Børneeventyr", i *Digt og Klogskab*, Høst & Søn 2003, pp. 54-57.

Rubow, Paul V.: *H.C. Andersens Eventyr. Forhistorien – Idé og Form – Sprog og Stil*, 2nd revised ed., Gyldendal 1943.

Shavit, Zohar: *Poetics of Children's Literature – The Notion of Childhood and Texts for the Child*, University of Georgia Press, 1986.

Simonsen, Inger: *Den danske Børnebog i det 19. Aarhundrede,* Nyt Nordisk Forlag 1942.

Skyggebjerg, Anna Karlskov: "Tingseventyret som genre og litteraturpædagogisk mulighed", in: *Pen og Blækhuus*, DPUs forlag 2004, pp. 97-110.

Sønsthagen, Kari and Torben Weinreich: *Leksikon for Børnelitteratur*, Branner og Korch 2003.

Tveden, Jesper: *Hvad sproget gør. H.C. Andersen og folkeeventyrene*, Dansklærerforeningen 2004.

Weinreich, Torben: "Poetisk skyllevand? – børnelitteraturen i 1800-tallet", in: *Digt og Klogskab. Et udvalg af 1800-tallets børnelitteratur*, Høst & Søn 2003, pp. 11-19.

Weinreich, Torben: "Skrev H.C. Andersen for børn?" www.hca2005.dk, 2004

Wentzel, Knud: "Folkeeventyr og kunsteventyr" in Øster, Anette et al.: *Det er ganske vist! Lærerens bog om H.C. Andersen*, Roskilde Universitetsforlag 2004, pp. 19-27.

Øster, Anette: "Børnenes H.C. Andersen", in Øster, Anette et al.: *Det er ganske vist! Lærerens bog om H.C. Andersen*, Roskilde Universitetsforlag 2004, pp. 11-18.

Øster, Anette: "H.C. Andersen i Erik Haugaards oversættelse", in *Sprogforum* nr. 33, 2005, pp. 20-27.

Øster, Anette: "H.C. Andersens eventyr på engelsk. Med udgangspunkt i Erik Haugaards oversættelse fra 1974", i *Nedslag i børnelitteraturforskningen 6*, Roskilde Universitetsforlag 2005, pp. 13-50.

Translation of this paper: Don Bartlett.

Childishness as Poetic Strategy

Mogens Davidsen

The work of Hans Christian Andersen displays many stylistic characteristics, we otherwise find in the art and literature of the 20th century. In the context of modern art, these characteristics have been labelled "naivism", "primitivism" or "exoticism", indicating that they resemble an articulation of a consciousness, different from or rather preceding that of the western civilized adult.

It can be fruitful to regard "Childishness" in the *oeuvre* of Andersen as a capacity, capable of grasping the same sort of potential and indeterminateness as the labels on modernistic expressions, mentioned above.

A considerable amount of cultural effort went into developing the concept of "Bildung" in the 19th century. One could say that the rationale of the artistic and aesthetic energy invested in Bildung was the creation of a framework to limit and contain the appropriate artistic articulation of a fixed view on life, or life-view, as the Danish "livsanskuelse" is translated in some books. The term is often seen in the *oeuvre* of Søren Kierkegaard, especially in the early part, when he is anxious to join the cultural and literary elite, and to present himself as a true follower of Johan Ludvig Heiberg's dominating ideas of a literary language in accordance with a claim to wring a meaning out of life, so to speak.

From the Papers of One Still Living

It is well known how Kierkegaard in his first book *From The Papers of One Still Living* from 1838 deprives Andersen of any capacity as a writer of novels whatsoever, primarily because Andersen lacks this "fixed life-view", in contrast to what Kierkegaard observes in the works of Thomasine Gyllembourg and St. St. Blicher.

Kierkegaard mainly treats Andersen's novel *Only a Fiddler* from 1837 with special regards to what is poetically true in the novel, as Kierkegaard states it. The main point of Kierkegaard's analysis is an understanding of "the life-view" as a precondition for as well the personal development of the writer as for the structure of the novel. Firstly, Kierkegaard deals with the psychological and social premises for the development of the writer of novels; secondly, he discusses – in the case of Andersen – the consequences of a lacking view of life, which manifests itself as a lack of epic development within the epic, a *contradictio in adjecto*.

Kierkegaard rejects Andersen's own theory of forfeiture (the musical protagonist Christian fails as an artist and dies in *Only a Fiddler*) as a valid view of life, partly because of the thus expressed distrust in life, partly because of the claim of "poetic truth" in the epic development and the claim of an immortal spirit surviving it all.

Then Kierkegaard investigates the "technique of it all" and lists a number of methods in Andersen's mode of expression that have in common that they are a manifestation of accidental occurrence, and hence lack any organic relation to the totality. Finally, we get a special discussion of *Only a Fiddler*, seeking answers to the questions if the protagonist of the novel, Christian, is depicted as a genius and – if he actually *is* a genius – we are presented with sufficient moments explaining the forfeiture of the genius in question. This search is made under the claim of poetic truth and as a verification of Kierkegaard's own view.

Initially, Kierkegaard looks for a focal point in the development of the main character, from which the character's entire progression can be embraced. He finds a scene in the novel, that could resemble such a focal point, but he doesn't regard it as fulfilling. Thus Kierkegaard is very troubled by the fact that he can't find a key point of interpretation for the protagonist of the novel, and he projects this textual circumstance to Andersen himself, seeing him as a person who lacks an Archimedean point in his view of life.

The background of Kierkegaard's characterization of Andersen as a writer of novels, he states as "the surely undeniable fact that any observant reader of Andersen's short novels will feel strangely disturbed by the double lightning (Zwielicht [twilight]) that prevails in all Andersen's novels as it does in the summer performances at our theatre."[1]

The double lightning is then traced back to Andersen's lacking ability to segregate the poetic from himself. The same joyless struggle, Andersen is fighting in life, his depressing considerations on life, are repeated in his poetry. His work weighs heavy as reality at the same time as his own reality evaporates into poetry. Furthermore

Kierkegaard makes the "general observation" that Andersen in his poetry must be regarded as "a possibility of a personality wrapped up in such a web of arbitrary moods and moving through an elegiac duodecimo-scale of almost echoless, dying tones just as easily roused as subdued, who, in order to become a personality, needs a strong life-development."[2]

In the optics of modernism – and from a Bergsonian point of view – it is striking that Kierkegaard calls Andersen a "possibility" of a personality, and this is not an altogether flattering characterization of Andersen.

As opposition to Andersen's novels Kierkegaard sets off *Hverdagshistorier* ("everyday life" stories) by Thomasine Gyllembourg – the mother of Johan Ludvig Heiberg – as an example of an epic well displayed view of life. For Kierkegaard, life itself yields such a view as a result of confidence in the world, a confidence it has caused fight to win; hence the "everyday life" stories gain an evangelical touch, which makes the reading an edifying study.

To Kierkegaard a life-view is the "transsubstantion of experience"; it is a conquered, unshakeable certainty, a backwards understanding of life through the idea. Concerning Andersen, he has not managed to "transsubstantiate" his experiences. They stick out as single sentences, singular phenomena, on which you might be able to produce, but not to fulfil the task of writing a novel. And Andersen's theory of forfeiture can not rightly be characterized as a life-view, because scepticism as such is not a theory of knowledge, and – as Kierkegaard states: "such a mistrust of life [...] at the same moment as it ends up as a final decision on life's questions it contains an untruth." Or – to state it in the Hegelian dialect, Kierkegaard used in *From the Papers of One Still Living*, the reflection has ended in negation.

Should one however admit the writer the right to name such – in reflection randomly stopped – consideration a life-view and let him produce novels, one would have to claim that in his novels he was able to unfold a number of consequences, all aiming at the fall of the hero. Then, the course of the novel would be "poetically true", and display an organic coherence. Yet, this is not the case with Andersen, hence Kierkegaard concludes, "that Andersen himself has not lived to the first power with poetic clarity since the poetic to the second power has not achieved greater consolidation in the whole."[3]

To Kierkegaard, Andersen's novels are characterized by coincidences. The entire mode of description and argumentation is accidental, because Andersen makes a number of insignificant comparisons, that don't lead to a deeper understanding of the matter for which the comparison was made. Furthermore, Andersen ascribes too much importance to individual, accidental incidents or gives external guarantees for the correctness of an a presumption. Moreover, Kierkegaard points out another type of coincidences; the "whole undergrowth of disturbing comments, which, for any tolerably attentive reader of Andersen's novels, makes the way in them impassable, I repeat impassable."[4] It is a striking application of metaphors, Kierkegaard uses to describe the difficulty of appropriating Andersen's novels, if we take into consideration, how Johan de Mylius points out Andersen's own understanding of himself as a *picarro*, the hero in a picaresque – pre-Bildung – novel (de Mylius does so in his book on the fairy tales *Forvandlingens pris*, 2004). The route of the picarro is also "impassable"; that is the main reason for his stopovers at all kind of impossible places, and his going through all kinds of bothers for the benefit of the reader.

Kierkegaard says about the protagonist Christian:

> Now, when the actual principal character appears before us in all his development, it would be desirable if somewhere there could be found a point of rest, a resting place, where we could collect ourselves and look back. But in this respect his path of development is by no means perspective. On the one hand, Andersen himself at times stops at some insignificant event, as if we were now at a turning point (a circumstance by which we must not let ourselves be led astray); on the other hand, the path is full of will-o'-the wisps, which sometimes induce one to believe that now the genius is awake, now he is matured, and which at other times are superseded by events that seem to witness to the contrary, until we again hear assurances that now the genius is matured etc. (p. 95)

Andersen administers what seem to be patterns of development "out of perspective"; a manner of orientation, the picaresque novel shares with modernistic representation, just as a course of events, associatively and capriciously arranged, is a presentation of perception, that thrives on each side of a massive block of enlightenment and "Bildung-thinking".

Kierkegaard also points out the long suite of epigraphs that open each chapter in *Only a Fiddler*:

Even if one does not share my view that an epigraph by its musical power, which to a certain extent it can well have without being verse, either ought to play a prelude, as it were, and thereby put the readers into a definite mood, into the rhythm in which the section is written [...] or it ought to relate piquantly to the whole section and not form a pun on one particular expression occurring once in the chapter or be an insipid general statement about the contents of the chapter. Even if one does not share my view, one will, however, surely grant me that it requires a good deal of taste, a high degree of inwardness in one's subject and in the temperature of the mood, to choose an epigraph that becomes a little more than an exclamation mark saying nothing or a figure like those the physiccians usually write above their prescriptions.

Now, Andersen does not possess these qualities. Through his long busying himself with poetry-making there is naturally at his disposal a large quantity of loci communes [commonplace remarks], of little verses etc., which, guided by a totally loose and exterior association of ideas, he now applies as best he can ...[5]

It is notable to observe, how Kierkegaard describes the character of Andersen's epigraphs, as he dismisses them as motivated: "a pun on one particular expression occurring once in the chapter", "an exclamation mark saying nothing", "little verses etc. [...] guided by a totally loose and exterior association of ideas".

Without making Andersen too "modernistic" or depriving his novels of real epic momentum, it is striking, how much Kierkegaard's negative statements about the kinship between the epigraphs and the content of the chapters, resemble the kind of relation between fragments of reality, that the modernistic collage – to choose an example – depicts. Art and literature in the 20th century extensively uses the breaking up and juxtaposing of elements, which *outside* the work of art, are hierarchically organized and arranged in accordance with epic, political and religious norms. In the modernistic work, however, other rules of kinship reign, and it is a central point in the modernistic work, that the synopses of the single parts or fragments correspond across habitual lines of connection. Thus, it could be lines of connection, "guided by a totally loose and exterior association of ideas" as Kierkegaard writes, or it could be a common "ring" to the words or a "pun", which relates parts of the text or picture, motivating a juxtaposition, that from a normative point of view or life-view. may seem either mocking or pure blather.

It often escapes the ethically rooted reader or beholder how it – always and also – is a serious aim of the modernistic work to challenge a habitual perception of reality, and to open for a sense of a certain nature of reality, which is usually overpowered by an acquired expectation of the task of art and literature.

But it actually doesn't escape Kierkegaard's attention! He ends his book of Andersen criticism in the following way:

> With regard to what I have to say in conclusion – prompted by the misrelation, certainly on the whole conceded to be factual, between a reading and a criticizing world's judgement of Andersen, insofar as this misrelation has also repeated itself in my consciousness – I could wish that I might succeed in speaking about this just as personally as I have tried to keep the foregoing free of any oblique relation to my personality. That is, as I reproduce the first stage [reading the book], the recollection of a variety of poetical moods with which every poetic life, even the most obscure (and this, in a certain sense, perhaps most of all), must be interwoven. And as I once again seek to retain every single one, the one displaces the other so rapidly that the totality of them assembles as if for departure in one single concentration, assembles in a present that nevertheless at the same moment feels in itself the necessity of becoming a past and thereby evokes from me a certain nostalgic smile as I consider them, a feeling of thankfulness as I recollect the man to whom I owe it all, a feeling that I would prefer to whisper in Andersen's ear rather than confide to paper. Not that at any moment it has been anything but a joy for me to be able to give him what is his due [...] because such an utterance is on the whole very exposed to misunderstanding, something, however, I hope that I shall be able to put up with if only Andersen, in order to avoid it, will hold what I have written with sympathetic ink up to that light which alone makes the writing readable and the meaning clear.[6]

Of course, Kierkegaard's ear or pitch for the world isn't inferior to that of Andersen! That is why he is anxious, towards the end of his criticism, to focus on the fact that his criticism of the novels strictly has followed the valid and current rules for this genre. He has spoken in the public space, hence he has couched his opinions accordingly; he has attended the norms of the literary authorities, the norms of Bildung and a life-view. If he – however – should value the work of Andersen as an ordinary, private reader, it would be quite another matter.

What does Kierkegaard mean by the statement that "the totality [...] assembles in a present ..."? Could he mean that the novel – in all its ambiguous and capricious ways of orientation – leaves the reader with a feeling of *presence*? If that is the case, one could say that Andersen's work of art is a pledge of life, no more no less. Unedited life, that is. The work of art is not a symbol of the world or a depiction of the world; it becomes reality in itself, displaying qualities of reality such as indeterminateness and potential.

"Andersen's first power must rather be compared to the flowers with male and female on one stalk, which is most necessary as a transition stage, but not suitable for productions in the sphere of the novel and short novel, which demand a deeper unity and consequently also presuppose a marked cleavage."[7] Kierkegaard says so in a note. He doesn't write it to suggest something about Andersen's sexual preferences. He writes it to characterize Andersen as representing a "transition stage", a dynamic state that has not yet found its final form, a stage characterized by possibility or potential. According to some of the theorists of modernism, primarily Henri Bergson, potential is the principal characteristic of reality as such – hence indeterminateness is a dominating quality of reality's manifestations in works of art if they were to function as objective correlations of the world's dynamics.

So Kierkegaard records that Andersen in his work is true to his ear for indeterminateness, even if such a "Kunstwollen" is completely alien to the time that Kierkegaard represents as a critic. But he actually likes what he reads, he whispers Andersen in the ear. And he is quite aware of the mental capacity one needs to activate, if Andersen's work is to be perceived in the right way; and it is not reason or common sense. Hence he writes his message with "sympathetic ink" to indicate the congeniality or congruence in way of perception he registers between Andersen and himself as a private person. In fact, he subscribes to what Bergson characterises as "instinct", a quality, typical of people of "negative capability".

If we look more deeply into Kierkegaard's later preoccupation with the paradox as an expression of the authentic possibility of life, then the paradox is characterized by qualities that do not fit into the predominant life-view of the golden age.

It is important in the occupation with Kierkegaard's paradox, whether it is the "ethical", the "intellectual" or the "absolute" paradox, to keep the original meaning of the Greek *paradoxos* in mind: against expectation, against the general opinion, unlooked-for, strange.

In general, on can think of the paradox as a practise of life, operating with a possibility outside the norm, because reality is conceived as richer and more complex than the mind can grasp. Thus, it is an orientation that threatens rational thinking or the mere constitution of rational thinking. If one therefore should point out an art-praxis similar to the orientation of the paradox, it would be one that expresses itself across semantic, rational meaning, determined by grammar, common sense or other "life alien" norms. It would be a modernistic form of art.

Negative Capability

But how does childishness fit into all that?

Well, if one regards modernity as a break up from the idea that it is possible to shape human beings in accordance with Bildung, because reality no longer can be assimilated in the personality in a meaningful way, we can consult Friedrich Hegel to get an idea of the consequences of modernity.

In *Phänomenologie des Geistes*, Hegel describes the process of Bildung as a process of alienation in the sense that the individual, as it transgresses towards what is new and different, is alienated from itself and to the outside world. The intention is, then that the individual should turn what is alien to something confidential by assimilating it. Hence the individual is emancipated from the basis of understanding, and can concentrate on a new beginning and a renewed understanding it has had till then with a broader and truer starting point. One has to make "homely" what is "unheimlich".

But what if it cannot be done? What if reality proves to be non-absorbable, so to speak, then you never get home. You are chronically alienated; you remain a visitor in a reality you cannot get to terms with.

Pär Lagerkvist, one of the modernistic pioneers in Scandinavia, published his novel *Gäst hos verkligheten – A Visitor in Reality* – in 1925. It has many features that can be characterized as "naivistic", which has been thoroughly and convincingly researched by Hans O. Granlid in "Det medvetna barnet", an article dealing with style and content in Lagerkvist's novel.

The novel is about Anders, and the reader experiences through him many decrees of life that for the reader are familiar and "safe" phenomena. Through the eyes of Anders, however, they gain a new dangerousness. Hence there is a kinship between the anxiety of the child towards the obvious, and the reader's relation with a modern world's manifestations that are impossible to interpret.

Granlid also compares the novel with naivism in art, and among other things he points out how naivistic painting displays awkwardness: insecure non-naturalistic drawing, flaws in the central perspective, pedantically applied local colour, a short-sighted additive manner of presenting things. This is similar to the literary use of a childish viewpoint, parataxis, ungrammatical broken syntax, simple vocabulary and accumulation of details. These are all part of the poetic strategy of *Gäst hos verkligheten* and we can easily detect them in Andersen's work as well. A strategy used to promote the feeling of being insecure and of indeterminateness.

Of course, alienation is an important theme of modernistic literature, but this obvious theme often overshadows a just as important rationale of modernistic art and literature. And that is to be an objective correlation for reality itself. Not to depict reality in a symbolic manner, but to work as reality, displaying reality's characteristics: indeterminateness and potential. Johan de Mylius has a chapter in his book *Forvandlingens pris*, called "Ubestemthed" – indeterminateness – where he states that indeterminateness is a fundamental capacity of a number of Andersen's texts. Furthermore, de Mylius writes that Andersen's fairy tales display indeterminateness to a larger extent than the folk tales (we all know the "Once upon a time"-opening as an example of the indeterminateness of the folk tale). De Mylius traces the quality of indeterminateness to an understanding of the picaresque character, and I have already made that view credible. However, I think it is possible to expand the application of indeterminateness to the quality of "negative capability".

If we should trace the capacity of negative capability back to its roots, we are led to John Keats. As is well known, Keats writes about it in a famous letter to his brothers, dated December 21, 1817:

> Several things dovetailed in my mind, & at once it struck me, what quality went to form a Man of Achievement especially in Literature & which Shakespeare possessed so enormously – I mean Negative Capability, that is when a man is capable of being in uncertainties, Mysteries, doubts, without any irritable reaching after fact & reason – ...

Probably with the enlightenment in his thoughts, Keats is anxious to keep art and literature clear of the criteria of probability and causality that human activity is based on from the enlightenment and onwards. Should we encircle the concept of negative capability further, we can characterize it negatively with the opposition or reaction against it: *positivism*, being the watchword of Continental intellectual life from August Comte's presentation of the ideas in the 1840s and on. This scientific movement that seeks to limit knowledge to the positively given experience breaks through in Scandinavia with Georg Brandes, and the scholarly character of the intellectual life has tremendous impact on the understanding of the origin and nature of art and literature until our time. The positivistic hero is one of distinct character with a strict course set out for his aims; he is in many ways the result of Bildung, just like Brandes himself.

In contrast to that, Keats suggests with his idea of negative capability a certain way of perceiving the World, free of prejudices and a fixed preconceived view. He is satisfied with not having a life-view, a consequent perspective.

In a letter dated November the 22, 1817, Keats writes to Benjamin Bailey, a student of theology at Oxford:

> Men of Genius are great as certain ethereal Chemicals operating on the Mass of neutral intellect – but they have not any individuality, any determined Character. I would call the top and head of those who have a proper self Men of Power. […] I am certain of nothing but of the holiness of the Heart's affections and the truth of Imagination – What the imagination seizes as Beauty must be truth – whether it existed before or not – for I have the same Idea of all our Passions as of Love they are all in their sublime, creative of essential Beauty. […] The Imagination may be compared to Adam's dream – he awoke and found it truth. I am the more zealous in this affair, because I have never yet been able to perceive how any thing can be known for truth by consequitive [consecutive, M.D.] reasoning – and yet it must be – Can it be that even the greatest Philosopher ever arrived at his goal without putting aside numerous objections – However it may be, O for a Life of Sensations rather than of Thoughts! It is 'a Vision in the form of Youth' a Shadow of reality to come – […] I scarcely remember counting upon Happiness – I look not for it if it be not in the present hour – nothing startles me beyond the Moment. The setting sun will al-

ways set me to rights or if a Sparrow come before my Window I take part in its existence and pick about the Gravel.[8]

There are several interesting passages in this quotation. First, Keats says that men of genius have no individuality (somewhere in the letters he says something similar about "the poetic character"). Second, he speaks of taking part in the activity of the smallest creation. I think he means something like that the poet is a depersonalised receptive being without an anchored and preconceived attitude towards life. At least not when art is to be made. Keats actually says that in order to be an artist you must *not* have a life-view, influencing the way in which you arrange reality in your work. In many ways, Keats anticipates the ideas of impersonality that were a foundation for a large amount of art in the 20th.Century, in particular, the ideas are attached to poetics of T.S. Eliot and Ezra Pound. Eliot launched the concept in his famous article "Hamlet and His Problems" from 1919, in which the concept of the objective correlation also is to be found.

Keats attaches a special way of conceiving to the aspect of impersonality: he picks "about the Gravel" when he sees a sparrow. Bergson would say that Keats through his intuition becomes one with the viewed object. To Bergson it is a central idea that a total understanding of an object can only happen through intuition, through synthesis, while all other kinds of mental activity is analysis, which only enlarges the distance to the regarded object because analysis is an attempt to understand the object as a function of what the object is *not*.

Another key statement in Keats' letter is the one about the "Life of Sensations" or imagination being a "Shadow of reality to come".

This is a very poetic version of another central idea with Bergson: the idea that the basis of reality, or reality's precondition, is of virtual nature; it doesn't contain any factual existence. If one seeks to trace the origin of the material reality, it is to be found in "élan vital", which is a condensed centre of power, where all tendencies and directions that a coming reality may follow, are included in one another. The reality, we know, is the realization of *some* of the possibilities of the core of existence, but certainly not all of them. Hence, the intangible basis of reality can very well be named a "Shadow of Reality to come", characterized by the quality of potential or possibility.

Kierkegaard characterizes Andersen in a similar way – "a possibility of a personality" – because he realizes that Andersen is a poet of negative capability, and I think it is fair at least to consider that Andersen might – subconsciously – have felt the need of his literature also to be an objective correlation of reality as much as a moral or religious statement. If that is the case, he would have to seek a certain form of literature – a form displaying indeterminateness, a form allowing parataxis and odd syntax, and a form allowing an alternative correspondence between the structural and semantic elements of the work. The fairy tale would live up to many of his claims, and perhaps that is why he chose childishness as poetic strategy.

The Flea and the Professor

If we were to try to detect the "modernistic" features of the early Andersen to his later work, it makes sense to compare the structure and strategy in the late text "The Flea and the Professor" from 1872 to the quintessential expressionistic poem from 1911, "Weltende", by the German poet Jakob van Hoddis.

Johan de Mylius has very convincingly stated how one of the leading subjects of "The Flea and the Professor" ("Loppen og Professoren") is the similarity between art and illusion or art and fraud.[9]

The professor in the story – son of a "fallen" balloonist – is not a real professor; his clothing and neat moustache just make him appear as a man of means and intelligence.

The professor gets himself a wife who is infatuated by his courtly appearance and title. She assists in his circus, where he performs as ventriloquist together with his wife in an act of illusion where she disappears before the eyes of the audience. But one day the wife fails to reappear after the act, and the illusionist – the artist – is left alone. However, he is capable of turning his loss and defeat into great art, because the wife has left him a bodily remnant of herself in the form of a flea. The flea becomes the dubious link between non-existing sexuality and profitable art.

The flea is trained by the professor to fire a cannon, "– a little one, of course", just as very little is left of the sexuality that the wife represented. However, it is enough to generate art and money, and eventually the little cannon is transformed into a big balloon that fulfils the professor's prestigious urge to climb to the stage of his balloonist-father.

But it is a strange path that leads from the cannon to the balloon.

The flea and the professor travel to the land of the savages where a little savage princess rules – her father isn't even referred to as a king;

because the charming and naughty kid governs, he is logically named princess-father, doing only what the child demands.

The flea and the professor are more or less kept in a childish luxury prison by the savages. The princess is in love with the flea and ties it to her earring; while the professor is kept behind sugar cane walls that he can lick all day, but they are nevertheless both prisoners.

The balloon that the professor and the flea eventually build – pretending to the savages that it is a cannon, becomes the final great act of illusion which gets them out of captivity.

The balloon is graceful art; it means uplift, elation (just as the Danish word "ballon" means balloon as well as the ballet skill of jumping glidingly). But in this story, we are told the tale of a "glide" that brings in money, esteem and glory. And this art is built on a deceit; it is a grand performance of illusion that leaves the audience gaping behind, waiting for the bang of the cannon.

And, as Johan de Mylius says:

> The actual story about how it all happened is by no means a fairy tale. It is a story that hardly takes the trouble of being a story at all. It is almost mere sleight of hand and optical illusion.
>
> Just watch how it is told: "There was a balloonist; he came to grief; the man fell and broke to pieces." [By the way, it is striking how English translations of "The Flea and the Professor" tend to narrate the abrupt, scarce syntax beyond the Danish instance. MD]
>
> This is how the story opens. Fragments of messages are blown into the face of the reader without any more ado. Here you are! And it continues in that way with short statements abruptly linked together, giving the story a character of absurd pantomime or dumb show instead of a continuous and calmly elaborated tale. [...]
>
> A jumping associative style, dropped remarks, repetitions and parallelisms form joining figures as replacement for the classic narrative with it's careful linking together of the told. [...]
>
> The style includes puns and other funny absurdities. [...]
>
> The story – because it is definitely not a fairy tale – is a linguistic performance of equilibristic nature. It is sleight-of-hand and plays of words, it mimes and gesticulates – and it is so enchantingly cynical in its occupation with all illusions. Including those the readers may have about the poet himself and his fairy tales.[10]

Johan de Mylius' characterization of the style of "The Flea and the Professor" shares many observations with those of Søren Kierkegaard concerning Andersen's early novels. Also in the late tale, words and expressions correspond across rational and semantic logic, and very disparate elements share a common nature (in Danish, "vild" both means "wild" and "savage", hence the balloon and the natives share qualities when transformed into art in the tale). And just as the "modernistic" features of the early novels can be regarded as the formal antithesis of the life-view of the golden age, the style of Andersen's late tale also serves to expose hollow "Bildung" and bourgeois behaviour; the civil, moral and religious norms of official normality become victims of Andersen's cynical and equilibristic story, disguised as a trivial tale for children. Furthermore, it exposes fame and fraud as true companions and registers the recognized and honoured manoeuvres of art and distinction to be rooted in sleazy sexuality and bodily filthiness.

World's End

In many ways, the aims and means of "The Flea and the Professor" are also present in the quintessential expressionistic poem from 1911 by German poet Jakob van Hoddis (1887-1942):

> Dem Bürger fliegt vom spitzen Kopf der Hut.
> In allen Lüften hallt es wie Geschrei.
> Dachdecker stürzen ab und gehen entzwei,
> Und an den Küsten – liest man – steigt die Flut.
>
> Der Sturm ist da, die wilden Meere hupfen
> An Land, um dicke Dämme zu zerdrücken.
> Die meisten Menschen haben einen Schnupfen.
> Die Eisenbahnen fallen von den Brücken.[11]

The English translation of the poem by Richard John Ascárate gives a rather good impression of the form and content of the German originnal version:

> Whisked from the Bourgeois' pointy head hat flies,
> Throughout the heavens, reverberating screams,
> Down tumble roofers, shattered 'cross roof beams.
> And on the coast – one reads – floodwaters rise.

> The storm is here, rough seas come merrily skipping
> Upon the land, thick dams to rudely crush.
> Most people suffer colds, their noses dripping
> While railroad trains from bridges headlong rush.[12]

Hoddis' poem is probably the most quoted example of expressionistic poetry. Although it is made in traditional iambic pentameter with an arrangement of rhymes that is anything but unusual or controversial, the poem immediately at its appearance struck the readers as strange and shocking.

The first expression that draws the reader's attention, with "The Flea and the Professor" fresh in mind, is probably the one about the roofers ("Dachdecker") that fall down and go to pieces ("entzweigehn"). It is almost the same non-human characterization that Andersen uses for the balloonist's faith in the beginning of his story.

This surreal feature together with the poem's general mood of distanced unconcern, cynicism and a feeling of pleasure with grotesque distortion, endow the poem with a cabaret-like quality. One could easily imagine the poem read aloud from a stage in Berlin and followed by an Andersenean ventriloquist as the next performance.

However, the preposterousness of the images and words causes disturbance and suggests that we are not confronted with an altogether harmless absurdity. The played down account of serious accidents together with trivial observations are at the same time ludicrous and uncomfortable (the already mentioned "breaking" of the roofers, the "merrily skipping" – "hupfen" – of the rough seas, and the somehow improper mentioning of the "dripping noses" – "Schnupfen" of most people), and it all contributes to the feeling of the confrontation with an alien universe where normal behaviour of matter and habitual hierarchy are suspended.

Hoddis' poem displays the disappearance of an emotionally experiencing subject in favour of a merely recording one. In that view it is easy to jump to a traditional modernistic interpretation of the poem as one that seeks to transmit the alienated feeling of metropolis and mechanical human relations to artistic expression. However, we must not forget the collage character of the juxtaposed observations, and for an interpretation that sees cynicism, irony and pathos as formal elements rather than expressions of a certain intellectual make-up, it is important to remember the mentioned character of modernistic art as an objective correlation of reality. Such an interpretation doesn't regard the images or statements of the poem as symbolic or mimetic representations; it focuses on the mental movement that is generated in the reader by the break up of normal hierarchies and linguistic or other expectations. For such an interpretation, it is vital to remember Bergson's description of the possibility of representing "élan vital":

> A single image can never replace the intuition of duration (la durée), but many different images, brought in from very disparate areas are in their co-operation capable of guiding the consciousness towards the certain point, where it is possible to grasp some intuition. By choosing the images as dissimilar as well possible, one prevents that a single of them "gets stuck" and takes up all the space for the intuition, it should yield to invoke, because other images will immediately contend for precedence with it and drive it away. Because all the images, in spite of their different forms, call for the same kind of attention by the thought, the same degree of tension so to say, the consciousness little by little gets accustomed to a very particular and precisely determined attitude, which is exactly the one the consciousness has to take up to break the veil that hides it from itself.[13]

La durée (duration) is of the same nature as the élan vital, but a weakened, more directional form of it. La durée, the psychical experienced time, is thus man's "bridge" to contact with the condensed dynamic life force that permeates and constitutes reality according to Bergson, and modernistic art can be seen as a means of encouraging the contact with its break-up and juxtaposing of habitual relations and hierarchies.

The former interpretation of Hoddis' poem and Andersen's late tale is part of an understanding of modernism, which sees the modernistic work of art as metaphor for collapse and disruption. Supported by a general conception of the depraved nature of the modern world, this understanding is based on an idea of human alienation towards big cities and modern war. To this understanding, human language broke its back at Somme and has never really recovered.

The latter interpretation, however, doesn't regard the modernistic syntax as powerless. On the contrary, it is part of an understanding of modernism that sees its artistic language as an attempt to grasp and answer the world's character of simultaneity, dissonance, vitality and indeterminateness. Qualities that are consequences of the hectic reality of modernity, but its artistic articulation is everything but a lamentation of lost consistence and lost communication of experience. It becomes a hitherto unseen encashment of reality's character of potential, possibility and life.

That both interpretations co-exist is a paradox, and thus they grant the works of Andersen and Hoddis a vital quality of existence.

Literature

Andersen, Hans Christian: "Loppen og Professoren", in *H.C. Andersens eventyr* V, Det danske Sprog- og Litteraturselskab, Hans Reitzels Forlag, Kbh. 1990

Andersen, Hans Christian: *Kun en Spillemand*, Det danske Sprog- og Litteraturselskab, Borgen, Kbh. 1988

Bergson, Henri: *Intuition og Verdensanskuelse* (Danish translation of *Introduction à la Métaphysique*, 1903), Kbh. 1914

Davidsen, Maria: "Poesie er Seier over Verden" in *Nordica*, bd. 12, Odense 1995

Granlid, Hans O.: *Det medvetna barnet*, Göteborg 1961.

Hoddis, Jakob van: "Weltende" in *Menschheitsdämmerung – Symphonie jüngster Dichtung*. (Herausgegeben von Kurt Pinthus), Berlin 1920.

Hoddis, Jakob van: "Worlds End" (translated by Richard John Ascárate), http://german.berkeley.edu/poetry/weltende.php

Keats, John: *The Letters of John Keats* 1814-1821, vol. I, Cambridge, Massachusetts, 1958.

Kierkegaard, Søren: *From The Papers of One Still Living* in *Kierkegaard's writings*, Edited and translated with notes by Howard V. Hong and Edna H. Hong (vol. 1: *Early polemical writings*. Edited and translated by Julia Watkin), Princeton University Press, Princeton, N.J. 1978-2000.

Mylius, Johan de: *Forvandlingens pris,* kbh. 2004.

Notes

1. Søren Kierkegaard: *From the Papers* ...p. 74.
2. Ibid., p. 70.
3. Ibid., p.84.
4. Ibid., p.88.
5. Ibid., p.93.
6. Ibid., pp.101-02.
7. Ibid., p.84.
8. The Letters of John Keats 1814-21, 1958, pp. 184-186.
9. Johan de Mylius: *Forvandlingens pris*, pp. 39-45.
10. Johan de Mylius: *Forvandlingens pris*, pp. 43-45 (my translation).
11. *Menschheitsdämmerung-Symphonie jüngster Dichtung*, p. 3.
12. http://german.berkeley.edu/poetry/weltende.php
13. From Henri Bergson: *Introduction à la Métaphysique*, 1903, my translation.

Father's Fault Concerning His Daughter

Asta Ivanauskaitė-Gustaitiene

Introduction

The thematic direction of the article was inspired by the idea of the famous Danish writer Villy Sørensen (1929-2002), who said that in Andersen's novels it is possible to see the manifestations of the positive explanation of the existing evil. The thing, which Leibniz in his *Essai de Theodicee* (1714), called *theodicee*.[1] And also by the idea of professor Johan de Mylius found in his most recent study, that Andersen's book *Picture Book without Pictures* (*Billedbog uden Billeder*) is "one of the central books in Andersen's entire creative work in general".[2] This idea is a good stimulus for the Andersenists to reread this book[3].

THEODICEE is a theological concept, which means the vindication of God (*gr*. Theos – God, dike – justice), the aim to explain how the existence of evil is reconcilable with the justice and goodness of God. Not only Christianity and other monotheistic religions, but also philosophy focuses on this problem. If God is good and almighty, why then do the catastrophes of nature take place, and why do innocent people have incurable diseases and die. There are especially many questions connected with the wrong (injustice) with respect to children: why are children snatched from the hands of their loving parents and die, why do they come to this world lame and sickly at all, why are they condemned to starvation, and so on.[4]

Andersen was interested in the problematics of theodicee in general. It can be seen in the orientation of his prose towards the representation of death, especially the death of children. Also the fact that the works on the topic of children's death Andersen wrote not only in order to explain this very-difficult-to-explain-problem by displacing it into the artistic reality, but also to comfort those who had to bury their juvenile children. For example, in 1847 he read his just written "The Story of A Mother" ("Historien om en Moder") to Henriette Collin to calm her, because she had lost two juvenile children over a period of four years.[5]

In the artistic reality of Andersen's short works of prose the amplitude of the manifestation of life's evil is very wide. Representing a child, Andersen often showed the evil manifested from the outside, without giving any reasons, as a part of the evil existing in the world – children's death, ailment, disease. And also evil rises through the child itself – as the expression of its own inner evil – the effect of original sin: "The Girl Who Trod on The Loaf", "The Read Shoes" ("Pigen, som traadte paa Brødet", "De røde Sko"). The genre of literary and also folk fairy tale, with which the name of Hans Christian Andersen is traditionally first of all connected, often *defeats* the existing evil, but does not explain it. For example, in the story "Five from One Pod" ("Fem fra en Ærtebælg") the pea, which falls and sprouts under the window of a sick girl, gives her strength to recover. Two objects – a book and a little bird in a cage – help the boy to start walking: "The Cripple" ("Krøblingen"). Looking at Andersen's short works of prose, it is evident, that God is often VINDICATED in the works which do not belong to the genre of fairy tale. In these works there is a suggestion that God's principles are stronger and more powerful than the pain experienced by the individual person, the injustice or humiliation done to this person; the death of children is justified, stating that it is better for a child to be dead: "The Story of a Mother" ("Historien om en Moder"); the pain experienced by a person acquires the status of the most precious pearl in "The Last Pearl" ("Den sidste Perle"). Bad children, who have disobeyed God's law, represented by the adults, and have violated the socially accepted norms of morality, are punished and through this punishment their spirits are purified, transformed, and their hearts are changed ("The Girl Who Trod on the Loaf", "The Red Shoes" ("Pigen som traadte paa Brødet", "De røde Skoe"). The mourning mother must "awaken", the girl who trod on the loaf receives hope, and the human principles of life triumph in their correspondence with the divine.

A child's death is experienced as the largest injustice, the evil of the world. First of all, it is a loss for the adult, i.e., an evil committed to the adult. Still, no less important to Andersen was the evil directly experienced by a child, especially the one that has a direct dynamics of cause and effect. (That evil in the stories can also be expressed indirectly, for example, nobody buys the matches offered by the girl in the story "The Little Girl with the Matches".

Still among all Andersen's short prose works there are only few, in which parents' wrongdoing to their children is directly expressed.

The text *Picture Book without Pictures* (*Billedbog uden Billeder*) was chosen for this analysis. The text consists of 33 pictures of reality, which are in essence independent, but all experienced by the moon.

In one fifth of the 33 'Evenings', a child is represented in one way or another, but only in few of them is the parents' wrongdoing to their children represented. And one of these pictures, the Second Evening, is chosen here for analysis. In this story, besides the authoritative gaze of the moon, the viewpoints of the child and the adult – a girl and her father – are revealed by the use of dialogue. The choice was motivated by Bo Grønbech's statement that in the reality of the short prose works the experience of the child reveals itself in different ways:

> When the perspective is not that of the child, one cannot expect the story to convey any new experience of the world, unknown to adults. That kind of experience, however, is present in other fairy tales. In "The Snow Queen" ("Sneedronningen"), "Ole Lukoje" ("Ole Lukøje", "The Old House" ("Det gamle Huus"), "Heartache" ("Hjertesorg") – just to mention the most important ones – the concepts of the adult world disappear, and we enter the world of children. In such texts we thus get a thoroughly authentic picture, which can be supplemented through other fairy tales which more sporadically and in glimpses show how the world appears to children. This is done through events and arguments that are only meaningful when seen within a child's horizon, whereas they are unreasonable from an adult point of view.[6]

The analyzed text presents three different perspectives and evaluations: the narrator's (the moon), the adult's (father), and the child's (the girl) –. Thus, it is possible straight away to make a supposition that this text can tell a lot about the realities of a child and adult and about the contact and the crossings of the worlds of a child and adults.

The main *objective* of this research is to discover the preconditions of the disharmony of the relationships between the father and his child and to reveal the father's fault with respect to the child. This detailed analysis of the text is presented in order to reveal the facts of the extra-artistic reality, focussing on the paradigmatic level of the text.

The chosen text is an inseparable part of the entire work, *Picture Book without Pictures*. Therefore, first of all this text is analyzed looking at the aspects of the general artistic principles and the manifestation of evil, supposing that the general principles of unity help to reveal the more subtle layers of meaning of the analyzed text. The Evenings of the *Picture Book without Pictures* are discussed using only the syntagmatic level of the text – the representation of the events.

The main concepts used are sin, breaking the law, and guilt, which are perceived theologically. These concepts are among the most important concepts of human reality and especially of Christianity. Sin is a violation of the order stated by God, and the perceived speaking of God, which is an absolute norm of morality, together with the person who breaks the law, cause its existence. Only God can consider something as a sin, thus only God's law can define what is evil and what is good. The concept "sin" (*hebr.* chata – to commit sin) means *an offence, deviation, fallacy or the missing of one's aim*. The breaking of the law is connected with the conscious ignorance of the known truths. Both sin and breaking of the law can call forth the feeling of guilt in a person – *guilt* (*gr.* Ophelema).

The hermeneutic analysis of the stories follows Paul Ricoeur's methodological approaches, referring to the conclusions of the research made by Erich Auerbach, Johan de Mylius, Jackie Wullschlager, and others.

Evil and Its Explanation: According to *Picture Book Without Pictures*

Andersen's text *Billedbog uden Billeder*[7] consists of 33 short stories, which differ in their genre, topic, problems and style. In terms of genre, they resemble a number of the socalled fairy tales, characterized by Johan de Mylius as "sketches, situations, pictures, moods, which are neither fairy tales, nor stories, but still were sent into the world as such"[8]. The coherence of the text comes from the fact that all the stories were written almost at once: at the end of 1839 the first 20 texts came to light, and the remaining texts the next year, in 1840. The idea of the title of the work is supposed to be borrowed from the composer Mendelssohn-Bartoldy's work *Lieder ohne Worte* (Songs without words).[9] Just after its publication in Germany and England this book became very popular. English critics called it *An Iliad in the Nutshell*[10] for its significance and compactness at the same time. In this text Andersen combines several of his scopes and sources of creative art – writer's and painter's, precisely and very insightfully fixing and *taking the photos* of the scenes – stopping the moments.

According to the thematic, problematic and stylistic analogy this work by Andersen is to be ascribed to the same paradigm as the works by Jean Paul, E.T.A. Hoffmann, Jeremias Gotthelf, and Adalbert Stifter, who seriously tried to go deeply into the social problems of their time (and not only their time). The works, which according to Erich Auerbach were left halfway in the sphere of the fantasy or idyll,[11] and the picture of economic, social and political world they represent is stagnant.[12]

In Denmark, and also in other countries, there was no serious academic approach and consistent analysis of *Billedbog uden Billeder* for a long time. And though solitary analyzes of this text, made by Niels Kofoed, Torben Brostrøm, and Jørn Lund in the last decades of the 20th century, studied certain aspects of the text, still they did not change its systematic evaluation. The text has been systematically evaluated only recently by Johan de Mylius.[13] His most recent study *Forvandlingens pris. H.C. Andersen og hans eventyr* presents an absolutely fresh new look at this book. Almost fifty pages of his study (the chapter "Billeder i det Uendelige") are devoted to the many-sided analysis of *Billedbog uden Billeder*.

This text is structured as the series of the moon's stories. Every evening the moon lights up the artist's face and opens the pictures of reality to him. The moon gives a promise to the artist that only by fixing such *little pictures* will the artist be able to create a new "*Thousand and One Nights story*". The comparison of pictures with the stories of *Thousand and One Nights* at once orient the texts towards universality, towards the attempt to embrace the vision of human existence as widely as possible. The orientation towards the creation of the universal situations is also seen in the words:

> The pictures presented here are not random, they follow a certain order, the same order, as that in which they were told. Some talented painter, poet or musician could create from them something more, if only he wished to. What I depict is only a few brief sketches, in haste inserting just one or two of my own thoughts among the rendered pictures, because the moon did not appear every evening – sometimes a cloud hid his face from me.[14]

In itself, a separate little picture does not seem very significant, and the *message* it carries is not very exceptional. Only the totality is important. The moon gives an opportunity for the creator to take his stand everywhere – it reveals the past and the present. The creator *sees* the dead towns of Italy – Pompeii, sees the Flood and Noah's

Ark, takes his stand in the epochs of Ancient Greece and 16th century Renaissance. Right here the present feeling of the creator is revealed, thus also his sadness, anxiety, and creative ecstasy are opened. The universality of the place – closed and open space, Denmark, Sweden, Germany, China, India, Italy, Paris, Israel, Greenland, Europe, Asia, and Africa. A yard, the room of the poor house, a theatre, the apartments of Louvre, a hill, the edge of a forest and a seacoast, the ruins of Pompeii, an editorial office, the barren land of Lüneborg, a graveyard, the ruins of the emperor's palace in Rome, a temple in China, a monastery, the basement of the church, an inn, and the prison.

In the pictures different people appear – unrestrained men, women, loving young people, an Indian woman, the Italian Renaissance poet Tasso, the famous Danish sculptor Thorvaldsen, rich landlords, farmers, emigrant peasants, the clown of the theatre Pulchinella, a cadet and an officer, a spinster, a dying wife, a dying husband, a nobleman with his wife, the mayor of the town, an old mother, a poor girl, a coachman, a singer, a painter, a poet, an editor, a merchant from the East, a chimney sweeper, a young priest, wandering musicians, a bride, a princess, and a prisoner.

It could be that Andersen consciously constructed his work as a universal archetypal image of human reality, created it from the real life episodes, pictures, and kaleidoscope of people of different social classes living in various times and in various places. The presented pictures are not connected with each other in any way. The only thing connecting them is the gaze of the same subject – the moon. The gaze, which, according to Johan de Mylius, is *from outside* and which is not neutral, but evaluating.[15] Besides, all the pictures called *Evenings* differ very much not only in their size, but also in their narrative technique. In some stories the plot is quite developed, in others it is very fragmented.

In his *Picture Book without Pictures* Andersen found the way to represent the depth of things and to perceive their essence.[16] Many stories in this text should be understood as allegories of life. And allegory is not only an artistic tool, but also a way to explain and perceive the world.[17] In this text the world is seen in two ways. The painter *sees* the world spontaneously, but with a narrow gaze, limited by the angle of the human eyes. Most often his look disappears altogether and only the sight of the moon figures in the *Evenings*. Only in some pictures, the narrative is structured as the painter's reminiscences. The moon renders a much wider vision of the world, there are no barriers, no borders, no time or space limits for the moon. Nothing limits the moon's look, and especially it is not limited by human nature – by the stereotypes, attitudes, and prejudices. Thus, the moon can reveal the most objective and precise picture of the world. The moon's sight is limited only by the time of "seeing" – the night, and the moon is localized and limited by the artificial barriers made by man, for example, curtains, not allowing the moon's light to penetrate into the room. The seeing of the painter and the moon could be compared with *mono* and *stereo* sounds, marking the character and quality of the sound. In this case *mono* would mark the painter's gaze, and *stereo* – the moon's. The moon lights up the most incredible situations of human reality, penetrating into the human house and soul, x-raying it in order to see in it the real essence of the things and objects. Nevertheless, creating expressive, pictorial pictures, the narrator emphasizes not the pictures, but what is hidden beyond them – the essence of the things covered as if by the medieval curtain – and reveals the most essential things – the maternal nature of the mother, the death of the dead or killed people in human memory, the suffering of the lovers and travellers. Thus, the *pictures* focus on the transformations – death, birth, marriage, cadet's becoming the officer, a poet achieving the status of a poet and the poet acquiring the status of a madman, the resignation of the unrecognized actor to suicide, the girl's becoming a beautiful woman, a married lady and a prostitute.

In some places the gazes of the moon and painter and their evaluation of the situation intermingle, especially in the 29th Evening. The light of the moon in this text lights up, purifies, and makes it urgent what is hidden or is considered to have no or very little significance.

What situations in the *pictures* does the Moon treat as the evils of life?

- Prostitution
- The child's suffering because of the parents being addicted to alcohol
- Poverty and the depreciation of human life
- Idleness, non-fulfilment of God's will on Earth, the vacancy of life
- Protectionism
- Social misery as the basis of emigration
- Existence "not in one's own place", bringing a person to suicide
- The duty, violating the human feeling
- Imprisonment

The best metaphorical description of the existing evil is presented in the very first *Evening*. Here a young Indian girl experiences a great joy, when she learns that her lover is alive – and at the same time she is secretly chased by the snake aiming at biting her.[18] The evil pursuing the child, from which even loving parents are not able to protect him, is rendered by the image of a bear in the 31st Evening. Children start playing with a bear, which steals into the room. They ignore any objective evil and do not feel any threat.

The evil of life in the pictures rivals the good. It is presented as a part of existence. The light of the moon from the skies lights everything up. The Moon lights up the reality as if a radiant eye of God. Evil exists, it most often is not vanquished, but only lighted up, i.e. it is seen.

The Faulty Moral of the Proverb: One's Own Children Have Wings, and Other People's Children – Horns

This chapter presents the analysis of the second *Evening* of the text *Billedbog uden Billeder*.

Johan de Mylius ascribes this *Evening* to the same paradigm as the texts of the 14th, 17th, 22nd, 31st and 33rd *Evenings*. These texts portray a child in childish situations in one way or another, and also reveal some dark sides of the adult reality. In many of these short texts about children the place of action is rather poor. The second *Evening* shows the inadequacy of idyllic colours of carefree childhood and the pain which a girl experiences, because she is unable to explain to the adult some things which are understood by children. Here arises, as Johan de Mylius calls it, the problem of *explanation* (forklaringsproblem).[19]

The second *Evening* of *Picture Book without Pictures* is interesting by its narrative technique, because the discussed elementary situation is "seen" and evaluated in three perspectives – the girl's, her father's and the moon's that sees everything. Reading the text, it can be felt immediately, but the study of the aspects of its extra-artistic reality helps to discover something more generalizing, more universally talking about the worlds of an adult and a child, father and daughter, a man and a girl in general.

As it has already been mentioned, the conflict between the girl and her father is reflected in three perspectives, thus it is read in three ways. In order to do it in an easier way, the Lithuanian proverb is chosen as the hypothetical variant for the possible conclusions. This proverb "One's own children have wings, and other people's – horns" characterizes the relationships between parents and their child, and between an adult and a child. It shows that a stranger evaluates the conduct of other people's children more strictly.

The father's law represents God's law to a small child. The Father acquires God's prerogative to punish or forgive.

The hermeneutic analysis of this short text is made referring to Paul Ricoeur's insights, when he talks about the differences between the meaning implied by the speaker and the meaning of utterance. He says that *the speech acts of any class – whether it is an order, a wish, a question, a warning, or assertion; – not only say something (locutionary act), but during the act something is done (illocutionary act) and this saying affects something (perlocutionary act)*[20].

The syntagmatic level of this short text is elementary. A small girl frightens a brood-hen several times and her father punishes her. When it becomes clear why the girl frightened the hen, the girl is reconciled with her father. Even the moon watching and evaluating the situation, approved the father's anger. Only when she was punished, did the girl say: "*I wanted – said she, – only to kiss the hen and to ask her for forgiveness for what I did yesterday, but I was afraid to tell you*"[21]. This story carries the message: *a person can be both better and worse than we think*. Many things are left hidden from our evaluation.

The Perspective of the Girl

To reveal the authentic feeling of a child is a very complicated task for an adult. In the work of art the grown up person tries to give a meaning to the child's feeling. The adult "diminishes" and restricts himself. And here the principle, to which formalists gave the term of *intentional fallacy*, starts working. It is done in order to see the world through the imaginary child's eyes. Nevertheless, it can be done only partly, because the adult never fully *gets under* the child's skin and really feels what the child feels. But on the other hand, for the child the adult is the one who can articulate the child's own thoughts, because differently from adults, who according to the famous Danish 20th century writer Karin Michaëlis, do nothing else, but verbalize their own sphere of consciousness. And a child differs from the adult, because a child is unable to explain and intelligibly reflect on its own experiences. The contemporary literary techniques of representation of a child make it possible to reveal the inner experience of a child rather well and to show the child's perception of the world. This can be done by the use of the inner monologue, stream of consciousness, and indirect discourse, in which the viewpoints and experience of the subject-adult and of the child intermingle and merge.

What techniques does Andersen use in order to reveal the feeling of the little girl? – He uses the characteristics of the moon, which evaluates the situation, and also relies on the dialogue.

The first lines of the analyzed text emphasize the fact that around the hatching hen a little pretty girl is capering about, who scares the hen with chickens, brooding nearby, and the girl's father punishes the girl. The word *little* is essential for the characteristic of the child, because it ultimately implies that the girl's age does not allow her fully to understand the motives of her action, and especially – the *Law*, as the system of consecutive rules. Not understanding the Law, she is also unable to break it, nor can she commit sin, and she is unable independently to feel guilty for it. Generally in the Christian view, a child is able to more or less understand his/her own guilt (sin), depending on the child's individual maturity, only at the age of around seven years. Not without reason, for example, is there a custom in the Catholic tradition of burying the baptized children – both boys and girls, who died under the age of five, wearing white dresses (as angels), believing that a child is innocent, because she or he *can not understand his/her guilt*. So the child's understanding of guilt is limited and restricted by his or her age. On the ground of this idea, it is possible to state that the girl did not understand the effect of her capering (game) – the scaring of the hen with its chickens because of her noisy game – as the breaking of the Law, because she did not know the Law itself, which is – it is not allowed to scare hatching hens.

To the child, father's law is God's law. It is directly confirmed in the Bible: "Children, obey your parents in the Lord: for this is right. Honour your father and mother" (which is the first commandment with a promise), "that it may be well with you, and you may live long on the earth. And, you fathers, do not provoke your children to wrath, but nurture the in the discipline and instruction of the Lord" (Ef. 6, 1-4).

In order to understand what is right, a little child must *hear* it and understand it *as a Law* from her father. In this text when the girl's father appears for the first time, he does not *remind his daughter about the law,* telling her for example, that it is not allowed to caper about the hatching hen, but he punishes her straight away – shouts at her ("han skændte"). The scolded girl does not comment or explain her behaviour in any way. Still, the further description of the girl's behaviour already shows its essential change. In the text it is marked by the words chosen for the description of the character of the girl's actions: "listede sig sagte hen ... smuttede ind til" (crept cautiously ... stole softly up to the). These words show the dynamics of the girl's behaviour – from merry and carefree game to the careful and not longer childish behaviour. The father's scolding (perlocutionary act) evidently causes the girl's behaviour. True, when the girl enters the hencoop she once more starts behaving in a childish way – she starts chasing the hen with its chickens. The multiplication of the same action straight away seems to the reader without reason and only the girl's final spoken sentence, "I just wanted to kiss the hen and to apologize for scaring her yesterday, but I was afraid to tell you this", verbalizes what was felt in the text implicitly. Two rather important aspects are revealed: the guilt that induced the girl to apologize to the hen, and the fear, which was marked in the text earlier by the words characterizing the girl's behaviour. In the girl's words her fear is already directly verbalized.

The sentence "around her (the hen – A.G.) a pretty little girl was running and capering about" shows that the girl's behaviour is absolutely spontaneous, maybe she does not even see the nearby hatching hen with its chickens. But the father's scolding actualizes the situation as if re-addresses it to the girl, in order that she could experience and re-evaluate the same situation anew. The father's words, his scolding evidently forced the girl to feel guilty. The inner feeling of guilt induces the girl to make it up with the hen, towards which she feels guilty. The means to get the forgiveness are taken from the adults' world – for them it is a kiss – an expression of reconciliation and love, but also of betrayal and untrue feelings. The parallel application of human rituals to the communication with animals seems comic.

The Viewpoint of the Moon

As it was mentioned, both in the whole work and also locally in this text *the Moon* has several functions: 1) it provides a look at the situation from the side; 2) it lightens up the situation and gives an opportunity for it to be seen in a new light; and 3) it evaluates the situation. In this text *the Moon* looks at the closed yard, which belongs to the family, in other words enters the closed space of family. The

Moon – or the Person looking at the situation with the eyes of the Other adult person – first of all as the child herself does not know the Law, which is represented and communicated to the child by the father, who articulates the rules of the Law. Thus, in fact the moon is unable to give an objective evaluation of the child's behaviour, because the moon does not know how much the child is allowed to do in general. The moon can only evaluate the child's behaviour according to her father's – as he is representing the Law. When the moon sees the conflict situation between the members of the family for the first time, the moon is a neutral watcher. The second time seeing the same situation the moon evaluates it the same way as the girl's father evaluates it. Still, the reaction of the moon to the situation is stronger, because seeing the particular situation the moon *makes a generalisation about the child's behaviour*, not separating the girl's behaviour and the girl as a person, but linking them. This is marked by the label, which the Moon puts on somebody else's child – *det onde barn* (the bad child). It is possible to state that the Moon evaluates the girl's behaviour the same way as a stranger, an adult who does not know the child, would evaluate it. In this artistic reality created by Andersen the Moon is a mirror reflection of the evaluations made by the child's father, transferring those evaluations to the level of generalisation. The viewpoint of the Moon would correspond to the second part of the Lithuanian proverb mentioned at the beginning of the chapter, that somebody else's (child – A.G.) has horns.

The Perspective of the Girl's Father

The girl's father is the one, according to the logic of the cited proverb, we could hope would interpret his child as a child with wings. It is he, the father, who must know his child, and reset her behaviour, according to the girl's individual character.

Still, as the text shows, her father behaves fatherly – he interferes when the child's game brings disharmony in the home environment. The father reacts to the disharmony he sees in the surrounding and behaves in the traditional manly way – he wants to solve the situation fast and radically. To do this, he needs to abolish the cause of the disharmony – to break off the child's game, to stop it, and to quiet the child. *To quiet,* in this case, means to punish. The father does not go deeply into the premise, that maybe the girl just does not know the law. It happens because the father *sees* the effect of his child's action

– the game, i.e., – the hen with its chickens is irritated. The father applies the principle that holds for the adults – where the law is concerned, you cannot plead ignorance in excuse of your conduct. This way the child is introduced into the adult's world drastically (because she is not ready, not prepared, and does not understand). When the same disharmony is repeated, it is natural that father's reaction is stronger: his scolding is stronger, he tames the transgressor of the *father's law* with his hands. The father, who represents the law, first of all punishes, but he does not ask or define the regulations of the law.

According to Adler, "it is very much evident, that we are influenced not by the facts, but by the way we interpret those facts".[22] Maybe the child's father punishes his daughter not for the particular crime. The disturbance of the rest of the hens does not seem to be a serious "crime" committed by the child. The famous children's psychologist Fritz Redlis would ascribe such kind of crime to the yellow sphere, to the conduct, "which is not desirable, but is tolerated for certain reasons".[23] It is the mistake made by the child, which only puts into disorder the peace, but in fact cannot bring harm to anybody. Father – the adult person – is angry, because he interprets the girl's behaviour as consciously negative. The adult person sees the fact, but not the circumstances. As the pastor in the novel Jonas (Lith.: Jūnas), written by the Norwegian writer Jens Bjørneboe (almost one hundred years later than Andersen's *Picture Book without Pictures* was written), said: "we, adults, are not able to understand those who are younger than us. The light, which teaches us to know the others, different from us, this light has already died away inside us. Even parents do not know their children".[24]

On the (Un)Happy Ending

Many researchers studying Andersen's writings – from Elias Bredsdorff to Johan de Mylius – have noted many times, that Andersen has difficulties in finding happy endings to his stories. Such endings made his stories sometimes sound unnatural. This was a case with "The Little Mermaid". Russian psychologists tried to explain this tendency.[25] According to Afanasjev,

> In fairy tales one "cannot recognize" Andersen (...) The optimistic endings of the fairy-tales were absolutely alien to Andersen, they

were *pasted* in contradiction to his own feelings, only sometimes obeying the requirements of genre. If only the genre allowed, then one of the most beautiful fairy tales by Andersen would be about the ugly duckling knowing that it is not for him to become a swan, and who in dark corners of the poultry-yard, in his solitude loudly cries about his knowledge and fate. Such is the real Andersen.[26]

This insight is important for the explanation of the happy ending of the analyzed text. The ending seems very positive: the truth is discovered, it wins, and adults reward the child with the kisses of reconciliation. According to Wayne C. Booth "the essential religious value – the vision of hope in the sight of the evil" is realized, and the reader can enjoy the fact that harmony returns to the relationships of the family. But such art interpretation of the text comes only when you read it for the first time. Rereading the text several times you perceive the dominance of the wrong done to the child, but not the reconciliation. Bitterness remains, when you imagine the pain the jostled and scolded, though kissed, child feels. The reconciliation "left" in the text is quite ambivalent – positively negative, indicating the potentially revealing conflicts between the girl and her father.

Conclusions

In modern literature for children and not only for children in the 20th and 21st centuries the problem of the parents' guilt towards their child is very interesting and is often explored. Many new or more recent literary works deal with this subject, e.g.: Jostein Gaarder *Sirkusdirektørens datter* or Herbjørg Wassmo *Det sjuende mote.*.

The analyzed short text marks the essential premises of the conflict between parents and children, and in a persuasive way reveals the threefold perspective of seeing the situation – the father's, the outsider's, and the child's. Everything has a very reduced measure. Andersen's inner approach is proved, which was fixed in the beginning of the *Picture Book without Pictures*: "some talented painter, poet or musician could create from them something more, if only he wished to." Even the analyzed text could be good material for further studies of childhood traumas and perversions. This text is useful for such interpretations, though it seems that the traumas described in the text are very simple and in everyday life are not being called traumas, but just misunderstandings. Nevertheless, the situation described in the text can be understood as a grain, as a precondition for such traumas to be born, because the text presents not only the blindness of one person, an adult, in respect to the child. Not only the father "does not see" and wrongly punishes the child. The moon, that has in fact an objective viewpoint, also justifies the punishment of the girl, her crucifixion, not questioning the evil of the situation. The moon everywhere and always sees the essence. He sees what is unseen with the naked but sophisticated artist's eye. The moon acquits and condemns rightly.' In other pictures of the book, the moon is able to see the essence. In this way the limited gaze of the adult, the principle "to look, but not to see", is even more sharpened and universalized. Thus, in this small text Andersen grasped the topic of the child traumatized by her parents' misunderstanding. A topic, which was not developed at his time. The drama arises not because of original evil, but is caused by the inadequacy of the child's world and adult world. The relationships between the child and adults, the understanding of each other are revealed as very complicated. So complicated that not only one adult person but even several adults cannot understand them.

Often the intelligent adults evaluate according to the outside – they are unable to investigate the hearts, because this is God's prerogative, thus they make inevitable and painful mistakes. They punish wrongly even an innocent child. And it is the fault not only of the inadequacy of childish and adult worlds, the difference of thinking.

It is possible to state that evil without reason, existing without anybody's bad will, and directed towards a child, is one of the difficult-to-explain-variants of evil, about which we could also ask why does God allow parents to spread evil to their own children, why does he not allow them to know their children till the end, why does he allow them to make mistakes. Andersen does not give an authoritative answer to these questions, because as it was mentioned the positive ending of the analyzed text is not persuasive. The evil of parents and children "is introduced" into the contexts of other forms of evil represented in pictures of life, and also other manifestations of evil are only lightened up.

Notes

1. Sørensen, Villy: "De djævelske traumer", in *Sørensen om Andersen*, København, Gyldendal. 2004. P. 109.

2. Mylius, Johan de. *Forvandlingens pris. H.C. Andersen og hans eventyr.* København, Høst & Søn. 2004. P. 182.
3. Andersen himself considered this text to be significant in his creative biography, because being love-sick for Jenny Lind, he chose this work to charm his sweetheart, especially the story about Pulchinelli. This story made his beloved cry (January 27, 1846).
4. According to Petersen, J. "Teodice: Lidelses problem som begrundelse for at New Age vinder frem på bekostning af kristendom", 2001, in http:// www.filosofi.net/artikler/ pedersen150101.html
5. Wullschlager, Jackie: *H.C. Andersen. En biografi.* København, Hans Reitzels Forlag. 2002. P. 315; Andersen's story "The Angel" (Engelen) is also inspired by the death of Edvard and Henriette Collins' child. (Ibid. p. 232.)
6. Grønbech, Bo. *H.C. Andersens Eventyrverden*, København, Hans Reitzels Forlag, 1945. Pp. 77-78.
7. In 2002 the first translation of this text into Lithuanian (from English) was published, with the title *What the Moon Saw* (in the book *Negirdėtos Anderseno pasakos* (*The Unheard Fairy Tales by Andersen*). Transl. Ingrida Matusevičiūtė. Kaunas, Vaiga. 2002). As Elias Bredsdorff indicates, a similar variant of the title is very characteristic of some English translations.
   Bredsdorff, Elias: Hans Christian Andersen. *A Biography*. Suffolk, Great Britain. 2001. P. 123.
8. Mylius, Johan de: *Forvandlingens pris. H.C. Andersen og hans eventyr.* København, Høst & Søn. 2004. P. 134.
9. Information from: H.C. Andersen. *Lykke-Peer, Digte, Billedbog uden Billeder, Reiseskildringer, Historier etc.* Aarhuus Stiftsbogtrykkerie a/s. 1928-1930. P. 130.
10. Ibid. P. 129.
11. Auerbach, E: *Mimezis*. Vilnius, Baltos lankos. 2003. P. 480.
12. Ibid.P.480.
13. Mylius, Johan de: *Forvandlingens pris. H.C. Andersen og hans eventyr.* København, Høst & Søn. 2004.
14. H.C. Andersen. *Lykke-Peer, Digte, Billedbog uden Billeder, Reiseskildringer, Historier etc.* Aarhuus Stiftsbogtrykkerie a/s. 1928-1930. P. 130.
15. Mylius, Johan de: *Forvandlingens pris. H.C. Andersen og hans eventyr.* København, Høst & Søn. 2004. P. 136.
16. In all his writing Andersen liked to depict the hidden, the unseen from the outside, and esoteric things, to reveal them in untraditional ways, to show them from a new angle, and to do their cross-section. Significant is not the fact that a princess kisses a swineherd, but who is she, if she kisses without love. Andersen was interested in showing what happened when a sign, in this case a kiss, loses its ordinary meaning. Not the actions, but their preconditions, the metaphysics of heart, were important to Andersen. Similarly, in the Gospel it is said that the hearts will be investigated, and Andersen seems to take this mission. Thus, he states at the beginning of "The Snow Queen": "... when we come to the end, we will know more, than we know now."
17. Naujokaitienė, E.: *Oskaras Milašius*. Kaunas, VDU leidykla. 2001. P. 125.
18. It is interesting that the same motive, as held where an Indian girl lets into water to flow a lightened lantern wanting to know if her beloved is alive, is

found in the most popular Lithuanian folktale "Eglė, žalčių karalienė" ("Fir-tree, the Queen of Serpents"). In Lithuanian fairytale "Eglė", lead by the same aim – to know if her beloved husband is alive – addresses the water, asking it to send a sign – a white foam if he is alive, or black foam of blood if he is dead.
19. Mylius, Johan de: *Forvandlingens pris – H.C. Andersen og hans eventyr*. København, Høst & Søn. 2004. P. 137.
20. Ricoeur, P. *Interpretacijos teorija*. Vilnius, Baltos lankos. 2000. P. 25.
21. *Billedbog uden Billeder*, P. 131.
22. Adler, A. *Social Interest: A Challenge to Mind.* New York: Capricorn. 1964. P. 26.
23. Cited from Ginott G. Haim. *Tarp tėvų ir vaiko: Nauji senų problemų sprendimai*. Vilnius, VIA RECTA, 1999. P. 73.
24. Bjørneboe, Jens. *Jūnas*. Vilnius, Lietuvos rašytojų sąjungos leidykla, 1999. P. 156.
25. A.J. Afanasjev, referring to Freud, Jung and the teaching of Campinskii about the informational metabolism, according to the dominant features of the psychic structure, character, and temper of the personality, defined 24 psychotypes, among which H.C. Andersen. This type is the most complicated and most difficult to bear especially for a man. The essence of that psychological type is weeping, girlishness, and disability to grow up. (Afanasjev A. Sintaksis liubvi. Moskva, Ostorožje. 2000.)
26. Afanasjev, Aleksandr. Sintaksis Liubvi (tipologija licnosti i prognoz parnych otnosenij), in http://treders.narod.ru/literature/texts/sin211.html

Dream and Reality:
"The Little Match Girl"
Seen in a Socio-psychological Perspective

Inger Lise Jensen

I will examine the "The Little Match Girl" from a social and psychological point of view. I will take in both the social and the literary contemporary time in connection with an analysis of the text. Further I will make use of different illustrations of "The Little Match Girl", some of which are made by children.

I will use the illustrations for a critical examination to elucidate the questions whether Hans Christian Andersen was writing for children and whether the story has something to say to children today.

Finally I will examine in what way "The Little Match Girl" has been used for example as Christmas cards, Christmas seals, illustrations for calendars, logos for institutions etc. This examination will be concerned with both the commercial use and a more idealistic use.

Introduction

"The Little Match Girl" may be the shortest story in the world, but nevertheless with a great content of feeling. The content tells us something about the time when it was written but also about the character of the individual. We must consider it a story and not a fairy tale because of its description of historical facts showing human and social relations.

"The Little Match Girl" is a well known and often translated text. From a list on the web, I have counted at least 10-12 different languages. I believe you could find many interesting illustrations in the translations, but most of the illustrations I will discuss here are made by Danish artists.

Why Did Hans Christian Andersen Write this Story?

Generally the fairy tales and stories by Hans Christian Andersen were inspired from within. But this story is inspired by a small, lovely drawing made by Johan Thomas Lundbye. How could just this picture trigger off the story about The Little Match Girl? To answer this question Hans Brix has in his thesis for the doctorate in 1907 pointed to a probable answer. He writes that Hans Christian Andersen's mother as she was a child was sent out to beg. She would not or dared not beg and she hid herself below a bridge across Odense Å (a small river). She fell asleep and when she came home in the evening she was reprimanded because she had not sold anything.[1]

Background for "The Little Match Girl"

In October 1845 Hans Christian Andersen set out on a one year study tour. He wanted to visit Germany, Italy, France and Switzerland. From November 12th to 21st he visited Duke Christian of Augustenborg at Gråsten Castle. In an atmosphere of magnificence and superfluity he wrote "The Little Match Girl" – a story about hunger, coldness and powerlessness, but also about religious submission.

While staying at Gråsten Castle Hans Christian Andersen received a letter with three woodcuts from xylographer Andreas Flinch in Copenhagen. Flinch asked if Hans Christian Andersen could write a fairy tale over one of the woodcuts. Andersen was at once inspired by the print, which shows a little girl holding a bunch of matches in her hand. On November 18 he wrote the story and the following day a fair copy was made of the story. We know this from his diary where he wrote that on November 18 he received a letter from Andreas Flinch with 3 pictures and on November 19 that he had made the fair copy and posted "The Little Match Girl".

The drawing for the woodcut was made by Johan Thomas Lundbye in 1843. The woodcut and printing were made by Hans Christian Henneberg almost at the same time. The print was for the first time used as illustration for "The Little Match Girl" in 1845 in *Folkekalender for Danmark, 1846* (Peoples Calendar for Denmark, 1846). The calendar was published in December 1845.[2]

Picture no. 1: Johan Thomas Lundbye, 1843.

Outlines from the Social and Literary Denmark at That Time

How Was Social Care in 19th Century Denmark?
A real social reform was not introduced in Denmark until 1933. It was directed towards people who could not provide for themselves. But through the centuries the Christian church had organised some welfare for poor people. The help consisted mainly of gifts, mostly natural produce.

In the Middle Ages (around 1200) the churches took care of the poor and even if there was plenty of money there was not money enough. Begging increased. The government disliked begging and had it prohibited. All people should work and earn their own money.

After the Lutheran reformation in Denmark (about 1530) the relief for the poor was transferred to the public. In the countryside the farmers supplied the poor people with foodstuffs, and in the towns lotteries and other forms of collection of money were arranged. It was not until around 1860 that the municipalities were forced to arrange or at least pay for the expenses for poor people. Thus, no organised welfare was available at the time when Hans Christian Andersen wrote the story.

In the little book by Erik Dal,[3] there is a small article with the headline: "Gjør vel, naar du giver." (Do well when you give gifts). According to this article, from *Almanak eller Huuskalender*, 1842, it is reprehensible to give alms to poor children. It will only support their desire for laziness and prevent a good upbringing and later on a good education. Lundbye's drawing was used for the first time to illustrate the article.[4]

How Were the 1840s, from a Literary Point of View?

The literary period and the political development are closely connected here. The years 1830-50 were a time of unrest and upheaval. From a literary perspective, we are in the Post-Romantic period and politically we have absolute monarchy in Denmark. Down through the 1830s there was a growing wish to replace absolutism by a new democratic constitution. Since 1660 the thoughts and ideas of absolute monarchy had been dominating and criticism was not popular here. Consequently many problems had been banned from the public discussion, for example the question of liberty of the press. Up to 1770 all printed matters were subject to censorship. Censorship was dropped for one year, but then partly reintroduced, and in 1799 censorship was intensified. From 1810 the political press was subject to censorship. In 1848 at long last the change of constitution was a reality and freedom of the press was introduced.

The movement characterizing literature from 1800 to 1870 was the Romantic Movement. In Denmark the movement is subdivided into some periods which overlap each other. The period that characterises the Danish Romantic Movement from 1830-50 is called "romantisme" (i.e. 2nd-generation Romanticism). This part of the Romantic period is characterised by disunion and extremes exceeding current standards. Hans Christian Andersen is part of this movement, but only to a certain degree. His figures never get really extreme, and his fairy tales and stories cannot be characterised in such terms.

Hans Christian Andersen came as we know from a poor family. He had no possibility to get economic help. The help a poor boy could obtain in those days normally came from kind, wealthy people, perhaps from the king if you were exceptionally skilful.

There was a foundation to benefit skilful but poor young artists, namely "Fonden ad usus publicos" ("Foundation of Public Utility"). Jonas Collin (1776-1861) in whose family Hans Christian Andersen was taken in was secretary of this foundation 1803-33. Because of that he had direct access to the king if he had something of special interest to discuss. He managed to get money for school education and later on money for study tours for Hans Christian Andersen. Probably in agreement with the other members of the management of The Royal Theatre in Copenhagen, Knud Lyne Rahbek, Frederik Conrad von Holstein and Gottsche H. Olsen.[5]

With this form of subvention given to Hans Christian Andersen and many other skilful young men, "the king" got a lot of support from those people. Consequently they did not often involve themselves in political matters or questions about the absolute monarchy as government.

The Story of "The Little Match Girl"

"The Little Match Girl" is divided in a realistic world and a fictional world, a world of dreams. First there is a realistic world where she feels hunger and a biting cold, and later in the story there is the fictional world with the dream or the vision, where she sees the food, the stove, the Christmas tree and the old grandmother.

This split in the story begins when the little girl slips over into her vision. The imagination, fantasy, slowly slips through the world of dreams where she sees the real things, and into the world of death. In the short time before she passes over into death she meets her grandmother. Her vision is psychologically understandable, based as it is on her thoughts about hunger, cold and loneliness.

Description of the Realistic World

What Does the Little Girl Look Like?
We do not know much about it, because her appearance is only described very briefly. Actually we have a frame into which the reader can put his own impression (imagination) of the girl.

But we know that she has long yellow hair which curls beautifully around the neck, and she looks subdued. She wears poor clothes, she does not have anything to cover her head, and her feet are without shoes and stockings. She has no gloves either, her hands and feet are blue with cold. She has an old apron around her and in this she wears her matches.

How is Her Family?
We understand that it is a very poor family. They are living in the loft at an unknown place and it is just as cold inside as outside because the roof is leaky. Perhaps the mother is a bit more kind to the girl than the father. She has given the little girl her own slippers as protection against the cold.

Picture no. 2: Aage Sikker Hansen, *Billedbog*, ca. 1939.

How Is the Weather?
We know it is New Years Eve and we know it is snowing and very cold. The little girl is freezing to death in the night. You can ask why the little girl is dying on New Years Eve. In our time we have a feast for the end of the old year, but it could also be the beginning of the new year. The first day of the year where everything will be new. It is an idea which Leif Ludwig Albertsen has in mind.[6]

What Are the Surroundings Alike?
We know that the little girl is in a town, walking in a street with many houses. The light is shining from the windows and the air is full of wonderful smells from cooking. The stoves are fired inside the houses, and the tables are beautifully decorated with roast goose and

other kinds of wonderful food. She sees decorated Christmas trees as well.

The little girl knows all these things, she knows that they are real. But they are in other people's homes, not in her home; in her family you do not find such wonderful things.

Picture no. 3: Svend Otto S., *Eventyrkalender 2002*.

Then comes the evening. The little girl is tired and freezing but she dares not go home. She has not earned anything; nobody wants to buy her matches. Her father will get very angry. She finds a comfortable place where two houses are joined and provide she has shelter for the wind.

Description of the World of Fantasy

Now we have had a look at the realistic world but what about the dream world. How does it come into existence?
The little girl is considering her situation, but defeats the fear of her father and lights a match. They were meant for sale and not for her private use. We now understand that the imagination is connected to the light. Every time she lights a new match she experiences an even more wonderful dream. In this dream world created through her imagination of the real matters which exist and the globe shaped light

from the matches, her body is released from basic needs. Now she no longer feels cold and hungry.

Picture no. 4: Christmas Card, ca. 2000.

Picture no. 5: Christmas Card, ca. 1960.

In this small limited world in the light globe from the match, everyday realities are absent. In her visions she sees a stove, a beautifully laid dinner table with roast goose, a Christmas tree with lots of lights, and finally her grandmother, the most wonderful vision to the little girl. When she sees her grandmother it means that she freezes to death.

Picture no. 6: Werner Wejp-Olsen, Cartoon, ca. 2003.

Picture no. 7: Werner Wejp-Olsen, Cartoon, ca. 2003.

Can Children Understand "The Little Match Girl" Today? Can They Understand the Contents (Matters) of the Text?

Yes, I think children understand the contents very well. Spontaneously they sense the feeling of pity and loneliness when the little girl sits down in the corner between the two houses.

Picture no. 8: Henry Heerup, Calendar Picture, 2005.

Picture no. 9: Axel Mathiesen, 1924.

To illustrate the questions in the headline I will show some drawings made by Polish school children. In the catholic school in Odense, in a Polish school, and in a Polish children's home, children at the age of 8 to 16 have worked with different kinds of illustrations for some of the fairy tales and stories of Hans Christian Andersen. Some of the illustrations were made for "The Little Match Girl". The drawings were shown in a big exhibition in the Town Hall of Odense.

The drawings I will comment on are made by three children at the age of 14 and one at the age of 11. Although the drawings are inspired by illustrations available in books, they contain some sensitivity. They show the religious aspect as well as the social aspect, namely the distress of the little girl. She is hungry and she feels cold. She is sad because nobody cares for her. The whole situation has elements which children can understand. Especially one of the pictures points to the religious aspect, the picture with the church, the grandmother, the match house and the little girl (no. 13, below).

The Little Match Girl may be a bit sentimental but because Hans Christian Andersen knows to describe elementary conditions as cold, longing and pain in a moving way, this little story will always say something to children.

The four Polish children have caught different feelings which adapt situations in the story.

Picture no. 10 focuses on the inward look of the girl's face, the Christmas tree in the window sill, the match in her hand and the matchbox in the street. She is obviously dreaming. Picture no. 11 shows a little girl deeply depressed. We notice a tear in her left eye.

She has a strong feeling of loneliness. She is excluded from social intercourse with other people, we know.

Picture no. 10.

Picture no. 11.

Picture no. 12 shows a girl in deep concentration. She looks at a burning match and has a vision of a beautiful Christmas tree. To the right are seen the street lamp, the moon, the stars, and the outline of a Christmas tree.

Picture no. 13 is very complex. It contains many elements. The matches are gathered to build a simple house, perhaps "The House of Dreams". In the background we see a church and in close connection with this, the girl's grandmother. From one of the matches in the match house a flame is burning; it connects the house of dreams with the church and the grandmother.

Picture no. 12.

Picture no. 13.

Was "The Little Match Girl" Meant to Be a Story for Children?

The little girl with the matches gets a very sad fate if one regards it as a real fate caused by a social problem. A remarkable thing is that the social aspect is pushed aside in favour of the religious aspect in connection with the death. You will see it in the happy reunion between the little girl and her grandmother. By this reunion Hans Christian Andersen gives one of the greatest griefs in life, when a beloved person dies, a gleam of optimism. This is only possible to do if you deeply believe.

In the 1800s an intensely believing person would never ask the question whether the deceased went to Heaven or not. And you would never doubt whether a child would go to Heaven. Hence, if you view the tale from a religious aspect it is a story for children. It should be regarded as a devotional story. When you die you will go to Heaven, free from all sorrow and pain. Death is something you should not fear; now you are in the hands of God.

Did Hans Christian Andersen write the story "The Little Match Girl" only for children? Actually I do not think so. I think he wrote it for grown-up people (as many other of his stories and fairy tales). Andersen seldom made up his mind clearly to social distinction and in this story his own opinion is blurred by the religious aspect. But – in "The Little Match Girl" he describes the social situation. He shows us that a child can die from hunger and cold without anyone taking pity on the little girl and helping her. By describing real distress and misery the little story points far beyond its own time.

What Does Hans Christian Andersen Want to Show Us With His Little Story?

Hans Christian Andersen involves himself in a very sensitive way with the dying child's visions. He includes basic elements as cold and hunger in relation to heat, food and beauty (the beautifully laid table and the wonderfully decorated Christmas tree). I think he wants to show the big differences in society by the contrasts in the story and so touch people emotionally.[7]

How Have the Different Artistic Works from "The Little Match Girl" Been Used?

Many people have been inspired by "The Little Match Girl" to different forms of artistic activities. It is particularly the emotions with the child and death which affect the grown-up illustrator. But there are few who clearly show the social conditions of the poor. You may find examples, see e.g. Aage Sikker Hansen (picture no. 2) and the postcard from the Association of the Disabled (picture no. 5)

I have chosen some illustrations which I consider to be the most interesting in connection with the story, not only illustrations from books by well known artists, such as Lundbye, Sikker Hansen and Axel Mathiesen, but also postcards for Christmas greetings, Christmas seals and pictures from calendars, and finally the drawings made by the Polish children.

Many other works have been made in other materials. Erik Cohrt has made a sculpture of the little girl in sandstone (picture no. 14). A material giving a soft and pleasant impression. And in the jubilee year of 2005, The Royal Copenhagen Porcelain made a plaquette with motif from the story (picture no. 15).

Picture no. 14: Erik Cohrt, Sculpture, 1949.

Picture no. 15: Jørgen Nielsen, Plaquette from Royal Copenhagen Porcelain, 2005.

In Finland a lot of matchbox illustrations have been made for stories and fairy tales by Hans Christian Andersen. "The Little Match Girl" is among those (picture no. 16). A cartoon has also been made by Werner Wejp-Olsen – a nice and in some way pleasant cartoon (pictures no. 6 and 7). You could almost forget the terrible conditions lying behind the story.

In 1930 the Danish post office published a Christmas seal with the "Little Match Girl" made by the artist Arne Ungermann. This Christmas seal is a quite sensitive print which show the little girl completely isolated and lost in her own thoughts (picture no. 17).

Picture no. 16: Finnish matchbox drawing.

Picture no. 17: Arne Ungermann, Christmas Seal, 1930.

The final illustration is from the organisation "Save the Children" – an organisation trying to help poor children all over the world.

Picture no. 18

Do the Artists' Works Intend to Improve Children's Situation?

Most of the pictures I have selected are not surprisingly made for sale but they are all made with great sensitivity. The nice sandstone sculpture made by Erik Cohrt is a work in which you can lose yourself, a sculpture you can enjoy several times. The logo for "Save the Children" with the little girl looking into the light globe of the match is one of the most idealistic works with inspiration from "The Little Match Girl".

The Danish Christmas seal from 1930 is meant for help to children. In 1904 the Royal Danish Post Office decided to publish new Christmas seals with different motives every year. The money which comes in from the sale is given to institutions for children with a.o. social problems, in Danish "julemærkehjem".

I almost forgot picture no. 5, the postcard from the association of the disabled (Vanføreforeningen). The association is also a relief organisation but the intention is to give help to children as well as to grown-up people.

Bibliography

Illustreret dansk Konversationsleksikon – Berlingske Forlag 1935.

Litteraturens veje. Red. Johannes Fibiger m.fl. Gads Forlag 1996.

Litteraturhåndbogen. Red. Ib Fischer Hansen m.fl. Gyldendal 1981.

H.C. Andersen. *Samlede eventyr og historier*, bind 1, "Den lille pige med svovlstikkerne". Gyldendals Tranebøger 1972.

Erik Dal. *Den lille Pige med Svovlstikkerne. Træk af et eventyrs forhistorie og skæbne*. Rosenkilde og Bagger 1956.

Jens Andersen. *Andersen, en biografi*, bind 1-2. Gyldendal 2003.

Johan de Mylius. *H.C. Andersen og Hertugdømmerne*. Grænseforeningens årbog 2005.

Johan de Mylius. *H C. Andersens liv, dag for dag*. Aschehoug 1998.

Leif Ludwig Albertsen. *Det grønne træ. Digteren og julen*. Privattryk 1982.

Litteratur, læring og dannelse. Forlaget ABC 1986.

Notes

1. Erik Dal: *Den lille Pige med Svovlstikkerne. Træk af et eventyrs forhistorie og skæbne* (The Little Match Girl. Features of the story behind a fairy tale, and its fate), p. 25.
2. Erik Dal: *Den lille Pige med Svovlstikkerne*, p. 17.
3. Erik Dal: *Den lille Pige med Svovlstikkerne*, p. 18.
4. "Gjør vel, naar du giver!"
   Det er vel i en vis Henseende ædelt og smukt, at dit Hjerte røres ved din Næstes Nød, at du villig aabner din Haand, naar du seer din Broder lider, at du føler Medlidenhed, naar din Næste klædt i Pjalter røstende og bævende anraaber dig om Hjælp og i Jesu Navn beder om en Bid Brød til at stille sin Hunger; men det er dog ogsaa kun i en "vis" Henseende smukt og ædelt. Jeg skal nærmere oplyse det ved et par Eksempler. Tænk dig f. Ex. et fattigt Barn

antastede dig paa Gaden, eller bankede paa din Dør, og bad: Giv mig en Skilling til en Bid Brød! tænk dig, at dette Barn var udsendt af slette, dovne Forældre, som intet gad bestilt, ei brød sig om deres Barns Opdragelse, men brugte det alene til Tiggeri; og spørg nu dig selv, spørg og undersøg ret alvorligt, om du virkelig gjør en god Gerning ved at give det fattige Barn. Understøtter du ikke derved Dovenskab, og gjør du ikke netop ved din Gave det umuligt for det fattige Barn, at erholde en god Opdragelse, befordrer du ikke derved Barnets timelige og aandelige Fordærvelse? Lukte du og lukte Alle Øret og Haanden for Barnets Klage, da vilde i de fleste Tilfælde baade Forældrene selv arbeide og tillige anføre deres Børn til nyttige Forretninger, hvorved de i sin Tid kunde blive brave og dygtige Folk; medens de nu ved din forkeerte Medlidenhed voxe op i Dovenskab, Uvidenhed og Synd!
(Do well when you give.
It is in a certain sense noble and beautiful that your heart is touched by the want of your neighbour, that you willingly open your hand when you see your brother suffer, that you feel pity when your neighbour, clothed in rags, in a quavering voice asks you for help, and in the name of Jesus begs a crust of bread to still his hunger; however, it is only 'in a certain sense' that this is beautiful and noble. Let me explain this further by means of a couple of examples. Imagine, for instance, that a poor child accosts you in the street or knocks on your door, asking, 'Give me a penny for a bit of bread'! Imagine that this child has been sent out by bad and lazy parents who don't bother to work, don't care about the education of their child, but only use it as a beggar; now ask yourself, ask and examine very seriously, if you are really doing a good deed by giving to the poor child. Do you not thereby support laziness, and doesn't exactly your gift make it impossible for the poor child to get a proper education, do you not in fact work for the corruption of the child, here as well as in the hereafter? If you and all others closed your ears and hands to the complaint of the child, then, in most cases, the parents would work themselves and also encourage their children to useful industry, by which in time they could become good and able people; whereas now, because of your misplaced pity, they grow up in laziness, ignoreance and sin!)

5. Jens Andersen: *Andersen - en biografi*, vol. 1, p. 64.
6. Leif Ludwig Albertsen: *Det grønne træ*, p. 74.
7. This understanding is also mentioned by Johan de Mylius in *H.C. Andersen og Hertugdømmerne*, p. 82.

Hans Christian Andersen's Flair to Communicate Basic Social Skills Naturally and Imperceptibly to National and International Readers

Eric J. Jones

Maria Montessori, the well-known educational philosopher, said in her Philosophies on educational, human development that a child's development comes from his/her environmental experience[1].

Each person, anywhere in the world is born into and grows up in a very unique environment. This development entails informal and formal education. Most children acquire the most basic social skills in the environment of the home and amongst family members closest to them in the initial formative years. At home they learn the skills of how to behave towards their elders, superiors, peers and strangers. Children, teenagers and later, young adults are taught either by example or by means of a formal, learning experience how to acquire acceptable and assertive social skills.

In our present whirlwind lifestyle much of the learning in the home is done by a nanny or a child minder as both parents choose to work away from home in order to live the way they want. In most instances it is no longer a matter of 'keeping up with the Joneses', but rather what can we achieve to outdo them. The children miss out on being taught how to behave and how to act under the most basic social situations in and around the home. Infants miss out on that very close relationship between child and parent and parent and child, in the initial stages of his or her development. The children get their first experience of the spoken or written word via the nanny or guardian. Both parents are too tired or too occupationally involved to keep the oral or reading culture alive. Fortunate are those youngsters who are being told or who listen to the reading of H.C. Andersen's *Fairy Tales* or any kind of folk tales in the initial stages of their mental and physical development.

Why then, it might be asked, should children have an early learning experience of the fairy tales of H.C. Andersen, for example? He succeeds in his plots, to make the children believe in the make-believe. If a child has never heard or seen how to behave to the persons in his/her immediate environment or towards strangers, the author will introduce them to those skills. This presentation aims at examining various social skills, which are revealed in some of H.C Andersen's *Fairy Tales*.

For the past two years I have been lecturing Communication in English to education students at the Cape Peninsula University of Technology. Out of the 300 students I lectured, 75% are non-English speakers from a disadvantaged background. Initially I discovered that the main problem with these students was the fact that they were unable to read. They did not know that reading could be fun; that a higher education learner should be able to understand reading in English, as English is the medium of instruction at the University. Lacking the skill of reading and misinterpreting the gist of English texts could have disastrous results, especially in understanding the contents of other subjects and in responding to tests and written assignment instructions and specifically in acquiring the skill of fluent speech, which is a crucial skill for the potential teacher, in the classroom.

To alleviate this problem I encouraged the students to begin reading Andersen's *Fairy Tales*. They were given the freedom of choice from finding stories at any library in their immediate living environment. Soon it was obvious that the most popular stories among the students were "Thumbelina", "The Tinder Box" and "Father Always Does What's Right".

In response to my question, why they liked these stories, the students commented that in these stories the main characters were always going on a journey or travelling for some reason or other.

Andersen Employs Social Skills in the Fairy Tales, "The Tinder-Box" and "Thumbelina", Convincing the Readers of the Usefulness of Such Skills

In "The Tinderbox", the readers are impressed by the polite and encouraging approach of the ugly witch to the soldier, returning from the war. She says

> God Aften, Soldat! hvor Du har en pæn Sabel og et stort Tornyster, Du er en rigtig Soldat! Nu skal Du faae saa mange Penge, Du vil eie!

> Good evening, soldier, she said, what a nice sword you've got, and what a big knapsack! You're a proper soldier. Now I'll show you how to get as much money as you want!

The young readers or listeners will accept the polite greeting notwithstanding Andersen's vivid description of her unsightly appearance. After all it is indeed very kind of her to greet the soldier, a complete stranger, who has just returned from the war, and she promises him much desired wealth. In addition they might be pleasantly surprised, as young readers are often led to believe that witches are evil and up to no good.

However, adult readers might suspect her true motive behind this obviously wheedling and scheming approach to achieve her own goal. She is not at all interested in the rich booty the soldier could find, but rather in the power she would gain if she possessed the tinderbox. A strategy, which eventually costs her her life and helps the soldier to woo the princess and become the new ruler of the country.

Andersen introduces the witch character in "Thumbelina" very differently. He allows the witch to serve the old woman in distress and liberates her from the depressing and frustrating condition of childlessness. Once again the woman makes her request in a believable, convincing and acceptable manner to the young reader or listener. One wonders if questioned or challenged, what explanation Andersen would have given: Why this witch, who might in the minds of children be regarded as evil and wicked, was endowed with such qualities of humane concern, believable wisdom and unconditional advice to the woman in distress.

> Jeg vilde saa inderlig gjerne have et lille Barn, vil Du ikke sig mig, Hvor jeg dog skal faae et fra?

> I would so dearly like to have a little child. Do please tell me
> Where I can find one.

Even more surprising is the witch's almost non-verbal guaranteed success and nonchalant response,

Jo, det skal vi nok komme ud af!

Oh that! Nothing easier.

Unlike in the case of the soldier's dealings with the first witch she is rewarded with a verbal expression of gratitude and a monetary reward.

Indeed a very believable employment of social skills such as fulfilling a request, receiving a vote of thanks and a reward, in the faith that the followed advice will do the trick. Somehow Andersen convinces readers of all ages of the fruitful possibility of a make-believe, wistful need, situation.

Therefore in both fairy tales, "The Tinderbox" and "Thumbelina", Andersen structures the plot with an adventurous journey. In the soldier's case it is all aimed at elevating his status and gaining material wealth. Whereas, in the case of Thumbelina, it becomes an adventurous, seasonal journey of survival.

Her physical beauty almost becomes a curse, as she is cherished and desired by a toad and a mole as a suitable bride. Despite the gloomy prospect of an undesirable marriage, the author presents her with opportunities to show compassion, be admired, aided and rescued from a most unacceptable fate.

After her compassionate rescue of the swallow, the tale is interspersed with the employment of the principles of common courtesy and apt expressions of gratitude; expressions which sustain the relationship between herself, the swallow, the little fish and finally the flower king. Examples are:

Goodbye, you lovely little bird, she said. Goodbye and thank you for your beautiful singing last summer when all the trees were green and the sun was so bright and warm.

Thank you my darling child, said the sick swallow. I'm lovely and warm now.

Ah, but it's so cold out of doors, she said. It's snowing and freezing. Stay in your bed; I'll look after you all right.

No, I can't, said Thumbelina. Goodbye, goodbye, you dear, kind girl, said the swallow, as it flew into the open sunshine.

Goodbye, bright sun! She said, throwing her tiny arms round a little, red flower standing near. Remember me to the dear swallow, if you happen to see it.

Tweet-tweet! She suddenly heard over her head. She looked up, and there was the swallow just passing. How delighted it was to see Thumbelina! She told the bird how she disliked having to marry the ugly mole and to live down under the earth where the sun never shone. She couldn't help crying at the thought.

Yes, I'll come with you, said Thumbelina.

That will be lovely, she said, clapping her little hands.

At the same time he asked her what her name was and whether she would be his wife; if so, she would become queen of all the flowers.

Goodbye, goodbye, said the swallow and flew away again from warm countries, far away, back to Denmark.

Hans Christian Andersen Uses Social Skills and the Principles of Common Courtesy of Understanding, Confidence, Trust, Respect, Loyalty, and Appreciation to Illustrate the Successful Interpersonal Relationship Between Husband and Wife, in the Fairy Tale, "Father Always Does What's Right"

Very likely the plot and ending of this tale will meet with the approval and acceptance of young readers and listeners.
    What a delight it would be to respond positively to the dialogue between the farmer and his wife towards the end of the tale.

    Ja, men Hønen byttede jeg bort for en Pose raadne Æbler!
    Nu maa jeg kysse Dig! sagde Konen.

    Yes, but I swapped the hen for a bag of rotten apples!
    Well, now I must give you a kiss! said the woman.

And miraculously this reaction from his trusting wife, after the farmer has gone to the fair to trade their horse for something more useful. Along the way he manages to exchange the horse for a cow, a sheep, a goose, a hen and finally for a sack of rotten apples.

When he relates his trading venture to two Englishmen, he meets at an inn, they make a bet with him that his wife will slaughter him if she finds out what he has accepted in exchange for their horse. On witnessing the wife's response and praise they remark:

Det kan jeg lide! sagde Englænderne. Altid ned ad Bakke og altid lige glad! det er nok Pengene værd! og saa betalte de et Skippund Guldpenge til Bondemanden, som fik Kys og ikke Knubs.

Now that's what I like! said the Englishmen. Always going down, but never downhearted! It's worth every penny of our money. And so they paid their bushel of gold coins to the farmer who got a kissing instead of a licking.

Although, in the mind of the adult reader, the tale has many improbable nuances, and although the very same readers might conclude that H.C. Andersen is wishfully idealizing the relationship between husband and wife, he succeeds well in convincing the young readers of a fascinating outcome of a make-believe story.

Note

1. Montessori, Maria. (1948). *To Educate the Human Potential.* Madras, India: Kalakshetra Publications.

Language for Children?
An Examination of the Language and Intended Readership of the Fairy Tales

Tom Lundskær-Nielsen

Despite all the efforts made by organisers of, and participants in, Hans Christian Andersen conferences over the years, and in particular by all those involved in celebrating the bicentenary of his birth this year, Hans Christian Andersen is still regarded chiefly as a writer of fairy tales, and as such as a children's writer, by the vast majority of people, especially those living outside Denmark. I am sure that we all want to change that perception, and many laudable attempts aimed at providing a more balanced picture have been made to achieve this objective, but rather than preaching the broader Andersen gospel, I would like to take as my point of departure the very notion of Hans Christian Andersen as a children's writer and look at some aspects of the language used in Andersen's fairy tales.[1]

If the fairy tales are really aimed at children, to what extent is that reflected in the language? Is the language, broadly speaking, the same throughout the almost four decades of fairy-tale writing, or does it change? And if it changes, in what way does it do so, and what does this say about the intended readership? These are the questions that I will try to address in this paper.

In order to carry out such an examination, there is only one place to start, namely with the first series of four fairy tales, published in 1835 under the telling title *Fairy Tales, Told for Children* (*Eventyr, fortalte for Børn*).

From the outset Andersen seems to have known the implications of what he was doing. A few months before their publication in May, he tells the writer B.S. Ingemann that he has started writing these tales and that he thinks he will succeed in his efforts. As he puts it in his letter, "Furthermore, I have begun some 'Fairy Tales, *Told* for Children', I think I will succeed with them. I have rendered a few of the fairy tales that made me happy to listen to as a child and which I think are not known."[2] And then he adds the following significant sentence, "I have written them completely as I myself would tell them to a *child*." On the eve of publication, he informed the German writer Adelbert von Chamisso that "in these [i.e. the first four tales] I think I have expressed the childish in a rather singular way".[3]

So the conscious emphasis on the spoken language (in a sense, not too different from Grundtvig's contemporary notion of "det levende ord" (the living word)) and a colloquial style as well as on children as the target audience is clear even before the publication of the first tales.

And yet, to what extent are the tales really for children, let alone solely or mainly for children? There can be no doubt that however much the aspects and features aimed specifically at children are stressed, Andersen was at the same time acutely aware of his "double audience". In the preface to the first collected edition of his Fairy Tales and Stories,[4] he managed to list in one sentence three of the key elements that make his tales unique by saying, "In style one ought to hear the narrator; these stories were made to suggest oral delivery; they were told for children but their elders should also enjoy listening to them." So here we have: (a) the visibility of the narrator; (b) the colloquial style of the spoken language; and (c) the double audience. In other words, the tales were never intended exclusively for children; that may initially have been a ruse on Andersen's part to make them seem more "innocent" and thus acceptable, or perhaps in order to test the water of contemporary criticism. But if the latter was the case, he failed miserably, for the earliest criticism in Denmark was almost unanimously fierce and unsympathetic, with the notable exception of P.L. Møller.

Much later, in his last and most comprehensive (though not most reliable) autobiography *Mit Livs Eventyr* (*The Story of My Life*), he appears almost apologetic about the early title pages – admittedly with the benefit of hindsight, but nevertheless echoing his pre-publication words – when he says somewhat cryptically, "In order to put the readers in their rightful place I had ... given the first books the title *Fairy Tales, Told for Children*." And he continues, "I had put my short tales down on paper in quite the same language and with the expressions in which I myself had orally told them to the little ones and had realised that all the different ages accepted this; the children mostly enjoyed what I would call the ornamental trappings, the older reader on the other hand was interested in the deeper meaning. The fairy tales became reading for children and adults, which I think, in our time, is the task for the writer of fairy tales. They started to find open doors and open hearts; and now I omitted "Told for Children" and let three books of *New Fairy Tales* follow the others..."[5]

If Andersen realised that the addition of "Told for Children" was a mistake, it took him quite a long time to remedy it. In fact, it happened 8 years and 23 fairy tales after the initial launch in 1835 when the first book of *New Fairy Tales* appeared in 1843, boasting four new tales of such high quality as "The Angel", "The Nightingale", "The Lovers" and "The Ugly Duckling". But does that mean that from now on the tales were written in a different way?

In attempting to answer this question, let us first take a look at some of the features that may be seen to appeal directly to children.

First of all we have interjections, often in the form of onomatopoetic expressions, such as the soldier's "een, to! een, to!" ("one, two! one, two!" or, in some translations, "left, right! left, right!") (p. 9) in the very first sentence of the first tale, "The Tinderbox", and later in the same tale, "Snik, snak!" ("Pish posh!") (p. 11) and the "Uh!" ("Ooh!"), "Eja!" ("Eeek!") and "Nej, det var ækelt!" ("Oh, how hideous!") (p. 10) of the soldier's initial reaction to the three dogs.[6] Such sound-imitating expressions are found in other early tales, e.g. the young toad in "Thumbelina" with his "Koax, koax, brekke-ke-kex!" (p. 34) and the swallow's "Kvivit! kvivit!" (p. 39) in the same tale, which is very similar to the lark's "kvirrevit!" in "The Daisy" (p. 107). However, they are not confined to the early tales. We have, for example, the street children's song "zizizi! klukklukkluk!" (p. 195) in "The Nightingale", where also the artificial bird goes "svup!" and "surrrrr!" (*ibid.*) when the mechanism inside it breaks, and in the rather late tale "The Toad", the toad itself just manages a last "Quak! ak!" (p. 857) before expiring in the beak of the stork. Nonsense rhymes, too, are common over a long period, as for example the "Snip snap snurre – Basselurre" (pp. 332/5) in "The Flax", the meaning of which is basically to indicate – to a child – that it is the end of something. In fact, as we shall see with other stylistic features, Andersen largely remains faithful to the kind of language that he used in his earliest tales.

Another feature of child-oriented language is the direct address by the narrator, especially in preparing the reader/listener for what is to come. It has frequently been remarked that Andersen not only uses a very colloquial style, but often intrudes in the narration to draw attention to the listening activity, as if he was reading the text aloud to a child. Hence the numerous instances of the word "hear".[7] It appears throughout his fairy-tale production right from the start with "The

Tinderbox" when the soldier, languishing in the prison, gets his tinderbox back and – well, what then? Or as Andersen puts it, "Well, now we'll hear" or "Now let's hear what happened", depending on how you translate the Danish expression "få at høre" (p. 13).

In "Little Claus and Big Claus", we are told at the end of the first paragraph, "Now we're going to hear how the two men got on, for it is a real story" (p. 15). In "The Swineherd", it comes after the first two paragraphs, as a simple, "Now we'll hear" (p. 181), and in "The Snow Queen" – at the end of the first story – it appears with the same wording (p. 218).

But sometimes there are variations. "The Daisy" has as its very first words, "Now you'll hear" (p. 106); "you" (the Danish informal singular form "du"), that is, the individual reader, or most likely a child, not the inclusive "we". And the very late tale, "What the Whole Family Said", opens with a question followed by a stalling answer, "What the whole family said? Well, listen first to what little Marie said" (p. 958).

A slightly less obvious rhetorical question appears at the beginning of "The Shepherdess and the Chimney Sweep" with its "Have you ever seen a really old wooden cupboard, quite black with age and with carved-out arabesques and foliage?" (p. 271), but the function of this is the same, namely to catch the attention of the listener from the start.

In fact, the need to tell a story at all may be queried in this way, as in "The Old Street Lamp", which begins with the question, "Have you heard the story about the old street lamp?" (p. 286), though the assumption is obviously that the answer will be in the negative.

There is wide variation in the ways that the narrator may choose to address the reader, particularly the young listener. For example, at the beginning of "The Daisy" the narrator states that "out in the countryside, close to the road, there was a cottage", and draws in the listener by appealing to an air of familiarity when he adds, "you yourself have surely already seen it" (p. 106), before going on to describe it.

A similar appeal to the comfort and cosiness claimed to be necessary for the proper enjoyment of the listening activity is seen in the arguably most famous opening of this kind, namely that of "The Snow Queen": "Now then! (Danish: "Se så!") Now we'll begin. When we come to the end of the story, we'll know more than we know now, for it was an evil troll" (p. 217).

Another type of narrator's intervention consists in commenting on the action, behaviour, looks or other aspects of a character. Here examples are legion. In "The Tinderbox" the narrator breaks in and comments on the soldier's habit of giving money to the poor by saying, "and that was very noble of him" (p. 11). In "The Daisy", when the peonies puff themselves up in order to be bigger than a rose, we are told by the narrator that "it is not really the size that matters" (p. 106), which may or may not have been intended as the *double entendre* that it would unquestionably be regarded as today.[8] A little later the narrator comments that "it was a good thing that the peonies couldn't talk" (p. 107), however absurd that may sound in the context of a talking lark and a thinking daisy, but a child may find it natural to observe such a distinction between birds and flowers. In "The Drop of Water" it reaches surreal proportions when we hear that "another old troll" did not have a name – and then are told that "that was the fine thing about him" (p. 319); and in "The Bell", when the third confirmand says that he never goes to any strange places without being accompanied by his parents and that he has always been a well-behaved child and will continue to be so even after his confirmation, we discern the morally indignant voice of the narrator in his "and that is nothing to poke fun at" (p. 252), though that was exactly what the others did.

The narrator's comments can also take the form of ostensibly supplying reasons for a character's actions or for anything else, though of course we should not always take these at face value. Again, "The Tinderbox" provides a good example. When the soldier has spent all the money he brought out of the hollow tree, he has to move into a tiny attic, and now none of his many friends from the time when he was rich come to see him, for – as we are told – "there were so many stairs to mount" (p. 11). Only a small child would accept that as a true explanation. In "The Travelling Companion", Johannes and his mysterious friend witness a comedy in the inn where they are staying. This has a king and a queen, both of whom wear golden crowns and long trains on their dresses, and in case we did not know, this is explained with the amusing words, "for they could afford that" (p. 49).

The little match girl, we remember, walks around freezing and dare not go home because "she hadn't sold any matches, not been given a single coin" (p. 279). In the Danish original, the use of the discourse particle "jo" ("hun havde jo ingen svovlstikker solgt, ikke fået en eneste skilling") adds to the intimate relationship between narrator and reader/listener by implying that they both know the reason, though to translate it into English by something like "as we know" sounds rather awkward and clumsy. Strictly speaking, the comment is completely superfluous since the same was said in the previous paragraph, namely that "nobody had bought anything from her the whole day, no one had given her as much as a small coin" (*ibid.*). So why the repetition? It can only be that it is aimed at a listening child. Once more, "The Drop of Water" provides us with an example that touches on the absurd. The first sentence of the second paragraph goes like this: "Now there once was an old man whom everybody called Creepy Crawley, for that was his name" (p. 319). We might have expected either a full stop after Creepy Crawley, or "an old man whose name was Creepy Crawley", but hardly the overt information that he was called that because it was his name. Stylistically, it comes near to being a tautology, and yet not quite. It is more in tune with the deadpan humour of the absurd that is a characteristic of some stand-up comedians of our own time.

Andersen's use of discourse particles (such as "da", "dog", "jo", "vel", etc.), like the "jo" just mentioned in "The Little Match Girl", constitutes a fertile hunting ground for text and language analyses of the fairy tales, and at the same time a nightmare for translators of the tales, not least when translating into English. This aspect of Andersen's fairy-tale language is well known,[9] but it is worth pointing out that discourse particles are predominantly used in the spoken language where they not only "colour" the clause in which they appear in a particular way (hence the alternative term, *modal adverbs*), but also imply a closer relationship between narrator and reader/ listener. Thus they offer almost unlimited opportunities for creating subtle nuances, which is something that Andersen exploited in a masterful way from beginning to end.

It is also possible to find combinations of comment and reason, and here too we need to exercise our critical faculties when we come across such examples. In "The Bell", when all the other people had almost literally fallen by the wayside, the prince and the poor boy decide to go their separate ways in their pursuit of the elusive bell. In practice, this presents a problem for the narrator since he cannot easily follow both of them, so he chooses to tell us that he will stay with the prince by stating, "and he is the one that we'll now follow, for he was a plucky lad" (p. 253). However, so is the poor boy, so can we really believe that this is the sole reason?

Examples of ambiguity are not difficult to find in the language of the fairy tales. The intimacy of the style often makes it far from easy to separate what are the narrator's comments or a character's thoughts. This fusion creates a mixture of inner monologue and authorial viewpoint. Take, for example, this passage from "The Red Shoes", which I have to quote in full:

> Then the Queen once travelled through the country, and she brought along her little daughter, who was a princess, and people flocked to the outskirts of the palace, and of course Karen was there too, and the little princess stood in a window in fine clothes and let herself be observed; she wore neither a train nor a golden crown, but lovely red morocco shoes; they were certainly prettier than those mother's shoemaker had sown for little Karen. Nothing in the world was after all comparable to red shoes! (pp. 264-65)

Is the construction "prettier than those mother's shoemaker had sown for little Karen" the words of the narrator, who is after all telling the story and here talks of "little Karen", or of Karen who is the only one that would naturally use the expression "mother's shoemaker"? It is difficult to tell as there seems to be a fusion of the two viewpoints.

A classic feature of folk fairy tales – and thus of children's subliminal perception – is the use of repetition (which we saw an earlier example of in "The Little Match Girl"). This reappears particularly in some of the fairy tales modelled on folk tales, often linked to the use of magic numbers. Thus there are three dogs in "The Tinderbox" and they bring the princess to the soldier on three consecutive nights. Little Claus fools Big Claus three times, the last time with fatal, but unmourned consequences, and each time Big Claus initially utters the same expression of surprise, "What on earth is this?" (Danish: "Hvad for noget?") (pp. 19, 21, 22). There are also three brothers in "Clod Hans" and hence three tests in front of the King's daughter, just as Johannes has to answer three questions in "The Travelling Companion".

One can hardly round off this part of the exemplification of features with special appeal to children without pointing to the obvious ploy of personifying not only animals, birds, trees and flowers, but also inanimate things from shirt collars and porcelain figures to darning needles and whipping-tops, and many others. What is interesting about these, from a language point of view, is the way they each appropriately express their experiences of their particular worlds and life experiences in very precise terms. They may occasionally deviate from this pattern, as when two porcelain figures in "The Shepherdess and the Chimney Sweep" climb up the chimney and then down again, with a third one trying to pursue them, but in general the individualisation of all these creatures and things within a world natural to them is certainly one of the elements that mark out Andersen as being very different from both his predecessors and contemporaries in the genre.

So far, I have looked at some of the language features that chiefly appeal to children, but since Andersen so obviously operates on (at least) two levels in his story-telling, it is very difficult to pin him down and isolate particular elements because they are usually intertwined with others. In the rest of this paper, I will briefly deal with some other stylistic elements typical of Andersen's fairy-tale language.

In my view, there are two overall characteristics of Andersen's language in the fairy tales that transcend attempts to pigeon-hole him as writing exclusively for children. They dominate the language of all his stories and fairy tales, even when these cannot possibly be chiefly aimed at children in terms of their content. For example, texts such as "The Ice Maiden" and "Auntie Toothache" are not in content children's stories at all, and yet the basic style used in them is quite similar to what it is in other stories and tales.

The first of these characteristics is the liberal use of direct speech. In its pure form, that is what makes up drama, and Andersen (himself a prolific playwright) certainly uses it with dramatic effect. It makes his tales livelier and his characters more vivid, and it does something else: it offers the narrator the opportunity to express himself indirectly by hiding behind the characters' words. Examples of this can be found in any tale.

It is true, though, that direct speech appears a little more sparingly in some of the stories, e.g. "A Story from the Dunes", than in most of the fairy tales proper. In the stories there are, for instance, more and longer passages of a descriptive nature.

But that is not true of the second main feature, namely the paratactic style that Andersen uses from beginning to end of his fairy-tale production. That does not mean that his sentences are short and staccato-like, though there are examples when this is the case. On the contrary, Andersen often writes long sentences – where the term "sentence" refers to what is written between two full stops – but he does not have many subordinate clauses in them. Instead of a linking subordinate conjunction, there is usually another main clause, separated from the previous one merely by a comma or a semicolon. This could be illustrated from any fairy tale. Let us just take a look at a few random and not very extreme instances. One is from "Thumbelina", describing her first happy moment away from her home when she meets the butterfly:

> A lovely, little, white butterfly kept circling her and finally settled on the leaf [of the water-lily], for it was so fond of Thumbelina, and she was so delighted, for now the toad couldn't reach her, and it was so lovely where she was sailing; the sun was shining on the water, it was like the most wonderful gold. (p. 35)

In this sentence there is just one short subordinate clause ("where she was sailing") among a string of main clauses, and this is the norm rather than the exception in Andersen's style. Another example is the long sentence from "The Red Shoes" quoted above, which contains only two subordinate clauses ("who was a princess" and "than those mother's shoemaker had sown for little Karen") but nine main clauses, and one can almost sense the breathless delivery when the text is read aloud.

Furthermore, unlike his use of direct speech, this feature does not change markedly with either time or the type of story he writes. We can find something similar in "A Story from the Dunes", for example in this sentence:

> The young man was sent by his king as an envoy to the imperial court in Russia, it was a post of honour, his birth and his knowledge gave him the right to this; he had a great fortune, his young wife had brought him another one no less great, she was the daughter of the richest and most distinguished merchant. (p. 639)

Here there is not even a linking "and"; main clause follows main clause without any connectors. It would have been in accordance with the language conventions of the day to have used either a few subordinate conjunctions and thus to have created subordinate clauses, or to have had one or more full stops. Both of these alternatives are – regrettably! – often found in translations of the stories and fairy tales into English, even by otherwise good translators, which has the unfortunate effect of "breaking up" Andersen's flowing style and thus the speed of delivery when read aloud.[10]

The effect of this innovative and at the time fairly revolutionary style was, as with the use of direct speech, to add to the liveliness of the language and make it more colloquial and hence "catching", especially for young listeners. But not only for the young: this was very much part of Andersen's aim at appealing to a double audience. He had clearly realised from the beginning, as we saw earlier, that this was a style that he not only felt comfortable with, but knew how to exploit to its maximum effect. It adds pace to the reading and oral delivery, and it can even lead to situations where we are thrown *in medias res* from the start. Such a moment is the beginning of the story "The Comet". It goes like this:

> And the comet came, shining with its body of fire and threatening with its sheaf; it was observed from the rich palace, from the poor cottage, by the crowd in the street and by the lonely wanderer crossing the pathless moor; everyone had their own thoughts about it. (p. 933)

Firstly, to begin a new sentence or paragraph, let alone a story, with the conjunction "and" (Danish: "og") was very uncommon then, except in one type of exalted style, namely that of the Bible. It is tempting to believe that this may have influenced Andersen, for he makes liberal use of "and" at the beginning of sentences, paragraphs and – as we saw – even of a whole tale.

Secondly, the use of the definite article "*the* comet" at the first mention of this phenomenon implies a kind of familiarity with the object that, strictly speaking, we cannot possibly possess. Nevertheless, it is yet another feature that creates closer intimacy between the narrator and the reader/listener and catapults us straight into the action.

To sum up, the answer to the question of intended readership that I posed at the beginning is not a straightforward one. There are undeniably typical child-oriented features in the language of the fairy tales, such as sound imitations, repetitions, interventions by the narrator and direct appeals to the listener, but although some of these appear more frequently in the early tales, most of them seem to have become inextricably bound up with Andersen's general fairy-tale style and are found throughout the fairy-tale production. Moreover, the pervading colloquial style, typified by frequent use of direct speech and parataxis, no doubt appeals to children by enlivening the text, but it is part and parcel of Andersen's particular way of writing fairy tales and is used as much to reach his double audience of children and adults alike. We know from Andersen himself that he was acutely aware of operating at different levels.

Some of the confusion concerning the intended readership may thus arise because, while the style (with certain modifications) remained fairly constant, the content of the stories and tales – roughly from "The Shadow" via "The Ice Maiden" to "Auntie Toothache" – increasingly displayed a darker side of life and a more resigned attitude on the part of Andersen. Ultimately, it is the combination of style and content that makes Andersen's fairy tales so revolutionary and so unique. This is as true now as it was during his own lifetime and it may help to explain his enduring popularity, which is likely to last well beyond the year of his bicentenary – and in view of all the competition from the modern visual media in particular, that in itself is almost a fairy tale.

Notes

1. The Danish edition of the stories and fairy tales used in this paper is: H.C. Andersen, *Samlede Eventyr og Historier*, ed. Svend Larsen, Jubilæumsudgaven, 2nd ed., Copenhagen: Hans Reitzel, 1997. All page references are to this edition. Unless stated otherwise, translations from the Danish texts are my own.
2. *Breve fra Hans Christian Andersen*, ed. C.St.A. Bille and Nikolai Bøgh, Vol. I., Copenhagen: C.A. Reitzel, 1878, (dated 10 February 1835) p. 292.
3. Poul Høybye, "Chamisso, H.C. Andersen og andre danskere", *Anderseniana*, 1969: 400. Chamisso is best known for his story *Peter Schlemihls wundersame Geschichte* (The Wondrous Story of Peter Schlemihl) (1814), which inspired, and is even referred to in, Andersen's "The Shadow", though here Andersen makes clear that the similarity is only superficial.
4. *Samlede Eventyr og Historier*, Copenhagen, 1862.
5. *Mit Livs Eventyr*, ed. H. Topsøe-Jensen, Copenhagen: Gyldendal, 1951 (first published in 1855), p. 290. Cf. also *The Fairy Tale of My Life. An Autobiography* (though, strangely, the title *The Story of My Life* appears at the top of every page) (no translator's name given), New York/London: Paddington Press, 1975, p. 204, but due to some inaccuracies there I have provided my own translation. (It is stated in the book, on the back of the title page, that it is "a reprint of the 1868 ed.", but the year appears to be erroneous, for 1871, Vol. 7 of Horace Scudder's "Author's Edition" (N. Y.) of *The Story of My Life*.)
6. Onomatopoetic terms are notoriously difficult to translate. In these examples, I have followed the translation by Tiina Nunnally in *Hans Christian Andersen. Fairy Tales*, ed. Jackie Wullschlager, Penguin, 2004. However, in the following examples no translation seems necessary as it would at best be very arbitrary. After all, what *do* swallows and toads, etc., really say in different languages?
7. For this aspect of the fairy tales, see also Johannes Møllehave, *H.C. Andersens salt. Om humoren i H.C. Andersens eventyr*, Copenhagen: Lindhardt & Ringhof, 1985, pp. 16-31.

8. Note that a similar expression is used in "The Dung-beetle" ("Skarnbassen"): "'First the big ones, then the little ones,' it said, 'however, it's not size that matters.' And then it stretched out its thin legs" (p. 680).
9. For a textbook treatment of discourse particles in Danish, see R. Allan, P. Holmes and T. Lundskær-Nielsen, *Danish: A Comprehensive Grammar*, London/New York: Routledge, 2002 [1995], pp. 365-68.
10. One of numerous examples of this tendency is Tiina Nunnally's rendering of the passage quoted from "The Red Shoes" in *op.cit.* (see note 6), pp. 207-08.

About Little Gerda, and Her "Moratoria"

James Massengale

That a considerable body of critical comment has grown up around Andersen's tale of "The Snow Queen" is understandable. It is one of the author's largest and symbolically richest constructs. Finn Barlby's statement, that it constitutes a "semantic magnet," is surely correct.[1] But that this "magnet" repels as much or even more than it attracts, I find more curious. It would seem that for the last fifty years, splinters from the nasty troll-mirror have flown up like dust when its pages are turned. This "love-hate" relationship can readily be observed in recent Danish scholarship; but the most marked example of it – as well as the most extensive analysis of the story – is Wolfgang Lederer's book-length, psychological-symbolic-biographical study.[2] Here is Lederer's dualistic conclusion, for example:

> [E]ven [Andersen's] best stories remained flawed, as *The Snow Queen* is flawed by its timorous, inconclusive ending ... And the whole body of his work, to the extent to which it survives, has been relegated by the brutal and perhaps justified verdict of time to the realm of "children's literature" ... But it was from his very failures, from the very flaws of his loving, that Andersen – poor, lonely oyster that he was – created the pearls he has left us.[3]

So what is it that Andersen in fact has left us? Is it a literary "pearl" or is it a "flawed, inconclusive" tale? Some years ago I jotted down a few notes in the form of "objections" to some of Lederer's points, and I have used these repeatedly in my own classroom. But my thoughts seemed hardly publishable in the beginning, and it appeared to me that a review by Pål Björby pointed clearly to the dangers in Lederer's attempt to equate Andersen's personal difficulties with his artistic personae, so I felt no need to make a public statement.[4] Gradually, however, my own notes began to congeal into a counter-argument, which is this paper. Lederer is still my chosen opponent, but I have become less interested in objecting to him than in supporting Andersen's construct on its own terms. The two past decades have also seen a blizzard of additional, well-formulated "Snow Queen" ideas, some of which I shall try to integrate here into my own train of thought – or respond to, if I find them impossible to integrate.

Although I refer to Lederer as my "opponent," I have to admit from the getgo that I have no intention of keeping the playing field level. My interpretation *cannot* treat Lederer's with impartiality, since it does not cater specifically to the biographical-psychoanalytical aspects of his approach. I am not interested in how mentally sick Andersen was (or was not); and I do not have the training to provide the sort of psychoanalytical discussion about the sickness issue, even if I *were* interested in the author's private interior development or lack thereof. My standpoint, like that of Bjørby, is based on a personal conviction that any author – even a self-centered one – can tell a story about something else than his own self-centeredness, at least every once in a while.[5] And this is what I contend has happened in the case of "The Snow Queen." But in order to demonstrate this, I am compelled to leave behind many of Lederer's psycho-biographical musings, and to set three procedural rules for my own argument. First, I shall attempt to stick to the text; second, I shall try to present a model in which all – or as many as possible – of Andersen's story symbols may be shown to work together as a single conceptual unit; and third, I shall try to do something with the psychology of the puberty issue as Andersen and his audience might have understood it, without relying upon a specifically Freudian or Jungian model. Only the third of these precepts puts me on a head-on collision course with Lederer, but he will be allowed to pop up, some might say straw-doggedly, throughout my discussion.

I also need to mention one caveat against my own rules, and attend to it from the beginning. Andersen, as we know, wrote his "First Story" about the "Troll Mirror" in November 1843, more than a year before he dashed off the remaining six stories of "The Snow Queen."[6] His statement, that the new (parts of the) narrative "danced across the pages" in December 1844, is also corroborated by the extant manuscript in Uppsala: there are only minimal corrections in the manuscript text, quite unlike the extensive substantive revisions often found in his papers in the Royal Library in Copenhagen.[7] Given the pause in the middle of the authorial process and Andersen's haste at the end in getting the tale to his publisher, we might expect some incongruity between the first story and the following six, and indeed some issues appear to need a bit of judicious editing: some larger pieces of the troll mirror, that were supposed to be used for window panes and spectacles, have no place in the "everyday" story. In addition, Andersen's use of Spitzbergen as a geographical goal for the quest immediately gives way to Lappland and Finnmark.[8] And, as several other researchers have noted, there is the matter of the disappearing parents, and the thing about the misquoted Brorson psalm text.[9] While these and a few additional *erreurs de plume*, if that is what they are, do not cause irrevocable damage to the story line, they can tip us off that the construct is not absolutely, hermetically tight. At the same time, there are strong indicators in the story of an exceedingly careful (or intuitively sure) authorial hand, even down to minute detail. The combination of minor sloppiness *and* careful precision is simply germane to the story as we have it. My caveat is that I must maintain what I consider a rigorous approach – while having to be a bit non-commital about the sloppy issues. I am well aware that another observer might consider my rigorous points to be evidence of Andersen's sloppiness, and my choice of Andersenian sloppinesses to be the central point of the story! This sort of unresolvable problem tends to make Andersen research quite open-ended, but I find no problem with that, either.

On one point, at least, virtually all researchers are agreed: "The Snow Queen" has to do with growing up. The scholarly division starts beyond that point: *do* the kids really grow up? does one of them grow up, but not the other? *how* or in what way does he or she grow up? and so on. Briefly stated, Lederer follows Gerda and Kay through a series of what he terms pubertal "moratoria."[10] Lederer's definition of the term, which he applies to both of the principal characters in the tale, is formulated most completely when introduced in regard to Kay's disappearance with the Snow Queen:

> At this stage in life – after the onset of physical-sexual maturity and drive, but before the readiness several years later to cope with the emotional involvements and the practical responsibilities that sexuality entails – a moratorium is generally needed.[11]

In my view, Andersen's story is rather structured on an *aberration* in pubertal development (represented by Kay), and not on a general pubertal principle, nor on a need. That Gerda is *not* depicted as aberrant is clear to me from the way the story unfolds. But what is then the nature of Gerda's quest, if it is not predicated upon a general rule of necessary developmental "moratoria"? To answer this, we have to trace Andersen's construct from the beginning. Assuming that my reader has the tale of "The Snow Queen" itself well in mind, I will not recount the tale itself, but use the space allotted me by concentrating on the symbols and their unifying principle.[12]

Starting with the troll mirror and its fragments: Lederer identifies the metaphysical beginning as the Fall, which starts with hubris and ends with the sorry state of mankind: "Therefore mankind was splintered (like the mirror) and alienated from itself."[13] Lederer's analysis derives three guiding principles from the assumption:

1. The story concerns itself basically with Hell and Sin ("Splintering is sinning is the opposite of loving – love being the force that unites", p. 7);
2. Forbidden knowledge (hubris or simply impertinence) is the driving force in "The Snow Queen" ("a thirst for forbidden knowledge ... is germane to our story", p. 8);
3. The nature of this forbidden quest is sexual ("Forbidden knowledge may be of two kinds, pertaining either to the sacred, or to the sexual ... And in our story, too, sex seems to be involved", p. 8).

This contains some good observation, but it is a conflation of two or three contradictory biblical passages, while Andersen's own construct has little to do with *any* orthodox notion of "the Fall."[14] Granted, Andersen works with *some* sort of a Fall-motif, and some adults, if they listened unreflectively to the "First Story" might have thought that the author was serving up a Bible-lesson adapted for the nursery. But the lesson will not hold up to scrutiny, and Andersen was well-enough acquainted with the Bible to be aware of this. The concept of the "First Story," simplistically expressed, works like this: once upon a time, the Devil and the Lord had an altercation, and as a result, the human world was divided into two types, like the rose bushes and the snails. The rosebushes never get it wrong, and the snails never get it right. The dichotomy that was so established is between a natural or original form of existence and a distorted one. There is no evidence of any existential choice leading the individual in either a rosebushy or a snailish direction. The message is something like: "splinters happen," and people are going to have to deal with this however they can. Lederer's point, "So we know that our story will have to do with sinning,"[15] might seem to have some support in the "First Story," but it certainly stops there; it is never corroborated anyplace else in the tale.

"The Snow Queen" tells us nothing about human sinning, that is, with any *actual* sinful human act.[16] Lederer subsequently acknowledges this when he correctly identifies the sum of Kay's rebellious activities: "He behaves, in short, like the typical adolescent."[17] And he adds, in an even more enlightened moment: "But we do recall that the splinters are to represent sinfulness; in what manner adolescent withdrawal into intellectuality may be a sin is not at all clear."[18] Exactly! The matter could have been cleared up at once if we had just noticed that neither the pre-pubertal children nor their projections are conceived of in terms of sin and expiation. Lederer instead defers his explanation of all this until the end of the story and of his book, when "we shall 'know more than we know now.'"[19] But do not hold your breath. All we shall learn by the end of Lederer's book is that Andersen himself failed to jump into a marital bed – however that might qualify as a sin.

The "Second Story" establishes the "everyday" premise of Andersen's construct: two children, a boy and a girl, who are inseparable playmates, make do in their poverty with natural and simple things. They are "rosebush" people, and Andersen uses the tiny rose garden and the Brorson psalm verse about roses and Christ to show this. But no clarification of the conjunction (between roses and Christ, in Andersen's own terms) is provided at this point in the tale. It is simply presented as a childhood fact. The children are companions; they play with roses (not so easy to do! but it works here as the preparation for a symbolic development); they have been taught a Christian psalm, and the psalm has something about roses in it that they take for granted. It is in this context that we meet Grandmother. The parents are mentioned only obliquely and never show themselves physically; in my view, they are not integral to the story construct.[20]

Now, into this idyll comes the Snow Queen. She has been variously described: Lederer (and with him, I fear, even several recent Danish critics) have linked her conceptually to figures in an early Andersen poem and the later tale of "The Ice Maiden" – or worse, to remarks attributed to Andersen's father. My point is: no matter how Andersen *learned* of this allegorical figure, no matter how he used it before or after the tale of "The Snow Queen," the tale has to be considered on its own terms. The Ice Maiden *is* an allegorical death figure in the story of that name. But Lederer finds her to be "identical with the Snow Queen," as "suggested by the common elements of the frosted window ..., by their [mutual] frigid nature, and by the kisses of death they bestow."[21] She also calls to mind "the goddess [sic]

Hel," the Grimm brothers' "Frau Holle," etc.[22] Now, since Kay is never *actually* killed by the Snow Queen, and since his "hibernation" is not one in which he *actually* sleeps, Lederer finally decides that the Snow Queen is most properly denoted as "the defensive-protective hibernation of the emotions during adolescence."[23] This is Lederer's definition (see above!) of a "moratorium." I do not see the Snow Queen as a moratorium. But I do find Andersen's use of her interesting and complex. I would like to start with the notion that she is nothing at all. She begins as an ironic, linguistic product of Grandmother's fantasy, in answer to little Kay's question about snowflakes:

"Det er de hvide Bier, som sværme," sagde den gamle Bedstemoder. "Har de ogsaa en Bidronning?" spurgte den lille Dreng, for han vidste, at imellem de virkelige Bier er der saadan en. "Det har de!" sagde Bedstemoderen. "Hun flyver der, hvor de sværme tættest ... Mangen Vinternat flyver hun gjennem Byens Gader og kiger ind af Vinduerne, og da fryse de saa underligt, ligesom med Blomster."
"Ja, det har jeg seet!" sagde begge Børnene, og saa vidste de, at det var sandt.[24]

["It's the white bees that are swarming," said the old Grandmother. "Do they have a queen bee too?" asked Kay, for he knew that real bees have such a thing. "Yes, they have!" said Grandmother. "She flies where they swarm the most ... Many a winter night she flies through the streets of the town and peeks in the windows, and then they freeze in such a strange way, as if there were flowers." "Yes, I've seen that!" said both of the children, and then they were sure that what she said was true.]

We recognize this narrative technique from "Little Ida's Flowers," where the Student's ironic fantasies are corroborated and accepted by the trusting child – much to the irritation of the Old Chancellor. Only in "The Snow Queen," we have no corrective voice to chide Grandmother for her nonsense. The parallel can be taken further, because Kay, like little Ida, also has a confirming experience during the night, when the Snow Queen "peeks in the window" and greets him for the first time. But *what* she represents, other than a remark and a child's lively imagination, is not made clear until Kay is struck by the two glass splinters, when he metaphorically turns "cold." Besides his normal beginning-pubertal traits (scientific observation, a longing for perfection) and his newly-acquired "aberrant" pre-pubertal tendencies (his rejection of roses and friends, his mocking attitude, his anti-authoritarian posturing), he is drawn toward the ice that he "contains." In this context, his memory of Grandmother's "Snow Queen fabrication" is conjured up and given power and a commanding personality (arguably projections of Kay in his aberrant state); and she is imbued with some pubertal aspects that Kay could be expected to comprehend only dimly, like an association of knowledge and sexuality. This seems to me to conform more closely to Andersen's construct than any attempt to connect the Snow Queen with "Dævelen" or "evil" or any heathen "soulless" creature who longs for humanity.[25] Note, however, the following issues, which *do* appear to be within the construct:

1. If Kay has gained something gratuitously (splinters), he has also lost something at the same time. He loses contact with the roses; he loses the warmth that un-splintered types have. He now contains a serious lack.
2. *After* the glass splinters take effect on Kay, the Snow Queen's power manifests itself. She appears to be an anthropomorphic projection of his own condition, and her palace a manifestion of his cold rationality, seen in terms of a geographical location.
3. Since Kay is a human being, however, his aberration is not permanent or irrevocable. This is represented by Andersen in terms of a conflict: he *wanted* to say his Lord's Prayer, but could not; he *wants* to spell "Eternity," but is unable, etc. The Snow Queen, his projection, only corroborates his own puffed-up and childish wish when she offers him "the whole world and a pair of new skates" if he spells the unfathomable word. Lederer's suggestion that this recalls the temptation of Christ is interesting as a free association, but it is not logically part of the construct here.[26]
4. While Gerda begins on the same level as Kay, acknowledging the Snow Queen's "reality" in front of Grandmother, she soon appears to forget the Snow Queen, and does not even call her to mind when Kay disappears on an icy night:

Hvor var han dog? – Ingen vidste det, Ingen kunde give Besked. Drengene fortalte kun, at de havde seet ham binde sin lille Slæde til en prægtig stor, der kjørte ind i Gaden og ud af Byens Port. Ingen vidste, hvor han var ...[27]

[But where was he? – Nobody knew, nobody could tell her. The boys just said that they had seen him tie his little sled to a great big one that drove into the street and out of the town gate. Nobody knew where he was ...]

5. But then comes an interesting twist: as Gerda gets into her quest, her *own* projected helpers will eventually make mention of the Snow Queen – strictly in terms of Kay and his "location." In analytical terms, Gerda must remember Grandmother's fabrication, and apply it (i.e. "understand it") in order to "find" the center of Kay's coldness, so that she may bring him back into the realm of her warmth.
6. So what does she find when she arrives at the Snow Queen's residence? Only a frozen Kay. The Snow Queen was always the aberrant Kay's thing. If he is no longer "aberrant," the Snow Queen no longer has any functional reality.[28]

I am clearly getting ahead of myself here. There is of course more to be said about the young people in the Snow Queen's palace. But first we have to address the matter of how Gerda gets there.

*

However little the *figure* of the Snow Queen has to do with Gerda, it is evident that the *tale* of "The Snow Queen" is Gerda's story. This may seem completely self-evident, but it is a matter of some psychological importance that has often been overlooked, not least by some post-Jungian scholars. As basic as the concept would seem (and as little as my own essay concerns itself technically with a Jungian point of view), the idea of Gerda *qua* anima-figure must be firmly rejected.[29] As fascinating a figure as Kay may seem, he is reduced for the bulk of the story to being the object of Gerda's quest, *not* an Andersenian alter-ego in this tale (not any sort of an ego-figure at all), and the narratological reason that he is placed in limbo is so that Andersen can focus our attention on his female protagonist. The fact that Gerda's journey begins and ends with the parties united does not alter this basic tenet of the construct.

That "The Snow Queen" as a journey is one which leads from childhood into puberty, may, as noted above, be taken for granted. That it is a *comprehensive* lesson in love is less often noted. And that it may be *our* lesson (and only to some degree Gerda's lesson) is an issue that separates my reading radically from that of Lederer. Here is how I think the process works.

The child Gerda is presented with a fundamental problem. In psychological terms, she has understood that Kay has isolated himself or (however one wishes to interpret this physically or psychologically) is "gone." Indeed, we, the adults, are told that he sits in complete isolation (in refrigeration, as Simon Grabowski has nicely said), with as his only companion – a cold, projected lack. What he lacks is of course Gerda, but since Gerda is his ticket to adulthood and love and he is *not* an adult and he lacks love, he has no understanding that he even lacks anything (this is a complicated way of explaining the "second kiss" of the Snow Queen). From Gerda's unsplintered perspective, she of course lacks Kay too, but she does not lack the *understanding* that she lacks Kay. On the other hand, she is a child. What does "a lack of Kay" even mean? Gerda needs no change of a quest object, what she needs is a quest. This is a hard thing to conjure up, if you do not know what it is. So she does her desperate thing, the sort of thing that only a desperate child can do. She weighs reasonable and unreasonable advice-givers, and chooses the latter as her guide. Andersen carefully balances the story situation between reality and allegory as he goes, never quite letting go completely of the everyday aspect.

In this way, Gerda's quest is constructed more "loosely" than the one in "The Story of a Mother." But there are strong similarities between the two tales.[30] In the Mother's tale, time is *explicitly* stopped (the old clock stops) and the allegorical part obviously begins as soon as she leaves the house.[31] In Gerda's case, the allegorical switch is more subtle. The realistic idea that Gerda asks people about Kay is balanced by the childlike notion that she asks the sun and the birds the same question.[32] The realistic act of running to the river gives way, then, to a "realistic absurdity" of her throwing her shoes in. But this absurdity – this challenge, if you will – causes the world to "open up" into allegory. Of course, it is also a psychological gesture, which is of interest to Lederer. He notes the Freudian aspects of the red shoe image and concludes: "Gerda makes the crucial – and Christian – decision to remain pure. She hopes ... to find Kay precisely because she is renouncing sexuality and choosing the path of virtue."[33] It can be a temptation for a post-Freudian to focus on the "red shoes" thing (menstrually colored, cup-shaped), especially in the intertextual light of Andersen's later story of that name, and lose track of the construct upon which this specific tale is based. But if Gerda rejects her (as yet dimly comprehended) sexuality, she logically rejects little Kay's as well, and might as well take off home. Her childish gesture is clearly both impractical and clueless, but as a challenge, it could just as well be sexually provocative: "Jeg vil forære Dig mine røde Skoe, dersom Du vil give mig ham igjen!"[34] ["I will give you my red shoes if you will give him back to me!"] So now her feet are naked, which is hardly a sign of de-sexualization. And the river's "response," ambivalent though it appears, starts her on her adventure. Maybe she is heading south, when Kay went north. No matter! She is moving, in the sense of the allegory, toward him, and the river offers her no prospect of a simple return. But this is fine for us adults to say! Gerda does not feel like a participant in an allegory, she feels like a foolish little child who may have made a fatal mistake. Her reaction – terror – also shows us that Andersen is sensitive to her psychological predicament. Her cries for help (her rejection of her bold act) "conjures" up what we could call a "helpful" projection, a "terror-reducer."

The "Ceres/Flora/Earth-Mother" person that answers Gerda's cry and hauls her in is correctly identified by Lederer, except that he *also* calls her a "goddess of organic death, just as the Snow Queen is the goddess of crystalline death."[35] She does not need this much analysis. She is a motherly Andersenian "wise woman," a kindly but not-too-clever witch whose human needs correspond temporarily to those of Gerda. She is also the first of Gerda's instructors, and the lesson she offers is one of love. And Gerda is no "flower" in her garden: Gerda is – simply – just Gerda, a pre-pubertal child who has run away to find her childhood friend, following a drive which she does not even fully comprehend, and which she (on some level) regrets. The problem, as at least one researcher has correctly pointed out, is that the particular type of love (the combing, sensual lulling into forgetfulness) the good witch exudes is *regressive* for Gerda.[36] It is also a deception. Andersen's symbolic portrayal of this, it seems to me, is as perceptive as it is narratologically satisfying. It involves a developmental conflict in the child, when the dimly understood drive toward an (unknown) sexuality is counterbalanced by fear and the desire for a (better understood) regressive substitute. The result is a kind of deceptive inertia. The benign witch whom she has conjured up makes every effort to end Gerda's striving, giving her a carressed, womblike and passive existence in which time and thought are erased. It is love's easiest manifestation. When Gerda's fear finally subsides, the (artificial) rose on the witch's sunhat becomes a psychological "trigger," which symbolically undoes the witch's magic, placing the "pact"-symbol ("pact" at this pont defined loosely or indefinitely) of Gerda and Kay in contrast to the form of love to which she has temporarily succumbed. The instant this realization is made, the witch is "left behind": she never chases Gerda, we never hear a cry of rage or pain from her, she simply disappears from the story, like a feeling of something superceded.

Gerda runs into the garden and resuscitates the sunken roses with her tears. Their words are an encouragement to Gerda to go on with her journey.[37] Thinking that flowers might be reliable in general, she accosts a whole series of other blossoms, about which the critical opinion has been mixed, to put it mildly.[38] Here is Lederer's assessment of the "flower pictures": "Indeed, these stories are not interesting. They are overly romantic and sticky; they are kitsch ... All this seems like dime-store fiction ... It makes perfectly good sense that Gerda, having kicked off the red shoes (sexuality) should now overact – as many girls do with their first brush with sex – and should withdraw to the safety of self-absorbed, narcissistic isolation."[39] *Pace*, Lederer, but for starters, Gerda has not even *had* sex, and her reaction to the flower stories is to insist that her quest is not at all like theirs, it is rather to find Kay – and this is no indicator of her mental isolation. But then, what *are* the flower stories good for? Andersen himself hardly considered them to be "kitsch." In fact, he was so concerned with the special quality and value of these six little sketches, he specified in his manuscript that the printer should use an in-set format for them, with a different typeface.[40] Each is a bit of word play (on the name or an aspect of the individual flower), and each story spins off from this to – (you would expect to hear this from me) – a tiny lesson in love. There is the tragic and also potentially illicit love of the Hindu wife; there is the lovesick maiden who waits for her knight who may never come; the dog! who longs to "belong" in the family, but is given a taunting rejection by the spoiled siblings; the three inseparable sisters who all died spinsters; the loving grandmother-granddaughter relationship; the narcissus who loved, but loved only itself. Designedly enigmatic, the pictures confuse and irritate poor Gerda. What does all this have to do with Kay? Of course, it has nothing to do with Gerda and Kay. Or, as Andersen's adult audience probably mused: it has *everything* to do with Gerda and Kay, but on a level that she cannot be expected to comprehend. The flowers answer Gerda's specific needs with allegories of *their* specific "needs." And this, of course, is of no help to Gerda, since she is not mature enough to make the connection. But the common denominator of the "flower pictures" is nonetheless the same as her own story. At some later, more mature point in her life, she might contemplate the similarities. For now, all she hears are the differences.

*

Lederer finds the "flower stage" that Gerda experiences in her interaction with the narcissus to be "the stage of development that follows upon the onset of puberty, [and] constitutes a moratorium for the girl."[41] If there is a hiatus in the "Third Story," six months of being combed to sleep seems more "moratory" to me than a half hour squabbling with flowers on your way out of the garden.[42] If we allow Gerda some sort of "moratorium" in the "Third Story," however, we shall have to explain why there should *not* be such things in the other stories as well. I shall leave it for the reader to decide who is right on this point.[43] The core of the "Fourth Story," as is well known, is the "Clod-Hans" tale, with its happy ending exhibited to Gerda, when she is escorted right into the prince's and princess' bedroom in the middle of the night. The Freudian analysis of the lily-bed bedroom need not greatly detain us.[44] Lederer finds it a confirmation of the sexual sterility of the author himself. A 19th-century family audience might, by contrast, find the situation a tad provocative. Gerda approaches the sleeping Prince on her bare feet, pulls the bedclothes back to look at his neck while holding the lamp over him, like a young Psyche. Meanwhile, Lederer provides no analysis of the inserted folktale, so I will have to do it on my own.

"Clod-Hans" (for all its rollicking good humor and in-your-face attitude) is a love story – a lesson in love, if you will. But it is not just *any* old love story. As would have been obvious to Andersen and his audience, it is *the* classic fairytale love story, the male wondertale with the princess and half the kingdom as a "prize" for the irresistible, undaunted underdog. But Andersen has manipulated the situation for us. Gerda *experiences* this fairytale love story in detail, but she experiences it vicariously. She associates with it (meaning, I think, with the implication of its successful outcome), which leads to a bit of nearly-pubertal thought, which could be expressed something like: now if *I* were the princess and *Kay* were the undaunted hero, what might be *our* outcome? But Andersen immediately imposes on this idea a second, more depressing thought: now if *Kay* were the undaunted hero and – *somebody else* were the princess, what would be *their* outcome? Gerda's reaction to this new possibility, seeing it more or less graphically displayed before her, is the most mature thought she has yet had. With the sweet pain of a budding erotic intuition, with an incipient sense of where and how the new love might be consumated, she lets Kay go: if he is happy, even if it means he is happy with somebody else, then she will be happy for him.[45] Unlike the confusing, enigmatic imagery of the flowers, this story and its erotic positioning are clear. It is evident that Gerda *understands* this story. But fast on the heels of her new discovery, she is once again corrected. The story of the prince and princess is only *their* story, not Gerda's at all, not the one that belongs to the "everyday reality" of the tale construct. And what *we* (adults) are shown in this context is the comparison between a *real* love story (Gerda's and Kay's) and a classic fiction.

Lederer interprets the "Fourth Story" in a different way: "Gerda is now encouraged to let herself be arrested at the next phase, that of the riddle princess ... This too constitutes a delay and a hesitation – a moratorium."[46] I find a number of difficulties with this idea. It would have been easy for Andersen to set up a situation in which Gerda had *found herself* stuck in the position of a riddle princess – with or without her wishing to be one – in order to be wooed by Kay or by some surrogate. In the story as we have it, there is no demand by the prince and princess that Gerda become a riddle princess herself, just because *they* have had such fun with the *topos*. Gerda has still found no concrete "directional information" as to Kay's whereabouts, but she is a step closer to her own pubertal initiation. She emerges from this strong bedroom lesson with a deepened sense of what growing up may entail and – quite naturally, she quickly asks leave to get on with her own journey.[47]

*

That brings us to the most daring of the adventures: the "Fifth Story" with the little robber girl, the tale that everybody in our generation likes best. Not only does the situation immediately turn brutal (the coachmen are murdered, Gerda threatened with being cooked and eaten, etc.), but it also turns a bit bizarre. Lederer gives us some solid and worthwhile ideas concerning the robber girl: "Her intimacies with Gerda are impetuously sensual and physical, and she constantly embraces and holds her. Her insistence on sticking her hands into Gerda's soft, warm muff, and her threat to 'stick my knife in your stomach' are sexually symbolic in a manner that must have been fairly transparent even in Andersen's repressed age."[48] I agree completely with this assessment. But I cannot go along with Lederer's conclusion about what it means: "This, then, would be the stage of the adolescent crush – of a girl's seduction by or infatuation with her girlfriends or older women."[49] I see no infatuation on Gerda's part, not even a repressed one. All I see is horror, the fear that she will be sexually assaulted, and, when an escape possibility presents itself, the determination to flee towards Kay. But what is eminently clear here is that Andersen paints a strong, graphic picture of a homosexual attraction on the part of the *robber girl*. The picture is sadistic and violently coercive – and yet I would insist that it too conveys a picture of love. Even the knife-wielding, murderous atmosphere is charged with the energy of love. Seen as a projection, it is truly like a dark mirror image of the erotic promise of the "Fourth Story." It is a love lesson that the virginal, borderline-pubertal Gerda may – indeed does – reject.[50] But at this point in the story, having just culled from the bedroom of the fairytale lovers an image of her future, she would appear to understand the robber girl's physicality, and she seems to have progressed to the point where she can fathom the physical implications of the love relationship which she is in the process of staking out for herself. A strong symbolic indicator of this is the concrete information about Kay's situation and geographical location, which is here conveyed to Gerda for the first time.[51]

*

The reindeer ride to the Lapp woman and the Finn woman is filled with enigmatic material, and Lederer admits having had difficulty in its interpretation: "It is not clear – at least to me – what function these steps are to serve."[52] To get going on this part, I would suggest another of those fairytale *topoi* that Andersen and his audience knew well: that of the arduous quest, in which the protagonist is aided by a trio of women, often sisters, each living isolated at the end of a frightfully long journey. According to this fairytale motif-complex, the protagonist seeks a lost lover, and each antiquated sister defers to an yet older one, as the one who finally has the power or knowledge to help.[53] But Andersen appears once again to have manipulated the *topos* in order to make a specific point: he has omitted the third of these helpers, leaving Gerda to fend for herself at the most critical point of her journey. The Finn woman tells the reindeer: "Jeg kan ikke give hende større Magt, end hun allerede har! seer Du ikke, hvor stor den er? Seer Du ikke, hvor Mennesker og Dyr maae tjene hende, hvorledes hun paa bare Been er kommen saa vel frem i Verden."[54] ["I can't give her more power than she already has! Don't you see how great it is? Don't you see how people and animals must serve her, how far she has come in the world on her own bare legs."] All of these attributes are part of the oldest-sister-motif, both the power and the command over the kingdom of animals. Here, in contrast to the situation in the "Fourth Story," Andersen appears to place Gerda *into* the *topos*, implying that she needs no additional helper or healer, she herself *is* the helper now.

So what is the source of Gerda's power? The Finn woman's formulation has irritated a number of critics, not only Lederer: "Hun maa ikke vide af os sin Magt, den sidder i hendes Hjerte, den sidder i, hun er et sødt uskyldigt Barn. Kan hun ikke selv komme ind til Sneedronningen og faae Glasset ud af lille Kay, saa kunne vi ikke hjælpe!"[55] ["She must not learn of her power from us; it lies within her own heart, it lies in (the fact that) she is a sweet, innocent child. If she herself cannot get to the Snow Queen and get the glass (splinter) out of little Kay, we certainly won't be able to help!"] That the power Gerda has accumulated over the course of her multiple lessons in love now lies in herself should be clear. That she is a "sweet innocent child" can convey the idea that she has not failed in her quest to this point, that she has not deserted her friend, that she has retained her innocence (the Danish term implies both moral blamelessness and chastity/virginity). But to read this phrase as if Andersen meant that Gerda should be regarded as the equivalent of a new-born infant – and that that should be considered some sort of power – is clearly at odds with the story construct. That the Finn woman would place Gerda at the confirmation altar is more to the point: you arrive at the altar as a "sweet innocent child" and leave it as an adult.

*

That puts us near the Snow Queen's palace, with no Snow Queen, and only one or two lessons to go. Gerda arrives at that far northern outpost with no mittens and no shoes, and faces a "regiment of snowflakes." She has no visible helper this time, when the reindeer turns back. But she finds herself in the "situation" of a religious legend, and it is her piety that both saves her from the cold and protects her from the deadly snowflake monsters. Andersen does not hesitate to use Catholic imagery: "Aanden blev tættere og tættere og den formede sig til smaa klare Engle, der voxte meer og meer, naar de rørte ved Jorden; og alle havde de Hjelm paa Hovedet og Spyd og Skjold i Hænderne; de blev flere og flere, og da Gerda havde endt sit Fadervor, var der en heel Legion om hende ... Englene klappede hende om Fødderne og paa Hænderne, og saa følte hun mindre, hvor koldt det var, og gik rask frem ..."[56] ["Her breath congealed more and more until it formed itself into small, bright angels, that grew larger and larger when they touched the ground; and all of them had helmets on their heads and spears and shields in their hands. There were more and more of them, and by the time Gerda had finished her Lord's Prayer, there was a whole legion of them around her ... The angels patted her feet and hands, so she didn't feel as much how cold it was and walked briskly forward ..."] Lederer is largely correct in his assessment of this: "Nothing, indeed, could save a person venturing in the Arctic without boots and mittens – nothing except a miracle: and this, apparently, Gerda confidently expects ... She goes into the Arctic as the Church fathers went into the desert, stripped of all ego, of all self, naked and humble before God ..."[57]

But if we have been attentive to this scene, we will have noticed two things: first, that this is again a lesson in love, in the religious sense that Andersen would have been quick to declare as the highest love of all – that of God; and second, that Gerda is not experiencing faith vicariously, but is a full participant, and knows (or accepts) that her secular quest has a sacred dimension or component. She has now finished her instruction in a plethora of forms, from the regressive or motherly love to the idealistic fairytale, to the violent, and on to the miraculous. She has experienced all of this – or projected it in a progressive form, if you would rather – in light of her own pubertal development, first in a confused and demoralized way, then vicariously, then more immediately, to arrive ultimately at the "cosmic" level, that God *is* love, that every manifestation of love may have its positive and negative side, but that love in its essence is nonetheless – mysteriously – positive. In Andersen's construct, this represents, at the same time, the manifestation of a drive toward Gerda's individual sexual maturity, which shares no outward traits with the other love stories she has heard or seen, but rests upon a common denominator. When it can be said in this way, Gerda is no longer a child. Her innocence is not to be confused with a lack of desire nor a lack of sexual potential.

This brings us to the meeting with Kay, and the "Seventh Story." Gerda and Kay embrace, and their bliss is so complete that the bits of ice dance with them and drop of their own accord into a pattern that spells out the word *Eternity*. Why "Eternity"? Where the word at an earlier point was only an enigma to the refrigerated little Kay, the *double-entendre* of a conjunction of the regeneration of the human race (secular "eternity") and the love of God (sacred "eternity") would now be clear to the adults in the audience, and Gerda (as "helper/healer," we will remember) is ready to teach Kay a crucial lesson which will bring him out of his pre-pubertal hiatus. If we need an allegorical confirmation ceremony preceding such an adult act, it would appear that the pieces of ice provide it.

> Og Gerda kyssede hans Kinder, og de bleve blomstrende; hun kyssede hans Øine, og de lyste som hendes, hun kyssede hans Hænder og Fødder, og han var sund og rask.[58]

> [And Gerda kissed his cheeks, and their color came back; she kissed his eyes, and they shone like hers; she kissed his hands and feet, and he was well and strong.]

When the Swineherd gives the Emperor's daughter eighty-six kisses in a row, no psychologist would hesitate to conclude that she is buying his rattle with her body. Why not allow this explicit text, with a barefoot girl covering the boy she loves with her kisses, serve as a completely adequate verbalization of a sex act? Is it the frigid ambiance? But if all the rest is an allegory, so is the ice pond, which would tell us that frostbite is not going to be an issue.

In light of the consummation of Gerda's quest, the return of the young people also makes logical sense. So much analytical energy has been expended on a supposedly happy ending that "just does not add up" (to which I will also object below), that some researchers have missed the slightly melancholy implication Andersen lends to the return trip.[59] In this light, let me add a few of my own comments as the young people retrace Gerda's "stations" in reverse order:

> da de naaede Busken med de røde Bær, stod Rensdyret der og ventede; den havde en anden ung Reen med ... og den gav de Smaa sin varme Mælk og kyssede dem paa Munden.[60]

> [When they got to the bush with the red berries, the reindeer stood waiting there; it had another young reindeer along ... and it gave the youngsters its warm milk and a kiss on the mouth.]

But what the reindeer do *not* do is tell stories, or give advice. They do give us a motherhood image, but this may be more of a gratuitous symbolic parallel than any sort of a lesson. Likewise, Kay and Gerda get warmth and clothing from the old wise women, but no mysterious rituals or predictions. Everything they do becomes a pedestrian leave-taking.

> "Farvel!" sagde de Allesammen. Og de første smaa Fugle begyndte at qviddre, Skoven havde grønne Knoppe, og ud fra den kom ridende ... den lille Røverpige, som var kjed af at være hjemme ... Hun kjendte strax Gerda, og Gerda kjendte hende, det var en Glæde. "Du er en rar Fyr til at træske om!" sagde hun til lille Kay; "jeg gad vide, om Du fortjener, man løber til Verdens Ende for din Skyld!" Men Gerda klappede hende paa Kinden, og spurgte om Prinds og Prinsesse. "De ere reiste til fremmede Lande!" sagde Røverpigen.

> ["Farewell!" they all said. And the first little birds began to cheep, the woods had green buds, and riding out of it came ..the little Robber Girl, who was tired of staying at home ... She recognized Gerda at once, and Gerda recognized her, it was such a pleasure. "You're a fine fellow to wander around!" she said to little Kay. "I'd like to know if you are worth the trouble, that people run off to the end of the world for your sake!" But Gerda patted her cheek, and asked about the Prince and the Princess. "They've gone travelling to foreign countries!" said the Robber Girl.]

The robber girl is de-clawed, her conversation fit for a bourgeois salon. The prince and princess are de-mystified as well, and have either joined the 19th-century tourist fad or (if we can still consider them as an allegory) have been *transmitted* to other faraway audiences. Even their remaining tame crow speaks "Vrøvl" [gibberish] now rather than communicating properly.[61] And when Gerda and Kay tell *their* story, the robber girl's only comment is: "Og Snip-snap-snurre-basselurre!" Which is to say, "Now *that* story is over," or perhaps: "and it was all nonsense anyway!"[62] Finally, the *first* of

Gerda's adventures (the good witch and her flowers) is omitted entirely from the backwards recapitulation, as if to corroborate the idea that there is nothing at all left of a regressive, magic garden in the tale. There is a matter-of-factness about this return, a lack of connection to magic in general, a grown-up attitude toward a childhood that is already fast receding. Narratologically, it is clear that every vestige of allegory has been removed. Everybody is once again "real." What better corroboration do we need that Kay and Gerda are no longer children, but are young lovers on the *other* side of a pubertal watershed?

*

This brings us at last to that "happy ending" and its problem! Let us follow the two young people home, assuming that they are post-pubertal lovers and not "children":

> Kay og Gerda gik Haand i Haand, ... og de kjendte ... den store By, det var i den de boede, og de gik ind i den og hen til Bedstemoders Dør, op ad Trappen, ind i Stuen, hvor Alt stod paa samme Sted som før ...; men idet de gik igjennem Døren, mærkede de, at de var blevne voxne Mennesker. Roserne fra Tagrenden blomstrede ind af de aabne Vinduer, og der stode de smaa Børnestole, og Kay og Gerda satte sig paa hver sin og holdt hinanden i Hænderne.[63]

> [Kay and Gerda went hand in hand, ... and they recognized ... the large city, that was the one they lived in, and they walked into town and up to Grandmother's door, up the stairs, into the living room, where everything was in the same place it had always been .... But as they walked through the doorway, they noticed that they had become grownups. The roses from the eaves' gutters were blooming in the open windows, and there stood the little children's chairs, and Kay and Gerda sat down on one each and held hands.]

It is the *contrast* that makes them realize that they have grown up. Now everything at home seems small and "childish."[64] They have grown, and their children's chairs – where Grandmother would expect them to sit – seem out of place. And then Grandmother (in her aged wisdom) "sad i Guds klare Solskin og læste høit af Bibelen: 'uden at I blive som Børn, komme I ikke i Guds Rige!'"[65] ["sat in God's bright sunshine and read aloud from the Bible: 'except ye become as little children, ye shall not enter into the Kingdom of Heaven!'"] So what do we expect Grandmother to do? For that matter, as long as Grandmother is looking, what do we expect the kids to do? And then the "children"-thing in the Bible, which would probably not have been misunderstood by an adult in Andersen's audience: to be a child at heart is not to be childish, any more than to think that "the Lord is my shepherd" means that we are supposed to be muddle-headed and wooly. This passage, like that of the Finn woman's whisperings, merely reflects Andersen's exegetic training, according to which "child-likeness" is commonly understood to mean "humility."

Lederer, for his part, makes a lengthy digression about how tough Andersen had it (which no one will deny), and then returns one last time to "The Snow Queen" to formulate his conclusion:

> Gerda manages not to get trapped [in her various *moratoria*], but she also manages not to learn anything. She goes through all her adventures essentially untouched and unimpaired, but also unenriched. She has, in fact, a veritable aversion to learning. What she refuses to learn, what she, in effect, represses, is what Andersen repressed. It is the very part of himself he had to deny. That part of him contained all he had always found unacceptable in himself ...With his childlike goodness he castrated himself, and he castrated, finally, his own body of work. It was this castration that constituted the basic misery and failure of nerve in his life.[66]

As my reader may have guessed, I would suggest a few corrections to this conclusion. "The Snow Queen" is not only an allegory concerning a successful pubertal maturation. It is a fanciful analysis of a set of psychological stages which contribute to this success. It seems clear to me, on the one hand, that Andersen was well aware of the physicality, of the sexual nature of the process, however carefully he concealed its implication by verbal pictures and ambiguities. But in addition, Andersen's model contains a *Weltanschauung* that provides an interesting counterpart to the religious systems for which Freud would later express such disdain.[67] As is well known, Freud eschewed any "cosmic" dimension for the puzzle-bits of psychological progress that formed a basis for his own "scientific" position. The implication of Freud's atheistic position was that real "science" had not been around for very long, but given time, it might well provide answers to the "cosmic" mysteries. In the meantime, conventional religion was an illusion, whose only effect was to impede the progress of the scientist's work. As I see it, Andersen's pre-Freudian formulation has a "cosmic" component that necessarily differentiates it from more recent theory, but which by no means undermines the acuity of the description of developmental changes in the progression of the child's libido. As presented allegorically and playfully in "The Snow Queen," it is neither a dogmatic, traditional Christian *Weltanschauung* nor a "Freudian" one. It presents a creative modification rather than an outright rejection of the Christian sphere, and at the same time, it raises a biological principle to the level of a "cosmic" rule. The "Snow Queen" model links the maturation process to a drive, a single inherent force within the (healthy) individual. This drive is given the dual function of sexual "pull" and a manifestion of "cosmic" regeneration. In this regard, Gerda's quest is the *opposite* of a "sin" or a "forbidden quest" – it is depicted as the highest good, the purest innocence. By contrast, it is the negative or "scientifically critical" Kay, whose sexuality turns aberrant or ultimately "cold" (unregenerative), and who needs to be "cured" of his condition, which is a way to equate (what Freud would later term) neurosis with a propensity for a useless, negative state, for which his only cure is the warmth of Gerda's kisses.

The construct also operates on a level which surpasses Gerda's knowledge from beginning to end. In our day, one can easily speak of "projections" emanating from her "sub-conscious." In Andersen's time, one might have posited a "hidden cosmic force" in her. However the interpretation is formulated, Gerda is never given an omniscient, authorial voice. She has her erotic limitation in Kay, and never supercedes this in the context of the tale. Andersen's construct in this case is significantly different from that of "The Little Mermaid," in which the very point of the story lies in the differing sets of "cosmic" principles and the instruction about these that the mermaid has to deal with.[68] In "The Snow Queen," it is the Finn woman who appears to be most cognizant of the "cosmic" dimension, when she says:

"Den lille Kay er rigtignok hos Sneedronningen, ... [men] han har faaet en Glas-Splint i Hjertet og et lille Glas-Korn i Øiet; de maa først ud, ellers bliver han aldrig til Menneske ..."[69]

["Little Kay is at the Snow Queen's palace, all right, ... [but] he has gotten a glass splinter in his heart and a little grain of glass in his eye. They have to be gotten out, because otherwise we will never become a human being ..."]

But she never says this to Gerda directly – the Finn woman is talking to the reindeer, in whispers. Andersen is careful *not* to give Gerda the "cosmic" rules (or at least, he lets them stay in a symbolic state below full consciousness), but rather to let her fight the whole thing out under her own steam, which must also mean: with those existential principles she herself can derive from her sequence of lessons in love. The tale comes to a close as the young couple faces their reproductive future. They may not be omniscient, but Gerda and Kay have made some significant progress.[70] They "suddenly understand" the old psalm text:

"Roserne voxe i Dale,
Der faae vi Barn-Jesus i tale."

["Roses grow in the dales,
There we shall get to speak with the Child Jesus."]

The point is that the secular implications of the drive that leads from childhood into puberty, and the sacred implications of "cosmic" regeneration, are linked as a form of communication. That is why Andersen in a happy moment can conclude for *their* sakes, whether or not for his own:

Der sad de begge to Voxne og dog Børn, Børn i Hjertet, og det var sommer, den varme, velsignede Sommer.

[There the two of them sat, both adults, and yet children, children in their hearts, and it was summertime, the warm, blessed summer.]

Notes

1. Barlby 2000, p. 6.
2. Lederer 1986, referred to in the rest of my text simply as "Lederer"; a reprint of two of its chapters appears in Lederer 2005, pp. 7-26 and 27-32.

3. Ibid., pp. 177-179. Grabowski 1974 contains a similarly dualistic conclusion, pp. 69-70.
4. Björby 1990.
5. My point – that Andersen does *not* place himself in the center of the story – is one I share with Michelsen 1940. Lederer tries (unsuccessfully) to co-opt Michelsen's position to support his opposite point of view (Lederer p. 227, footnote 2).
6. See Andersen 1964, 7, pp. 91ff.
7. The autograph manuscript at Carolina (UUB, Handskriftsavdelningen V. 286), was donated to a Swedish acquaintance, and thus did not end up among the papers willed to the Collin family.
8. Andersen 1964, 2, p. 69 (line 28). The discrepancy is noted in Johansen 2000, p. 115.
9. See, for example, Christensen 2000, pp. 46ff. Whether or not Andersen *meant* to misquote Brorson is an issue that has not been resolved in the literature I have read, nor will it be resolved in this essay.
10. Kay's is discussed in Lederer, p. 30; Gerda's on p. 43, 51, the potential for one on p. 57, the emergence of both from a "moratorium" p. 67, Gerda's "stages" in general as moratoria p. 175.
11. Ibid. p. 30.
12. This might prove exasperating to the reader whose recollection of the tale is not fresh. If that is the case, I would recommend following along with Andersen 1964, 2, 49-76, since I refer to this definitive edition when quoting from the tale in this essay.
13. Lederer, p. 8.
14. Besides the famous passage in Genesis 3, there is a different sort of Fall in Isaiah 14:12-15 and yet another in Revelations 12:7-9; all of these have oblique and conflicting things to say about how the Devil relates to humankind. Andersen would probably have read them all at some point, and his story of "Troldespeilet" corresponds to none of them.
15. Lederer, p. 7.
16. The ability to recite the "Lord's Prayer" (present in Gerda, temporarily absent in Kay) provides the tale with a sinless-sinful dichotomy; but the external origin of Kay's condition make it more like a disease than a "sin"-concept.
17. Lederer, p. 27.
18. Ibid., p. 28.
19. Loc.cit.
20. See Andersen 1964, 2, p. 50: the parents are noted briefly (line 30-38); their "permission" is referred to on p. 51 (line 7). After Grandmother has been introduced, the concept of "permission" may be relegated to her, and all mention of the parents disappears.
21. Lederer, p. 29.
22. Lederer, p. 29. Lederer's "free association" technique gives him ample room to appeal to our fantasy, but also leads to contradictions in meaning that are difficult to resolve.
23. Ibid., p. 30.
24. Andersen 1964, 2, p. 51 (line 21-29).

25. Cf. Lederer's shifting definitions noted above, some of which analysis is connected to the "First Story" and some of which is not.
26. Lederer, p. 65.
27. Andersen 1964, 2, p. 55 (line 14-17).
28. Nyborg, by contrast, finds it "utilfredsstillende, at titelpersonen således forsvinder uden videre" (Nyborg 1962, p. 153). Lotz 1988, p. 213, notes (correctly, as I see it) that what Andersen does here "understreger ..., at Gerda ikke løser Kay fra kvindens fangenskab men fra hans egen forblindelse."
29. Lederer, p. 174, and Nyborg 1962, p. 144 refer to Gerda as *anima*; and Rubow 1940, p. 21 to Kay as an Andersenian alter-ego.
30. This has already been pointed out in Rubow 1940, p. 19.
31. In Gerda's tale, the events are framed in *oblique* relation to time. There are physical signs that the Mother is aging, but "everyday" time is both foreshortened and extended in her tale – one cannot be sure which. In Gerda's tale, time appears to be symbolically presented as a sequence of psychological or directional "seasons." In Brix 1907, p. 209, the idea is suggested that the seasons progress in "real time," which would then allow for a sexual maturation as "Aarene rulle."
32. The child's natural interaction with inanimate objects, plants and animals is a talent which is not shared by adults. Cf. Massengale 1993.
33. Lederer p. 37.
34. Andersen 1964, 2, p. 55 (line 33-34).
35. Lederer p. 41.
36. Nyborg 1962, pp. 142f.
37. The perceptive reader will have noted that there is no "rose picture" among the flower pictures. One interpretation: the rose's story *is* Kay and Gerda's story, which is not complete until the end of the tale.
38. Nyborg 1962, p. 146, has a notation that "de intet har med den egentlige handling at gøre." Cf. Bøggild 2000, p. 141. On the other hand, Johan de Mylius takes the "flower pictures" much more seriously (Mylius 2000, p. 30).
39. Lederer pp. 42f.
40. Andersen 1964, p. 58 (line 23, footnote).
41. Lederer, p. 43.
42. I would prefer "regression" as a term to "moratorium" in this case, since it denotes a particular developmental issue rather than an unspecified one.
43. Hans Henrik Møller appears to side with Lederer on some level, when he terms the stories "forsinkelser i handlingens gang" (Møller 2000, p. 13).
44. However, Ib Johansen adds a Freudian touch to the analysis here which seems most apt: the dream horses and the carousel are "et erotisk spil mellem prins og prinsesse" (Johansen 2000, p. 112). This stands in marked contrast to Lederer's notion of the "unconsummated" marriage and the "chaste nature" of the bedroom (Lederer, pp. 50f.).
45. The comment in Duve 1967, p. 181: "Men hennes Kay ligger ikke i ektesengen – og den som er glad er Gerda" – is clearly a misreading. But I am not happy with Villy Sørensen's either, when he speaks of Gerda's love as "uerotisk: hun bliver ligefrem ked af det, da hun opdager at det ikke er Kay der har vundet prinsessen" (Sørensen 2004, p. 73).
46. Lederer p. 51.

47. Her hosts do fit her out like a princess, as if to indicate that she may now go and be a riddle princess herself. But she loses this fictional image, along with the coach and jewels, within the first four lines of the "Fifth Story."
48. Lederer pp. 56f.
49. ibid. p. 57.
50. Bøggild 2000, p. 160 (perhaps building on Nyborg 1962, p. 150), refers to the robber girl as a "troldspejling" of Gerda. This good idea could be approached in Jungian terms: Gerda has "advanced" sufficiently toward adulthood and individuation to be able to project a "Shadow"-figure that contains the negation of the positive sexuality she has learned about in the "Fourth Story."
51. A "directional" helper Gerda finds here is the wood-dove, as Nyborg has pointed out: the bird is known to be "viet til kærlighedsgudinden Afrodite" (Nyborg 1962, p. 150).
52. Lederer p. 59.
53. Aarne-Thompson 1964, Type 400, V *The Search* and 425, IV, *Search for Husband*.
54. Andersen 1964, 2, 72 (lines 24-27).
55. Loc. cit. (lines 28-30).
56. Ibid. p. 73 (lines 18-26). Andersen's interest in Catholic imagery for storytelling purposes is noted in Massengale 1999, 565ff.
57. Lederer p. 63.
58. Andersen 1964, 2, p. 75 (lines 17-19).
59. Lederer p. 69.
60. Andersen 1964, 2, p. 75 (lines 25-28).
61. This point is also made in Bøggild 2000, p. 163, footnote 17.
62. In Lederer's book, p. 219, the robber girl adds: "So everything came out all right," which is *not* what the Danish phrase means.
63. Andersen 1964, 2, 76 (lines 18-28).
64. Cf. Grabowski 1974, p. 59. However, Grabowski's own "love-hate" argument continues with the statement that "Kay never obtains any fundamental insight into himself and the potential integrative resources of his own psyche" (p. 65). This in turn appears to anticipate Lederer's less nuanced formulation. My argument is that Kay's development is largely omitted from the story, since it is constructed from Gerda's point of view.
65. Andersen 1964, 2, p. 76 (lines 30-31). Nyborg 1962, p. 154, citing Brix 1907, p. 260, finds that the older meaning of "blive" = "forblive" (remain) could have bearing on the problem. In my reading, this undoubtedly correct linguistic nuance makes no difference in terms of Andersen's construct, in which I find no "stagnation" (Nyborg's term).
66. Lederer pp. 176-8.
67. Freud 1933, esp. pp. 195-216.
68. See Massengale 1999.
69. Andersen 1964, 2, p. 72 (lines 16-20).
70. After which, of course, it may all be headed downhill. Andersen has nothing to say in *this* tale about the problem of individual immortality, which otherwise constituted a considerable thorn in his side.

Works Cited

Aarne-Thompson 1961: Antti Aarne and Stith Thompson, *The Types of the Folktale*, 2nd revision (Helsinki: FF Communications, 1961).

Andersen 1964: *H.C. Andersens Eventyr*, ed. Erik Dal, with commentary by Erling Nielsen (København: Hans Reitzel, 1963-67). 7 vols. ("The Snow Queen", 2, 1964, pp. 49-76).

Barlby 2000: *Det (h)vide spejl. Analyser af H.C. Andersens "Sneedronningen"*, ed. with an introduction by Finn Barlby (Dråben, 2000, Bibliography pp. 215-20).

Bjørby 1990: Review of Lederer 1986 in *Scandinavian Studies*, 62, 1990, pp. 491-495.

Brix 1907: Hans Brix, *H.C. Andersen og hans Eventyr* (new edition) (København: Gyldendal, 1970).

Bøggild 2000: Jacob Bøggild, "Fortællingens arabeske allegori i 'Sneedronningen,'" in Barlby 2000, pp. 137-64.

Christensen 2000: Erik M. Christensen, "Een på brillen," in Barlby 2000, pp. 35-53.

Duve 1976: Arne Duve, *Symbolikken i H.C. Andersens eventyr* (Oslo: Psychopress, 1967).

Freud 1933: Sigmund Freud, "The Question of a *Weltanschauung*," in *New Introductory Lectures on Psycho-Analysis*, transl. James Strachey (reprinted: New York: Norton, 1989), pp. 195-225.

Grabowski 1974: Simon Grabowski, "The Refrigerated Heart," in *Anderseniana*, II, 1, pp. 50-70 (1974).

Johansen 2000: Ib Johansen, "En vinterrejse: *Quest*-struktur og sort og hvid magi i H.C. Andersens 'Sneedronningen,'" in Barlby 2000, pp. 89-136.

Lederer (1986): Wolfgang Lederer, *The Kiss of the Snow Queen. Hans Christian Andersen and Man's Redemption by Woman* (Berkeley: U. Cal. Press, 1986). A reprint of two chapters (Lederer 2005) appears in *Hans Christian Andersen*, ed. with an introduction by Harold Bloom (Philadelphia: Chelsea House, 2005), pp. 7-26 and 27-32.

Massengale 1993: James Massengale, "A Divided World: A Structural Technique in Andersen's Original Tales," in *Andersen og verden*, ed. Johan de Mylius (Odense: Odense Universitetsforlag, 1993), pp. 262-75.

Massengale 1999: James Massengale, "The Miracle and A Miracle in the Life of a Mermaid," in *H.C. Andersen: A Poet in Time*, ed. Johan de Mylius et al., (Odense: Odense Universitetsforlag, 1999), pp. 555-76.

Michelsen 1940: William Michelsen, "Symbol og Idé i 'Sneedronningen,'" in *Anderseniana*, 8 (København: Munksgaard, 1940), pp. 35-56.

Mylius 2000: Johan de Mylius, "Forvandlingens billeder," in Barlby 2000, pp. 71-88.

Møller 2000: Hans Henrik Møller, "Hvordan staver man til evighed?" in Barlby 2000, pp. 7-20.

Nyborg 1962: Eigil Nyborg, *Den indre linie i H.C. Andersens eventyr* (København: Gyldendal, 1962).

Rubow 1940: Paul v. Rubow, Et "Vintereventyr," in *Reminiscenser* (København: Munksgaard, 1940), pp. 7-47.

Sørensen 2000: Villy Sørensen, "Vintereventyr," reprinted in *Sørensen om Andersen*, ed. Torben Brostrøm (København: Gyldendal, 2004), pp. 70-74.

Hans Christian Andersen's Stories: The Southern Africa Perspective

Vincent Mhlakaza

Introduction

All three so-called 'Synoptic gospels' give an account of how our Lord on his final, pre-crucifixion journey from Galilee to Jerusalem subjected the front-liners among his disciples to an oral examination. The examination consisted of just two questions. "Who do the people say the son of man is?" was the first. If I should frame a similar question, "Who do book lovers and literary critics say Hans Christian Andersen was?" I would expect a variety of answers. Some may say he was a modernized Geoffrey Chaucer, others a Danish Counterpart of Charles Lamb, others Confucius, the great ancient pedagogue reborn, or one of the greatest fiction writers this world has ever known. The second question was, "Who do you (his apostles) in particular say I am?" This exposition addresses the second question to me: who do I, a Southern Africa writer say Andersen was?

My use of a Biblical image in opening this essay can neither sanctify nor defile the tales and short stories of Andersen. It merely serves to illustrate how a look at a writer of the stature of Andersen gives rise to a chain of comparisons. But before I come to grips with the appreciation of Andersen and his tales, a fairy tale or a tale as a literary genre calls for analysis.

An average hearer or reader of a tale absorbs it as a story which though remote from realities of nature is nevertheless symbolic of some truth in life. Characters in a tale be they humans, animals, birds or inanimate objects, often exhibit attributes they naturally do not possess. In a tale for example, a hare may outwit a lion as if it were a genius; storks can speak and converse like human beings; a mole defends its queer subterranean habitation with the force of a homo sapiens. Tales such as those of Andersen and those found in the folklore of Southern Africa peoples are, therefore, thematic short stories either didactic or etiological in purpose or merely providing amusement and enhanced by introduction of some magical or supernatural powers. The supernatural is represented by goblins, ogres, ghosts and witches. In the list of role players the Bantu tale has the dreaded "modimo", the cannibals, in addition to the above.

Sometimes a clear miracle forms the art of the story, giving leverage to the underdog so that the big and arrogant is defeated. This generates humour in a tale because the audience enjoys seeing the bully humiliated.

One more interesting characteristic of a tale is the so-called "deus ex machina" whereby some part of the body of the person killed, an animal or a bird emerges to expose the evil-doer. The "deus ex machina" is often found in the Southern Africa tales.

Critical Context

Now we can proceed to the stories of Andersen specifically, highlighting their similarity and dissimilarity with those found in literatures of Southern Africa peoples. In this paper I shall prefer to use the term Bantu to designate Black peoples of Southern Africa. These are Ndebele, Northern Sotho, Southern Sotho, Swati, Tsonga, Tswana, Venda, Xhosa and Zulu.

I have before me a copy of the voluminous, *The Complete Illustrated Stories of Hans Christian Andersen*, London: Chancellor Press, 2001. Thanks to the diligence of H.W. Dulcken whose translation made the stories accessible to the English speaking world to which I belong. A content of 139 stories in all is proof offhand of how quality and quantity blended in the mind of Andersen whose 200 years we are joyfully celebrating.

My classification of the stories on the basis of characterization yields the following:

human characters
birds and animal characters
mixed characters
super-human and sub-human characters.

For the sake of economy of space, from the category of tales involving human characters, I shall outline and discuss just two, namely, "Great Claus and Little Claus" (*Complete Illustrated Stories,* pp. 24-33), and "The Emperor's New Clothes" (pp. 60-64). Mentioning these two stories makes me feel sentimental because the first time I heard them told I was below seven or six years of age and the narrator, my own mother! A few years ago before my mother passed away in the year 2003, I asked her about her sources for these and she told me that during those early days a number of Andersen's tales had found their way to primary school readers. Either the publishers or my mother made a slight alteration of the names in the form of the two stories, that is Groot Piet for Great Claus and Klein Piet for Little Claus. The appellations 'groot' and 'klein' are Afrikaans words meaning 'great' and 'little' respectively.

A summary of the details of the plot of the first story is as follows: Great Claus who is a more prosperous farmer than Little Claus, cruelly kills the only horse of Little Claus. The latter cleverly uses the hide of his dead horse to perform magic, which earns him a bushel of money. Great Claus notices the newly acquired wealth of Little Claus who fools him by saying the money is the price of the hide of his horse. Great Claus then stupidly kills all four horses of his, so as to get hides to sell and gain four times the money Little Claus possesses. But lo, tanners and shoemakers wouldn't buy a horse's hide for a bushel of money. When Great Claus realises Little Claus has fooled him he decides to go and chop off his head whilst in bed. Fortunately, the day he comes to do this Little Claus has laid the corpse of his grandmother on his bed and the sharp axe of Great Claus hits the head of the already dead old lady.

Little Claus then devises another trick to trap the unwary. He dresses his dead grandmother in her Sunday clothes, and drives to an inn whose manager is notorious for his fiery temper. The manager is angered when the old lady fails to respond to his offer of a drink and smacks her. In this way he again becomes the victim of the tricks of Little Claus who makes him believe that he has killed his grandmother. Little Claus claims compensation of a bushel heaped with money. Great Claus is amazed to see Little Claus he believed he had killed but now richer than ever before, and when Little Claus tells him he got this other bushel of money by selling the corpse of his grandmother, Great Claus goes forthright to kill his own grandmother and to sell her corpse in town. The townfolks are appalled to hear someone advertising the sale of a corpse and warn him, but since they believe he is mad, they let him go. On reaching Little Claus's farm he seizes him and ties him inside a sack with the intention of throwing him into a river to drown in retaliation.

The journey to the river is long and the burden of Little Claus in the bag heavy. So as he passes by a church he stops to rest a little and enjoy the playing organ and beautiful psalms sung by worshippers. Coincidentally an old shepherd passes at the spot and stumbles against the sack containing Little Claus left outside the church yard. Little Claus persuades him to untie the bag and he, now freed convinces the old drover that should he creep into the same sack he would march into heaven directly. This done, Little Claus leaves the old man tied tightly inside the sack and drives the cattle of the drover to his own farm.

When the church singing is over Great Claus returns to his sack and proceeds to the river where he dumps it thinking that Little Claus is inside. But to his great surprise he meets Little Clause at a crossroad driving a large herd of fat cows and oxen: Little Claus tells him the cattle are a gift from "the loveliest maiden" dwelling at the bottom of the river where Great Claus attempted to drown him. Great Claus believes what he hears and changes roles with Little Claus because he too wants to be rich if not richer than Little Claus. Little Claus carries him to the river and drops him into it; he sinks and drowns and there ends the story.

Someone who accepts without question that he has killed a person by just pouring a glass of mead over her face and clapping her! People who agree to be tied in a sack and thrown into a deep river believing it is either the way to walk directly to heaven or to reach strange sea-cattle in a land of green grasses under a river bed! That is a tale par excellence. But Andersen deserves a distinction mark for the amount of humour with which he managed to fill this story. I remember my mother's narration of this story interrupted several times because she choked in laughter and we children listening laughing until our tiny bellies ached. The hideous events of the desecration of the dead body of Little Claus's grandmother, the drowning of the innocent old drover and that of Great Claus forming part of the plot of this story are all covered by the heavy blanket of the humour created by Andersen and induce no bad feeling in the reader or hearer. I will quote one part for illustration: the dialogue between the old drover and Little Claus,

> "Oh, dear!" sighed Little Claus, "I'm so young yet, and am to go to heaven directly!"
>
> "And I, poor fellow," said the drover, "am so old already, and can't get there yet!"

"Open the sack," cried Little Claus; "Creep into it instead of me, and you will get to heaven directly." (*Complete Illustrated Stories*, p. 32).

Andersen's story about "Great Claus and Little Claus" is therefore a rare instance in literature where tragedy and comedy overlap; something achieved only by writers of rare skill.

There is a tale in the Bantu folklore bearing some noteworthy similarities to the story about the Clauses. It is the tale of a legendary giant called Dimo and a little girl named Tselane. The giant was also a cannibal. Great Dimo is as gullible as Great Claus, an interesting point of similarity. The parents of Tselane move to a new place but Tselane at her own request remains at the old home. Dimo who has been keenly watching happenings comes at an opportune moment to grab Tselane in the absence of her parents, forces her into a sack and carries her away. Confining a person inside a sack is another parallel. In the same way Great Claus stopped by a church to enjoy the singing and organ music, Dimo stopped by a house where people were drinking. The owner of the house suspicious that Dimo might be carrying a human being in his sack cleverly sends him on an errand to fetch some water from a well a little distance from the house. She gives him a container with little holes at the bottom. Dimo gets to the well and fills the container with water. Midway from the well however, he discovers that all water has run out. He returns to the well to refill the container. In the meantime the owner of the beer house gets a chance to secretly open the bag of Dimo wherein she finds Tselane whom she recognizes. Tselane is quickly taken out of Dimo's sack. Then snakes, bees, wasps and scorpions are collected to fill the sack. At length great Dimo comes back, and taking his sack he realises it isn't as heavy as it was before although his anger prevents him from checking for the contents. On arrival at his hut he chases his wife away with the excuse that she did not help him carry the bag so she would not have a share of the tender meat of his prey. After shutting the door and preparing fire for the roasting of Tselane he opens the sack and is fiercely attacked by the snakes, stung and bitten by bees, wasps and scorpions. He does not even see the doorway and escapes through a window and runs until he plunges into a pond where he drowns. So, like Great Claus of Andersen, Great Dimo of the Bantu tale perished by drowning.

Now I divert my attention to the style of Andersen. Andersen's art is primarily typified by constant employment of dialogue. He lets his characters speak to one another, confide or argue and sometimes engage in soliloquy whilst he as a third person narrator stands aside. This style does not only break the monotony of an extended narration but more importantly enhances the dramatic value of his stories.

From the year 1988 up to 1998 I was an English Lecturer at a college in the Eastern Cape Province of South Africa training future primary school teachers. There I used to guide my trainees in selection of parts of several stories by Andersen for short sketches they dramatized with their pupils. This fitted well into the scheme of applying the "Communicative approach' to the teaching of English as a second language. Further, on certain social occasions my students staged a full show of what we termed 'popular theatre' constructed with extracts from Andersen's tales. I pray custodians of Andersen's writings who may happen to hear this honest confession of plagiarism not to take me to a court of law! I wouldn't be able to defend myself as I cannot speak Danish. Once more I am tempted to give the story of "Great Claus and Little Claus" as an example of such a reconstruction:

SCENE ONE: AT THE HOUSE OF LITTLE CLAUS
Little Claus deplores the death of his horse (soliloquy)
Sharpens his knife for flaying the dead horse
He is assisted and consoled by his grandmother
Leaves the stage to go and flay the horse (end of Scene One)

SCENE TWO: AT THE FARMHOUSE BY THE ROAD
It is evening; lights are on
Little Claus acts as a stranger
The use of the hide for conjuring
(verbatim extracts, *Complete Illustrated Stories*)
Little Claus leaves happily with his bushel of money
(end of Scene Two)

SCENE THREE: (IN THE STREET NEAR THE CHURCH)
Dialogue between Little Claus and the drover
(*Complete Illustrated Stories*)
Other actors simulate cattle of the drover
The drover gets into the sack and is left in the lurch
Little Claus sprightly driving away cattle inherited from the drover

> Great Claus arrives at the scene and carries the bag containing the drover to the river. (end of Scene Three)

It goes without saying that whatever modifications of Andersen's story I and my former students made to suit Popular Theatre requirements, Little Claus remained the protagonist and Great Claus the antagonist.

Casting an eye on the second story, "The Emperor's New Clothes", awakens once again my childhood memories. In the Bantu world of Southern Africa, a tale is told in the evening while children sit by the hearth waiting for supper. Our family house was small and very often the burning fire made us children feel so warm that we stripped off our shirts. I recall then, the strange sensation when mother gesticulated during the course of her narration and gently brushed my bare abdomen and chest in the manner of the 'cheats' touching the undressed body of the Emperor as they exclaimed,

> "Oh how well they look! How capitally they fit! What a pattern! What colours! That is a splendid dress!" (*Complete Illustrated Stories*, p. 63)

All that I have said about "Great Claus and Little Claus" can be repeated in the context of "The Emperor's New Clothes". But the humour in "The Emperor's New Clothes" is seasoned with a grotesque satire ridiculing people who so much valued retention of their high positions that they would not speak the truth and by so doing would not make the Emperor avoid the shame of parading the streets of the city totally naked; worse still the Emperor himself who dared not say he saw nothing splendid when he looked at himself in the mirror.

Perhaps a new string I may now harp upon is that of themes. Although the theme and sub-theme of "The Emperor's New Clothes", are on the surface and transparent, they are equally quite complex and therefore different readers are likely to view them from differing angles such as:

> The world full of deceit.
> Flattering of the high and mighty.
> Dishonest preservation of one's status quo.
> The evil of dissembling.
> People occupying positions they don't deserve.
> Innocence and frankness of the child.

To elaborate a little on the last but one above I may quote from William Shakespeare's play *Twelfth Night*, "Some are born great, some achieve greatness, and some have greatness thrust upon them." If "The honest old Minister," whom the Emperor considers, "He can judge best how the stuff looks, for he has sense and no one understands his office better than he," failed to warn the Emperor that the weavers he had hired move nothing, then this world, indeed, is devoid of honest people; everyone in a high position must be listened to with a feeling of mistrust or doubt.

Andersen unravels the plot of this tale by the intervention of a little child who in the midst of pretentious men and women cried out,

"But he has nothing on!" (*Complete Illustrated Stories*, p. 63)

So, a humble little child becomes the hero of the day and rescuer of the miserable Emperor and the exposer of the dishonesty of the same Emperor's highly positioned men and women. Herein lies the subtheme of the story, which may be expressed as follows:

Small is great.
Small is virtuous.
The small, young or despised outweighs the big.

As hinted in the introduction, the theme of the small contrasted favourably with the big bully or the pompous is frequently employed not only in the tales of Andersen but also in the Bantu tales. One of the most famous tales of Andersen, "Thumbelina", confirms this; yes, the fairy Thumbelina, so tiny as to be hardly more than an inch in height is made the admirable spectacle of beauty; her minute heart a vessel of true love and mercy (*Complete Illustrated Stories*, p. 39).

Other themes dealt with in Andersen's stories are,

Greed for wealth ("The Tinder Box", pp. 18-23)
Wisdom as opposed to brute force ("Great Claus And Little Claus", pp. 24-33)
Jealousy ("The Thorny Road of Honour", pp. 489-493)
Disobedience and unfaithfulness ("Put Off Is Not Done With", pp. 885-899)
Crime does not pay ("The Wicked Prince", pp. 198-200)

These and many others form the spirit of Bantu tales as well.

Closely related to themes of stories are morals. It is true that a great deal of the tales of Andersen are meant for amusement especially of children. A few others are etiological in purpose, meaning, they explain how certain phenomena began. A good example of the latter is the story of "The Storks" which explains why migratory birds change countries according to seasons and how they train their young ones for the long flights across countries (*Complete Illustrated Stories,* p. 149).

Many others, however, underpin important moral issues. A mere scanning of what I have listed above as major themes show how prominent a feature didacticism is in both Andersen's and the Bantu tales.

For illustration purpose I choose to single out a story whose moral lesson is straightforward, "The Goblin and The Huckster" (*Complete Illustrated Stories,* pp. 457-60). Here is a summary of this short story:

A rich huckster owned a house part of which was used as a shop for selling his stocks. He had a goblin very loyal to him because he fed him well; on top of that the mannikin was assured of a special treat every Christmas eve. The huckster's wife had a long tongue. One inmate of the house was a student who because of his meagre economic means rented just the garret of the house. The student, as should be expected, valued books.

One day the student descended from the garret to buy some cheese and the huckster tore a page from an old poetry book to wrap the cheese bought. That annoyed the student extremely. To him the book was sacred and should be handled as such. So to show his disapproval of the act of the huckster he returned the cheese he had bought and bought the torn book instead.

The goblin witnessed the dispute between the two and naturally took the side of the huckster. But having stealthily followed the student to his abode – and after seeing how absorbed the student was in reading the torn book, the goblin was converted and realised that the written word was precious indeed. Manifestation of that conversion occurred when the house next to theirs caught fire. All panicked and rushed here and there in attempts to save their valuables such as jewellery and money but the goblin ran to the garret with the intention of saving his friend's dilapidated book!

Andersen, in this story, in the manner of a professional writer, hides behind the back of the principal character and formulates the moral, spelling it out poignantly,

> "Give me the book instead of the cheese: I can eat my bread and butter without cheese. It would be a sin to tear up the book entirely." (*Complete Illustrated Stories*, p. 458).

Read the story, "The Thorny Road of Honour" (*Complete Illustrated Stories*, pp 489-493) and see how Andersen at times went beyond the limits of a story-teller and assumed the stance of a preacher. Although literary critics may not praise Andersen for this, it proves beyond doubt that he strove with his pen and tongue to rid the world of jealousy, rash judgement, aristocracy, hatred, cruelty and the like. It is in this respect that Andersen may be compared to Confucius, the great teacher, moralist and philosopher.

Let us turn the page and go to tales of Andersen involving ghosts, fairies, sea maidens, goblins, witches, animals and birds. These bring Denmark of the times of Andersen nearer to Southern Africa of the present where magical beliefs are deeply embedded in the minds of Nguni, Sotho, Venda and Tsonga peoples of this sub-continent. It appears that stories of this category make up the bulk of the works of Andersen and I wonder how and where to begin.

All Bantu peoples believe in the after-death life represented by ancestral spirits who reveal themselves to the living in dreams where they impose their will on the living. Fortunes as well as misfortunes befalling their relatives are attributed to them. So, apparitions described in Andersen's stories such as that of "The Child in The Grave" (*Complete Illustrated Stories*, pp. 493-497) strike the Bantu more as a reality than a mere tale. The numerous stories of a mischievous very short man called Tikoloshe by the Nguni and Thokolosi by the Sotho compare well with goblins in the stories of Andersen. The cruel Tikoloshe to whom strangling people is a sport is used by sorcerers and would be visible only to his victims. He enters closed doors or drops from the ceiling to do his work. The goblin who made fun with the tongue of the huckster's wife in "The Student and the Huckster" would be understood by the Bantu as Thokolosi. The Bantu witch who during daytime leads the life of ordinary men and women and at night flies around riding naked on a broom is a counterpart of the ghastly witch of Andersen capable of performing untold superhuman acts. Perhaps the Bantu tale misses only the mermaid or the sea-maiden and this is understandable because the Bantu generally inhabit the interior of Southern Africa where the natural environment consists only of forests, grasslands and mountains.

Yet Andersen is at his best when he tells stories about animals and birds. Take once more the fairy-like story of "Thumbelina" as an example. Beautiful description of the life habits of the swallow, the mole, the field mouse, the cockchafer and the adventures of the tiny Miss Thumbelina are spell-binding. The kindness of Thumbelina towards the half-dead swallow contrasted with the selfishness of the mole reminds us of the important moral found in Shakespeare's play, *The Merchant of Venice*: that true love and kindness are always rewarded.

The "tweet, tweet" from the throat of the swallow; the "cluck, cluck," of the old man's fowl (*Complete Illustrated Stories*, p. 123) the rhyme of the naughty boys in the story of "The Storks" (*Complete Illustrated Stories,* p. 149) are fine examples of the application of a technique of a short tune in the middle of a story by Andersen and so common in the Bantu tale. The technique has a two-fold advantage, namely to amuse the audience and to arrest its attention especially if the story is long.

Integrative Conclusion

Then who do I say Hans Christian Andersen was after this lengthy exposition? I dare say he was a Danish writer whose patriotism was so healthy as to be inclusive and not exclusive: a writer whose stories move a reader from Denmark to Sweden, then across the Atlantic to America and across the Mediterranean to Africa. The content of his stories displays the profundity of his knowledge of mankind, his environment, of other beings, the physical as well as the metaphysical and yet so humble as to be a favourite of children if not their pal! His ideologies 200 years ago in Denmark are as fresh and compelling as ever in Southern Africa.

Surely if Andersen's stories were read today with a purpose, we would find ourselves better human beings in a better world. I wish this August event of celebration of 200 years of Hans Christian Andersen may direct our thoughts, among other things, to a new appraisal of the educational value of his tales.

Hans Christian Andersen – a Young Poet? Considerations about a Textbook

Ivy York Möller-Christensen

A large number of Educational Institutions are moving forward at a rapid pace these days, an extremely rapid pace. Many of you will already know that, amongst other initiatives, a reform will take place in Danish grammar schools, just beginning in these august-days of 2005. This reform will imply a change of rules, which is supposed to lead the young generations into a new era. A six month period of introduction which consists of "almen studieforberedelse", "naturvidenskabeligt grundforløb" og "almen sprogforståelse" ("general study preparation", "introduction to natural sciences" and "general understanding of languages") will lead to a high level of general understanding of a wider range of subjects. This new grammar school should also develop a general range of socalled personal competencies. These new demands to the educational system open up to a broad spectrum of advantages and possibilities, but these also challenge the institutions to implement considerable changes to the school structure, to the materials used in teaching, and to the teachers themselves and their competencies.

The world today is undergoing constant changes, as is the world of the youngsters. We cannot, as the ancient saying of Heraclitus goes, step into the same river twice. Everything is in constant movement. But in actual fact it is probably more of an existential fundamental condition than it is a cause for amazement. The challenge is to work on the change and to work with the new technical possibilities as these can help to create a kind of order and connectivity in the minds of the youngsters. An appreciation of the link of subjects and their connection to each other even across the subjects, across the languages; across the faculties, and especially – something which has long needed a more prominent presence – a sense of historical consciousness, which for example lets the young person sense that an absolute monarchy followed after the Athenian democracy and the belief of the God of thunder and his rumbling reign of the sky.

I will choose to call this an idealistic – and hopefully not too naive – approach to educational constructivism that from my point of view should be considered a positive and highly important challenge to the development in modern schools. Teachers with everyday contact to young people again and again realize that the pupils and the young students are living existentially on shaky foundations due to their lack of coherence and structure – whether it is in their family lives, in their spare time or in school. It's my a priori assumption that reality does not in itself deliver the stuff for coherent experience of reality and of life. On the contrary. Reality is in itself without any meaning. Reality is chaotic and senseless. But humanity implicates the possibility and the ability to construct, to create or to build meaning. In German you talk about Bildung – etymologically coming from the "Althochdeutsch" and meaning Schöpfung and Verfertigung, but also Bildnis and Gestalt. So this so called educational constructivism is connecting a pure modern and in a way nihilistic understanding with a strong will to create meaning, which is greatly bound by tradition.

Many teachers hope that the ideas and the ideals are not only unrealistic dreams. But how can one, as a Danish tutor, text book author and publisher of an anthology, modestly and from ones own little corner, contribute even an ounce of meaning and connection in order to create some connectivity? This is the actual background for what is to follow. First I want to show you the content of the textbook, which has just been published by the "Systime" Company, catering especially for grammar schools and colleges of education.[1] As you will see, my introduction – of about 30 pages – is followed by seven sections, each devoted to one theme. The sections are:

1. Rejsen (The Journey)
   Det danske, det kosmopolitiske, og den globale åbenhed (The Danish, the cosmo-politan, and the global openness)

2. Kunstneren (The Artist)
   Mytedannelse, selviscenesættelse og tvivl (The creation of myths, self-promotion and doubt)

3. Barnet og det barnlige (The child and childlike behaviour)
   Naivitet, genialitet og uskyld (Naivety, genius and innocence)

4. Lysten (Lust)
   Seksualitet, drift og køn (Sexuality, sexual urge and gender)

5. Fattigdommen (Poverty)
   Nød og udstødelse (Need and rejection)

6. Døden (Death)
   Angst, frygt og frelse (Fear and release)

7. Fremtiden (The Future)
   Natur, udvikling og teknik (Nature, advance and technology)

The texts within these areas have been compiled in a way so that the scope of the oeuvre is expressed very clearly with the emphasis on those texts in which Andersen is particularly advanced for his time and which seem especially relevant to the young readership of today. The topics are labelled with different numbers, and several of the texts can also be read for other purposes than those that have been underlined in the particular chapter. For example, the fairytale "Ib og lille Christine" (Ib and Little Christine) (1855) has been used in the chapter entitled: "Barnet og det barnlige" (The child and childlike behaviour), but has also been drawn upon as examples in chapters 1, 4 and 6. In this sense the anthology is flexible in its uses.

The attempt to find connections are utilized – as well as the goal to show the entire Hans Christian Andersen – in very concrete ways in the edition, for example by involving foreign languages, in the book itself as well as in those texts which are to be found on the internet in connection with the homepage of the book (they are marked with "W"). Thus one will find the fairytale "Den lille Pige med Svovlstikkerne" (The little Matchgirl) in English, German, Spanish and French as well as in Danish. Such a compilation opens to themes of translation as well as to different understandings and cultures within the relevant languages. Under each specific language one can work with its linguistic building blocks and their relevant foundations. These can be discovered in comparative studies. For instance the texts under chapter 7 called "The Future" can contribute to projects concerning industrial development and techniques – also in connection with ethical questions. In addition, other examples of Hans Christian Andersen texts in foreign languages have been included. For example a German critique of an Andersen text and an extract of the English translation of *Mit Livs Eventyr* (*The Fairy Tale of My Life*). This is in order to show that Andersen's works should not simply be seen as entirely national but have their roots entwined internationally as well.

In this manner it is possible in your work to establish connections to cultural and artistic motions within other languages.

The workbook related to the Andersen texts opens to the possibility of co-operation between a large number of grammar schools subjects. And in addition computers and the internet are also encouraged as a means of attaining relevant information, as are knowledge and search bases for communication, for example power-point presentations. Here, the principle for education is that the learning and the communication of the student ought to be interconnected. It is no longer only the teacher who is communicating knowledge because the process in itself encourages better learning. Communicating knowledge forces one to analyze the material and to ask oneself the question, what is relevant here, and what is not? Communicating knowledge requires that you explain it, and by explaining it you understand it yourself too.

Mentioning the importance of the skill of communication of knowledge, I come to an important didactical criterion of this anthology, namely to impel the young people to use their creativity through a number of working papers – for instance by creating mind-maps, essay-writing, power-point presentation of results of discussions in class, rhetorical exercises and free writing.

In relation to this textbook with its introduction, I wanted to enlarge the general knowledge about the poet. To show a picture of this famous poet, which is professionally acceptable because it is representative of the author's entire artistic work. So many years in schools and in the literary world have been spent by simply clinging to the picture of the ugly duckling, which turns into the most beautiful swan, clinging to the myth of Hans Christian Andersen. Awe of the man has inspired a sense of fear of painting a less perfect picture of this national treasure that is Hans Christian Andersen. The result has been that we have consciously or sub-consciously clung onto the image of the unproblematic and biedermeier-like poet, this clean and innocent incarnation of a child-like personality that was so strongly connected with the romantic movement and the myth about the poet which Andersen himself worked very hard to create and maintain. It has been mostly ignored that there are deeply modern and divided traits in his literature. Only in the last couple of decades has the focus been turned to this area. The first real attempt at this was as a matter of fact made by the poet-philosopher Villy Sørensen in his revolutionary book titled *Digtere og Dæmoner* (Poets and Demons, 1959) where he analyzes both Kierkegaard and Andersen and takes a closer look at

"Skyggen" ("The Shadow", 1847), "Tante Tandpine" ("Auntie Toothache", 1872) and "Sneedronningen" ("The Snow Queen", 1845) in a much more modern way than had been done before. So both aspects of Andersen – namely on the one hand the strong connection to tradition and on the other hand the obvious modernity should be shown.

Two centuries have now passed since the birth of the poet, and the one-sided picture of him has become rather outdated. For me it was important to show the young readers that behind the glorious swan on the shiny and blank water, there was hiding a little ugly and insecure duckling. Just as it is probably the case with all of us. And just this leads to the crucial point in relation to young people and their meeting with especially older literature, where the language and orthography are often experienced as somewhat inconvenient: namely the possibility of identification and the possibility through fantasy to live out unknown fates.

And just that makes Andersen a poet about whom you still ask questions, and whom it is interesting to work with, also for the modern reader and for youngsters. The truth in Andersen's works is never straight-forward, it is complex. Light and darkness are complement each other, like yin and yang. And that discussion or existential dialectics which is shown in the author's works are worth occupying oneself with. It is what makes it personally appealing and importantly credible to young readers.

Literary tuition, in short, is meant to contribute to a way of establishing a flow of serious and believable, artistic works which deal with basic human conditions, texts which allow the students to use their imagination in order to draw conclusions which have perhaps not been drawn before. This develops identity and it is educational – and education is strongly connected to the narrative. The tale is essential by a place where one may select components for real understanding. Components, which can be tied together, constructing meaning and sense.

Today's so-called post modern reality is so fragmented that the loss of the actual meaning is not even considered a travesty because it is often not understood what the loss actually consists of. In short: The experience of chaos is for many young people non existent, because the understanding of chaos also requires an understanding of order. One of the most important purposes for young people's education in human arts and especially in literature is through stories and through narratives to identify, to experience different ways of understanding life, and to experience engagement and passion – human com-passion.

Note

1. Ivy York Möller-Christensen (ed.), *H.C. Andersen – tradition og modernitet*. Systime (68 texts, introduction pp. 9-39; study assignments pp. 184-201.) Århus, 2005.

Strong Minded and Strong Willed Girls in Hans Christian Andersen's Fairy Tales Found in "The Snow Queen" (1844); "The Little Match Girl" (1845); "Clod Hans" (1855) and "The Swamp King's Daughter" (1858)

Inger M. Olsen

"Literature not only names the maze that confronts characters and readers, it also holds out a thread by which both may better find their way," wrote Stephen G. Nichols, (PMLA 432) in his article "Writing the New Middle Ages." This statement could be the motto for this paper, an attempt to draw attention to a group of almost overlooked girls in H.C. Andersen's fairy tales. That is, the strong-minded and strong willed ones.

In "The Snow Queen" (1844) H.C. Andersen (1805-75) wrote about two girls who fit this category. Gerda and the robber girl both display these character traits in regard to their notions of doing what must be done. In Gerda's case it is to find Kay. Before she set out, she "kissed her grandmother, who was asleep, put on her red shoes and walked all alone out through the town gate." (Conroy & Rossel 113) On her way she encountered several natural phenomena and people who each in turn attempted to delay her and her quest, but she prevailed. However, when she encountered the robbers she had to use her powers as a storyteller to escape.

At first the robber girl seemed to be working against Gerda but she proved otherwise when she kept Gerda as her pet or playmate in order to save her from the grown-ups. Because "'They're not going to slaughter you' ... 'You shall sleep tonight with me and all my little pets!'" (Conroy & Rossel 128) The next day, after hearing Gerda's story she sent her to explore the route taken by Kay when he had gone off together with the Snow Queen, out of Gerda's neighborhood. And so the little robber girl equipped Gerda, on her own, for the trip to the

North Pole to the Snow Queen's palace and supplied her with a reindeer, food and warm clothing.

When Gerda had successfully completed her quest, found Kay and liberated him from the Snow Queen's spell she encountered the robber girl once more. She and Kay saw, "a young girl riding a magnificent horse. ... She had a shining red cap on her head and pistols in her belt. It was the little robber girl, who had gotten bored staying at home." (Conroy & Rossel 138) Their meeting was joyous and friendly although the robber girl stated she was not sure Kay deserved all of Gerda's efforts. She furthermore had news about all the creatures and people who had furthered Gerda's trip. The robber girl had matured, if not into a caring young woman, then into a more balanced person who parted from Gerda and Kay to venture out and explore the world, whereas the two childhood sweethearts were going home.

In 1845 H.C. Andersen again touched upon the theme. This time it was the little girl in "The Little Match Girl". She may seem an odd example of someone displaying a strong will.

When, however, one takes a closer look at her actions it becomes apparent that she, in the face of inevitable punishment at home, takes matters in her own hands, burns all the matches to get some pleasure and a tiny bit of warmth. She is driven purely by her own will into a display of strong-mindedness, which leads to visions of her grandmother,

> When she appeared in the light of the burning matches the little girl exclaimed, "Grandma take me with you! I know you'll be gone when the match goes out. ... And she quickly struck all the rest of the matches in the bunch." (Conroy & Rossel 159)

The grandmother had been the little girl's only comfort and the only person who had shown her love. The little girl's subsequent death from starvation and cold, it would appear to the people passing her, came as a byproduct of her situation.

From the city H.C. Andersen went to the countryside and to court in order to create the milieu for his next example. This girl was neither poor nor oppressed. She was a princess who could speak for herself.

The king's daughter said in "Clod Hans" (1855), "'Now you're talking!' ... 'Why you've got the answers!'" (Conroy & Rossel 185) The princess was looking for a husband. She had at last found a fellow who could talk and meet the measure of her tests and expectations. As a consequence of his answers he was deemed fit to be her husband. Traditionally we have viewed Clod Hans as a tale about the unlucky shortchanged youngest brother who ends as the lucky one who gains the princess as his wife. However, the interlude with the princess deserves a closer look. It is the princess who does the encouraging and she is the one who joins Clod Hans in his rebellious acts toward the stiff court. He joined her in her attempt at rebellion against the societal rules. Consequently she felt he would teach her how to stand up to the court regulations. At once he delivered an example of his abilities. He gave the alderman his best act of defiance when "he emptied his pockets and threw mud in the alderman's face." This made the princess declare, "That was well done!" ... "I couldn't have done it, but I'm certainly going to learn now!" (Conroy & Rossel 186) The princess, we must assume, had a large pent up measure of frustration with stiff court manners, which had now found a release in Clod Hans. Even though we have it "straight from the alderman's newspaper – and you can't believe a word in it." (Conroy & Rossel 186)

From court the poet moved to distant times but he kept his girl royal.

"The Swamp King's Daughter" (1858) is still another example of someone who is outside the norm. This fairy tale made the poet B.S. Ingemann (1789-1862) write to H.C. Andersen,

> De er et lykkeligt Menneske! Naar De rager i en Rendesteen, finder De straks Perler og nu har De jo fundet en Ædelsten i – Dyndet. Det er en velgjørende Phantasie, der saaledes holder os Roser for Næserne, hvor det stinker værst i Verden, og viser os en kongelig Herlighed og en smuk Prindsesse i Dyndet. (Brevveksling, II, 420)

> You are a lucky person! When you stir about in a gutter you immediately find pearls and now you have indeed found a jewel in the mud. It is a refreshing imagination which thus is holding roses in front of our noses where it stinks the worst in the world and shows us royal splendor and a beautiful princess in the mud. (Brevveksling, II, 420)

He had chosen a girl who, however, was not totally strong willed by her own choice. Her dual nature, a human being by day and a toad by night, was the cause of many of her daredevil acts such as diving into wells and jumping off cliffs into the ocean. She was driven by instincts, which in turn caused her to display behavior which did not lead to happiness for her and her surroundings. She took delight in scaring her foster mother with her wild stunts. As a consequence, in the story, the mother stork is annoyed with the father stork who had rescued the little girl from the swamp. He should have left her in the bog. As it was she and her tricks had become a menace to everybody, including the storks. The girl's character traits propelled her into the situation of unforeseen consequences. They lead to displacement and her disappearance on her wedding night, which leave the storks to keep her memory alive. She becomes part of the stork family's story passed on from one generation to the next. The fairy tales itself gave food for thought when the writer on the occasion of the French translation of this fairy tale said the following about the Danish language,

> Vort danske Modersmaal har en Farverigdom, en Afvexling i Udtryk, der betegner de forskellige Stemninger. Jeg var glad ved mit Modersmaals Rigdom; hvor er det blødt og klangfuldt, naar det tales, som det skal tales. I Locle paa Jurabjergene kom jeg til denne Erkjendelse. (*Mit Livs Eventyr* II 232)

> Our Danish mother tongue has a richness of color, a variety in expression which marks the various moods. I was happy about the richness of my native tongue; how soft and melodious it is when spoken as it should be spoken. In Locle in the Jura Mountains I arrived at this realization. (Mit Livs Eventyr II 232)

These feelings Andersen shared with Søren Aabye Kierkegaard (1813-55) who said,

> Jeg føler mig lykkelig ved at være bundet til mit Modersmaal, bunden som maaske Faa er det, ... bunden til et Modersmaal, der er rigt i indre Oprindelighed ... et Modersmaal, der fængsler sine Børn med en Lænke, som er let at bære – Ja! men tung at bryde. (Kierkegaard 364)

> I feel lucky to be tied to my mother tongue as perhaps few are, tied to a native tongue which is rich in inner originality ... a mother

tongue which imprisons its children with a chain which is easy to bear – Yes! But hard to break. (Kierkegaard 364)

Having given the poet such food for thought it is interesting to note that she and the other girls mentioned lived with the results of their actions in the cases of the princess in Clod Hans, the swamp king's daughter, Gerda and the robber girl. Or they die from it, as was the fate of the little match girl.

H.C. Andersen was an innovator. He was ahead of his time pointing to a female figure based on Kierkegaard's notion of a modern hero(in) "who stands and falls entirely on her own actions." (*Either-Or*, 1843, I, 141)

Women's movements had not made their marks on society yet. The Danish Women's Society ("Dansk Kvindesamfund") was not founded until 1871. Female writers hid behind their male counterparts as did, e.g., Thomasine Gyllembourg (1773-1856) who did not write let alone publish in her own name because that was not proper. Instead, Gyllembourg used her son Johan Ludvig Heiberg as her shield. Heiberg made one attempt at championing a young woman writer when in 1851 he wrote a foreword to Mathilde Fibiger's (1830-72) work *Clara Rafael. Tolv Breve* (Twelve Letters) but he did not have the fortitude to maintain his support of the young woman writer.

Andersen did not act as a champion of any one young girl and her work but he had insight which made it possible for him to introduce a girl figure who was not just a sweet, proper, well-behaved and loved child and not a Grimm fairy tale girl who would be under a spell when behaving badly only to emerge as the perfect, pretty girl when the spell was broken as in, e.g., "King Thrush Beard" ("Kong Drosselskæg"). The princess is humiliated and laughed at only to find that her husband was behind it all in order to propel her into finding and becoming her inner good self. Andersen pointed forward to what Simone de Beauvoir (1908-86) wrote in her work *The Second Sex* that

> Man finds again in woman bright stars and dreamy moon, the light of the sun, the shades of grottoes; and, conversely, the wild flowers of thickets, the proud garden rose are women. Nymphs, dryads, sirens, undines, fairies haunt the fields and woods, the lakes, oceans, moorlands. Nothing lies deeper in the hearts of men than this animism. (Beauvoir 176)

As women had started to test society's mood and willingness to put up with their stretching of the boundaries of accepted modes of behavior H.C. Andersen likewise placed some of his girls in situations where they acted contrary to the expected norms and mores but in accordance with new notions which would lead them to greater personal freedom which in turn would liberate society. The girls mentioned are by no means the only examples one can find in his fairy tales.

And H.C. Andersen did not leave it at that. Just as he was pioneering a new view of girls and their mode of behavior he slipped social criticism into "The Little Match Girl". What can be more painful and indicting to a society than a story about a little girl forced to sit outside during the Christmas season, on New Year's Eve to be specific, and freeze to death. However, the social criticism went unnoticed and unheeded, as did Andersen's pointing out that girls could take matters in their own hands.

Works Cited

Andersen, H.C. *Mit Livs Eventyr* I-II. Ed. H. Topsøe-Jensen. København: Gyldendal, 1996.

Beauvoir, Simone de. *The Second Sex*. Trans. & Ed. H.M. Parshley. New York: Vintage Books, 1952.

Conroy, Patricia L. & Sven H. Rossel, trans. & eds. *Tales and Stories by Hans Christian Andersen*. Seattle & London: University of Washington Press, 1980.

H. C. Andersens brevveksling med Lucie & B.S. Ingemann, I-II. Ed. Kirsten Dreyer. København: Museum Tusculanums Forlag, 1997.

Kierkegaard for dig og mig, I. Ed. F.J. Billeskov Jansen. 4 vols. København: Rosenkilde og Bagger, 1989.

Kierkegaard, Søren Aabye. Trans. David F. Swenson and Lillian Marvin Swenson. *Either/Or*, I. 2 vols. Princeton: Princeton University Press, 1944.

Kofoed, Niels. *H.C. Andersen og B. S. Ingemann. Et Livsvarigt Venskab*. København: C.A. Reitzel, 1992.

Nichols, Stephen G. "Writing the New Middle Ages." *PMLA* 120 (2005): 432.

Note

The quotations are translated by Inger Olsen.

"The Snow Queen" by Hans Christian Andersen: "Weltanschauung" and the Imaginative Mind

Inge Lise Rasmussen

The Fourth International Hans Christian Andersen Conference aims at establishing the collocation of Hans Christian Andersen's work between children's stories and adult literature. It may first be noted that in certain genres such as novels, theatrical plays and travel literature, H.C. Andersen undoubtedly addresses an adult audience. As concerns his fairy tales, it may be said that they address both a very young and an adult audience. In fact, their very value lies in the fact that they can be read with great joy both by adults and children. I think this was exactly what H.C. Andersen wanted to do in his fairy tales: to create something that could enthrall children but at the same time contain a message for adults.

In the best of his fairy tales he succeeded splendidly in this. As an example I have chosen "Sneedronningen. Et Eventyr i syv Historier" (The Snow Queen. A Tale in Seven Stories).[1] This fairy tale is in my opinion able to capture the interest of children and at the same time it may give parents something to think about too. This is because the sublime universe of the tale takes us to the level of a very poetic animated cartoon and simultaneously attains a highly intellectual level of existential philosophy very similar to that found in the Danish philosopher Søren Kierkegaard's work.

In the middle of the nineteenth-century Copenhagen was only a small town where everybody knew each other. Seen from today's perspective, two of its inhabitants stood out among the others and in any way became famous, not only in Denmark but in the entire world. One of these was obviously H.C. Andersen, whose greatness we are celebrating here. The other was Søren Kierkegaard.

Interestingly, these two great minds did not get along with each other. This was due to their very different personalities, but no less to the fact that Kierkegaard became famous following his long, critical review of a novel by H.C. Andersen, who was already renowned.

This review was to bring the philosopher notoriety. The novel in question was *Kun en Spillemand* (*Only a Fiddler*), a book which Kierkegaard completely demolished in his 1838 work, *Af en endnu Levendes Papirer* (*From the Papers of One Still Living*).[2]

Kierkegaard thought that H.C. Andersen was unable to write novels because he did not have a *Weltanschauung* and that instead of evolving, he produced a sort of inner void under variegated images.[3] It is easy to understand that Andersen was unhappy about the review and that it was very difficult for him to forgive the philosopher. In any case, the diaries repeatedly show that he read Kierkegaard's books (26th June 1852 and 13th October 1862). It may however be excluded that he read them diligently just to keep track of his "enemy". Andersen simply tried to keep an open mind concerning everything that went on around him. That he did not agree with Kierkegaard is obvious from his entry dated 13th October 1862, when together with Jonas Collin he gathered material for his travel book *I Spanien* (*In Spain*). On this occasion he wrote as follows: "I read at home in *Begrebet Angest* (*The Concept of Anxiety*), where he talked about the secret way of a genius, the presence of destiny, and that God in Heaven, (in a certain sense) does not understand geniuses! I said that it was unholy ..."[4] Two years later, on 10th December 1864, during a dinner at Hartmann's house, the host was said to "compare Wagner in the world of music with Kierkegaard in the world of literature, because they both demolish without creating something themselves."[5]

Of course it should be stressed that "The Snow Queen" was written a long time prior to the dairy passages quoted above. Andersen got the inspiration for the story in 1843 and started writing it in Maxen near Dresden where he stayed from the 12th to the 18th of July 1844. The story was finished by 8th December of the same year. Only two days later he signed a contract for a new collection of fairy tales with his publisher C.A. Reitzel. On the 19th he proofread it for the last time, and only three days later he was able to give copies of the new collection to his friends. The publishing house did not waste time: evidently it hoped that the book would sell well as a Christmas gift.

In 1844 Kierkegaard had not finished working on his philosophical system. His *Enten-Eller* (*Either-Or*) had appaeared in 1843, but *Sygdommen til Døden* (*The Sickness Unto Death*) did not appear until 1849. I will in any case investigate whether it is possible to transfer some of Kierkegaard's philosophical concepts to the fairy tale by H.C. Andersen.

The introduction to the fairy tale, "First Story. Which Has to Do with a Mirror and its Fragments", can be understood as an allegory which tells how evil entered the world. It might also be interpreted as the entrance of original sin into the world. In "Second Story. A Little Boy and a Little Girl" Kay gets a piece of glass from the mirror in his eye with the result that he has to leave the Garden of Eden, where he had lived with Gerda, and where the Grandmother, like some sort of God, had kept an eye on them. In the Bible God had forbidden Adam and Eve to eat the fruit from the tree of wisdom. In this fairy tale there is no such prohibition. But Gerda shows her dread of the Snow Queen and consequently asks the Grandmother whether she might be able to enter the house. When the Grandmother fails to reply, Kay confidently suggests that if the Snow Queen got in, he would put her on the stove till she melted. Upon hearing such talk the Grandmother stroke his hair, as if she very well knew what was to come.

Just like the snake in Paradise, the shard of mirror manages to harden the heart and open the eyes of Kay. The two children were sitting and enjoying a book with illustrations of animals and birds, just as Adam and Eve in Eden had once enjoyed the creations of God. We then read:

> "Oh! Something hurt my heart. And now I've got something in my eye." The little girl put her arm around his neck, and he blinked his eye. No, she couldn't see anything in it. "I think it's gone," he said. But it was not gone. It was one of those splinters of glass from the magic mirror. You remember that goblin's mirror – the one which made everything great and good that was reflected in it appear small and ugly, but which magnified all evil things until each blemish loomed large. Poor Kay! A fragment had pierced his heart as well, and soon it would turn into a lump of ice. The pain had stopped, but the glass was still there. (32-33)

The goblin's glass was demoniacal in the sense that it was thaumaturgical and invested with evil spirit. According to Kierkegaard anything demoniacal is linked with original sin, desperation and sickness unto death. For Kierkegaard this demoniacal nature was a particular sort of fear: namely the fear of facing the good. This fear was to be found in people subject to the sorcery of the sin, who are no longer able to fight for good. They have given up fighting and have become entranced by the fear of good, so they want to remain in a state of nonfreedom. We might say that for Kierkegaard, fascination with sin is a binding relationship with evil, while the demoniacal state represents a fear of the good. In Kierkegaard a demoniacal person is vanquished, falls into sin and in his desperation respects the consequences of evil. When somebody who is stronger than him in good will tries to save him from the wilderness of sin, he prays in the hope that this time he will not again become weak.

The innocent child's soul embodied by Kay has been damaged and he no longer wants to look at the illustrated book of animals. He is no longer able to enjoy the rose trees together with Gerda and the Grandmother. He starts to kid and to ape, making fun of everything. At the same time he becomes very clever and starts to prefer snow-flake flowers to real flowers. Because of his boldness the Snow Queen is able to attract him, and by the time he understands what has happened it is too late, and he can remember nothing more than the multiplication tables.

We might say that Kay is about to grow up and starts to move toward the borderline that in Kierkegaard's philosophy divides the aesthetic and ethical order, coinciding with the order of humor. Concerning the sense of abstraction in Kay, Kierkegaard normally uses the words "number" and "quantity" to indicate something untrue and abstract, such as all those things which are unlike the religious acts of a single individual. In the very beginning it is difficult for Kay to break from his faith acquired during childhood, but then he is kissed by the Snow Queen and she lets him creep under her fur, and he feels as if he is sinking into a snow drift so that he no longer feels the cold. This means that he ceases to fight and lets himself glide into the demoniacal cold of rationality. He now forgets everyone from his former life and starts to tell the Snow Queen that he can do mental arithmetic as far as fractions, and also that he knows how many square miles there are in the country, and what the population is. Hearing this, the Snow Queen smiles and flies with him into a wide-open space where it is black and cold, and where wolves howl. His misfortune is enormous, but the demoniacal cold has made him so insensible that he does not grasp the desperation of the situation. Kay no longer knows that he has a self, and that is a sort of sin which is a sickness unto death.

In the "Third Story. The Flower Garden of the Woman Skilled in Magic" Gerda first stays at home waiting for Kay, but as he does not show up she finally decides to go into the unknown world. With the help of the river she arrives in the cherry orchard. Here lives an old woman wearing a large sun hat decorated with painted flowers and leaves. At first Gerda is rather afraid of the old woman, but after having eaten some of the cherries and looked at the flowers, which were more interesting than any picture-book because each of the flowers told its own story, she follows the woman into her cottage. Here it happens that Gerda forgets everything about her past and fully enjoys her new fairy tale world, letting all the flowers tell their stories. Such was also the case with the moon in *Billedbog uden Billeder* (*Picture Book without Pictures*), which could tell a wonderful fairy tale and so create a beautiful animated scene every time it paid a visit to the young poet. Instead, the old woman was able to cast spells and very much wanted to keep Gerda in her house and garden forever. And since she knew that the roses might awake some memories in Gerda, she found a way to let them sink into the earth. The rose can be seen as a symbol of self in Gerda. In the first chapter of the fairy tale we encounter the roof garden with two small rose trees which grow vigorously and may be compared to the two small children. But the old woman has forgotten that on the painted hat there still is a rose. One day Gerda sees it, and now she starts to seek the roses in the garden, but she looks in vain. Then she sits down and cries desperately. Her tears sink into the earth just where the rose bushes had stood, and they immediately spring up in full bloom. And so she kisses the roses and thinks of the roses at home and of little Kay. The old woman, indeed, did not want to harm the girl, but she casts a spell on her because she egoistically wanted to keep her there in a sort of aesthetic prison where Gerda demoniacally forgot herself, her own eternal self. As the little girl is gripped by fear, she flies far away from the garden with its never-ending summer back into the wide world. She realizes that she has wasted her time. Outside the garden the weather is cold and rough. It might be said that she enters the ethical world of grown-ups with their responsibilities.

The "Fourth Story. The Prince and the Princess" ironically takes Gerda back into the real world, where people get married and prosaically find their place in life. First we meet the helpful couple of crows, who gain a permanent appointment and get married. But also the princess, who has already learned all the newspapers in the world and forgotten them again, is looking for a husband. It should be recalled that Kierkegaard did not have a very high opinion of newspapers.

In the fourth story there is a passage which can make us think of "Thickheaded Jack" ("Klods-Hans"), namely where the man who speaks most eloquently will be chosen to marry the princess. Gerda, who is enamored of her Kay because he is able to calculate sums and fractions, does not doubt that he will win the hand of the princess. Therefore during the night she takes a private staircase into the royal palace. But both to her joy and sorrow she finds out that the newly-married young man is not her Kay. She needn't be jealous, but at the same time she must admit that she has not found her Kay.

In the "Fifth Story. The Little Robber Girl" our little heroine passes from the royal castle to the terrible house of the thieves. Only with difficulty does she avoid being killed and eaten by the old robber queen and ends up in the hands of the rough and rude robber girl. But even in a world full of general envy, thievery, violence and killing Gerda is able to survive, because in her goodness she moves directly towards her goal. And now she even gets help from the wood-pigeons, who know where Kay is to be found. And the little robber girl gives Gerda her reindeer, so that she can go up to the North Pole and pick him up.

When in the "Sixth Story. The Lapp Woman and the Finn Woman" the reindeer asks the Lapp Woman to give Gerda a potion which will make her as strong as twelve men so that she may be able to conquer the Snow Queen, the Lapp Woman explains why Gerda in spite of the nearly inhuman situation has fared so well. She says the following to the reindeer:

> No power that I could give could be as great as that which she already has. Don't you see how men and beasts are compelled to serve her, and how far she has come in the wide world since she started out in her naked feet? We mustn't tell her about this power. Strength lies in her heart, because she is such a sweet, innocent child. (27)

A pure heart, or a strong consciousness of self in fact helps the girl so that she only needs to say the Lord's Prayer and out come little angels to take her side in the terrible battle against the Snow Queen's army made out of snowflakes cold as ice which take the shapes of intrinsically ugly figures. But little Gerda has very clear ideas, and after these tragic events she has now fully reached the religious order.

With the "Seventh Story. What Happened in the Snow Queen's Palace and What Came of it" we again find Kay blue, almost black with cold. But the Snow Queen had kissed his sense of cold away, so he does not feel the cold in the over one hundred chambers of her palace lit by the Northern lights. Right in the center of the endless hall the Snow Queen is sitting on her so-called mirror of reason on a frozen lake while Kay tries to make sharp, flat pieces of ice fit together. As with a Chinese puzzle he tries to create the word *Eternity*, but even if he makes the cleverest shapes and designs he is not able to do it. The Snow Queen has told him that if he can make out that word he shall be his own master and she will give him the whole world along with a pair of new skates.

For Kay there might be hope, since the word *Eternity* fascinates him. He is cold but not dead, and looking for a solution that he might never be able to find. He is in a tragic situation of desperation and needs a push, so that he will be able to make a leap into the religious order.

The push is given by Gerda through her example. With the help of a prayer she made her way into the Snow Queen's palace and now she will find Kay. She cries with delight and the warm tears fall on his head and on his breast, and they sink into his heart till the ice is melted and the piece of glass is washed away. Then she sings:

> Where roses bloom so sweetly in the vale,
> There shall you find the Christ Child, without fail.

And now also Kay cries and the piece of glass swims out of his eye. As a consequence of this act of love the pieces of ice dance about for joy; and when they get tired they fall of their own accord into the very word which the Snow Queen had bid him make out: *Eternity*. The faith of Kay has suddenly been found and he is now free and can go home. The demoniacal has no longer any power over him, and he is not desperate anymore.

The word eternity can here be understood in two ways, namely as a lapse of time without any limits or as a being without time, which is not subordinated to any definition of time. For Kierkegaard the second definition is not only a negation of time, but it also refers to a qualitatively different form of being, which has both a religious and an ethical essence. In this way another paradox emerges, because faith is divided into two forms, namely faith in eternity as eternity, and secondly faith in eternity as growth over time.

Happy to have found one another, the two start their journey back. Home again, they enter the living-room of their childhood, and through confrontation with grown-up figures they understand that they have become adult. Here they find the Grandmother, who sitting in the sunshine reads aloud out of her Bible and reminds them "Except ye become as little children, ye shall not enter into the Kingdom of Heaven" and sings the old hymn about the roses which bloom so sweetly in the vale. The room of childhood in this way becomes a figure of eternity, where the children grow in time but manage to remain part of something beyond time.

With this short interpretation I do not intend to say that H.C. Andersen has written his fairy tale referring directly to the categories of Kierkegaard. In the world of H.C. Andersen it is more typical to talk about children's faith and providence than about existential philosophy and *Weltanschauung*. However, the two men lived in the same period and some of their philosophical thoughts might therefore be the same. What I want to stress is that Andersen is a great and genuine writer because an interpretation of this fairy tale in the light of Kierkegaard's concepts is equally successful. It happens to H.C. Andersen just as it happens to Kay, that the paradox is not solved through intellectual speculation. The paradox, so to say, solves itself, just as it happened to the pieces of ice that dancing around for joy found the right solution. But also in Kierkegaard's philosophical work a paradox has to be solved through a leap from one order to another.

So we may say that H.C. Andersen in his work faces existential problems and intuitively understands how to solve them. As an example we have tried to read the text with regard to the philosophy of Søren Kierkegaard. But we might also have read it with regard to the psychoanalytical methods of Carl Gustav Jung and the result would have been the same. The equation would have been solved. This matter of fact must satisfy even the most critical adult reader. At the same time it can incite something in the child, or plant a seed, which over time can develop and finally become ripe.

In my introduction I mentioned that the fairy tales of H.C. Andersen can also be experienced as a sort of animated cartoon in which each fantastic scene makes way for another. In my book *Øjets sekraft og billedets fødsel* (*The Eye's Force of Vision and the Birth of the Image*)[6] I provided examples of how he built on his experience from the worlds of theatre, painting and sculpture when he described his many wonderful scenes so rich with colour.

The most variegated chapter in "The Snow Queen" is without doubt the third story, where Gerda lives spellbound in the garden. Here every flower dreams its own fairy tale and tells it. Or rather, we may say that every flower is capable of painting or putting a scene into an animated cartoon. For example, the tiger-lily tells the following story:

> Do you hear the drum? *Boom, boom*! It was only two notes, always *boom, boom*! Hear the woman wail. Hear the priests chant. The Hindu woman in her long red robe stands on the funeral pyre. The flames rise around her and her dead husband, but the Hindu woman is thinking of that living man in the crowd around them. She is thinking of him whose eyes are burning hotter than the flames – of him whose fiery glances have pierced her heart more deeply than these flames that soon will burn her body to ashes. Can the flame of the heart die in the flame of the funeral pyre?

The reaction of little Gerda is that she does not understand it. And that is natural, because in order to conceive it one needs to know something about the old Indian ritual of burning the widows together with their dead husbands. And one must also know something about impossible love. But even without such preparation, the image has a very strong effect with its wonderful sound associations and the red flames that cover the still-living Indian woman. We are in an exotic country very far away and in only a few lines we have a sort of movie about life and death and love.

The little snowdrop's story is as follows:

> Between the trees a board hangs by two ropes. It is a swing. Two pretty little girls, with frocks as white as snow, and long green ribbons fluttering from their hats, are swinging. Their brother, who is bigger than they are, stands behind them on the swing, with his arms around the ropes to hold himself. In one hand he has a little cup, and in the other a clay pipe. He is blowing soap bubbles, and as the swing flies the bubbles float off in all their changing colours. The last bubble is still clinging to the bowl of his pipe, and fluttering in the air as the swing weeps to and fro. A little black dog, light as a bubble, is standing on his legs and trying to get up to the swing. But it does not stop. High and low the swing flies, until the dog loses his balance, barks, and loses his temper. They tease him, and the bubble bursts. A swinging board pictured in a bubble before it broke – that is my story.

This scene has many Nordic colours. Concerning the sounds, we can hear the dog barking and we can imagine the sound of the swing and of the wind which makes the green ribbons and the soap-bubbles move. It is all very delicate. White and green dominate. And then we have the black spot of the dog and the many colours of the bubbles.

This kind of image is close to a European imagination. And because of its childish content it is easy to understand for a child. I think that a poetic image like this would be a success in any modern cartoon.

The same may be said of the scene with the hobgoblin's mirror flying around, or of the scene with the Snow Queen sitting in her palace, etc. They are all timeless in the sense that they are unbounded by history. Instead, in the second story in which Kay and Gerda are small we have a clear reference to the nineteenth century, and so they have a patina that makes it difficult for a modern child to recognize himself in such surroundings. This might keep some young readers away from H.C. Andersen, while an adult normally finds such a historical distance interesting.

In essence, "The Snow Queen" is all about how good defeats evil. This theme is found in many other fairy tales. And this theme is always a good way to enthrall children and adults alike. But the story also shows us that H.C. Andersen had an elaborate *Weltanschauung* which in his best fairy tales works very well together with his use of images. Not less because the many colours create a very poetic and pictorial universe, a delightful atmosphere, where even children can be made to contemplate life with a new perspective.[7]

Notes

1. Andersen, Hans Christian, "The Snow Queen. A Tale in Seven Stories". In: *The Complete Andersen*. Transl. by Jean Hersholt. The Limited Editions Club, New York, 1949.
2. Kierkegaard, Søren, "Af en endnu Levendes Papirer. Om Andersen som Romandigter, med stadigt Hensyn til hans sidste Værk "Kun en Spillemand" (From the Papers of One Still Living. On Andersen as a Novelist, with Continuous Regard to his Last Work "Only a Fiddler")". In: *Samlede Værker*. Vol. 1. Gyldendal, Copenhagen, 1962. Pp. 11-57.
3. Kierkegaard, p. 32.
4. *H.C. Andersens Dagbøger*. Vols. 1-12. Gads Forlag, Copenhagen, 1971-90. Quotation from Vol. 5, p. 256.
5. *H.C. Andersens Dagbøger*, Vol. 6, pp. 163-64.
6. Ramussen, Inge Lise, *Øjets sekraft og billedets fødsel. Artikler omkring H.C. Andersen* (*The Eye's Force of Vision and the Birth of the Image. Articles about H.C. Andersen*). . C.A. Reitzel, Copenhagen, 2000.
7. See also H. Topsøe-Jensen, "Sneedronningen". In his: *Buket til Andersen. Bemærkninger til femogtyve eventyr*. G.E.C. Gad, Copenhagen, 1971. Pp. 92-102.

Hans Christian Andersen – Writing for Children?

Torben Weinreich

When Hans Christian Andersen in 1835 published his first four fairy tales, "The Tinder Box", "The Princess and the Pea", "Little Claus and Big Claus", and "Little Ida's Flowers", in a humble booklet, they had the title *Fairy Tales, Told for Children* on the front page. Until 1842 and four booklets later his fairy tales were in the same way "told for children".

Nevertheless it is frequently discussed if Andersen wrote his 156 fairy tales for children – or at least some of the fairy tales, and at least until 1842, when he himself used the words "told for children".

We are in discussions like this confronted with both very specific and more general and abstract questions.

1) Did Andersen write his fairy tales or at least some of them for children?

2) Will we still – today – about 150 years later – be able to argue that the fairy tales (or some of them) should be considered as children's literature?

Those are the more specific questions. And then to the more general question, which is – when we are talking about children's literature – also a meta-theoretical question:

3) What is the imperative condition or qualification if we want to designate a literary work as children's literature?

Those are the questions I will try to answer in this paper. And I shall from the beginning emphasize that we are not only talking about Hans Christian Andersen – though I will use Andersen's texts as examples. I shall here remind you of the similar discussions about the peculiarity of works like Lewis Carroll's *Alice's Adventures in Wonderland* (1865) and A.A. Milne's *Winnie-the-Pooh* (1926). Perhaps we could involve E.T.A. Hoffmann's *Nussknacker und Mausekönig* (1816), too.

I will start with the meta-theoretical discussion: What is the imperative condition or qualification if we want to designate a literary work as children's literature? Who decides?

Let us start with a literary work, e.g. H.C. Andersen's "The Tinder Box". This work is allegedly written – and published – for children. We know that from the book's title ("told for children") and from statements by the author.

And here comes the reader, an adult, and he (or she) reads the work and understands it, likes it and is enriched. What happens now? The adult reader says:

1. I understand it.
2. I like it.
3. Ergo: It is written for me.
4. And then perhaps: It's not for children?

But the adult is here making a great mistake. And a fundamental one, too. What he is doing here is an example of what we in philosophical terms could call "naive empiricism": "What I like is made for me!"

Let me – in order to describe this "naive empiricism" more distinctly – present two other examples of "naive empiricism". And again it is about children, adults and "something good", e.g. literature:

Situation no 1: An adult is sitting together with a small child, who is only 9 months old and very hungry. Present in this situation is also a little bottle with mashed banana and a spoon. Before giving the child the mashed bananas, he tastes it and finds it excellent, a wonderful taste. Is the conclusion now that the bottle with mashed banana is made for adults? And is it then not for children? Or is it so that sometimes adults like things made for children?

Situation 2: A child finds and reads a book written and published for adults. And now the child is arguing:

1. I understand it.
2. I like it.
3. Ergo: It is written for me.
4. And then perhaps: It is not for adults.

I will not comment on the two situations here and now, but add: It is all about intentionality – also when we define children's literature, and when we decide whether a specific literary work should be considered children's literature or not.

Intentionalities

So let me introduce you to this general view of intentionalities, using Umberto Eco's terms from *Lector in Fabula* (1979) and *Interpretation and Overinterpretation* (1992). He distinguishes between:

intentio auctoris
intentio operis
intentio lectoris

Intentio auctoris means that the author decides if the work is for children, and intentio lectoris that the reader decides. Intentio operis is a little more controversial: Because here the work itself *is* or *is not* for children. It is for children if the author (perhaps without being aware of it) has inscribed a children's reader in the work; it is what Umberto Eco calls a "lettore modello" and Walker Gibson "a mock reader" in Jane P. Tompkins (ed.): *Reader-Response Criticism,* (1980).

I think that two intentions more should be added to Umberto Eco's intentio-model, as I have done in my own book *Children's literature – art or pedagogy* (2000):

Intentio mediatoris (1)
Intentio mediatoris (2)

Intentio mediatoris (1) is among others the publisher, who can decide that this book is (and therefore should be sold as) children's literature. Perhaps even with the age of the intended reader printed on the book.

Intentio mediatoris (2) comprises among others librarians, who decide where the book should be placed in the library – and perhaps say to children: this book is good for you, and this one is not.

Let's now go back to Andersen and his fairy tales.

Writing for Children?

When Hans Christian Andersen's first fairy tales came out in Denmark in 1835, he was criticised on a number of accounts. The stories were said to be immoral and potentially harmful for children. Andersen wrote in a style unaccustomed for readers. He used the spoken language, including the spoken language of children. One critic wrote: "One may not put words together in print in the same disorganised way that one does when speaking."

In 1842 when Andersen was firmly established as a writer of fairy tales in the public consciousness, another critic wrote: "To write fairy tales for children or common people in some peculiar manner, or to imitate *in art* the common people's natural but at times also longwinded and not infrequently clumsy, incoherent narrative style, or in what we recognise as a *childlike* style and tone is to corrupt children in a tasteless, incomprehensible way."

Despite the criticism, Andersen continued to write in his own style. He described this written style as "natural". He wrote in his diary 27. March 1834: "Let me follow my natural instinct. Why should I follow a fashion and go at a trot? If I amble around, it's because it's my natural pace."

And nature is what it was all about at the beginning and in the middle of the 1800s when Romantic philosophy and Rousseau's views of nature and children set the tone. Rationalist educationalists were concerned at this tendency. In 1792 a Danish critic, J.C. Tode, wrote in the magazine *Iris* no. III:

> It has now become customary for most children's writers to retain the language that children use. They allow the characters to speak like children and they allow them to offend against grammar and common sense to imitate nature. This is an error that will damage children because it will encourage them to use an unpolished, uncorrected, slapdash tone. It is already a problem of their age and must be avoided.

It is frequently overlooked that one of Andersen's great virtues as an innovator within children's literature is his use of the spoken language in the written genre. It was a revolution! Andersen put his feelings into words himself, almost as a kind of poetics: "You should be able to hear the narrator in any writing; therefore the language should reflect the spoken form. The stories are for children but adults should be able to listen, too." Notice the last part.

But what did Andersen himself say about writing for children? This question has – as I said in the beginning – quite often been raised.

The truth is that a considerable number of the stories *were* written and published for children. The very first issue from 1835 and the following issues until 1842 were called "Fairy Tales, Told for Children". Then the reference to children vanished. From 1852 he began to refer to his fairy tales as "stories". In his memoirs, *The Fairy Tale of My Life* from 1855, he says: "The most appropriate name in our language for my fairy tales in terms of their style and essence is *stories*."

Andersen also – in the beginning – stresses in his letters to friends that his fairy tales are written for children and accounts for his reasons when, for example, he writes to his friend the Danish poet B.S. Ingemann in February 1835:

> Furthermore I have begun a few "Fairy tales *told* for children" and I think they work. I have put in a couple of the fairy tales I liked when I was young and which I do not consider to be well-known. I have written them just as if I was telling them myself to *a child*.

As far back as New Year's Day in 1835 Andersen told his good friend Henriette Hanck that he was writing some fairy tales: "I am trying to win over the new generations you know!"

Andersen was very much aware that his tales would be *read aloud* to children, and that adults would be present. In a letter to Ingemann in 1843 – and that was after he had finished using the words "told for children" in the titles of his fairy tales – he wrote that he had finally come clean about his fairy tales, and he added:

> Now I tell stories from my own head, I take an adult idea and then tell it to children while remembering that mother and father are often listening, and you have to consider them.

In modern research in children's literature we would talk about the "ambiguity" of a children's story and perhaps "double address", that is, that we can have more than one reader or listener inscribed in a work for children.

Here I have to add that: Andersen's stories were very early translated into English. However, the English versions were often sentimentalised and amended – out of consideration for children. It was thought that children could not understand Andersen's irony and that some of the fairy tales were too hard-hitting. You can say that the translators – about 150 years ago – took part in the discussion that I am talking about in this paper: Is Andersen writing for children? Obviously not childish enough, they said. Accordingly, some fairy tales were simply changed, such as "The Little Match Girl" (1848) in some editions in which the girl does not die but is invited inside and saved.

There is an image of Hans Christian Andersen as "the Children's Friend", rather than someone who merely wrote stories for children. This was of great irritation to Andersen himself, especially in his later years, and he turned against this image of "Andersen, the Children's Friend" at the same time as it became increasingly clear that he did not write his fairy tales or "stories" *only* for children.

"The Bell"

Let us now go to another thing, which could indicate that Andersen had children in mind when he was writing. He first published some of his fairy tales and children's poems in children's magazines, even after 1842. The fairy tale called "The Bell", considered by many to be a story for adults, appeared for the first time in the Danish "Monthly Magazine for Children" in 1845, and the poem "The Woman with the Eggs", which has later on become a firm favourite in anthologies used in Danish schools, first appeared in a children's magazine in 1839.

But here we have to think hard: could the reason for publishing his works in children's magazines be that Andersen was asked, perhaps pressed? Perhaps he just needed the money.

And then we are back in the more general discussion: When does a literary work become children's literature? Before I answer this question a very short summary of the plot in "The Bell":

> In a big town one can every evening, when the sun is setting, hear the beautiful sound of a bell. "It was as if the tones came from some church in the secret depths of the forest." A little group of children decided to find the bell, but only two of them do not grow tired and do not return to town.
>
> One of the boys is a king's son; the other one is very poor. They split and we follow the king's son farther and farther into the woods, and he – at last – finds the bell and the church.

But at the same moment arrives from the other side the poor boy with his short sleeves and wooden shoes. They have *both* found the bell and the church – at the same moment, and "they ran towards each other, and held each other by the hand in the great tabernacle of Nature and Poetry, while above them sounded the invisible, holy bell". And it all ends with a "hallelujah".

If we here – in the model – go to the level of intentio mediatoris (1) we can claim that at the moment a work is *published* as children's literature, and the author does not protest, then it *is* children's literature. And then "The Bell" became children's literature at the moment it was published in the magazine.

But who is to decide, whether "The Bell" is children's literature or not?

– Andersen? (perhaps he wrote something about "The Bell" in his letters or diaries, which could answer this question; I do not know)
– The publisher?
– Teachers or librarians?
– The reader?

And if we say the reader, what shall we then do with the adult, reading it and saying: "I understand and I like it, and *it is not* for children?" And with the child reading it, too, saying: "I understand it and I like it, and *it is* for children?"

The conclusion is: Andersen wrote in a variety of genres and for a broad audience. Children were a part of it. He knew this – and he told us about it, as I have shown it.

Let us go back to "The Bell" and ask: Is it children's or adult's literature? I will conclude, using this table where C is children's literature and A adult's literature:

"The Bell"	C	A
1. Intentio auctoris	?	?
2. Intentio mediatoris (1)	X	(X)
3. Intentio operis		X
4. Intentio mediatoris (2)	(X)	X
5. Intentio lectoris	(X)	X

1. I do not know the exact intention. What I know is that Andersen gave "The Bell" to the children's magazine.
2. It was published in a children's magazine.
3. According to my analysis, the inscribed reader is a sophisticated reader (and an adult).
4. If we look at anthologies used in school, we can see, that teachers do not use "The Bell" in the primary school very often.
5. "The Bell" has – as far as we know – only a few children-readers. At the Centre for Children's Literature in Copenhagen, Anette Øster has a made a survey about young people and Andersen's fairy tales – showing that most children do not even know about "The Bell".

To explain the parenthesis:

2. "The Bell" is seldom represented in modern books for children with fairy tales by Andersen.
4. Some teachers use the text in primary school and with success.
5. Some children read, understand and like "The Bell".

It looks as if we have to distinguish between *normal* and *sophisticated* readers, also when we are talking about children. One could add: Of course we have to. But very often we are talking about children-readers as represented by a statistical norm.

Conclusions

If we follow this path – that is, that a book is a children's book if some children-readers understand and like it – we will find that *every* book in this world is a children's book, because some children are what I call sophisticated readers.

But we cannot use these sophisticated readers when we define children's literature. On the other hand: If we decide that children's literature is what children *read* (and not only a few sophisticated children), and that adult literature is what adults *read*, then *perhaps literature is just literature!?*

Children's literature is often defined as literature written and/or published for children, and with a child-reader inscribed in the work. And I agree. But this still leaves us with the question: Is Hans Christian Andersen's "The Bell" children's literature? The answer is
   yes
   and no
   and perhaps.
   Why should it be so easy?

"Look! Now we'll begin. When we have got to the end of the story we shall know more than we do now"

Ejnar Stig Askgaard

It is curious to stand in Munkemøllestræde in Odense and contemplate the childhood home of Hans Christian Andersen. And it is difficult to dwell on his memory there – for the street is a very busy one. So for safety's sake, it is a good idea to stick to the narrow pavement and flatten oneself against the wall of the telephone building opposite in order to get a good impression of the small home, where only the first two bays were actually part of the modest scenario of the childhood home: the living room and the kitchen. Everything has changed. New buildings dominate the scene. Only the childhood home, with a commemorative plaque on the gable, where the house juts out, and the further progression of the building round the corner towards Horsetorvet, are left as a relict of the time when the writer was a child. Where the telephone building now stands Eilskov's dwelling once was, where Hans Christian made the acquaintance of Shakespeare's works thanks to widow Bunkeflod. The gateway Munkemølle Port, which determined military service for those who lived outside and those who lived inside respectively, has also disappeared. For those interested in the writer there is only this interrupted sight of the childhood home, lovingly restored to its original state in 1930. So lovingly was it restored that there is still an alley between the childhood home and the more recent building it has as its northern neighbour, where the baker of rye bread once lived. This narrow alleyway is hidden by a little wall that links the two properties, although it can be guessed at behind the brickwork and the zinc plates that follow the slope of the roof. It is here we are to begin. For precisely here, in the gable of the childhood home facing the rye-bread bakery, Anne Marie Andersdatter – Hans Christian Andersen's mother – had her small Adonis garden, the semi-Persian garden that Hans Christian describes in *The Fairy Tale of My Life*:

> By means of a ladder it was possible to go from the kitchen on to the roof, and there, in the gutters between it and the neighbour's house stood a box of soil with chives and parsley growing in it; – it was all the garden my mother had ...[1]

This small garden commands our interest, as the author continues: "in my story of 'The Snow Queen' that garden still blooms."

In "The Snow Queen", then, the writer had the modest garden of this childhood as his point of departure. In his tragic novel *Only a Fiddler* Andersen gives us a more detailed picture of it:

> In the market towns every house normally has a small garden, yet this house had none – but one must have some sort of garden, even if no bigger than for a handful of chives and some purslane. So it came about and was, if one dare call it so, one of Scandinavia's hanging gardens, as owned by the poor. A large wooden box filled with soil made up their garden; it was placed high up on the gutter between the next-door houses, where the ducks could not fly up and do it harm. If anything was to be picked, the ladder had to be fetched, placed in the kitchen between the rows of tins and the chimney, with one person holding the wobbling ladder while the other climbed up it to the ceiling, where a hatch was opened and one could reach the box with the top half of one's body. It was a treat for the little boy to go up there; once he had even been allowed – floating between his mother's hands out of the hatch – to place his feet on the edge of the box.[2]

The garden from which so many dreams originated had so solid a position in Andersen's universe that it was able to form the framework of his creative writing. Other vivid flashes of memory can also be made out as beacons in the literary landscape that Andersen's tale of the Snow Queen so richly spreads out for us.

I would, however, like to dip into the time a dozen years prior to the writer conceiving his tale. In 1832, Andersen was actually in Odense on a visit. In a letter to Henriette Wulff dated 7 July he reports as follows:

> It makes a strange impression on me to see the places where I played as a child. It is as if I were dead and were now returning to

a world where, in another incarnation and under other conditions I had lived and played.³

By means of this excellent formulation, Andersen was able to express that he found it difficult to recall the life he had lived as a child in Odense almost 13 years earlier. He could not recognise himself as a child. Childhood belonged to a world that he was unable to completely return to – via his reason. Something impenetrable lay between the life he now lived and the one he had lived. This is hardly surprising. For if one reads the writer's reminiscences paying particular attention to his childhood years, one gradually discovers that they were characterised by a quite different understanding of the world than the one he as a writer and we as present-day readers are part of. There are a few brief glimpses: When Hans Christian fetched buttermilk from Hunderup and, terrified, passed Nonnebakken on his way home, he did not calm down until he had passed Odense River "since I knew that no trolls or ghosts could get past water".

St. John's Wort used to be stuck in the creaks between the beams, and their growth would reveal the owner's state of health. Andersen mentions his St. John's Wort with the words: "mine thrived and promised me a long life", while hereby indirectly pointing to his father's sorry fate. Andersen provides us with a fine portrait of his father, who died when only 33 years old. Unlike both wife and child – indeed, unlike those in the neighbourhood – he was an enlightened man who, with his fine abilities, yearned for learning and new ideas. His mental gaze was towards the future – he was not only intelligent but also a freethinker, and with his knowledge, insight and reason he had a weight of common sense that made him somewhat condescending when confronted with, for example, his wife's superstitious nature. In his first reminiscences, written down by Andersen shortly after the letter just quoted – the so-called *Levnedsbog* [Autobiography] – the writer recalls a situation: One evening his father declared that he did not share the same belief as his wife and boy, nor the whole neighbourhood for that matter. He was of the opinion that Christ was only a human being, although a wonderful human being, that the Bible was not exactly by God, and that there could be no hell. "'I am a freethinker!' he said, and never has any word gone straight through my soul like that one; I did not exactly know what it was, but felt it was something that was out of the ordinary." After that, Andersen writes:

My father's reasonable words did not help and when one morning he awoke and had a bad gash in his arm that could have been caused by a nail or a pin, my mother and the woman next door assumed and declared that the gash came from the devil because my father refused to recognise him.[4]

Later, as an old man, Andersen told his young friend Nicolaj Bøgh that his mother, having heard his father utter these intrepid words, threw a scarf over him and said: "It was the devil that was here in this room and said that, Hans Christian, not your father, and you are to forget what he has said, for he did not mean it." Then both of them had cried and prayed the Lord's Prayer together. In the last tale he ever wrote – "What old Johanna told" – we find this childhood memory once more. We also hear from Nicolaj Bøgh's reminiscences that the story of the gashes on his father's arms (and legs) took place when his father lay dead: "There, Hans Christian, you see," his mother had said. "The Evil One has caught hold of him and wanted to have him because he said what he did about Christ."[5]

It is difficult for us nowadays to imagine what such a conceptual world was like. It is easy to pass lightly over Andersen's words, because we are unable to follow the idea of the devil catching hold of the father; it is easier to grasp as a piece of poetic imagery. But that was not how it was meant – there was no talk of poetic turns of phrase. It was meant completely literally. Superstition and piety mingled in his childhood world to form one whole. If we look closer at the terrible days when his father lay dying, we hear via Andersen:

One morning he awoke with wild hallucinations, talked of campaigns and of *Napoleon*; he believed he was taking orders from him and was himself commanding. My mother immediately sent me out for help, but not from the doctor, no, from a so-called "wise old woman" who lived three miles from Odense. I arrived out there, the woman asked me several questions, then took a strand of wool, measured my arms, made strange signs over me and finally, on my chest, laid a green branch, of the type of tree on which *Our Lord* was crucified, she said, adding: "Now follow the river on your way home! Should your father die this time, you will meet his spectre!"

You can imagine my fear, I who was so full of superstition and lived under the power of fantasy. "And you did not meet anyone?" my mother asked when I arrived home; with pounding heart I assured her, "No!" The third evening my father died. His body was left laid out on the bed; I lay with my mother outside, and throughout the night a cricket chirped. "He *is* dead!" his mother said to it. "You don't need to sing for him, the Ice Maiden has already taken him!" I understood what she meant – the previous winter, when all our windows had frozen over, my father had pointed out that the pane had frozen over in the form of a maiden with both arms outstretched. "She wants to have me!" he had said jokingly. But now, as he lay dead in his bed, my mother recalled that, and what he had said occupied my thoughts.[6]

It is quite impossible for us today – as children of the Enlightenment – to fully understand the conceptual world and perception of reality in which Hans Christian lived when a child. It was also difficult for the writer himself when – having received an education and his consciousness having matured – he was once again confronted with the world he had left behind. "It is as if I were dead and were now returning to a world where, in another incarnation and under other conditions I had lived and played."

"The Snow Queen" has the land of childhood as its point of departure, and it is tempting to focus on the flashes of memory Andersen makes use of in the tale. There is the small roof-garden in the gable of the childhood home in Munkemøllestræde, there is the Snow Queen that takes the beloved Kay, like the Ice Maiden took his beloved father – even the writer's paternal grandmother who tended the garden at Grey Friars' Hospital seems to peep out of the fairy tale as the old woman in the flower garden. "I was allowed to play there with her," Andersen writes about his grandmother in his reminiscences from 1832, "to look at the lovely flowers, and I especially liked to kiss the roses – a desire I still have each time I see one that is really beautiful and red," which immediately makes one think of little Gerda, who in the flower garden embraces and kisses the roses that her tears have produced. The fairy tale is resonant with the land of childhood – by Gerda's walk alongside the river in search of Kay who is to be found and cured we are reminded of 11-year-old Hans Christian walking alongside Odense River with a strand of wool round his wrist and the sprig of "The Tree of Christ's Cross" on his way home to his father's deathbed. Andersen was able to use this experience from real life in the service of art, but "The Snow Queen" is not a poetic biography because of that. The writer had something else to say, and in the following I will attempt to show that the purpose of his return journey to the land of childhood was to formulate what he was unable to put into words in his letter to Henriette Wulff in July 1832.

Andersen began this tale "in seven stories" in 1843 – and the following year it was included in *New Tales*, which contains the richest collection of the writer's fairy tales, those which were really to cement his mastery of the genre. The first story – the introduction or, perhaps, the argument of the narrative – was conceived and written around November 1843, while the rest of the tale – the anecdotal implementtation of the argument of the introductory story – was written the year after and completed in December 1844. The first time we hear of the fairy tale is in a letter to B.S. Ingemann of 20 November 1843, where Andersen writes that two new tales are as good as finished. The one is called "The Elder-Tree Mother", the other "The Magic Mirror", which he does not consider unfortunate:

> One day the devil invents something that gives him great pleasure – he creates a mirror that has the ability to cause everything beautiful and wonderful in it to shrink and become small, while every fault and weakness grows and becomes more prominent. If a good thought passes through a human breast, a laugh goes through the mirror. After the earth has seen its reflection, the devil flies up to heaven, so that God and the angels can be reflected in it, but then the mirror laughs more and more as it approaches heaven, so that it quivers and falls out of the devil's hands. It crashes down to earth and smashes into millions of pieces, each of which fly into people's eyes and then they rather see the weak than the excellent; if a shard enters their heart they are turned into laughing people who only laugh, and at everything! Now the story comes into the tale, how such comes about and how only by crying deeply and gazing into the nature of God can the splinter of glass be cried out again! ... I believe, and it will delight me if I am right that I have found the knack of writing fairy tales! ... I have lots of material, more than for any other form of writing; it often seems to me as if every piece of fence, every little flower was saying take a look at me and my story will come to you. And if I do so, well, then I have the story![7]

The letter makes it clear that Andersen already had his introductory story, and that this was to form the basis of a number of tales. The remark about the stories of the flowers that are revealed to the writer seems to point forward to the fourth tale, where the flowers tell their stories to little Gerda. But for some unknown reason Andersen let the tale lie unfinished. It is not until December 1844 that his almanac reveals he is busy on it once more. He writes on 5 December: "At work on The Snow Queen", and 8 December: "At work on The Snow Queen, read it and The Fir Tree at Miss Bülow's. Completed the tale." In a letter to Ingemann from January 1845, the author also writes: "My latest fairy tale, The Snow Queen, [...] has been a pleasure for me to write, it so penetrated my thoughts that it danced over the paper …" So the writer worked on his tale for a long time in his mind before, in a rush of poetic frenzy, committing it to paper. He remained faithful, however, to the idea he had formulated the previous year: After the story about the Magic Mirror come six stories that develop and give expression to the idea "to cry deeply and gaze into the nature of God". Andersen's subtitle for the tale underlines this: "A Tale in Seven Stories". Via the subtitle Andersen is also referring to E.T.A. Hoffmann's *Meister Floh*, which has the subtitle "Ein Märchen in sieben Abenteuern zweier Freunde". In Hoffmann's tale we also find the theme of how the insignificantly small can have overwhelming significance. In "The Snow Queen", it is the eye and the heart that are most cruelly affected by the pieces of glass from the crushed mirror, and thereby Andersen's introductory words gain a strong, ironic – though also witty – nature, since he lets his tale begin with the word "look":

> "Look! Now we'll begin. When we have got to the end of the story we shall know more than we do now."

By means of this brilliant introduction, where the word "Look!" is even in the imperative, the next sentence anticipates the end of the fairy tale: "When we have got to the end of the story we shall know more than we do now", which is true enough – utterly banal, for by then we have of course read the entire story – but also in a particularly sophisticated way, for by then sight – the clear overview and awareness – has returned and conquered both for the child characters of the story and for readers and listeners, who of course identify themselves with Kay and Gerda. And the sentence continues:

> [When the story is done you shall know a great deal more than you do now] because it was a terribly bad hobgoblin, a goblin of the very wickedest sort, it was the "divil" himself!

Already at this early stage the confusion arises that is guaranteed by the magic mirror in the tale: For what are we dealing with? Is it a goblin or the devil? Does the devil belong to the horde of goblins, or is the devil himself the worst of them? If you read the fairy tale instead of listening to it, you find a code that only the reader can grasp. The "divil" is placed in quotation marks, which means that the word should not be taken at face value, but is more of a label. Furthermore, "divil" [Danish: Dævelen] rather than "devil" [Danish: Djævelen] signals popular wisdom and superstition. Before long, the confusion is complete, for now the goblin and the devil are renamed one and the same: "the goblin devil". Parallel with these linguistic codes is launched the story of the magic mirror that distorts everything and turns the world upside-down. Piety causes the mirror to laugh – it shakes and quivers so much with laughter on its way up to God and the angels that it falls out of the goblins' hands and on hitting the earth smashes into thousands of pieces and fragments that turn the heads of all those they come into contact with. Because of the crushed mirror, the earthly scenario is turned into a confused space where doubt prevails as to what is true and what is false. It is in this scenario the narrative perspective is situated and the rest of the story takes place. The world is dazzled by a delusion. We can no longer see. What are we to do? Andersen anticipates yet again, and in masterly fashion, the course of the story via his language, for the final sentence of the first story provides the answer. When the eye can no longer be relied on, another sense must be made use of. The sentence is:

Now we shall hear

By means of this fantastically well-constructed introductory story the stage has been set: the mirror has been crushed and seven years' bad luck are turned into seven stories. The scenario has been laid out: there is a life on earth and there is God's heaven, but there is also something in-between – a supernatural world. For there is no devil, there is a "devil" or a "goblin devil", i.e. a demonic world that is situated between life on earth and the divine. This supernatural world is that of delusions – and it gets in the way of humans and their understanding of true nature and existence.

This scenario comes into force for the main characters of the tale in its second story: that of the little boy and the little girl, Kay and Gerda. They find themselves neither on earth nor in heaven, although in both places at the same time – namely in the small paradise-like roof-garden, high up above the earth and under heaven: "The children held each other by the hand, kissed the roses, looked up at the Lord's bright sunshine, and spoke to it as if the Christ Child were there". And what Andersen wants us to hear is revealed in the second story. It is the song of children, Brorson's hymn: ["Jeg er en Rose i Saron"] "Den yndigste rose er funden", which is repeated time after time. In Andersen it sounds like this:

> Roserne voxe i Dale,
> Der faae vi Barn-Jesus i Tale!

> [Where roses bloom so sweetly in the vale,
> There you will find the Christ Child, without fail.]

Brorson wrote:

> Ach søger de nædrige Stæder
> I Støvet for Frælseren græder
> Saa faar I vor JEsum i Tale,
> Thi Roserne voxer i Dale.[8]

> [Oh, seek the lowliest places,
> Weep for the Saviour in the dust,
> Then you will find Jesus,
> For the roses bloom in the vale]

Brorson was a forgotten writer during the Romantic period in Denmark. His hymns are nowhere to be found in the Evangelical-Lutheran hymn book, and it was actually only in Southern Jutland and in Moravian circles that his hymns had its devotees. He was not at all known in Copenhagen – Grundtvig, for example, asked Rahbek in 1816 if he knew who had actually written this hymn. Andersen, however, knew of him. As early as his poem-cycle *The Twelve Months of the Year* from 1832 we find "The fairest Rose" reproduced in "The Month of November" in three slightly adapted versions, and at the end of the tragic novel *Only a Fiddler*, Christian on his sick-bed reminds Luzie of the hymn by quoting this famous passage. Andersen possibly knew of the hymn via his friend and private tutor Ludvig Christian Müller, who in 1831 included the hymn in his *Selection of Danish Hymns*.

By referring to Brorson's hymn, Andersen makes it clear that the fairy tale "The Snow Queen", despite all its phantasmagoria, has a religious purpose and a Christian message. That Andersen in adapting the hymn makes use of the third and fourth lines of the verse and thus omits mentioning the cathartic force of tears on the path to salvation – which he does mention in his letter to Ingemann – is quite deliberate, for it is precisely weeping that has the decisive role to play in the fairy tale of the Snow Queen, and since tears have the eye and the heart as attributes, the eye and the heart are the essential linguistic factors in the tale. The fairy tale of the Snow Queen is all about seeing and understanding – and about understanding with the heart. In terms of language this purpose is evident in Andersen's way of constructing his story.

Before little Gerda teaches Kay the hymn, however, unrest has disturbed the paradise-like idyll. A winter scene has got in the way, and the grandmother explains that the snowflakes are white bees. They do have a queen, however, who is to be found where the swarm is at its thickest, she tells them. This story excites young Kay, who soon after sees it all for himself. One evening the half-dressed boy looks through a small peephole that he has made with a heated coin in the ice-coated window-panes. Outside, the snowflakes are swarming like bees and alighting on the flower-boxes, where they become thicker and thicker until the Snow Queen appears. This excites the boy. On the one hand he is attracted, on the other repulsed:

> A few snowflakes were falling, and the largest flake of all alighted on the edge of one of the flower boxes. This flake grew bigger and bigger, until at last it turned into a woman, who was dressed in the finest white gauze which looked as if it had been made from millions of star-shaped flakes. She was beautiful and she was graceful, but she was ice-shining, glittering ice. She was alive, for all that, and her eyes sparkled like two bright stars, but in them there was neither rest nor peace. She nodded toward the window and beckoned with her hand. The little boy was frightened ...

This small erotic scene, which might remind one of the story of the birds and the bees, marks an imminent change in the harmony and the course of the story. Summer comes once more, the children sing the hymn and praise the summer: "How wonderful the summer days were, how blessed it was to be outside next to the fresh rose-bushes that never seemed to want to stop flowering". One is almost tempted to say with Faust "Verweile doch! du bist so schön!" But then the idyll is suddenly cut short when "The clock struck five from the great church tower" – one chime for each of the five senses Kay is robbed of when at the same instant he gets the splinters from the magic mirror in his eye and heart.

From that moment his personality changes. He becomes malicious and mocking, and when winter arrives the Snow Queen comes and takes Kay off with her, who is no longer able to say the Lord's Prayer and can only remember his arithmetic tables. The magic world that now seduces him is represented by "The Snow Queen" – the goddess of winter and the cold heart. After this, the stage is left completely to Gerda, and her story, which is dealt with in the rest of the fairy tale, must therefore be considered the main story. We follow the girl through all sorts of trials and tribulations until her mission – to recover Kay – is successfully completed. It is Gerda's persistent, fervent belief that ensures that the story can only have a happy ending.

It is providence that drives little Gerda, and the story can therefore be understood only from a Christian point of view. "The Snow Queen" is no story of personal fate. Against faith, hope and love fate does not stand a chance. In Andersen's universe, determinism must give way to providence. In non-Christian narratives there are, however, stories of personal fate that strikingly resemble "The Snow Queen", namely the fertility myths – and the template on which "The Snow Queen" has been built does not substantially differ from the average fertility myth. The essential difference is precisely that the eternal recurrence of the myth is broken, stretched out, so that in the service of providence it points towards the coming of paradise, Judgment Day, not towards the yearly pulsing cycle of life and death. It would seem as if "The Snow Queen" is a religious version – a "literary myth" – of the fertility myths, so it would seem natural to investigate a version of such a myth in Norse mythology, e.g. the one found in the tale of Balder's death ("Balder's Dream" in the *Edda*). Balder is the son of Odin and Frigg. He is the favourite of the gods, and Frigg enters into a pact with everything living and dead that no one is to hurt Balder. The only thing she does not enter into a pact with is the mistletoe, because it is too young for anyone to demand an oath from it. Loke assumes the form of a woman and elicits the secret of the mistletoe out of Frigg. He then gets Balder's blind brother Høder to shoot the mistletoe at the otherwise invulnerable Balder. And Balder dies.

"'Tis the white bees swarming!" Illustration by Dugald Stewart Walker in *Andersen's Fairy Tales*, Garden City, New York, Doubleday, Page & Company, 1914.

After this, the story of Balder's cremation is told, but also the story of Balder's third brother, Hermod, and how he attempts to bring back Balder from the kingdom of the goddess of death, Hel. Hermod rides

Odin's horse Sleipner over the river Gjal (the Styx of the North), which is the river that divides the world of the living from the dark underworld. Here Hermod finds Balder enthroned. The next day Hermod explains his mission, and Hel promises to release Balder if everything both alive and dead is prepared to weep for him. Hermod rides back to Asgård and relates what the conditions are for Balder's release. Everyone then weeps for Balder, with the exception of Tøk, a giantess. Tøk, it transpires, is one of Loke's many guises. So Balder has to remain with Hel.

The parallels with this myth are the Greek variant about Adonis, the Egyptian about Osiris and the Celtic about Aeddon. They share the common feature of describing the yearly cycle (summer-winter-summer-winter). That the whole world weeps for Balder is of course the poetic image of the steam that rises from cold objects when warmed. Balder (light/heat/summer) is killed by the mistletoe (an evergreen small parasitic plant) via Høder (blindness/the dark) behind whom stands Loke (the evil one/cold/winter). Hermod (who is driven by love/heat/summer) seeks to ensure Balder's release from Hel (the North/cold/winter); the whole world joins in and weeps (thaw/spring-summer), but Loke resists and Hel keeps what is hers (winter once more). That is how the circle eternally recurs. This circuit has its finale in "The Völuspa" – the story in the *Edda* about Ragnarok – for here Balder returns, and with blind Høder as well, to a new world where peace reigns (light and dark in conflict-free coexistence).

If one compares in terms of narrative "The Snow Queen" and the story of Balder in the *Edda*, one will be considerably surprised. This can be illustrated schematically as follows:

1. Division has been sown in the world, but it operates unseen (the goblin devil's crushed mirror/Loke)
2. The dangerous weapon appears to be harmless (fragments of the mirror like gains of sand/the mistletoe). The dangerous weapon is a parasite: It is worth nothing without a host (the mirror fragments as well as and the mistletoe need a host)
3. The loved one is removed from the world of the living (Kay/Balder)
4. He is missed, but only one person has courage enough to find him (Gerda/Hermod). This attempt is made out of love. The act offers no personal gain
5. A supernatural animal aids him (talking swallows, crows, wood pigeons, but in particular the reindeer/Sleipner)
6. The journey goes northward
7. A river is passed (The river outside the city gate/Gjal). This river marks the transition from the natural to the supernatural/the land of the living and the underworld

8. Someone on guard sits by the river, whose task it is to stop living people passing (the good old lady, who knows magic and tries to stop Gerda/Modgun)
9. Gerda arrives at the garden of the Snow Queen. She forces her way through "a whole regiment of snowflakes", the outposts of the Snow Queen/Hermod comes to Hel's fief. He forces Hel's Gate with the aid of Sleipner
10. Gerda enters the hall of the Snow Queen's palace. She finds Kay sitting with the game of ice-cold reason/Hermod enters Hel's hall. Here he finds Balder enthroned
11. Kay is saved by Gerda because she weeps. The riddle of the game of ice-cold reason is solved by tears and hymn-singing and this gives Kay his 'letter of release'/Hermod returns to the land of the living with hope. For there is one solution for Balder's salvation: tears
12. Kay and Gerda can return home from the Queen's palace/Loke ruins hope and the mission fails. Balder does not return home – only Hermod. Hel keeps her own.

If these twelve items are considered, striking similarities will be found between "Balder's Dream" and "The Snow Queen" – except for the last item. But it is precisely here that Christian providence shows its strength – that the world can be changed by faith in the Christ Child. The only significant difference between the two stories is the result of the rescue operation: Hermod fails, while Gerda is successful. Even so, Balder does return in Norse mythology (the *Edda*'s Völuspa). This takes place at Ragnarok, the end of the world in Norse mythology. At both Ragnarok and the Day of Judgment the old world comes to an end, time ceases to exist and there is a transition to the new kingdom where peace and friendliness reign: in "The Snow Queen" Kay has the chance to free himself from the Snow Queen by solving the game of ice-cold reason. The pieces of ice have to be laid out so they form the word "Eternity". Kay does not solve the riddle himself; it is the happy reunion between Kay and Gerda that causes the pieces of ice to form the word. "Eternity" occurs when temporality ceases – in that way the end of life and the world is signalled at the same time as the establishing of a new world-order: what follows after death – the Day of Judgment and Ragnarok. In "The Snow Queen" the motifs in Gerda's piety and Kay's salvation, Balder's death and Ragnarok are elegantly linked. Firstly, via the riddle of "Eternity" already mentioned; secondly, in the final scene of the sixth story, where Gerda fights her way forward to the Snow Queen's palace:

> She ran as fast as ever she could. A whole regiment of snowflakes swirled toward her, but they did not fall from the sky, for there was not a cloud up there, and the Northern Lights were ablaze.

> The flakes skirmished along the ground, and the nearer they came the larger they grew ... They were the Snow Queen's advance guard ... little Gerda said the Lord's Prayer, she could see her breath freezing in front of her mouth, like a cloud of smoke. It grew thicker and thicker, and took the shape of little angels that grew bigger and bigger ... All of them had helmets on their heads and they carried shields and lances in their hands.

Outside the Snow Queen's palace a violent battle is then fought between the queen's "outposts" and those of heaven. Gerda leaves the battlefield and enters the queen's palace. When she and Kay later leave the palace the surroundings have changed: "... the wind died down and the sun shone out ...".

It is the forces of the earth and the "air" ("spirit") that fought in the same way as in the Völuspa. Here the gods and giants (the gods of "sky" and "earth") fought a battle in which practically all of them perish along with the old world. The few surviving and significant figures that hereafter live in the new and better world represent the forces that previously opposed each other. There is now peaceful co-existence. Two humans also enter the new world: Lif and Lifthrase, in the same way as a new Kay and Gerda leave the battlefield.

In "The Snow Queen" it is made clear that God never perishes. On the face of it, there would seem to be an importance difference between Ragnarok and the Day of Judgment, for the highest ase-god – Odin – dies along with the old world. But the difference is only apparent: for Odin – and the Norse gods in general, for that matter – although they represent the forces of good as opposed to the giants, are not heavenly gods. The Norse ase-gods are linked to the qualities of earthly life that are charged with positive value. The creative god does not perish in Ragnarok. N.M. Petersen in his *Norse Mythology* (1869) and Hans Christian Andersen in "The Marsh-King's Daughter" (1857) call this god – very aptly – "the unnamed god"/"the unnameable god".

In "The Marsh-King's Daughter" the theme of Balder's death reappears. And it is interesting that in this tale Andersen also makes use of motif material and expressions from "The Snow Queen". "The Marsh-King's Daughter" concretises the connection of the fairy tale with Norse mythology, as is not the case in "The Snow Queen", and furthermore the poetic image is organised in a more sophisticated way: here it is one and the same person – the girl Helga – who possesses the opposing forces – the double nature.

Helga is the product of a conspiracy. Her mother – the daughter of the Pharaoh, also of "fairy stock" – who comes from the southern part of Egypt, has travelled all the way North to try and find the lotus flower, the medicinal plant that can save her father's life. But she is betrayed by her retinue: they tear her swan's guise to pieces "so the feathers whirled around like a flurry of snow", as it says in the tale. The mother sinks into the marsh down to the marsh-king – he is kindly disposed towards her – she has a daughter by him: Helga on the lotus flower.

In this way, the negatively charged earth-underworld principle is united with the positively charged heavenly principle in little Helga, who thus has a double nature: during the daytime she has a beautiful human appearance, but an ugly, obdurate nature; at night she has the appearance of an ugly frog, but is good-natured. There is then a blend of the Kay and Gerda characters, but one that is linked to a healing principle, the Lotus Flower – in the same way as the Rose is such a principle in "The Snow Queen". Throughout the tale we follow Helga's contending nature during the day and her sorrowfully repenting nature at night. Her entire existence lies in the hands of the Viking woman, who believes in her salvation from the magic spell. In the Viking woman we have the element of providence that Gerda possesses in "The Snow Queen". But in "The Marsh-King's Daughter" the element of providence is also concretised in the young Christian priest who makes his decisive entry into the story. Via his faith and self-sacrificing demonstration of Christian love the lotus comes into flower, the petals unfold to the rays of the sun: the frog's skin falls off Helga and she stands there as her innermost, true being, posing as beauty and love for the reader of the fairy tale. In the same way, the ice-shell breaks off Kay in "The Snow Queen" when he is confronted with Gerda's supreme love.

Christian love is of crucial importance in "The Marsh-King's Daughter", but Helga too, like the lotus flower, is the healing element for the apparently dead Pharaoh as well as the saving element for the mother trapped in the marsh, who – like Kay – is "apparently dead" – reckoned by all non-believers to be dead. Helga and her mother return to Egypt [travel south] to their grandfather [cf. the grandmother in "The Snow Queen"], who revives. And now the whole dramatic story seems, as in "The Snow Queen", to have been like a "long, heavy dream".

The two fairy tales are basically variants of each other. However, in "The Marsh-King's Daughter", the antagonistic forces are simply embedded in double natures and portioned out in a clever physical and mental mosaic. So it is interesting that the reader of "The Marsh-King's Daughter" is presented via the Viking woman with the thematic starting point of the story. For the Viking woman has a prophetic dream while Helga's salvation is being won:

> ... darkness reigned outside. A storm blew up ... Beside the terror-stricken dreamer, little Helga seemed to crouch on the floor, in the ugly frog's shape. She shuddered, and crept close to her foster mother ... The air resounded with the clashing of swords and clubs, and the rattle of arrows like a hailstorm upon the roof. The hour had come when heaven and earth would perish, the stars would fall, and everything be swallowed up by Surtur's sea of fire. Yet she knew there would be a new heaven and a new earth ... Then the god whose name could not yet be spoken would reign at last, and to him would come Balder, so mild and loving, raised up from the kingdom of the dead.

Here what had been left out of "The Snow Queen" is mentioned – the basic motif. In "The Marsh-King's Daughter" the statement is legitimate because the action is fixed in time – it actually takes place during the Viking Age. Andersen is well aware of "the unnameable god", and so his choice of words reveal the insight that the mythological gods of the North are not the creators of the world, but gods in the world.

The Educational Journey

"The Snow Queen" also becomes interesting bearing Andersen's dissertation in mind: for what Andersen is describing is a journey that is one of inner development and that ends in an understanding:

> Kay and Gerda looked into each other's eyes, and at last they understood the meaning of their old hymn.

This educational journey is, so to speak, that of humanity – from a spontaneous but not expressed monotheism, via a supernatural polytheism where all phenomena contain a mystery that transcends their objective surface, finally arriving at a concluding monotheism – God's omnipresence and man's link to God via providence and purity of heart.

At the beginning of the tale, spontaneous but unreflecting monotheistic religiosity is illustrated: the children sit beneath the triumphal arch of the blessed rose trees and look into "God's bright sunshine". With the splinter from the mirror – and thereby the hegemony of reason – a journey starts where the children, so to speak, founder in a polytheistic universe (but a false one, it should be noted), where every nook and cranny seems to have autonomous divinity. And the journey ends with the conscious embracing of Christianity.

As far as Kay is concerned, the polytheistic period begins with the entry of the splinter into his eye. This gives him "double vision" – his view of the world is characterised by credible delusion and a lack of any deep understanding, as I have described above.

Kay is fascinated by the snowflake pattern, which, like his own vision, reflects uniformity in kaleidoscopic fashion. Kay is dazzled by the ice-cold accuracy; he binds himself to what is earthly, but also to the cold and the static. His connection to the Snow Queen becomes the poetic expression of this alliance. What can disturb Kay's fascination is changeability – love and warmth and what points towards an order that does not immediately announce its presence in physical nature – God's order. Kay mentions it himself:

> "Now look through the glass," he told Gerda. Each snowflake seemed much larger, and looked like a magnificent flower or a ten-pointed star. It was marvellous to look at.
> "Look, how artistic!" said Kay. "They are much more interesting to look at than real flowers, for they are absolutely perfect. There isn't a flaw in them, until they start melting."

The danger to this unreal accuracy is the influence of heat: it will be able to melt the snowflakes. Kay's psyche is thus bound up with winter, the cold, the Snow Queen and the snowflake, whereas Gerda's is bound up with summer, heat, the heavenly, love and the rose.

Kay, now bewitched, resists then the phenomena and the established symbols of history that do not reflect an "earthly" logic but point beyond the earthly towards the heavenly order. He becomes hostile towards Gerda's warm-heartedness and mockingly imitates – as if himself was the magic mirror – the grandmother and people in the street. And the roses – the metaphorical link between the earthly and the heavenly – rouses his loathing:

> "Ugh! that rose is all worm-eaten. And look, this one is crooked. And these roses, they are just as ugly as they can be. They look like the boxes they grow in." He gave the boxes a kick, and broke off both of the roses.

Kay's insight into the world has stiffened and the alliance with the Snow Queen is described shortly after, when he attaches his sledge to hers and is transported far away from the town square to her palace.

As far as Gerda is concerned, the lack of insight expresses itself as the polytheism that accompanies her on her search for Kay. The surroundings acquire supernatural powers: swallows, crows, wood pigeons, reindeer, sun and flowers can all communicate with her. Apart from the sorceress and the women with magic powers in Finland, the natural surroundings also acquire supernatural status. She finds herself in a cherry orchard where eternal summer reigns. Despite the polytheistic universe in which Gerda finds herself during her search for Kay, elements exist that describe a greater power than others: the sun and the rose. It is the sun that first speaks and that tells Gerda Kay is probably not dead. It is the rose missing from the cherry garden that causes Gerda to stay there. But the roses spring up, stimulated by Gerda's tears, and like the sun they can tell her that Kay is not dead. This makes the rose a significant element once again, for the other flowers are only able to tell their own stories – they are like the mirror in the sense that they demonstrate vanity, self-centredness and the enclosed, fathomless abyss.

Gerda is linked to the sun and roses. Her face is described as a rose, she is led by the sun and the blessed sunshine. Gerda's dreams are blessed and the dreams fly to her like God's small angels. Something similar occurs in the sixth story, where her Lord's Prayer breath materialises as angels. The coach she receives from the prince and princess in the fourth story also gleams "like bright sunshine".

Even though Kay and Gerda find themselves in a polytheistic universe, there is a difference between them. Kay is the static one, driven by simple logic, whereas Gerda is the dynamic one, driven by irrational religious providence. Also, Kay is the one who has broken the connection with the heavenly, whereas Gerda is driven by this connection.

"I can give her no greater power than she possesses already: don't you see how great that is?" Illustration by Katharine Beverley and Elizabeth Ellender in The Snow Queen, E.P. Dutton & Co., Inc., New York City, 1929.

Hans Christian Andersen had a thorough knowledge of Norse mythology. In 1830, he presented his specialised knowledge in a dissertation with which he – unsuccessfully – attempted to win the university's aesthetics prize.[9] Despite this, the writer's excellent dissertation gives us an interesting impression of how he interpreted the mythological material. His point was that humanity in its "childhood" had a conception of one god and was thus monotheistic in orientation. This conception, with the development of the human mind and the recognition of natural forces, was replaced by polytheism, in which divinity was ascribed to every niche in the natural scenario. As the mind matured and insight and knowledge were gained into the nature, cause and interrelationships of physical phenomena, polytheism – the demonisation of existence – was once more replaced by monotheism, a reflective monotheism – this thought can be recognised from Heinrich Steffens' romantic philosophy. According to Andersen, the religious conceptions are directly proportional to cultural evolution and the insight into the laws of natural forces. Superstition and paganism describe a colourful but uneducated insight.

In "The Snow Queen" it is possible to rediscover Andersen's theory of cultural evolution. The two children, Kay and Gerda, are presented at the beginning of the tale as innocent beings that live in a non-reflective monotheism. The magic mirror destroys this idyll. The two human beings now enter into a world that is demonised, one where every aspect of nature acquires supernatural qualities (polytheism). It is not until the Christian message has been fervently accepted that this demonised existence disappears "like a heavy dream". It is with a matured mind and reason that superstition loses its hold and the Christian message can be accepted. The ending of "The Snow Queen" underlines this:

> Grandmother sat in God's good sunshine, reading to them from her Bible: "Except ye become as little children, ye shall not enter into the Kingdom of Heaven."
> Kay and Gerda looked into each other's eyes, and at last they understood the meaning of their old hymn:
>
> *"Where roses bloom so sweetly in the vale,*
> *There shall you find the Christ Child, without fail."*

And they sat there, grown-up, but children, still children at heart. And it was summer, warm, glorious summer.

Andersen writes the following about his childhood in *The Fairy Tale of My Life*: " ... I listened to everything superstition told me on all sides – for me it ranked alongside the holiest belief ... I grew up pious and superstitious ... I ... was so full of superstition and lived in the power of fantasy." When in 1832 the writer, his mind now mature, once again saw the places where he had played as a child, it is hardly surprising that the world of childhood seemed to him to be a heavy dream. The demonised world he had lived in as a child had now completely disappeared – or rather: Andersen, with his matured reason and insight was no longer able to recall the mental space in which he had moved as a child, considering it simply as "a world where, in another incarnation and under other conditions I had lived and played". In the same way as Kay and Gerda noticed "that they had become grown-up persons" when they returned and entered the door to the land of their childhood, Andersen probably also noticed that he had become grown-up in the same way when in 1832 he saw the town of his birth. With "The Snow Queen", Andersen shaped and formulated this experience; he was able to install certain childhood memories in his literary universe, but most important of all, his acquired knowledge, his understanding, insight and Christian belief. In "The Snow Queen", this awareness grows with every single word of the narrative until the reader, just like Kay and Gerda, finally understands the words of the hymn-writer. This is what the writer promised us when he opened his tale with the words: "When the story is done you shall know a great deal more than you do now."

Notes

1 H.C. Andersen: *Mit Livs Eventyr*, ed. H. Topsøe-Jensen, Gyldendalske Boghandel, Nordisk Forlag, København 1951, p. 28.
2 H.C. Andersen: *Kun en Spillemand*, ed. Ole Jacobsen, H. Topsøe-Jensen, Det Danske Sprog- og Litteraturselskab, Gyldendal 1944, p. 10.
3 *H.C. Andersen og Henriette Wulff. En Brevveksling*, ed. H. Topsøe-Jensen, vol. I: 1826-1848, Flensteds Forlag, Odense 1959, p. 79.
4. *H.C. Andersens Levnedsbog*, ed. H. Topsøe-Jensen, Det Schønbergske Forlag, København 1962, p. 30.
5. Nicolaj Bøgh: "Fra H.C. Andersens Barndoms- og Ungdomsliv" in *Personalhistorisk Tidsskrift*, 5. rk., II, p. 62.
6. H.C. Andersen: *Mit Livs Eventyr*, ed. H. Topsøe-Jensen, Gyldendalske Boghandel, Nordisk Forlag, København 1951, p. 40-41.
7. *H.C. Andersens brevveksling med Lucie og B.S. Ingemann*, ed. Kirsten Dreyer, vil. I: 1820-1853, Museum Tusculanum, København 1997, p. 191.
8. H.A. Brorson: Nogle Jule-Psalmer Gud til Ære Og Christne-Siæle i sær siin elskelige Meenighed til Opmuntring Til den forestaaende Glædelige Jule-Fest Eenfoldig og i Hast sammenskrevne, Tundern 1732, p. 20.
9. Ejnar Stig Askgaard: "En akademisk borger" in *Anderseniana* 2000, p. 79-90, followed by transscription of H.C. Andersen: "At udvikle de græske og nordi-

ske Mythers Forskjellighed i Lighederne og deres Overeenskomst i Forskjellighederne" [1830], pp. 91-124.

The texts are translated by John Irons, fairy tale translations by Jean Hersholt/ John Irons

The Toll of Andersen's Bell – From Neo-Platonism to New Age – Ways of Understanding and Interpreting the Great Writer's Spirituality

Vera Gancheva

Hans Christian Andersen's bicentenary is an event of great significance not only because of the wide range of opportunities it affords for a new approach to, and a reassessment of, some important and surprisingly modern aspects of his work and personality, but also because it has become an integral part of the world's global cultural *poly-logue*. Such a *poly-logue* meaning a discourse encompassing a wide communicative space presupposing and creating active contacts among all parties in it is no modern phenomenon at all; since time immemorial it has been generated by the peoples' necessity to evolve in an environment of interaction, accomplished at some points in human history without the mediation of mass communication and modern technologies as it is nowadays, but no less real for that. For millennia, the naturally born body of world mythology, or "man's first mental dictionary", as Italian historian and philosopher Giambattista Vico (1668-1744) calls it, has represented an open universe, filled with countless gods and heroes. The similarity in terms of plots, characters and attributes between the myths of diverse and usually remote peoples is not as surprising as it might seem. In fact, it confirms the truth that mankind's development could be seen as the evolution of a certain type of communication. It testifies to mankind's intrinsic aspiration for another world; a world of high ethical and spiritual values; a world at many removes above the quotidian; a world transcendental in relation to the one we inhabit. Mircea Eliade (1907-86), an eminent scholar of world religions, refers to this world as an *absolute reality*. According to Eliade, it is the norms and values of this reality that lead human existence, lending the quality of meaning to it and affording the key to man's spiritual potential. It helps us formulate quite a few truths about man, about human beings but in order to grasp these truths, we ought to penetrate the sacral dimensions of the myth, which convey its allegorical and symbolic message. The decoding of the latter could draw upon a particular type of knowledge, but it could also be based on an insight into the creative power of art, which operates with its own language, structure, imagery, and rhythm.

It appears that Andersen's works, both in their entirety and each of them in particular, are similar to mythology in terms of their impact. They are obviously intransient and resist unequivocally rational definition. Andersen's texts possess a quality comparable to magic, to a three-stage initiation; an introduction of those in touch with them into the secrets of sacred wisdom and the art of mental and psychological maturation. There is no denying that Andersen's works, especially his fairy-tales, provide their readers, regardless of the age, nationality or epoch they live in, with a profound knowledge of human nature; deep knowledge about man's fusion with the *universum*, with countless and dynamic sets of entities, phenomena, ideas, events and processes, brought together in a non-geocentric unity. Man's belonging to this unity means a chance of evolution beyond the limitations of his earthly nature. It also involves great responsibility, both individual and collective. In Andersen's work, one can clearly see the *mythological tradition*, instituted and followed for centuries by distinguished representatives of world literature such as Dante, Shakespeare, Goethe, Melville, Joyce, Kafka, T.S. Eliot, Thomas Mann, Tolkien, Borges, the list being, of course, far from exhaustive. For all these writers and thinkers mythology is not only a cultural heritage but also a poetics and a philosophy. It is far from being a simple matrix for them or even for the most eminent creators of the cyber-culture today – the intellectual gurus of the rising World Wide Web generation whose sacral "cosmic allegories" and techno-utopias should also be set within the boundless "Realm of the Spirit", *Aandsriget*, into which Andersen initiates us in his first book, entitled *Youthful Attempts* (*Ungdoms Forsøg,* 1822), and signed with the pseudonym William Christian Walter wedging his own name between the names of two great writers – Shakespeare and Scott – who have reaffirmed with their work the immortality of mythology as a source of artistic insight. As early as that stage, the young author, hardly 17 years of age, transports the reader into an unusual world, where the borderline between dream and reality is effaced. The folklore of Funen encircles within its frame pictures of the island's remote past, legendary images and events, ancient cults. The latter are endowed with the quality of universal validity owing to the conscious use of the unconscious, triggered by the contact with *magna mater* – Nature as a universal mother; but also Nature as supreme reason. The validity of the message is also due to the transfer of motifs and experiences from myths into the context of the quotidian and vice versa. It is quite easy to detect the influence of the three great figures of Danish literature at that time – Adam Oehlenschläger, Jens Baggesen, and Bernhard Severin Ingemann. Andersen is definitely impresssed by the three writers' aspiration towards fusion between the real and the ideal; towards recreation of the oneness in the nexus between idea, man and phenomenon. This set of ideas bears the imprint of Neo-Platonism, as well as of Friedrich Schelling's conception of Nature as a visible "idea of organic entity", *organismetanken*, directed to the co-ordination of everything in existence. Andersen, as we shall see later, evolves these ideas into a system of thought, which has a mythic-mystical tint and links to Nature Philosophy. His conceptual framework projects in a peculiar way the system put forward by physicist Hans Christian Ørsted (1777-1851), not only a scientist who discovered electromagnetism but also a Romantic philosopher well known for his lectures on cosmology, in his book *The Spirit in Nature* (1850). The book gives Andersen an impetus towards an even more active search for a really thorough synthesis between art, myth, religion and science. This synthesis could be perceived as a supreme stage in the development of individual and collective consciousness, a synthesis intensifying man's creative potential, the aesthetics of the future and enhancing also the spiritualizing of all natural laws into laws of intuition and thought (Schelling).

In "The Bell" ("Klokken", 1845*)*, for instance, we can detect a pronounced echo of the Romantics' ecstatic reverence for Nature, which is seen as the epitome of universal truth and eternal harmony; their veneration for the universal almighty spirit which permeates Nature, regulating and adding meaning to its countless forms, adding meaning to life itself. These are ideas to which Ørsted attached the concretion of a theory applying the method of a scientist and the skill of the researcher. In fact, it would be tempting to juxtapose Ørsted and another eminent physicist, our contemporary, Fritjof Capra (b. 1939) whose parallels between science and theology, his reflections on man and Nature, on energy and matter, on the non-linear dependences in originating and solving global problems, have contributed to shaping the radically new outlook of a few generations of intellectuals (as well as of a broader public) in the second half of the 20th century. His ideas have ushered in a new stage in the extension of the philosophical and social scope of science, opening up unexpected alternatives and horizons.

I am convinced that those who have read Andersen's tales, even at a tender age, have become aware, in a profound and multifaceted way, of the direct and indirect links in the nexus *evolution-cosmos-man*. These links lie at the core of the principles put forward and advocated by Capra, Prigozhin, Hawking and other scientific luminaries, principles considered no less esoteric than myth, which the above mentioned scientists (and many others) cite as a possible basis for their researches and observations.

However, in "The Drop of Water" ("Vanddraaben", 1848), a fantastic story, expressly devoted to Ørsted, the friend and admirer, who was the first to fully believe in the writer's genius, Andersen adds some apocalyptic overtones to his (Ørsted's) otherwise optimistic thesis on the unity of man, spirit, and Nature. He accurately identifies the danger stemming from man's inability to achieve and preserve his unity with the natural and the spiritual. One manifestation of this danger is urbanization, which is synonymous with man's violation of original harmony. We possess the means of our own survival, Andersen suggests. He recommends that hardship and anxiety be overcome with faith in the universal unity of which man constitutes a part. This faith should be based, following the example of Nature, on love and awareness of the divine.

The popular Danish motto "What is outwardly lost, should be inwardly regained", which charged the Danish nation with courage and confidence in its own powers in the difficult decades of the 19th century, assumes in Andersen's works the form of an artistic principle. This is manifested, for example, in the technique drawing upon the metamorphoses of Nature, whose order determines the order of the social world. For Andersen, social reality is horizontal, responsive to the mobility, which he himself, as it were, had mastered. In his tales we find a mostly relative hierarchy ("The Bell" even suggests opportunities for a social idyll, natural and attainable within the temple of the universe). This hierarchy is impartial and static, since it corresponds to the order established in Nature – an eternal order manifested in the sea, the sun and all powers symbolizing the absolute essence of the universe and its values, its comforting immutability. The sanctioning powers that Nature wields are the wind and water, and when they fuse into snow, cold and ice, this is painful and destructive, but not overwhelmingly so, because a heartfelt religious song can stop the avalanches of the Snow Queen; in fact, man can truly be the lord of Nature, as stated in the wonderful essay "The Muse of the New Century" ("Det nye Aarhundredes Musa", 1861*)*. This essay testifies to some deviation from the Romantic cult of Nature as the locus of a sublime spirit and providence, as an endless source of imagination and inspiration. It is important to note, however, that this tendency should not be seen as Andersen's deviation from transcendental idealism as an outlook and an aesthetic platform.

The warning flags in "The Drop of Water", as well as in many others of Andersen's tales and stories, are raised more than a century before the publication in 1962 of Rachel Carson's book *Silent Spring*. Although it would be far-fetched to describe Andersen as an ecologically minded writer in the modern sense of the word, we should be aware of his ambivalent attitude to scientific and technological progress, which was picking up momentum at the time when he lived. His enthusiastic response to technological developments does not prevent him from mistrusting utilitarianism and industrialization and its attending reforms. Andersen interprets and comments on the realities of the day with a peculiar form of mysticism. He fervently advocates his belief in the immortality of the soul, which adds a metaphysical dimension to progress. Progress seems to be provocative to man, but at the same time it gives him the confidence of the lord of Nature, although attended by the sense of doubt, guilt and even doom.

Andersen's unorthodox religious thought subdues this pessimism and attracts readers with a combination of mysticism and realism, paganism and Christianity, religious humbleness and triumphant outbursts of elation over people's almightiness. Almightiness provided by modern technology, which opens up new horizons, affords opportunities for contact with other worlds, and makes possible a victory over the irreversibility of time (as in the myth).

In "The Great Sea Serpent" ("Den store Søslange", 1871) for example, the telegraph cable, running along the sea bed to connect Europe and America, is likened to a huge serpent girdling the earth, or to be more accurate, the human world. In ancient Scandinavian mythology, this is Midgårdsormen, one of the monsters hostile to the gods of the Scandinavian pantheon and one of the most terrifying fighters against them in the last struggle of Ragnarok. Such ambivalence, which from a certain perspective, seems to be part of the game of reducing (and in highest degree) the distance between writer and reader, is interpreted by some scholars as a manifestation of the collisions in Andersen's inner world; a manifestation of the complexity of his personality expressed also in the inclination towards mixing reality and myth, the exciting and the scary.

At the same time, it is worth noting that over the last 150 years a number of revolutionary scientific and technological inventions, for all their utilitarian value and undeniable materiality, have trained people to communicate with, as it were, non-existent partners, to leave the zone of the real, to see and hear the occupants of a "ghostly beyond". The 19th century marked the beginning of a restructuring of society into a series of institutions abstract for the average individual and organs of power, with which immediate contact is unthinkable. Telegraphic transmission of messages and all types of information, telephone connections, which squeezed the whole planet into their network, the boom of radio programs after World War I and of TV shows after World War II, radically transformed the cultural environment, both in terms of quantity and quality. This transformation should be seen as a cutting off from physical space, which until then used to be the arena of all political, social, economic and artistic processes together with all facts and sets of actions or events, originating from and determining them. Of course, today we should add to the list cell phone messages, emails, these hallucinogenic 3-dimensional phantoms of virtual space, which travel at the speed of light along the so-called *Information Superhighway*. Like Andersen's serpent-cable, they seem to have emerged from a cosmogonic (or eschatological) myth oddly enough stripped of narrative and embedded in modernized models of identification through them.

The French philosopher, theorist of culture and historian Michel Foucault (1926-84) speaks about dissociation of the subject under the pressure of empirical circumstances. He suggests that there has been a change in the subject's status and his location in terms of the real and the imaginary. This change has been brought about by *panopticism*, i.e. the ubiquitously activated order of supervision, the original intention being to alter people's habits and thinking in accordance with the exigencies of a new age. Subsequently, however, the new order has become identical to a distorted application of the otherwise rational ideology of social organization and discipline. Under this new order, the things seen are opposed to the things said and done. Continual total supervision has become synonymous to patronage and pressure, to brutal authoritarianism oppressing the masses. "An archeologist of humanitarian culture", as he also dubs himself, Foucault still reflects on a social environment verging on the technotronic order, while the evolution of today transcends the scope of writing/écriture and the visual and acoustic *traces* left by us in its space build up a particular culture and outlook, quite different from the then dominant ones.

Another distinguished French philosopher, Jacques Derrida (1930-2004), has rooted his reflections in a situation characterized by an *intensification of the spectral*, according to his own formulation. This involves the past being infiltrated into the present in a way that makes the future predictable, or downright visible. However, the future still remains ghostly, to no lesser degree than what has already happened or what is happening. As far as modern technologies are concerned, according to Derrida, they expand and enhance the power of phantom appearances; they consolidate this power with their miraculous achievements and almost esoteric effects. If spectrality means "the regard that watches me without responding to my regard", then this concept signifies (from both a philosophical and historical perspective) a *trace* in the sense of non-presence; the non-presence of the thing that is not there but still exists in its own dimension, as Derrida suggests. Along with a number of writers (Balzac, Twain, Gorky, Dickens, Proust, Kafka, Huxley, Gibson) and literary theorists, Derrida contributes to consolidating the view that technological progress generates a world which is increasingly created and re-created by traces, by signs and non-presence, by allegories and analogies. To such a degree that a body or an object, either physical or imaginary, does not necessarily serve as a confirmation of reality. Instead, it confirms the *metaphysics of absence.*

In other words, this is a universe characterized by its vacuum of ideas and emotions. Andersen's works fill this vacuum with humour and imagination, transformed by the great writer into a means of self-protection for human beings also in our epoch. Their author's humour and imagination serve as a shield against the invasion of shadows, those inevitable simulacra of reason, which let irrationality take possession of reason's realm; a shield against our becoming humanoids, albeit of flesh and blood. The artistically shaped and philosophically conveyed conviction that only spirituality can bring redemption and "ontological safety" is yet another explanation of the never-ending appeal of Andersen's works. In them, through a "synergetic" amalgamation of fiction and reality, he objectifies the otherwise subjective discourse typical of literature. In fact, he assumes control over the literary by using the power of the direct, pre-literary impact, typical of ancient Icelandic sagas or pre-historical myths. Andersen subjects the literary to his imagination, finding a perfect material expression for the idea that childhood is a gravitational centre of all existence.

He advocates this idea as a supreme moral and aesthetic norm. Not a binding norm, but one that stems from the perception of the ultimate unity of spirit and Nature, life and universe, miracle and triviality.

There is the popular image of Andersen as a writer who can spin a good tale; the image of a man of humble origin with a number of inhibitions; the image of an eccentric personality which fits his undoubted genius; the image of a man who has achieved public recognition but has failed in his private romantic relationships. All these stereotypical constructs might be partly accurate but they can hardly account for the powerful and lasting effect of his work on both adults and children, whose attitudes have been shaped by different historical (and geographical) circumstances. By the way, it is worth noting that the age we live in – a crucial and complex age of upheavals – is in many respects similar to the age which coincides with the great writer's physical existence. I mean his *physical* existence because spiritually he spans centuries. He has adopted, both intuitively and intellectually, the idea of the *correspondences*, the links between ideas, phenomena and human beings, of a common spirit, *en fælles ånd*, and the unity of all origins in Nature. These ideas are attended by his conviction that human existence is only a link of the *Great Chain of Being*; that it is part of a universal organism, and that humans have been assigned the mission to work, within this organism, towards their own and its improvement and are bound to lend harmony to their immediate surroundings.

In fact, Andersen's ideas are reminiscent of the rich, palette-like outlook of Neo-Platonism, a philosophical and aesthetic movement which contains almost a millennium of thought. Multifaceted and definitely human-oriented, this movement combines three types of rationalism: the religious, the esoteric and the scientific. The combination makes for a system allowing new impulses and ideas, which particularly appealed to the Romantics, as they, like Renaissance thinkers, aspired to achieving a universal worldview. A worldview that combines metaphysics (ontology) with crucial questions concerning existence, knowledge, experience, art. In its original form, as designed and developed by Plotinus in the 3rd century A.D., Neo-Platonism is an objective idealist system, putting forward a peculiar type of *panpsychism*, according to which the soul of the cosmos is like a sea. The natural world is immersed in this sea, and the body is within the soul.

Plato's *Nature Philosophy* and the impact of Pythagorean teachings about the cosmos in his dialogue *Timaeus* attracted the interest of

Renaissance thinkers and artists. They were also attracted by the orientation of the individual towards liberation from an enslaving sensitivity; towards introspection and ecstasy as a means of achieving spirituality and reaching for supernatural dimensions. In the Renaissance, Plato's ideas were assimilated through the mediation of Augustine and the mystics from the School of Chartres, who laid the foundations of Europe's natural sciences, and introduced concepts like Natura, Genius, Poesia. In all their doctrines they highlighted their faith in the immortality of the soul (which by the way is not mentioned in the Bible, nor is it a subject for mediaeval theologians). Also, Neo-Platonists advocated their view that the soul's function is to fuse *the situated above and the situated below in creation*, as well as the belief that love is the power guiding and directing the soul. Their ambition was to create a universal philosophy and a universal language, which would express the subtlest shades of human thought and discourse; a language that would be beautiful and gratifying to people all over the world. Some Neo-Platonists went even further than that and suggested the possible unification of all world religions.

There could be no more convincing artistic incarnation of such Neo-Platonic ideas than Andersen's tales, where they vibrate in the rhythm of the beautiful; where we are confronted with the pantheistic view that God is ubiquitous; where we are enlightened by the belief that death is no ending at all – instead, it is a new beginning. Andersen's tales suggest that life is not a biologically determined process but a road leading further and further up. Life is also an inexhaustible treasury of miracles. Faith abolishes sorrow and transforms it into bliss, into the joy of existence, and amazement at the balance of forces in it. All these messages are conveyed in an exquisite language, accessible to all. A language as intelligible as magic, as graspable as love, no matter how inept the translation might be. (By the way, it is well known that Andersen's works are considered to be among the texts that are most difficult to translate in European literature.)

Neo-Platonism does not preach a doctrine. Instead, it represents a conglomerate of ideas, based on extensive experience and a quest for the spiritual, spanning from Antiquity, ideas combined with views that have taken shape in the course of the progress of culture and science over the centuries. Neo-Platonism has contributed to building up the radically new worldview and intellectual-emotional balance of Europeans. It has offered an enriched and tolerant set of values and has also created the corresponding vision of an individual endowed with a powerful and sophisticated mind; an individual of multiple interests and a peculiar sensibility; an individual thirsty for knowledge; an individual who has gained the insight of the erudite into many fields.

The concept of Platonic love, for example, introduced by Marsilio Ficino, one of the most eminent representatives of the Neo-Platonic School, has become emblematic in the European social, ethical, and cultural tradition. It has come to be associated with the aspiration to an ennobling spiritual friendship, based on a shared attraction to purity, truth, and fusion with God. Without being quite specific on the issue of its connection to sexual intercourse, Marsilio Ficino's theory has changed our perception of human relationships, extending their scope beyond the confines of eroticism and bi-sexuality. It has had an enormous impact on literature and art, especially in the Age of Romanticism (1790-1840). For the Romantics, Platonic love implies sublimity and an insight into the mysteries of being and the essence of its meaning. This insight is reminiscent of initiation where love is the other face of death, and the only power that can redeem us from it.

The concept has also reverberated in science, especially in some more philosophically oriented quarters. This tendency is manifested, for instance, in Ørsted's already mentioned book *The Spirit in Nature*, whose title in itself suggests a definition of the author's holistic view about the absolute integrity of universal being. This view is complemented by the optimistic belief that contrasts and contradictions are not insurmountable; that they can merge into a unified, all-encompassing principle of life.

The androgynous personifies the integration of two opposites, as we know from Antiquity, and from some works of, say, Goethe, Almqvist, Andersen, Balzac, Gautier, among many other great writers. For them, this peculiarity is a prerequisite for genius. Søren Kierkegaard (1813-55) and Georg Brandes (1842-1927) have positively identified such ambivalence in Andersen. The former discusses it in a sarcastic vein. The latter, however, sticks to a benevolent and analytical tone, pointing out that as an artist Andersen combines the best aspects of the psychological setup and the abilities of both male and female, which lends a unique quality to his talent of a fairy-tale writer, because children are not aware of distinctions between the two sexes, and tend to perceive people as such, rather than as representative of a particular sex.

Novels, plays, poems, short stories, travelogues, diaries – all these genres are part of Andersen's impressive legacy, but it is universally recognized that they are not nearly as popular and charming as his fairy-tales, which have contributed to the spiritual education and development of millions of people over the last two centuries. Kierkegaard's reproach that Andersen lacks philosophical depth and originality is hardly justifiable, given the fact that while it might not be theoretically oriented, even today his work expands the mental horizons of its readers, irrespective of their age. It has a transformational impact; it makes its readers acutely responsive to the wisdom and morality it communicates; it tunes its readers' spirit in the key of emotions, but also in the key of ideas; it makes its readers part of a solid century-long tradition in world civilization; it initiates them into the realm of knowledge through feeling, which is as esoteric as it is simple, quotidian, and consequently comprehensible and useful for all. A spontaneous, organic mystic, rather than a well schooled theorist, Andersen, as it were, volunteers to serve as our guide to Jacob's ladder, which reaches as far above as the sky, where we can also end up charged with divine energy if we choose to follow him upwards. On account of his magnetism as a storyteller some compare him to St Francis of Assisi. Another great Scandinavian writer, the Swede August Strindberg (1849-1912), likens him to Orpheus and aligns him with his teachers, Schiller and Goethe, Victor Hugo and Charles Dickens and the French occultist Sar Péladan (1858-1918).

Cosmopolitan by nature, a cosmologist by vocation, Andersen remains fundamentally bound up with his northern motherland; he poeticizes its folklore and its people's peculiar worldview; he indicates the dramatic intensity and the specific colour of a unique artistic heritage, attaching universal validity to it and charging it with fresh energy. Actually, according to Carl Gustav Jung (1875-1961) this is what the role of a myth in world culture amounts to. Andersen uses his artistic talent to demonstrate how significant the particle is for the whole, how significant every individual is for humanity. His genius is typically Scandinavian – it transforms the negative aspects of life into positive energy, and sets for itself a pragmatic purpose, which it then pursues with persistence and achieves with determination. This achievement is equal to a feat, whose dimensions do not necessarily look epic to the layman's eye. Superficially, Andersen bears no resemblance to the belligerent, bizarre and taciturn heroes of the Poetic Edda for instance – Odin's offspring or "protégés" who have sensed the sweet flavour of victory and the bitterness of defeat. As we know, Romanticism rediscovers these heroic figures and makes them supernaturally and, as it were, ultimately invincible. No matter how different Andersen might be from these heroes, his complex life, filled with suffering and battles, seems like the projection of a saga or a lay about some of them. Because, albeit by different means and in a different age, Andersen also fought his fights and conquered the world.

In fact, some say that Andersen and Freud are the first to have opened wide the secret door to the chamber of childhood, which we slam closed (supposedly forever) once we leave its space. The writer performs this through the key of symbols; the neurologist uses the key of science. Of course, Andersen was not aware of the work of Freud and Jung, but his achievement as a psychologist is comparable to the achievement of these psychoanalysts and psychiatrists, philosophers of culture, who studied its processes as well as the structure of personality. Although he was no theorist or practicing researcher, Andersen's merit consists in the fact that with his works he achieves a therapeutic effect by means of a peculiar type of *psycho-synthesis*. He penetrates deep into the subconscious; he cleanses it and cathartically washes away all those impure sediments of reality; he cures it of its traumas; he helps it bring to light and make use of universal and individual archetypes; he goes into the analogies between these archetypes and the phenomena they generate; he interprets and suggests their symbolic meanings.

According to the Danish critic Jens Andersen (b. 1955), whose two-volume biography (2003) of the writer has deservedly received public recognition, there are two channels (or more exactly, corridors) that could help us reach the core of Andersen's fairy-tale world: the first one is that of the royal-court or Biedermeirian bourgeois *salon*, and the second one is that of the *children's room*. I would add a third channel, which binds Andersen's work with the traditions of European *mysticism*; with the hermetic-magic worldview, combined with the visions of Romanticism; a worldview that draws upon the legacy of the East; a worldview based on humanistic and theological priorities; a worldview that has enriched literature and art with ideas, imagery, and allegorical constructs, receiving in return its "legitimacy" as a philosophic and aesthetic trend. The evolution of this worldview over the centuries reflects also the respective stages of the evolution of mankind, and follows the direction of liberation from the confining etymology of its denomination – from the Greek word μυστικός (mysterious, enigmatic, hidden).

And if we assume that the contemporary Danish writer Stig Dalager (b. 1952), author of a novel about Andersen (*Journey in Blue*, 2004), is right in claiming that Andersen's artistic disposition makes him akin to modern painters like Pablo Picasso and Asger Jorn, who have made the childish and the naïve into a key feature of their aesthetic creed, we could then also establish a similar kinship between Andersen and, say, Iamblichus, Meister Eckhart, Jacob Böhme, Carl Linnaeus, Emanuel Swedenborg, William Blake. All of them are distinguished thinkers and Gnostics, who share the conviction that divinity speaks through the child; that the child possesses a radically transforming potential.

In the 20th century, we discover traces of Neo-Platonism in such interesting manifestations of the synthesizing might of the European spirit as Bauhaus, Rudolph Steiner's cosmology, Nicolas Roerich's philosophical system "Living Ethics", surrealism, abstractionism, as well as in the work of a number of writers, especially poets, composers, and even pedagogues. We could assume that the large-scale mystical movement, referred to as New Age, has also been inspired by the plurality of Neo-Platonic philosophical ideas. In its essence, New Age is a Romantic response to the de-humanization of today's hi-tech society; a response to the computerization of our culture and to the alienation of the average individual from its élitist trends. By means of para-sciences, various cults, teachings and esoteric practices, advertised in countless books and sites, the movement provides its followers with the opportunity to fill the emptiness within their souls and the chance (often more illusory then real) to find answers to main existential questions. It offers them a complex and often contradictory amalgam of neo-paganism, theosophy, Jungian theory, myths (the myth of Atlantis being the central one among them), astrology, chakras, aura and re-incarnations, contact with the beyond, I Ching, Ayurveda, among many others. The movement rose in the 1970s in California as an expression of the aspiration towards the creation of "an ecology of the spirit". It represents an attempt to revive mankind's traditional ambition to penetrate the secrets of God; an attempt to trigger a revolutionary turn in individual and mass consciousness through the revival of mythological parabolas, or through the realization, at least partly, of the socalled *anthropic principle*. (In other words, cosmology is anthropologized, and anthropology assumes cosmic dimensions, in order to achieve a synchronic and diachronic influence of the Cosmos over man.) Whether the irrational vein, which this movement contributes to the global cultural *poly-logue* in the conditions of hi-tech society, is as fruitful and philosophically motivated as that similar stream which undermined the absolute dominance of reason at the end of the 18th century, remains to be seen. This should be the subject of a separate study, which would probably be hampered by the extreme heterogeneity of the phenomenon, as well as by its aggressive comercialization, which keeps pace with its growing popularity (including in Russia and the countries of the former Soviet bloc over the last 15 years).

But while this movement's system of views and principles may not be well motivated and always intellectually elevated, its wide currency all over the world and compactness of a planetary religion attests to the need for such ideas; the need for emotional intensity, intuition and fantasy, without which the really human life, the art and the literature would be unthinkable. Consequently, the rise of this movement attests to people's need for Andersen's work, whose impact is rightly described as the most long-lasting in the history of world literature. Also, it is important to note that his work helps us understand and assimilate these ideas; it raises a protective wall against their possible abuses, the consequences of which have been, and can be, dangerous. So the toll of his mysterious bell keeps reverberating from the very bosom of Nature; it awakens and redeems those who are ready to hear it, of course.

Literature

Andersen, H.C. *Samlede Eventyr og Historier*. Cph. 1994.

Carsten Bach-Nielsen & Doris Ottesen (ed.) *Andersen & Gud. Teologiske læsninger i H.C. Andersens forfatterskab*. Cph. 2005.

Andersen, Jens. *Andersen: en biografi*. Bd 1, 2. Cph. 2003-04.

Brovst, Bjarne Nielsen. *H.C. Andersen*. Bd 4, *Den ensommes lod*. Cph. 1998.

Capra, Fritjof. Sagesse des sages. Paris 1988.

Dansk litteraturhistorie. Bd 2. Cph. 1965.

Denmark. An Official Handbook. Cph. 1970.

Duve, Arne. *Symbolikken i H.C. Andersens eventyr*. Oslo 1967.

Enquist, Per Olov. *Från regnormarnas liv*. I En triptyk. Sthlm. 1981.

Enquist, Per Olov. *H.C. Andersen. Författarnas litteraturhistoria. De utländska författarna*, II. Sthlm. 1980.

Hans Christian Andersen. A Poet in Time. Papers from the Second International H.C. Andersen Conference. Odense 1999.

Jørgensen, Aage. *Idyll & Abyss. Essays on Danish Literature and Theater*. Aarhus 1992.

Jørgensen, Jens. *H.C. Andersen: en sand myte*. Cph. 1987.

Kofoed Niels. *H.C. Andersen: den store europæer*. Cph. 1996.

Litteraturhåndbogen. Cph. 1989.

Mylius, Johan de. *H.C. Andersen: liv og værk. En tidstavle 1805-1875*. Cph. 1993.

Mylius, Johan de. *Forvandlingens pris*. Cph. 2005.

Nielsen, Erling. *Hans Christian Andersen*. Cph. 1963.

Nyborg, Eigil, *Den indre linie i H.C. Andersens Eventyr. En psykologisk studie*. Cph. 1962.

Wullschlager, Jackie. *Hans Christian Andersen. The Life of a Storyteller*. London 2000.

Trivializing Trauma(s): Carnivalesque-grotesque Elements in Hans Christian Andersen's "The Happy Family" (1847, 1848), "Heartache" (1852), and "The Goblin and the Grocer" (1852)

Ib Johansen

Introduction

Grotesque elements in Hans Christian Andersen's fairy tales (and other literary works) have been pointed out by quite a few scholars – in Denmark for instance by Jens Aage Doctor and Niels Kofoed.[1] In the present paper I intend to focus on three fairy tales and their carnivalesque-grotesque elements, i.e. "The Happy Family" ("Den lykkelige Familie", Eng. 1847, Dan. 1848), "Heartache" ("Hjertesorg", 1852), and "The Goblin and the Grocer" (or as it is occasionally entitled "The Goblin at the Grocer's", i.e. "Nissen hos Spekhøkeren", 1852). What these three stories offer can be said to be three different *versions* of the (Romantic or post-Romantic) grotesque: in "The Happy Family" the focus is thus on a kind of low-key and/or ironic reading of a Biedermeier scenario – with an ironic emphasis on its would-be *utopian* and festive elements – whereas "Heartache", with its serio-comic portrayal of (human/animalistic/cosmic) *mortality*, downsizes or trivializes the process of mourning, for the little girl who is excluded from getting access to Puggie's [the lap-dog's] grave and therefore "burst[s] into tears"[2] can be said to carry a disproportionately heavy emotional load, compared to what can be expected of a child (or for that matter: an adult person); and in "The Goblin and the Grocer" the definitely Romantic opposition between spirit and matter – in this case exemplified by the Student and the Grocer respectively – can be said to be submitted to an ironic *twist*, i.e. to the extent that the Goblin is unable to choose between the ideal sphere on the one hand (represented by the high ideality of the Student's *book*) and on the other hand the material world and all its needs and necessities (represented here by the *porridge* offered to the Goblin by the Grocer on Christmas Eve as an exemplary gift or what Bataille might term an instance of *potlach*); in spatial terms the opposition is between the *heights* and the *depths*, i.e. between the Student's *garret* and "the tattered old book he had brought upstairs with him"[3] on the one hand and on the other hand the (literally) down-to-earth *store*, where the Grocer sells his "butter" and other victuals (!).

In twentieth-century literary theory two major approaches to the grotesque can be identified, i.e. on the one hand that of Mikhail Bakhtin in his *Rabelais and His World* (1965, 1968) and on the other Wolfgang Kayser's classic approach in *Das Groteske. Seine Gestaltung in Malerei und Dichtung* (1957, 1960). Whereas Bakhtin's study is mainly concerned with the Middle Ages and the Renaissance – and the controversial relationship between high culture and popular culture – Kayser's emphasis is primarily on the Romantic and post-Romantic period (going up to the twentieth century ["Das Groteske in der Moderne"]), with a primary focus on "[die] entfremdete Welt" or the *estranged world* of late eighteenth- or early nineteenth-century literature, which means that there is an element of self-alienation at play in the majority of the literary examples thematized in Kayser's work, while Bakhtin's focus is rather on the joyful relativity of carnival culture, where the high and the low – or the comic and the serious – are constantly light-heartedly turned *upside-down* or *inside-out*, i.e. we may here precisely bear in mind two of the Russian scholar's favourite *topoi* or rhetorical ploys in his book on Rabelais...[4]

Or as it is formulated by the Danish literary theorist Helge Nielsen in his book on the grotesque (*Det groteske. Begrebshistorie. Litterær kategori. Grotesteorier*, 1976), where he focuses on the theoretical opposition between the two scholars: "In contrast to the demonic-diabolical, das Urgrauen, which the artist of the grotesque according to [Wolfgang Kayser] invokes and at the same time attempts to overcome, making laughter give in to terror in the experiencing subject, [in Bakhtin] it is laughter, universal and all-embracing laughter, overcoming fear and creating an authentically human community, that is the essential thing. Common to both [theorists] is the [element of] ambivalence."[5]

As a matter of fact, those who have reflected on the aesthetic category of the grotesque have often noticed its *oxymoronic* character. According to Byron Jennings, "[t]he Grotesque object always displays a combination of *fearsome* and *ludicrous* qualities – or to be more precise, it simultaneously arouses reactions of fear and amusement in the observer".[6] As a matter of fact, this oscillation between diametrically opposed reader responses to the grotesque – characteristic of the said literary form, if we are to believe Byron Jennings – has precisely left its impact on the *theoretical* attempts to come to terms with a poetics of the grotesque; and it is reflected directly in the groundbreaking work of the two major theorists in this field: Wolfgang Kayser and Mikhail Bakhtin (cf. what Helge Nielsen has observed with regard to the opposition between Kayserian *Urgrauen* and all-embracing Bakhtinian *laughter*).

According to Bakhtin, "Time [itself] plays and laughs! It is the playing boy of Heraclitus who possesses the supreme power in the universe ('domination belongs to the child')".[7] (In this context we are actually reminded of Hans Christian Andersen's "The Naughty Boy" (1835)!). What is celebrated by Bakhtin in the passage just quoted is "the gay and free laughing aspect of the world, ... its unfinished and open character, ...[and] the joy of change and renewal".[8] And Bakhtin similarly focuses on *the divine child*, an archetypal figure presented to the reader in positive terms by Heraclitus in his fragment number 109 (cf. note 7): "A lifetime [or, eternity] is a child playing, playing checkers; the kingdom belongs to a child".[9] In this context Bakhtin's characteristic emphasis on *playfulness* and on the *extempore* character of medieval festivities or carnival culture (on *homo ludens*) can be contrasted with the poetological focus on precisely the notion of *temporality* in deconstructive theory (de Man's "rhetoric of temporality") – and in this perspective it is no wonder that de Man himself was extremely skeptical with regard to the Bakhtinian notion of dialogue (or dialogism), a skepticism that could easily be transferred to Bakhtin's theory of carnival, too. Whereas to Bakhtin, in Matthew Roberts' words, "the phenomenon of meaning is born, renewed, and augmented in dialogue",[10] and whereas Bakhtin actually stresses *the ecstasy of communication* (to use a Baudrillardian term somewhat out of context),[11] focusing on "the people's growing and ever-victorious body that is 'at home' in the cosmos",[12] "[f]or de Man – and, he argues, for the Romantics as well – the figures of allegory and irony designate a common awareness of the 'temporal void', at once the disjunction of sign and referent and the 'nothingness' or fictionality of a self which is really no more than 'a succession of discontinuous moments'" (Matthew Roberts).[13] Thus the fullness of time, such as it is envisaged in the Bakhtinian notion of carnival, is emphatically opposed to the "temporal void" of de Man's reading of the epistemological crisis of Romantic poetry. However, what de Man tends to regard as a kind of *neue Sachlichkeit*, characteristic of poets like Wordsworth and Shelley, is, in Bakhtin's view, rather symptomatic of a sort of global *Verfallsgeschichte*, influencing, on a deep-structural level, the whole history of Western culture since the seventeenth century.[14]

Friedrich Schlegel's "Gespräch über die Poesie" (1800) can be regarded as an important source of inspiration to Wolfgang Kayser. But on the other hand, Kayser argues that something is *missing*, i.e. "the abysmal quality, the insecurity, the terror inspired by the disintegration of the world".[15] According to Kayser, "[w]e are so strongly affected and terrified [when we are confronted with the grotesque] because it is our world which ceases to be reliable, and we feel that we would be unable to live in this changed world. The grotesque instills fear of life rather than fear of death ..."[16] This notion of the grotesque as a representation of "THE ESTRANGED WORLD"[17] makes the said category more closely related to the Todorovian fantastic (with its emphasis on the inability of the subject or reader to decide whether a given phenomenon belongs to the purely natural or to the supernatural sphere) than to the Bakhtinian version of the grotesque (however, there are *also* links between the two categories in a Bakhtinian perspective, in particular if we include the Russian scholar's book on Dostoevsky with its reflections on Menippean satire).[18]

Kayser's sombre and sinister version of the grotesque leaves little space for freedom and gaiety, but on the other hand the purely *artistic* quality of the grotesque work of art does, in a certain sense (i.e. on an aesthetic level), bring about "a secret liberation. The darkness has been sighted, the ominous powers discovered, the incomprehensible forces challenged. And thus we arrive at a final interpretation of the grotesque: AN ATTEMPT TO INVOKE AND SUBDUE THE DEMONIC ASPECTS OF THE WORLD".[19]

In Hans Christian Andersen's attempt to develop his own particular version(s) of the (Romantic or post-Romantic) grotesque in narratives like "The Happy Family", "Heartache", and "The Goblin and the Grocer" there are obvious links to both the Bakhtinian grotesque – with its roots in popular/oral culture and its types of discourse – and to the more sinister versions of the grotesque theorized by Wolfgang Kayser. As far as the *formal* aspects of Andersen's grotesque are concerned, we should perhaps also bear in mind Ludmila A. Foster's article "The Grotesque: A Method of Analysis" (1967), where she (like Byron Jennings) focuses on the *oxymoronic* character of the grotesque, to the extent that it "requires a juxtaposition, a duality, a coexistence of opposite or in some way incompatible elements".[20]

Biedermeier *in extremis* – Reflections on "The Happy Family" (1847, 1848)

In a famous article from 1968[21] the Danish scholar Erik Lunding has argued that within the mid-nineteenth-century Danish canon "extreme" versions of Romanticism were few and far between; what is missing here is the kind of *Zerrissenheit* we come across so often in Germany (or for that matter, in other European countries); writers like E.T.A. Hoffmann, Novalis or Tieck represent in this respect a far more *transgressive* ethos than Danish "parsonage culture" ("[p]ræstegaardskulturen i Danmark")[22] would permit. Instead *Biedermeier* culture – and Biedermeier literature – triumph, which means that violent contrasts are banished and with regard to *style* what we encounter is a "demand for moderation and sobriety, implying that in terms of language more spectacular archaisms and provincialisms are avoided, and dialects are not allowed to flourish either".[23]

In "The Happy Family" we notice that this harmonizing strategy is submitted to a de-constructive *turn*, insofar as (what looks like) an extreme version of bourgeois self-centredness or self-complacency is here exposed to the acid bath of ruthless irony: "The old white snails [the protagonists of the narrative] were the finest folk in the whole world – they knew that the forest [i.e. 'a veritable forest of burdocks' ['[e]n heel Skræppeskov']] existed entirely for them, and the manor-house existed for them to be boiled and laid on a silver dish".[24]

The thematic universe of "The Happy Family" emphasizes the opposition between on the one hand extreme old age (exemplified here by "the last two snails, both extremely old"),[25] i.e. whatever is dated, senescent, and/or *moribund*, and on the other hand the forces of (self-)renewal or rejuvenation, in Bakhtinian terms inherent in the sheer exuberant vitality or *joie de vivre* of popular culture as such.

According to Mikhail Bakhtin, "... destruction and uncrowning are related to birth and renewal. The death of the old is linked with regeneration; all the images [in Rabelais' work as well as in carnival culture in general] are connected with the contradictory oneness of the dying and reborn world".[26] And in "The Happy Family" we are presented with a somewhat diminished version of this grand/cosmic theme, i.e. to the extent that the old snails (like Roderick and Madeline Usher in Poe's story) represent the decline and fall of (late) feudal culture, the setting sun of the *ancien régime*, whereas their (adopted) *descendents* (the young snail and his bride) exemplify precisely such a sheer *surplus* of would-be Nietzschean will power that we come across over and over again in carnival culture, where "[t]he victory of the future is ensured by the people's immortality. The birth of the new, of the greater and the better, is as indispensable and inevitable as the death of the old. The one is transferred to the other, the better turns the worse into ridicule and kills it".[27] In "The Happy Family" the final *wedding* signalizes such a decisive peripety, where Mother Snail makes "a charming speech ... [and] [w]hen the speech was over, the old snails crawled into their houses and never came out again; they went to sleep. The two young ones took charge of the forest and raised a large offspring. But they were never boiled or laid on a silver dish, so they came to the conclusion that the Manor must have fallen into ruins and that everybody in the world had died out; and as no one contradicted them, it must have been true".[28] Even though the ending has a somewhat apocalyptic ring to it, it nevertheless seems as if the utopian *Biedermeier* world is truly capable of swallowing up everything, even the pitfalls and/or atrocities of ordinary everyday life, where the well-established customs of the past are mercilessly discontinued and the spectacular *lit-de-parade* of their ancestors (including being boiled and laid on a silver dish) is never taken up again – for better or for worse! Instead their descendents seem to be compelled to confront the Darwinian struggle for life and survival of the fittest!

Mourning and Its Discontents – Double Plot in "Heartache" (1852)

In Hans Christian Andersen's "Heartache" we are confronted with not only one, but *two* stories – even if the second story is presented to the reader as more essential than the "prelude" (or "Forhistorien"). In this context it is interesting to notice that Hans Henrik Møller has recently presented us with a reader-response interpretation of the story, where "Heartache" is essentially viewed as a kind of meta-poetical fable – and the main focus is on the *problematic* relationship between the text and its audience/readership. As a matter of fact, in this reading the position of the narrator vis-à-vis the narrated events remains *undecidable*.[29]

Anyway, it is obvious that the story demands an extraordinary effort on the part of the reader in order to be comprehended – and at the same time the very position of the reader is *undermined* by the narrative, for it is explicitly stated that "anyone who doesn't understand [the story] had better go and buy shares in the widow's tannery".[30]

If we take a look at the beginning of the story, we can easily see how the narrator *manipulates* his (narrative) materials – but his *objective* when he adopts such a strategy nevertheless remains somewhat mysterious: "This is really a story in two parts that we present you with here; the first part might just as well be left out – but it provides us with preliminary knowledge ('Forkundskaber'), and that is useful!"[31] What is essential and what is un-important thus remains un-decided – and for all that (in practical terms) un-*decidable*. The first part of the story has two protagonists: the Madam/Matron (who owns a tannery) and her pug-dog ("Moppen"). Both of them visit a manor-house, and the widow attempts to make the (absent) owners of the manor-house interested in buying shares in her tannery. What is focused here is thus what looks like a simple business transaction.

The second (and nominally more *important*) part of the story begins with the solemn words: "'*The pug died!*' – that is the second part."[32]

What the rest of the story focuses on is the burial ceremony and the attempt on the part of the widow's grandchildren to turn the pug's grave into a profitable enterprise – for "[t]he charge for admission [to the grave] should be a trouser-button – that was something every boy would have and could also pay for the little girls with".[33] However, one little girl is not provided for – apparently she does not know a boy with a trouser-button and thus she is simply *excluded* from the good company. An outsider or a social *pariah*.

The narrator's position is allegedly synonymous with a bird's-eye view of childhood itself and its sorrows and misfortunes – with seeing everything "from above" ("We saw it from above – and seen from above – this, like so many of our own griefs and those of others – yes, then we might laugh at them!").[34] But this Olympian position nevertheless appears to be difficult to maintain – there is always the un-acknowledged scapegoat, i.e. the person who does not fit into the scheme of things and cannot come to terms with his or her own destiny. And just as the widow is baffled by the sheer length of the landowner's title ("*Generalkrigskommissær, Ridder, etcetera*"),[35] the reader is left to his/her own devices with regard to the deeper *meaning* of the narrative, for "anyone who doesn't understand it had better take shares in the widow's tannery".[36] It appears that capital(ism) is simply essentially stupid! Or at least it is one hundred percent insensitive to the subtleties of the art of storytelling.

Anyway, mourning itself is simultanously envisaged in carnivalistic terms as a festive celebration, where "[t]he children danced around the grave ...",[37] and associated with civilization and its discontents, i.e. with the profound unease provoked in the individual by being exluded from the social world and its routines and practices (exemplified by the little girl, whose "heartache" has given the story its title). The grotesque discrepancy between this heart-felt response and its *object* is certainly in accordance with Ludmila A. Foster's definition of the grotesque mode, when she refers to "a juxtaposition, a duality, a coexistence of opposite or in some way incompatible elements".[38] This *oxymoronic* structure is definitely also present in "Heartache"!

Juggling the Heights and the Depths – Schizophrenic Consciousness in "The Goblin and the Grocer" (1852)

At the beginning of this story the Goblin (i.e. the protagonist) knows very well where he belongs – what is his position in the scheme of things. He stays with the Grocer, for "here every Christmas Evening he was given a bowl of porridge with a big lump of butter in it! the Grocer could provide that; and the Goblin remained in the store, and that might teach you a lesson".[39]

However, the world-view of the Goblin is challenged by the Student, who lives in the attic, and who seems to appreciate books and learning in a manner that the Goblin is thoroughly unfamiliar with. Whereas the Grocer sticks to the values of *material culture*, the Student satirizes his materialism by drawing his attention to "an old book, full of poetry" and the alternative value system that it stands for: "You are a splendid person, a practical person, but poetry you do not know anything about – in fact, no more than this tub!"[40]

The Goblin is thoroughly dissatisfied with this remark on the part of the Student, for "this was a very naughty remark, especially vis-à-vis the tub, but the Grocer laughed and the Student laughed, for it was said kind of jokingly. But the Goblin was annoyed, for how dare anyone say this about a grocer, who was also a landlord and sold the best butter."[41]

The Goblin decides to put everything to the test, and this he does by carrying out a kind of *enquête* or opinion poll among all the kitchen utensils and other household objects he is familiar with: "When it grew dark, the store was closed and everybody had gone to bed, except the Student, the Goblin entered the room and picked up the Matron's gobbledygook ('Madammens *Mundlæder*'), for she did not need it when she was asleep, and wherever he placed it on any object, it spoke up for itself, and it could express its thoughts and feelings just as well as the Matron, but only one at a time could have it, and that was a blessing, for else there would have been Babylonian confusion in there."[42]

The grotesque strategy in this narrative is based on the discrepancy between (on the one hand) the extreme – or would-be extreme – *talkativeness* of the object-world (possessing to an extraordinary degree the gift of the gab) and (on the other hand) the supernatural *aura* of the project of Enlightenment – represented here by the Student and his book: "... out of the book there emerged a bright ray, which became a trunk, a mighty tree, raising its head so high and spreading its branches above the Student's head. Every leaf was so fresh and every flower was the head of a lovely girl, some of them with eyes so dark and luminous, others so blue and marvellously bright."[43] The pathos of the Enlightenment project – with a mystical aura or halo added to it – is thus undermined or de-constructed by the trivialities of the purely material life-world, i.e. by its sordid, abject, and excessively counter-productive atmosphere!

According to Bakhtin, "[f]emale chatter [similar to the Matron's gobbledygook or *Mundlæder* in "The Goblin and the Grocer"] is presented in the "Cackle of Fisherwomen" (*Caquets des Poissonières*), 1621-22, and in the "Cackle of the Women of Faubourg Montmartre" (*Caquets des Femmes du Faubourg Montmartre*), 1622 . The seventeenth-century dialogues are interesting historical documents reflecting [a general degeneracy in cultural life]; the frank talk of marketplace and banquet hall were transformed into the novel of private manners of modern times. And yet a tiny spark of the carnival flame was still alive in these writings."[44] I would argue that it is also still alive in the chatter of tub, coffee-mill, till, and buttercask in Hans Christian Andersen's "The Goblin and the Grocer"!

As it is pointed out by Wolfgang Kayser in his study of the grotesque, in E.T.A. Hoffmann's romantic universe a striking contrast between the angelic beauty of some of his female characters and both grotesque-animalistic and "demonic" qualities in other characters is thematized over and over again[45] – and in "The Goblin and the Grocer" a similar thematic contrast can certainly be pinpointed (!), exemplified here by the opposition between the quasi-celestial book on the one hand and the trivialities of the Matron's *Mundlæder* and the humble household utensils on the other.

The Goblin is induced to choose between what Gaston Bachelard in his *The Poetics of Space* (1958, 1964) has termed "the rationality of the roof" and "the irrationality of the cellar" – or between the aerial and the terrestrial.[46] He is split between the heights and the depths – the Student's attic and the Grocer's *store* (a down-to-earth setting). When he has *saved* the Student's book – during a fire, where it later turns out that it is the house next door that is threatened – he appears to have opted for the higher, ideal sphere. But in the end he remains faithful to the earth – "yes: 'I will divide myself between them [i.e. the Student and the Grocer]', he said: 'I cannot altogether let go of the Grocer for the sake of the porridge'."[47]

And as it is summed up by the narrator at the end: "And this was quite human! – we, too, have to go to the Grocer – for the sake of the porridge."[48] The material bodily lower stratum – to adopt a Bakhtinian term – thus ultimately triumphs over the rationality of the roof and the would-be superior *spiritual* sphere – or so it seems!

Notes

1. Cf. for instance Jens Aage Doctor: "H.C. Andersens karneval", in: *Andersen og Verden*. Redigeret af Johan de Mylius, Aage Jørgensen og Viggo Hjørnager Pedersen (Odense: Odense Universitetsforlag, 1993), pp. 410-19, and Niels Kofoed: "The Arabesque and the Grotesque. Hans Christian Andersen Decomposing the World of Poetry", in: *Hans Christian Andersen. A Poet in Time*. Edited by Johan de Mylius, Aage Jørgensen and Viggo Hjørnager Pedersen (Odense: Odense University Press, 1999), pp. 461-69.
2. Cf. http://www.andersen.sdu.dk/Print.html?ps=vaerk/hersholt/Heartache_e.html &title=H..., p.2.
3. Cf. http://www.andersen.sdu.dk/vaerk/hersholt/TheGoblinAndTheGrocer.html
4. Cf. Wolfgang Kayser: *The Grotesque in Art and Literature*. Translated from the German by Ulrich Weisstein (New York and Toronto: McGraw-Hill Book Company, 1966), p. 184, where it is explicitly stated: "THE GROTESQUE IS THE ESTRANGED WORLD". Cf. Wolfgang Kayser: *Das Groteske. Seine Gestaltung in Kunst und Literatur* (Oldenburg und Hamburg: Gerhard Stalling Verlag, 1957), p. 198: "... *das Groteske ist die entfremdete Welt*" (Kayser uses spatialization instead of italics). On the "grotesque in the twentieth century" cf. Wolfgang Kayser, *The Grotesque, op. cit.*, pp. 130-78, and in the German version [cf. above the reference to "[d]as Groteske in der Moderne"], cf. *Das Groteske, op. cit.*, pp. 140-92. Cf. also Mikhail Bakhtin: *Rabelais and His World*. Translated by Helene Iswolsky (Cambridge, Massachusetts, and London,

England: The M.I.T. Press, 1968), e.g. p. 424, where there is a reference to expressions in Rabelais that are "turned inside out" – and *passim.*

5. Cf. Helge Nielsen: *Det groteske. Begrebshistorie. Litterær kategori. Grotesk-teorier* (Copenhagen: Berlingske Forlag, 1976), p. 67 (my translation): "I modsætning til det diabolsk-dæmoniske, das Urgrauen, som grotesk kunstneren if. WK [i.e., Wolfgang Kayser] besværger og samtidig forsøger at overvinde, og som hos opleveren får latteren til at vige for rædslen, er her latteren, den universelle og altfavnende latter, som overvinder frygten og skaber et ægte menneskeligt fællesskab, det centrale. Fælles er ambivalensen."

6. Cf. Lee Byron Jennings: *The Ludicrous Demon. Aspects of the Grotesque in Post-Romantic German Prose* (Berkeley and Los Angeles: University of California Press, 1963), p. 10: "We may say that the grotesque object always displays a *combination of fearsome and ludicrous qualities* – or, to be more precise, it simultaneously arouses reactions of fear and amusement in the observer" (Jennings' italics).

7. Mikhail Bakhtin: *Rabelais and His World, op. cit.*, p. 82.

8. *Ibid.*, p. 83 (my ellipses).

9. Cf. *A Presocratics Reader. Selected Fragments and Testimonia.* Edited, with Introduction, by Patricia Curd. Translations by Richard D. McKirahan, Jr. (Indianapolis/Cambridge: Hackett Publishing Company, Inc., 1996), p. 40.

10. Cf. Paul de Man: "Dialogue and Dialogism", in: *Rethinking Bakhtin. Extensions and Challenges.* Edited by Gary Saul Morson and Caryl Emerson (Evanston, Illinois: Northwestern University Press, 1989), pp. 105-14. The *quotation* is from Matthew Roberts' article on Bakhtin and de Man, "Poetics Hermeneutics Dialogics. Bakhtin and Paul de Man", in: *Rethinking Bakhtin, op. cit.*, p. 124 (cf. note 13).

11. Cf. Jean Baudrillard: "The Ecstasy of Communication", in: *Postmodern Culture.* Edited by Hal Foster (London and Sydney: The Pluto Press, Second impression 1985 (first published as *The Anti-Aesthetic* in 1983)), pp. 126-34.

12. Cf. Mikhail Bakhtin, *op. cit.*, p. 341. When we take into consideration to what extent *homelessness* and *estrangement/alienation* have been explicitly thematized in nineteenth- and twentieth-century fiction (and, in a philosophical perspective, in particular the way in which these notions have been put-into-discourse in Marxism and existentialism), it is worth-while paying attention to this contrapunctal emphasis on "the people's growing and ever-victorious body that is '*at home*' in the cosmos" (my italics). From the eighteenth- and nineteenth-century *Bildungsroman* to Kafka and Camus such a thematic preoccupation (i.e. such an emphasis on *Entfremdung*) has remained a structural *constant* in the Western world.

13. Cf. Matthew Roberts: "Poetics Hermeneutics Dialogics. Bakhtin and Paul de Man", in: *Rethinking Bakhtin, op. cit.*, pp. 128-29.

14. Cf. Mikhail Bakhtin, *op. cit.*, p. 101, where Bakhtin refers to historical changes within the cultural sphere in seventeenth- and eighteenth-century Europe as "this process of laughter's degradation". Cf. also what I write about this problematic in "The Semiotics of Laughter", in: *Signs of Change. Premodern → Modern → Postmodern.* Edited by Stephen Barker (Albany: State University of New York Press, 1996), pp. 7ff.

15. Wolfgang Kayser: *The Grotesque, op. cit.*, p. 52. Cf. Wolfgang Kayser: *Das Groteske, op. cit.*, p. 53: "Aber es fehlt eines: die Bodenlosigkeit, die Abgrün-

digkeit, das sich einmischende Grauen angesichts der zerbrechenden Ordnungen."
16. Wolfgang Kayser: *The Grotesque, op. cit.*, pp. 184-85 (my ellipsis). Cf. Wolfgang Kayser: *Das Groteske, op. cit.*, p. 199: "Das Grauen überfällt uns so stark, weil es eben unsere Welt ist, deren Verlässlichkeit sich als Schein erweist. Zugleich spüren wir, dass wir in dieser verwandelten Welt nicht zu leben vermöchten. Es geht beim Grotesken nicht um Todesfurcht, sondern um Lebensangst."
17. Cf. Wolfgang Kayser: *The Grotesque, op. cit.*, p. 184: "THE GROTESQUE IS THE ESTRANGED WORLD". Cf. Wolfgang Kayser: *Das Groteske, op. cit.*, p. 198: "*[Das] Groteske ist die entfremdete Welt*" (Kayser uses spatialization instead of italics). Cf. note 4.
18. According to Tzvetan Todorov, "the fantastic is that hesitation experienced by a person knowing only the laws of nature, confronting an apparently supernatural event". Cf. Tzvetan Todorov: *The Fantastic. A Structural Approach to a Literary Genre*. Translated from the French by Richard Howard (Cleveland/London: The Press of Case Western Reserve University, 1973), p. 25. Cf. also Mikhail Bakhtin: *Problems of Dostoevsky's Poetics*. Edited and Translated by Caryl Emerson. Introduction by Wayne C. Booth (Minneapolis: University of Minnesota Press, Second printing, 1985), p. 114: "We emphasize that the fantastic here [i.e. in Menippean satire] serves not for the positive *embodiment* of truth, but as a mode for searching after truth, provoking it, and, most important, *testing* it. To this end the heroes of Menippean satire ascend into heaven, descend into the nether world, wander through unknown and fantastic lands, are placed in extraordinary life situations..." (Bakhtin's italics, my ellipsis).
19. Cf. Wolfgang Kayser: *The Grotesque, op. cit.*, p. 188. Cf. Wolfgang Kayser: *Das Groteske, op. cit.*, p. 202: "Bei aller Ratlosigkeit und allem Grauen über die dunklen Mächte, die in und hinter unserer Welt lauern und sie uns entfremden können, wirkt die echte künstlerische Gestaltung zugleich als heimliche Befreiung. Das Dunkle ist gesichtet, das Unheimliche ist entdeckt, das Unfassbare zur Rede gestellt. Und so gibt sich eine letzte Deutung: *die Gestaltung des Grotesken ist der Versuch, das Dämonische in der Welt zu bannen und zu beschwören*" (Kayser uses spatialization instead of italics).
20. Ludmila A. Foster: "The Grotesque. A Method of Analysis", *Zagadnienia Rodzajów Literackich*, Vol. 9 (1967), p. 80.
21. Cf. Erik Lunding: "Biedermeier og romantismen", *Kritik 7* (1968), pp. 32-67.
22. *Ibid.*, p. 55 (my translation).
23. *Ibid.*, p. 59 (my translation).
24. Cf. *H.C. Andersens Eventyr*, II: *1843-55*. Ved Erik Dal (København: Hans Reitzels Forlag, 1964), p. 157 (my translation): "De gamle hvide Snegle vare de fornemste i Verden, vidste de, Skoven var til for deres Skyld, og Herregaarden var til for at de kunde blive kogt og lagt paa Sølvfad."
25. *Ibid.*, p. 156 (my translation): "[og derinde boede] de to sidste, inderlig gamle Snegle."
26. Cf. Mikhail Bakhtin: *Rabelais and His World, op. cit.*, p. 217 (my translation): "... destruction and uncrowning are related to birth and renewal. The death of the old is linked with regeneration; all the images [in Rabelais] are connected with the contradictory oneness of the dying and reborn world" (my ellipsis).
27. Cf. *ibid.*, p. 256.

28. Hans Christian Andersen: *80 Fairy Tales*. Published in co-operation with Hans Christian Andersen House, Odense. Translated from the original Danish text by R.P. Keigwin. Illustrations by Vilhelm Pedersen and Lorenz Frølich reproduced from the original drawings in the Andersen museum at Odense (Copenhagen: Høst & Søn, 2004), pp. 225-26 (my ellipsis). Cf. *H.C. Andersens Eventyr*, II, *op. cit.*, pp. 158-59 ("Og efter at den Tale var holdt, krøb de Gamle ind i deres Huus, og kom aldrig mere ud; de sov. Det unge Snegle-Par regjerede i Skoven og fik en stor Afkom, men de blev aldrig kogte, og de kom aldrig paa Sølvfad, saa sluttede de deraf, at Herregaarden var faldet sammen. og at alle Mennesker i Verden vare uddøde, og da Ingen sagde dem imod, saa var det jo sandt ..." (my ellipsis).
29. Cf. Hans Henrik Møller: "Mellem afstand og nærhed. H.C. Andersen og det moderne". In: *H. C. Andersen. Modernitet & modernisme. Essays i anledning af Annelies van Hees' afsked fra Amsterdams Universitet*. Redigeret af Aage Jørgensen og Henk van der Liet. (Amsterdam: Scandinavisch Instituut/Universiteit van Amsterdam, 2006, pp. 85-106. Also in: *PLYS 20* (2005), pp. 173-94.
30. Cf. Hans Christian Andersen: *80 Fairy Tales*, *op. cit.*, p. 238 (in this translation the story is called "Heartbreak").
31. Cf. *H.C. Andersens Eventyr*, II: *1843-55*. Ved Erik Dal (København: Hans Reitzels Forlag, 1964), p. 245 (my translation): "Det er egentligt en Historie i to Dele, vi her komme med; første Deel kunde gjerne være borte, – men den giver Forkundskaber, og de ere nyttige!"
32. *Ibid.*, p. 246 (my translation, Andersen's italics): "'*Moppen døde!*' det er anden Deel" (Andersen's italics).
33. Cf. Hans Christian Andersen: *80 Fairy Tales*, *op. cit.*, p. 237.
34. Cf. *H.C. Andersens Eventyr*, II: *1843-55*, *op. cit.*, p. 246 (my translation): "Vi saae det ovenfra – og ovenfra seet – denne, som mange af vore og Andres Sorger, – ja saa kunne vi lee af dem!"
35. Cf. *ibid.*, p. 245 (Andersen's italics). In Jean Hersholt's translation the circumstantial title of the owner of the manor house becomes "General War Commissary, Knight,' etc." Cf. http://www.andersen.sdu.dk/Print.html?ps=vaerk/hersholt/Heartache_e.html&title=H ..., p. 1.
36. Cf. note 30.
37. Cf. *H.C. Andersens Eventyr*, II: *1843-55*, *op. cit.*, p. 246 (my translation, my ellipsis): "Børnene dandsede rundt om Graven..." (my ellipsis).
38. Cf. note 20.
39. Cf. *H.C. Andersens Eventyr*, II: *1843-55*, *op. cit.*, p. 255 (my translation): " ... her fik han [i.e. Nissen] hver Juleaften et Fad Grød med en stor Klump Smør i! det kunde Spekhøkeren give; og Nissen blev i Boutiken og det var meget lærerigt" (my ellipsis).
40. Cf. *ibid.*, p. 255 (my translation): "'... De er en prægtig Mand, en practisk Mand, men Poesi forstaaer De Dem ikke mere paa, end den Bøtte!'" (my ellipsis).
41. Cf. *ibid.*, pp. 255-56 (my translation): "Og det var uartigt sagt, især mod Bøtten, men Spekhøkeren loe og Studenten loe, det var jo sagt saadan i en Slags Spøg. Men Nissen ærgrede sig, at man turde sige sligt til en Spekhøker, der var Huusvært og solgte det bedste Smør".
42. *Ibid.*, p. 256 (my translation): "Da det blev Nat, Boutiken lukket og Alle tilsengs, paa Studenten nær, gik Nissen ind og tog Madammens *Mundlæder*, det

brugte hun ikke naar hun sov, og hvor i Stuen han satte det paa nogensomhelst Gjenstand, der fik den Mund og Mæle, kunde udtale sine Tanker og Følelser ligesaa godt, som Madammen, men kun een ad Gangen kunde faae det, og det var en Velgjerning, for ellers havde de jo talt hverandre i Munden".

43. *Ibid.*, p. 256 (my translation, my ellipsis): "... der stod ud af Bogen en klar Straale, der blev til en Stamme, til et mægtigt Træ, som løftede sig saa høit og bredte sine Grene vidt ud over Studenten. Hvert Blad var saa friskt og hver Blomst var et deiligt Pigehoved, nogle med Øine saa mørke og straalende, andre saa blaa og forunderlige klare" (my ellipsis).

44. Mikhail Bakhtin, *Rabelais and His World*, *op. cit.*, pp. 105-06 (my ellipsis).

45. Cf. Wolfgang Kayser: *The Grotesque*, *op. cit.*, pp. 105-06. Cf. also Wolfgang Kayser: *Das Groteske*, *op. cit.*, pp. 113-14.

46. Cf. Gaston Bachelard: *The Poetics of Space*. Translated from the French by Maria Jolas. With a new Foreword by John R. Stilgoe (Boston: Beacon Press, 1994 [first published in French under the title *La poétique de l'espace*, 1958]), p. 18 and p. 22.

47. Cf. *H.C. Andersens Eventyr*, II: *1843-55*, *op. cit.*, p. 258 (my translation): "ja: 'jeg vil dele mig imellem dem! sagde han [i.e. Nissen]: "jeg kan ikke reent slippe Spekhøkeren for Grødens Skyld!'."

48. *Ibid.*, p. 258 (my translation): "Og det var ganske menneskeligt! – Vi andre gaae ogsaa til Spekhøkeren – for Grøden."

The Bed of Procrustes:
An Analysis of Hans Christian Andersen's "The Fir Tree"

Paul A. Bauer and *Lone Koldtoft*

Hans Christian Andersen's fairy tale "The Fir Tree" (1844)[1] and Søren Kierkegaard's "The Unhappiest One" (1843)[2] are two very different texts, both in terms of form and content. One thing they have in common, however, is that they both examine the relation between time and existence, that is, the way in which being human is bound up with relating oneself, not just to the present, decisive moment, but also to one's past and future. In both works, this relating is presented from a negative perspective, in that the personalities depicted are unable to establish the presence necessary for happiness.

"The Unhappiest One", which is part of "A's papers" in *Either-Or*, is a speech that is the rather unlikely vehicle for some complex philosophical considerations, starting with grammar and leading into an examination of the nature of unhappiness. The speaker uses four grammatical tense forms and the notion of presence to develop a theory of unhappiness in an attempt to determine the person most deserving of the title The Unhappiest One.

Andersen's "The Fir Tree", is written in an entirely different genre, *i.e.*, fable, and concentrates on a single figure, a fir tree. We follow the fir tree's inner deliberations throughout its unhappy life, from the forest, *via* its life's great moment, to its wretched death. Despite the differences between the two texts, we believe that describing the fir tree in terms of the speaker's theory of unhappiness can bring new clarity to the fir tree's plight. We will therefore sketch the theory of unhappiness as it is found in "The Unhappiest One" and then discuss it in relation to Andersen's unhappy fir tree.

The Unhappy Winner and the Award

In literary terms, "The Unhappiest One" is panegyric; it is the text of a speech that enthusiastically praises its eponymous subject. We must imagine that the speech is given on the occasion of an award ceremony. It is a quite remarkable person who is given the award and the award itself is just as remarkable; the prizewinner is the unhappiest person on earth and the prize consists of an empty grave.

We are not given much information about the identity of the speaker, but he exercises a certain demonic power over his audience. "I do not say: Give me your attention, because I know I have it; I do not say: Lend me your ears, for I know they belong to me." It is also he that has the authority to decide the winner and to award the empty grave on the audience's behalf. It is perhaps not too much of a stretch to say that the speaker is Satan himself (or at least A speaking from this perspective).

The audience, addressed as the *symparanecromenoi* [Fellowship of the Dead] are a kind of hellish counterpart to the hosts of heaven,[3] having distinguished themselves by triumphing over the fear of death. They wander ceaselessly over the earth, bearing the sense of being in the world but apart from it, fearing only the coherence and continuity of a life being lived. "We who ... live as aphorisms in life, without association with men, having no share in their griefs and joys; we who are not consonants in the clamor of life but are solitary birds in the stillness of night, assembled together only once to be edified by representations of the wretchedness of life ... we who do not believe in the game of gladness nor the happiness of fools, we who believe in nothing but unhappiness."[4] All of these are nominated for the award, but it becomes clear, as the selection process proceeds, that few present at the gathering are worthy candidates.

The Theory of Unhappiness

At the outset, the speaker reminds his audience that it is Hegel who has written the paragraph on unhappiness and renders Hegel's idea thus:

> The unhappy one is the person who in one way or another has his ideal, the substance of his life ... his essential nature, outside himself. The unhappy one is the person who is always absent from

himself, never present to himself. But in being absent, one obviously can be in either past or future time. The whole territory of the unhappy consciousness is thereby adequately circumscribed.[5]

The obvious inference from this quotation is that one is truly happy when one is present to oneself in the present moment. The speaker then adds a few grammatical insights of his own:

> So, then, the unhappy one is absent. But one is absent when one is in either past or future time. This expression must be insisted upon, for it is obvious, as philology also teaches us that there is a *tempus* [tense] that is present in past time and a *tempus* that is present in a future time, but this same science also teaches us that there is a *tempus* that is [past perfect], in which there is no present, and a [future perfect] that has the same feature. The[s]e are the hoping and the recollecting individualities.[6]

Thus the speaker attempts to refine Hegel's unhappy idea by saying that one is unhappy by degrees. He has apparently seized upon the German designations of what in English is called the simple past and simple future, *i.e.*, *Präsens der Vergangenheit* and *Präsens der Zukunft*, as indicating that these forms denote a certain identity with the action or event described. One is unhappy in the looser, milder sense when one is present to oneself in either some past or future moment. Unhappiness in a stricter sense is when this presence to oneself is lacking.

	Past recollection	Future hope
Presence – loose sense	*Präsens der Vergangenheit* Simple past	*Präsens der Zukunft* Simple future
Absence – strict sense	Past perfect	Future perfect

A primary characteristic of presence is what the speaker calls 'reality'. Kierkegaard usually uses the word reality in a general sense, *i.e.*, to "indicate that a thing or concrete circumstance is present in the world without specifying how it came to be."[7] Here, however, we see that the reality of a thing has a strong subjective component, in that a thing must be a reality for the individual. In addition, reality can be either gained or lost. As we shall see, much puzzlement about this use of reality gets resolved when the speaker later spills the beans and calls it 'meaning'. In the following remarks, the two terms will be used synonymously.

The speaker says, "In order for the hoping individuality to become present in future time, it must have reality or, more correctly, it must acquire reality for him; in order for the recollecting individuality to become present in past time, it must have had reality for him."[8] He makes it clear that just having an active imagination is not sufficient to establish the reality of a thing and first offers a counter-example: "If ... an individual became absorbed in antiquity or in the Middle Ages or in any other time, or he became absorbed in his own childhood or youth in a way that had *decisive reality* for him, then ... he would not be an unhappy individual [in the strict sense]."[9] But on the other hand, "If I were to imagine a person who had had no childhood himself, since this age had past him by *without real meaning*, but who now, by becoming a teacher of children, discovered all the beauty in childhood and now wanted to recollect his own childhood, always stared back at it, he would certainly be a very appropriate example [of unhappiness in the strict sense]."[10] That is, he would be trying to recollect something that he had not originally experienced: the meaning of his childhood. He would always be in the position of imposing a meaning on remembered events, rather than drawing meaning from them.

One might ask the question, "How is it possible to find decisive reality in antiquity or the Middle Ages, which one has not experienced, but not possible to find this reality in one's own childhood, which one has experienced?" It may be simply a quirk in Kierkegaard's personality that led him to write this, but on the other hand he may be thinking that the writings and historical accounts of past ages are pre-digested experience; the chaos and confusion of actual experience has been distilled and the meaning of it has been made more readily accessible for the reader, thus making it easier to have an immediate sense of "being there".

It is important to emphasize that for the speaker "*decisive* reality" and "*real* meaning" are very lofty concepts and that not any old Harry Potter- or Lord of the Rings-universe suffices to provide them. The object of hope or recollection must have such reality or meaning that if the subject "receives a blow", *i.e.*, if the reality of the object is lost to it, then he or she gives up, not just on the object, but on hoping or recollecting altogether. But if the one tense becomes inhospitable, then perhaps the other tense will do: "We also see from this that one blow, be it ever so hard, cannot possibly make a person into the unhappiest one. That is, one blow can only either rob him of hope and thereby make him present in recollection or rob him of recollection and thereby make him present in hope."[11]

As an example of such a blow, the speaker invokes the figure of Niobe, whose loss of her twelve children [*i.e.*, her hope] at the hands of Artemis and Apollo is continually before her, living eternally in her moment of grief [*i.e.*, in recollection]. "The world changes, but she knows no change, and time comes, but for her there is no future time."[12]

So being happy means having a "place to rest, nearest yourself". True happiness is resting in the present; resting in either the recollected past or anticipated future is unhappiness, but in a mild sense (although the speaker determines the future as the happier of the two, because the future is approaching the present, whereas the past is unhappier, because it is receding).

The speaker then proceeds to the categories that constitute unhappiness in the strict sense, namely absence in the past or future, which are characterized by a half-hearted yearning for rest in one or the other tense: "If [one who hopes] cannot become present to himself in hope but loses his hope, then hopes again, etc., then he is absent from himself, not merely in present but also in future time, and thus we have a form of unhappiness [in the strict sense]."[13] A bit later the speaker says, "But when the hoping individuality wants to hope for a future that nevertheless can acquire no reality for him, or the recollecting individuality wants to recollect a time that has had no reality, then we have essentially unhappy individualities ... he hopes for something that he himself knows cannot be realized [*i.e.*, have decisive meaning for him]."[14] One is perhaps reminded of the atheist who pathetically wishes he or she could believe in God anyway.

The culmination of unhappiness is what the speaker calls a "combination" of the hoping and recollecting forms of strict unhappiness. For this individuality it is "recollection that prevents him from becoming present in his hope and it is hope that prevents him from becoming present in his recollection." In this form of unhappiness, the object is not lost when it receives a decisive blow, rather it is put in doubt. At first glance, it might seem worse to lose the object of one's happiness than to have it cast in doubt, but this is not necessarily so:

the families of soldiers missing in action often find the strain of not knowing more corrosive to the soul than learning the unhappy result. For these families, the future is in doubt: alive or dead? The speaker's combined form of unhappiness, on the other hand, heightens the tension by also putting the past in doubt as well: a young girl approaches the speaker to tell her tale of woe. She cannot grieve because she cannot be certain her lover, her life and breath, has been unfaithful and she cannot hope because he was an enigma. Are all her joyful memories of him an illusion, because he is a deceiver? Or will she find marital bliss in his arms? She is stretched on her own bed of Procrustes, between the uncertainties of hoping and recollecting, unable to find solace in either.

Although we have claimed that the combined form of unhappiness is the highest form, the speaker does in fact imply that the unhappiness of The Unhappiest One is of an even higher degree, in a realm where the terms describing happiness and unhappiness become confused and render it unintelligible. We will therefore content ourselves with the lower, intelligible forms.

So, on the speaker's account, unhappiness is an interaction between a subject and its object of essential interest. Reality is the meaning the object has for the subject, and rest is the certainty, or rather certitude, that the subject has concerning the being of the object. The subject can have certitude, either that the object *is*, in which case it hopes, or that the object *is not*, in which case it recollects. In either case, rest and reality meet and the subject is (unhappily) present in the relevant tense.

But if either rest or reality is lacking, then the subject is absent in the relevant tense. The families of soldiers missing in action, for example, have the reality (their children mean everything to them), but they lack certitude (alive or dead?). The opposite is true of the atheist who wishes he or she could believe in God. He or she has the certitude (that God does not exist), but lacks reality (God cannot have decisive meaning). How then does "The Fir Tree" measure up?

"The Fir Tree"

"The Unhappiest One" is a baroque and absurd comedy, a kind of *Screwtape Letters* with an aesthetic twist. Andersen's "The Fir Tree", on the other hand, is written as a sad and at times tragicomic fable, that begins in an idyllic forest and proceeds to the home of a wealthy family. We follow the fir tree's progress through the stages of life – childhood/youth, maturity, old age and death.

We meet the fir tree for the first time in the forest, as it is growing from a seedling and into a young tree. It has within it a burning desire to be full grown; grand ideas about the future consume it completely. Will it sail the oceans of the world as a ship's mast? Will it be a Christmas tree, standing proudly in a warm living room? It is clearly a fantasist, intensely engaged in the objects of its imagining. In its yearning to grow tall and strong, it fails to notice that its youth is slipping away, despite being admonished from several quarters. "'Rejoice in your youth,' said the sunbeams, 'rejoice in your supple growth, in the young life within you.' And the wind kissed the tree and the dew shed tears upon it, but the fir tree didn't understand what they meant."[15]

Only when the tree reaches maturity and is chopped down, does its fantasy life fail it for a time. In this moment of transition – from youth to adulthood – the fir tree realizes that it is losing its previous life and it retreats into its past.

> The tree gave out a sigh as it fell headlong to the ground. It felt faint with pain and could not think any happy thoughts. It was sad that it would be taken away from its home in the forest. It knew that it would never again see its dear old friends, the little bushes and flowers round about – perhaps not even the birds.[16]

The fir tree doesn't feel at all at home in recollection, however, and as soon as circumstances change, it livens up and again entertains visions of a grand and glorious future. This time its longing is so intense that its branches tremble and its bark aches. It is placed in a warm living room and decorated with Christmas ornaments. The evening doesn't proceed as anticipated; made dizzy by its finery and its longing for experiences on an ever grander scale, and dismayed that it is considered little more than a stage prop, Christmas Eve passes the fir tree by almost unnoticed. Later, it vacillates between disappointment and a somewhat dampened hope for the future. "Tomorrow I will not tremble," it decided, "I will enjoy my splendor to the fullest."[17] But there is no splendor the next day or ever again. The next morning, the tree is taken up to the attic and placed in a dark corner to wait out its days.

Abandoned by humans, the fir tree at first continues to entertain hopes that something new and exciting will happen. But gradually these hopes fade and it slips into memories of its days in the forest. It never entirely gives up hope, however. A story that it heard read aloud Christmas Eve occasionally occupies its thoughts, the story of Klumpe-Dumpe,[18] who gets the princess even though he stumbles (down a staircase) at the start. Adopting this story as the template for its life, the fir tree believes there is still a grand future ahead of it, even though it has stumbled thus far.

Mostly, it is given to reminiscences of bygone days. After a time, a few mice show up and listen attentively as the fir tree tells them stories from its life. The mice challenge it several times to admit that its best days are behind it, but the fir tree will have none of it.

"Oh," said the little mice, "how happy you have been, you old fir tree!"

"I am not old at all," said the tree. "It was only just this winter that I was taken from the forest! I am in the prime of my life, I've just stopped growing!"[19]

But after a while, the mice lose interest in the stories and leave the fir tree alone to vacillate between hope and recollection.

One beautiful spring day the fir tree is brought down from the attic and into the yard. "'Now life begins again! ... Now I will live again!' it cried joyfully."[20] In the clear light of day, however, it finds that its branches are withered and yellow and it is thrown among the weeds and contemptuously trampled on by the children and robbed of its star. "The tree looked at all the beautiful flowers and the freshness of the garden and then looked at itself and wished it had stayed in its dark corner of the attic."[21] The truth finally dawns upon the fir tree and it despairs: "My life is over and done! If only I had enjoyed it while I could! Now it is over, all over!" and the fir tree ends its days in the fire, absorbed in its memories. "With every popping sound, the tree sighed deeply and thought of a summer day in the forest, a winter night as the stars shone down. It thought of Christmas Eve and Klumpe-Dumpe, the only story it had ever heard and knew how to tell – and then it was all burned up."[22]

The Bed of Procrustes

So how are we to evaluate the poor fir tree in the light of the speaker's categories of unhappiness? It is quite clear that while in the forest, the fir tree is a fantasist, completely present in its dreams of future happiness. It is thus unhappy in the loose sense. Despite the brief, fateful lapse into recollection as it is taken from the forest, the fir tree continues being present in the future as it is brought inside and decorated for Christmas Eve by the servants, devoting itself, if possible, even more intensely to its future joys. But Christmas Eve is a rude shock and in the silence of the night after the celebration, the tree acknowledges that it has gone about things in the wrong way and vows to do better next time.

But there is no "next time" and the isolation of the attic deals the double blow that sends the fir tree into unhappiness in the strict sense. Like the young girl who cannot grieve because she cannot be certain her lover has been unfaithful and who cannot hope because he was an enigma, the fir tree is caught, unable to determine whether the object of essential interest, its life's greatest moment, lies ahead (and it should live in hope) or whether it lies behind (and it should live in recollection). It cannot rest in its future, because the future is in doubt: It believes that it will get the princess despite having stumbled; on the other hand, it finds the darkness and stillness of the attic oppressive and, goaded by the mice, it cannot rid itself of the suspicion that it has grown old, that there are no more Christmas Eves in store. And for precisely the same reasons it cannot rest in its past: Perhaps this Christmas Eve was its life's greatest moment and it should try to remember it in the best way; on the other hand, new and even more exciting experiences may await it. It has reached the depths of unhappiness, stretched on the procrustean bed of the combined form of strict unhappiness and unable to find rest in either hope or recollection.

The fir tree's time in the yard is nasty, brutish and short. Here in the bright light of day, its newly-awakened hopes are totally dashed; like a medieval execution that is intended to make the soul penitant before death, the fir tree is humiliated, it is trampled and tortured, it is forced to see its wretchedness and, after acknowledging its condition, it is allowed to die – chopped to bits and burned on the cleansing pyre. We might thus imagine that its dying memories connect and reconcile it with its life in a kind of "fulfilled moment" of salvation, a view that is current in Andersen scholarship.[23] But because these memories did not have reality for it while it lived, they cannot sustain it in death. Unlike Niobe, whose memories of her children sweeten and sharpen her eternal sorrow, the fir tree can only cling to the pallid memories of a past it has not truly lived. The final "fulfilled moment" can at most cut off the avenue of hope, throwing it out of the combined form of strict unhappiness and into the category of absence in the past (which is also a form of unhappiness in the strict sense). There is no retrieving a lost life.

"The Fir Tree" is a fable whose simple plot and "Carpe diem!" moral belie a more complex dynamic of presence and absence, which the theory of unhappiness is able to illuminate. We hope, in an introductory way, to have directed scholarly attention to the usefulness of this theory as yet another tool in the literary workshop.

Notes

1. *H.C. Andersens Samlede Værker, Eventyr og Historier I, 1830-1850,* eds. Klaus P. Mortensen, Laurids Kristian Fahl, Esther Kielberg, Jesper Gehlert Nielsen with the assistance of Finn Gredal Jensen. Copenhagen: Det Danske Sprog- og Litteraturselskab and Gyldendal 2003. Abbreviated hereafter: SV. All passages from "The Fir Tree" are translated by the authors.
2. Søren Kierkegaard, *Either-Or: Part I* in *Kierkegaard's Writings, III,* eds. and trans. Howard and Edna Hong. Princeton: Princeton University Press, 1987. Abbreviated hereafter: EO.
3. It seems evident from *Søren Kierkegaards Skrifter* K2, 137.6, p. 142, that Kierkegaard intended *symparanecromenoi* to be a perversion of the New Testament idea of dying in Christ.
4. EO, p. 220.
5. Ibid. p. 222.
6. Ibid.
7. Gregor Malantschuk, *Nøglebegreber i Søren Kierkegaards tænkning,* eds. Grethe Kjær and Paul Müller, Copenhagen: C.A. Reitzel 1993, p. 210. Authors' translation.
8. EO, p. 224.
9. Ibid. Emphasis added.
10. Ibid. Emphasis added.
11. Ibid. p. 223.
12. Ibid. p. 227.
13. Ibid. p. 223.
14. Ibid. p. 224. The speaker claims that the same dynamic holds for "absence in the past", but does not give any details.
15. SV. p. 296.
16. Ibid. p. 297.
17. Ibid. p. 299.
18. "Klumpe-Dumpe" has been translated into English as "Humpty-Dumpty". The two figures have nothing to do with each other, however, except for having fallen down. "Klumpe-Dumpe" developed later into the figure "Klods-Hans".
19. Op. cit. p. 300.
20. Ibid. p. 301.

21. Ibid. p. 301.
22. Ibid. p. 301.
23. Johan de Mylius has advanced this idea in a few articles and in his recent book, *Forvandlingens Pris: H. C. Andersen og hans eventyr*, Copenhagen: Høst & Søn, 2004, p. 111.

Approaching Fear in Hans Christian Andersen's Fairy Tales Through Sigmund Freud, Julia Kristeva and Melanie Klein

Cynthia Mikkelsen

In the dawn of the 21st century the study of fairy tales seems to be more popular than ever since this genre has proved to be of the most time-resistant. Many studies attempt to interpret fairy tales from all over the world using several scientific theories (ethnological, psychoanalytical, sociological, etc.) in order to examine their effect on children's psyche. Through Sigmund Freud, Melanie Klein and Julia Kristeva's psychoanalytical readings, this paper attempts a psychoanalytical approach and interpretation regarding the element of fear in six of H.C. Andersen's most popular fairy tales.

To begin with, one ought to underline some of the reasons that justify the importance of studying fear in H.C. Andersen's fairy tales and in particular in the following six fairy tales which are considered to be of his most popular: "The Little Match Girl", "The Steadfast Tin Soldier", "The Ugly Duckling", "The Snow Queen", "The Wild Swans", "The Little Mermaid".

First of all, their plot and evil factor should be briefly presented:

"The Little Match Girl"

In "The Little Match Girl" evil and consequently fear derives from society that margins the Other, the Different. The girl is poor and frightened, abandoned by everyone familiar and unfamiliar, in other words her own family and society in general. She tries to find comfort in her fantasies and in God by striking matches in order to warm herself and at the end she finds happiness in death where she is united with her grandmother, who can be interpreted as the good mother's substitute.

"The Steadfast Tin Soldier"

"The Steadfast Tin Soldier" is the Other, the peculiar one that cannot be accepted by its environment due to its handicap: it has only one leg. When it falls in love with a beautiful ballerina, the other toys seem to envy it. Its fear of rejection, due to its handicap, makes it suppress its erotic desire which somehow explains its steadfastness. As a result (thought not mentioned clearly in the text), it suddenly finds itself in an adventure, where it confronts rats, ends up in a fish belly, suffers a lot till it returns to its place, next to the ballerina. However, its misfortune doesn't end with its return since at the very end of the tale it ends up in a fire and gets destroyed, along with its beloved ballerina, who due to her loneliness lives a life in vanity.

"The Ugly Duckling"

"The Ugly Duckling" is accidentally born in an alien environment and finds itself captured among ducklings that don't cease to make fun of it, underestimate it and humiliate it. At the beginning its mother defends it but pretty soon she also turns against it in order to gain her environment's acceptance. The story focuses on the trials and the misfortunes the little duckling comes across in its quest of self identification and approval, through its mother's abjection, till it finds itself among the swans, its actual species.

"The Snow Queen"

In "The Snow Queen" evil makes its appearance from the very opening scene where "an evil troll", a goblin, constructs a mirror that "had the quality of making everything good and fair that has reflected in it dwindle to almost nothing. The loveliest landscapes looked like boiled spinach in it, and the best people became nasty or stood on their heads without stomach". A mirror that "broke into a hundred billion – and even more – fragments". After the primal scene, the tale focuses on the lives of two small children, Kay and Gerda, Kay's misfortunes after he has got one of the mirror's fragments into his eye and another into his heart, Gerda's quest after Kay's abduction by the Snow Queen (the evil mother substitute) and her trials and adventures during her long journey to the Snow Queen's palace where she confronts evil and defeats it, gaining back her friend and entering maturity.

"The Wild Swans"

This is a story regarding love and devotion that narrates the triumph of Good over Evil. A wealthy king, after his wife's death marries a gorgeous but mean woman who is jealous of his twelve children, eleven boys and a girl. After having already sent the little girl away from home, she uses dark magic and, by mistake, turns the boys into swans instead of mute, small birds. Despite the father's love, the wicked stepmother always manages to manipulate the king and sends away the girl, who finds herself in the middle of many adventures. But, being a loving person, she manages not only to break the spells and transform her brothers into humans again but also to defeat the mean and evil archbishop, who tries to accuse her of witchcraft to the prince that loves her and finally marries her.

"The Little Mermaid"

In this tale, which can be read as an ambiguous autobiography or an allegory of the author's own life, we find ourselves in an underground kingdom where a widower merman lives with his family. The story's main concern is the youngest mermaid's strange impulses which are deviant with respect to her family. Despite her home's stability and comfort she decides to leave it for the human world although she learns about the enmity there is between merfolk and humans as mermaids are considered to provoke human's death. The minute she turns fifteen and swims to the human world, the affection she felt for the boy's statue she had in her garden becomes love for the handsome prince she comes across. As a result, she decides not to apply the basic "mermaid rule" – according to which she can get the Prince and take him down to her garden, dead – and saves him from drowning. Something which is pretty peculiar for a mermaid. Returning to her kingdom she learns from her grandmother the difference between human and mermaid qualities and decides, after overcoming her immortality problem, to abandon everything for the sake of her love and have herself mutilated by the Sea Witch, the evil figure – who is horribly described – in order to obtain legs instead of tail. Despite her sacrifices in order to become human-like, and the dilemmas she overcomes, she loses everything and turns into a daughter of the air.

Why Study the Element of Fear in Fairy Tales, and Why Approach it Through Psychoanalysis?

Since the terrorists' attack on September 11th in New York and the most recent in the heart of Europe, in London, not to mention all the others that take place worldwide from time to time, mankind lives in a constant condition of unspecified fear. Even the perception of evil and fear has changed as mankind no longer knows or even supposes the exact face of the enemy in order to be on the alert. As a result, thousands of innocent people daily lose their lives in vain, in the name of peace and liberty, since there seems to be a crusade against terrorism, the unknown evil, in order to somehow conjure people's fear. In other words, nowadays fear and its various "faces" (specified or not, personal or universal) is more "in season" – if this phrase may be used – than ever before.

Within this context, the element of fear ought to be studied and in particular, one should examine the means through which symbolic narrations, myths, legends, fairy tales, and "writing" in general attempt to assemble their own universe, suggesting simultaneously emulations and answers to a non-answerable question: What is fear and how does it affect people's conscious and unconscious life?

Many definitions have been given of fear, among which the most appropriate for this study are the following:

- being afraid or feeling anxious or apprehensive about a possible or probable situation or event; being afraid or scared of; being frightened of;
- an emotion experienced in anticipation of some specific pain or danger (usually accompanied by a desire to flee or fight);
- concern: an anxious feeling;
- being uneasy or apprehensive about.

Having defined evil, fear and their frequent appearance in tales, one might ask: Why use psychoanalysis in the interpretation of fairy tales? Simply because each and every fairy tale, considered as a system that attempts to describe the most complex and difficult psychic fact, the Self, as individuality and as expression of the collective unconscious, pictures the procedure of the formulation of the Self, emphasizing some of its different phases. After all, psychoanalysis has to do with aesthetics, meaning not only the theory of beauty but also the theory of the qualities – positive and negative – of feeling and in particular of a very specific province of our mental life. Therefore, given that Andersen's tales are acceptable as such, with the difference that they are addressed to both children and adults,[1] psychoanalysis can be applied to them too, although many theorists have argued that his fairy tales constitute the portrait of an oppressive person: The author H.C. Andersen himself!

Jung, one of the most popular psycho-analysts worldwide, made an effort to interpret fairy tales, trying to appease fear by rationalizing it and thus getting it under our consciousness' control. According to him, fairy tales are considered to be the purest and simplest expression of collective unconscious psychic processes, since in them there is much less specific conscious cultural material than in legends or myths, and therefore they mirror the basic patterns of the psyche very clearly. In other words, fairy tales represent the archetypes in their simplest, barest and most concise form.

One can choose to interpret a fairy tale by focusing on either one of the four functions of consciousness (thought, feeling, sensation and intuition) or a combination of the four. In order to somehow translate into intellectual terms – even though according to Jung's theories this is impossible – the unknown psychic factor of the fairy tales' archetypes on evil and fear, this paper attempts to conduct a comparative study and refers basically to Sigmund Freud's "uncanny", Julia Kristeva's "abjection" and Melanie Klein's psychoanalytic theory on children. In other words, it shall try to bear out their impact on the formulation of these fairy tales, circumscribing them of course on the basis of one's own psychological experience. After all, interpretation is an art which depends on one's studies, personality and inspiration.

According to the famous psychoanalyst Bruno Bettelheim who specializes in the impact fairy tales have on children:

> Evil, that which is morally bad or wrong or has the nature of vice, causing harm or destruction or misfortune, is not without its attractions [...] and often is temporarily in the ascendancy. It is not that the evildoer is punished at the story's end which makes immersing oneself in fairy stories an experience in moral education, although this is part of it. In fairy tales, as in life, punishment or fear of it is a limited deterrent to crime. The conviction that crime

does not pay is a much more effective deterrent, and that is why in fairy tales the bad person always loses out. It is not the fact that virtue wins out at the end which promotes morality, but that the hero is most attractive to the child, who identifies with the hero in all his struggles. Because of this identification the child imagines that he suffers with the hero his trials and tribulations, and triumphs with him as virtue is victorious. The child makes such identifications all on his own and the inner and outer struggles of the hero imprint morality on him.[2]

It is obvious therefore that Andersen's fairy tales don't resemble to the majority of fairy tales and the rest of folk tales and particularly not the Scandinavian ones, where evil is personified and is almost always defeated by the brave and virtuous hero, as the romantic genre demands according to Northrop Frye.[3] Only a few of Andersen's tales have good, optimistic endings. For example, three of the six fairy tales in question end with the hero's "defeat". The Little Match Girl at the end dies and flies upwards to God. The Steadfast Tin Soldier is reduced to a mere lump in the fire, losing its loved ballerina. The Little Mermaid, somehow betrayed by Love, turns into a daughter of the air constantly seeking to gain an undying soul. Precisely this tragedy of the heroes' destiny is claimed to cause fear and inconvenience to whoever reads these tales since fairy tales are expected to have happy endings in order to help children identify with the hero and gain strength in order to struggle through life.

Vladimir Propp, who in his book *The Morphology of Folktales*[4] tries, by breaking down a large number of Russian folk tales into their smallest narrative units – narratemes – and arrives at a typology of narrative structures, has proved that there were thirty-one generic narratemes in the Russian folk tale. In other words, Propp argued that all fairy tales were constructed of certain plot elements – functions – which occurred in a uniform sequence. By studying them, he noted that most folk tales and fairy tales dwell on evil and the fear it provokes to their heroes, making use, among other things, of the mother and father figure, the shadow experience, the abjection and the uncanny.

At this point it would be helpful to try and define the terms "uncanny" and "abject" that Freud and Kristeva use in their effort to explain fear and its origins. Of course, the implementation of their theories in H.C. Andersen's fairy tales has caused, from the very beginning, the appearance of many obstacles. First of all Freud himself characterized Andersen's fairy tales as being far remote from the uncanny, from that which is familiar and peculiar at the same time. What could be more difficult then, than the attempt to implement a theory, the creator of which has expressed his opposition in any application of this specific theory to Andersen's fairy tales? At this point I believe that it would be helpful to quote Jack Zipes who argues that "the very fact of reading a fairy tale is an uncanny experience in that it separates the reader from the restrictions of reality from the onset and makes the repressed unfamiliar familiar once again."[5]

First of all, what is the meaning of the word "uncanny"?[6] The uncanny, although the English translation is not the exact equivalent of the German "unheimlich", is strongly related to what is frightening, to what arouses dread and horror. According to Freud's description the uncanny "derives its terror not from something externally alien or unknown but – on the contrary – from something strangely familiar which defeats our efforts to separate ourselves from it" (Morris). But, in order to use a special conceptual term such as the "uncanny", there must be present a special core of feeling that diversifies the uncanny from what is merely frightening. Jentsch, in "Zur Psychologie des Unheimlichen"[7] (1906), ascribes the essential factor of the feeling of the uncanniness to intellectual uncertainty. He believes that a particularly condition for awakening uncanny feelings is created when an inanimate object becomes too much like an animate one. A remark that one can easily refer to, when reading Andersen's tale "The Steadfast Tin Soldier". In this fairy tale an inanimate object, a tin soldier, is presented as alive and furthermore, as a creature with a heart that falls in love with another inanimate object. Even though by narration, one doesn't feel inconvenient or awkward by the fact that toys come into life every night, it is beyond doubt that this phenomenon does not coincide with our everyday experience and therefore it causes at least an uncertainty and an ambiguous feeling.

Freud's definition derives even from our everyday experience: The uncanny is that class of the frightening that leads back to what is known of old and long familiar. As we already know from experience, what is novel, can easily become frightening and uncanny, since it is unknown and unfamiliar. But, can something familiar cause horror? According to Freud yes! The uncanny he refers to is something old and familiar that people have somehow come to terms with, till the day it transforms to something uncanny through the addition of magic, animism, sorcery, omnipotence of thoughts, and other elements that one can come across sometimes even in real life but certainly in fairy tales.

By studying various definitions of the word, one can quite easily see that, among its different shades of meaning, the German word "heimlich" – which in English is translated as homely – is sometimes identical with its opposite, "unheimlich". And that is the core of Freud's theory! The fact that "heimlich" belongs to that set of ideas which, without being contradictory, are quite different. In our case, the word "heimlich" means what is familiar and agreeable and, at the same time, what is concealed and kept out of sight. Therefore, unheimlich is used as the contrary of the first significance. In this context, Schelling[8] defined "unheimlich" as the name of everything that ought to have remained secret and hidden but has come to light. In brief, the word's meaning develops in the direction of ambivalence till it coincides with its opposite as a kind of sub-species.

In the fairy tale "The Little Match Girl", by clinging to her fantasies where even dead people, such as her grandmother, appear and become visible as spirits, the girl affirms the belief that dead men's appearances on improbable and remote conditions arise that emotional attitude which is very close to the definition of uncanny. In this fairy tale the striking of a match – an improbable and remote condition – causes the appearance of the deceased grandmother, a familiar / unfamiliar figure that causes at the very same time, horror and warmth to the little girl that doesn't believe her eyes. Subject and object of fantasy come so close and the lack of distance allows the girl's entrance in the abjection phase.

In the fairy tale "The Steadfast Tin Soldier", the sudden animation of the toys, of something inanimate, that takes place every night, is likely to cause fear to the child listening to the tale because what is long familiar to it, its toys, suddenly acquire another dimension. Even the soldier, during the tale, feels terrified. In the tale, there is a personified "bad" figure, the jealous goblin. With no specification within the narration one might imagine that the tin soldier's fall – "terrific descent" from the third storey that led to a terrible adventure and finally its destruction was caused by the goblin, the evil that manages to triumph.

Even "The Ugly Duckling" confronts uncanniness when his own mother, a figure so close to him and so remote and cruel as well, denies him due to his appearance. A familiar figure becomes suddenly unfamiliar and hostile causing pain to the duckling. The unreceived though expected mother's love generates anger and depression to the duckling that leaves home searching for the love of which its mother deprived it. A rejection and denial caused probably by abjection.

The same goes for "The Little Mermaid". The world that is familiar to her suddenly seems to transform into her own prison because she has chosen to deny her past and identity and her environment is the only attachment to them. She cannot easily escape her past and when she does, she is defeated by fate or God, just like in ancient Greek tragedies.

The uncanniness in "The Wild Swans" and "The Snow Queen" has to do with the mother figure which is represented as the evil stepmother and the witch.[9] Even though they are both supposed to be caring and loving due to their "mother" role, they both cause harm and their victims seem at least at first, incapable of resisting. Furthermore, in this tale fear arises also due to the fact that both children are actually called to mature and leave behind any trace of childishness and purity. In other words, the fear of Death is relevant to the fear of Life and Eros.

In *Powers of Horror. An Essay on Abjection*,[10] Kristeva asserts that the first abjection we experience is at the point of our separation from the mother, where there is no distance between object and subject. This idea is drawn from Lacan's psychoanalytical theory which obviously underpins her theory of abjection. She asserts that abjection represents a revolt against whatever gave us our own existence or state of being. At this point the child enters the symbolic realm or the law of the father. In other words, the roles of the abject and of the abjection help define and re-define the borders of the subject. Placed in opposition to the symbolic, the abject threatens to draw the subject into an 'abyss' where 'meaning collapses'. When we as adults confront the abject we simultaneously fear and identify with it. It provokes us into recalling a state of being prior to signification (or the law of the father) where we feel a sense of helplessness. The self is threatened by something that is not part of us in terms of identity and non-identity, human and non-human. Kristeva expresses this succinctly when she says: "The abject has only one quality of the object and that is being opposed to it". The abject is what "disturbs identity, system, order. That which does not respect borders, positions, rules. The in-between, the ambiguous, the composite".[11]

When we enter into the world of the abject, our imaginary borders disintegrate and the abject becomes a tangible threat because our identity system and conception of order is being disrupted. Kristeva's theory of abjection is concerned with figures that are in a state of transition or transformation ("The Ugly Duckling", "The Little Mermaid", "The Wild Swans").

In most of the fairy tales studied Kristeva's theory applies easily. The Steadfast Tin Soldier was the exception to all tin soldiers made by tin, the Other that ought to be margined, especially after falling in love with the ballerina that represented the world of beauty and normality from where it was cast out: "All the soldiers were alike with one exception, and he differed from the rest in having only one leg". By being isolated, separated by the other tin soldiers and by its beloved one, the hero is called upon a mission of self identification which derives even from falling in love. The Little Match Girl "did not dare to go home for she had not sold any matches, and had not earned a single penny. Her father would beat her …". She is abjected not only from society but even from her own father. Being incompetent of living on her own she is constrained to live in an ambiguous dead end situation, completely at the border and, by her dreams, subject and object become one and distort normality. The Little Mermaid "was a curious child, quiet and thoughtful, and while the other sisters decked out their gardens with all kinds of extraordinary objects which they got from wrecks, she would have nothing besides the rosy flowers like the sun up above, except a statue of a beautiful boy". "Nothing gave her greater pleasure than to hear about the world of human beings up above". In other words, the little mermaid, driven by her love for the unknown, the human's world at first, and afterwards by the love she felt for the prince (what Kristeva described as "jouissance" which is a sensation akin to joyousness) decides to reject her identity, subverting all boundaries, laws, and conventions her world had. Abjecting and being abjected from her world, she finds herself rejected from the other world, the human one as well and ends up, having lost every sense of identity, in becoming a daughter of the air, for ever seeking immortality. And the same goes for the Ugly Duckling that was "a monstrous ugly, big duckling" that looked like no other, an abject that, after its separation from its mother, tried to find its own identity, not standing being a burden. By marginalizing the duckling, the Other, the ducks' community retains its own identity and order and the fear of deconstruction ceases to exist. In other words, in the tale the duckling experiences abjection by separating from its mother that rejected it and tries to construct its own identity and borders. The little girl and its brothers are the abjects in "The Wild Swans" since they threaten the order of the stepmother so their identity is doomed to alter. At the same time they experience abjection by separating from each other and from their father, substitute of the good mother, the objects that provided their identity, and enter in the symbolic order trying to construct their identities through adventures that end up in their maturity.

The good and bad mothers and women who appear in the tales are representations of the primary understanding of women, motherhood and the constant friction between the desire to pull away from what threatens one's borders and the desire to give in to those boundaries. The grandmother in "The Little Mermaid" is an excellent example. In some tales this suggests a possible motivation for mothers' evil actions. After all, tales are believed to relate mostly to the child's subconscious fear of being consumed by the parent, and are aimed at providing successful ways to manoeuvre oneself out of the alliance the mother (or anti-mother) seeks at all costs to manifest for herself. In each case in the tales, autonomy for the child comes with the death of the mother, which as Kristeva asserts is both a "biological and psychic necessity, the first step on the way to becoming autonomous". One should underline that the mothers who are mean in the tales are characterized as either step-mothers or witches, placed at a distance from the true maternal (even though they may be symbolic of the "true maternal"). A theory well applied to the stepmother of the tale "The Wild Swans" and the witch in "The Little Mermaid".

As far as Melanie Klein's theories[12] are concerned, it should be outlined that, while a full discussion of all of her theoretical applications is beyond the scope of this project, some of her theories are particularly useful in the analysis of fairy tales. One of Klein's major propositions is that "the neonate brings into the world two main conflicting impulses: love and hate". Each of these conflicting impulses must be dealt with, usually by either "bringing them together in order to modify the death drive with the life drive or expelling the death drive into the outside world". Along with this conflict arises the conflict of a primary relationship with the mother, a relationship both satisfying and frustrating, further complicated with the addition of the father. In the case of "The Little Mermaid" the grandmother substitutes the deceased mother, being at the same time over-protecting and depressive, with her advice acting as an obstacle, the little one has to overcome in order to turn into a human being. She loves and hates her at the same time as she reminds her of her own identity. The bad mother, who generously offers the transformation and in return makes her mute, is the witch, who reflects one half of the imaginary split mother, and poses danger to the child since she transforms her into something totally other than herself, even depriving her of language and preventing her from entering the symbolic order. In "The Little Match Girl" the deceased grandmother, though not evil, deprives the girl of any desire to live and devours her by letting her abandon life.

Therefore, besides love and hate, there is the "good" and "bad" mother, the mother as symbolic of both life and death, the symbolic (paternal) and semiotic (maternal), total oneness and total autonomy. The mother and the infant/child's perception of the mother figures heavily in each of these sets. In fact, the curious "split" nature of the infant's perception of the maternal figure recalls a kind of doppelgänger, a doubling of the maternal (in positive and negative incarnations) that itself can be seen as abject as Kristeva demonstrates.

Sheldon Cashdan in *The Witch Must Die. How Fairy Tales Shape Our Lives* (1999) states that the tales themselves reflect the infant/child's need to "combat sinful tendencies in the self", and he generally works to provide an alternative to a psychoanalytic reading. He does nevertheless discuss the idea of the split mother as character: "Over time, the realities of infant life force the child to face the unsettling realization that the person responsible for its survival is both consistent and inconsistent, both gratifying and frustrating – both good and bad". That is the case of the ugly duckling's mother, who at first, is very loving and supporting but finds herself wishing that the duckling would be miles away in order to regain the acceptance of the other animals in the mansion. As far as "The Little Mermaid" is concerned, the bad mother is the Sea Witch and the confusing mother, the grandmother that, with her advice, causes pain and suffering to her beloved grandchild. In "The Wild Swans" the father plays the role of the good mother but due to his paternal being he is very weak and unable to save the children from the bad mother. For that reason, when looking at fairy tale representations it is essential to see the effect of the maternal (or female) characters whose actions most clearly affect the child's life. The father in these tales is presented as less powerful, at times even weak. It is only after the clash between child and mother that the father begins to gain power in the tales.

Another important aspect of Klein's theory is her understanding of the differences between the boy and girl child's experiences and connections to their mothers. This has a direct impact on analyzing both the roles of girl/boy children in the tales, and understanding of the female child/adult as being specially connected to fantasies. For Klein, the boy's experience of the mother is always tainted or influenced by his castration fears. In *The Psycho-Analytic Play Technique*

(1955) she states that for boys, "the connection of these [castration] anxieties with castration fear can be seen for instance in the phantasy of losing the penis or having it destroyed inside the mother". Thus in the child's imaginary, the mother stands in as a potentially castrating image, as well as representing the figure who (for all infants) first satisfies and then frustrates, and threatens to consume.

The tale "The Snow Queen", apart from the obvious fear it provokes by the story of a hobgoblin's magic mirror and its fragments that, once inserted in ones eye, turn the heart so cold as if it were a lump of ice, confirms Klein's theory. The Snow Queen in the homonym tale represents the mother for the boy causing both satisfaction and frustration to him whereas at the same time provokes Kay's passion and sexual awakeness. She takes care of him but at the same time she cuts him off from anything familiar and close to him. The same goes for the Mother Thief. When Gerda finds Kay he is hostile as if he was threatened by her, representing a long lost world and an invader in his new world. Kay represents the uncanny at that time for Gerda since he provokes uncertainty: he looks like her old boyfriend but acts like a stranger. He is "heimlich" and "unheimlich" at the same time and the same goes for Gerda.

To conclude, why should one torment oneself by trying to apply all the above mentioned theories in the interpretation of fairy tales? Wouldn't it be easier to let oneself simply enjoy the "magic" impact each and every single fairy tale has in our soul? In one sense, conceptualizing and rationalizing everything, deprives our lives of every joy and childishness and we might find ourselves tied down for good to the ugly duckling stage that all of us face, without transforming into the swans we can become. Therefore, one should be aware and try to remove the glass from one's eyes as soon as possible, before the life's match dies away and one finds oneself alone and mute, looking far away in the ocean waiting for the appearance of a swan to save the day ...

Bibliography

Bettelheim, Bruno, *The Uses of Enchantment. The Meaning and Importance of Fairy Tales*, New York: Vintage Books 1977.

Cashdan, Sheldon, *The Witch Must Die. How Fairy Tales Shape Our Lives*, New York: Basic Books 1999.

Freud, Sigmund, *The Standard Edition of the Complete Psychological Works of Sigmund Freud. Volume XVII: An infantile Neurosis and Other Works*, (transl. James Strachey and Anna Freud), Vintage: The Hogarth Press 2001.

Klein, Melanie: *The Psycho-analytic Play Technique*, 1955

Klein, Melanie, *The Psycho-analysis of Children*, New York: W.W Norton 7 Company Inc Publishers 1932.

Klein, Melanie, *Envy and Gratitude*, New York: Dell Books 1977.

Klein, Melanie, *Love, Guilt and Reparation*, New York: Dell Books 1977.

Kristeva, Julia, *Powers of Horror. An essay on Abjection*, (transl. Leon S. Roudiez), New York: Columbia University Press 1980.

Kristeva, Julia, *Desire in Language: A Semiotic Approach to Literature and Art*, (transl. Thomas Gora, Alice Jardine, and Leon S. Roudiez), Oxford: Basil Blackwell 1982.

Northrop, Frye, *Anatomy of Criticism*, New York: Atheneum 1968.

Propp, Vladimir, *Morphology of the Folktale*. Austin: University of Texas Press 1968.

Zipes, Jack, *Fairy Tales and the Art of Subversion*, New York: Routledge 1983.

Notes

1. Andersen in fact confessed to a friend [letter to B. S. Ingemann, 20 November 1843] that "he always writes his stories bearing in mind that they shall be heard also by adults".
2. Bettelheim, Bruno, *The Uses of Enchantment. The Meaning and Importance of Fairy Tales*, New York: Vintage Books 1977
3. Northrop, Frye, *Anatomy of Criticism*, New York: Atheneum 1968.
4. Propp, Vladimir, *Morphology of the Folktale*. Austin: University of Texas Press 1968.
5. Zipes, Jack, *Fairy tales and the Art of Subversion*, NY: Routledge 1983.
6. Freud, Sigmund, *The Standard Edition of the Complete Psychological Works of Sigmund Freud*. Volume XVII: An infantile Neurosis and Other Works, (transl. James Strachey, Anna Freud), Vintage: The Hogarth Press 2001.
7. Ernst Jentsch: "Zur Psychologie des Unheimlichen", in *Psychiatrisch-neurologische Wochenschrift*, 1906, Vol. 8, pp. 195 ff. Quoted in Freud "Das Unheimliche" (1919), in: *Gesammelte Werke,* vol. 12, Frankfurt a M. 1986, pp. 229-68.
8. James Strachey (ed, trans), *The Standard Edition of The Complete Psycological Works of Sigmund Freud*, Vol XVII, The Uncany, p. 224.
9. The Snow Queen is read by me as a witch since she has the "magic" power of seducing Kay and keeping him "hostage".
10. Kristeva, Julia, *Powers of Horror. An essay on Abjection*, (transl. Leon S. Roudiez), New York: Columbia University Press 1980.

11. Kristeva, Julia, *Powers of Horror: An Essay on Abjection,* (tans Roudiez, Leon S.), New York: Columbia University Press 1980, p. 1.
12. Klein, Melanie, *The psycho-analysis of children*, New York: W.W Norton 7 Company Inc Publishers 1932.

The Soul of Things. Literary Forms and Popular Motifs in the Tales of Hans Christian Andersen

Leander Petzoldt

> "All the world's a stage,
> And all the men and women merely players;
> They have their exits and their entrances;
> And one man in his time plays many parts ..."
> (Shakespeare, *As you like It*, II, 7)

Hans Christian Andersen is famous, well-known and popular particularly for his fairy tales, less so however, for his autobiographic writings and travel descriptions, romances and plays, diaries and his letters.

Thomas Mann, the author of the novel *Der Zauberberg*, repeatedly referred to Andersen as the poet who had influenced him the most. Of course Andersen was not the Biedermeier period idyll enthusiast, he is known as by the masses. He was deeply troubled by tormenting contradictions and self doubts: A man from proletarian background, who unfolded before his inner eyes a dream world, who remained unaffected by elite educational experiences, and became the famous poet, who in the literary world of the 19th century had rank and name.

He shares the fate of many poets with only a very few works in their oeuvre that have become really popular.

Out of the more than 200 fairy tales of the brothers Grimm only a very small number became common heritage in the sense that their titles would be named spontaneously when asked for (Little Red-Cap, Little Snow-White, Rumpelstilzchen, Rapunzel, and others). Similarly out of Andersen's 156 fairy tales only about 30 are known on a supraregional level, especially in the Anglophone and German areas, nevertheless the complete tale collection thus been repeatedly translated into these languages. In Germany many of these fairy tales are even frequently attributed to the brothers Grimm. So for instance "The Steadfast Tin Soldier", "The Little Match Girl" or "The Princess on the Pea". These, of course, are fairy tales that Andersen had partly taken from the narrative tradition of his Danish homeland. This means that they are international types of folk tales, which, as for instance "The Travelling Companion" known under the title "The Grateful Dead", reaches back to the story of Tobias in the Bible, as far as the motif is concerned.

The story of "The Snow Queen" shows characteristics of the genuine fairy tale, too. The humans in the fairy tale operate with the supernatural characters as if they were of their own kind. Max Luethi has called this procedure "mono-dimensional" ("Eindimensionalität") as the facts of the other world do not scare the human actors. Frequently Andersen implied also motives of folk legend, as for instance in "The Marsh King's Daughter" the motif of the "hurry of the time": Three minutes in heaven are 300 years on the earth.

Typically popular motives, as the treasure guarded by a dog with eyes "as large as mill-wheels", are modified by him in a humorous way: "you are not to look at me all the time", said the soldier to the dog, "your eyes could hurt from it".

One should not forget – as already Elias Bredsdorff stated – that the majority of Andersen's fairy tales are not "folk tales" of the kind which the brothers Grimm, Asbjørnsen, Grundtvig and Moe collected. Andersen was inspired as much by popular tradition as by high literature, by Icelandic Sagas, the French "contes de fées", from Spanish narrations of the Conde Lucanor ("The Emperor's New Clothes"), Boccaccio's "Decamerone", Shakespeare, and eastern fairy tales ("the Flying Trunk"), up to the German Romantic era: Tieck ("Puss in Boots" / "The Princess on the Pea"), Chamisso ("The Shadow" / "Peter Schlemihl"), E.T.A. Hoffmann, Musäus, La Motte-Fouqué and Brentano. It was clear that he developed a special relationship with the poets of the Romantic period, whose intellectual profundity and irony certainly impressed him.

In his short story "The Shadow" he even gives indirect reference to his source, to Chamisso's "Peter Schlemihl": "And this annoyed him ..., because he knew that there was a story of a man without shade, which was known to all the people at home in the cold countries. And if the learned man came home and told his own story, they would say, he had only copied it, and he would not stand for that."

Already Georg Christensen proved in his source-critical study (1906) that in what Andersen himself called folk tales can be found only folk tale motives, "however, no folktale as a whole can be proven to be underlying". Thus in the end only seven tales remain, which can be called ordinary folk tales according to the type listing of Aarne-Thompson. But here too, as in "The Travel Companion" and "The Wild Swans" he individualized and changed the texts by interferences and additions (Pulmer 1980, 105). The other tales are such, in which pranks and merry tendencies prevail, and give a far more homogenious impression than the so-called "tales of magic". "Seemingly was the world view of the prank fairy tale, in which the tale's hero owes his luck not to the marvellous intervention of supernatural powers, but his own wit and own cunning intelligence and capability, for Andersen less problematic than the one of the tale of magic ..." (Pulmer 105).

Against the usage of today's editors, Andersen himself did not call his fiction "folkeventyr", which corresponds with the German "Volksmärchen", but "Eventyr og Historier". However, less than a dozen stories are to be counted among the "eventyr", while the overwhelming majority of more than 140 stories cannot be considered to be fairy tales. Regardless of the fact that they contain fairy tale and legend motives, here we have independent literary works that make use of the poet's allowance to collect impressions and to digest them in his texts. Thereby he developed an unmistakable style, coined by the use of onomatopoetic words, neologisms, direct speech and particularly by fairy tale structures (the youngest/stupidest brother wins the princess).

The folktale abstracts and describes types, which, to a certain extent like silhouettes, do not have relations or backgrounds, but have the potential to connect themselves with everything, as Max Luethi has observed, Andersen's characters are taken from real life and act in the contemporary reality of the author. He addresses his listeners, who were certainly not always children, directly. Among the most important characteristics of Andersen's style the "animation of things" ("Dingbelebung") can be mentioned: needles, rags, collars of paper, boots, lighter, a pottery jug, brooms, plates, buckets, a tea pot, porcelain figures, a feather, and a trinket, speak and behave like humans, which leads to grotesque constellations and amusing situations.

Especially "The Flying Trunk" is one of Andersen's most well-known narratives, praised rightfully as one of the most imaginative stories which tell a fairy tale in artful cross-setting. As in the text "The Darning Needle", here the animation of objects has become the most important "plot" of the narration. One could almost speak of animism as social and cultural anthropology does and which can be observed in indigenous peoples (of course with a magic-demonic component). Here, however, the term of the "insight" seems more adequate. "Andersen has a comprehension for the mute nature of all the things", writes G.K. Chesterton. With the term "insight" ("Hineinsehen") Oswald A. Erich named the inclination and/or ability of humans to understand in dead forms of utility or coincidence anthropomorphic or theriomorphe characters and to animate them in a certain sense. The recognizing of human or animal forms in roots, clouds, ink spots, is named "Pareidolie" in psychology. The fact that this ability, similarly to the eidetic ability, is particularly diffused among indigenous peoples and simple, non-scholarly educated persons, especially children, however, is well-known. As Jean Piaget has proved in the development of cognitive structures in infancy, the child animates its environment, toys, dolls and other things, when it reaches symbolic thinking as a result of internal imitation. Furthermore, in his work *The Construction of Reality in the Child* (1975), where he describes the formation of a concrete action-referred world view in the child, Piaget points to the fact that the child goes through an animistic phase, which is completed with the twelfth year of age. "His (the child's) understanding of the relations of physical cause and effect (is) a magic-phenomenistic one." Based on Piaget's research, Bruno Bettelheim speaks of the necessity of the magic world for the child. "The child trusts what the fairy tale tells because its world view agrees with his own." And further: "For the child there is no sharp boundary between liveless objects and living beings; and what is alive, has a life very similar to our own."

A further characteristic of Andersen's style is the linkage of his stories with reality. Indeed, the reality stimulated him to the production of his stories, as shown by the example of "The Dryad" where he writes: "All this happened and was experienced. We saw it ourselves, at the (World) Exhibition of Paris in 1867, in our time, in the high, wonderful time of fairy tale."

Still, "The Gardener and the Noble Family" is an example for his sense of reality. The story is set on a Danish manor and describes the relationship of the aristocratic family with their gardener Larsen. This relationship is characterized by condescension, envy and praise, as the gardener brings to the table always new creations of flowers and fruits: "But they were not proud of it at all", writes the poet, "they only felt as the lordship that could fire Larsen ..."

The animation of objects, even the personification of *abstracta*, like the "concern", the *"vertigo"*, the "seasons", does not really stand in contradiction to the reference to reality in his narrations. "Andersen's world of fairy tales is populated by a number of living, personal, individual powers: Humans, animals, things, nature phenomena – all equally valuable, all equally alive, still everything in its own way. They all have strength, or if one wants to say so, a soul", writes Bo Grønbech, "and this is primary, the shape only secondary" (11).

But in the end all these occurences are rooted in reality. In the interaction of the animated objects, the human reactions and the bourgeois reasons are those that control the field and despite their sometimes exotic alienation thus are stories of humans (Grønbech). Here he celebrates the sentimental culture of the internal, as developed in the bourgeois society of his epoch and which was established as an example by employment of the medium literature (Pulmer 108).

This connects also with the moralization of the plot as well as the moralizing and romanticizing of poverty and his sentimental relationship to nature, – all these things are extraneous to the folk tale. This way Andersen adapted consciously or not his "fairy tales", or better narrations, to the taste of upper class culture, a social stratum in which he felt good and had successes. Thus he developed a completely new form on the basis of an old genre. These shared only the name and some tendencies. It was a genuine poetic innovation, which made him one of the greatest writers of Denmark. "His singular achievement consisted in the fact that he transplanted the characters and terms of popular religion and folk narrative into this distinguished, officially recognized literature and that it could develop here in a completely new way" (Grønbech, 5).

Thus it becomes clear why in his "fairy tales" magic elements are absent. "The Flying Trunk" reacts not to a magic formula or a ritual, but to the push of a button. Here, a dream of mankind is anticipated, and also the folk tale tries to put this dream into effect – however, with magic means.

Many of the magic means used in fairy tales are based on the desire to overcome space and time effortlessly. Magic flying devices, as for instance a wooden eagle in the Russian folk tale or a flying horse manufactured from ebony and ivory, suggest flying machines from the earliest period of technology, which proceeded from a theriomorph appearance. More evident is the magic character in a fairy tale from the South Seas. Here the hero carves "from a tree that bleeds when being cut, a bird ... sticks on feathers. Then his foster mother revives it by hitting the ground with a palm branch and saying magic formulas. And with this he brings back his wife." Here besides elements of animistic animation of nature we find the magic-ritual custom and the magically loaded word in the spell. Magic formulas, spells with an appellative character are literally quoted in the fairy tale. Like other verses in the tale, they usually belong to the oldest, constant components of a tale type. Especially in the Nordic fairy tale such formulas, whose application was connected originally with the simultaneous scratching into rune sticks, have been preserved: "I practise magic so that you are not moderate in travel nor flight, till you reach my brother in the underworld", speaks the giantess in the stone boat. Another Nordic giantess uses the following spell: "Each body that is on earth or in earth, as well as all the spirits I call doomed." The word's inherent power, connected with the decided instruction, cause the magic change.

Of all that nothing is to be found in Andersen's "fairy tales". Also here he remains in the real world, to a large extent and his marvellous events are not caused by magic.

If one reads his stories so to speak between the lines, behind the fairy tale façade, a lot of darkness, satire and sometimes malicious irony may be found. This does not concern his social criticism as manifested in "The Dryad", in "The Gardener and the Noble Family", or in "Everything in its Proper Place". Andersen's transitions from the realistic to the peculiar are often divided by a narrow line, often however, he passes the line in an almost destructive way and thereby destroys the harmony. These are fairy tales without a "happy end", which in the tradition of European folk tales is almost impossible. Certainly, here are reflected oppressing, if not to say neurotic, memories of the fears in childhood, despair, and embarrassment, of a world of suppression and a hierarchic class society that trouble even the aging poet's dreams. In his private writings these tormenting fears, the anxiousness of becoming mad, but also his strange relationship to his sexuality are manifested.

His fears were countless. As many people of his time he feared being buried alive. On his bedside table he placed a sign at night saying "I'm only apparently dead". And the rope which he always took along on his journeys, so that in case of a fire in the hotel he could let himself down, can still be admired in his museum. A portrait by Günter Grass shows a "slightly self-complacent looking face of a puritan", as a journalist has written. Perhaps Grass as an artist, writer and painter has intuitively recognized the man behind the writer Andersen.

Bibliography

Andersen 1990: *Hans Christian Andersen, Meines Lebens Märchen*. Hanau 1990.

Bredsdorff 1980: Elias Bredsdorff, *Hans Christian Andersen. Des Märchendichters Leben und Werk*. München/Wien 1980.

Christensen 1906: Georg Christensen, "Andersen og de danske Folkeventyr", in: *Danske Studier* (1906) pp. 103-12 and 161-74.

Grimm 1818: J. u. W. Grimm, *Deutsche Sagen* (ed. L. Petzoldt). Hildesheim 2002, vol. I, Einführung, pp. 5-50. [Berlin 1818.]

Grønbech 1956: Bo Grønbech, "Das Märchengut von Hans Christian Andersen", in: *Die Freundesgabe*, II. Rheine 1956.

Klotz 1985: Volker Klotz, *Das europäische Kunstmärchen*. Stuttgart 1985.

Lüthi 1981: Max Lüthi, *Das europäische Volksmärchen*. Achte Aufl. Bern/München 1981.

Mayer 1975: Hans Mayer, *Aussenseiter*. Frankfurt/M 1975, pp. 224-33.

Nielsen 1995: Erling Nielsen, *Andersen*. Vierte Aufl. Hamburg 1995.

Odenius 1954: Oloph Odenius, "De tacksamma döda", in: *Arv* 10 (1954) pp. 97-108.

Petzoldt 1989: Leander Petzoldt, "Zaubertechnik und magisches Denken. Erscheinungsform und Funktion magischer Elemente im Märchen", in: Ders.: *Märchen, Mythos, Sage*. Marburg 1989, pp. 1-12.

Pulmer 1980: Karin Pulmer, "Vom Märchenglück zum Bürgeridyll. Zu H.C. Andersens Volksmärchenbeschreibungen", in: *Skandinavistik* 10 (1980) pp. 104-17.

Tismar 1981: Jens Tismar, *Das deutsche Kunstmärchen des zwanzigsten Jahrhunderts*. Stuttgart 1981.

"Now Then! We Will Begin ...": Communicative Strategies in Hans Christian Andersen's Fairy Tales

Margarita Slavova

The folklore and mythological "memory", embedded in the genesis and the immanent characteristics of the fairy tale as a genre, determine its literary existence. And, in spite of the inevitable transformation under the pressure of literary conventions, it secures its genre continuity. At the same time, the genre acquires new characteristics in the literary context that makes qualitative changes in its form and function.

As is well known, the institutionalizing of the literary fairy tale began in the Parisian salons during the 17th and 18th centuries and arose out of the need of aristocratic women to elaborate and conceive alternatives in society to the ones prescribed for them by men. These women began telling the tales as a type of parlor games in which the teller was to make the tale "seem" as if it were made up on the spot and as though it did not follow prescribed rules. Improvisation and experimentation with known folk and literary motifs were stressed. Most of the elaborate tales they told and then wrote are set within a conversational frame that reproduces the milieu and the carefully formulated repartee that was part of salon culture.

> The *conteuses* do sometimes write stories based on traditional material; they also occasionally echo traditional formulae that seem to define women as the oral conduits of popular culture ... But, much more often, and usually simultaneously, the *conteuses* place their tales in the complex and playful ambience of salon conversation. The "oral" for them is not primarily naive and primitive, but rather a highly-charged, high cultural event. [1]

In that way Mme D'Aulnoy, Mlle L'Heritier, Mme de Murat and others established the convention that many later writers of fairy tales (women and men) follow: the creation of a conversational frame for the tales as a device in the poetics of the genre with a communicative effect.

By framing their tales with traces of salon conversation, the French women writers represented the fairy tale as part of an *aristocratic* oral culture – countering the attempts of their contemporary Charles Perrault to create the illusion that he reproduced story-telling the way it existed in the *popular* oral culture of his day (which is shown in the title of his book *Les contes de ma Mere Loye* as well as by the simulation of the voice of the traditional story-teller in its style).

Simulating orality of the popular culture or referring to folk tradition became the dominant style and ideology of the fairy tale in the 19th century, when it was confirmed and developed as a valuable literary genre mainly by the German Romantics. It was then that its social function changed. As Jack Zipes notes, this process began in the 18th century in France, when

> the literary fairy tale's major reference point was another literary tale or an oral tale and was intended to amuse and instruct the isolated reader, or perhaps a reader who read aloud in a social situation ... At the same time, writers began to introduce didactic tales and fairy tales with a strong message for children in primers and collections intended for young audiences of the aristocracy and bourgeoisie.[2]

When the fairy tale was recognized as instructive but amusing reading, it was also institutionalized as reading for children. Along with some of the German Romantics who contributed to the writing of fairy tales for children in the first half of the 19th century (e.g. E.T.A. Hoffmann and W. Hauff), Hans Christian Andersen took a very active part in this process.

The renewed social and aesthetic function of the literary fairy tale influenced its poetics, as well as its communicative strategies.

Primarily addressed to children, the new literary fairy tale tries to find a way to its audience by secondary updating of the reminiscence of its oral existence through the "memory" of the genre – recalling the times when it "lived" in the oral presentation of people, endowed with talent and authority, for an audience of mixed age. The authorial tale too, even though it is fixed in a written text, reaches the child in the oral performance of an adult reader, who acts as the necessary mediator in the communication chain "author – text – addressee". And the child appears to be a recipient-listener who does not care for the aesthetic distance and the mediation of the performer. Most commonly the child identifies the person reading aloud with the author and her/himself with the protagonist.

That's why the act of telling a fairy tale – auto-reflexive for the artistic consciousness of the literary tale – is included in its poetics as a narrative strategy with communicative effect.

In folklore the situation of telling a tale is primarily marked by the initial and final fairy tale formulae, and secondly by the speech gestures in the narrative style of the narrator, who communicates by direct contact with the listener and spectator, and because of this is presented neither in the pre-text nor in the text itself.

However, the literary fairy tale either explicates the act of telling in a paratext where the participants in the communicative situation and the circumstances that have caused it are presented, or simulates direct communication – by an introductory sentence in the text or in a compositional frame. In this way the author strives to evoke credibility in the fairy tale. This sort of credibility is related to the shared concepts of life and moral values typical of the traditional type of narration.

> The narrator announces his story and explains its procedure, continually involving the reader by addressing him directly all the while,

the German scholar Hans-Heino Ewers writes.[3] The aim is to create an impression for oral face-to-face communication and the story itself to be identified by the addressee as an act of this type of communication.

By abandoning his anonymity, the author claims his presence but outside the story line by questions, exclamations, addresses, promptings to the implied listener, nominatively marked as such in the addresses or by second person pronouns and verb forms. Andersen's fairy tales abound in examples of initial introduction of the narrator in the text: *"Now listen to this!"* ("The Daisy"); *"Now then! We will begin."* ("The Snow Queen"); *"Have you ever heard the story of the old Street Lamp? It's really not very amusing, but you might listen to it for once."* ("The Old Street Lamp"); *"Have you ever seen a very old chest, black with age, and covered with outlandish carved ornaments and curling leaves? Well, in a certain parlor there was just such a chest, handed down from some great-grandmother."* ("The Shepherdess and the Chimney Sweep"); and *"Where did we get this story? Would you like to know?"* ("Auntie Toothache").[4]

The simulation of an oral speech act directed to auditory perception is achieved by the sound, grammatical and syntactical organization of the text as a whole. Manfred Menzel offers some interesting observations in his article "Elements of Orality in the Fairy Tales of H.C. Andersen". The author quotes in the original those of Andersen's works in which the feigned orality of the fairy tale style is achieved by sound-oriented fragments (such as alliterations, rhythmic and rhymed repetitions, onomatopoetic devices, and so on): "The Wind Tells about Valdemar Daae and His Daughters", "The Bell Deep", "What Old Johanne Told", and others. At the same time he pays attention to such grammatical peculiarities as repetition and lower lexical variability, a tendency toward parataxis and fragmentation of the syntax, mixing tenses (changing from simple past to present tense) in order to create the impression of immediacy, and interposing spontaneous comments, which are also considered features of an oral utterance of the language (that of the face-to-face communication).[5] We should note that the translations of the works preserve the mentioned peculiarities only to a certain extent. That's why, in this case, we should trust the conclusions made on the basis of the original texts.

The type of narration in which there is a story frame, which is enlarged to a tale of everyday life, becomes popular in the fairy tale fiction for children too. The floor is given to a character who is at the same time a narrator too – this is either an adult from the family (grandmother, grandfather, uncle), or from the patriarchal community (a loquacious person from the inn), or a travelling stranger (a road-companion, a fun-fair actor) – a character who has the characteristics of a traditional folk narrator and has his manner of story-telling. The narrative subject also is a fantastic character of folk type, bearer of collective experience and wisdom.

The listeners are personages too – sometimes specified with names and individual features, but more often typologised as addressees of a fairy tale narrative by which they are being amused or put to sleep in the traditional style of telling. In this way the appellative orientation of the narrative to a recipient-listener is stressed, and the processes of identification in the actual receptive act are stimulated.

Andersen's fairy tales that exemplify the first category are "Grandmother" (where the grandmother is introduced as a seemingly skilful storyteller by the words of her grandchild), "The Old Tombstone" (where the storyteller is the oldest member of the family), "Ole the Tower-Keeper" (in which the storyteller is duplicated by his old friend Ole, the tower keeper), and "The Bond of Friendship" (written as a story told in 1st person narration by the shepherd). And to exemplify the second category we have the stories "The Bell Deep" (where the story is told by the bell), "The Wind Tells about Valdemar Daae and His Daughters" and "The Garden of Paradise" (in both of them the role of narrator is entrusted to the wind), "The Marsh King's Daughter" (where the storks tell the story to their youngsters). The most popular fairy tale "Ole Lukøie" is among these too, where the compositional scheme of the narrative includes seven bedtime fairy tales that seem "attached" in chain by the appearance in the nursery of the Nordic guardian of sleep who works wonders. Actually, this is a simplified, "children's" adaptation of the archetypal narrative model of *The Arabian Nights*, which finds its continuation and development in children's fairy tale fiction.

As is well-known the chain principle of framing separate fairy tale stories, related not by single ones but by several narrators, had been introduced as early as the earliest European collections of fairy tales – these of Straparola and Basile. It had been used later in Wilhelm Hauff's fairy tale almanacs. But the multiplicity of narrative voices presupposes multiplicity of social and evaluative positions expressed through them too, which distances such narrative types from the child addressee. In the context of children's literature, where the fairy tale is institutionalized as the dominant genre, from the evaluative point of view, the monological narrative mode is preferred, since it simply affirms, through separate stories, a conventional and generally established system of values. And even when it articulates various narrative voices, this is done more on the principle of complementation and not that of dialogue. In this way the storytelling, used as a narrative model connected with the oral existence of the genre and its auditory perception by non-reading children, preserves its "initiation" ("rite-of-passage") function also as a form of literary communication.

It is exactly this function of the narrative scheme of storytelling/ listening to fairy tales that has been used in Andersen's fairy tales.

Storytelling as a motif and *the story* as a catalyst of change and success in the redemptive journey are brilliantly incorporated in the structure of "The Snow Queen". Its composition is organized as "a fairy tale in seven stories" but it is actually consists of many smaller stories, each of which reveals the existential problem of its narrator. In such a way the narrative form articulates human experience from different, but at the same time complementing points of view, irrespective of whether the character is a flower, a bird, an animal or a person. And the ever-repeated story of Gerda marks the initiation (rite-of-passage) "movement" of the heroine in search of and reaching the existential meaning.

> A story is that which is alive and active and which causes catharsis for those who participate in it,

writes Sue Misheff.[6] Gerda's story – a story which searches for balance between innocence and knowledge, sense and reason through the shared experience – proves to be the means of finding and rescuing Kay, who is deprived of feelings in the kingdom of reason. It is so because the articulated word, organized in a story, which finds an involved public obtains magical power. Both narrator and listeners are subjected to it. This is the power of innocence, enriched by knowledge, and of reason led by an "informed heart".[7]

The unspoken word has similar "magical" power in fairy tales, which is discussed by Ruth Bottigheimer in her interesting study on *Fairy Tales for Children* by The Grimm Brothers.[8] Muteness as a meaningful activity of characters and listening as a kind of action relevant to storytelling are functionalized in the poetics of the literary fairy tale – this is connected mainly to German social and cultural tradition.

As we have already mentioned, the fairy tale of Andersen utilizes, above all, the storytelling as a side of the verbal act of communication by endowing with "magical speech" not only people but natural phenomena and elements /the Sun and the wind/, plants, animals, objects, supernatural creatures. Being transformed in this way into subjects of fairy tale narration, their presence has become explicit in the compositional frame and also by the comments and the intonation of the narrator's voice and is always directed to the imaginary reader as if she/he were hearing and seeing the story live, here and now. Even when the storyteller himself is impersonalized, he does not give up the conversational style of presenting the story by using direct reference to the reader/listener (involving her/him as a witness to the story), as well as rejoinders and comments. In such a way Andersen's fairy tale "*is being born by life itself*" and is incorporated into it not as a relict from past times. His model of a fairy tale is a narrative form with a communicative potential to discuss contemporary issues of interest to readers of all ages.

The fact that the target readers for Andersen are not children alone, we know from particular statements of his. But the dual addressee is set in the appellative structure of the fairy tale narrative too, as well as in those meta-narrative remarks and comments that presuppose "a dialogue" with an adult reader well versed in literature.

Andersen found such recipients, like the French women writers of fairy tales from the 17th and 18th centuries, in the aristocratic and bourgeois salons of those towns he visited during his many travels throughout Europe. But in contrast to the salon conversational style of his distant predecessors for whom the story was a verbal play for the refined public, Andersen plays with the conventions and the communicative strategies of the genre without giving up the techniques of folk storytelling and not forgetting the most grateful public of all – children.

> Andersen carefully crafted the narration of his tales to evoke the power of oral storytelling, yet the narrative voice is a distinctive one, not the impersonal voice of most folk tales,

concludes Terri Windling. And she looks for explanation for this in that fact of Andersen's biography, which has attracted the attention of others too:

> He perfected his stories by reading them aloud within his social circle, and many a dinner party ended with children and adults alike clamoring for a story.[9]

Did the shoemaker's son resort to the memories of his own childhood, when he had listened to the stories of old women in Odense? Or had he compensated, in this way, not only the unrealised actor's talent but also his pursuit of social prestige and literary fame? Whatever the psychological motivation of Andersen the creator was, it undoubtedly resulted in a unique literary fairy tale and narrative form that has immortalized his name and has flourished in the field of children's literature after him.

Notes

1. Elizabeth W. Harries. "Simulating Oralities: French Fairy Tales of 1690s", *College Literature,* 23 (June 1996), p. 105.
2. Jack Zipes. "The Origins of the Fairy Tale for Children or How Script Was Used to Tame the Beast in Us". – In: Avery, Gillian (ed.), Briggs, Julia (ed.). *Children and Their Books*: A Celebration of the Work of Iona and Peter Opie. (Oxford: Clarendon, 1989), pp. 130-131
3. Hans-Heino Ewers. "Children's Literature and the Traditional Art of Storytelling". *Poetics Today*, 13:1 (Spring 1992), p. 173.
4. All quotations of H.C. Andersen's fairy tales in English are made according to Jean Hersholt's *The Complete Andersen*, web-edition: www.andersen.sdu.dk/vaerk/hersholt/om_e.html
5. Manfred Menzel. "Elements of Orality in the Fairy Tales of H.C. Andersen". – In: *Hans Christian Andersen. A Poet in Time.* (Odense: Odense University Press, 1999), pp. 383-395.
6. Sue Misheff. "Redemptive Journey: The Storytelling Motif in Andersen's 'The Snow Queen'". *Children's Literature in Education*, Vol. 20, No 1, 1989, p. 6.
7. Bruno Bettelheim: *The Informed Heart: Autonomy in a Mass Age.* Glencoe, IL: Free Press, 1961.
8. Ruth B. Bottigheimer [Рут Ботигхаймер. "Мълчи, Гретел ...", или Занемелите жени в *Приказки за деца* на братя Грим". – *Деца. Изкуство. Книги,* № 3, 1990].
9. Terri Windling. "Hans Christian Andersen: Father of the Modern Fairy Tale". http://www.edicott-studio.com/jMA03Summer/hans.html